International Conference on Cognition and Exploratory Learning in Digital Age (CELDA 2023)

Porto, Portugal
15-18 July 2023

Editors:

Demetrios G. Sampson
Dirk Ifenthaler
Pedro Isaías

ISBN: 978-1-7138-8470-5

Printed from e-media with permission by:

Curran Associates, Inc.
57 Morehouse Lane
Red Hook, NY 12571

Some format issues inherent in the e-media version may also appear in this print version.

Printed with permission by Curran Associates, Inc. (2024)

For permission requests, please contact International Association for Development of the Information Society (IADIS) at the address below.

International Association for Development of the Information Society (IADIS)
Rua Sao Sebastiao Da Pedreira
No. 100, 30, 1050-209
Lisbon, Portugal

Phone: 351 21 3151373
Fax: 351 21 3151244

secretariat@iadis.org

Additional copies of this publication are available from:

Curran Associates, Inc.
57 Morehouse Lane
Red Hook, NY 12571 USA
Phone: 845-758-0400
Fax: 845-758-2633
Email: curran@proceedings.com
Web: www.proceedings.com

TABLE OF CONTENTS

FULL PAPERS

VISUALIZATION ONBOARDING DESIGNED BY USERS: AN EMPIRICAL STUDY 3
Margit Pohl, Benjamin Potzmann, Christina Stoiber, Wolfgang Aigner

SCORE PREDICTION FROM PROGRAMMING EXERCISE SYSTEM LOGS USING MACHINE LEARNING 11
Tetsuo Tanaka, Mari Ueda

THE EFFECTS OF AGE AND LEARNING WITH EDUCATIONAL ROBOTIC DEVICES ON CHILDREN'S ALGORITHMIC THINKING 18
Charoula Angeli, Panayiota Diakou, Vaso Anastasiou

INTEGRATING LARGE LANGUAGE MODELS IN ART AND DESIGN EDUCATION 25
Alberto Giretti, Dilan Durmus, Massimo Vaccarini, Matteo Zambelli, Andrea Guidi, Franco Ripa Di Meana

EXPLORING INFRANODUS: A TEXT ANALYSIS TOOL 34
Irina Tursunkulova, Suzanne De Castell, Jennifer Jenson

IMPLICIT EPISTEMOLOGY - THE BELIEFS OF STUDENTS OF EDUCATION SCIENCES 43
Anita Gramigna, Giorgio Poletti

ON THE PREDICTORS OF COMPUTATIONAL THINKING SELF-EFFICACY 51
Josef Guggemos

ONLINE PRESENCE, METACOGNITION, AND COURSE DESIGN WITHIN THE COMMUNITY OF INQUIRY 60
Larisa Olesova, Ayesha Sadaf

THE USE OF METACOGNITIVE STRATEGIES IN STORYTELLING TO EXAMINE PRESCHOOL CHILDREN'S LISTENING COMPREHENSION SKILLS 67
Mahani Abdul Malik

RELATIONSHIP BETWEEN TEACHING PRESENCE AND SHARED-METACOGNITION IN ONLINE CASE-BASED COURSES 77
Ayesha Sadaf, Stella Yun Kim, Adrie Koehler

THE APPLICATION OF FUZZY DELPHI METHOD IN CONTENT VALIDITY ANALYSIS 84
Mohd Azli Jailani, Chong Kim Loy

HYBRID SIMULATION OF A SCIENTIFIC CONFERENCE: INQUIRY-BASED LEARNING TO ENABLE MASTER'S DEGREE STUDENTS TO ACQUIRE RESEARCH SKILLS 91
Patricia Brockmann

PATTERN ELEMENTS IN HIGHER VISUAL ART EDUCATION 99
Antonina Korepanova, Kai Pata

THREE FRAMEWORKS FOR DATA LITERACY 107
Stephen Downes

STUDENT CENTERED METHODS, SOFT SKILLS AND COMPETENCY BASED LEARNING FROM THE VIEW OF ENGINEERING AND TECHNICAL TEACHER STUDENTS 116
Ibolya Tomory

POTENTIAL OF ADAPTIVE E-LEARNING FOR KNOWLEDGE HETEROGENOUS GROUPS OF STUDENTS IN ENGINEERING DESIGN EDUCATION 125
Frederike Kossack, Eike Uttich, Beate Bender

CAPACITY BUILDING ACROSS HIGHER EDUCATION AND RURAL YOUTH IN WINNOVATORS SPACE 133
Kai Pata, Kristi Jüristo, Matej Zapušek, Nathalie Leiba, Sanja Popovic Pantic, Vladan Devedzic, Sonja Radenkovic, Mirjana Devedzic, Marija Blagojevic, Danijela Miloševic

PRIVACY CONCERNS DURING REMOTE EMERGENCY LEARNING IN HIGHER EDUCATION IN QATAR 142
Byrad Yyelland, Alan S. Weber, Robert Bianchi, Wajdi Zaghouani, Khawla Kittaneh, Ryad Ghanam, Selma Fejzullaj, Huda Iqbal, Afreena Niaz

TAP OR SWIPE: INTERACTION'S IMPACT ON COGNITIVE LOAD AND REWARDS IN A MOBILE MENTAL MATH GAME 153
Patrick Jost, Sebastian Rangger, Andreas Künz

ARE NEWLY UNDERGRADUATES SELF-DIRECTED, RESILIENT, AND SKILLFUL DURING ONLINE LEARNING? 163
Mohd Tajudin Md Ninggal, Rohaizak Omar, Azleen Ismail

THE IMPACT OF A PROJECT-BASED LEARNING ENVIRONMENT ON THE DEVELOPMENT OF UNDERGRADUATE STUDENTS' DIGITAL LITERACY SKILLS 171
Ourania Miliou, Charoula Angeli

MATHEMATICAL PROBLEM-SOLVING BY MEANS OF COMPUTATIONAL THINKING AND PROGRAMMING: A USE-MODIFY-CREATE APPROACH 179
Nils Kristian Hansen, Said Hadjerrouit

HOW TO DEAL WITH AI-POWERED WRITING TOOLS IN ACADEMIC WRITING: A STAKEHOLDER ANALYSIS 187
Michael Burkhard

ANALYSING AFFORDANCES OF TH E-ASSESSMENT SYSTEM NUMBAS IN MATHEMATICS EDUCATION FROM AN ACTIVITY THEORY PERSPECTIVE 199
Said Hadjerrouit, Celestine Ifeanyi Nnagbo

HOMOGENEITY OF TOKEN PROBABILITY DISTRIBUTIONS IN CHATGPT AND HUMAN TEXTS 207
Dragica Ljubisavljevic, Marko Koprivica, Aleksandar Kostic, Vladan Devedžic

THE "FERNSTUDENT". ENHANCING THE POTENTIAL OF HYBRID TEACHING BASED ON USER-CENTERED DESIGN 214
Daniel Ullrich, Andreas Butz, Sarah Diefenbach

USING GRAPH-BASED HEURISTICS TO ANALYZE A SYSTEMATIC LITERATURE REVIEW AND VALIDATE AN EXPERT-BASED TAXONOMY 223
Nadine Schlomske-Bodenstein, Bernhard Standl, Pablo Pirnay-Dummer

MINING, ANALYZING, AND MODELING THE COGNITIVE STRATEGIES STUDENTS USE TO CONSTRUCT HIGHER QUALITY CAUSAL MAPS 233
Allan Jeong, Hyoung Seok-Shin

ANCHORING CONCEPTS INFLUENCE ESSAY CONCEPTUAL STRUCTURE AND TEST PERFORMANCE 241
Roy B. Clariana, Ryan Solnosky

"I'M AFRAID TO FAIL THE TEST" - MOTIVATIONAL ORIENTATION, STATISTICS ANXIETY AND ACADEMIC DISHONESTY 249
Yovav Eshet, Pnina Steinberger, Keren Grinautsky

EFFECTS OF AN IMMERSIVE, MULTILINEAR FUTURE SCENARIO FOR EDUCATION PURPOSES 257
Flurina Hilber, Thomas Keller, Elke Brucker-Kley

GROUPING STUDENTS' LEARNING PATTERNS WITH MANABA'S LOG DATA BY K-MEANS 265
Kai Li

EDUCATION TO PREVENT HUMAN MECHANISATION IN A FACULTY OF INFORMATICS: DEVELOPING LEARNING MATERIALS TO IMPROVE STUDENTS' VERBAL COMMUNICATION SKILLS 273
Mari Ueda, Isoharu Nishiguchi, Hiroshi Tanaka, Kazunori Matsumoto, Tetsuo Tanaka

TEACHING REFLECTIVE USE OF TECHNOLOGY: A PILOTED WORKBOOK BASED ON EVACUATIONS 280
André Greubel, Julia Wenkmann, Hans-Stefan Siller, Martin Hennecke

VALUE AND CHALLENGES IN DEVELOPING OUTCOMES-BASED STUDENTS-CENTRED PROGRAMME 289
Aliza Ali

POTENTIAL CHALLENGES AND SUPPORT MECHANISMS FOR STUDENTS TRANSITIONING TO UNIVERSITY LIFE 297
Liga Zvirgzdina, Anda Zeidmane, Natalija Sergejeva

SYSTEMATIC LITERATURE REVIEW OF THE EFFORT OF GAMING ELEMENTS ON E-LEARNING PLATFORMS 305
Tobias Harald Popp, Heidi Schuhbauer

THE TRIGGER-BASED DISCUSSION-ORIENTED CONTINUOUS LEARNING MODEL 313
Dina A. Zekry, Gerard T. McKee

KEYBOARD AS A STIMULATOR IN TIMBRE RECOGNITION TRAINING 321
Adam Rosinski

EVALUATING POPULAR MOOC PLATFORMS BY GENERATIVE ARTIFICIAL INTELLIGENCE (AI) ROBOTS: HOW CONSISTENT ARE THE ROBOTS? 329
Victor K. Y. Chan

CHARACTERIZATION OF PHYSICAL COMPUTING DEVICES BY ATTRIBUTES FROM A PEDAGOGICAL PERSPECTIVE 337
Eric Schätz, Alke Martens

LEVERAGING EMOTIONS TO ENHANCE LEARNING SUCCESS IN ONLINE EDUCATION: A SYSTEMATIC REVIEW 345
Nicolai Plintz, Dirk Ifenthaler

AUGMENTED REALITY AND VIRTUAL REALITY IN PRESERVICE TEACHER PREPARATION: A SYSTEMATIC REVIEW OF EMPIRICAL LITERATURE 353
Joan Ann Swanson

LEGAL ISSUES AND RISKS OF INSTRUCTION VIA MASSIVE OPEN ONLINE COURSES (MOOCS): SMALL MACAO VS. SOME MAJOR JURISDICTIONS 361
Victor K. Y. Chan

CHATGPT AND BARD IN EDUCATION: A COMPARATIVE REVIEW 369
Gustavo Simas Da Silva, Vânia Ribas Ulbricht

FOSTERING PROBLEM SOLVING AND CRITICAL THINKING IN MATHEMATICS THROUGH GENERATIVE ARTIFICIAL INTELLIGENCE 377
Alice Barana, Marina Marchisio, Fabio Roman

<u>SHORT PAPERS</u>

MAIN FACTORS FOR IMPROVING THE EFFECTIVENESS OF MATHEMATICS STUDIES 389
Anda Zeidmane, Natalija Sergejeva

SHAKING THE "FOUNDATIONS OF EDUCATIONAL TECHNOLOGY" 393
Suzanne De Castell, Jennifer Jenson

APPLICATION OF MOBILE EEG FOR COGNITIVE TESTING IN NEURODEVELOPMENTAL DISORDERS 397
Natalia Georgara, Spyridon Doukakis

HIGHER EDUCATION TRAINING ACTIVITIES IN INTERNATIONAL ENVIRONMENTS FOR DEVELOPING SKILLS OF CIVIL-MILITARY COOPERATION 402
Antonino Cambria, Marina Marchisio, Enrico Spinello

THE EFFECTS OF LEARNING ANALYTICS-BASED FEEDBACK ON KNOWLEDGE ACQUISITION: THE ROLE OF FEEDBACK LITERACY 407
Mustafa Tepgeç, Joana Heil, Dirk Ifenthaler

PROMOTING SOCIO-EMOTIONAL LEARNING WITH A VIRTUAL ROBOT FACILITATOR OF SMALL GROUP DISCUSSIONS: A CROSS-CULTURAL STUDY 411
Goren Gordon, Laura Di Giunta, Chiara Riccioni, Clementina Comitale, Giulia Gliozzo, Carolina Lunetti

USAGE OF AND ATTITUDES TOWARDS AI-TECHNOLOGY IN THE LEARNING PROCESSES OF FIRST-YEAR STUDENTS 417
Jan Delcker, Joana Heil, Dirk Ifenthaler, Sabine Seufert, Lukas Spirgi

PROFESSIONAL DEVELOPMENT OF FOREIGN LANGUAGE TEACHERS: OPPORTUNITIES, CHALLENGES AND DEVELOPMENT PATHWAYS 421
Zhang Yajuan, Maria Da Piedade Vaz Rebelo, Maria Augusta Pereira Nascimento

STUDY ON THE TRAINING TO IMPROVE EMPLOYEES' EMOTIONAL WELL-BEING AT WORKPLACE 427
Anna Vintere

MOBILE SYSTEM FOR SIMULATION OF PHYSICAL CIRCUIT OPERATION AND APPLICATION TO EDUCATION INVOLVING CIRCUIT CONSTRUCTION 433
Atsushi Takemura

EARLY CONCEPT FOR A GENERIC AND DOMAIN AGNOSTIC SERIOUS GAME FRAMEWORK 439
Daniel Atorf, Sergius Dyck, Ehm Kannegieser

REFLECTION

THE POWER OF DIGITAL PLATFORMS: FACILITATING THE COLLABORATION OF UNDERGRADUATE COMPUTER SCIENCE PROJECT TEAMS 445
Margaret R. Scaturro Heil

Author Index

FULL
PAPERS

VISUALIZATION ONBOARDING DESIGNED BY USERS: AN EMPIRICAL STUDY

Margit Pohl[1], Benjamin Potzmann[1], Christina Stoiber[2] and Wolfgang Aigner[2]
[1]*Vienna University of Technology, Austria*
[2]*St. Pölten University of Applied Sciences, Austria*

ABSTRACT

Visualizations have become more complex in recent years so that users need to learn how to use these systems. Onboarding systems can help users to learn how to interact with a visualization efficiently. Simple tutorials are often not sufficient. There are still open questions on how to design such onboarding systems. So far, a few usability studies have been conducted to clarify this issue. We decided to adopt an approach using sketching. We conducted a study with 29 participants. Possible users of onboarding systems were asked to develop prototypes of an onboarding system based on sketches. The process of developing these prototypes and the results were analyzed in a qualitative study. We can show that onboarding systems should follow a step-by-step approach and be integrated into the visualization. In addition, it seems that questions, tasks, and examples should be part of an onboarding system, so that users can try out how to use the system on their own.

KEYWORDS

Visualization Onboarding, Qualitative Evaluation, Prototyping, Sketching

1. INTRODUCTION

Information visualization (InfoVis) is becoming mainstream, especially since the COVID pandemic (Grammel et al., 2010). The general audience got in touch with diverse data visualizations presenting medical data such as reproduction numbers, COVID-19 cases, hospitalizations, etc. Using data visualization effectively can be demanding for first-time and inexperienced users (Börner et al., 2016). Having a low level of visualization literacy (Boy et al., 2014; Börner et al., 2016; Galesic and Garcia-Retamero, 2010) leads to incorrect conclusions and to frustration or rejection of otherwise powerful data visualizations (Börner et al., 2016). Onboarding systems can assist users to interact with visualizations more efficiently. Approaches from educational psychology can help to create successful onboarding systems.

While there is some research on how to design onboarding systems (Stoiber et al., 2022a,c, 2021; Chundury et al., 2023), there are still some open questions. Some empirical evidence indicates that onboarding systems integrated into the visualization (in-situ onboarding) are more acceptable to users than external onboarding systems, and step-by-step approaches also seem advantageous (Stoiber et al., 2022c). On the other hand, it is not yet clear whether users would, for example, appreciate videos for onboarding or whether an abstract approach that explains only the functionality of the system without any concrete examples is better than an approach using a concrete data set. To clarify the open questions and get additional support for the existing results, we conducted a study inspired by constructive visualization (Huron et al., 2014a; Huron, 2014; Grammel et al., 2010). We developed a concept for an investigation based on the observation of study participants explaining a visualization to other study participants. The idea was that one group of participants (group A) should learn a visualization called Netflower (Stoiber et al., 2019) by themselves and then explain Netflower to participants from another group (group B). Participants from group B were supposed to sketch a prototype for an onboarding system based on their experience in a Zoom meeting.

Netflower (Stoiber et al., 2019) is a visual analytics tool in the form of a web application that was developed primarily for data journalists. It visualizes network flows, such as the number of asylum seekers between countries, using a Sankey diagram and multiple bar charts, shown in Figure 1. It provides various filtering options and interactive features, including hovering and click-for-detail interactions, which may not be immediately obvious to users.

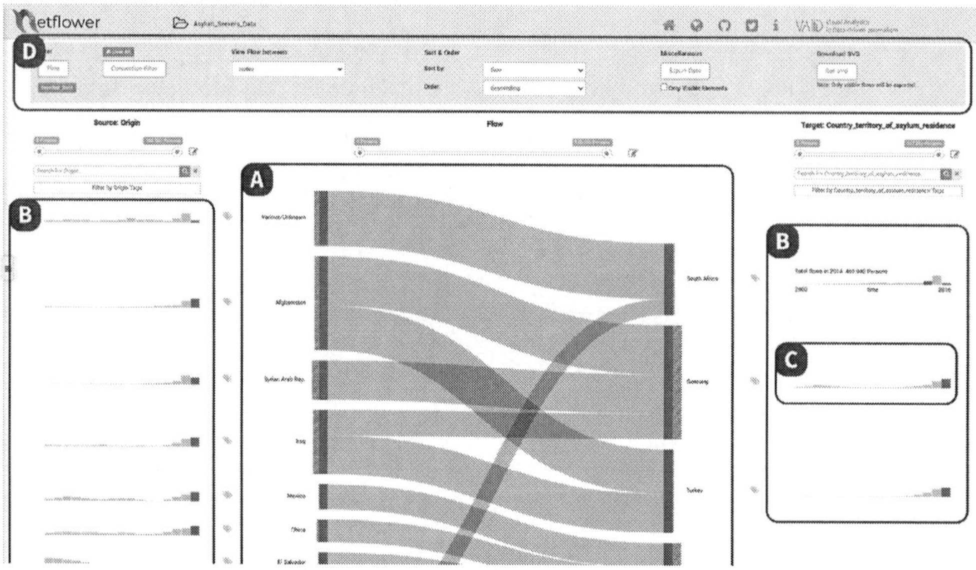

Figure 1. Key Features of Netflower. The main visualization consists of a Sankey diagram **A**, showing the flows between nodes. It is read from left to right, as the left nodes represent the origins of the flows, and the right nodes represent the targets. It is supported by bar charts **B** to the left and right, showing the development of all flows to or from one node along the time axis. Hovering over a bar **C** in this chart reveals the labeling of the time axis, as well as the exact value for the sum of flows for this node at that time. The global filtering and sorting options, as well as the export features, are concentrated in the grey section **D** at the top. Not pictured are the buttons to show more flows in the Sankey diagram.

2. RELATED WORK

2.1 Educational Approaches for Visualization Onboarding

Visualization onboarding methods (Stoiber et al., 2022c) aim to support end users in comprehending data visualizations and taking full advantage of the tools at hand. In this context, different educational approaches have been suggested (e.g., constructivism, and especially scaffolding).

In the current literature, Tanahashi et al. (2016) investigated *top-down* and *bottom-up teaching methods* and *active* or *passive learning types*. The bottom-up teaching method ("textbook approach") (Zeid et al., 2011) focuses on small, detailed pieces of information that students then combine to get a better understanding. Conversely, a top-down teaching method is given when a broad overview first helps to understand the abstract, high-level parts of an idea/topic, which then provide context for understanding its components in detail (Tanahashi et al., 2016). Furthermore, a distinction can be made between active and passive learning types. Passive learning means that students only receive the information without participatory dialog. In contrast, active learning describes an active participation (Tanahashi et al., 2016).

In their comparative study, Kwon and Lee (2016) explored the effectiveness of *active learning* strategies. Three tutorial types—static, video-based, and interactive —were used to support the learning of parallel coordinates plot visualizations. They observed that participants who used interactive and video tutorials outperformed those who used static or no tutorials. Their analysis indicates that top-down exercises were more effective than bottom-up and active learning types, with top-down tasks being the most effective.

Ruchikachorn and Mueller (2015) found out that the *learning by analogy* concept is helpful as participants in their study could entirely or at least significantly understand the unfamiliar visualization methods better after they observed the transitions from the familiar counterpart. The authors also describe another advantage of learning-by-analogy over other forms of demonstrations, such as textual or oral descriptions: the power of visuals, as they bridge any language barriers.

Stoiber et al. (2022c) developed four onboarding concepts (a step-by-step guide, scrollytelling, a video tutorial, and an in-situ scrollytelling). They conducted two quantitative comparative user studies with MTurk workers and a qualitative comparative user study with students. The main aim of these studies was to investigate the effect of onboarding on user performance and evaluate the subjective user experience. They proposed guidelines for the design of visualization onboarding methods, in particular, (1) onboarding systems should be integrated into the visualization tool; (2) use of an easy-to-understand data set and concrete examples on how to read the charts is vital, they support and increase comprehension; (3) to-the-point descriptions make it easier to absorb information (step-by-step); (4) Some users tend to ignore onboarding systems, even if they struggle. These users have to be motivated to use onboarding. Additionally, the authors explored abstract and concrete onboarding instructions and assessed them in a quantitative comparative user study with students (Stoiber et al., 2022a).

2.2 Involving Users in Visualization Creation

There is increasing research on how non-expert users create information visualizations. This kind of research has been inspired to some extent by the work of Seymour Papert (2020). Papert assumes that learners should interact with concrete objects to discover their properties (discovery learning) rather than learn in a more abstract way. One approach has been to investigate the sketching processes of non-expert users (Grammel et al., 2013). The authors argue that, while novices might be reluctant to express their ideas using a software product, they had fewer problems producing a sketch of a visualization. Sketching also yields interesting results because it may reveal the users' thought processes. Roberts et al. (2015) use sketching as a method to teach visualization design to students. They aim to enable students to study a large range of different solutions and, in that way, encourage their creativity.

Another approach that is better able to represent dynamic visualizations is constructive visualization (Huron et al., 2014a). Constructive visualization states that users should engage in the construction of their own visualizations by using familiar objects. Huron (2014) argues that non-expert users often have difficulties creating appropriate visualizations when they use off-the-shelf software. A possibility to overcome this problem is to use tangible tokens (e.g., Lego bricks or beads), that is, physicalization. This is the main idea of the constructive visualization approach. Huron et al. (2014b) observed users develop their own visualizations. This kind of research clarifies how the visual mapping process of non-expert users works. Their research indicates that this process deviates significantly from the processes suggested by commercial software to develop visualizations.

The idea of constructive visualization inspired our own approach. However, it should be pointed out that adopting physicalization for developing an onboarding system would be difficult. Therefore, we decided to use sketching (in combination with written explanations) to develop prototypes of onboarding systems. Despite the criticism, sketching can provide interesting insights into potential users' ideas about how to design such systems. From prototypes developed by our study participants, we aim to derive design recommendations for onboarding systems.

3. INVESTIGATION

3.1 Study Design

There were two groups of participants. Group A participants had to explain Netflower to group B participants. First, participants from group A had to fill out a questionnaire with open-ended questions. This questionnaire mainly contained questions about how they intended to convey information to participants from group B. It provided us with information about the educational theory they wanted to adopt. Basically, there are two different approaches: a cognitivist approach (Ertmer and Newby, 2013) based on an expository teaching style or a constructivist approach (Sawyer and Greeno, 2009; Duffy et al., 1993) based on solving examples or gamification. We wanted to know which approach the participants wanted to use.

Second, we conducted Zoom meetings where group A participants explained Netflower to group B participants, and we recorded these Zoom meetings. We assume that the analysis of the recordings of these meetings can provide us with insights into how participants would go about conveying information about visualization in a face-to-face setting.

Third, participants from group B had to fill out a questionnaire with open-ended questions and develop a prototype for an onboarding system. The prototypes consisted of sketches with explanations of the functionality of the system. In previous studies, participants tested existing onboarding systems. It might be argued that this is restrictive because participants can only decide about these existing systems. When they design the onboarding system, they can express their ideas and preferences without constraints.

This is a report about ongoing research. We will present results from the questionnaires completed by group A and the prototypes developed by group B. We will not present the results from the analysis of the recordings of the Zoom meetings. We used qualitative content analysis (Schreier, 2012) to analyze the data from these two sources.

We will address the following two research questions:

RQ1: What kind of educational approach do participants adopt to teach Netflower to another participant?

RQ2: What kind of prototypes do participants develop for onboarding purposes?

The answers to these two research questions should enable us to get more detailed information about designing efficient onboarding systems.

3.2 Participants

The persons participating in this investigation were students of computer science who were enrolled in a master's program. This means they had some previous knowledge about various diagram types and that they had experience using visualizations.

21 participants identified as male, and 8 identified as female. Of 29 subjects, we randomly assigned 15 subjects to group A and 14 to group B. However, we excluded one participant from group A and one from group B, as they did not submit reasonable input. After removing their answers from the data set, we have 14 documents from group A and 13 documents from group B. We base our results on the analysis of these documents.

4. RESULTS

The following results are based on the developed prototypes and the answers to the questionnaires. We used qualitative content analysis (Schreier, 2012) to interpret the results. Two of the authors conducted this analysis. We primarily used codes based on previous research (Stoiber et al., 2022a,b), but a few additional codes were developed during the coding process. The analysis was pursued until an agreement between the two authors was reached. The results of the most interesting topics will be discussed in the following. The main issues addressed by the participants are highlighted in the discussion of the results.

4.1 Results Group A

Group A had to learn Netflower themselves and then teach it to participants from group B. They had to fill in a questionnaire with open-ended questions on how they learned Netflower and how they planned to teach it to the participants from the other group. We wanted to know what educational approach they would use to teach Netflower.

How did you proceed with learning the tool Netflower? Eight participants started with the tutorial and then solved the tasks. Four participants ignored the tutorial and just explored, and two participants ignored the tutorial and just solved the tasks. In general, participants from group A learned about Netflower in a very interactive and explorative manner. P12 said about the tutorial, *"I first tried to read the tutorial, but I found it* *a bit tedious and dull without having the visualisation directly in front of me. Therefore, I eventually skipped the tutorial, opened the visualisation and started by trying to solve the tasks right away."*

Will you start your explanation with the visualized data or with features of the tool? Starting with the data implied that a concrete dataset was used as an example (e.g., the asylum seeker dataset in our example), in contrast to a procedure where the functionality was explained without referring to a concrete dataset and on a more abstract level. An abstract explanation would just state, for example, that a Sankey diagram shows flows from an origin to a destination without reference to any concrete data. Ten participants said they would start with examples using domain data. Four said they would start with a brief abstract introduction about the tool and then talk about the application examples using domain data. Participants apparently preferred to use the dataset provided by Netflower to explain its functionality. Nobody wanted to adopt a completely abstract approach.

What approach do you want to adopt when you teach Netflower to the participants from the other group? Nine participants said they would present information and then answer questions. Four participants said they would instead work through tasks together. However, all participants planned to present examples from the currently loaded data set during their explanation. The participants' ideas about how to teach Netflower to other participants rather follow a cognitivist approach, mainly consisting of presenting the system and answering questions.

4.2 Results Group B

Group B participants had to develop prototypes for visualization onboarding systems. Again, we were especially interested in what kind of educational approach participants would choose for their prototype and whether they would rather suggest tutorials or more interactive kinds of prototypes.

What are the main ideas for an onboarding system of the participants? Most of the participants described onboarding systems based on a step-by-step system (mentioned six times). As a motivation for this, P3 explained, *"If I had to follow a tutorial instead of having it explained to me by someone else, I would like it to have a similar structure. That is, showing different parts of the visualization one by one, explaining what they represent and how they can be interacted with".* This step-by-step system was usually opened within the Netflower system (in-situ). This approach was often combined with a feature providing hints to the users when they needed advice (mentioned seven times). Only three participants described an onboarding system that was primarily a video tutorial. One of these solutions was a video tutorial integrated into Netflower (in-situ). The other two solutions suggested having first a short video tutorial before using Netflower and then solving interactive examples. It should be mentioned, however, that some of the other prototypes also contained videos, but only as supplementary material.

Two participants suggested tutorials. One of these solutions is not in-situ but suggests that users open Netflower simultaneously and solve an example. The other tutorial consists of a brief introduction to the system before starting Netflower, and then users should solve an example. One participant suggested using gamification to teach Netflower. It is an open question whether gamification is an efficient approach for onboarding.

It is obvious from this overview that participants are skeptical about classical tutorials that should be read before using the system. This does not seem to be a solution that the users appreciate. Most of the systems are integrated into the Netflower system (in-situ), use a step-by-step approach, and use some form of interactive examples. Most of the prototypes rather follow a constructivist educational approach, so users have to develop their own mental model about the system Netflower actively.

Did they integrate elements of the explanations they got in the Zoom meetings? The answers concerning this question are very heterogeneous. Three participants mentioned that the step-by-step approach in the Zoom meetings inspired them also to adopt a step-by-step approach. Three other participants said they did not make use of their experience in the Zoom meetings. All other ideas originating from the Zoom meetings were only mentioned once (e.g., explaining through examples, focusing on hard-to-understand areas, and videos with explanations instead of text).

Did the participants use data-oriented (with examples) or abstract onboarding instructions? It is still not clear whether explanations in onboarding systems should rather be abstract or use examples with specific data. The participants of our study predominantly developed systems that are data-oriented and not abstract. There is only one person who used an abstract approach.

Was onboarding provided before or during interaction with Netflower? All participants stated that onboarding should take place while users work with Netflower. There are two special cases where the participants planned to have a short video tutorial before the users started to work with the system. In one case, the tutorial and Netflower were supposed to be open simultaneously.

Did participants design in-situ or external onboarding? Participants also found that onboarding should take place within the system (in-situ) and not be offered as a stand-alone system (external). Only one participant suggested an external system, and two suggested a combination of both approaches. These are the same exceptions as the one described in the previous paragraph.

Did onboarding support defined steps or free-to-browse options? Several participants planned for a step-by-step onboarding system. The idea is to follow steps in a pre-defined order. Eight participants adopted this approach. Three participants suggested a hybrid approach where it is possible to skip some of the steps. One participant suggested that users should be completely free to browse the system, and another did not specify whether to use defined steps.

Explanation of "reading the chart," "interacting with the chart," and "using the chart". The structure of onboarding explanations is based on work by Stoiber et al. (2022c, 2021). The onboarding stage "Reading the chart" explains the visual encoding (e.g., size, color); "Interacting with the chart" helps the user to understand the interaction concept. "Using the chart" guides the user towards further insights (e.g., making comparisons, identifying value, etc.). The analysis of our data shows that participants planned for explanations concerning "reading the chart" (12), interacting with the chart (12), and using the chart (7).

How did onboarding support interaction (Tasks/Questions; Worked Examples)? We wanted to know whether participants included tasks, questions, or examples in their prototype. A specific case would be worked examples, that is, examples where a path to a solution and the solution are provided. This category also included cases where the onboarding system gave hints to the users on how to solve a task. Nine users included questions or tasks in their onboarding system, seven included worked examples. Only two users did not use any kind of tasks or examples. P10 explained why s/he appreciated examples *"Following along an example does not only explain what you can do but also why you should do it"*. P14 explained why it was so important to use examples: *"I think that these tasks greatly impacted my decision on how to present Netflower. Because I worked through these tasks in exactly that order I had already a strategy for "learning" Netflower which is very similar to the tasks and the tutorial."*

Features: (multimedia, possibility to skip, possibility to repeat later, pop-ups, progress bar) Multimedia: We defined the category multimedia broadly. Everything apart from the text was coded as multimedia. Eight participants wanted to use multimedia in their system (mainly video or animation), and five only wanted to use text. Possibility to skip: We wanted to know whether the planned onboarding systems would force the user to study the whole system or provide the possibility to look at just the material that interested them. It is a bit surprising that many of the participants intended to force users to work through the whole material (8), and only a minority (4) allowed the users to skip material they did not need. It might be argued that it makes sense for users to access only the information they need in an onboarding system.

Discard previous prototypes: We wanted to know whether participants explored possible solutions. Six of the participants stated that they had discarded previous solutions. The first drafts were generally less sophisticated and contained less interaction than the final drafts. One user started with a pre-recorded tutorial but mentioned that s/he wanted to involve the user more. Another one first developed a system with a step-by-step wizard that was not integrated into Netflower and was not interactive. Again, this was modified so that the final version was interactive and integrated.

5. DISCUSSION: LESSONS LEARNED AND LIMITATIONS

The current investigation provides some possible recommendations for the design of onboarding systems. It suggests that a step-by-step system integrated into the visualization is the most appropriate solution. Traditional tutorials or videos are not seen as an attractive possibility. Furthermore, the investigation indicates that questions, tasks, and examples should be introduced into onboarding systems to help users familiarize themselves with the visualization if needed. Participants also favored a more concrete approach, using concrete datasets as examples. For an overview of the results see Table 1.

Based on our investigation, we can answer our proposed research question presented in Section 3.1.

Table 1. Summary of the results of our analysis of the responses of the questionnaire

Group A	
Learn Netflower	tutorial, solve tasks
Teach Netflower to Group B	primarily domain data (concrete) Didactic approach: present information, answer questions, examples
Group B	
Main Ideas	step-by-step system, in-situ, interactive
	data-oriented, referring to data visualized
	defined steps
	use tasks or worked examples

RQ1: What kind of educational approach do participants adopt to teach Netflower to another participant? Participants suggest a cognitivist approach to teaching Netflower: presentation, questions, and answers. Besides, they would use concrete onboarding instructions to refer to the data visualized.

RQ2: What kind of prototypes do participants develop for onboarding purposes? In contrast, the prototypes for visualization onboarding developed by group B participants follow a rather constructivist approach. They would integrate interactive step-by-step (defined steps) onboarding instructions, which are integrated into the onboarding system (in-situ). Additionally, concrete onboarding instructions are preferred.

We present ongoing research in this paper. We have not yet analyzed the recordings of the Zoom meetings. It is possible that this analysis may clarify some of these open issues. There are other limitations, that we would like to point out. So far, we have only analyzed the results of participants with some prior knowledge about visualizations. It would be interesting to investigate whether participants with more domain knowledge and less knowledge about visualizations behave differently.

6. CONCLUSION

We conducted an investigation to clarify how onboarding systems for visualizations should be designed. This investigation was inspired by constructive visualization approaches and used sketching for the development of prototypes for onboarding systems. The investigation yields some interesting new results. This indicates that the approach using sketching is able to clarify issues that were not previously identified.

ACKNOWLEDGEMENT

This work was funded by the Austrian Ministry for Transport, Innovation and Technology (BMVIT) under the ICT of the Future program via the SEVA project (no. 874018).

REFERENCES

Alpern, B. and Carter, L., 1991. The hyperbox. *Proceedings of the 2nd Conference on Visualization '91, VIS '91*, pp. 133–139. IEEE Computer Society Press. ISBN 0818622458.

Börner, K. et al, 2016. Investigating aspects of data visualization literacy using 20 information visualizations and 273 science museum visitors. *In Information Visualization*, 15(3): pp. 198–213, 2016. ISSN 1473-8716. doi: 10.1177/1473871615594652.

Boy, J. R. et al, 2014. A principled way of assessing visualization literacy. *In IEEE Transactions on Visualization and Computer Graphics*, 20(12), 2014, pp. 1963–1972. ISSN 1077-2626. doi: 10.1109/TVCG.2014.2346984.

Chundury, P. et al, 2023. Contextual in situ help for visual data interfaces. *In Information Visualization*, 22(1) 2023 pp. 69–84. doi: 10.1177/14738716221120064.

Duffy, T.M. et al, editors, 1993. *Designing Environments for Constructive Learning*. Nato ASI Subseries F:. SpringerVerlag, Berlin, Heidelberg, Germany. ISBN 978-3-642-78071-4.

Ertmer, P.A. and Newby, T.J., 2013. Behaviorism, cognitivism, constructivism: Comparing critical features from an instructional design perspective. *In Performance Improvement Quarterly*, 26 (2), 2013, pp. 43–71. ISSN 1937-8327. doi: 10.1002/piq.21143. URL http://onlinelibrary.wiley.com/doi/10.1002/piq.21143/abstract.

Galesic, M. and Garcia-Retamero, R., 2010. Graph Literacy: A Cross-Cultural Comparison. *Medical Decision Making*, 31 (3):444–457, 2010. doi: 10.1177/0272989X10373805. URL https://journals.sagepub.com/doi/10.1177/0272989X10373805. Publisher: SAGE PublicationsSage CA: Los Angeles, CA.

Grammel, L. et al, 2010. How information visualization novices construct visualizations. *In IEEE Transactions on Visualization and Computer Graphics*, 16(6), 2010, pp. 943–952. ISSN 2160-9306. doi: 10.1109/TVCG.2010.164.

Grammel, L. et al, 2013. A survey of visualization construction user interfaces. *EuroVis (Short Papers)*, pp. 019–023, Eindhoven, The Netherlands, 2013. Eurographics Association.

Huron, S., 2014. *Constructive Visualization: A token-based paradigm allowing to assemble dynamic visual representation for non-experts*. PhD thesis, Université Paris Sud-Paris XI, 2014.

Huron, S. et al, 2014a. Constructive visualization. *Proceedings of the 2014 conference on designing interactive systems*, pp. 433–442, Association for Computing Machinery.

Huron, S. et al, 2014b. Constructing visual representations: Investigating the use of tangible tokens. *In IEEE Transactions on Visualization and Computer Graphics*, 20(12) 2014, pp. 2102–2111. doi: 10.1109/TVCG.2014.2346292.

Kwon, B.C. and Lee, B., 2016. A comparative evaluation on online learning approaches using parallel coordinate visualization. *Proceedings of the SIGCHI Conference on Human Factors in Computing Systems*, CHI '16, pp. 993–997. ACM Press. ISBN 978-1-4503-3362-7. doi: 10.1145/2858036.2858101.

Papert, S.A., 2020. *Mindstorms: Children, computers, and powerful ideas*. Basic books, New York, NY.

Roberts, J.C. et al, 2015. Sketching designs using the five design-sheet methodology. *In IEEE transactions on visualization and computer graphics*, 22(1) 2015, pp. 419–428.

Ruchikachorn, P. and Mueller, K., 2015. Learning visualizations by analogy: Promoting visual literacy through visualization morphing. *In IEEE Transactions on Visualization and Computer Graphics*, 21(9) 2015, pp. 1028–1044,. ISSN 1077-2626. doi: 10.1109/TVCG.2015.2413786.

Sawyer, R.K. and Greeno, J.G., 2009. Situativity and learning. In Murat Aydede and P. Robbins, editors, *The Cambridge Handbook of Situated Cognition*. Cambridge University Press, Cambridge, pp. 347–367.

Schreier, M., 2012. *Qualitative content analysis in practice*. Sage publications, Newbury Park, California.

Stoiber, C. et al, 2019. Netflower: Dynamic Network Visualization for Data Journalists. *In Computer Graphics Forum (EuroVis '19)*, 38(3) 2019, pp. 699–711. doi: 10.1111/cgf.13721. URL https://doi.org/10.1111/cgf.13721.

Stoiber, C. et al, 2021. Design and comparative evaluation of visualization onboarding methods. *Proceedings of the 14th International Symposium on Visual Information Communication and Interaction*, VINCI '21, New York, NY, USA, 2021. Association for Computing Machinery. ISBN 9781450386470. doi: 10.1145/3481549.3481558. URL https://doi.org/10.1145/3481549.3481558.

Stoiber, C. et al, 2022a. Abstract and concrete materials: What to use for visualization onboarding for a treemap visualization? *Proceedings of the 15th International Symposium on Visual Information Communication and Interaction*, VINCI '22, New York, NY, USA, 2022a. Association for Computing Machinery. ISBN 9781450398060. doi: 10.1145/3554944.3554949. URL https://doi.org/10.1145/3554944.3554949.

Stoiber, C. et al, 2022b. Visualization Onboarding Grounded in Educational Theories. In *Visualization Psychology*. Springer Nature, n.p. URL http://arxiv.org/abs/2203.11134.

Stoiber, C., 2022c. Comparative evaluations of visualization onboarding methods. *In Visual Informatics*, 6(4) 2022, pp. 34– 50. ISSN 2468-502X. doi: https://doi.org/10.1016/j.visinf.2022.07.001.

Yuzuru Tanahashi, Nick Leaf, and Kwan-Liu Ma. A study on designing effective introductory materials for information visualization. *Computer Graphics Forum*, 35(7):117–126, 2016. ISSN 1467-8659. doi: 10.1111/cgf.13009.

Zeid, A. et al, 2011. CAPSULE: An Innovative Capstone-Based Pedagogical Approach to Engage High School Students in STEM Learning. *Proceedings of the ASME 2011 International Mechanical Engineering Congress and Exposition*, 5, pp. 305–314. doi: 10.1115/IMECE2011-62187.

SCORE PREDICTION FROM PROGRAMMING EXERCISE SYSTEM LOGS USING MACHINE LEARNING

Tetsuo Tanaka[1] and Mari Ueda[2]
[1]*Dept. of Information and Computer Sciences, Faculty of Information Technology, Kanagawa Institute of Technology*
1030 Shimo-ogino, Atsugi, Kanagawa, 243-0292, Japan
[2]*Dept. of Information Media, Faculty of Information Technology, Kanagawa Institute of Technology*
1030 Shimo-ogino, Atsugi, Kanagawa, 243-0292, Japan

ABSTRACT

In this study, the authors have developed a web-based programming exercise system currently implemented in classrooms. This system not only provides students with a web-based programming environment but also tracks the time spent on exercises, logging operations such as program editing, building, execution, and testing. Additionally, it records their results. For educators, the system offers insights into each student's progress, the evolution of their source code, and the instances of errors. While teachers find these functions beneficial, the method of providing feedback to students needs improvement. Immediate feedback is proven to be more effective for student learning. If the final course score could be predicted based on early data (e.g., from the 1st or 2nd week), students could adapt their study strategies accordingly. This paper demonstrates that one can predict the final score using the system's operational logs from the initial phases of the course. Furthermore, the score predictions can be revised weekly based on new class logs. We also explore the potential of offering tailored advice to students to enhance their final score.

KEYWORDS

Programming Exercise, Score Prediction, Effective Feedback, Operation Log, Log Analysis

1. INTRODUCTION

The digital learning environment is expanding. Within programming education, services such as Google Colaboratory, paiza.io, and Replit have emerged, which enable students to program directly in browsers without constructing personal programming environments. On these digital platforms, student activity logs and learning histories are automatically recorded. Research utilizing these datasets to pinpoint areas where students struggle has been conducted [Ohno 2022]. Furthermore, dashboards have been designed to consolidate various learning metrics, offering valuable insights to both educators and learners [Kia 2020; Sedrakyan 2019; Susnjak 2022; Khulbe 2023]. Such dashboards have evolved into essential feedback tools [Raubenheimer 2021] that substantially influence academic outcomes.

However, a challenge persists: programming courses often report high failure rates. Early performance prediction has been proposed as a remedy for the same [Carter 2019; Quille 2019; Liu 2023; Sobral 2021]. Score prediction stands out as a potent feedback tool. Early identification of underperforming students enables educators to intervene with timely advice. This anticipatory feedback allows students to understand their current academic standing, adjust their study schedules, and even redefine their learning goals. Such feedback is pivotal for strategic study planning.

We have designed and implemented a programming practice system used in real-world classrooms [Satoh 2022; Tanaka 2023a]. Presently, our system provides educators with insights into overall class trends and individual student exercise statuses via a dashboard. However, the student dashboard remains limited, and its feedback capabilities are not yet fully realized. We aim to augment the system with more effective feedback mechanisms. Our prior work [Tanaka 2023b] delved into preliminary analyses of programming exercise logs to enhance student feedback. This paper delves deeper, focusing on predicting final exam scores based on those preliminary findings.

Immediate feedback has emerged as most effective for students. If one can predict a course's final score based on early-stage data (e.g., from the 1st and 2nd weeks of a term), students can recalibrate their learning approaches accordingly. Conversely, if students receive unfavorable predictions early on, it might demotivate them, causing them to resign prematurely. To circumvent such setbacks, it is crucial to ensure that the students remain motivated. They should understand that even if initial projections are unsatisfactory, dedicated efforts can reverse the tide. We demonstrate that the final score can be predicted using early course system logs and that these predictions can be regularly revised as new weekly logs are generated. Additionally, we explore strategies for tailored advice to improve final scores.

Moving forward, Section 2 delves into the system's architecture, while Section 3 elaborates on the methodologies and outcomes of score prediction.

2. PROGRAMMING EXERCISE SYSTEM OVERVIEW

As depicted in Figure 1, the developed programming exercise system offers students an online programming environment and provides instructors with insights into their coding status [Satoh 2022; Tanaka 2023a]. Whenever a student interacts with a programming environment—be it through keyboard inputs, clicks on execution buttons, or any other actions—the system logs various details on a server. This includes the specific time of each action and the content displayed within the editor, console, standard output, and output files at that instance. The system formats the log and presents a list of practice situations for each student to the teacher. Currently, the system exclusively supports the C programming language.

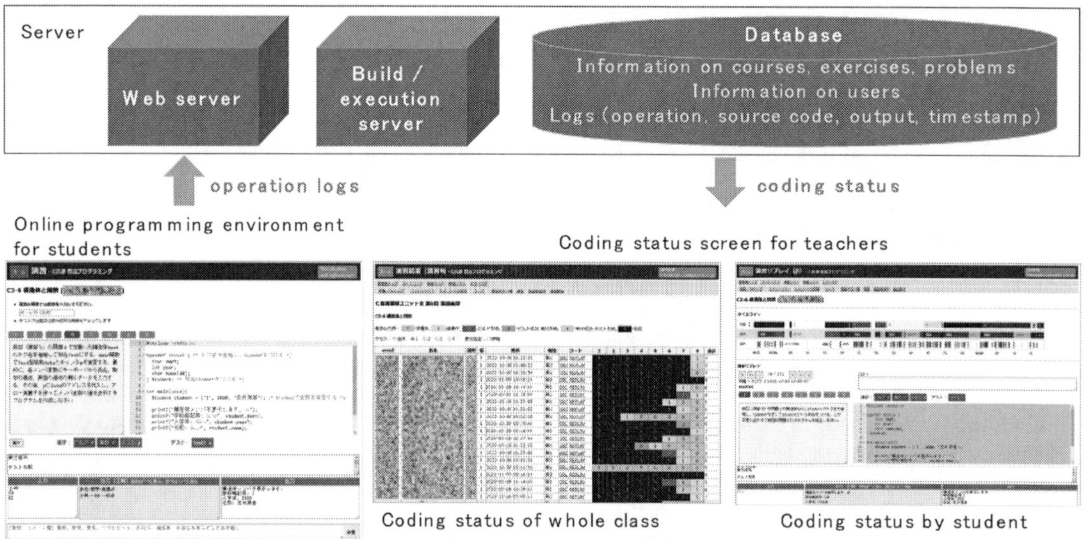

Figure 1. Programming exercise system overview

The logged data comprise various details, as listed below.

- Exercise information: course ID, exercise ID, problem ID
- User details: user ID, email, name
- Operational data and outcomes, which include the following.
  - Operation type (e.g., display, problem switching, blur, edit, copy and paste, build/execute/test)
  - Coding status indicators (e.g., not started, editing, build failed, execution failed, test failed, test successful, specific test cases passed or failed)
- Contents of the editor, console, standard output and error outputs, output files, and timestamps of each operation.

On the educator's dashboard, as illustrated in Figure 1, a comprehensive list comprising the coding statuses of the entire class is displayed. It provides details such as user ID, username, seat number, class, last update timestamp, and the progression status of each problem being worked on. The progression is categorized as *not started*, *editing*, *build failed*, *build succeeded (but execution failed)*, *execution succeeded (but test failed)*, and *completed*. Furthermore, hyperlinks to the latest snapshot of a student's practice situation and a link showcasing a chronological animation of their practice history are also available. This layout aids teachers in identifying students who might be struggling, even if they have not explicitly sought help.

Additionally, the system offers instructors a real-time glimpse into each student's coding scenario. On this screen, educators can directly execute the student's code and inspect the outcomes. This feature enables teachers to review the specific code written by students and diagnose the types of errors that might be appearing on their respective devices, be it PCs or tablets. Another highlight of the system is its ability to present a dynamic representation of a student's coding journey. Here, the system portrays an animated timeline, detailing the problems tackled, their progression stages (like editing, executing, testing), and a chronological record of user interactions and results.

3. SCORE PREDICTION

To utilize the operation logs of the programming practice system for effective feedback to students, we conducted a preliminary log analysis. This analysis confirmed that variables such as the total working time, the total number of program executions, and the total number of completed programs influenced the prediction results [Tanaka 2023b].

Providing feedback to students immediately is most effective. Predicting the final course score based on early data (from the 1st or 2nd week) can empower students to adjust their learning habits and study plans as required. However, there is a potential downside: predictions of poor scores at an early stage can demotivate students and lead to them giving up. To prevent such a scenario, the students must be reassured that, even with a less-than-ideal initial prediction, they can improve with continued effort and further learning.

In this study, our goal is to predict the final score on a weekly basis by using the accumulated data, and thus provide weekly feedback to students. Our initial approach involves creating a multiple regression analysis model using data from actual classes conducted in the latter half of the 2022 academic year.

3.1 Analysis Target

During the 3rd and 4th quarters (spanning seven weeks each) of 2022, our system was employed in the "C language unit" classes at the Department of Information and Computer Science, Faculty of Informatics, Kanagawa Institute of Technology, Japan. Here are the specifics.

- The system served approximately 230 students, predominantly first-years, in a 90-min seminar class.
- The units included C language unit II (one class), C language unit III (four classes), and C language unit IV (one class).
- Examples of answers are published after each class.
- The class sizes varied, ranging from 10 to 45 students
- In a single 90-minute class, each student generated 250 to 300 logs. This count doubled to 500 to 600 logs when considering independent study post-class.

For the analysis, our data targets were set as follows.

- Course: C language unit III, which has the highest student enrollment.
- Log acquisition period: 3rd quarter of 2022.
- Student Cohort: 145 first-year students who enrolled in C language unit II in the 2nd quarter and unit III in the 3rd quarter.
- Log Types Analyzed: We considered various parameters, including the score from C language unit II, time spent, number of execution attempts, number of problems tackled, and number of programs completed. These were aggregated both during class and post-class.

3.2 Prediction Method

In the 3rd and 4th quarters of 2022, we implemented the system in real-world classes. From this data, we developed a multiple regression analysis model with the following parameters.

- The objective variable is defined as the final examination scores from the C Language Unit III in the 3rd quarter of 2022.
- Explanatory variables comprise the final examination scores from C Language Unit II in the 2nd quarter of 2022 and five types of logs from the 3rd quarter. These logs include the time spent, number of trials, number of attempted problems, number of completed problems, and the average time to completion, both during class and post-class.
- We used Python and Scikit-learn for analysis. The explanatory variables were standardized using sklearn.preprocessing.StandardScaler, and then trained using sklearn.linear_model.LinearRegression.
- Predictions began based solely on the scores from C Language Unit II from the previous quarter. We then added logs incrementally from each successive class, from the first to the seventh.
- Model evaluation metrics include the mean squared error (MSE), the coefficient of determination (R^2), p-value Prob(F), adjusted coefficient of determination Adj.-R2, and partial regression coefficient for training data and test data.

3.3 Prediction Results

Table 1 presents the prediction results. Results (1)–(8) detail predictions starting solely with the scores of C Language Unit II followed by results obtained after adding logs from each class, up to the seventh class. The table data are used to generate a scatterplot of the predicted vs. actual scores, the MSE of the training data, R^2, the p-value (Prob(F)) of the test, adjusted R^2 (Adj.- R2), and the MSE and R^2 for the test data.

The Prob(F) statistic, derived from the training data for each model, is notably low, highlighting the utility of each model. Additionally, the adjusted R^2 for each model exceeds 0.5, suggesting good accuracy—though it is neither stellar nor poor. Conversely, as more class data gets incorporated into predictions, the accuracy of the model augments for the training data but declines for the test data, evidenced by the increasing MSE and decreasing R^2. Notably, post the fifth model—which incorporates 4th lesson logs—R^2 falls below 0.4. The scatterplots reflect this trend, showing test data predictions significantly diverging from actual values and thus indicating overfitting.

Table 2 lists partial regression coefficients for model (2), grounded on C2 scores and the logs of the first class. Only two variables, C2 score and the number of attempted problems during class, registered p-values under 0.05. Given the observed correlation among variables, addressing multicollinearity is imperative; this will be addressed in future research.

These findings affirm the feasibility of early-stage predictions and feedback regarding students' final exam scores, especially at the course's outset (the 1st and 2nd weeks), despite extant challenges.

Table 1. Prediction results

	(1) C2 score only	(2) C2 score, logs of 1st lesson	(3) C2 score, logs of 1st–2nd lessons
Scatter plot	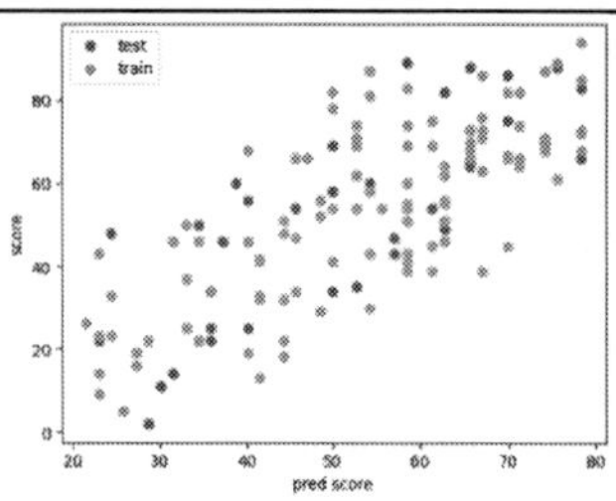	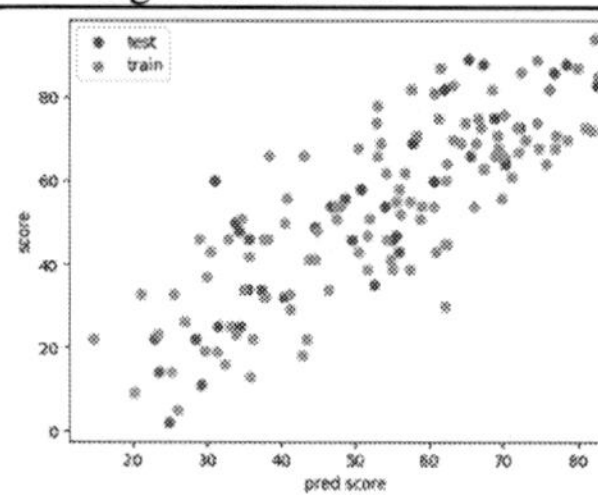	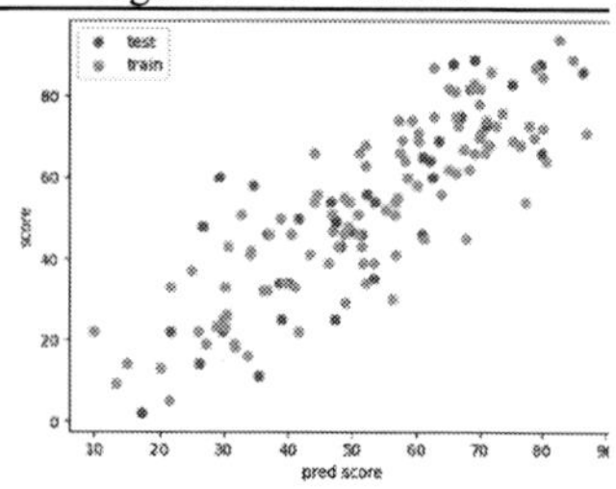
Training	MSE: 188.5 R^2: 0.561 Prob(F): 1.2e-20 Adj. R^2: 0.556	MSE: 151.9 R^2: 0.646 Prob(F): 3.0e-17 Adj. R^2: 0.605	MSE: 114.2 R^2: 0.734 Prob(F): 9.4e-17 Adj. R^2: 0.669
Test	MSE: 213.3 R^2: 0.592	MSE: 142.0 R^2: 0.731	MSE: 165.4 R^2: 0.684

Table 1. Prediction results (continued)

	(4) C2 score, logs of 1st–3rd lessons	(5) C2 score, logs of 1st–4th lessons	(6) C2 score, logs of 1st–5th lessons
Scatter plot	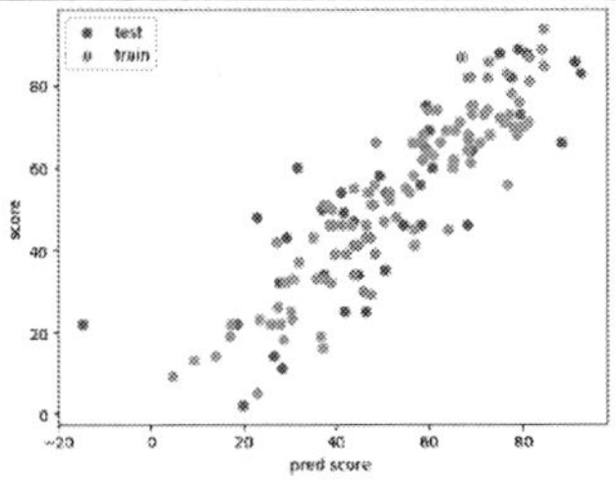	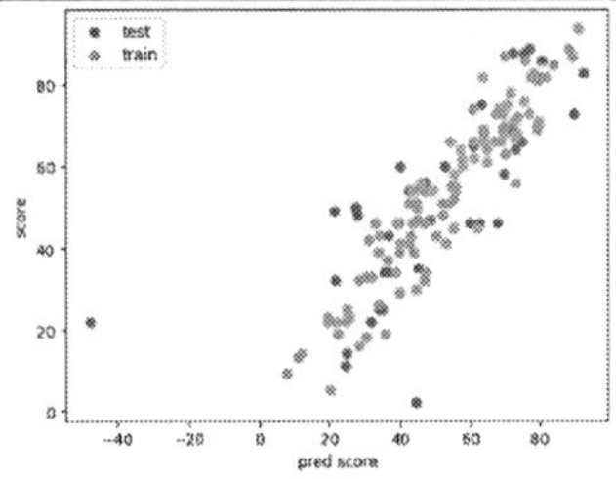	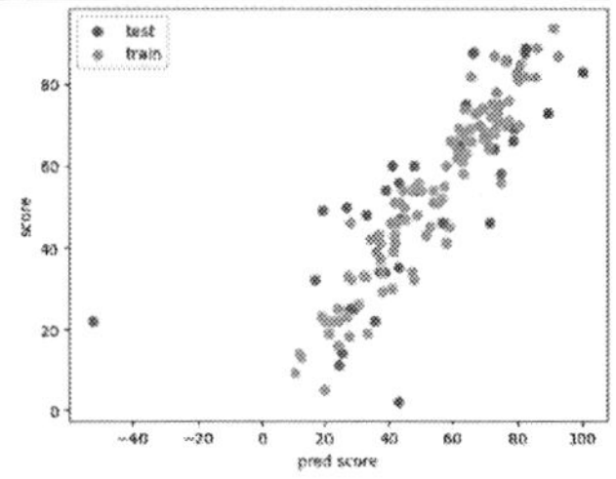
Training	MSE: 74.0 R^2: 0.828 Prob(F): 2.30e-18 Adj. R^2: 0.757	MSE: 52.4 R^2: 0.878 Prob(F): 7.8e-18 Adj. R^2: 0.802	MSE: 44.8 R^2: 0.896 Prob(F): 1.6e-14 Adj. R^2: 0.800
Test	MSE: 201.9 R^2: 0.615	MSE: 331.4 R^2: 0.367	MSE: 362.2 R^2: 0.309

	(7) C2 score, logs of 1st–6th lessons	(8) C2 score, logs of 1st–7th lessons
Scatter plot	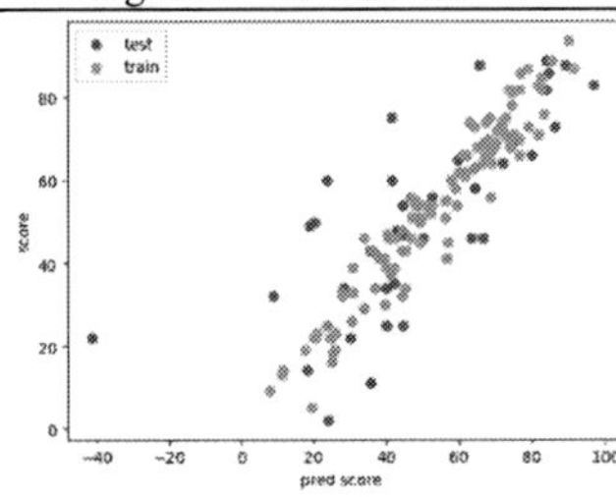	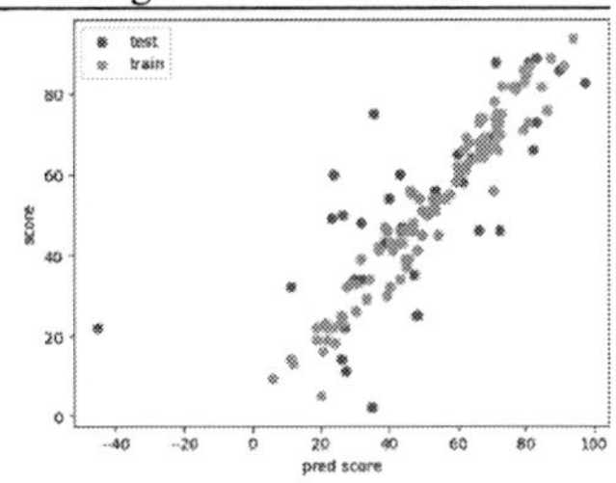
Training	MSE: 31.6 R^2: 0.926 Prob(F): 4.8e-13 Adj. R^2: 0.829	MSE: 24.4 R^2: 0.943 Prob(F): 3.2e-10 Adj. R^2: 0.830
Test	MSE: 357.2 R^2: 0.318	MSE: 395.5 R^2: 0.245

Table 2. Summary of model (2), which is based on the C2 score and the logs of the 1st class

	coef	std err	t	P > |t|	[0.025	0.975]
Const	53.4722	1.258	42.506	0	50.975	55.969
C2 score	12.7118	1.475	8.619	0	9.784	15.639
During class						
Time spent	1.1715	2.64	0.444	0.658	−4.069	6.412
Number of trials	−4.1953	2.613	−1.606	0.112	−9.382	0.991
Number of attempted problems	7.0018	3.086	2.269	0.025	0.877	13.127
Number of completed problems	−1.0812	3.01	−0.359	0.720	−7.057	4.895
Average completion time	0.8762	1.596	0.549	0.584	−2.292	4.044
During and after class						
Time taken	0.4645	3.882	0.120	0.905	−7.242	8.171
Number of trials	2.2258	2.705	0.823	0.413	−3.144	7.595
Number of tried problems	3.7181	5.040	0.738	0.462	−6.286	13.722
Number of completed problems	−5.2563	4.989	−1.054	0.295	−15.159	4.646
Average of completion time	−4.2947	3.852	−1.115	0.268	−11.94	3.351

3.4 Changes in the Predicted Scores of Students with the Same Initial Predictions

An initial low prediction based on the previous quarter's C2 scores could demotivate students or lead them to consider dropping the subject. To counter this potential discouragement, demonstrating that, even if the early-stage predicted score is low, significant improvement can be achieved through subsequent efforts is crucial.

To this end, Figure 2 displays the evolving predicted scores of seven students (A–G) who all started with an initial prediction of 50 points. Moreover, Table 3 highlights the number of problems students tackled during class—a significant determinant of the score. The numbers enclosed in parentheses in the table beneath Figure 2 represent actual scores, while column C2 displays scores predicted solely from C2's score (consistently 50 points). Columns 1 to 7 show predicted scores with the logs from each subsequent lesson incorporated. The average difference between the predicted and actual scores is 3.2 points. The sequence of predicted scores mirrors the order of actual scores, indicating a commendable predictive accuracy. Students A, B, E, and F are part of the training data from Section 3.3, while students B, D, and G are in the test dataset.

A comparison of the evolving predicted scores against the number of attempted problems (as depicted in Table 3) reveals that diligent effort tends to amplify the predicted score. Conversely, less effort is often accompanied by a decline. From these insights, alongside the predicted score, educators can offer targeted feedback, encouraging students to maintain their current momentum or suggesting that they tackle more problems during class. They might also advise seeking assistance from teachers or teaching assistants when required.

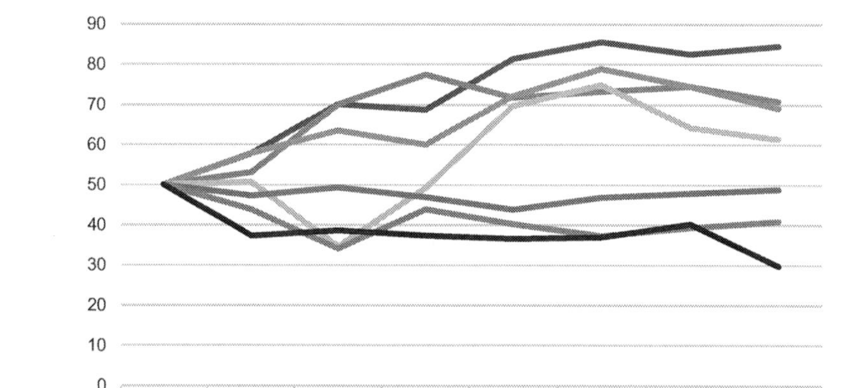

	C2	1	2	3	4	5	6	7
A (82)	50	57,7	70,1	68,7	81,4	85,6	82,6	84,5
B (78)	50	53	70	77,5	71,7	73,3	74,5	70,8
C (69)	50	57,8	63,5	60	72,2	78,9	74,5	69
D (58)	50	50,7	34,6	49,2	69,7	74,9	64,2	61,3
E (54)	50	47,3	49,3	47	43,8	46,8	47,9	48,8
F (41)	50	43,8	34,1	43,9	40,2	37,3	39,4	40,9
G (34)	50	37,3	38,7	37,4	36,6	37	40,2	29,7

Figure 2. Changes in the predicted scores of students with the same initial predictions

Table 3. Number of attempted problems during class

	1st class	2nd class	3rd class	4th class	5th class	6th class	7th class
A	8	6	6	5	8	7	6
B	3	6	6	6	6	6	6
C	8	7	6	5	8	7	6
D	5	0	8	7	6	7	0
E	4	5	5	5	5	6	5
F	0	0	5	4	0	6	7
G	1	5	2	5	5	6	6r

4. CONCLUSION

To utilize the programming exercise system's operation log for effective student feedback, we constructed and evaluated a multiple regression analysis model. We verified that a student's final score can be reasonably predicted from early course system logs. Furthermore, this prediction can be refreshed on a weekly basis based on the logs of each class; accordingly, pertinent feedback can be provided to each student. However, we noted an escalation in overfitting as the number of incorporated classes increased. We also deliberated on the potential for offering tailored advice aimed at enhancing the final scores of each student.

Moving forward, our intention is to consistently gather logs and reaffirm our findings through multiyear data analysis. We also plan to explore data from other courses, such as C Language Units II and IV, as well as Software Fundamentals. Our efforts will address the issue of multicollinearity and pinpoint strategies to improve the students' final scores, focusing on areas beyond in-class challenge frequency.

ACKNOWLEDGMENT

We are grateful to Professor Tsuyoshi Miyazaki, Lecturer Nozomi Nakakawaji, Lecturer Hidetoshi Okazaki, and other educators responsible for the C language class. We appreciate the invaluable feedback, bug reports, and enhancement suggestions provided by them and their students. This work was supported by JSPS KAKENHI Grant Number JP23K02747.

REFERENCES

Carter, A. et al. (2019). Leveraging the integrated development environment for learning analytics, The Cambridge Handbook of Computing Education Research. Cambridge Univ. Press, Cambridge, U.K. ch 23, pp. 679-706.

Kia, F. et al. (2020). How patterns of students dashboard use are related to their achievement and self-regulatory engagement, *Proceedings of LAK'20*, pp. 340-349.

Khulbe, M. et al. (2023). Mediating teacher professional learning with a learning analytics dashboard and training intervention, *Technology, Knowledge and Learning*, vol. 28, pp. 981-998.

Liu, E. et al. (2023). Early prediction of student performance in online programming courses. *Wang, N. et al (eds) Artificial Intelligence in Education*. Posters and Late Breaking Results, Workshops and Tutorials, Industry and Innovation Tracks, Practitioners, Doctoral Consortium and Blue Sky. AIED 2023. Communications in computer and information science, vol 1831. Springer, Cham.

Ohno, A. (2022). Evaluating the usefulness of C language learning support system as a learning analytics tool, *IIAI Information Engineering Express*, vol. 8, no. 1, pp. 1-12.

Quille, K. et al. (2019). CS1: How will they do? How can we help? A decade of research and practice, *Comput. Sci. Educ.*, vol. 29, nos. 2-3, pp. 254-282.

Raubenheimer, G. et al. (2021). Toward empirical analysis of pedagogical feedback in computer programming learning environments, *Proceedings of ACE'21*, pp. 189-195.

Satoh, A et al. (2022). Prototype of programming exercise support system able to visualize coding status, *Proceedings of 11th International Congress on Advanced Applied Informatics*, pp. 256-259.

Sedrakyan, G. et al. (2019). Guiding the choice of learning dashboard visualizations, *Linking dashboard design and data visualization concepts*, vol. 50, pp. 19-38.

Susnjak, T. et al. (2022). Learning analytics dashboard: A tool for providing actionable insights to learners, *International Journal of Educational Technology in Higher Education*, vol. 19, 12.

Sobral, S. et al. (2021). Predicting students performance in introductory programming courses: A literature review, *Proceedings of 15th International Technology, Education and Development Conference,* pp. 7402-7412.

Tanaka, T. et al. (2023a). Programming exercise system to ascertain students' coding status, *Proceedings of 11th International Conference on Information and Education Technology*, Fujisawa, Japan, pp. 204-209.

Tanaka, T. et al. (2023b). Preliminary analysis of programming exercise logs to provide effective feedback to students, *Proceedings of 12th International Congress on Advanced Applied Informatics*, Koriyama, Japan, 4 pages.

THE EFFECTS OF AGE AND LEARNING WITH EDUCATIONAL ROBOTIC DEVICES ON CHILDREN'S ALGORITHMIC THINKING

Charoula Angeli, Panayiota Diakou and Vaso Anastasiou
Department of Education, University of Cyprus
The Crosspoint Building
Corner of Kallipoleos and Hypatia 1
Nicosia, 1071, Cyprus

ABSTRACT

Educational Robotics is increasingly used in elementary-school classrooms to develop students' algorithmic thinking and programming skills. However, most research appears descriptive and lacks experimental evidence on the effects of teaching interventions using robotics to develop algorithmic thinking. Using the robots Dash and Dot, this study examined algorithmic thinking development in groups of children aged 6, 9, and 12. The results showed a statistically significant main effect between the age of students and algorithmic thinking skills and a statistically significant main effect between intervention and algorithmic thinking. In conclusion, the findings underscore the necessity of providing learners with structured, scaffolded activities tailored to their age to effectively nurture algorithmic thinking skills when engaging in Dash and Dot activities.

KEYWORDS

Algorithmic Thinking, Robotics, Dash and Dot, Young Children

1. INTRODUCTION

In an increasingly technology-driven job market, algorithmic thinking and programming skills are in high demand (Semeraro, Griffiths, & Cangelosi, 2023). Early exposure equips students with essential tools for future careers in STEM-related fields. Developing algorithmic thinking and programming skills in elementary education is thus becoming increasingly recognized as a crucial aspect of preparing students for the digital world they will navigate.

A promising area for developing algorithmic thinking is the rapidly developing field of Educational Robotics (ER). Multiple studies found that robotics activities facilitated the development of algorithmic skills in young learners in various formal and informal learning contexts (Author). Hence, ER is increasingly used in primary classrooms to create interactive and engaging learning environments for developing algorithmic thinking in children (Su & Yang, 2023). Nonetheless, while the existing body of research includes a large number of descriptive studies reporting on children's interactions with robots (Merino-Armero et al., 2022), the field lacks systematic evidence on the experimental design and effects of interventions on the teaching of algorithmic thinking considering learners' age.

To this end, the study sought to examine the development of algorithmic thinking skills of 146 primary-school children aged 6, 9, and 12 during problem-solving activities with the robotic devices Dash and Dot within the context of two teaching interventions and a control group. Accordingly, the research sought to answer the following questions:

1. Given their initial performance on the pretest, did teaching intervention differentially affect children's performance on algorithmic thinking tasks?

2. Given their initial performance on the pretest, did age differentially affect children's performance on algorithmic thinking tasks?

3. Given the initial performance on the pretest, was there an interaction effect between teaching intervention and age on children's performance on algorithmic thinking tasks?

2. THEORETICAL FRAMEWORK

Algorithmic thinking involves breaking down complex problems into smaller, manageable steps (decomposition), designing step-by-step procedures to accomplish a task (algorithms), and debugging (recognition and correction of errors) (Sengupta et al., 2013). Algorithmic thinking also involves iterative problem-solving, where individuals test and refine their algorithms based on feedback and outcomes (Sengupta et al., 2013). In computer science, algorithmic thinking is fundamental to programming and computational problem-solving.

The framework for teaching algorithmic thinking leverages educational robots to enhance students' computational thinking skills and problem-solving abilities. This approach involves engaging students in hands-on activities where they program the robot to perform specific tasks and follow sequences of actions. This practical approach allows students to see the direct impact of their code on the robot's behavior, fostering a deeper understanding of algorithmic thinking (Hsu et al., 2019). Providing scaffolding and differentiated instruction is crucial in supporting students' learning.

In this study, the authors examined the effects of two teaching interventions with different types of scaffolds to develop elementary-school students' algorithmic thinking skills. Scaffolds included programming Dash with the help of Dot and Blockly, a programming application, and embodied learning activities facilitated by the researcher and Dot to teach about algorithmic thinking skills by performing bodily movements.

3. METHOD

3.1 Participants

One hundred forty-six participants aged 6, 9, and 12 participated in this study. The participants were recruited from different private and public schools in rural and urban areas in a European country. The participants' parents provided consent forms before their children participated in the research, and permission for the research was granted. All the participants had no previous experience with programming nor learning with the robots Dash and Dot.

3.2 Teaching Interventions

Each age group was randomly assigned into two intervention groups and a control group. Children participated in a 3 (age 6, 9, 12) X 3 (groups Dash and Dot, Dot and Researcher, Control) research design study. Group A (GA) and Group B (GB) formed the experimental groups, and Group C formed the control group (CC). The two teaching interventions involved problem-solving tasks by using robots. The CC had to execute the same tasks without receiving any teaching intervention. Each child worked individually in all phases of the research. In GA, children interacted with Dash and Dot and were guided by Dot on how to program Dash, using the Blockly application, to make Dash execute a task. In GB, children followed instructions given by Dot and interacted with the researcher by performing various bodily movements to form algorithms. On the contrary, the CC children had to explore Dash and Dot alone in a free-style play activity.

3.3 Research Materials

GA used Dash and Dot, the iPad applications *Go* and *Blockly*, and a city-mat for Dash to execute the tasks. GB children only had the mat and Dot at their disposal. In this group, the researchers used printed arrow cards to explain the steps in writing an algorithm. The students in the CC used Dash and Dot in an exploratory free-play fashion to discover their functions. The researcher used specific scripts for all phases to ensure consistent data collection and kept a researcher diary.

3.4 Dash and Dot Robots

Dash and Dot, shown in Figure 1, are two different robots with different features. Dot is a smaller robotic device with a spherical blue shape, one eye and two ears. Dot can speak, change eye and ears color, make noises, and reproduce recordings through programming using *the Go* application. Dash is larger than Dot, has a blue color, and has the shape of four spherical parts - three parts on the bottom and one part on the top. The robot has one eye and two ears on its head, which can change colors through programming. Dash can be programmed using the *Blockly* application.

Figure 1. Dash and Dot

3.5 The Mat and Problem-Solving Tasks

Students in all three groups solved the same tasks. All tasks involved using a floor mat, visually representing a city with various locations such as a school, post office, bank, department store, playground, and residences. Students had to figure out the commands of a path to move from one location to another. Participants in the Dash and Dot group followed instructions from Dot to program Dash to move from one location to another. Students in the Dot group used Dot as a buddy to instruct them to walk using their bodies on the mat and move from one location to another. Finally, students in the control group followed written instructions on a script to move on the mat from one location to another in a free-style play activity.

3.6 Instruments

All participants completed a pretest before the interventions and a posttest at the end of the study. The time allowed to complete the test on each occasion was 30-min. The pretest and the posttest were the same and consisted of four sections on aspects of algorithmic thinking. Each part had two different problem-solving subtasks. The first part evaluated sequencing, the second part evaluated decomposition, the third part focused on the skill of debugging and the fourth part on the skill of repetition (control flow).

3.7 Research Procedures

Data collection for the experimental groups was completed in three phases: A, B, and C. The control group completed only phases A and C. Phase A lasted for 20 minutes and was an exploration phase for all children to become familiar with the materials and the robots. Phase B was the intervention phase for GA and GB and lasted for 40 minutes. GA children were instructed by Dot how to use the application *Blockly* to write and code algorithms so that Dash can execute a task. On the contrary, GB children followed instructions by Dot and the researcher and used bodily movements by stepping and moving on the mat to simulate the algorithm and used printed arrow cards to visualize the steps of the algorithm. Finally, phase C was the assessment phase for all groups (30 minutes). Children were asked to write the steps of an algorithm or show the steps of the algorithm using the printed cards. For each phase, the researcher recorded the child's number of efforts to develop the correct algorithm and the extent to which the child used the skills of decomposition and debugging.

4. RESULTS

The researchers developed the rubric shown in Table 1 to assess participants' algorithmic thinking. The rubric evaluated the solutions participants proposed for each problem-solving task, considering various factors such as the number of failing attempts, decomposition of commands, and debugging. Analytically, children's algorithmic thinking was assessed based on the correctness of their sequences of instructions expressed in *Blockly* command language (i.e., *MOVE FORWARD, MOVE BACKWARD, TURN LEFT, TURN RIGHT, REPEAT)* and other symbolic systems they used to express the steps of an algorithm. Table 1 shows the rubric that emerged from the inductive data analysis.

Table 1. Algorithmic thinking rubric

Code	Description	Points received
1	Success without decomposition from first attempt	21
2	Success with decomposition into two from first attempt	20
3	Success with decomposition into three from first attempt	19
4	Success with decomposition into four from first attempt	18
5	Success without decomposition from second attempt	17
6	Success with decomposition into two from second attempt	16
7	Success with decomposition into three from second attempt	15
8	Success with decomposition into four from second attempt	14
9	Success without decomposition from third attempt	13
10	Success with decomposition into two from third attempt	12
11	Success with decomposition into three from third attempt	11
12	Success with decomposition into four from third attempt	10
13	Success without decomposition from fourth attempt	9
14	Success with decomposition into two from fourth attempt	8
15	Success with decomposition into three from fourth attempt	7
16	Success without decomposition from fifth attempt	6
17	Success with decomposition into two from fifth attempt	5
18	Success with decomposition into four from fifth attempt	4
19	Success with decomposition into three from sixth attempt	3
20	Success without decomposition from seventh attempt	2
21	Success with decomposition into two from seventh attempt	1

Table 2 shows descriptive statistics for students' scores on the pretest, posttest, and the tasks in the third phase of the research. As shown in Table 2, 12-year-old students' scores were higher than all other scores, whereas 6-year-old students' scores were the lowest. Also, as shown in Table 2, students in the Dash and Dot group outperformed all other groups.

Table 2. Descriptive statistics for pretest, posttest and performance in Phase 3

	Intervention											
	Dash and Dot			*Dot and Researcher*			*Control*			*Total*		
	Pretest											
Age	*Mean*	*SD*	*n*	*Mean*	*SD*	*n*	*Mean*	*SD*	*n*	*Mean*	*SD*	*n*
6 years	9.40	3.16	24	8.91	3.12	28	8.33	3.28	18	8.93	3.15	70
9 years	11.75	3.35	16	10.75	2.83	14	10.47	3.91	15	11.01	3.37	45
12 years	11.70	3.22	10	10.06	2.21	9	12.83	2.32	12	11.66	2.78	31
Total	10.61	3.38	50	9.62	2.97	51	10.24	3.70	45	10.15	3.35	146
	Posttest											
Age	*Mean*	*SD*	*n*	*Mean*	*SD*	*n*	*Mean*	*SD*	*n*	*Mean*	*SD*	*n*
6 years	11.02	3.34	24	9.96	3.48	28	9.51	4.01	18	10.21	3.58	70
9 years	13.97	2.26	16	12.93	2.32	14	12.60	3.09	15	13.19	2.60	45
12 years	14.75	1.51	10	12.78	2.39	9	13.83	1.99	12	13.82	2.07	31
Total	12.71	3.16	50	11.27	3.31	51	11.69	3.70	45	11.89	3.42	146
	Phase 3 performance											
Age	*Mean*	*SD*	*n*	*Mean*	*SD*	*n*	*Mean*	*SD*	*n*	*Mean*	*SD*	*n*
6 years	332.67	45.79	24	311.96	62.51	28	286.72	72.69	18	312.57	62.01	70
9 years	360.75	24.19	16	368.71	31.33	14	315.33	64.22	15	348.09	48.59	45
12 years	363.00	38.91	10	343.78	28.55	9	335.25	37.77	12	346.68	36.58	31
Total	347.72	40.69	50	333.16	55.87	51	309.20	64.15	45	330.76	55.95	146

A MANCOVA was then conducted to examine whether there were statistically significant differences in the phase 3 performance and scores on the posttest between the three age groups across all three research groups taking into consideration the scores on the pretest. The results showed that performance on the pretest was a statistically significant covariate for both phase 3 performance ($F(1, 146) = 10.47$, $p<.05$) and posttest scores ($F(1, 146) = 117.46$, $p<.05$). The results also revealed statistically significant differences between the three age groups for both phase 3 performance ($F(2,146) = 4{,}81$, $p<.05$), and posttest scores ($F(2, 146) = 9.58$, $p<.05$). In regards to the age differences on phase 3 performance, 12-year-old-students, and 9-year-old-students outperformed 6-year-old-students. Regarding statistically significant differences in the posttest performance, the same results were observed, namely that 12-year-old students and 9-year-old students outperformed 6-year-old students.

The results also revealed statistically significant differences between the two interventions and the control group for both phase 3 performance ($F(2,146) = 7,40$, $p<.05$) and posttest scores ($F(2, 146) = 2.31$, $p<.05$). Specifically, the Dash and Dot group outperformed all other groups, and the Dot and Researcher group outperformed the control group.

5. DISCUSSION

The study's findings demonstrated statistically significant main effects between the age of students, intervention, and algorithmic thinking. The findings concur with recent research on robotics activities with Dash and Dot that reported on the importance of structured, scaffolded activities over free play in fostering algorithmic thinking skills. For example, a study by Mabie, McGill, and Huerta (2023) found that learners engaged in structured, scaffolded activities with Dash and Dot showed notable improvements in algorithmic thinking abilities. In contrast, learners participating in free-play activities demonstrated limited progress in algorithmic thinking. This finding is also consistent with a study by De Santo et al. (2022), which emphasized the significance of scaffolded interventions in enhancing algorithmic thinking skills in robotics.

Additionally, age has been identified as a critical factor influencing the development of algorithmic thinking skills with Dash and Dot. The study's findings align with the research findings reported by Kanaki and Kalogiannakis (2022), revealing that older learners showed higher levels of algorithmic thinking proficiency as their cognitive capabilities and problem-solving strategies matured with age.

In conclusion, these findings underscore the necessity of providing learners with structured, scaffolded activities tailored to their age to effectively nurture algorithmic thinking skills when engaging with robotics activities involving Dash and Dot. Educators can utilize these findings to design age-appropriate curricula and instructional strategies, promoting meaningful learning experiences that empower students in their technological journey.

6. CONCLUSION

In the dynamic interplay between technology and education, robots like Dash and Dot offer a glimpse into the future of learning. However, to harness their full potential, a structured approach is crucial. Scaffolded interventions, tailored to children's needs and paced to their learning trajectories, ensure that algorithmic thinking isn't just a buzzword but a tangible skill that they internalize and carry forward. In this blend of technology, pedagogy, and structured support, lies the promise of an empowered generation, ready to navigate and shape the digital landscapes of the future.

REFERENCES

De Santo, A., Farah, J. C., Martínez, M. L., Moro, A., Bergram, K., Purohit, A. K., ... & Holzer, A. (2022). Promoting Computational Thinking Skills in Non-Computer-Science Students: Gamifying Computational Notebooks to Increase Student Engagement. *IEEE Transactions on Learning Technologies*, *15*(3), 392-405.

Hsu, Y. C., Irie, N. R., & Ching, Y. H. (2019). Computational thinking educational policy initiatives (CTEPI) across the globe. *TechTrends*, *63*, 260-270.

Kanaki, K., & Kalogiannakis, M. (2022). Assessing algorithmic thinking skills in relation to age in early childhood STEM education. *Education Sciences*, *12*(6), 380.

Mabie, A. K., McGill, M., & Huerta, B. (2023, June). A systematic literature review examining the impacts of integrating Computer Science in K-5 settings. In *2023 ASEE Annual Conference & Exposition*.

Merino-Armero, J. M., González-Calero, J. A., & Cozar-Gutierrez, R. (2022). Computational thinking in K-12 education. An insight through meta-analysis. *Journal of Research on Technology in Education*, *54*(3), 410-437.

Semeraro, F., Griffiths, A., & Cangelosi, A. (2023). Human–robot collaboration and machine learning: A systematic review of recent research. *Robotics and Computer-Integrated Manufacturing*, *79*, 102432.

Sengupta, P., Kinnebrew, J. S., Basu, S., Biswas, G., & Clark, D. (2013). Integrating computational thinking with K-12 science education using agent-based computation: A theoretical framework. *Education and Information Technologies*, *18*, 351-380.

Su, J., & Yang, W. (2023). A systematic review of integrating computational thinking in early childhood education. *Computers and Education Open*, 100122.

INTEGRATING LARGE LANGUAGE MODELS IN ART AND DESIGN EDUCATION

Alberto Giretti[1], Dilan Durmus[1], Massimo Vaccarini[1], Matteo Zambelli[2], Andrea Guidi[3] and Franco Ripa di Meana[4]

[1]*Università Politecnica delle Marche, Via Brecce Bianche, 60131 Ancona, Italy*

[2]*Università degli Studi di Firenze – Dipartimento di Architettura – DiDA, Via della Mattonaia, 8, 50121 Firenze, Italy*

[3]*Queen Mary University of London - Centre for Digital Music - Mile End Road E1 4NS London, UK*

[4]*Academy of Fine Arts, Via di Ripetta, 222 – 00186 Roma, Italy*

ABSTRACT

This paper provides a possible strategy for integrating large language artificial intelligence models (LLMs) in supporting students' education in artistic or design activities. We outline the methodological foundations concerning the integration of CHATGPT LLM in the educational approach aimed at enhancing artistic conception and design ideation. We also present the knowledge and system architecture for integrating LLM in the °'°Kobi system. Finally, this paper discusses some relevant aspects concerning the system's application in a real educational context and briefly reports its preliminary assessment.

KEYWORDS

Large Language Models, Art Education, Design Education, Creativity, Associative Thinking

1. INTRODUCTION

Artificial Intelligence (AI) has the potential to address some of the biggest challenges in education today, innovate teaching and learning practices. However, rapid technological developments inevitably bring multiple risks and challenges, which have so far outpaced policy debates and regulatory frameworks (UNESCO 2019). Generative AI models for natural language have created a new set of opportunities in the realm of creativity (Berns & Colton, 2020; Bown, 2012; Dwivedi et al., 2023; Hughes et al., 2021; Zhang et al., 2018).

Large language models (LLMs) are AI applications that are trained on enormous amounts of textual data. They are generative mathematical models of the statistical distribution of tokens found in the huge corpus of human-generated text, where tokens include words, graphemes, single letters and punctuation (Shanahan, 2023; Tunstall et al., 2022). LLMs such as BERT and GPT are becoming more common as a support in idea generation tasks due to their ease of use and strong generative capabilities, as they offer impressive abilities to answer questions, write perfectly contextualized or imaginative stories and even sustain a conversation (Raiyyan, 2023). The underlying technology is key to further innovation, and despite critical views and even restrictions in communities and regions, it is beyond dispute that LLMs will endure (Davenport & Mittal, 2022; Papp, 2023).

LLMs capabilities have both potential benefits and negative influences in educational applications from the perspective of students and teachers. There is no doubt that students' unstructured use of AI's generative capabilities through trivial copy-and-paste operations hinders the development of autonomous critical capacities. However, to the extent that generative capacities can be integrated within a well-defined didactic experience, they can serve as a tool for expanding imaginative capacities, thus amplifying the power of the creative practice. From the teachers' point of view, the rapidity of these technological advances and the increasing complexity of the pedagogical problems they raise call for reflection on the development of innovative solutions that can integrate these technologies into a well-funded pedagogical background (Alam, 2021; Liang et al., 2021).

In this article, we illustrate an initial attempt of integrating an LLM in the pedagogical framework for design and art education provided by the °’°Kobi system, a knowledge-based system aimed at eliciting and sharing knowledge in communities of practice, and at fostering reflective and divergent thinking in creative processes (Giretti, 2022). We will illustrate preliminary experiences conducted in two design courses at the University of Florence, and a directing course at the Academy of Fine Arts in Rome, where the °'°Kobi system, was introduced as an aid to collaborative ideation processes. On that basis, the article discusses the possibilities for the integration of LLM into the °’°Kobi educational framework.

Section 2 will briefly describe the relevant educational context and the role of the °'°Kobi system. Section 3 will offer a more abstract analysis of the knowledge cycle supported by the system, and Section 4 will discuss the integration of LLMs' language skills in that context. Section 5 will describe some preliminary experiments, and section 6 will discuss summarize the results and limitations briefly illustrate future developments.

2. THE °’°KOBI SYSTEM IN ART AND DESIGN EDUCATION

°’°Kobi is a knowledge-based system aimed at fostering creative thinking throughout reflection, associative thinking, and multiculturality as the key dimensions to be supported in creative education, to complement and enhance the apprenticeship practice. A thorough description of the °’°Kobi framework can be found in (Giretti, 2022). The main °’°Kobi features are:

a) *Supporting reflective thinking* - by means of Knowledge Mapping interfaces that foster the creation of new critical and interpretative structures through abstract conceptualization and reflective observation, as well as reformulation and reinterpretation of contents (Wexler, 2001).

b) *Supporting associative thinking* - by implementing large knowledge domains, arranged as shallow relational structures, encompassing multiple semantic contexts. °'°Kobi uses both computational linguistics principles (Mitkov, 2022) and gestalt principles (Köhler, 1967) to establish semantic associations among texts or images belonging to the same or different semantic fields (Speer et al., 2017; Mednick, 1962).

c) *Implementing the multicultural dimension* - by developing an ecosystem that integrates multidisciplinary contents based on well-defined semantics from the different disciplines and linguistic domains. °’°Kobi generates what is commonly called a knowledge ecosystem (Szoniecky, 2018).

So far °’°Kobi has been used as a collaborative design tool in two design methods courses at University of Florence and in one Direction course at the Fine art Academy of Rome. Different courses reflect the various teaching context, saying educational objectives, background knowledge, teaching styles, the cultural dimensions of the students, etc. Students and teachers used the Miro© frontend as a shared whiteboard to annotate their work in knowledge maps using different strategies, either following teachers’ recommendations (e.g., brainstorming, the six hats method, the issue-concept-form) or in a free style (Figure 1 left). At present, the class has produced an ecosystem with more than 8,000 nodes representing a consistent core of shared knowledge to which the experiences produced by subsequent classes in the coming years will be added (Figure 1 right).

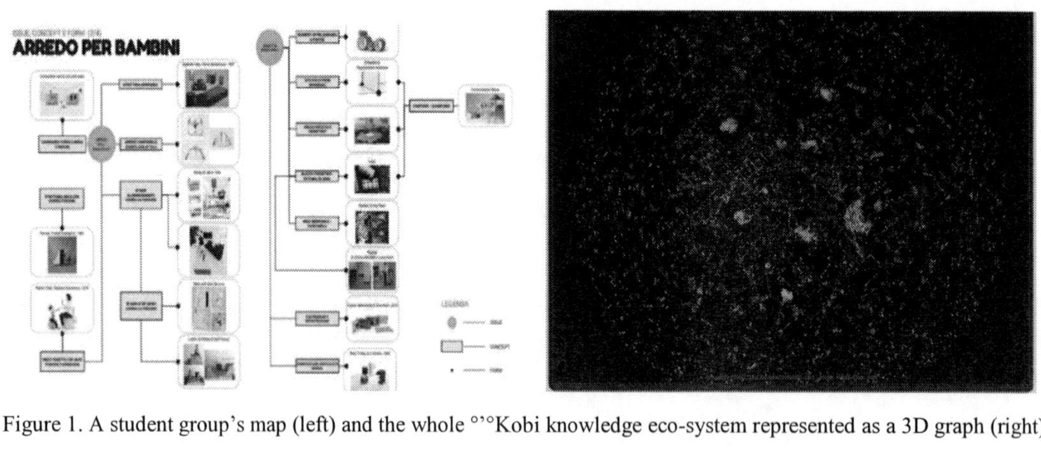

Figure 1. A student group’s map (left) and the whole °’°Kobi knowledge eco-system represented as a 3D graph (right)

In °'°Kobi, contents of different users are semantically related according to the principles discussed above, thus generating a knowledge eco-system that has multiple educational roles and relevance. First, each knowledge map naturally generates a linguistic domain or semantic field because it naturally reflects the terminology and the associations proper to the topic at hand. Syntactic associations between terms belonging to different linguistic domains tend to generate a polysemous or sometimes metaphorical shifts that are extremely relevant for creative thinking (Mednick, 1962). Our experience show that knowledge maps developed within a class share a rather well-defined semantic domain. We mean that the terminological field, the concepts, and their relationships are in great part shared among different student groups belonging to the same class. On the contrary, semantic relations that qualify shared words among different classes are significantly diverse (Figure 2).

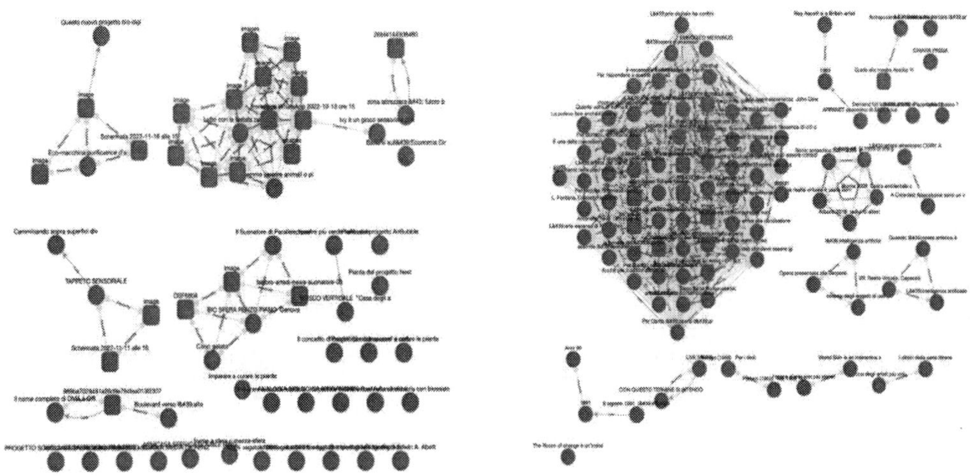

Figure 2. The semantic domain of the word *'plane'* in a design class (left) and in a directing class (right)

3. THE KNOWLEDGE CYLCES IN THE °'°KOBI SYSTEM

°'°Kobi can be used as a supporting tool in any experiential learning activity (Morris, 2020) seeking to emphasize reflective observation and abstract conceptualization within the concrete experience and the active experimentation of the atelier practice (Giretti, 2022). Knowledge is therefore the principal dimension of °'°Kobi and will the main dimension of the LLM integration as well. Hence, to introduce the strategies for integrating LLM into °'°Kobi it is necessary to specify the main knowledge cycles that are supported by °'°Kobi in the educational contexts in which it is used. Figure 3 shows the main knowledge cycles of the °'°Kobi system.

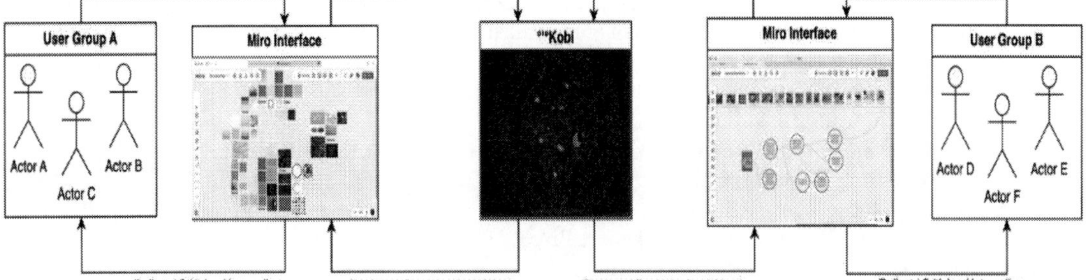

Figure 3. °'°Kobi main knowledge cycles – different user groups share their work through the °'°Kobi ecosystem

The first knowledge cycle (Externalize/Visualize) <=> (Reflect/Criticize/Internalize) is typical of a knowledge mapping system such as Miro© and has been extensively studied as a means of amplifying the learner's critical capabilities (Schön, 1983). The second cycle (Analyse/Memorize/Share) <=> (Retrieve/Contextualise/Adapt) can be traced back, if preferred, to a Case Based Reasoning protocol (CBR) (Kolodner, 2014). However, in °'°Kobi it is conducted at the level of loosely structured, variable-grain knowledge fragments, rather than in well-structured fixed grain knowledge structures, as in CBR.

Retrieving contents form the web is indeed a diffuse practice among students of design and art courses to get inspiration for their work. The quality that distinguishes °'°Kobi from a simple web search is the consistency of semantic context that is maintained during the search. A search in °'°Kobi always produces a semantic context, similarly to what is shown in figure 2. Therefore, the fragments of knowledge provided to the student have an intrinsic semantic consistency and implicitly underlie a critical profile. Thus, the large volume of multimedia material available and its semantic arrangement produces a semantic focus that cannot be achieved with traditional web search engines. On the other hand, °'°Kobi also supports divergent thinking by expanding the semantic context during research. In this way °'°Kobi broadens the search domain by including semantic fields that are only terminologically related to the student's current focus, so that possibly divergent semantic structures are brought to attention. Again, this is a more sophisticate approach to divergent thinking than the naive divergence obtained as a side effect of the juxtaposition of disparate information in web searches.

4. EXPANDING THE REFLECTION CYCLE THROUGH LLM

The first (reflection) knowledge cycle in °'°Kobi visually arranges project clues and its main contents. This cycle indirectly generates embryonic conceptual structures that are then analyzed and encoded in °'°Kobi's knowledge base. °'°Kobi primarily aim is, in fact, to capture the embryonic knowledge structures generated as a side effect of the reflection cycle. These structures generally lack linguistic coherency and a perfectly clear semantics. In other words, they are mostly unfinished because they are part of an on-going process. In that sense they are embryonic, because their relations are not perfectly qualified.

We believe that LLMs are a key technology in the exploration and in the qualification of these semantic structures. The impressive linguistic proficiency displayed by LLM systems underlies an equally large semantic base that is implicit in the huge sets of neural weights of their hidden layers. However, the LLMs implicit knowledge can be made explicit each time through well-defined dialogic interactions. Hence, the idea is that, if the interactions are based on the current semantic context the student is involved in, perfect synergies can be implemented by simply triggering the necessary generative or analytical processes in the LLM through appropriate questions. This is essentially what we have pursued.

The LLM has been used to implement two further AI based knowledge cycles in °'°Kobi (Figure 4):

- *Expansion*: given a set of concepts, the process of expansion generates a paraphrase of the set of concepts. This paraphrase can be objective, that is, aimed at preserving as much as possible the initial conceptual context, or imaginative, that is, aimed at generating unlikely connections. Expansion uses the text generation function of LLMs.
- *Conceptualization*: give an extended text, conceptualization lists and defines the concepts underlying the text. This function uses a complex mix of summarization capabilities of LLMs.
- As mentioned, using LLMs with Text2Text generation function, the activation of both functions is solved by asking appropriate questions (Huggingface, 2023). Figure 4 shows how °'°Kobi knowledge cycles have been enriched using LLM linguistic capabilities.
- *Conceptualization* is used to make explicit the conceptualization of long texts (usually contained in pdf documents) so that each document can contribute to the associative exploration of the knowledge eco-system in a more consistent and rich way. In fact, each document is preprocessed and divided in paragraphs. Then each paragraph is conceptualized. The set of concepts are finally memorized in the knowledge eco-system and linked to the document.

- On the other side, *Expansion* is the process of enriching the associations of concepts that are encountered in an explorative step. Expanding a concept structure means asking the LLM to generate objective or fictional text and importing it as reflection material in the working space (i.e. Miro interface). This material then provides seeds for further steps.

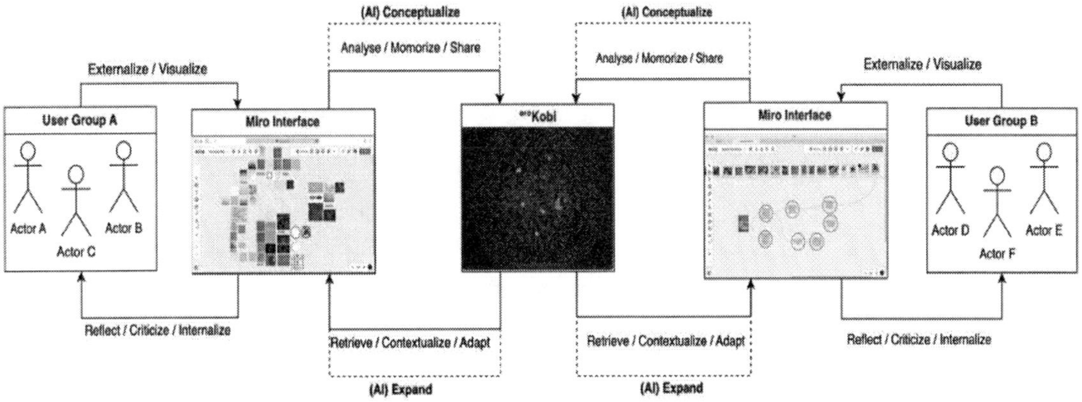

Figure 4. °'°Kobi AI enriched knowledge cycle – AI provides conceptualization of long texts as well as explanation of concept clusters or ideation based on a well-defined semantic context

All in all, °'°Kobi acts as a semantic broker between the students and the LLMs, with the goal of managing students' ideational journeys by exploring semantic pathways through structures of meaning that are retrieved, expanded or newly generated on demand during the creative process.

5. AN EXAMPLE

To corroborate what was discussed in the previous section, we will illustrate some exploration steps in the °'°Kobi system using the knowledge base provided by the students in the courses.

Table 1 shows the transcript of the interaction between a student and the °'°Kobi system that triggers the expansion and conceptualization processes based on the functionality of the LLM. The first step of interaction is through Kobi's search engine, which retrieves one or more semantic contexts, depending on the selected search scope. Figure 2 shows a graphical display of the two semantic contexts retrieved from the search using the word 'plane'. The student can expand the contexts retrieved by search engine using the LMM. In that case, the textual nodes of the contexts are pre-processed to obtain a set of tokens to be used for querying the LLM. The first step (right column in Table 1 first row) shows a subset of the generated tokens. The student then selects some tokens and uses a standardized question that triggers a textual expansion process (step 2 in table 1). The answer produced by the LLM consists of an articulated text that implicitly contains many new concepts. The student can then ask the LLM to succinctly enucleate the concepts in the text, again through a standard question form (step 3 in table 1). The answer, as shown in the right column, contains a much more explicit conceptual structure. Finally, the student can interact with the LLM in free form, asking for further insights (step 4 in table 1). The °Kobi system tracks all interactions and, if requested, stores the exploratory path in its knowledge ecosystem.

Table 1. The transcript of a user interaction that engages AI functionalities and generates new conceptual structures

n	Step	Concept/Question	Answer
1	(°'°) Search	plane	- **Biosphere** RENZO PIANO Genoa - Normal operation we need to move from the empirical plane - The Seattle Central Library - In the Jussieu Library, the technique used by OMA is based on horizontal rings - OMA reconfigures the typical layout of libraries by giving them new vertical surfaces - The sections of each floor are manipulated - The Jussieu Library - Embassy of the Netherlands - A city with urban elements - **New urbanised public space** - Vertical that are manipulated - Wood with upper levels - Connect with those above - **Generative processes** …
2	(AI) Expand	Explore the relations among the following concepts: **biosphere**, **generative processes** and **new urbanized public space**.	The biosphere, generative processes, and new urbanized public spaces are interconnected concepts that relate to environmental systems, societal development, and urban design. Here's an exploration of their relationships: 1. **Biosphere:** The biosphere refers to the part of the Earth's surface and atmosphere where living organisms exist. It encompasses all ecosystems and includes interactions between organisms and their physical environment. The biosphere plays a crucial role in sustaining life on Earth, providing essential resources, regulating climate, and maintaining ecological balance. 2. **Generative processes:** Generative processes refer to the natural or human-driven mechanisms that create or generate something new. In the context of the biosphere, generative processes can include biological evolution, natural selection, ecological succession, and ecosystem dynamics. These processes drive the diversity and adaptation of organisms, shaping the functioning of ecosystems and the overall biosphere. 3. **New urbanized public space:** New urbanized public spaces are areas within urban environments that are specifically designed for public use and recreation. They can take various forms, such as parks, plazas, pedestrian zones, waterfront promenades, or green roofs. These spaces contribute to the quality of urban life, providing opportunities for social interaction, leisure activities, and access to nature. Now, let's explore the relations among these concepts: • **Biosphere and generative processes:** The biosphere is shaped by generative processes that operate on various scales and timeframes. Natural selection and evolutionary processes drive the adaptation and diversification of species within ecosystems. Ecological succession allows for the development and transformation of ecosystems over time. These generative processes are fundamental to the functioning and resilience of the biosphere, maintaining its biodiversity and ecological balance. • **Generative processes and new urbanized public space:** Generative processes can also be applied to the creation and development of new urbanized public spaces. Designers and urban planners use generative processes to shape these

			spaces, considering factors such as community needs, environmental sustainability, and the integration of natural elements. By utilizing generative processes in the design process, new urbanized public spaces can be dynamic, adaptable, and responsive to the evolving needs of the urban environment and its inhabitants. • **Biosphere and new urbanized public space:** New urbanized public spaces have the potential to contribute to the preservation and enhancement of the biosphere. Thoughtful design and management can integrate ecological principles and sustainable practices into these spaces. For example, incorporating green infrastructure, such as trees, green walls, or rain gardens, can provide ecosystem services like air purification, stormwater management, and wildlife habitat. Additionally, creating accessible green spaces in urban areas can help improve human well-being, promote physical and mental health, and foster a sense of connection to the natural world. In summary, the biosphere, generative processes, and new urbanized public spaces are interconnected through their influence on ecological systems, societal development, and urban design. Understanding and considering these relationships can lead to the creation of sustainable, vibrant, and inclusive urban environments that support both human and environmental well-being.
3	(AI) Conceptualize	Find the main concepts of the text above.	The main concepts of the text above are: 1. Biosphere 2. Generative processes 3. New urbanized public space
4	(AI) Expand	Can you suggest architects that used the above concepts as design clues?	1. **Ken Yeang:** Ken Yeang is an architect known for his innovative approach to ecological design and bioclimatic architecture. His designs often incorporate principles of the biosphere by integrating greenery, natural ventilation, and energy-efficient strategies into buildings. Yeang's projects aim to create sustainable urban environments that harmonize with the natural ecosystem. 2. **Stefano Boeri:** Stefano Boeri is an Italian architect known for his work on vertical forests and urban reforestation. His projects, such as the Bosco Verticale in Milan and the Vertical Forest in Nanjing, China, integrate extensive greenery into high-rise buildings. Boeri's designs promote biodiversity, air purification, and the creation of new urban habitats, emphasizing the importance of the biosphere within urban contexts. 3. **Bjarke Ingels:** Bjarke Ingels is a Danish architect renowned for his innovative and sustainable approach to urban design. His firm, BIG (Bjarke Ingels Group), has developed projects that emphasize generative processes and adaptability. For example, the Amager Bakke waste-to-energy plant in Copenhagen incorporates a ski slope and a climbing wall, transforming a functional infrastructure into a dynamic public space that generates energy while offering recreational opportunities. 4. **Jan Gehl:** Jan Gehl is a Danish architect and urban planner known for his influential work on creating people-oriented, pedestrian-friendly urban spaces. His approach emphasizes the importance of designing cities for human scale, social interaction, and public life. Gehl's designs prioritize the creation of new urbanized public spaces that promote

<table>
<tr><td></td><td></td><td></td><td>walkability, connectivity, and livability, considering the needs and behaviors of people within the urban environment.
These architects have explored and implemented innovative design approaches that align with the concepts of the biosphere, generative processes, and new urbanized public spaces, pushing the boundaries of sustainable and human-centric architecture.</td></tr>
<tr><td>5</td><td>(°'°) Memorize / Share

A new conceptual structure is generated in the Kobi knowledge ecosystem (solid lines)</td><td></td><td>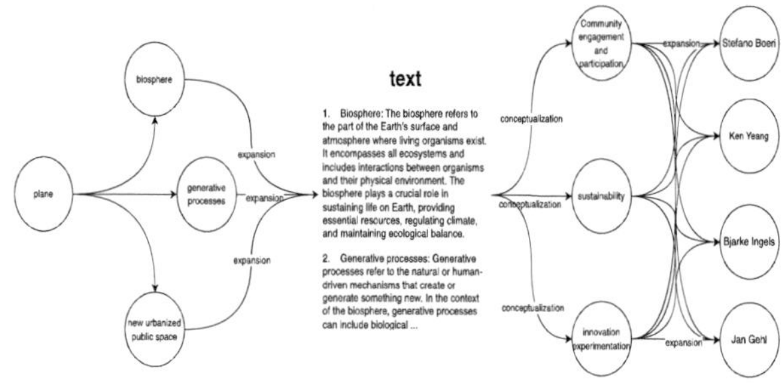
</td></tr>
</table>

Therefore in °'°Kobi the students' interactions with the LLM occur within an exploratory path that has a well-defined semantic basis. The student is prompted to reflect on the conceptual structure underlying the possibly complex answer obtained from the LLM. Explaining this structure also allows such content to be stored within the knowledge ecosystem, becoming a primary object of the system, an object that will be able to interact according to the semantic principles of °'°Kobi with all other materials produced and displayed in the interface.

6. CONCLUSIONS

°'°Kobi reinterprets the Knowledge Mapping paradigm (Wexler 2001) as the requirement of sharing the rich conceptualizations underlying the production of educational materials and students' homework, by indexing, storing, and retrieving them in a flexible and semantically rich manner. In this paper, we have discussed how the integration of Large Language Models (LLMs) in art and design education can be integrated to this purpose. We have outlined the methodological foundations concerning the integration of CHATGPT LLM in the educational approach aimed at enhancing artistic conception and design ideation and presented the knowledge and system architecture for integrating LLM in the Kobi system. We have also discussed some relevant aspects concerning the system's application in a real educational context and briefly reported its preliminary assessment. Using the LLM ability to create associations on a semantic level, °'°Kobi improve the effectiveness of what is commonly called a knowledge ecosystem (Szoniecky 2018).

However, there are limitations to the research presented in this paper. First, the experiments were conducted in a limited number of laboratory tests at specific institutions, and therefore the results may not be generalizable to other educational contexts. Additionally, the experiments focused primarily on text-based ideation and did not explore the potential of LLMs in sound and image generation. Finally, the experiments have been limited to the knowledge generation and elicitation phases. In fact, during the tests, the system showed limitations in the usability of the interfaces. This would interfere in the evaluation of the entire knowledge cycle. Therefore, future work could include improving interface usability, extending the °'°Kobi system to incorporate sound and image generation capabilities, as well as conducting experiments in a wider range of educational contexts to further explore the potential benefits and limitations of integrating LLMs in art and design education. Overall, the integration of LLMs in art and design education has the potential to revolutionize the creative process and enhance students' ability to generate innovative solutions to the most pressing problems of our time.

REFERENCES

Alam, A. (2021). Should Robots Replace Teachers? Mobilisation of AI and Learning Analytics in Education. 2021 International Conference on Advances in Computing, Communication, and Control (ICAC3), 1–12. https://doi.org/10.1109/ICAC353642.2021.9697300

Berns, S., & Colton, S. (2020). Bridging Generative Deep Learning and Computational Creativity.

Bown, O. (2012). Generative and Adaptive Creativity: A Unified Approach to Creativity in Nature, Humans and Machines. In J. McCormack & M. d'Inverno (Eds.), Computers and Creativity (pp. 361–381). Springer. https://doi.org/10.1007/978-3-642-31727-9_14

Davenport, T. H., & Mittal, N. (2022, November 14). How Generative AI Is Changing Creative Work. Harvard Business Review. https://hbr.org/2022/11/how-generative-ai-is-changing-creative-work

Dwivedi, Y. K., Kshetri, N., Hughes, L., Slade, E. L., Jeyaraj, A., Kar, A. K., Baabdullah, A. M., Koohang, A., Raghavan, V., Ahuja, M., Albanna, H., Albashrawi, M. A., Al-Busaidi, A. S., Balakrishnan, J., Barlette, Y., Basu, S., Bose, I., Brooks, L., Buhalis, D., … Wright, R. (2023). "So what if ChatGPT wrote it?" Multidisciplinary perspectives on opportunities, challenges and implications of generative conversational AI for research, practice and policy. International Journal of Information Management, 71, 102642. https://doi.org/10.1016/j.ijinfomgt.2023.102642

Giretti, A., Lemma, M., Zambelli, M., & di Meana, F. R. (2022). Knowledge Mapping for Creative Thinking, in Sampson D.G., Ifenthaler D. and Isaías P. Eds 19th International Concference on Cognition and Exploratory Learning in the Digital Age (CELDA 2022), pg. 193-200, ISBN: 978-989-8704-43-6

Huggingface. (2023, March 28). Models—Hugging Face. https://huggingface.co/models

Hughes, R. T., Zhu, L., & Bednarz, T. (2021). Generative Adversarial Networks–Enabled Human–Artificial Intelligence Collaborative Applications for Creative and Design Industries: A Systematic Review of Current Approaches and Trends. Frontiers in Artificial Intelligence, 4. https://www.frontiersin.org/articles/10.3389/frai.2021.604234

Köhler, W. (1967). Gestalt psychology. Psychologische Forschung, 31(1), XVIII–XXX. https://doi.org/10.1007/BF00422382

Kolodner, J. (2014). Case-Based Reasoning. Morgan Kaufmann.

Liang, J.-C., Hwang, G.-J., Chen, M.-R. A., & Darmawansah, D. (2021). Roles and research foci of artificial intelligence in language education: An integrated bibliographic analysis and systematic review approach. Interactive Learning Environments, 0(0), 1–27. https://doi.org/10.1080/10494820.2021.1958348

Mednick, S. (1962). The associative basis of the creative process. Psychological Review, 69, 220–232. https://doi.org/10.1037/h0048850

Mitkov, R. (2022). The Oxford Handbook of Computational Linguistics. Oxford University Press.

Morris, T. H. (2020). Experiential learning – a systematic review and revision of Kolb's model. Interactive Learning Environments, 28(8), 1064–1077. https://doi.org/10.1080/10494820.2019.1570279

Papp, S. (2023, April 23). Unlocking the Limitless Creativity of Generative AI: How It's Already Changing Our World. Medium. https://medium.datadriveninvestor.com/unlocking-the-limitless-creativity-of-generative-ai-1ddb56437069

Raiyyan, S. M. (2023, April 8). Unlock GPT-4 Potential: 69 Tools & News for Top 1% AI Enthusiasts! Medium. https://medium.com/@smraiyyan/unlock-gpt-4-potential-69-tools-news-for-top-1-ai-enthusiasts-33f0d4cca705

Schön, D. A. (1983). The reflective practitioner: How professionals think in action. Basic Books.

Shanahan, M. (2023). Talking About Large Language Models (arXiv:2212.03551). arXiv. https://doi.org/10.48550/arXiv.2212.03551

Speer, R., Chin, J., & Havasi, C. (2017). Conceptnet 5.5: An open multilingual graph of general knowledge. In Proceedings of the thirty-first AAAI conference on artificial intelligence, San Francisco, California, USA.

Szoniecky, S. (2018). Ecosystems Knowledge: Modeling and Analysis Method for Information and Communication. John Wiley & Sons.

Tunstall, L., Werra, L. von, & Wolf, T. (2022). Natural Language Processing with Transformers. O'Reilly Media, Inc.

UNESCO (2019). Outcome document of the International Conference on Artificial Intelligence and Education 'Planning education in the AI era: Lead the leap' 16 – 18 May 2019 Beijing, People's Republic of China. https://unesdoc.unesco.org/ark:/48223/pf0000368303

Wexler, M. N. (2001). The who, what and why of knowledge mapping. Journal of Knowledge Management, 5(3), 249–264. https://doi.org/10.1108/EUM0000000005868

Zhang, Y., Sun, J., Yang, Z., & Wang, Y. (2018). Mobile social media in inter-organizational projects: Aligning tool, task and team for virtual collaboration effectiveness. International Journal of Project Management, 36(8), 1096–1108. https://doi.org/10.1016/j.ijproman.2018.09.003

EXPLORING INFRANODUS: A TEXT ANALYSIS TOOL

Irina Tursunkulova[1], Suzanne de Castell[2] and Jennifer Jenson[1]
[1]*Faculty of Education, University of British Columbia, Canada*
[2]*Faculty of Education, Simon Fraser University, Canada*

ABSTRACT

The exponential growth of scholarly publications in recent years has presented a daunting challenge for researchers to keep track of relevant articles within their research field. To address this issue, we examined the capabilities of InfraNodus, an AI-Powered text network analysis platform. InfraNodus promises to provide insights into any discourse, uncover blind spots, and enhance a scholar's perspective by representing text as a network graph with relevant topical clusters and their relations. To understand the tools' effectiveness in analyzing scholarly articles, we used a set of 15 abstracts and 15 full papers. Our findings revealed that InfraNodus could indeed create topical clusters and meaningful patterns from abstracts, but its generated questions and summaries lacked relevance and coherence with the content. A deeper understanding of how the AI operates within the tool would benefit researchers seeking to optimize their literature review processes.

KEYWORDS

InfraNodus, Text Analysis, Literature Review, AI

1. INTRODUCTION

In 2014, Smithsonian Magazine reported that in roughly 28,000 scholarly journals, 1.8 million articles were published each year (https://shorturl.at/cLO35). These numbers have been increasing for the past decade. According to Academia (www.academia.edu), there were 684,708 full text papers on digital games and learning in April 2023; 689,912 by August 2023. Google Scholar identified 18,200 scholarly publications on digital games and learning published in 2022. The proliferation of large numbers of articles published by scholarly journals of varying caliber creates unprecedented challenges for scholars aspiring to keep abreast of established and emerging research and theory in their fields of study. It is the expectation underlying that ubiquitous requirement imposed upon scholars and researchers for a comprehensive "review of literature" relevant to one's research question, an expectation that is, quite simply, no longer realistic and no longer realizable. Might the very tools that have created this unmanageable glut of scholarly publication be harnessed to manage and even control it?

2. EXPLORING AN AI TOOL

A positively reviewed AI-driven tool that appeared promising for academic text analysis, InfraNodus (https://infranodus.com/) was chosen for this exploratory study. When InfraNodus first became available, its developers positioned it as a text network analysis platform able to "generate insight and new ideas using AI and network thinking" (https://infranodus.com/) with capabilities to "overview… any discourse, reveal the blind spots, enhance a scholar's perspective". According to InfraNodus developers, the tool both represents texts as networks, and provides graphical representations of the most relevant topical clusters and the relations between them. It utilizes network analysis algorithms to visualize information as a graph and extract meaningful patterns from it. The InfraNodus website advises that the tool can work with "ideas, articles, books, Google search results, surveys, tweets, spreadsheets", so we were confident the platform could also analyze scholarly articles. Could that kind of tool mobilize AI to sift through a body of texts and identify core concepts and recurrent conceptual relationships within them? We designed a small exploratory study expressly to answer that question, and this paper describes that study and its findings.

Our exploration of the tool's capability to assist scholarly literature reviewing and research-based hypothesis generation was guided by 3 sub-questions: (1) How well does InfraNodus enable a valid analysis/representation of the web of topics/connections resident within the extensive literature on game-based learning (the topic of our current research program)? (2) Can it 'generate', from its AI-based analysis of the research literature, useful questions/filters for a more focused and (humanly) manageable literature review? (3) How does InfraNodus manage the volume of abstracts, let alone full texts, for the thousands of publications on game-based learning, and can it help users do the epistemic surveying and mapping of an academic literature review? Or might we have come to a point where we need new understandings of what a "review of literature" has come to mean?

For the initial round of tool exploration, we used the first 15 articles of a contextualizing literature review on digital games and learning that we needed to carry out preliminary to a study focusing on microgames and language learning. We wanted to see what this AI-driven text analysis/representation tool might do to essentially 'sift' more efficiently through a daunting, and burgeoning, number of games and learning papers, in order to identify work whose questions and methods could inform the study we were embarking on. Since the current proliferation of academic publications, more and less loosely demarcated, is a state of affairs very much technologically produced, could it be resolved, or at least better-managed, using AI-based analytical tools? After all, many of the things that human reviewers do are pretty basic, like scanning for particular words, particular demographics, or specific authors, or journals, and skimming through abstracts.

Research skills are challenging to teach in a way that is meaningful to students and has ongoing impact in research practice. This paper investigates constructivist and experiential strategies for effective learning and deep understanding of postgraduate research skills and proposes a game-based learning (GBL) solution. A (non-digital) game called *How to Fail Your Research Degree* was designed and iteratively developed. Gameplay loop analysis identifies various learning and game mechanics and contextualises them in relation to GBL theory. Evaluation of gameplay (n = 127) demonstrates effective transmission of intended learning outcomes and positive game experience based on Keller's Attention-Relevance-Confidence-Satisfaction (ARCS) model. Discussion proposes that the game has high cognitive authenticity, relies heavily on tutor facilitation, can create tension between knowledge and confidence, and is applicable to multiple domains and learning situations. GBL is proposed to be an original and effective approach to teaching high-level, functional learning outcomes such as academic research skills.

Figure 1. Abbott, D. (2019). Game-Based Learning for Postgraduates

As new users of InfraNodus we first looked at a single abstract by Abbott (2019), to learn what functionalities the tool offers. According to InfraNodus' developers, it is capable of visually representing an abstract in the form of a network whose main topical groups are created from conceptual 'nodes' identified through the application of AI analysis of that text.

As of September, 2022, abstract wording was limited to 136 words, requiring that the abstract be split into two or more text boxes.

Multiple texts derived from the same abstract were included as separate abstracts in the web created by InfraNodus. The results are displayed in figure 2.

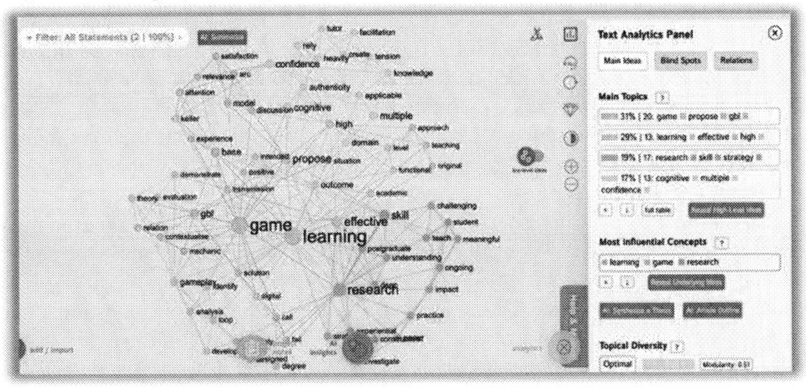

Figure 2. Text analysis network based on Abbott's (2019) article created by the AI

Next, still using this one (split up) abstract, we tested the tool's ability to generate questions using its GPT-3 AI, the third generation "Generative Pre-trained Transformer". GPT4, now widely in use, is already being progressively integrated, though GPT3 is still used for InfraNodus' lower subscription levels as of this writing.

The first question that the AI generated was *"What is the most effective approach to teaching that results in high academic outcomes?"* (see figure 3).

To assess the salience and fidelity to the abstract of the AI question generator, we tried the "more questions" feature. Figure 4 illustrates how the next question generated differed from the first.

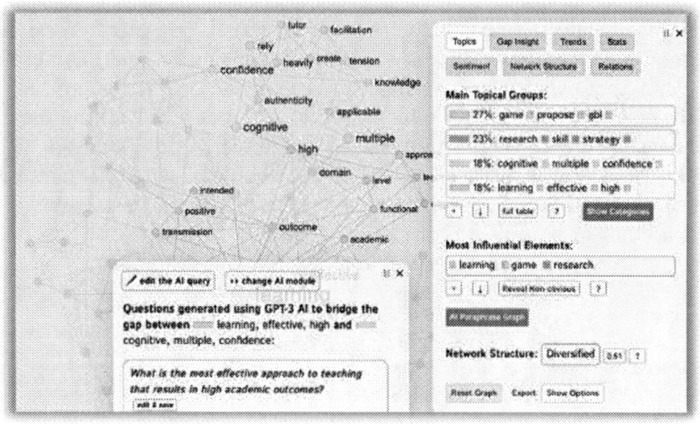

Figure 3. Question generated by InfraNodus based on Abbott's (2019) article

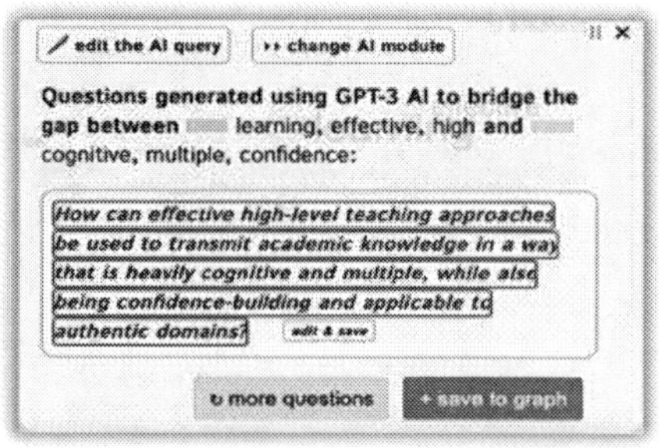

Figure 4. Additional questions generated by the AI

Questions can be regenerated until the AI starts producing the same questions; this happened after the third activation of "more questions". The questions AI generated were, however, concerningly dissimilar in terms of meaning. For instance, while the first question asked "what teaching method is the most efficient in producing high academic results", the second question focused on "how effective advanced teaching methods can be utilized to impart academic knowledge in a manner that is highly cognitive and diverse, while also fostering confidence and practical application in real-world contexts".

Another feature available in InfraNodus is creating summaries of inserted text. When we activated that option, InfraNodus suggested the following summary for the Abbott (2019) abstract: "*This paper investigates constructivist and experiential strategies for effective learning and deep understanding of postgraduate research skills and proposes a game-based learning (GBL) solution.*" This is literally identical to the second sentence in the abstract, not a summary of it. In constructing the summary of the Abbot's (2019) abstract InfraNodus focused on its first two sentences, including information about the purposes of the study, ignoring details about the study's methods, findings and proposed solutions, all of which are described in the abstract (see figure 1).

After exploring what InfraNodus could do with a single abstract, we added fourteen more abstracts from GBL scholarly articles. To fit within the tool's upload restrictions, n=15 articles were manually combined into one pdf, which was then converted to .txt file before being uploaded into the InfraNodus platform. The abstracts were uploaded as one text document, however the tool splits longer abstracts into smaller chunks, making the total number of text boxes 27. Finding no explanation of how many words each text box could have, we counted the maximum number of words in boxes. We found that the maximum number of words a box included at that time was n=156, however one textbox with n=146 words had been split mid-sentence into two text boxes (see figure 5).

Hoping to better understand the criteria for, and implications of, the tool's automatically splitting longer abstracts into separate text boxes, we reached out to InfraNodus Labs to ask how the separation of an abstract impacts the analysis the AI does.

InfraNodus creator Dmitry Paranyushkin, generously responding to our questions, explained that "*There are not really word limits, but it can't process more than 3 Mb at once (and we don't recommend it, because the graph becomes too big). When the statements are split, the last word of the statement won't be connected to the first one of the next statements. This is the way the analysis is affected" (*Paranyushkin, personal communication. All subsequent italicized quotes are from this same source). However, if the textual units input to the system have been systematically structurally skewed, preserving the conceptual integrity only of short abstracts, and dismembering (and replicating) longer ones, it stands to reason that the system' outputs will be limited accordingly.

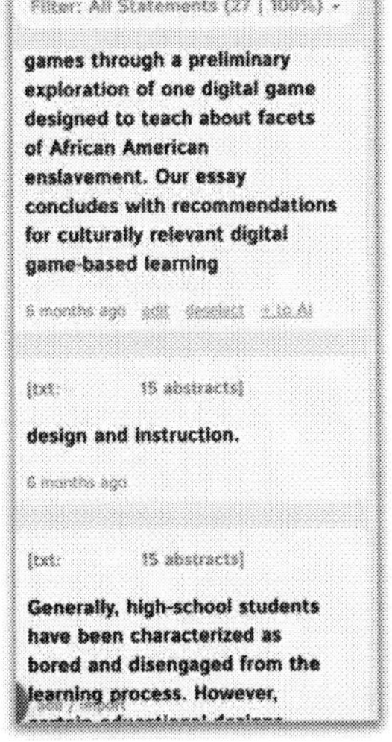

Figure 5. The tool splits articles into smaller texts

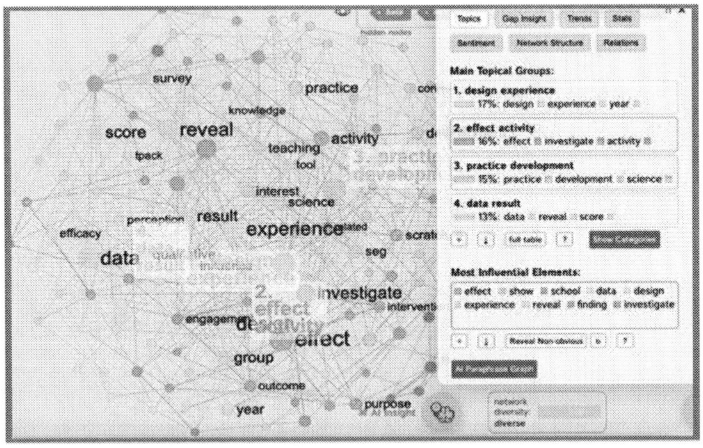

Figure 6. The topical network based on fifteen abstracts

Based on 15 abstracts, InfraNodus identified as **main topical groups**: design experience, effect activity, practice development, and data result, as seen on the right side of the image (figure 6). By default, the AI hid some **non-obvious nodes** to show **important** nodes. The user can opt for *showing* or *hiding* **influential nodes**, which will reconfigure the topical groups displayed. The tool allows the user to manually hide or show specific nodes, and the main topical groups change accordingly. It's worth noticing that single words are the primary semantic currency, not compound nor complex conceptual 'nodes'. And this is important for thinking about limitations, but also about how this kind of software might be most useful. We posed 3 questions to InfraNodus's developer: (1) how are "important" Nodes identified; (2) how are "important" nodes distinguished from "obvious" or "influential" ones; and (3) what criteria are used to make this differentiation.

Developer Dmitry Paranyushkin reponded that InfraNodus *"uses a betweenness centrality measure to identify the most important nodes. You can also switch in your settings to use the node's degree instead. The most important = influential in our case = obvious".* Betweenness centrality is concerned with control over information flow and meaning. He shared an article *Betweenness Centrality: Topical Brokers* published on the InfraNodus blog website, from which we learned that central nodes in a discourse are those topics that most frequently interact with and that most frequently interrupt, other topical connections (Paranyushkin, 2023). But does the AI identify nodes in a discourse, and therefore also topical connections, conceptually or lexically? Word and concept are not homologous, concepts do not map neatly on to linguistic tokens, and not all words are names, so the frequency of a term's appearance may bear no necessary relationship to the importance, influence, or impact of the concept it points to.

By March, 2023 when the same abstracts were reviewed, again, the "Reveal Non-Obvious [nodes]" feature had been changed to "Reveal Underlying Ideas". Despite the update in the feature's name from "non-obvious nodes" to "underlying ideas", in both cases the designated function was to "remove the most influential nodes from the graph to reveal the important topics behind". If "most influential" topics are the same as "most important" topics, then on what basis does the graph change after the "reveal underlying ideas" (previously "non-obvious nodes") feature is applied?

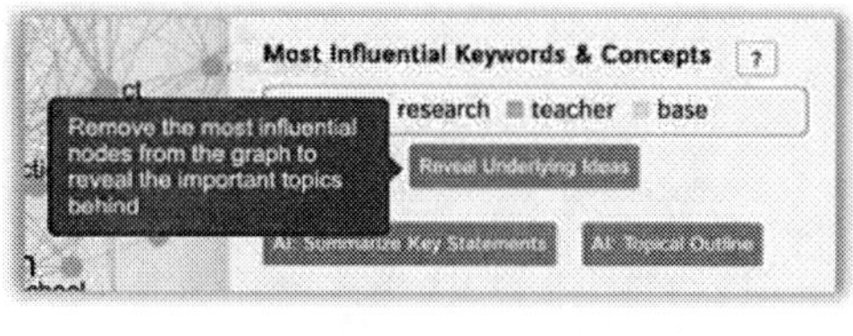

Figure 7. Most influential concepts offered by the tool through "Reveal underlying ideas" feature. Previously this feature was called "Reveal Non-obvious"

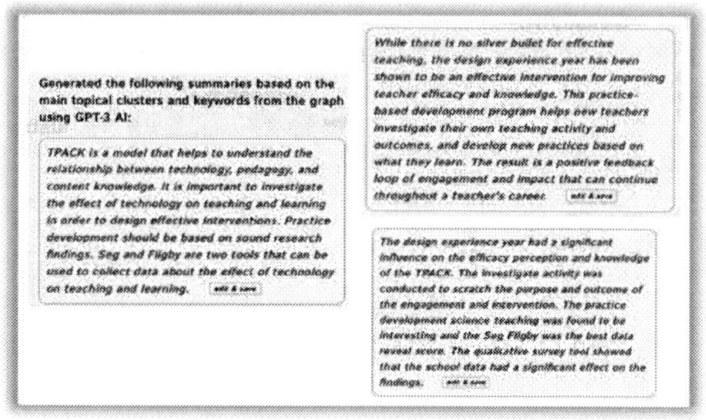

Figure 8. Summaries generated using fifteen article abstracts

As we tested the tool's ability to create and regenerate summaries of several abstracts inserted as one document, we found at times that the regeneration of summaries led to different phrasing and significantly different meaning from the abstracts being summarized.

For example, according to the InfraNodus summary on the left, Seg and Fligby are considered to be two tools for collecting data. According to the abstract, however, "FLIGBY is a serious game initially developed with the objective of simulating the business management process and the application of Flow theory in a business context" (Almeida and Buzady, 2019). SEG, mentioned in that summary, stands for Serious Educational Games, and while SEG was the primary focus of Annetta et al. (2014), it was not mentioned in any of the other abstracts. TPACK was the framework used in Açikgül, K (2020) article, but had otherwise no connection with the previous two abstracts. InfraNodus' GPT-3 AI-generated summaries were looking so different from the original abstracts, we increasingly doubted the validity and reliability of its summaries, and so addressed three further questions to its developers: (1) Through what processes, and using what data sets, is the GPT-3 trained? (2) How does it learn to transform abstracts into summaries? and (3) What is meant by "transforming"? The developer proposed that these were questions properly concerned with GPT-3 AI, and suggested we ask them to OpenAI, the creators of GPT-3, not to InfraNodus.

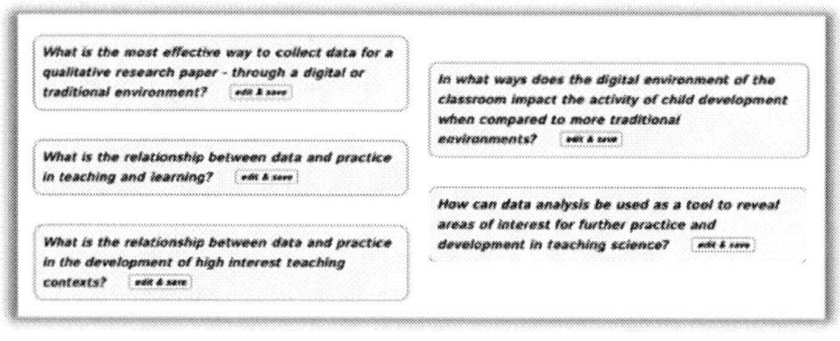

Figure 9. Questions created by InfraNodus based on the 15 abstracts

These considerations impact another feature offered by InfraNodus, that of "question generation". This option can be used to 'generate' useful questions/filters, a function we supposed might inform and guide a more focused and manageable literature review. The questions generated by the AI differed until, after five consecutive regenerations, the same questions recurred. Again, the length of the abstract text and diversity of topics within one long text impacted the variety of question the AI generated: when only one abstract was used, the AI generated only three more or less similar questions before repeating itself, whereas with fifteen abstracts it generated five different questions. When creating these questions based on 15 abstracts, however, InfraNodus did not generate questions relevant to all abstracts, but rather only to (what appear to be) randomly selected abstracts, drawing wording (phrases) from only these abstracts. As with the summary-generation feature, this question-generation option raises questions about its usefulness in the analysis of research materials.

When we asked InfraNodus creator Paranyushkin what the AI bases the questions it generates (and "re-generates") on, he responded that "It actually shows in the *AI Insight* box — on the basis of structural gaps". It makes sense to base questions on structural gaps, since questions mostly concern what we don't yet know. What isn't clear is what a "structural gap" consists in, and by what criteria it is identified.

While the Home page of the tool identifies its capabilities as including the ability to identify main topics, and generate summaries and research questions through the use of GPT-3 AI, its developer does not know, or cannot say, how those are accomplished by the GPT-3 core InfraNodus depends upon. Not knowing, or not perhaps not being able to explain to a non-specialist, the algorithms behind the topical maps, summaries and questions supplied by the GPT-3 is not the main issue. The main issue is that the questions and summaries generated appeared only superficially and literally connected to the texts purportedly being summarized and questioned.

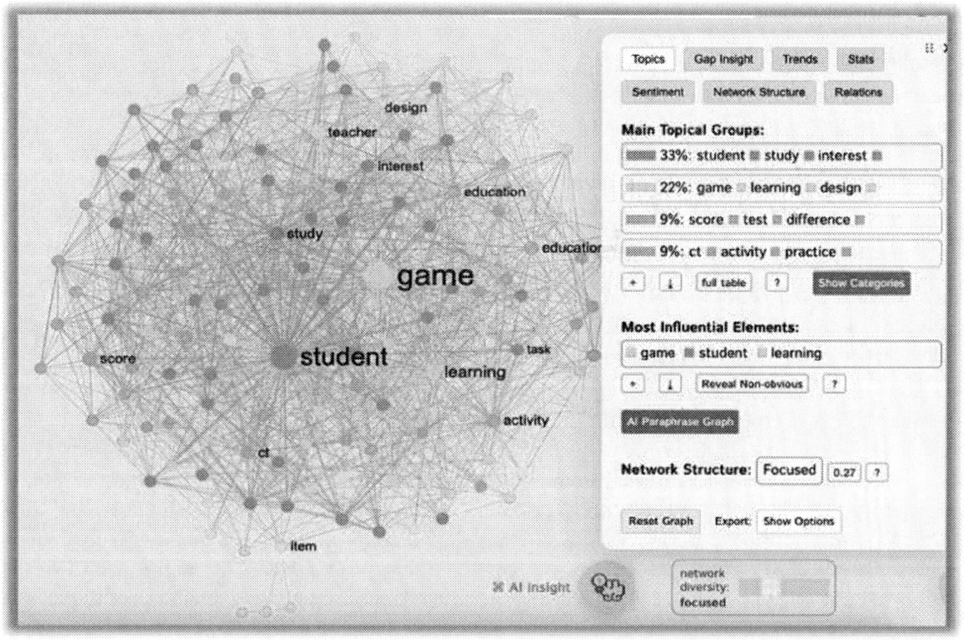

Figure 10. The topical network based on fifteen full papers. Note that 'ct' and 'item' are identified as 'nodes'

Initial attempts to upload all 15 articles were unsuccessful due to difficulties in merging and compressing the PDFs of the articles. Visuals and signatures in the files made it challenging to compress the files to the required size. At the end, all files were copied and pasted in .txt format. Inconveniently, that method of file preparation prior to uploading the document is time consuming: over an hour to merge and convert 15 articles for upload. Not only do users need a tool to easily and quickly convert files from PDF to .txt format, it is unclear how a paper's references, tables and picture descriptions might affect the analysis. This is something that is not mentioned anywhere on InfraNodus website.

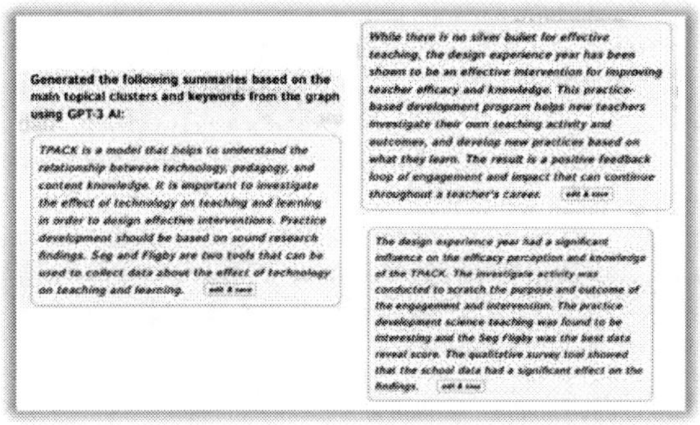

Figure 11. Summaries based on 15 abstracts

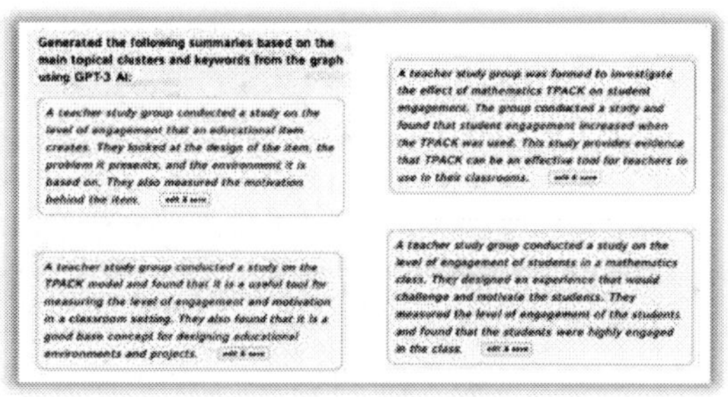

Figure 12. Summaries based on 15 full articles

The analysis of the 15 full articles showed how the inclusion of some references and all graphs, tables, and pictures description might impact the outcome. InfraNodus offered several different summaries of these 15 full articles. The four summaries presented below were randomly chosen from 8 consequent attempts at regenerating. After the 9th attempt, the summaries were repeated. Evidently the more input the tool has, the more questions and summaries it can generate prior to regenerating repetitive ones.

There is a notable difference between the summaries generated from the 15 abstracts, and those generated by the 15 full articles. The summaries generated from the full articles used more exact phrases from those articles. The summaries generated from the abstracts of these articles appeared randomly to combine terms and phrases from different articles.

Further explorations of this tool to see how differences between abstract summaries and paper summaries impact Infra Nodus' knowledge representation (and "idea generation") require comparing summaries of articles with references and without them, to identify how the names of the cited articles impact the summaries and research questions that AI creates, and looking at the differences between articles with abstracts, tables and images and graphs, and articles without these elements.

Network visualization is a key feature of InfraNodus. Its function is to reveal a text's main topics and blind spots. When a set of abstracts encompasses several different topics, with one topic mentioned in many more abstracts than other topics, that directs the AI analysis of the set towards that more frequently mentioned topic, overlooking other less often mentioned topics that may actually be more important. However, frequency of mentions is no guarantee of significance (if we have learned anything from Xwitter), and this is where a reasonably informed human reviewer has the edge. The tool can only at the very best re-present the text input, including all its intellectual fashion accessories and detritus, things a human reviewer would filter out of a representation of the discursive field.

2.1 How Much Text can InfraNodus Manage?

Our study's last question was concerned with InfraNodus' scalability: what could be the usefulness of this software for sifting through the enormous numbers of publications graduate students and researchers routinely encounter nowadays in undertaking a review of literature, which, in our own sub-field of digital game-based learning, for example, means at least 18,000 full papers. The tool's website states that InfraNodus can perform text analysis, but it does not specify the upper limit to the quantity of text it can analyze. The maximum input varies with level of subscription: Cloud, with 1 Mb upload limit for 9 euros monthly; Pro, with 1.2 Mb upload for 29 euro monthly, and Premium/Enterprise with 3Mb upload limit for 79 euros monthly, with Pro and Premium now using GPT4. For the purposes of analyzing academic texts, however, even the Premium plan offers very limited capability.

The developer explains, "*More is not recommended as the graph becomes too dense and unreadable. This is a tool for visual analysis. If you just want to get a list of keywords from a document you can use another tool but then of course the insight you get is quite boring*". So, is InfraNodus a primarily aesthetic visual "analysis" tool, rather than a tool that might reasonably be expected to help a user manage even a cursory or preliminary text analysis? What, in that case, do its visualizations tell us? When just 15 articles are split into 6,319 text boxes, they are well and truly "deconstructed". Recall the tool developer's explanation: "w*hen the statements are split, the last word of the statement won't be connected to the first one of the next statements. This is the way the analysis is affected*". Six months after this study's initial exploration of InfraNodus, the tool appears to allow more words within a box, but sentences are still split, and that splitting still influences text analysis. Even as we embrace multi-modality and applaud growing cultural and educational recognition of the value and importance of media and technologies for knowledge-representation beyond textual ones, it is difficult not to conclude from this study's exploration that such visual representations are conceptually problematic, generating kind of surface-structural plausibility at best, and complete nonsense at worst. For example, in an extension of the study reported here, we analyzed a set of self-authored publications hoping to see more clearly how the AI processed data and produced its representations, summaries and questions. The 'table of contents' it created to summarize one of those papers presented this word salad:

II. Aspect Development Detail Educationally Argue Question Content Infuse
A. Overview of aspect development
B. Detail educationally argue question content
C. Infuse into education

2.2 Literature Review as "Big Data"?

We conclude this small but in-depth look at ways the academy is being invited to engage AI 'solutions', for what promised benefits, and at what actual costs, by circling back to the question that led us here: how do researchers contend with a (*technologically produced*) proliferation of published scholarship that now far exceeds human capabilities to carry out what used to be standard expectation of graduate students and academics: a comprehensive and up-to-date review of literature contextualizing the research undertaken. Scoping out possible uses of AI as a technological solution to a technologically-generated problem, InfraNodus, according to its developers, offered a promising first step: "It provides a clear and actionable visual analysis of any text. Great to use as a writing assistant or to understand a new field or topic. Based on network analysis it can also indicate structural gaps in any discourse to help generate new ideas." (https://www.g2.com/products/infranodus/reviews)

Based on our attempt at using InfraNodus to analyze a set of 15 texts, all game-based learning research papers, we conclude that there appear, at this point, reasonable grounds for caution about the kinds of understanding and the quality of new ideas such a tool enables, raising questions about its usefulness in generating and graphically representing the (dynamic) structure of a conceptual network analysis. What are we actually looking at, and what is its validity as a representation of the discursive network?

It needs always to be borne in mind how rapidly technological change can happen. In this developer's case, the expectations set out initially for the software have been both modified and extended, the tool itself has been fine-tuned, and this rate of research and development is bound to continue. The question that matters most, however, is which things can be modified (like implementing a way to ensure whole sentences remain in the same text box, or multiple textboxes accommodating a single sentence are treated as one sentence, or removing references from papers and providing a separate way to analyze these), and which problems are *technologically* insurmountable, just as the viral proliferation of academic 'information' is insurmountable by humans.

What can we do that a machine cannot and, much more importantly, what MUST we do because, otherwise, a machine can think it can? If the AI can only connect concepts that utilize the same words, then it is almost certainly missing out on connections that articulate the same or similar concepts in different words. Given the almost limitless existence of synonyms in language, this is a massive limitation. The whole point of AI is that it is supposed to be able to 'understand' the meanings of words and even images, but if it cannot connect corresponding ideas expressed through variable lexicon, how is it more than a glorified Google search.

According to Korab (2021), InfraNodus now readily accepts pre-configured data such as Twitter feeds, Google trends, RSS News feeds, and research papers abstracts and titles. However we have not yet been able use InfraNodus efficiently to input "new", minimally pre-processed, data (specifically academic research papers), in a way that differentiates and manages elements standard in academic texts, such as reference lists, footnotes, charts and graphs and images, even if that's just to separate them from the text 'body' prior to its analysis. And, to this point, although the tool appears to allow larger numbers of words in a text box, it still fragments sentences to fit its words into length-limited textboxes, and texts remain fragmented and disconnected. "Words" here operates more like "names", and appear to be treated as elements conceptually disconnected from communicative context (even at a sentence level)---except when, inexplicably in our own closer look, an entire sentence is selected and quoted from among its textual relatives in service of 'summarizing' the text as a whole or, equally inexplicably, concepts are juxtaposed in ways that appear conceptually random or 'off-kilter', whether grammatically or semantically or both. The tool appears to combine together terms and phrases from different abstracts, themselves appearing randomly selected, and as was shown in Figure 10, included as topical 'nodes' terms like 'ct' and 'item' and 'graph' that surely appear in the text, but have nothing to do with its meaning. It's not clear how "influential nodes' are identified and quantified, beyond word frequency, or whether internodal 'relationships' such as "betweenness centrality" (Paranyushkin, 2023) depend upon more (and other) than textual proximity and co-occurrence.

3. CONCLUSION

This exploration used InfraNodus as a beginner's way to assess the capabilities AI tools more generally might offer us to contend with a humanly insurmountable problem. That problem resulted from, and would not have been possible without, AI, in its earlier processing/storeage machine incarnations. Researchers now must contend with a burgeoning and indeed, viral pandemic of publication, including publication of academic research and scholarship that, even with the most cursory 'scoping out' kind of reading, exceeds a human lifespan, let alone a doctoral fellowship. It seemed reasonable to look to AI for help, however we found InfraNodus neither accurate nor therefore useful. It proved, as this study attests, severely limited in its ability not only to identify and represent conceptual networks across a large number of texts, but as well even within a single text, leaving us with serious reservations about the kind of knowledge-representation any such GPT-enabled 'big data' analysis of academic research and scholarship would, or could, produce.

REFERENCES

Abbott, D., 2019. Game-based learning for postgraduates: An empirical study of an educational game to teach research skills. *Higher Education Pedagogies*, vol. 4, no. 1, pp.80-104.

Abdusselam, M.S., 2020. The Effect of Serious Games on the Awareness of Energy Sources Consumption. *International Technology and Education Journal*, vol. 4, no. 1, pp.36-42.

Açikgül, K., 2020. The Effect of Technological Pedagogical Content Knowledge Game Activities Supported Micro-Teaching Practices on Preservice Mathematics Teachers' Self-Efficacy Perception Levels. *Acta Didactica Napocensia*, vol. 13, no. 2, pp.157-173.

Acosta, M. M., & Denham, A. R., 2018. Simulating Oppression: Digital Gaming, Race and the Education of African American Children. *Urban Review: Issues and Ideas in Public Education,* vol. 50, no. 3, 345–362.

Admiraal, W., Huizenga, J., Akkerman, S. and Ten Dam, G., 2011. The concept of flow in collaborative game-based learning. *Computers in human behavior*, vol. 27, no. 3, pp.1185-1194.

Ak, O., & Kutlu, B., 2017. Comparing 2D and 3D game-based learning environments in terms of learning gains and student perceptions. *British Journal of Educational Technology,* vol. 48 no. 1, pp. 129–144.

Akpinar, Y., & Aslan, Ü. (2015). Supporting Children's Learning of Probability Through Video Game Programming. *Journal of Educational Computing Research*, vol. 53, no. 2, pp. 228–259.

Aleven, V., Kay, J., Rowe, J. P., Shores, L. R., Mott, B. W., & Lester, J. C., 2011. Integrating Learning, Problem Solving, and Engagement in Narrative-Centered Learning Environments. *International Journal of Artificial Intelligence in Education (IOS Press),* vol. 21, no. 1, pp. 115–133.

Almeidea, F., & Buzady, Z. 2019. Assessment of Entrepreneurship Competencies through the Use of FLIGBY. *Digital Education Review,* vol. 35, pp. 151–169.

Altanis, I., Retalis, S., & Petropoulou, O., 2018. Systematic Design and Rapid Development of Motion-Based Touchless Games for Enhancing Students' Thinking Skills. *Education Sciences,* vol. 8, no. 1, p. 18.

An, Y.-J., & Cao, L., 2017. The Effects of Game Design Experience on Teachers' Attitudes and Perceptions regarding the Use of Digital Games in the Classroom. TechTrends: *Linking Research & Practice to Improve Learning,* vol. 61, no. 2, pp. 162–170.

Annetta, L., Vallett, D., Fusarelli, B., Lamb, R., Cheng, M.-T., Holmes, S., Folta, E., & Thurmond, B., 2014. Investigating Science Interest in a Game-Based Learning Project. *Journal of Computers in Mathematics & Science Teaching*, vol. 33 no. 4, pp. 381–407.

Anyaegbu, R., Ting, W., & Li, Y., 2012. Serious Game Motivation in an EFL Classroom in Chinese Primary School. *Turkish Online Journal of Educational Technology - TOJET,* vol. 11, no. 1, pp. 154–164.

Arnold, U., Söbke, H., & Reichelt, M., 2019. SimCity in Infrastructure Management Education. *Education Sciences*, vol. 9, no. 3, p. 209.

Asbell-Clarke, J., Rowe, E., Almeda, V., Edwards, T., Bardar, E., Gasca, S., Baker, R. S., & Scruggs, R., 2021. The development of students' computational thinking practices in elementary- and middle-school classes using the learning game, Zoombinis. *Computers in Human Behavior,* vol. 115.

James, K., Horst, R., Takeda, Y. P., & Morales, E., 2020. The Patch: An artful syn (aes) thetic mapping of linguistic data through collaborative digital/analogue literacy processes. *McGill Journal of Education,* vol. 55, no. 3, pp. 641-665.

Korab, Peter (2021) InfraNodus: An Excellent Tool for Textual Data Analysis https://towardsdatascience.com/infranodus-excellent-tool-for-textual-data-analysis-2b4839e6cd10

Paranyushkin, D. (2018). Measuring discourse bias using text network analysis. Towards Data Science. https://towardsdatascience.com/measuring-discourse-bias-using-text-network-analysis-9f251be5f6f3

Paranyushkin, D. (2023). *Betweenness centrality: Topical brokers - Nodus Labs Support Center.* Nodus Labs Support

IMPLICIT EPISTEMOLOGY - THE BELIEFS OF STUDENTS OF EDUCATION SCIENCES

Anita Gramigna and Giorgio Poletti
University of Ferrara, Italy

ABSTRACT

The purpose of this research is to understand the mental states of the students of Educational Sciences around the educational phenomenon, which also includes the knowledge of emotion and feeling (Zohar & Dori, 2012). To this end, a questionnaire was administered, analyzed in the light of a quantitative-quantitative methodological approach. In fact, the beliefs around the educational emergencies of our time condition the learning of our students in the main disciplines studied during study. Consequently, it is useful to know these representations to formulate a more effective training proposal as more aware of the receptive and processing characteristics of our young interlocutors. There is a similarity between cognition and implicit epistemology, this research wanted to make some of its fundamental structures explicit (Santoianni, 2019).

KEYWORDS

Implicit Epistemology, Youth Anthropology, Training, Hermeneutics, Learning

1. INTRODUCTION

The relationship between the behaviors and learnings of our children, like that between knowledge theory and educational choice, are organic to the processes of structuring, demarcation, and composition of the cognitive field (Sternberg, 1997). This is the starting hypothesis.

Technology has introduced epochal changes, both in social dynamics and in the processes of construction of Knowledge, and, finally, in the elaboration of thought (Gramigna, 2018).

Digital natives weave with new technological devices a relationship that involves all areas of their existence: play, cognition, social and friendly relationships, affectivity (Ferri, 2011). The consequence is that it has contributed to forging anthropology and therefore the mentality of our young people who respond to new training needs (Galimberti, 2018).

In fact, as a result of the massive use of technology both in the field of play and in communication, the youth mentality is highly conditioned by a technical rationality. The meaning attributed to learning and, in general, to education is extremely far from what we teachers attribute to it. Finally, the learning styles of our students, whether global or analytical, visual, or verbal, reflective, or impulsive, converging, or divergent, are decisively affected by the new socio-cultural context of modern technologies. It is in this context that young people start the processes of building their own identity, the anthropology of the new generations.

Hence, the importance of knowing the beliefs of our students around the most current educational issues. It is precisely the implicit epistemology, that is, the idea that children have of Knowledge and of themselves that solicits and guides the dynamics of their learning. The idea that young people have of education, its processes and ends have a lot to do with their cognitive self, that is, with that conceptual domain where those same mental representations operate. In this sense, this conceptual domain represents the basis for the organization of many cognitive activities. For this reason, it is especially important to know the beliefs of our students for the active role they play in the processes of knowledge construction. The cognitive self is structured around the attitude that the subject has towards learning, its motivations, the imaginary that concerns training, fantasies, desires, expectations of gratification or not on the achievement of educational objectives. The feeling, the perception of the self is a basis for the organization of every cognitive activity, it has to do with an explicit dimension of the self, but it does not end with it.

In fact, it is especially important in the mechanisms of learning optimization, because it can strategically help to organize content and methods in the light of that context of meanings. The exploration, awareness and deepening of the sense of self helps to structure knowledge, to organize associative networks, to increase logical connections (Chalmers, 1999). In fact, how to deny that the ideas we have about our mental processes influence the construction of knowledge, the elaboration of cognitive strategies, memory itself. Implicit theories, not fully connoted and not conscious, act on our way of learning and processing knowledge.

Hence the importance of knowing implicit epistemology and, broadening the discourse, of knowing Knowledge (Morin, 1989).

The epistemic and consequently methodological assumptions of our research are the following:

- the parameters by which we evaluate the impact that the beliefs of Educational Sciences students exert on motivation and expectations
- the epistemological presuppositions, including the implicit ones of procedures that have a hermeneutic, qualitative-quantitative character
- methodological consistency with these assumptions
- the conceptual tools, the theoretical background in the international debate around implicit epistemologies
- the theories of reference: constructivism and cognitivism (Piaget, 1962; Vygotsky, 1987)
- the criteria for a constant review of the research model and its strategies: coherence and consequentiality
- the means of observation, collection, cataloguing and documentation: questionnaires using scale Likert for a measurement of attitudes for both a qualitative and quantitative evaluation of the mental states of students of Educational Sciences at the University of Ferrara, Department of Humanities taking into account that the educational phenomenon it is also understood and constituted by the knowledge of emotion and feeling (Damasio, 1995); it was chosen to use a scale with an even number of values, 6 (from 0 to 5) to avoid neutrality and "force" a choice of field for each of the statements of the questionnaire. The choice of statements and terminologies that may be, at first reading, excessively technical are chosen according to the target of the research, students of Educational Sciences who have in the use and contextualization of these terms one of their types of knowledge;
- the tools for verifying and evaluating the results of our research in relation to the objectives, assumptions and means that we have been able to use clarity of data in relation to the objectives and their correspondence with the expected results;
- the coherence between all these elements and the possibility of a readjustment of the research design during construction.

2. MATERIAL AND METHODS

2.1 Motivation and Identification of the Problem

The generational gap in mentalities due to the massive use of new digital technologies, as well as the high index of change and complexity in the social structure of Western countries, is a salient problem in the field of training (Bencivenga, 2020). Today more than ever it is crucial to study the anthropology of the younger generations to analyze the specificity of their educational needs and, consequently, to elaborate an effective training proposal for the context in which they live. The study we present identifies some salient guidelines of the youth mentality whose analysis allows us to structure our training offer more effectively. The identification and analysis of the elements characterizing contemporary youth anthropology is fundamental to orient the processes of knowledge construction both in teaching and learning (Gramigna, 2021). Gardner (2004) explains that the two cognitive postures lead to resonance, or the belief or not of having arrived at a good knowledge that does not require further investigation. But the prejudicial role of activated cognitive operations is dominant and can be significant in forms of learning difficulty or resistance.

2.2 Objective

This research aims to understand the implicit epistemologies of the undergraduate students of Educational Sciences of the three-year degree course.

The survey aims to analyze the mentality of our young interlocutors to better intercept their pre-judgments around issues of immense importance both for the course of study they have chosen, and for the profession they intend to conduct.

To this end, we will try to clarify the areas of signification of the concept of Education.

Contents

Therefore, an attempt has been made to highlight beliefs, often not fully conscious, about the meaning of the educational phenomenon. Specifically, these thematic nodes have been identified as we believe that they are formative emergencies of contemporaneity:

- responsibility in the educational relationship
- learning and the role of modern technologies
- the educational response to violence and suffering

These problems are interconnected with each other because of the educational implications that cross them.

The solicitation we have placed on our students puts in place a first essential process of auto reflexivity through a practice of applied hermeneutics that is represented by the process of analysis of the questions administered with the relative answers.

2.3 Epistemic Frame

The epistemic frame is autofermenters and auto reflexiveness, both in the disciplinary side and in the personal one, are those techniques of self-construction that Foucault (1988) had already partly illustrated to us in the story of himself. In fact, as Bateson (1979) teaches us, the epistemological structure of our reflection determines the questions we ask ourselves and the procedures we follow to find answers, to build solutions to problems, to elaborate innovative ideas, to teach and to learn. The epistemic framework refers to a hermeneutic conception of knowledge that is here conceived as a relational process in continuous construction. Within this framework lies the constructivist and cognitivist conception of learning (Bruner, 2000). Any learning is therefore considered a construction because it operates a structural change in complexity and depth in the configuration of mental representations as in their enrichment.

2.4 The Quantic-Qualitative Methodology

In the sciences of education in general, like the methods we are dealing with, need to confront each other on innovative epistemological bases so as not to have to depend passively on the uniqueness of approach of the dominant hard sciences. Innovation is also measured by the ability to expand the number of stakeholders involved in the screening of meaningful information and discussion on the key issues of science and technology. Specialists often lack the humility to relate to everyday life, for them only the "laboratory" is a place appropriate to science. And, however, it seems a suggestive hypothesis to reconsider the task of the "experts" to leave adequate space for the "concerned", who usually suffer the decisions from above both for school reforms and for organizational changes in the world of work. In the last decade, an idea of post-normality has made its way that moves according to a precautionary principle, to concentrate the greatest number of opinions and verify the legitimate aspirations that have the formative factor at heart.

Post-normal intelligence, which should be put to the test, implies a systemic strategy, a willingness to confront difference, to respond to a deep desire that until now has not found effective and credible solutions. Post-normal intelligence wants to prefigure the future, it feels the desire to undertake, to give shape: for this reason, it would be important to reconsider the role of techniques that involve a wise use of the hands that, in our youth world, have become almost inert. The formation aimed at taking charge of the new intellectual processes will have to diverge from the normal image still prevalent, based on the hierarchies of disciplinary areas.

The concatenation of the questions posed by the questionnaire focus on the relationship between the phenomena and on the phenomena themselves that in fact can only be understood in the context and the context is made up of relationships. Therefore, our analysis methodology, while using quantitative data, refers to a qualitative system that considers the numerical data in the systemic relationship with the identified context (Poletti, 2020)

Statistical sample

Having to analyze the students of a specific degree course and setting the goal of understanding the mental states of the students of Educational Sciences in relation to the educational phenomenon, we opted for the administration of the questionnaire to the entire population of students attending the course, collecting eighty-six questionnaires.

2.5 Expected Results

The expected results will allow us to formulate our teaching proposal in the light of their beliefs, both to make them explicit to their own eyes, and to help them problematize the themes. Finally, we will have valuable information on the motivations of learning as well as on the expectations towards the course of study and professional prospects.

2.6 Evaluation

The research project was evaluated in the light of these criteria:

- consistency between objectives, assumptions, and categories used
- between these elements and the possibility of their readjustment during construction
- achievement of the expected results

In the light of this verification, the positive evaluation led us to present this report for publication. In drafting the research design, in fact, we clarified the epistemological assumptions, even implicit, of the procedures we used, relating to the formulation of the questionnaire, its administration, collection, documentation and analysis of information. To this end, we have evaluated from time to time, the operational congruence of our heuristic behaviors, but in the light of a system, albeit dynamic and reticular reference (Morin, 2007).

On the other hand, the problem of "naive theories" on learning had already been highlighted by Bruner, 2000) who nevertheless referred to teachers, but it is important here to point out the importance of the conditioning that common sense plays in educational processes.

2.7 Results

In line with the objectives and methodologies illustrated, anonymous questionnaires were completed through a Google Form, in which no profile data were collected but we wanted to focus attention on the level of sharing of 15 statements that aim to describe and highlight the beliefs of students in relation to learning and the underlying implicit epistemologies. The questionnaire asked to give a value to the level of sharing of fifteen statements on a scale from 0 (total disagreement) to 5 (total agreement) without having the possibility of having a neutral position but "taking sides" with respect to the statements.

The fifteen statements on which it was asked to express a value of sharing are, in the order in which they were proposed:

1. Educational responsibility is shared between teacher and student
2. Today's children are much smarter than those of the past
3. The bully is not a victim of society
4. Suffering is an inescapable existential experience
5. Logic is not the only form of directionality accredited to build knowledge
6. Knowledge is not transmitted.
7. Innovative technologies are hermeneutic
8. Studying eventually is a very tiring matter.
9. Children need to be educated to become smarter

10. Poor academic performance is the responsibility of teachers
11. Bullying is the fault of the carelessness of school and family
12. Suffering must be avoided at all costs
13. The teacher transmits knowledge
14. Innovative technologies have made us smarter
15. The best thing is to know without having to study

The data collected are summarized in Table 1.

Table 1. Summary of valuation data against proposed claims

Claims	*0*	*1*	*2*	*3*	*4*	*5*
Educational responsibility is shared between teacher and student	0	5	19	17	23	22
Today's children are much smarter than those of the past	13	22	20	20	9	2
The bully is not a victim of society	25	31	13	11	3	3
Suffering is an inescapable existential experience	2	12	12	14	24	22
Logic is not the only form of directionality accredited to build knowledge	0	3	17	14	18	34
Knowledge is not transmitted.	53	17	9	5	2	0
Innovative technologies are hermeneutic	3	10	29	25	14	5
Studying eventually is a very tiring matter.	3	12	21	23	16	11
Children need to be educated to become smarter	6	27	19	19	9	6
Poor academic performance is the responsibility of teachers	8	21	30	22	5	0
Bullying is the fault of the carelessness of school and family	4	12	16	20	23	10
Suffering must be avoided at all costs	38	23	10	8	3	4
The teacher transmits knowledge	6	10	20	22	24	4
Innovative technologies have made us smarter	14	23	27	18	2	2
The best thing is to know without having to study	42	21	12	9	2	0

At a first quantitative observation it is interesting to note, combining the values 0-2 and 3-5 how the answers show a strong polarization (see Table 2) either towards agreement or towards disagreement except for the statements:

- Innovative technologies are hermeneutic
- Studying eventually is a very tiring matter
- The teacher transmits knowledge

Table 2. Summary of the data relating to the valuations with respect to the proposed statements, summarized in percentages highlighting Agreement and Disagreement with the statements

Affirmation	*Disaccord*	*Accord*		
Educational responsibility is shared between teacher and student	24	62	28%	72%
Today's children are much smarter than those of the past	55	31	64%	36%
The bully is not a victim of society	69	17	80%	20%
Suffering is an inescapable existential experience	26	60	30%	70%
Logic is not the only form of directionality accredited to build knowledge	20	66	23%	77%
Knowledge is not transmitted.	79	7	92%	8%
Innovative technologies are hermeneutic	42	44	49%	51%
Studying eventually is a very tiring matter.	36	50	42%	58%
Children need to be educated to become smarter	52	34	60%	40%
Poor academic performance is the responsibility of teachers	59	27	69%	31%
Bullying is the fault of the carelessness of school and family	32	53	37%	62%
Suffering must be avoided at all costs	71	15	83%	17%
The teacher transmits knowledge	36	50	42%	58%
Innovative technologies have made us smarter	64	22	74%	26%
The best thing is to know without having to study	75	11	87%	13%

Where there is a substantial and here vision in the two segments, particularly evident in "New technologies are a hermeneutic" where there is a 49% of disagreement and a 51% of agreement with a prevalence of values 3 on the one hand and 4 on the other to underline an uncertainty and a probable difficulty of instantiation of the term hermeneutics.

The quantitative analysis of the data also shows a strong propensity to disagree with the statement Knowledge is not transmitted (92%) which is certainly supported, in its credibility by the fact that there is a decisive disagreement with the statement The best thing is to know without having to study (87%).

To be noted, from a quali-quantitative analysis a further congruence is detected by analyzing the result relating to the statement: Educational responsibility is shared between teacher and student who points out a 72% concordant attitude, with 53% of 4 and 5 (complete sharing) and at the same time there is a substantial disagreement (69%) on the affirmation Poor academic performance is the responsibility of teachers. The only element of perplexity is the propensity to agree that the teacher transmits knowledge where knowledge is not transmitted, but this can detect the awareness of the substantial difference between knowing and knowing, that is, detecting and highlighting relationships.

The data for this reason reveal a hermeneutic context and implicit beliefs that enhance and allow to structure increasingly effective educational paths.

The data reveal, even if still in a non-clear way, that students have the concept of knowledge and how emotional and relational elements also converge in it, not only cognitive.

3. CONCLUSION

This survey has led us to reconfigure in a global sense our own reflections on training practices and their models, finally on the consequences, not always explicit, that both have towards the learning behaviors of our students and the values they attribute to study practices. We have noticed that there is a tendency to find information but not to process knowledge that can also be spent in contexts other than those in which it was found. The idea of knowledge on which we teachers have been trained, with the related learning strategies, have nothing to do with the conscious requests of the students. It is not only an anthropological phenomenon, but also and a cognitive problem. The social image of knowledge as an "encyclopedia" has been replaced by that of "context".

We have come to the conviction that the mindset we must educate must include both procedural and finalistic aspects. From this study it emerges that the criterion of judgment with which our students evaluate knowledge is marked by pragmatism. This means that they consider the study based on a practical relational model for the life lived. Knowledge, for them, must solve problems in a concrete and inexpensive way. Hence the drifts of much school policy and not little didactics.

Yet, shift the focus of attention to metacognitive mechanisms, draw their attention and soon realize that they can approach studies with greater satisfaction.

For this reason, in the light of the results of our research we can affirm that the conception of knowledge cannot concern only the field of acquired knowledge as it contemplates its matrices and its implicit cultural roots. Knowledge, in fact, constructs the correlations that connect reality to our system of representation, or to what we believe to be reality itself and knowledge. This has important implications on our training proposals because we must teach to evaluate, from time to time, the operational congruence of cognitive behaviors, in the light of that system, albeit dynamic reference that we have called epistemology, or theory of Knowledge. In fact, to know a phenomenon means to understand it, to have a clear awareness, and to be aware of oneself, in relation to the problems posed by that phenomenon. This goes far beyond the goal of passing an exam.

Teaching involves setting up contexts that promote cognition through targeted interventions. A first step of this set-up is in the analysis of the implicit beliefs of our students through the observation of their behaviors both socially and cognitively. This process of consciousness will help the students to understand the nature of certain difficulties and to use, in a metacognitive sense, their talents (Margiotta, 2015). Hence the emphasis on those themes to intercept and build links of signification, interactions, virtuous dialogues between disciplinary, scientific, cultural, and anthropological environments often wrongly considered incommunicable with each other.

For this reason, it is essential to know the processes and mechanisms of knowledge, to be able to build "other" knowledge and transfer skills from different areas and times. Epistemology can read entropy, the disorder that generates uncertainty, anxiety, difficulty in studying. What? building a domain of coherence, that is, extending in time and space a network of significant relationships between the phenomena that characterize the context in which we live. In this perspective, the school or university environment cannot be considered just a sort of scenario, background or inert envelope that welcomes a being who determines himself independently of his presence. It can only be understood as a network of relationships whose nodes refer to other networks that surround and intertwine in the subject. Its network of structures is like an elastic, dynamic, strongly integrated and, at the same time, open hierarchy.

It is an organizational scaffolding of knowledge with which we interpret and build, therefore it has an active and concrete tension. Active, because it acts on reality and concerns both processes, acquisition, construction, organization of cognitive data. And it is concrete, because it refers to the way we see the world, to the questions that we ask ourselves when we act and that direct our conduct, it concerns the hypotheses of our research and its procedures.

This constitutive state does not concern only the teaching-learning processes, which is easily inferred, but also and above all the quality of the reactions that these processes trigger in the subjects involved and, through them, in the environments that relate to them, and vice versa, in a continuous circle of interdependencies.

The administration of the questionnaire allowed to establish associative chains within the thematic context of their own beliefs around knowledge and learning. In this way the structure of a learning can be highlighted to their own eyes. Selecting the salient data of implicit epistemology favors the organization of its mental representation, which is the first step to monitor the processes of obstruction of knowledge (Flavell, 1979). Selection and organization are two essential functions of intelligence that can thus be encouraged.

In short, we need to help our students understand how we represent ourselves and how, with learning, we can produce more effective problem-solving representations. To this end, with the questionnaire, we have drawn cognitive lines of action according to the principle of coherence. Monitoring one's learning is the first step to learning to learn (Margiotta, 2013). The next steps are self-knowledge, the salient characteristics of one's cognitive field, one's motivations, the best strategies to adopt and their combination. And then, learn that reflection that evaluates the phases of the cognitive process and that puts the boy in a position to recalibrate it (Feuerstein R., Feuerstein R. S., Falik L. H., Rand Y. 2013).

The awareness of the mechanisms of knowledge construction, of the active role of the ideas we have of it, the implicit theories that we manufacture, the prejudices, finally, the possibility of controlling, at least in part, the progress of cognitive processes, has important repercussions on learning because it orients us – or disorients us – in the use as in the invention of the tactics we implement when we learn. Strategies for organizing data, content and information, association paths, mnemonic references, in fact, play a crucial role in the processes of optimization of learning. This is what we mean when we talk about learning to learn, when we say that we need to learn to translate knowledge, content, methods, codes and languages from different contexts and times. Creativity has a lot to do with the ability to invent, develop, elaborate, and learn strategic learning plans. In short, all this is intricately linked to our metacognitive competence. Both the choice and the invention of learning strategies, and finally the productive use of error, depend, to a considerable extent, on the metacognitive knowledge that we are accumulating, processing, organizing.

Consciousness makes perceptible the sense of self to us that we reflect on it.

Here, then, following the thread of reasoning, we can reach a further consequence in our considerations on consciousness and its educational implications: consciousness is sense of self in knowledge. It enhances the reach of the mind because it allows it to develop its abilities.

To this end, we believe that any type of teaching requires preparation of an epistemological nature, because the knowledge we intend to build with our students aims at processing information and not simply at receiving it. This elaboration requires knowing how thought works while it learns. This is the existential meaning of knowledge that in epistemology binds the individual to science. Therefore, the formative philosophy that, in this brief conclusion we wish to propose, consists in linking the study of gnoseological processes to reflective dynamics, therefore, to the critical knowledge of personal epistemologies as well as those implicit both of common sense and of ideologies. The objective of this training is in the construction of "ability to manipulate the models of explanation, execution and regeneration of mastery systems related to the expert development of the areas of experience and culture studied" (Margiotta, 1997, p. 76). The school, the university, the research centers, the various educational institutions, the work should contribute to elaborating a description always elastic but satisfactory (that is, able to provide us with an orientation map) of the contemporary. We need a dynamic and ecological conceptual system of the socio-cultural context to which we belong.

For this reason, it is important, with the boys, to reason around their idea of knowledge and education, but also of the existential knots that accompany the growth of each one. Hence the questions about the educational emergencies of our time.

REFERENCES

Bateson, G. (1979). *Mind and Nature: A Necessary Unity*, Dutton, London.

Bateson, G. (1997). *Una sacra unità. Altri passi verso un'ecologia della mente*. Adelphi, Milano.

Bencinvenga, E. (2020). *Critica della ragione digitale*. Feltrinelli, Milano.

Bruner, J. (2000). *La cultura dell'educazione*. Feltrinelli, Milano.

Chalmers, D. (1999). *La mente cosciente*. Mc-Graw Hill, Milano.

Damasio, A. R. (1995). *L'errore di Cartesio. Emozione, ragione e cervello umano*. Adelphi, Milano.

Ferri, P. (2011). Nativi digitali. Bruno Modadori. Milano.

Feuerstein, R., Falik, L.H. et al. (2013). *LPAD Learning Propensity Assesment Device*. Erickson, Trento.

Flavell, J. H. (1979). *Metacognition and cognitive monitoring: A new area of cogni-tive– developmental inquiry. American Psychologist*, 34, 10), 906-911, 1979.

Foucaul, M. (1988). *Technologies of the self*, in L. H. Martin, H. Gutman e P. H. Hutton , curated by), Technologies of the Self. A seminar with Michel Foucault, University of Massachusetts Press, Amherst.

Galimberti, U. (2018). *La parola ai giovani*. Feltrinelli, Milano.

Gardner, H. (2011). *Cambiare idee. L'arte e la scienza della persuasione*. Feltrinelli, Milano.

Gramigna, A. (2018). *RoboticaMente: metacognizione e innovazione nella scuola dei* talenti in "Formazione & Insegnamento", a. XVI, n.2, 2018, pp. 305-320.

Gramigna, A. (2021). *La fabbrica delle idee. A proposito di educazione e intelligenza*. Biblion, MIlano

Margiotta, U. (1997). *Dopo Piaget: equivalenza delle competenze e modelli di apprendimento*, in U. Margiotta, a cura di, Pensare in rete. *La formazione del multialfabeta*. CLUEB, Bologna.

Margiotta, U. (2013). *Neuroplasticy and cognitive modifiability* in AA.VV. , Feuerstein Institute), Neural Plasticy and cognitive modifiability, pp. 5-10. Medimond.

Margiotta, U. (2015). *Teoria della formazione. Ricostruire la pedagogia*. Carocci, Bologna.

Morin, E. (1989). *La conoscenza delle conoscenze*. Feltrinelli, Milano

Morin, E. (2007). *Il Metodo 3, La conoscenza della conoscenza*. Cortina, Milano

Piaget, J. (1962). *Il linguaggio e il pensiero*. Giunti Barbera, Firenze

Poletti, G. (2020). *Teoria e metodologia della ricerca educativa*. Volta la carta, Ferrara.

Santoianni, F. (2019). *Brain Education Cognition. La ricerca pedagogica italiana, RTH - Research Trends in Humanities*. Education & Philosophy, 6, 44-52.

Sternberg, R. J. (1997). *Thinking styles*. Cambridge University Press, Cambridge.

Vygotskij, L. S. (1987). *Il processo cognitivo*. Bollati Boringhieri, Torino.

Zohar, A. & Dori, Y. J. (Eds.) (2012). *Metacognition in Science Education: Trends in current research*. Vol. 40. Springer Dordrecht.

ON THE PREDICTORS OF COMPUTATIONAL THINKING SELF-EFFICACY

Josef Guggemos
University of Education Schwäbisch Gmünd, Oberbettringer Str. 200, 73525 Schwäbisch Gmünd, Germany

ABSTRACT

Computational thinking (CT) is an important 21st-century skill. This paper aims at investigating predictors of CT self-efficacy among high-school students. The hypothesized predictors are grouped into three areas: (1) student characteristics, (2) home environment, and (3) learning opportunities. CT self-efficacy is measured with the Computational Thinking Scales (CTS) that comprises five dimensions: creativity, algorithmic thinking, cooperativity, critical thinking, and problem solving. N = 202 high-school students act as the sample, linear regression as the analysis method. The best prediction is possible for algorithmic thinking ($R^2 = .511$). For cooperativity, the explanatory power of our model it is weak ($R^2 = .146$). Across all five CTS dimensions, CT self-concept is the best predictor for CT self-efficacy.

KEYWORDS

Computational Thinking Scales, Gender and Home Environment, Cognitive Dispositions, Motivation, Learning Opportunities

1. INTRODUCTION

Computational thinking (CT) has emerged as a promising resource for solving problems across various subjects and work environments (Buitrago Flórez et al., 2017; D. Barr et al., 2011). Wing (2006, p. 33) conceptualized CT as "solving problems, designing systems, and understanding human behavior, by drawing on the concepts fundamental to computer science". As a concept, CT may still be in its infancy (Shute et al., 2017; Tsarava et al., 2022). To contribute to a better understanding of CT, the purpose of our research is *prediction* (Newman et al., 2007), i.e., we test the association of CT with variables that might predict CT.

In previous work, we relied on a performance test to operationalize CT (Guggemos, 2021). Performance tests are often regarded as superior to self-assessment instruments. However, self-assessments are not by nature inferior to performance tests (Scherer et al., 2017). Rather, the validity of a measurement depends on its intended use (AERA et al., 2014). Self-assessment instruments tend to capture self-efficacy, which could be a good predictor for behavior (Scherer et al., 2017). Moreover, CT is a complex construct. Focusing solely on its cognitive nature may be an oversimplification (Kafai & Proctor, 2022). Román-González et al. (2019) argue that it is unlikely to capture a complex construct such as CT with a single measurement instrument.

Durak and Saritepeci (2018) utilized a cross-sectional sample of 156 students from grades 5 to 12 for investigating predictors of CT. To measure CT, Durak and Saritepeci (2018) relied on the Computational Thinking Scales (CTS) (Korkmaz et al., 2017). CTS is an established self-assessment instrument (Shute et al., 2017). Following ISTE (2015), it comprises five dimensions: creativity, algorithmic thinking, cooperativity, critical thinking, and problem solving. As multidimensionality implies, it may be problematic to aggregate the five dimensions using an overall (sum) score. This assertion is supported by (Guggemos et al., 2023). Using confirmatory factor analysis, they showed that a higher-order model with an overall CT-factor does not converge. Furthermore, the correlations among the five dimensions vary substantially; in some cases, they are not significantly different from zero, e.g., between algorithmic thinking and cooperativity. Durak and Saritepeci (2018) reported educational level (grade), mathematics and science class performances, and ways of thinking as significant predictors of CT. Building on this study, it is beneficial to also consider students' CT motivation and family background because those factors may be important when investigating CT (del Olmo-Muñoz et al., 2020; Fraillon et al., 2019; Repenning et al., 2015).

Overall, investigating the association of each of the five CTS-dimensions with potential predictors may contribute to a better understanding of CT. Our research question is:

What are the predictors of high-school students' CT self-efficacy, i.e., creativity, algorithmic thinking, cooperativity, critical thinking, and problem solving, at the individual level?

To answer this research question, section 2 presents hypotheses on predictors of CT. These hypotheses are identical to those in (Guggemos, 2021). We focus on high school students and the individual level, i.e., we do not consider the classroom or school context.

2. THEORETICAL BACKGROUND AND HYPOTHESES

2.1 Conceptual Framework

The conceptual framework of the International Computer and Information Literacy Study 2018 (ICILS) structures our hypotheses (Fraillon et al., 2019). It distinguishes antecedents and processes. "Antecedents are exogenous factors that condition the ways in which (...) learning takes place" (Fraillon et al., 2019, p. 6). Antecedents comprise student variables, such as gender, and home environment variables, such as parents' socioeconomic status. "Processes are those factors that directly influence (...) learning" (Fraillon et al., 2019, p. 6). Such CT learning opportunities can be either formal or informal in nature (Grover & Pea, 2013; Wing, 2008).

2.2 Antecedents – Student

CT research has consistently underscored the significance of gender differences (Shute et al., 2017). Such differences in CT may be due to differences in self-efficacy and interest, which might be attributed to gender stereotypes (Master et al., 2016). The ICILS reports significantly higher CT scores for males in comparison to females for the overall sample. Román-González et al. (2017), using Spanish secondary students as a sample, found an increasing gender CT gap in favor of males as students age. Since our study is in the realm of high-school education, we expect: **H1.** The gender 'male' positively predicts CT.

CT is conceptualized as a problem-solving methodology across subjects (V. Barr & Stephenson, 2011; Wing, 2006). In light of this, it may be strongly related to reasoning skills (Ambrosio et al., 2015; Buitrago Flórez et al., 2017; Wüstenberg et al., 2012). Román-González et al. (2017) reported a medium correlation of CT with reasoning ability. We assume: **H2.** Reasoning skills positively predict CT.

According to Wing (2006, p. 33), CT may be an analytical ability, like "reading, writing, and arithmetic". In terms of mathematics skills, Wing (2008) claimed that CT and mathematical thinking share the same general way of approaching problems. Durak and Saritepeci (2018) reported higher CT levels for students with higher academic success in mathematics. Concerning language skills, V. Barr and Stephenson (2011) argued that CT concepts are also present in the language arts. In their literature review, Zhang and Nouri (2019) showed that reading is regularly regarded as a part of CT. Román-González et al. (2018) reported a medium positive correlation between CT and verbal ability. In sum, we hypothesize: **H3.** Mathematics skills positively predict CT; **H4.** Language skills positively predict CT.

The relationship between programming and CT is often thematized. Israel et al. (2015) regard the use of computers to model ideas and programming as an integral part of CT. Buitrago Flórez et al. (2017), as well as Lye and Koh (2014), argue that by means of programming, several core facets of CT can be addressed. Shute et al. (2017) concluded there is a close relationship between CT and programming skills due to similar underlying cognitive processes. Hsu et al. (2018) reported, based on their review of the literature, that programming is widely used to teach CT. We expect: **H5.** The ability to program positively predicts CT.

Many authors, including Wing (2006), emphasize that computer literacy is distinct from CT. However, the question remains whether computer literacy is conducive to CT or not. Since CT aims to represent a problem in such a way that a computer can solve it (Israel et al., 2015; Wing, 2006), knowledge about the capabilities of computers may be beneficial. Moreover, CT is often taught using computers and technology (Hsu et al., 2018). The ICILS also found a strongly positive correlation between information and computer literacy and CT. Against this background, we hypothesize: **H6.** Computer literacy positively predicts CT.

According to the expectancy-value model (EVM) by Wigfield and Eccles (2002), the expectation of success and subjective task value drive the level of achievement motivation. The expectation of success depends on the person's self-concept, which can be broadly defined as the perception of oneself (Shavelson et al., 1976). Drawing from this, CT self-concept could be defined as the perception about oneself in the area of CT. A core element of self-concept is the perceived competence (Bong & Skaalvik, 2003). As such, it may be closely related to self-efficacy. Indeed, domain specific self-concept and self-efficacy are often hard to separate (Bong & Skaalvik, 2003). The main difference might be the time orientation: self-concept is relatively stable whereas self-efficacy is malleable. In line with Retelsdorf et al. (2011), we rely on the self-concept and hypothesize: **H7.** CT self-concept positively predicts CT.

The second component of the EVM addresses the perceived task value. Following Wigfield and Eccles (2002), the individual perception of usefulness plays a central role. Students who regard CT as more important for their academic and personal success are expected to put more effort into CT learning. This is also expected from students who enjoy engaging in CT tasks and are interested in them, regardless of external incentives. The described elements of perceived task value are consistent with the self-determination theory (Ryan & Deci, 2000); they may be manifestations of self-determined motivation. We hypothesize: **H8.** 'Self-determined motivation' positively predicts CT.

2.3 Antecedents – Home Environment

Educational outcomes have often been linked to the home environment (Rutkowski & Rutkowski, 2013). An important aspect of home environment is 'Socioeconomic and Cultural Status' (SECS), which comprises parental income, parental education, parental occupation, and the availability of cultural goods at home. The rationale is that families with a higher SECS are able and willing to provide more favorable learning environments (Retelsdorf et al., 2011). In terms of empirical evidence, the ICILS consistently reported higher CT scores for students from families with a higher SECS. We hypothesize: **H9.** SECS positively predicts CT.

Another important aspect of home environment might be migration (OECD, 2015). Reasons for the lower performances of students from families with migration background could be due to language-related issues. The ICILS reported a significantly lower CT score for students from immigrant families in comparison to those from non-immigrant families. Hence, we hypothesize: **H10.** A migration background is negatively associated with CT.

2.4 Processes – Learning Opportunities

Both formal and informal learning opportunities may be necessary to foster CT (Grover & Pea, 2013; Wing, 2008). Although CT could be part of every subject, it is deeply rooted in computer science education (Grover & Pea, 2013) and draws on basic concepts of computer science (Wing, 2006). Hence, we regard computer science instruction as a formal learning opportunity for CT and hypothesize: **H11.** Computer science instruction positively predicts CT.

Besides formal learning opportunities, CT could also be fostered in informal settings, i.e., outside of school courses. Durak and Saritepeci (2018) hypothesized that the use of information and communication technology (ICT) and the internet has a positive influence on CT. However, both hypotheses were rejected. A reason for this could be that students use digital devices like smartphones to a great extent for leisure activities (Fraillon et al., 2019). These activities might not be conducive to CT. In light of this, the use of computers (PC and laptop) may be a better indicator for informal learning opportunities. We therefore hypothesize: **H12.** Duration of computer use positively predicts CT.

3. METHOD

3.1 Sample and Data Collection Process

Our sample comprises N = 202 students from the 11th (second last) grade of three 'Gymnasium Helveticum' (high schools) in German-speaking Switzerland. The students are nested in twelve classes. Data were collected using Questback Unipark. The class teachers supervised the students and ensured a suitable test environment. The allotted time was 90 minutes, but all students were allowed to finish their work. All students fully answered the questions. On average, the students were aged 17.23 years (SD = 0.85 years); 56% were female. They reported 2.89 hours (SD = 1.20 hours) of computer science instruction in the past. Of the student, 77% claimed to be able to program in languages such as Java or Python.

3.2 Measures

We operationalize CT self-efficacy using a validated short German version of CTS. The short version comprises three items for each of the five CTS dimensions. Table 1 reports sample items for all five dimensions of this short version. For all CTS items in the short version, refer to Guggemos et al. (2023).

Table 1. Sample items of the used CTS short version.

Creativity	"I believe that I can solve possible problems that may occur when I encounter a new situation."
Algorithmic thinking	"I can mathematically express the solutions for the problems I face in daily life."
Cooperativity	"I like solving problems related to a group project together with my friends in cooperative learning."
Critical thinking	"I make use of a systematic method while comparing the options at hand and while reaching a decision."
Problem solving	"I cannot apply the solutions I plan respectively and gradually." (R)

Note. Items taken from Korkmaz et al. (2017, p. 565). Measured on a 7-point rating scale ranging from 'not true at all' to 'entirely true'. R = reverse coding.

3.3 Data Analysis

We use linear regression to predict CT self-efficacy. Measurement error can bias the results. Therefore, we adopt the approach of Savalei (2019) to consider measurement error. We calculate sum scores for each of the five CT dimensions. Then we restrict the residual variance of these five dependent variables to an error variance corresponding to a reliability of .9. Such reliability might be a reasonable upper limit. This aligns with the actual observed values of α and ω, as presented in Table 2. We employ manifest variables for the independent variables (Retelsdorf et al., 2011). The analyses are performed with the package lavaan 0.6-9 (Rosseel, 2012).

4. RESULTS

4.1 Quality of Measurement Instrument – Dependent Variables

Table 2 displays the reliability as well as convergent validity of the five dimensions: α and $\omega > .7$, AVE > .5. Discriminant validity is also ensured as the heterotrait-monotrait ratio is smaller than 0.71. Overall, these figures indicate a decent quality of the measurement instrument (Hair et al., 2019).

Table 2. Validity and reliability assessment of the German CTS short version (N = 202)

					Manifest correlations, square root of AVE on diagonal				
Construct	M (SD)	α	ω	AVE	(1)	(2)	(3)	(4)	(5)
(1) Creativity (3 items)	5.4 (1.2)	.87	.87	.75	.87				
(2) Algorithmic thinking (3 items)	3.9 (1.7)	.90	.90	.73	**.28**	.85			
(3) Cooperativity (3 items)	4.5 (1.6)	.89	.80	.70	.19	.13	.84		
(4) Critical thinking (3 items	4.9 (1.2)	.80	.80	.57	**.59**	**.53**	**.19**	.75	
(5) Problem solving (3 items)	5.3 (1.6)	.78	.78	.54	.17	-.00	-.14	.13	.73

Note. Items measured on a 7-point rating scale. λ = standardized loading, α = Cronbach's alpha, ω = Revelle's Omega Total, AVE = average variance extracted. Figures in bold represent correlations significant at the 5% level.

4.2 Quality of Measurement Instrument – Independent Variables

Table 3 summarizes the used variables and instruments for operationalizing the predictors. Sample items are provided. As can be seen, (where applicable) internal consistency reliability is achieved.

Table 3. Operationalization of predictors, assessment of reliability, and taken actions

Predictor	Instrument	Scale	Reliability	(Sample) item
Gender	self-report (Konsortium PISA.ch, 2018)	male = 1, female = 0	n/a	What is your gender?
Reasoning ability	6-items performance test (Heydasch et al., 2017)	binary, multiple-choice	ω = .76, α = .70 ✓	Preview available here: https://ww2.unipark.de/uc/HOT_preview/ospe.php?SES=39f1d2b152f885e494fd8ea5c6bd3fb6
Mathematical skills	self-report grade	1 (worst) – 6 (best)	n/a	What was your grade in Mathematics last school year?
Language skills	self-report grade	1 (worst) – 6 (best)	n/a	What was your grade in German last school year?
Ability to program	1-item self-evaluation	binary	n/a (single-item)	Are you able to program (e.g., Java or Python)?
Computer literacy	20-item performance test (Richter et al., 2010)	binary, multiple-choice	ω = .79, α = .76 ✓	You want to prevent other people from following your navigation behavior on the Internet. What measure contributes to this?
CT Self-concept	6-item self-evaluation (Köller et al., 2000)	rating 1 – 7	ω = .93, α = .88 ✓	Generally, solving that kind of tasks is easy for me. (Samples are provided)
Self-determined CT motivation	9-item self-evaluation (Prenzel et al., 1998)	rating 1 – 7	ω = .95, α = .93 ✓	Performing such tasks is fun for me (Samples are provided)
Parents' socioeconomic and cultural status (SECS)	self-report (Konsortium PISA.ch, 2018): scaled to M = 50, SD = 10	3 components: ISEI father, ISEI mother, no. books	n/a (formative measurement)	What does your mother do for a living? (open-ended question)
Migration background	self-report: at least one parent born outside of Switzerland (Retelsdorf et al., 2011)	yes = 1, no = 0	n/a	Were both your parents born in Switzerland? (reverse coding)
Past computer science instruction	self-report (Konsortium PISA.ch, 2018)	number of lessons	n/a	How many computer science lessons have you had in the past?
Duration of computer use	self-report (Konsortium PISA.ch, 2018)	rating 1 – 7 ranging from 0 – more than 6 hours/day	n/a	How long do you use the computer (PC or laptop) on a normal day?

Note. ISEI = International Socio-Economic Index of Occupational Status derived from parents' occupation (Ganzeboom et al., 1992). ω = Revelle's Omega Total, α = Cronbach's Alpha. ✓ = sufficient reliability. Self-report = fact is reported. Self-evaluation = (subjective) evaluation necessary. Rating scales 1 – 7 ranging from entire disagreement to entire agreement.

4.3 Regression Analysis

Table 4 depicts the results of the regression analysis.

Table 4. Linear regressions with the five CT self-efficacy dimensions as outcome variables (N = 202)

		CT dimensions									
		Creativity		Algorithmic Thinking		Cooperativity		Critical Thinking		Problem solving	
H	Predictor	Est.	s.e.[a]	Est.	s.e.[a]	Est.	s.e.[a]	Est.	s.e.[a]	Est.	s.e.[a]
1	Male gender	-0.19	0.15	0.27	0.19	-0.03	0.20	-0.17	0.14	0.10	0.16
2	Reasoning ability	-0.02	0.04	0.05	0.06	***-0.15***	***0.05***	-0.05	0.05	-0.04	0.05
3	Mathematical skills	***-0.19***	***0.09***	**0.57**	**0.12**	-0.04	0.15	-0.00	0.10	-0.00	0.13
4	Language skills	0.25	0.16	-0.21	0.15	-0.09	0.19	0.18	0.15	0.23	0.15
5	Ability to program	0.04	0.16	**0.53**	**0.18**	0.36	0.21	0.30	0.17	0.25	0.21
6	Computer literacy	0.01	0.02	-0.01	0.02	-0.01	0.03	0.02	0.02	0.03	0.02
7	CT self-concept	**0.30**	**0.08**	**0.28**	**0.10**	0.09	0.10	**0.47**	**0.08**	**0.23**	**0.10**
8	Self-determined CT motivation	0.08	0.07	**0.19**	**0.08**	0.05	0.08	**0.13**	**0.06**	***-0.22***	***0.09***
9	Parents' SECS	-0.00	0.01	0.01	0.01	0.02	0.01	**0.02**	**0.01**	-0.01	0.01
10	Migration background	-0.12	0.14	0.19	0.16	-0.12	0.17	-0.01	0.14	-0.13	0.16
11	Past computer science instruction	-0.08	0.07	-0.07	0.09	**0.23**	**0.11**	-0.14	0.08	0.10	0.09
12	Duration of computer use	-0.07	0.05	-0.09	0.06	-0.18	0.08	***-0.23***	***0.05***	-0.02	0.06
	R^2	.215		.511		.146		.467		.165	

Note. Figures in bold indicate significance at the 5% level; figures in italic indicate results contradicting the hypothesis.
[a] cluster robust standard error (cluster = class).

None of our hypothesis was fully supported. Hypotheses with mixed results are H1, H3, H5, H7, H8, H9, and H11. The hypotheses not supported by our evidence are H2, H4, H6, H10, and H12.

5. LIMITATIONS, DISCUSSION, AND IMPLICATIONS

5.1 Limitations

Our study is not without limitations. The associations reported cannot be interpreted as causal since omitted variables might account for the relationships. We attempted to mitigate this risk through a comprehensive review of variables that influence CT from a theoretical point of view. Our sample has a narrow scope, including only students from German-speaking Switzerland and specifically from one school type, the Gymnasium Helveticum. The dependent variable, CT, is measured using a short version of CTS. However, employing the full version could introduce problems related to discriminant validity (Guggemos et al., 2019).

5.2 Discussion

As Table 4 shows, the association between the CT predictors and CT self-efficacy varies considerably depending on the CTS dimension. Hence, our results may complement the work of Durak and Saritepeci (2018) who used CTS to form a single outcome variable. Contrary to our hypothesis, the male gender is not positively related to CT self-efficacy. This is consistent with the findings of Durak and Saritepeci (2018). Against this backdrop, the assertion that female students' lower CT can be attributed to lower self-efficacy may be doubtful. Across all five dimensions of CTS, CT self-concept appears to be the best predictor. This might not be surprising as self-concept and self-efficacy are closely related (Bong & Skaalvik, 2003). Self-determined motivation is also a significant predictor for algorithmic and critical thinking; this may point to the overall importance of motivation, as captured by the EVM, for predicting CT self-efficacy.

Other than in the ICILS, variables from the area *home environment* and *learning opportunities* can explain hardly any variance. The reason may be that the ICILS used a performance test instead of a self-assessment instrument to measure CT. Overall, the best prediction is possible for algorithmic thinking. The explained variance equals 51.1%, which may be a moderate proportion (Hair et al., 2019). For cooperativity, on the other hand, the explanatory power of the model is weak with an explained variance of only 14.6%.

There were also four findings contrary to our hypotheses that we will discuss in the following. Mathematics skills negatively predict creativity. The meta-analysis of Bicer et al. (2021) reports a positive association of general creativity and mathematical achievement ($r = .39$). However, the constructs in this meta-analysis are captured with performance tests. Students with higher mathematical skills may perceive their creativity as low although this might, in fact, not be the case. Further research may elaborate the nature of computational thinking creativity and develop test instruments for this construct. Developing such a domain specific concept may be promising. Bicer et al. (2021) showed that the association of mathematical achievement is higher with mathematical creativity ($r = .53$) than with general creativity ($r = .39$).

The association between reasoning ability and cooperativity is negative. Reasoning ability is a core facet of general intelligence. In light of this, the findings may be contrary to findings of more intelligent people are more capable of cooperating (Jones, 2008). Again, the reason for the negative association may lie in the nature of the CTS. Cooperativity in the sense of the CTS focus on the willingness to collaborate with friends and classmates. Intelligent students may deliberately choose who they work with. In a classroom setting, they may have had unfavorable experiences in the past, e.g., with group phenomenon such as free riding. This may have reduced their willingness to cooperate in such a setting. Further research may focus on the ability to cooperate in a broad context, i.e., not restricted to friends and classmates. The small correlation of cooperativity with the other four dimensions of CTS may also indicate a different nature of this construct.

Critical thinking is negatively associated with duration of computer use. However, McMahon (2009) reported a positive correlation between the length of time spent within technology-rich environments and the development of critical thinking skills. Again, our contrary finding could be attributed to the different nature of self-reports and performance tests as used by McMahon (2009). Another reason may be that students in their free time do not use computers for pedagogically meaningful purposes. Since free time is limited, heavy computer users might have less time for activities that are reportedly conducive to critical thinking, e.g., reading books and newspapers (Carr, 1988).

Problem solving is negatively associated with self-determined CT motivation. The reason may be the measurement of problem solving. Guggemos et al. (2023) argue that the operationalization of this dimension by CTS is problematic: all the items that capture problem solving are reversely coded. Hence, the factor problem solving may be a methodological artefact. At the content level, there is no obvious reason why self-determined CT motivation negatively predicts problem solving. Again, this finding might indicate the need to revise CTS.

5.3 Implications

Our work has three main implications: 1) Further elaboration on the CTS might help clarify the nature of the constructs and their operationalization. Specifically, the dimension *problem solving* could be problematic as it comprises only reversely coded items. 2) Aggregating the five CTS dimensions into a single CT-score seems problematic. Results vary significantly when each of the five dimensions is treated as a dependent variable. 3) Of all five CTS dimensions, algorithmic thinking may be at the core of CT self-efficacy, as the conceptually based predictors can explain the greatest proportion of variance.

REFERENCES

AERA, APA, & NCME. (2014). *Standards for educational and psychological testing.* American Educational Research Association. https://eric.ed.gov/?id=ED565876

Ambrosio, A. P., Xavier, C., & Georges, F. (2015). Digital ink for cognitive assessment of computational thinking. *IEE Frontiers in Education Conference*, 1520–1526. https://doi.org/10.1109/FIE.2014.7044237

Barr, D., Harrison, J., & Conery, L. (2011). Computational thinking: A digital age skill for everyone. *Learning & Leading with Technology*, *38*(6), 20–23. https://eric.ed.gov/?id=EJ918910

Barr, V., & Stephenson, C. (2011). Bringing computational thinking to K-12. *ACM Inroads*, *2*(1), 48–54. https://doi.org/10.1145/1929887.1929905

Bicer, A., Chamberlin, S., & Perihan, C. (2021). A Meta-Analysis of the Relationship between Mathematics Achievement and Creativity. *The Journal of Creative Behavior*, *55*(3), 569–590. https://doi.org/10.1002/jocb.474

Bong, M., & Skaalvik, E. M. (2003). Academic self-concept and self-efficacy: How different are they really? *Educational Psychology Review*, *15*(1), 1–40. https://doi.org/10.1023/A:1021302408382

Buitrago Flórez, F., Casallas, R., Hernández, M., Reyes, A., Restrepo, S., & Danies, G. (2017). Changing a generation's way of thinking: Teaching computational thinking through programming. *Review of Educational Research*, *87*(4), 834–860. https://doi.org/10.3102/0034654317710096

Carr, K. S. (1988). How can we teach critical thinking? *Childhood Education*, *65*(2), 69–73. https://doi.org/10.1080/00094056.1988.10522400

del Olmo-Muñoz, J., Cózar-Gutiérrez, R., & González-Calero, J. A. (2020). Computational thinking through unplugged activities in early years of primary education. *Computers & Education*, *150*, online first. https://doi.org/10.1016/j.compedu.2020.103832

Durak, H. Y., & Saritepeci, M. (2018). Analysis of the relation between computational thinking skills and various variables with the structural equation model. *Computers & Education*, *116*, 191–202. https://doi.org/10.1016/j.compedu.2017.09.004

Fraillon, J., Ainley, J., Schulz, W., Friedman, T., & Duckworth, D. (2019). *Preparing for life in a digital world: IEA International Computer and Information Literacy Study 2018 international report*. International Association for the Evaluation of Educational Achievement (IEA). https://www.iea.nl/publications/study-reports/preparing-life-digital-world

Ganzeboom, H. B., Graaf, P. M. de, & Treiman, D. J. (1992). A standard international socio-economic index of occupational status. *Social Science Research*, *21*(1), 1–56. https://doi.org/10.1016/0049-089X(92)90017-B

Grover, S., & Pea, R. (2013). Computational thinking in K-12: A review of the state of the field. *Educational Researcher*, *42*(1), 38–43. https://doi.org/10.3102/0013189X12463051

Guggemos, J. (2021). On the predictors of computational thinking and its growth at the high-school level. *Computers & Education*, *161*, 104060. https://doi.org/10.1016/j.compedu.2020.104060

Guggemos, J., Seufert, S., & Román-González, M. (2019). Measuring computational thinking - adapting a performance test and a self-assessment instrument for German-speaking countries. *Proceedings of the 16th International Conference Cognition and Exploratory Learning in the Digital Age (CELDA)*, 183–191. https://doi.org/10.33965/celda2019_201911L023

Guggemos, J., Seufert, S., & Román-González, M. (2023). Computational Thinking Assessment – Towards More Vivid Interpretations. *Technology, Knowledge and Learning*, *28*, 539–568. doi.org/10.1007/s10758-021-09587-2

Hair, J. F., Risher, J. J., Sarstedt, M., & Ringle, C. M. (2019). When to use and how to report the results of PLS-SEM. *European Business Review*, *31*(1), 2–24. https://doi.org/10.1108/EBR-11-2018-0203

Heydasch, T., Haubrich, J., & Renner, K.-H. (2017). The short version of the Hagen Matrices Test (HMT-S): 6-Item induction intelligence test. *methoden, daten, analysen*, *7*(2), 183–202. https://doi.org/10.12758/MDA.2013.011

Hsu, T.-C., Chang, S.-C., & Hung, Y.-T. (2018). How to learn and how to teach computational thinking: Suggestions based on a review of the literature. *Computers & Education*, *126*, 296–310. https://doi.org/10.1016/j.compedu.2018.07.004

Israel, M., Pearson, J. N., Tapia, T., Wherfel, Q. M., & Reese, G. (2015). Supporting all learners in school-wide computational thinking: A cross-case qualitative analysis. *Computers & Education*, *82*, 263–279. https://doi.org/10.1016/j.compedu.2014.11.022

ISTE. (2015). *Computational thinking: leadership toolkit*. https://www.iste.org/computational-thinking

Jones, G. (2008). Are smarter groups more cooperative? Evidence from prisoner's dilemma experiments, 1959–2003. *Journal of Economic Behavior & Organization*, *68*(3-4), 489–497. https://doi.org/10.1016/j.jebo.2008.06.010

Kafai, Y. B., & Proctor, C. (2022). A Revaluation of Computational Thinking in K–12 Education: Moving Toward Computational Literacies. *Educational Researcher*, *51*(2), 146–151. https://doi.org/10.3102/0013189X211057904

Köller, O., Daniels, Z., Schnabel, K. U., & Baumert, J. (2000). Course selections of girls and boys in mathematics: The role of academic self-concept and interest. *Zeitschrift für Pädagogische Psychologie*, *14*(1), 26–37. https://doi.org/10.1024//1010-0652.14.1.26

Konsortium PISA.ch. (2018). *Schülerinnen und Schüler der Schweiz im internationalen Vergleich [Students in Switzerland in international comparison]*. Konsortium PISA.ch. https://www.sbfi.admin.ch/dam/sbfi/de/dokumente/2019 /12/bericht-pisa-2018.pdf.download.pdf/pisa-2018-bericht_d.pdf

Korkmaz, Ö., Çakir, R., & Özden, M. Y. (2017). A validity and reliability study of the computational thinking scales (CTS). *Computers in Human Behavior*, *72*, 558–569. https://doi.org/10.1016/j.chb.2017.01.005

Lye, S. Y., & Koh, J. H. L. (2014). Review on teaching and learning of computational thinking through programming: What is next for K-12? *Computers in Human Behavior*, *41*, 51–61. https://doi.org/10.1016/j.chb.2014.09.012

Master, A., Cheryan, S., & Meltzoff, A. N. (2016). Computing whether she belongs: Stereotypes undermine girls' interest and sense of belonging in computer science. *Journal of Educational Psychology*, *108*(3), 424–437. https://doi.org/10.1037/edu0000061

McMahon, G. (2009). Critical thinking and ICT integration in a Western Australian secondary school. *Educational Technology & Society*, *12*(4), 269–291. https://www.jstor.org/stable/10.2307/jeductechsoci.12.4.269

Newman, I., Ridenour, C. S., Newman, C., & DeMarco, G. M. P., Jr. (2007). A typology of research purposes and its relationship to mixed methods. In A. Tashakkori & C. Teddlie (Eds.), *Handbook of mixed methods in social & behavioral research* (167-188). Sage.

OECD. (2015). *Immigrant students at school: Easing the journey towards integration*. OECD. https://doi.org/10.1787/9789264249509-en

Prenzel, M., Drechsel, B., & Kramer, K. (1998). Lernmotivation im kaufmännischen Unterricht: Die Sicht von Auszubildenden und Lehrkräften [Learning motivation in business education: the perspective of trainees and teachers]. *Zeitschrift für Berufs- und Wirtschaftspädagogik, special issue 14*, 169–187.

Repenning, A., Webb, D. C., Koh, K. H., Nickerson, H., Miller, S. B., Brand, C., Her Many Horses, I., Basawapatna, A., Gluck, F., Grover, R., Gutierrez, K., & Repenning, N. (2015). Scalable game design: A strategy to bring systemic computer science education to schools through game design and simulation creation. *ACM Transactions on Computing Education*, *15*(2), 1–31. https://doi.org/10.1145/2700517

Retelsdorf, J., Köller, O., & Möller, J. (2011). On the effects of motivation on reading performance growth in secondary school. *Learning and Instruction*, *21*(4), 550–559. https://doi.org/10.1016/j.learninstruc.2010.11.001

Richter, T., Naumann, J., & Horz, H. (2010). A revised version of the Computer Literacy Inventory (INCOBI-R). *Zeitschrift Für Pädagogische Psychologie*, *24*(1), 23–37. https://doi.org/10.1024/1010-0652/a000002

Román-González, M., Moreno-León, J., & Robles, G. (2019). Combining assessment tools for a comprehensive evaluation of computational thinking interventions. In S. C. Kong & H. Abelson (Eds.), *Computational thinking education* (pp. 79–98). Springer. https://doi.org/10.1007/978-981-13-6528-7_6

Román-González, M., Pérez-González, J.-C., & Jiménez-Fernández, C. (2017). Which cognitive abilities underlie computational thinking? Criterion validity of the Computational Thinking Test. *Computers in Human Behavior*, *72*, 678–691. https://doi.org/10.1016/j.chb.2016.08.047

Román-González, M., Pérez-González, J.-C., Moreno-León, J., & Robles, G. (2018). Extending the nomological network of computational thinking with non-cognitive factors. *Computers in Human Behavior*, *80*, 441–459. https://doi.org/10.1016/j.chb.2017.09.030

Rosseel, Y. (2012). lavaan: An R package for structural equation modeling. *Journal of Statistical Software*, *48*(2), 1–36. https://doi.org/10.18637/jss.v048.i02

Rutkowski, D., & Rutkowski, L. (2013). Measuring socioeconomic background in PISA: One size might not fit all. *Research in Comparative and International Education*, *8*(3), 259–278. https://doi.org/10.2304/rcie.2013.8.3.259

Ryan, R. M., & Deci, E. L. (2000). Self-determination theory and the facilitation of intrinsic motivation, social development, and well-being. *American Psychologist*, *55*(1), 68–78. https://doi.org/10.1037/0003-066X.55.1.68

Savalei, V. (2019). A comparison of several approaches for controlling measurement error in small samples. *Psychological Methods*, *24*(3), 352–370. https://doi.org/10.1037/met0000181

Scherer, R., Tondeur, J., & Siddiq, F. (2017). On the quest for validity: Testing the factor structure and measurement invariance of the technology-dimensions in the Technological, Pedagogical, and Content Knowledge (TPACK) model. *Computers & Education*, *112*, 1–17. https://doi.org/10.1016/j.compedu.2017.04.012

Shavelson, R. J., Hubner, J. J., & Stanton, G. C. (1976). Self-Concept: validation of construct interpretations. *Review of Educational Research*, *46*(3), 407–441. https://doi.org/10.2307/1170010

Shute, V. J., Sun, C., & Asbell-Clarke, J. (2017). Demystifying computational thinking. *Educational Research Review*, *22*, 142–158. https://doi.org/10.1016/j.edurev.2017.09.003

Tsarava, K., Moeller, K., Román-González, M., Golle, J., Leifheit, L., Butz, M. V., & Ninaus, M. (2022). A cognitive definition of computational thinking in primary education. *Computers & Education*, *179*, 104425. https://doi.org/10.1016/j.compedu.2021.104425

Wigfield, A., & Eccles, J. (2000). Expectancy-Value Theory of achievement motivation. *Contemporary Educational Psychology*, *25*(1), 68–81. https://doi.org/10.1006/ceps.1999.1015

Wing, J. M. (2006). Computational thinking. *Communications of the ACM*, *49*(3), 33–35. https://doi.org/10.1145/1118178.1118215

Wing, J. M. (2008). Computational thinking and thinking about computing. *Philosophical Transactions. Series A, Mathematical, Physical, and Engineering Sciences*, *366*(1881), 3717–3725. https://doi.org/10.1098/rsta.2008.0118

Wüstenberg, S., Greiff, S., & Funke, J. (2012). Complex problem solving — More than reasoning? *Intelligence*, *40*(1), 1–14. https://doi.org/10.1016/j.intell.2011.11.003

Zhang, L., & Nouri, J. (2019). A systematic review of learning computational thinking through Scratch in K-9. *Computers & Education*, *141*, 103607. https://doi.org/10.1016/j.compedu.2019.103607

ONLINE PRESENCE, METACOGNITION, AND COURSE DESIGN WITHIN THE COMMUNITY OF INQUIRY

Larisa Olesova[1] and Ayesha Sadaf[2]
[1]*University of Florida*
618 SW 12th ST, Rm. 2821, Gainesville, FL 32601, USA
[2]*University of North Carolina Charlotte*
9201 University City Blvd, Charlotte, NC 28223, USA

ABSTRACT

This study examined students' perceived metacognition and online presence within the Community of Inquiry (CoI) framework in online courses. Forty students participated in this study. Data were collected through the CoI survey instrument and shared metacognition questionnaire. The findings revealed students rated teaching presence as the highest while social presence was the lowest among the three presences. Students rated individual metacognition higher than group metacognition. Students identified readings, discussions, and application activities as the most contributing course elements to their critical thinking. Students shared that the instructor's feedback was the most encouraging facilitation technique for critical thinking. The findings of this study will be helpful for researchers and practitioners who design and teach asynchronous online courses for undergraduate students to promote metacognition.

KEYWORDS

Community of Inquiry, Metacognition, Online Presence, Asynchronous

1. INTRODUCTION

There is a need to understand undergraduate students learning in asynchronous online courses (Garrison and Akyol 2015). Research suggests that understanding how metacognition manifests in a shared learning environment can help select effective course designs to guide deep learning outcomes (Garrison 2022). Previous studies examined how group activities can impact students' individual metacognition to self-regulate critical thinking (DiDonato 2013; Koehler et al. 2020). DiDonato (2013) found that group interactions can contribute to individual metacognition when students were given a complex semi-structured task. However, Koehler et al. (2022) found that students did not have effective regulation strategies to deal with the complexity of group ownership. Researchers suggested that group activities should be thoughtfully designed to help students individually and collaboratively regulate their learning. Koehler et al. (2020) noted that further research is needed to determine how students can regulate learning. Similarly, Garrison (2022) noted that the role of metacognition in online courses has not been enough examined yet. It is not clear enough how critical thinking should be structured in shared contexts when students participate in group activities, i.e., discussions.

Therefore, this study is an attempt to fill this gap by providing an examination of undergraduate students' perceptions of online presence and metacognition when they participate in asynchronous online course group activities, i.e., discussions or role-play. The following research questions guided this study:

1. What are student perceptions of online presence (teaching, social, and cognitive) in asynchronous online courses?
2. What are student perceptions of metacognition in asynchronous online courses?
3. What course design elements contributed to student learning and what course aspects encouraged perceived critical thinking?

2. BACKGROUND

The Community of Inquiry (CoI) framework has been created to help examine the construction of individual and group learning experiences in asynchronous online courses (Garrison 2022). The framework consists of three overlapping presences: cognitive presence, teaching presence, and social presence (Garrison et al. 2010a). In this study, we define them as the study constructs. The construct of cognitive presence guides the construction of meaning through reflection and discourse; it is operationalized through the Practical Inquiry model that supports the dynamics of reflective thinking and a collaborative inquiry process (Garrison et al. 2001). The construct of social presence can enhance students' cognitive processes through social interactions in asynchronous online environments; it also can predict students perceived cognitive presence (Akyol and Garrison 2008). The construct of teaching presence is defined as "the design, facilitation, and direction of cognitive and social processes to realize personally meaningful and educationally worthwhile learning outcomes" (Anderson et al. 2001, p.5). This type of presence is essential to establishing and maintaining an effective social and cognitive presence (Garrison et al. 2010b). In addition, teaching presence contributes to the creation of an online community of learners to provide opportunities for social interactions.

According to Garrison and Akyol (2015, p. 67), teaching presence can help "understand metacognitive development by encouraging students to take personal responsibility for their learning through facilitating discourse and resolving misunderstandings collaboratively." Metacognitive development or metacognitive construct is defined as "a set of higher knowledge and skills to monitor and regulate cognitive processes of self and others" (Garrison and Akyol 2015, p.184). Metacognition is a required cognitive ability to achieve deep and meaningful learning that must be viewed from both an individual and social perspective.

Garrison, Anderson, and Archer's (2000) Community of Inquiry (CoI) was used as the theoretical framework to understand students' perceptions of online presence and metacognition in asynchronous online courses. The CoI framework provides a model of cognition that operationalizes online learning with the perspective of understanding metacognitive processes in the asynchronous online learning environment (Garrison 2022). The CoI framework was used as a guide to examine how students deal with multiple opportunities to be self-reflective and communicative to support and sustain metacognition in the asynchronous learning environment (Garrison and Akyol 2015). The commonality between metacognition and the CoI is the interplay between internal knowledge construction and course learning activities. The CoI framework was used because it emphasizes both the personal and shared worlds of a learning experience, which is consistent with metacognition in the shared online learning environment and the integration of the personal and shared view of metacognition (Garrison et al. 2010a).

3. METHODS

A descriptive research design was used to provide exploration regarding the perceived online presence construct (teaching, cognitive, and social) and metacognitive construct in asynchronous online courses for undergraduate students. Forty students from a public university located in the Mid-Atlantic area of the U.S. participated in this study. The sample was majority female (80.0%, n = 32; male: 17.5%, n = 7; unknown: 2.5 %, n =1) and approximately more than half (67.5%, n = 27) of them were in the age of between 18 and 25 years. The majority (75.0%, n=30) of the participants have taken more than four online courses, and most (62.5%, n=25) of them rated themselves as being very comfortable with participating in online courses. The sample was included in the study because students were enrolled in the Psychology Undergraduate Online Program courses in summer, 2022 and voluntarily completed the survey. The courses in this study were designed following the COI principles for collaborative learning including problem-based approach, case-based learning, role-based discussions, project-based approach, peer review facilitation, and scenario-based learning.

3.1 Data Sources

Data were collected by using the CoI Survey instrument and the metacognition questionnaire survey. The online surveys were administered to students at the end of the summer semester 2022 through Qualtrics. The CoI survey was developed by Arbaugh et al. (2008) to measure students' perception of teaching presence (TP), social presence (SP), and cognitive presence (CP). The survey consists of 34 five-point, Likert-type items (TP: 13- items, SP: 12 items, CP: 9 items). The CoI survey was validated with Cronbach's Alpha yielded internal consistencies equal to 0.94 for Teaching Presence, 0.91 for Social Presence, and 0.95 for Cognitive Presence (Arbaugh et al. 2008).

Students' perceptions of metacognition were measured using the metacognition questionnaire developed by Garrison and Akyol (2015) which includes 26 five-point, Likert-type items in two dimensions: Self-regulation and co-regulation. Each item employs a 5-point Likert-type scale, with 1 = strongly disagree and 5 = strongly agree. The metacognitive construct survey conducted by Garrison and Akyol (2015) needs further validation of the shared metacognition instrument with a larger sample size. The instrument was validated for 292 participants and the researchers did not find a correlation between the factors (individual monitoring and managing; group monitoring and managing) and self and co-regulation (Garrison and Akyol 2015, p.68). However, the instrument confirmed the metacognitive construct and has the potential to continue developing future research.

Simple demographic information was also collected such as gender, age, prior experience with online courses, and the courses to which a student was enrolled. Students were asked to respond to three sets of survey questions: with a reflection on their CoI, individual self-regulation, and co-regulation. The survey data were analyzed through descriptive statistics using means and standard deviations.

4. RESULTS

The findings for the first research question showed that students rated three presences as the following: cognitive presence (M=4.15, SD=.21); teaching presence (M=4.32; SD=0.22), and social presence (M=3.70; SD=0.33). Among the three online presences, teaching presence was rated as the highest while social presence received the lowest rating among students (M=3.70; SD=0.33). Further analysis of teaching presence revealed that students rated as the highest (M=4.63; SD=0.49), the item that the instructor provided clear instructions on how to participate in course learning activities (Table 1). It seems the online courses provided a clear and well-structured explanation of all course activities and assignments. However, the item of whether the course instructor helped identify areas of agreement and disagreement on course topics that helped students to learn received the lowest rating (M=3.92; SD=0.96). It seems that undergraduate students needed more help and support from their course instructor while participating in online course activities, i.e., online discussions or course projects.

Table 1. Students' perceptions of teaching presence in asynchronous online courses (n=40)

Teaching Presence Items	M	SD
The instructor clearly communicated important course topics.	4.54	0.64
The instructor clearly communicated important course goals.	4.56	0.60
The instructor provided clear instructions on how to participate in course learning activities.	4.63	0.49
The instructor clearly communicated important due dates/time frames for learning activities.	4.51	0.76
The instructor was helpful in identifying areas of agreement and disagreement on course topics that helped me to learn.	3.92	0.96
The instructor was helpful in guiding the class towards understanding course topics in a way that helped me clarify my thinking.	4.36	0.90
The instructor helped to keep course participants engaged and participating in productive dialogue.	4.24	0.85
The instructor helped keep the course participants on the task in a way that helped me to learn.	4.33	0.77
The instructor encouraged course participants to explore new concepts in this course.	4.41	0.72
Instructor actions reinforced the development of a sense of community among course participants.	4.13	0.84
The instructor helped to focus discussions on relevant issues in a way that helped me to learn.	4.24	0.85
The instructor provided feedback that helped me understand my strengths and weaknesses relative to the course's goals and objectives.	3.97	0.97
The instructor provided feedback in a timely fashion.	4.28	1.02

When we analyzed cognitive presence items to understand students learning, we found that students rated high (M=4.33; SD=0.70) the item that they were able to apply the knowledge created in the course to their work or other non-class-related activities (Table 2). However, the lowest rating was the item "Online discussions were valuable in helping me appreciate different perspectives" (M=3.67; SD=1.24).

Table 2. Students' perceptions of cognitive presence in asynchronous online courses (n=40)

Cognitive Presence Items	M	SD
Problems posed increased my interest in course issues.	3.77	1.04
Course activities piqued my curiosity.	4.08	0.84
I felt motivated to explore content-related questions.	4.10	0.91
I utilized a variety of information sources to explore the problems posed in this course.	4.29	0.84
Brainstorming and finding relevant information helped me resolve content-related questions.	4.11	0.86
Online discussions were valuable in helping me appreciate different perspectives.	3.67	1.24
Combining new information helped me answer questions raised in course activities.	4.26	0.64
Learning activities helped me construct explanations and solutions.	4.26	0.75
Reflection on course content and discussions helped me understand fundamental concepts in this class.	4.26	0.72
I can describe ways to test and apply the knowledge created in this course.	4.37	0.59
I have developed solutions to course problems that can be applied in practice.	4.13	0.88
I can apply the knowledge created in this course to my work or other non-class-related activities.	4.33	0.70
Overall, I was satisfied with an online course.	4.32	0.87
I learned much from an online course.	4.28	0.72

Among social presence items, the highest rating was for the item "I felt comfortable participating in the course discussions" (M= 4.14; SD=0.99) (Table 3). Students rated the lowest the item "Online or web-based communication is an excellent medium for social interaction" (M=3.18; SD=1.32).

Table 3. Students' perceptions of social presence in asynchronous online courses (n=40)

Social Presence Items	M	SD
Getting to know other course participants gave me a sense of belonging in the course.	3.38	1.18
I was able to form distinct impressions of some course participants.	3.44	1.17
Online or web-based communication is an excellent medium for social interaction.	3.18	1.32
I felt comfortable conversing through the online medium.	4.03	0.99
I felt comfortable participating in the course discussions.	4.14	0.99
I felt comfortable interacting with other course participants.	4.00	1.03
I felt comfortable disagreeing with other course participants while still maintaining a sense of trust.	3.82	1.02
I felt that my point of view was acknowledged by other course participants.	3.82	1.12
Online discussions help me to develop a sense of collaboration.	3.54	1.23

The results for the second research question revealed that individual metacognition items (Table 4) showed higher ratings than the group metacognition (Table 5). For example, students rated the item "I am aware of my effort" for self-regulation as the high (M=4.69; SD=0.47) while the item "I question my thoughts" as the lowest (M=4.21; SD=0.80). This explains that students are more confident about their learning efforts while rarely questioning their thoughts. The group metacognition showed a lower rating than the individual. This is when students share metacognition and create group knowledge together. They rated the two items "I pay attention to the ideas of others" (M=4.36; SD=0.63) and "I listen to the comments of others" (M=4.36; SD=0.74) highest while the item "I monitor the learning of others" received the lowest rating (M=2.90; SD=1.19). This explains that students focused more on their learning and rarely contributed to helping others to learn. Interestingly, when students were asked to identify the course design elements that helped them learn, the majority (n=28; 70.0%) reported that the course readings and 60% (n=24) identified discussions as the design elements that helped them learn. However, reflection on learning and practice received the lowest rating (n=4; 10%).

Table 4. Students' perceptions of individual metacognition in asynchronous online courses (n=40)

Metacognition Items Individual	M	SD
I am aware of my effort	4.69	0.47
I am aware of my thinking	4.62	0.54
I am aware of my level of motivation	4.59	0.50
I question my thoughts	4.21	0.80
I make judgments about the difficulty of a problem	4.33	0.66
I am aware of my existing knowledge	4.41	0.75
I am aware of my level of learning	4.36	0.90
I assess my understanding	4.46	0.64
I change my strategy when I need to	4.33	0.62
I search for new strategies when needed	4.36	0.58
I apply strategies	4.38	0.63
I assess how I approach the problem	4.26	0.69
I assess my strategies	4.31	0.69

Table 5. Students' perceptions of group metacognition in asynchronous online courses (n=40)

Metacognition Items Group	M	SD
I pay attention to the ideas of others.	4.36	0.63
I listen to the comments of others	4.36	0.74
I consider the feedback of others	4.26	0.82
I reflect upon the comments of others	4.28	0.83
I observe the strategies of others	4.08	0.94
I observe how others are doing	3.92	1.11
I look for confirmation of my understanding from others	4.15	0.90
I request information from others	3.54	1.10
I respond to the contribution that others make	3.97	0.81
I challenge the strategies of others	3.49	1.02
I challenge the perspectives of others	3.51	0.97
I help the learning of others	3.62	0.94
I monitor the learning of others	2.90	1.19

The analysis of students' answers to open-ended questions revealed that students found that application activities contributed to their learning because they were able to apply their knowledge, i.e., role play. Other frequently mentioned course aspects that contributed to learning were instructional videos and well-organized course structure. Among the least contributed course aspects to learning were responding to others in discussions and completing quizzes through the lockdown browser. Interestingly, when students were asked to share suggestions on further course improvements, students shared that they wanted more interactive discussions and more role-play activities. When asked about what encouraged their critical thinking, students mentioned that the course design, engagement, and course topics encouraged them to learn. Among instructor facilitation techniques that encouraged or discouraged students' critical thinking, some students mentioned that the instructor's feedback encouraged them while others shared that minimal or no instructor's feedback discouraged their critical thinking.

5. DISCUSSION

To facilitate higher-order learning among undergraduate students, instructors need to structure group activities in a way to help undergraduate students move from individual metacognition (self-regulation) to shared (group) metacognition. Students in this study still did not perceive others as the way to learn and develop critical thinking. They still focused on their learning and probably they were not ready to contribute to group knowledge. We consider that these specific findings are advantages of this study. Specifically, how students perceived their learning to contribute to the learning of others.

The findings also revealed that social presence is low in asynchronous online courses. However, students shared they wanted more engagement and fun activities, i.e., Kahoot or Zoom discussions. This suggests that the findings of this study can be applied to practice, such as instructors may pay more attention to supporting social interactions to promote cognitive presence and help students move to group-shared metacognition to build collaborative knowledge. More engagement strategies and well-designed group activities are still needed to support undergraduate students learning, especially for discussion-based activities.

6. LIMITATIONS

This study has several limitations due to the specific conditions of the data collection. The sample was not randomized because the participants were not randomly selected, and no control measures were used for comparison. Therefore, the results are not differentiated in the effect of the course design on three presences and metacognitive constructs. The sample size in some courses was low, so, the results may not be representative. Finally, the students who participated in this study were from summer courses enrolled in one online program. More data will be collected from other courses and programs.

7. CONCLUSION

This exploratory study contributed to the field of online teaching and learning to understand undergraduate students learning. Moreover, the findings of this study found evidence that undergraduate students still need instructor support in asynchronous online environments, specifically when they participate in group activities, i.e., discussions or role-play. This study also found that students needed more instructional videos and instructional feedback to promote critical thinking. More research is needed to explore the type of courses, course design, assignment tasks, and the type of students to understand how metacognitive processes manifest within the Community of Inquiry collaborative environment.

REFERENCES

Akyol Z. and Garrison D. R. (2008). The development of a Community of Inquiry over time in an online course: Understanding the progression and integration of social, cognitive and teaching presence. *Journal of Asynchronous Learning Networks*[online], 12 (3-4), pp.3-22. Available from: https://doi.org/10.24059/olj.v12i3-4.1680 [accessed 10 September 2023].

Anderson T., Rourke L., Garrison R. and Archer W. (2001). Assessing teacher presence in a computer conferencing context. *Journal of Asynchronous Learning Networks* [online], 5(2), pp 1-17. Available from: https://doi.org/10.24059/olj.v5i2.1875 [accessed 10 September 2023].

Arbaugh J. B., Cleveland-Innes M., Diaz S. R. D., Garrison R., Ice P., Richardson J.C. and Swan K.P. (2008). Developing a Community of Inquiry instrument: Testing a measure of the Community of Inquiry Framework using a multi-institutional sample. *The Internet and Higher Education* [online], 11(3-4), pp. 133-136. Available from: https://doi.org/10.1016/j.iheduc.2008.06.003 [accessed 10 September 2023].

DiDonato N. (2013). Effective self- and co-regulation in collaborative learning groups: An analysis of how students regulate problem-solving of authentic interdisciplinary tasks. *Instructional Science* [online], 41(1), pp 25-47. Available from: https://doi.org/10.1007/s11251-012-9206-9 [accessed 10 September 2023].

Garrison D. R. (2022). Shared metacognition in a Community of Inquiry. *Online Learning* [online], 26 (1), pp 6-18. Available from: https://doi.org/10.24059/olj.v26i1.3023 [accessed 10 September 2023].

Garrison D. R. and Akyol Z. (2015). Toward the development of a metacognition construct for communities of inquiry framework. *Internet and Higher Education* [online], 24, pp 66–71. Available from: https://doi.org/10.1016/j.iheduc.2014.10.001 [accessed 10 September 2023].

Garrison D. R., Anderson T. and Archer W. (2001). Critical thinking, cognitive presence, and computer conferencing in distance education. *American Journal of Distance Education* [online], 15 (1), pp 7-23. Available from: https://doi.org/10.1080/08923640109527071 [accessed 10 September 2023].

Garrison D. R., Anderson T. and Archer W. (2010a). The first decade of the community of inquiry framework: A retrospective. *The Internet and Higher Education* [online], 13(1–2), pp 5–9. Available from: https://doi.org/10.1016/j.iheduc.2009.10.003 [accessed 10 September 2023].

Garrison D.R., Anderson T. and Archer W. (2000). Critical inquiry in a text-based environment: Computer conferencing in higher education. *The Internet and Higher Education* [online], 2 (2–3), pp 87–105. Available from: https://doi.org/10.1016/S1096-7516(00)00016-6 [accessed 10 September 2023].

Garrison D.R., Cleveland-Innes M. and Fung T.S. (2010b). Exploring causal relationships among teaching, cognitive and social presence: Student perceptions of the community of inquiry framework. *The Internet and Higher Education* [online], 13(1-2), pp 31-36. Available from: https://doi.org/10.1016/j.iheduc.2009.10.002 [accessed 10 September 2023].

Koehler A.A., Cheng Z., Fiock H., Janakiraman S. and Wang H. (2020). Asynchronous online discussions during case-based learning: A problem-solving process. *Online Learning* [online], 24(4), pp. 64-92. Available from: https://doi.org/10.24059/olj.v24i4.2332 [accessed 10 September 2023].

Koehler A.A., Cheng Z., Fiock H., Wang H., Janakiraman S. and Chartier K. (2022). Examining students' use of online case-based discussions to support problem solving: Considering individual and collaborative experiences. *Computers & Education* [online], 179. Available from: https://doi.org/10.1016/j.compedu.2021.104407 [accessed 10 September 2023].

THE USE OF METACOGNITIVE STRATEGIES IN STORYTELLING TO EXAMINE PRESCHOOL CHILDREN'S LISTENING COMPREHENSION SKILLS

Mahani Abdul Malik
Faculty of Education, Open University Malaysia
Malaysia

ABSTRACT

Listening comprehension is necessary for successful learning and communication in this modern digital age. Studies have shown that early exposure to listening activities can significantly impact the development of listening comprehension skills, especially in preschool children, as their cognitive and linguistic abilities rapidly develop. The purpose of this qualitative study is to explore the use of metacognitive strategies in storytelling to examine preschool children's listening comprehension skills in preschool children in Kepong, Malaysia. Data was collected through the checklist and anecdotal observation to observe six children's engagement in 3 storytelling sessions. The study was done in 2 phases: Phase 1 involved data collection of the teacher's current teaching instructions and challenges faced during teaching and learning. Phase 2 involved designing appropriate metacognitive strategies to examine children's English listening comprehension skills. The study showed metacognitive strategies could help preschool children with listening comprehension skills.

KEYWORDS

Metacognitive Instructions, Storytelling, Listening Comprehension Skills, Preschool Children

1. INTRODUCTION

Stories have existed since cave drawings as far back as 30,000 years. Now storytelling has become an important component of education as it has many advantages as a teaching technique. Storytelling can motivate children (Kasami, 2021), assist children in remembering new words (Wood, 2016), encourage learning English (Isbelle, 2022), and have access to low-cost media to teach rich language experiences (Wright, 2008). Children can develop early literacy through reading and storytelling and simple games such as letter games, listening for sounds and words and looking for pictures, letters, and words in the environment (Lasim & Andy, 2017). Storytelling can also address literacy development by improving listening, oral language, reading comprehension, and writing. According to Abdul, Luqman and Zaini (2017), stories are useful materials teachers can use to develop listening comprehension and literacy in their first and second language. This reinforces Mello (2001) research on how storytelling could enhance fluency, vocabulary, writing, and recall literacy.

Lately, research has shown that children in Malaysia perform poorly in English language examinations due to their inability to comprehend the language (Hazita, 2016; Kaur, 2014). This was further confirmed in Ho's (2016) study on the relationship between speaking, reading, and writing skills and listening comprehension skills. Despite beginning to learn English at a young age, Ho's research revealed that many Malaysian children lack the listening and speaking abilities necessary for fluency. Storytelling is an effective method for listening activities recommended in the National Preschool Standard-Based Curriculum (NPSC). Although the NPSC learning standards clearly state that children should listen, respond, and talk about the story told, teachers only use the storybooks to read as a fun activity to create interest in the language without any specific task to enhance listening comprehension. Studies have shown the benefit of storytelling in improving children's attention span, comprehension and listening skills (Koroglu, 2020).

According to research, listening comprehension is a complex cognitive process that involves various cognitive and linguistic skills, such as attention, memory, inference, and knowledge of vocabulary and syntax

(Goh, 2010). Studies have shown that early exposure to listening activities can significantly impact the development of these skills, particularly in preschool-aged children (Hakuta & Ramos, 1986; Lems, 1999). Therefore, it is crucial to instil listening comprehension skills early, particularly in preschools, when children's cognitive and linguistic abilities rapidly develop. Furthermore, children exposed to listening activities and language-rich surroundings tend to perform better academically and grow cognitively (Hart & Risley, 1995; Ramani et al.,2017). If listening comprehension involves complex cognitive processes, could metacognitive strategies be a good strategy to help children improve their listening comprehension as it helps to make individuals aware of their thought processes?

Kao and Wang (2018), in their research on college-level EFL learners in Taiwan, found that students who were taught using metacognitive strategies showed significant improvement in their listening comprehension skills compared to those who did not. In addition, Cross (2010) explains metacognition can assist listeners in coordinating, regulating, and controlling their listening processes. Since preschool children are still too young to be aware of their thought processes, it would be timely to explore if metacognitive strategies used during storytelling can help children in their listening comprehension skills. Therefore, the research objective of this study is to examine preschool children's listening comprehension skills when metacognitive strategies are used during storytelling.

2. METACOGNITIVE STRATEGIES AND LISTENING COMPREHENSION SKILLS

Recent years have seen a rise in interest in the study of metacognition as a topic of particular significance in educational research due to its capacity to provide students with the vocabulary and abilities to monitor, manage, and hopefully improve children's thinking processes (Vandergrift, 2019). However, much of this research was for older children, and not many involved preschool children. However, de Boer et al. (2018) say metacognitive knowledge and skills emerge early. Still, it takes time, explicit teacher teaching, scaffolding, modelling, and plenty of practice for students to become proficient metacognitive adults. There was also much evidence supported by various meta-analyses showing a strong relationship between metacognitive strategies and children's achievements (de Boer et al., 2018).

With this in mind, research has shown that experienced listeners use twice as many metacognitive strategies as less-skilled listeners (Vandergrift 2003). Their strategies are more towards comprehension monitoring, a combination of questioning and world knowledge, and logical possibilities, unlike less-skilled listeners who tend to use more mental translation. This is not surprising if we revert to Imhof's (2010) definition of listening, which states that listening is an intentional action that requires self-regulation. This would clearly explain why metacognitive strategy improves listening skills.

Hence, preschool teachers must make children aware of what they are listening to. Teachers that use metacognitive strategies can explain to students why they are learning a concept, how it relates to other concepts, what they are expected to accomplish, how to do it, and what success looks like. This strategy is doable for preschool children. They should also be given the time and space to clarify their comprehension, ask questions, and get precise, useful feedback on various performance-related areas. These kinds of strategies can be used in storytelling sessions to examine preschool children listening comprehension skills.

In this study, the researcher used metacognitive strategies such as connecting to children's schemata (prior knowledge), explaining the storytelling's objective, predicting and using questioning techniques and scaffolding. These strategies were used during pre and post-storytelling sessions to examine preschool children's listening comprehension skills.

3. LISTENING COMPREHENSION PROCESSES

Listening comprehension is a complex cognitive process that involves the interaction between the speaker's message, the listener's background knowledge, and the listener's attention and memory processes. It involves many processes that many second-language learners with low-level languages, such as preschool children, find difficult. However, native and proficient second-language speakers have no problem understanding complex speech comprehension. According to Pourhosein and Ahmadi (2011), despite second-language learners' problems, they can control their learning and listen actively. He further explains this can be done by relying on listening strategies to overcome incomprehension.

Most listening combines top-down and bottom-up processes to increase listening comprehension, called interactive processing. Applying prior knowledge, contextual information, and linguistic information makes comprehension and interpretation easy. If the content is familiar to the listener or the listener is listening to topics stored in long-term memory, then the long-term memory can assist the listener in understanding. Prior knowledge can be used to predict and eventually understand the input (Vandegrift, 2019). However, if the content is unfamiliar to the listener, he depends solely on his linguistic ability, especially lexical and syntactic knowledge, to understand information (Pourhosein & Ahmadi, 2011). Preschool children, especially in Malaysia's interior and rural areas, are rarely exposed to English aural/oral language in their lives. These children will have difficulty recognising word segmentation and word and grammar form. If teachers could trigger children's prior experience, this would assist them in their listening comprehension skills. With this in mind, metacognition strategies would help hasten the bottom-up and top-down processes. According to Vandergrift (2019), self-regulation strategies become procedural knowledge when listeners are aware of their metacognition. One way to improve children's metacognition abilities is to expose children to listening sequences in the first two years of language learning (Vandergrift, 1999).

This research split the storytelling session into three parts pre, while and post-listening. Pre-listening is a phase for the preparatory activity to make the content explicit and explain objective and foreground roles, procedures, and listening goals. This activity aims to make children retrieve their prior knowledge and make the listener, speaker and thinking on a common level, making listening comprehension easier (Iliyas, 2017). While listening, the teachers told the story with the help of compensatory mechanisms such as pictures to help children compensate for their lack of knowledge of the target language. Post-listening is a follow-up to pre-listening meant to check comprehension and evaluate listening skills and strategies (Saha & Talukdar, 2000).

This study would be beneficial as previous research has always used metacognitive strategies with older children or adults (Cao & Lin, 2020; Du Toit & Kotze, 2009; Gaylo & Dales, 2017).

4. CONCEPTUAL FRAMEWORK

Figure 1 explains the conceptual framework of the research. In the storytelling, the researcher used four metacognitive strategies: connecting the concept of the story to the schemata (children's prior knowledge), explaining the objective of the storytelling, using questioning techniques and scaffolding (giving options, moment-to-moment feedback and chunking information). This would help the children in their listening comprehension skills. The children's listening comprehension was assessed using the following activities: retelling the story, arranging the story's sequence using pictures, completing oral questions with options given (read aloud from the worksheet), and justifying the answers given and justifying the given answer.

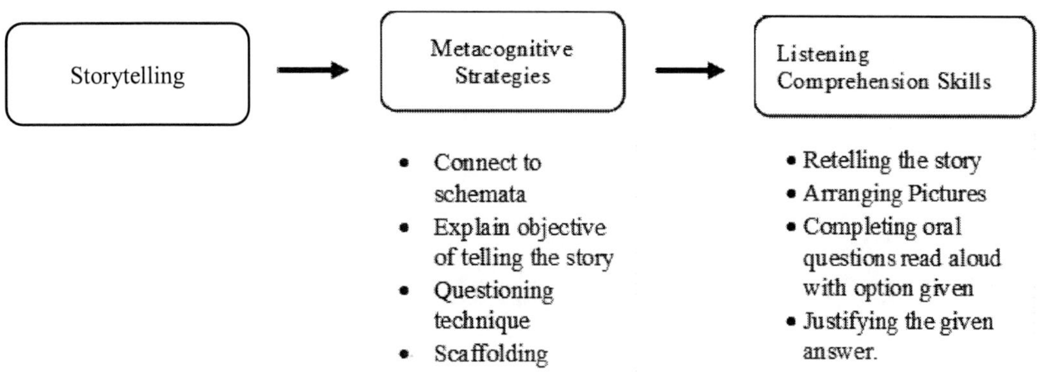

Figure 1. Conceptual framework

5. METHODOLOGY

This research employed a qualitative research approach and a case study as its research design. This approach was chosen to help the researcher comprehend what was practiced in the natural setting. Checklists and anecdotal reports were the primary methods for collecting data on children's listening comprehension skills. The research was done in 2 phases to allow the researcher to understand better what is being practiced in the natural setting. In the first phase, it was essential to understand private preschool teachers' current teaching strategies and the difficulties faced when developing children's listening comprehension skills. The teachers were interviewed, and the data were transcribed verbatim. The transcription was then coded, and common themes were extracted. This stage was crucial because it provided insights into practitioners' perspectives on the issues and strategies used during storytelling. The practitioner's perspectives were essential for developing acceptable and helpful strategies to improve the children's listening comprehension skills during storytelling. The researcher created three lesson plans in the second phase based on the information gathered in phase one, the National Preschool Standard-Based Curriculum (NPSC), listening and learning theories. Preschoolers need a systematic approach to improve their listening comprehension skills. The study employed the Mastery Learning Model, Metacognitive strategies, and cognitive Constructivist theory as a framework to create the teaching strategies needed in the three lesson plans. Three subject-matter experts reviewed the teaching strategies used in the three lesson plans. Each lesson's duration was 45 minutes, as preschool lessons were generally between 30 to 45 minutes in Malaysian preschools. Before implementing the lesson, the teachers underwent 3 hours of briefing. A dry run was done to foresee potential problems during the lessons. The lessons were recorded using two cameras placed at different classroom corners. The decision to use three lessons was based on previous research done by Santos (2018) to study children listening comprehension skills. Three storybooks chosen for this research were based on the complexity and familiarity of the books to the children, as the respondents were Chinese-speaking children who lacked the vocabulary and were more familiar with Asian culture.

Table 1. List of Storybooks

Lesson	Title of Storybooks	Author
1	1. The Blue Balloon	Mick Inpen (2019)
2	2. The Ugly Duckling	Hans Christian Anderson (2019)
3	3. My Monster and Me	Nadiya Hussain (2019)

Each storytelling was divided into three parts: pre-listening, while-listening and post-listening. Metacognitive strategies were used in all three stages. In the pre-listening stage, the teacher discusses the book cover to help children understand the concept of the story and link it to their prior knowledge, build interest in the story, explain difficult words found in the story and inform the children of the objective of listening to the story. This is especially important for inexperienced listeners such as preschool children. The while-listening stage was the storytelling session, where the teachers used facial and body expressions, proper speed in telling the story, and cues and pictures to help them understand the story. The teachers also gave facilitation and support through scaffolding throughout the lesson. Scaffolding is an essential component in metacognitive instruction as it helps children realise their thinking processes and give children the knowledge to complete their listening task and motivate them (James 2010). Post-activities were carried out to reinforce and help teachers assess children's understanding. Refer Table 2.

Table 2. Implementation of the lesson

Stages	Activities
Pre-listening Stage	The teacher showed the cover of the book: • Discuss and ask questions about the book cover and explain how it relates to children's experiences. • Using their prior knowledge, children make predictions about the plot and the characters in the story. • Go over the meanings and appropriate usage of challenging words. • The children were made aware of the purpose of listening to the story.
While-listening Stage	• The teacher told the story using varying intonations and facial expressions. Point to pictures and tell the story with excitement.
Post-listening Stage	• The teacher encouraged the children to retell the story. Children's thought processes were aided by repetition, scaffolding in the form of immediate feedback, dividing the narrative into smaller components, questioning, and encouragement. • Small-group post-listening exercises included rearranging picture cards, role-playing, drawing, and short questions in worksheets that were done orally as a group.

6. SAMPLE

A private registered preschool in Kepong, Kuala Lumpur, Malaysia, provided the data for this study. The researcher chose this preschool because it satisfied various study requirements. The National Preschool Standard-based Curriculum, which is the school's primary curriculum, qualifies this preschool as appropriate because it would provide the researcher with a thorough picture of the actual scenario. Since the researcher wanted to ensure the study was conducted in a realistic preschool setting, using the National Preschool Standard-Based Curriculum was vital. Due to the limited sample size, non-probability sampling was used in this case study. The study aimed to investigate a real-world phenomenon rather than draw any generalisations from the data (Yin, 2009).

In this study, six preschool children from two classes were selected purposively, four children were males (M), and two were females (F). The children were grouped into advanced, average and weak groups based on the children's English progress report. These children were in the same age group and were born in 2014 (6 years). Refer Table 3. Qualitative data were collected using anecdotal observation.

Table 3. Demography of Participants

Class	Preschool Children	Mastery of English	Gender	Language Spoken at Home
Class 1	Child 1	Good	M	English & Mandarin
	Child 2	Average	M	English & Mandarin
	Child 3	Weak	F	Mandarin
Class2	Child 4	Good	M	Mandarin
	Child 5	Average	F	Mandarin
	Child 6	Weak	M	Mandarin

7. METHODS OF DATA ANALYSIS

This research used the checklist to record the children's listening comprehension. In addition to the checklist, anecdotal data were gathered to provide a more comprehensive understanding of the children's listening comprehension abilities. Anecdotal data provides qualitative observations and descriptions of children's behaviour, engagement and interactions during the storytelling sessions. Triangulating the data with anecdotal data allows a more holistic assessment of children's listening comprehension skills.

Two video recorders were placed at different corners during the teaching and learning session to record the teachers conducting their lessons and the engagement of the six children in the study. After each session, the researcher immediately watched the video and recorded the observation using the checklist and anecdotal records.

8. RESULT

The research used metacognitive strategies in storytelling to examine children listening comprehension skills. A checklist was developed to assess children's listening comprehension skills by observing their abilities in doing three main tasks: retelling the story, organising the sequence of the story using picture cards and answering oral questions with given options. The checklist had nine items based on the three main tasks, and the children's abilities were assessed on a scale from 1 to 5. (Refer Table 4).

Table 4. Scale used in checklist

1 Cannot Perform	2 Poor	3 Average	4 Good	5 Excellent
Unable to do the task even with assistance given	Able to do the task with many missing information or mistakes or with a lot of assistance	Able to do the task with some missing information or mistakes or with some assistance	Able to do the task with very little missing information or mistakes or able to do with little assistance	Able to do the task well without any assistance

Anecdotal observation was also done during the storytelling session. This was used to triangulate the data from the checklist to allow for a more holistic assessment. The researcher looked for reoccurring behaviours, interactions or responses that stood out and were aligned with the research objective. The observation was coded and grouped in the anecdotal record to facilitate looking for common patterns or themes. This would give a deeper understanding of how they may influence the children's listening comprehension abilities. The data were then compared and contrasted to the checklist data. The children were categorised into three levels of English competencies based on their class English performance. The result of this study will answer the research objective of examining preschool's children listening comprehension skills. The result will be presented based on the three levels the children were categorised in.

8.1 Advanced Children

Child 1 and Child 4 were categorised as Advanced children. Child 1 is fluent in English language and speaks both languages at home. Child 4, on the other hand, even though he is fluent in English, only speaks Mandarin at home. Referring to the checklist, Child 1 scored 5 for retelling for all three sessions. He had no problem retelling the story in all three lessons but Child 4 scored 3 in the first session and 4 in the other two. He had issues in the first session in retelling the main events and key details. He always missed out on relevant information. Both children had no problems with the story sequence during the retelling session. Based on the anecdotal report, child 4 always seem to be in haste when retelling the story. However, when Child 4 was questioned and asked to justify his answers, he could answer confidently. This showed Child 4 did comprehend the story but left out relevant information due to his haste. He, however, manages to give the gist of the story. Both children had difficulty inferring in the third story as it needed extra thinking, as the monster is a metaphor for the boy's emotions. Child 1 could not infer story 3 at the beginning; however, when the teacher broke the information into chunks and gave moment-to-moment feedback, he could provide an accurate answer confidently. The anecdotal report showed both children were very responsive and actively answering questions, especially in the third storytelling session. Both children were active and dominant during the post-listening activities, especially during the card activity, where the children arranged the picture cards according to the sequence of the story.

8.2 Average Children

Child 2 and Child 5 were categorised as average children. Child 2 is timid, does not speak much English in school, and only speaks Mandarin at home. Child 5 is a fun boy who likes interacting with friends. He converses primarily in Mandarin in school and only Mandarin at home. Child 2 scored 1 in the first storytelling session and scored 4 in the second, and 3 in the third. In the first storytelling session, Child 2 could not retell the story but looked blankly at the teacher. Being a timid child and having to retell the story for the first time, the experience could be too overwhelming for her. She could not say anything even when the teacher tried to coax her. The second story was more manageable as she heard the story before. In the third session, Child 2 retelling abilities improved although it was a new story, she could retell part of the story with assistance. Child 2 showed improvement in her ability to tell the story's sequence and could answer specific questions. Child 2 showed noticeable improvement in listening comprehension. Child 5 scored 2 for retelling the first and third story and 3 for the second story. However, he got the sequence of the story correct. Child 5, although he listened attentively to the story, he did not seem to understand the story completely. Refer Table 5. Child 5, however, was confident in answering the questions as options were given to assist him in answering the questions. This showed that although he had some understanding, it was difficult for him to communicate what he understood due to his limited vocabulary.

Table 5. Transcribed data on anecdotal records for average children

Observation	Sub Category	Source
Although the teacher read the sentence several times, Child5 continued to misunderstand until she explained the sentence in Mandarin to everyone (Child 5)	Unable to understand	C5AR3

8.3 Weak Children

The weak children were Children 3 and 6. Both children could speak mainly in Mandarin but could understand English and respond when needed. Child 3 is very passive and has a limited vocabulary. He had difficulty retelling the story. In the first session, he could not retell the story and just said I forgot (refer Table 6). However, in story sessions 2 and 3, the teacher got him to continue retelling the story after assisting with the first part. This strategy helped the child (refer to Table 7). Child 6 also had a problem retelling the stories. However, she did put in effort when assistance was given. Both children could arrange the pictures with assistance from the teacher. Both children could answer the questions as options were given to assist them. This showed that some understanding did occur.

Table 6. Transcribed data on anecdotal records for weak children

Observation	Sub-category	Source
Child 3 could not retell the story. When the teacher encouraged him, He explained in Mandarin that he had forgotten. (Child 3)	inability to understand	AR L 22-L23
The teacher tries to scaffold by asking," What happens when the monster gets smaller"? Bob answered while looking at the space," The boy says with the monster and the monster will do". (Child 3)	inability to understand	AR L32-L33

Table 7. Checklist

Lesson	1						2						3					
Child	1	2	3	4	5	6	1	2	3	4	5	6	1	2	3	4	5	6
Retell the main events and key details from the story	5	1	1	3	2	1	5	4	2	4	3	3	5	3	2	4	3	2
Include relevant information while retelling the story	5	1	1	3	4	1	5	4	2	4	4	3	5	3	2	4	3	3
The sequence of the event in the retelling was accurate	5	1	1	5	5	1	5	4	3	4	5	5	5	4	2	5	4	4
Identified the beginning, middle and end of the story based on the picture sequence	5	1	4	5	5	4	5	4	4	5	5	4	5	5	4	5	5	3
Able to explain why the pictures were arranged in a particular order	5	1	4	5	4	4	5	4	4	5	4	4	5	4	3	5	4	4
Answered specific questions about the story accurately	5	3	4	5	5	4	5	4	4	5	4	4	5	3	4	5	3	4
Provide evidence, infer or give details from the story to support their answers	5	1	2	4	5	2	5	4	3	4	5	2	3	2	2	2	3	2
The child understood the vocabulary used in the question and responded appropriately	5	3	2	5	3	2	5	4	3	5	3	3	5	3	2	5	3	2

9. DISCUSSION

This qualitative study involved six preschool children in a private preschool in Kepong, Malaysia. The research objective was to examine private preschool children listening comprehension skills when metacognitive strategies were used during storytelling. The result indicated metacognitive strategy had a positive result on the listening comprehension of the six preschool children. This result tallied with (Heong, 2018) study, where metacognitive strategies were applied to Advances program students at the Thai Nguyen University of Technology and (Hashiemian & Farhang-Ju, 2020) study, where metacognitive strategies were tested on L2 learners listening comprehension skills in Iran.

Although the results were not apparent for the weak students, they showed some improvement according to the teachers, as previously they could not answer any questions. This study showed that a successful strategy was needed to facilitate second-language listening comprehension, especially for these children with little English mastery. Metacognition is a difficult strategy for young children; however, it managed to help them in their listening comprehension. Metacognition strategies used during the pre-listening skills helped the children acquire the top-bottom process quickly. They were given specific instructions and made aware of the objective of listening and linking the story to their prior knowledge.

Furthermore, the study introduced difficult words in the pre-listening stage, which helped the children. Children who are poor speakers of English tend to translate what they listen this will overemphasise the bottom-up process (Goh,2000). Furthermore, studies by (Goh, 2000; Liu, 2003; Osada, 2001) suggest that L2 listeners must develop better word recognition skills and resist mentally translating and overemphasising bottom-up skills, which delay the children's comprehension. Even the teachers said they felt the translation of words helped the children understand better.

The result of this study has a significant impact on teaching listening skills in preschools. It does not only assist children but also preschool teachers. It significantly impacts teachers' existing practices in teaching listening skills to preschool children. Malaysian preschool teachers' pedagogical knowledge of teaching listening skills is limited (Rezaei & Fatimah, 2013). Teachers must be aware that listening is an essential skill, and if not mastered, it will affect children's mastery of speaking, reading and writing (Hassan, 2008). Teachers' pedagogical content knowledge in teaching English needs to improve with periodical training. Teachers must be exposed to different strategies to develop listening comprehension skills. This study's teaching strategy can be used as a reference to the parties involved with planning, developing, and implementing the curriculum to improve the existing curriculum, especially in approach and listening skills. Changes must be made to make English language learning at the preschool level more effective.

Using digital technology could also be the way forward in helping children to increase their listening comprehension, such as using digital storytelling and using gamification as post-listening activities. However, technology-based learning resources can be ineffective in and of themselves; if they are not flexible, authentic, and engaging, neither teachers nor students will find much value in them. This means they won't be as effective as intended unless good instructional practices are employed with technology or multimedia (Jones, 2008). Digital tales, in particular, and internet-based technology often encourage L2 learning. Additionally, they introduce novel linguistic constructions, syntax, vocabulary, phrases, and formulaic speech within a significant and organised context that aids in understanding the story world.

This study produced a teaching strategy that could increase children's interest in learning English. Through the activities and strategy used in the study to develop children listening comprehension skills, the children showed interest and better comprehension of the stories.

Future research could also look into digital storytelling and integrating gamification into storytelling, especially in the pre-listening stage.

10. CONCLUSION

This qualitative study was interesting as not much research was done on listening comprehension skills at the preschool level, especially in Malaysia. The study showed although listening comprehension skills involve a complex multistep procedure, providing metacognitive instructions helped enhance preschool children's listening comprehension skills. The children showed interest and better comprehension of the stories, which was impossible before. Developing listening comprehension skills also allows children to be active listeners, which is essential in communication, especially in the digital era.

REFERENCES

Abdul, Q.; Luqman , B.; Zaini, M. M. (2017). Developing material of listening comprehension for the department student. *Journal on English as a Foreign Language*. 6(1), 1-20.

Cao, Z. & Lin, Y. (2020). A study on metacognitive strategy use in listening comprehension by Vocational College students.*English Language Teaching*. 13(4)ISSN1916-4742

Chen, S.-C., & Lin, H.-Y.(2021). Using storytelling as a teaching strategy to promote language learning for preschool children. *Education Sciences*, 11(3), 131https://doi.org/103390/educsci11030131

Cross (2010). Raising L2 listeners' metacognitive awareness: A sociocultural theory perspective. *Language Awareness, 19,* 281-297.

Du Toit, S., & Kotze, G. (2009). Metacognitive strategies in the teaching and learning of mathematics. *Pythagoras*, *0*(70). https://doi.org/10.4102/pythagoras.v0i70.39

Goh, C. C. M. (2010). Listening comprehension and strategy use: A longitudinal exploration. *System*,38(2), 185-193.

Hakuta, K., & Ramos, M. (1986). Preschool children's English proficiency and change in English language proficiency over time.*Applied Linguistics*, 7(2), 110-132.

Hart, B.,& Risley,T. R. (1995). *Meaningful differences in the everyday experiences of young American children*. Baltimore Paul H. Brookes Publishing.

Hasan, A. S. (2008) Making input comprehensible for foreign language acquisition. *Damascus University Journal*, 24(2), 31-53.

Hashiemian, M., & Farhang-Ju, M. (2020). Effects of metacognitive on intermediate L2 learners' listening comprehension . *retieved from https://www.researchgate.net/publication/360849952*

Ho, S. H. (2016). The effect of listening comprehension on ESL learners' English language proficiency. *Malaysian Journal of ELT Research.*12 (2). 15-30.

Hazita, A. (2016). Implementation and challenges of English language education reform in Malaysian Primary schools. *3L: language, linguistics, literature.* Vol *22*(3), 65-78.

Imhof, M. (2010). What is going on in the mind of a listener? The cognitve Pschology of listening.In Wolvin,A.D. *Listening and human communication in the 21st century* (pp97-126). Wiley-Blackwell

Isbell, R. T. (2022). *Telling and Retelling Stories Learning Language and Literacy*. Retrieved June 9, 2023, from https://www.naeyc.org/sites/default/files/globallyshared/downloads/PDFs/resources/pubs/isbell_article_march_2002.pdf

James (2010).The use of metacognitive scaffolding to improve college students' academic success *Journal of College Teaching & Learning,* 7 (2010), pp. 47-50.

Jones, R. D., Marrazo, M. J., & Love, C. J. (2008). *Student engagement—creating a culture of academic achievement.* Rexford, NY: International Center for Leadership in Education.

Kasami, N., (2021). Can Digital Storytelling Enhance Learning Motivation for EFL Students with Low Proficiency and Confidence in English? *The EuroCALL Review*, 29(1), 68-80. https://doi.org/10.4995/eurocall.2021.12754

Kuo, L.-J., & Anderson, R. C. (2010). *Beyond comprehension: The role of text in cultivating the habits of thoughtful reading*. Abindon-on -Thames, Routledge.

Lasim, M & Andy (2017). Teaching proficiency through reading and storytelling(TPRS) as a technique to foster student speaking skills. *Journal of English and Linguistic Studies*.4(1) 19-36.

Lervåg, A., & Aukrust, V. G. (2017). Listening comprehension and its relation to reading skills in children from diverse linguistic backgrounds: A systematic review. *Educational Research Review*, 20, 1-24 doi:10.1016/j.edurev.2016.11.003

Liu, N. F. (2003). *Processing problems in L2 listening comprehension of university students in Hong Kong*. (PhD dissertation), Hong Kong: Polytechnic University.

Mello, R. (2001). Building bridges: How storytelling influences teacher and student relationships. In *Proceedings, storytelling in the Americas conference.* St. Catherine, ON: Brooks University Press ERIC Document Reproduction Service No. ED457088).

Pourhosein G. A.; & Ahmadi, M. R. (2011). A study of factors affecting EFL learners English listening comprehension and the strategies for improvement. *Journal of Language Teaching and Rese*arch, *2(*5) 977-988.

Ramani, G. B., Jaeggi, S. M., & Levine, S. C. (2017). Early exposure to parents' beliefs relates to children's beliefs about intelligence: Evidence from India. *Journal of Experimental Child Psychology*, 161, 116-131.

Razaei, A., Fatimah, H. (2013). Impact of awareness-raising about listening micro-skills on the listening comprehension enhancement: An exploration of the listening micro-skills in EFL classes. *Australian Journal of Teacher Education,38(*8), http://dx.doi.org/10.14221/ajte.2013v38n8.4

Osada, N. (2001). What strategy do less proficient learners employ in listening comprehension? A reappraisal of bottom-up and top-down processing, *Journal of the Pan-Pacific of Applied Linguistics 5,* 73-90.

Saha, M. & Talukdar, A. R. (2000).Teaching listening as an English language skill, Retrieved from *www.articlebase.com*

Santos, R. S. (2018). Improving young learners' listening skills through storytelling. *Corpus* 10150122460

Tham, T. H (2018) Applying metacognitive strategies in teaching listening comprehension to Advanced Program Students at Thai Nguyen University of Technology. *International Journal of Humanities*. 5(3).

Vandergrift, L. (1999). Facilitating second language listening comprehension: acquiring successful strategies. *ELT Journal, 53(3)*, 168-176.

Vandergift, L. (2019). Listening: theory and practice in modern language competence. *Subject Centre for Languages, Language and Area Studies Good Practice Guides*. Retrieved from http://www.llas.ac.uk/resources/gpg/67

Wood, J. D. (2016). Using stories to help children learn a foreign language. Retrieved from: difibug.ugr.es/bitstream/handle/10481/46235WOOD_TFGLearnLanguage.pd?sequence=1&isAllowed=y

Yin, R. K. (2009). *Case study research: Design and method* (4th ed.) California: Sage.

RELATIONSHIP BETWEEN TEACHING PRESENCE AND SHARED-METACOGNITION IN ONLINE CASE-BASED COURSES

Ayesha Sadaf[1], Stella Yun Kim[1] and Adrie Koehler[2]
[1]*University of North Carolina Charlotte*
9201 University City Blvd, Charlotte, NC 28223, USA
[2]*Purdue University*
610 Purdue Mall, West Lafayette, IN 47907, USA

ABSTRACT

This study investigated student perceived shared-metacognition–self-regulation and co-regulation–as explained by three teaching presence sub-elements–*Instructional Design, Direct Instruction, and Facilitation*–in an online case-based course. 113 online graduate students enrolled in an advanced instructional design course participated in the study. Data were collected through the Community of Inquiry survey and a shared metacognition questionnaire survey. The findings revealed that students perceived *Direct Instruction* as a significant predictor of their shared-metacognition (self-regulation and co-regulation) in online case-based courses. The findings highlight the importance of teaching presence for *Direct Instruction* to increase self and co-regulation for maximizing the quality of online case-based instruction. The findings of this study will be helpful for researchers and practitioners who design and teach online courses to promote metacognition.

KEYWORDS

Shared-Metacognition, Case-Based Instruction, Online Courses, Online Learning

1. INTRODUCTION

Rapid growth of online learning and access to information communication technologies has led to a growing need to understand the process of collaborative thinking and learning in an increasingly connected world (Garrison & Akyol, 2015). Yet, instructors struggle with issues of quality due to the "requirement of higher-level self-directed learning skills and greater difficulties in enabling effective human interactions" (Xu & Xu, 2019, p. 26). To enhance the quality of online courses and to create a meaningful experience for students, it is important to understand strategies that can support the development of students' metacognitive processes in shared learning environments (Garrison, 2022).

Metacognition is an important intellectual skill that plays a critical role in enhancing student online learning outcomes through monitoring and regulating their own learning. However, online instructors face the challenge of using strategies to help students regulate and manage their learning in a collaborative online learning environment. Effective teaching presence can provide guidance in encouraging students to take responsibility for their learning through facilitating discourse and resolving issues collaboratively (Garrison & Akyol, 2015). Researchers suggest a need for more research on how to develop the awareness and regulatory strategies to monitor and manage learning process that enhance student learning outcomes (Garrison, 2022; Sadaf et al., 2022). Therefore, the results of this study will enhance the quality of teaching and learning used in online courses and provide guidelines for instructors looking to enhance shared metacognition to guide the improvement of online case-based instruction.

2. LITERATURE REVIEW

Metacognition is defined as "a set of higher knowledge and skills to monitor and regulate cognitive processes of self and others" (Garrison & Akyol, 2015, p.184). It requires learners to set their learning goals and monitor their progress towards those goals (DiDonato, 2013; Akyol, 2013). According to Kizilcec et al. (2017), metacognitive strategies assist learners to plan, monitor, and regulate their learning process to accomplish goal setting, self-monitoring, and self-evaluation. Metacognitive reflection and discourse with self and co-regulation can inform students how they can improve their approach to learning (Garrison, 2022). Studies have examined metacognitive processes in collaborative learning contexts recognizing the importance of individual and social regulatory processes within a community of inquiry (Kilis & Yildirim, 2018; Koehler et al., 2022). Collaborative learning environment requires more engaged approaches to help learners construct new meaning and share understanding with others (Garrison & Akyol, 2015). Therefore, Garrison (2022) emphasized the importance of exploring shared learning environments and strategies that can support the development of students' metacognitive processes.

Teaching presence is one of the core elements of the community of inquiry (CoI) framework that provides the theoretical and methodological tools to understand the complexities of metacognition in collaborative learning environments (Garrison & Akyol, 2015). Teaching presence is defined as "design, facilitation, and direction of cognitive and social processes for the purpose of realizing personally meaningful and educational worthwhile learning outcomes" (Anderson et al., 2001, p. 5). Teaching presence within the CoI framework has been conceptualized by the following elements (See Table 1):

1. Instructional design and organization refer to the designing and planning the online course structure, process, the interactions between students, and assessment components (Anderson et al., 2001). Examples could include developing course materials, designing course activities, and organizing the course.
2. Direct instruction refers to providing subject matter expertise to support students' learning rather than directly lecturing students. According to Anderson et al., (2001), direct instruction can be achieved through facilitating reflection and discourse by organizing content, and using various forms of assessment and feedback.
3. Facilitating discourse focuses on facilitating learning to "maintaining the interest, motivation and engagement of students in active learning" (Anderson et al., 2001, p. 7.). Examples could include working to achieve consensus and understanding, sharing meaning, and ensuring the efficacy of the process (Miller et al., 2014).

Table 1. Subcategories or indicators of the main elements of teaching presence

Elements of Teaching Presence	Subcategories of teaching Presence
Instructional design/organization	Setting curriculum
	Designing methods
	Establishing time parameters
	Utilizing the medium effectively
	Establishing netiquette
Direct instruction	Presenting content and questions
	Focusing the discussion
	Summarizing the discussion
	Confirming understanding
	Diagnosing misperceptions
Facilitating discourse	Identifying areas of agreement and disagreement
	Seeking to reach consensus and understanding
	Encouraging, acknowledging, and reinforcing students' contributions
	Setting the climate for learning
	Drawing in participants and prompting discussion

Adapted from Shea et al. (2003)

While teaching presence within the CoI framework is not limited to course instructors only but can rather be distributed across teachers and students, for the specific purpose and questions of our study, we focused on teaching presence behaviors of online course instructors.

With regards to metacognition, the *Design* component focuses on design for critical reflection and discourse to provide a metacognitive map of the learning process; *Facilitation* component relates to the implementing and supporting metacognition; and *Direct Instruction* focusses on improving collaborative learning through the awareness and management of learning processes leading to higher levels of academic achievement (Garrison, 2022). Therefore, teaching presence can help in establishing and maintaining social and cognitive process of learning that can lead to metacognition (Garrison et al., 2010). Vaughan & Wah (2020) concluded that teaching presence should "intentionally design, facilitate, and direct a collaborative constructive learning environment in order for students to learn how to co-regulate their learning (metacognition)" (p.1). Vuopala, et al., (2019) concluded that "prompting regulation activities among students, such as task-related monitoring, teachers can support students to engage in metacognitive processes that are related to high-level knowledge co-construction" (p. 247).

Although, there have been studies suggesting a strong association of students' perceived teaching presence and learning outcomes in online courses (Arbaugh, 2008; Caskurlu et al., 2020), there is only one study exploring the relationship between three presences (teaching, social, and cognitive) and shared metacognition in an online case-based course (Sadaf et al., 2022). The results showed that teaching presence revealed no statistically significant relationship with metacognition suggesting that students with higher perceived teaching presence are relatively less likely (or unlikely) to have higher metacognition. Although Sadaf et al., (2022) study shed some light on the relationship between teaching presence and shared metacognition, research focused all three presences and on students enrolled in one course/program. Specific focus on teaching presence elements and considering the perspectives of students enrolled in varied courses/programs might provide more insight and strengthen the results of the previous studies.

2.1 Theoretical Framework

The Community of Inquiry was used as the theoretical framework because it emphasizes both the personal (reflective) and shared (collaborative) worlds of a learning experience (Garrison et al., 2001). The CoI framework has been created to help examine construction of individual and group learning experiences in online and blended learning environments (Garrison, 2022). The CoI assumes that learning occurs at the intersection of the three presences– social presence, teaching presence, and cognitive presence (Garrison et al., 2001). In addition, self-regulation and co-regulation are seen as important mediators among the three presences. For this study, we focused on the relationship between teaching presence and shared-metacognition in online learning. The predictive effects of students' perceived teaching presence on their metacognition will help online instructors use pedagogical strategies to design and facilitate courses.

2.2 Purpose of the Study

The purpose of this study is to explore students' perceptions of the role of teaching presence in determining their shared metacognition (self-regulation and co-regulation) in an online case-based course. The following questions guided this study: To what extent are students' perceptions of shared metacognition (self-regulation and co-regulation) explained by teaching presence (course design, facilitation, and feedback) in online CBI?

1. To what extent are students' perceptions of self-regulation explained by the sub-elements of teaching presence in online CBI?
2. To what extent are students' perceptions of co-regulation explained by the sub-elements of teaching presence in online CBI?

3. METHODS

3.1 Participants

A purposeful sample of 113 graduate students (19 males and 90 females) enrolled in an Instructional Design course were selected to participate in this study. The sample was included in the study because students were enrolled in the online graduate course designed based on a case-based instruction to learning instructional design (ID). About half (n = 52) of them were more than 36 years old. The majority (n=98) of the participants had taken more than 3 online courses. All of the participants rated themselves as being very comfortable with participating in online courses.

3.2 Context of the Study

"Advanced Instructional Design" is a course required for students in the Learning Design and Technology graduate program. In this course, students engage in authentic design activities via participation in an online community of inquiry and participate in two instructor-facilitated case studies at the beginning of the term, followed by participation in four student-led case discussions. Prior to participation in the case discussions, students complete individual case analyses in which they reflect on and respond to a number of specific prompts. The prompts are designed for students to give key issues careful consideration before participating in the whole class discussions. Then, students participate in weekly discussions and propose/develop relevant solutions to the issues presented in a case. Finally, at the end of the course, students reflected on their expertise in solving cases. Course activities and assignments were designed to help students develop the knowledge, strategies, and attitudes needed to become effective instructional designers. Learning experiences revolved around two major activities: 1) The analysis and synthesis of, and reflection on, instructional design case studies and 2) Ongoing reflection on the development of students' instructional design expertise. The course is designed for students to take responsibility for their own learning by identifying their own learning goals, finding and utilizing resources to help them meet those goals, and continually monitor their progress.

3.3 Data Collection and Analysis

Data were collected from an online survey administered at the end of Spring/Fall 2021 semesters and Spring 2022. Students' perceived teaching presence was measured using CoI survey questions and metacognition was measured using the shared metacognition questionnaire survey. Each item employs a 5-point Likert-type scale, with 1 = strongly disagree and 5 = strongly agree. Simple demographic information was also collected such as gender, age, prior experience with online courses, and the program to which a student belongs. Students were asked to respond to three sets of survey questions including teaching presence, self-regulation, and co-regulation.

A series of multiple linear regressions were performed with the three sub-elements of teaching presence as an independent variable and self-regulation and co-regulation as dependent variables in the model. Ratings on each of self-regulation and co-regulation was represented by 13 items. For teaching presence, "Design and Organization" was measured with 4 items, "Facilitating Discourse" was with 5 items, and "Direct Instruction" was assessed using 4 items. The assumptions of linearity, homoscedasticity, and no presence of outliers were tested and found to be met by data. Stepwise regression was used to achieve the parsimony of the final model, while selecting the most significant predictors.

4. RESULTS

4.1 Students' Perceptions of Self-Regulation Explained by Teaching Presence

Results of stepwise multiple linear regression showed that *Direct Instruction* was significantly related to self-regulation, explaining 13.4% variance of the outcome variable, F(1, 111) = 17.154, $p < .001$ (see Table 2). The other two variables, *Design and Organization*, and *Facilitating Discourse* were not found to be a significant predictor of self-regulation. The estimated standardized beta coefficient indicated that one unit increase in *Direct Instruction*, on average, led to .366 unit increase in self-regulation ($t = 4.142$, $p < .001$). This suggests that students participating in an online CBI course perceive *Direct Instruction* to increase their self-regulation.

Table 2. Summary of regression analysis (Model 1)

Analysis of Variance	Dependent variable: Self-Regulation			
Source	**Sum of Squares**	**DF**	**Mean Square**	**F**
Model	553.497	1	553.497	17.154***
Residual	3581.565	111	32.266	
Total	4135.062	112		
Predictors	**Estimate (standardized)**	**Std. Error**	**t**	**Prob > $\|t\|$**
(Intercept)	47.029 (-)	2.524	18.630	.000***
Direct Instruction	0.618 (.366)	0.149	4.142	.000***

Note. $*\, p < .05,\ **\, p < .01,\ ***\, p < .001; R = .366, R^2 = .134, adjusted\ R^2 = .126$

4.2 Students' Perceptions of Co-Regulation Explained by Teaching Presence

Similar to the results of self-regulation, results of co-regulation identified *Direct Instruction* as the only significant predictor. This variable alone explained 12.7% of the variance of co-regulation, R^2=.127, $F(1, 111)$ = 16.501, $p < .001$ (see Table 3). Specifically, one unit increase in *Direct Instruction* led to .356 unit increase in co-regulation on average (standardized coefficient beta, $\hat{\beta}$ = .356, t < 4.014 p < .001). This shows that students perceive *Direct Instruction* helps them better monitor and manage shared learning dynamic or co-regulated learning during CBI.

Table 3. Summary of regression analysis (Model 2)

Analysis of Variance	Dependent variable: Co-Regulation			
Source	**Sum of Squares**	**DF**	**Mean Square**	**F**
Model	611.945	1	611.945	16.111***
Residual	4216.055	111	37.982	
Total	4828.000	112		
Predictors	**Estimate (standardized)**	**Std. Error**	**t**	**Prob > $\|t\|$**
(Intercept)	43.255 (-)	2.739	15.793	.000***
Direct Instruction	0.650 (.356)	0.162	4.014	.000***

Note. $*\, p < .05,\ **\, p < .01,\ ***\, p < .001; R = .356, R^2 = .127, adjusted\ R^2 = .119$

5. DISCUSSIONS

Students participating in an online CBI course perceive *Direct Instruction* – presenting content and questions, focusing the discussion, confirming understanding, and diagnosing misperceptions – to increase their shared metacognition. According to Garrison (2022), *Direct Instruction* focusses on improving collaborative learning through the awareness and management of learning processes leading to higher levels of academic achievement.

Findings of this study show that students perceive *Direct Instruction* to help them better monitor and manage shared learning dynamic in both self-regulated as well as co-regulated learning during CBI. This can be due to the strategies instructor used that required students to co-analyze instructional design problems, develop solutions to real problems via cases, and give and receive constructive feedback from peers and instructor. Students completed individual case analyses in which they reflected on a number of specific prompts designed for students to consider key case issues and their conscious choices for solving those issues before participating in the whole class case-discussions. Through these reflective strategies, students contributed to case-based inquiry to develop self and co-regulatory metacognition processes (Garrison & Akyol, 2015). This finding is aligned with Koehler et al. (2020) who found that within the CBI context, students rely on instructor-set course requirements to guide their solutions and trust instructor's feedback.

Results of this study are supported by other studies that found CBI can help in facilitating deep and meaningful learning through shared collaborative experiences (Koehler et al., 2022; Sadaf, et al., 2021) where students can be aware of (monitor) and regulate (manage) thinking through the shared inquiry processes. The analysis and reflection on instructional design case-studies and ongoing reflection on the development of students' instructional design expertise helped students increase their self-regulation that led to better monitoring and managing co-regulated learning during CBI. Koelher et al., (2020) suggested that instructors need to support other students' engagement and progression in their case learning process and train them so that they can gain the benefits of the CBI. Students may need more instructional encouragement or support to become metacognitively aware and active in terms of monitoring and managing the inquiry process depending on their experiences (Garrison & Akyol, 2015).

6. CONCLUSION

This study makes a significant contribution in terms of student perceptions of shared metacognition (self-regulation and co-regulation) as explained by three sub-elements of teaching presence–planning, direct instruction, and facilitation–in an online CBI, as framed by the CoI framework. First, *Direct Instruction* is a significant factor contributing to students' self and co-regulated learning. Second, this study sheds light on teaching presence attributes instructors can use to positively influence self-regulation and co-regulation in an online CBI. This study, therefore, serves as a base for further studies and opens up new directions to explore the types of *Direct Instruction* strategies instructors can use to improve shared metacognition in online CBI.

Looking at the results, one may conclude that students participating in an online CBI course perceive *Direct Instruction* to increase their self-regulation. In addition, students perceive *Direct Instruction* helps them better monitor and manage shared learning dynamic or co-regulated learning during CBI. In this regard, online instructors can use case-based instructional strategies that ask students to explore the problems, find and justify their solutions to facilitate high-levels of cognitive presence that may lead to deeper constructivist learning among students. Instructors can use strategies to prepare students to take responsibility of their own learning by identifying their own learning goals, finding and utilizing resources to help them meet those goals, and continually monitor their progress. Taking responsibility will enable students to reflect on each other's contributions to the developmental progress toward the intended goals while they are engaged in discourse (Akyol & Garrison, 2011). Overall, the findings in this study are valuable because they contribute to further effective design of online courses through the use of case-based scenarios for real-world learning.

This study has some limitations that may lead to future research efforts. First, this study is limited in generalizability of findings due to the sample of participants representing only one program and two universities. Follow-up studies could utilize large sample size with data collected across programs or institutions to further refine the results and implications of this study. In addition, researchers can explore strategies other than CBI to see how teaching presence plays a role in facilitating self and co-regulation. Additionally, research investigating the relationship between students' perceptions of the impact of teaching presence (course design, facilitation, and feedback) on shared metacognition (self-regulation and co-regulation) in online courses across different disciplines would be a promising direction for future studies.

REFERENCES

Akyol, Z., & Garrison, D. R. (2011). Understanding cognitive presence in an online and blended community of inquiry: Assessing outcomes and processes for deep approaches to learning. *British Journal of Educational Technology*, *42*(2), 233-250.

Akyol, Z. (2013). Metacognitive development within the Community of Inquiry. In Z. Akyol & D. R. Garrison (Eds.), *Educational communities of inquiry: Theoretical framework, research and practice* (pp. 30–44). IGI Global.

Anderson, T., Rourke, L., Garrison, D. R., & Archer, W. (2001). Assessing teacher presence in a computer conferencing context. *Journal of Asynchronous Learning Networks, 5*(2), 1–17.

Arbaugh, J. B., Cleveland-Innes, M., Diaz, S. R., Garrison, D. R., Ice, P., Richardson, J. C., & Swan, K. P. (2008). Developing a community of inquiry instrument: Testing a measure of the community of inquiry framework using a multi-institutional sample. *The internet and higher education*, *11*(3-4), 133-136.

Caskurlu, S., Maeda, Y., Richardson, J. C., & Lv, J. (2020). A meta-analysis addressing the relationship between teaching presence and students' satisfaction and learning. *Computers & Education*, *157*, 103966.

DiDonato, N. (2013). Effective self- and co-regulation in collaborative learning groups: An analysis of how students regulate problem solving of authentic interdisciplinary tasks. *Instructional Science*, *41*(1), 25–47. https://doi.org/10.1007/s11251-012-9206-9

Garrison, D. R. (2022). Shared metacognition in a Community of Inquiry. *Online Learning, 26*(1), 6–18. https://doi.org/10.24059/olj.v26i1.3023

Garrison, D. R., & Akyol, Z. (2015). Toward the development of a metacognition construct for the community of inquiry framework. *Internet and Higher Education*, *24*, 66–71. https://doi.org/10.1016/j.iheduc.2014.10.001

Garrison, D. R., Anderson, T., & Archer, W. (2001). Critical thinking, cognitive presence, and computer conferencing in distance education. *American Journal of Distance Education,15*(1), 7– 23.

Garrison, D. R., Cleveland-Innes, M., & Fung, T. S. (2010). Exploring causal relationships among teaching, cognitive and social presence: Student perceptions of the community of inquiry framework. *The Internet and Higher Education*, 13(1–2), 31–36. https://doi.org/10.1016/j.iheduc.2009.10.002

Kilis, S., & Yıldırım, Z. (2018). Investigation of community of inquiry framework in regard to self-regulation, metacognition and motivation. *Computers & Education, 126*, 53–64. https://doi.org/10.1016/j.compedu.2018.06.032

Kizilcec, R. F., Pérez-Sanagustín, M., & Maldonado, J. J. (2017). Self-regulated learning strategies predict learner behavior and goal attainment in Massive Open Online Courses. *Computers & education*, *104*, 18-33.

Koehler, A. A., Fiock, H., Janakiraman, S., Cheng, Z., & Wang, H. (2020). Asynchronous Online Discussions during Case-Based Learning: A Problem-Solving Process. *Online Learning*, *24*(4), 64–92.

Koehler, A. A., Cheng, Z., Fiock, H., Wang, H., Janakiraman, S., & Chartier, K. (2022). Examining students' use of online case-based discussions to support problem solving: Considering individual and collaborative experiences. Computers & Education, 179, 104407. https://doi.org/10.1016/j.compedu.2021.104407

Miller, M. G., Hahs-Vaughn, D. L., & Zygouris-Coe, V. (2014). A confirmatory factor analysis of teaching presence within online professional development. *Journal of Asynchronous Learning Networks, 18*(1).

Sadaf, A., Kim, S. Y., & Wang, Y. (2021). A comparison of cognitive presence, learning, satisfaction, and academic performance in case-based and non-case-based online discussions. *American Journal of Distance Education*, *35*(3), 214-227.

Sadaf, A., Kim, S. Y., & Olesova, L. (2022). Relationship between metacognition and online Community of Inquiry in an online case-based course. *Online Learning, 26*(4), 1-16.

Shea, P. J., Pickett, A. M., & Pelz, W. E. (2003). A follow-up investigation of "teaching presence" in the SUNY Learning Network. *Journal of asynchronous learning networks*, *7*(2), 61-80.

Vaughan, N., & Wah, J. L. (2020). The Community of Inquiry framework: Future practical directions-shared metacognition. *International Journal of E-Learning & Distance Education*, *35*(1), 1–25.

Vuopala, E., Näykki, P., Isohätälä, J., & Järvelä, S. (2019). Knowledge co-construction activities and task-related monitoring in scripted collaborative learning. *Learning, Culture and Social Interaction*, *21*, 234–249. https://doi.org/10.1016/j.lcsi.2019.03.011

Xu, D., & Xu, Y. (2019). The promises and limits of online higher education: Understanding how distance education affects access, cost, and quality. https://files.eric.ed.gov/fulltext/ED596296.pdf.

THE APPLICATION OF FUZZY DELPHI METHOD IN CONTENT VALIDITY ANALYSIS

Mohd Azli Jailani[1] and Chong Kim Loy[2]
[1]*Faculty of Social Sciences and Humanities, Open University Malaysia*
47301 Petaling Jaya, Selangor, Malaysia
[2]*UNITAR Graduate School, UNITAR International University*
47301 Petaling Jaya, Selangor, Malaysia

ABSTRACT

Validity is one of the essential criteria for an instrument to be used in counselling and educational learning instruction. Several components of validity requirements need to be validated before using the instrument. One of those components is content validity. As mentioned in the literature, content validity is a qualitative assessment. However, using qualitative assessment to analyse collective agreement among panel experts would create some issues. A few suggestions were made to find a seamless solution to overcome the problems. Among the suggestions is to use quantitative analysis rather than qualitative. Thus, this study aimed to explore an alternative approach to testing the content validity of an instrument. For this reason, a newly developed counselling needs assessment instrument was used to quantify the 16-panel experts' agreement. The instrument has 126 items, and the Fuzzy Delphi Method (FDM) was used to verify the panel experts' consensus on the instrument's content validity. The results have shown that out of 126 items, two items, item 62 and item 115, were discarded from the list as the items scored less than 0.5 of the defuzzification threshold value.

KEYWORDS

Validity, Content Validity, Learning and Instruction Assessment, Counselling Assessment, Fuzzy Delphi Method

1. INTRODUCTION

Testing has been regarded as a fundamental component in counselling services. This is because counsellors constitute a major group of test users (Anastasi, 1992; Leppma & Jones, 2018). The nature of counselling work that need to deal with different types of client's populations would require counsellors to use various types of instruments, which include measurements of cognitive and affective behaviour, self-administered inventories, computerised testing and several other approaches or methods. The same scenario in learning and instruction, the assessment provides educators with valuable information about students' knowledge, skills, and progress. It serves multiple purposes, including evaluating learning outcomes, identifying areas for improvement, and informing instructional decision-making.

To ensure the assessments can truly benefit clients in counselling and students in learning, the instrument itself need to meet certain types of requirements. One of the essential requirements is validity. According to Taherdoost (2016), validity simply can be defined as measure what it supposed to measure. Fraenkel and Wallen (2008, p.147) defined validity as "the appropriateness, meaningful, correctness and usefulness of the inferences a researcher makes." Without validity, a phenomenon such as intelligence cannot be explained and described by an intelligent test because the test did not measure what it supposed to measure.

In general, validity is divided into four different types of categories, firstly, face validity, secondly, content validity, thirdly, construct validity and fourthly, criterion validity (Taherdoost, 2016). Yaghmale (2003) delineated that measuring content validity of instruments are important because it gives confidence to the readers and researchers about the instruments. Muhamad Saiful Bahri Yusoff (2019) defined content validity as the degree to which elements of an assessment instrument are relevant to and representative of the targeted construct for a particular assessment purpose.

Heale and Twycross (2015) mentioned that content validity is a subset of face validity. Therefore, Drost (2011), Yaghmale (2003), and Fraenkel and Wallen (2008) described content validity as a qualitative type of validity rather than quantitative. The procedure of measuring content validity usually involves a group of panel experts who will be given an evaluation form which contains several open-ended questions for them to highlight their comments or responses about the items of an instrument. However, as explained by Rubio et al. (2003) and Ramlan Mustafa and Ghazali Darusalam (2018), this procedure depicted some limitations. Among the limitations are that experts' feedback is subjective; thus, it is prone to be biased, especially when senior experts deliberate their comment, the tendency to accept the comment would be almost certain as compared to a comment which is made by junior lecturers, even though their comment were profound.

The other limitation of measuring content validity via the qualitative method is that the feedback produced cannot be calculated since it is qualitative. Therefore, it is challenging to reduce errors or inconsistencies in the comments made by the panel experts (Ramlan Mustafa & Ghazali Darusalam, 2018).

2. PROBLEM STATEMENT

To overcome the problems mentioned above, a quantitative approach may be seen as the best approach to conduct content validity studies as an alternative to the conventional or qualitative approach.

One of the quantitative methods is the Fuzzy Delphi Method (FDM). Mohd Nazri Abdul Rahman et al. (2016) explained that FDM is not a new technique but an innovated technique from the traditional Delphi method. The traditional Delphi method is an expert opinion survey built with three features: anonymous response, iteration and controlled feedback, and statistical group response. However, this procedure requires researchers to conduct the survey several times, which could delay the research progress and increase the overall costs. To overcome the problems, FDM, as explained by Yu et al. (2010), was introduced to quickly get the consensus from the experts without going through many rounds of survey exercises. The method eliminates ambiguity caused by expert panels' differences in meaning and interpretation.

To identify whether FDM could deliberate information on content validity, a newly developed counselling needs assessment instrument was used to quantify the consensus of the panel experts over the instrument. The counselling needs assessment instrument blueprint, which consists of 126 items, was developed to assist school counsellors in determining the priorities of their guidance and counselling programmes or activities. In this study, FDM was deployed to verify whether the 126 items could assess students' counselling needs under the six components of needs, namely Academic needs, Emotional needs, Personal Development needs, Career needs, Peer Relationships and finally, Family needs.

2.1 Research Objective

To validate the content validity of a newly developed counselling needs assessment instrument through the Fuzzy Delphi method (FDM).

2.2 Research Question

What is the content validity status of a newly developed counselling needs assessment instrument as analysed through the Fuzzy Delphi method (FDM)?

3. LITERATURE REVIEW

Content validity is of significant importance in both counselling assessment and learning and instruction. It ensures that the content covered in assessments and instructional materials accurately represents the knowledge, skills, and competencies that are relevant and necessary for effective counselling and learning outcomes. This section explores the importance of content validity in counselling assessment and learning and instruction, supported by relevant citations.

Content validity is crucial in counselling assessment to ensure that the assessment tools accurately measure the constructs they intend to assess. In the context of counselling, content validity ensures that the assessment instruments cover the relevant areas of motivations, needs, personalities, interests, skills, and attitudes necessary for effective counselling practice (Hays & Erford, 2014). Assessments with high content validity in counselling provide reliable and meaningful information about clients' psychological functioning, facilitating appropriate interventions and treatment planning.

In learning and instruction, content validity ensures that the instructional materials align with the desired learning outcomes. It ensures that the content covered in textbooks, lesson plans, and other instructional resources is relevant, accurate, and representative of the knowledge and skills that learners need to acquire (Messick, 1996). When instructional materials possess high content validity, they promote meaningful and effective learning experiences, allowing students to acquire the intended knowledge and skills.

Subject Matter Experts (SMEs) play a crucial role in establishing content validity. They possess in-depth knowledge and expertise in the specific domain being assessed. SMEs evaluate the relevance and appropriateness of the content to ensure it adequately represents the construct being measured (Downing, 2006). Their input and judgment are invaluable in determining the content's validity.

Content validity assessment is the most appropriately conducted through a qualitative approach (Brod, Pohlman & Waldman, 2014). The process began when a group of SMEs was selected, and they were asked to review the content thoroughly and provide their qualitative feedback based on the defined content domain. However, some experts, for example, Downing (2006), Messick (1996), Lynn (1986) and Merriam (2009), have deliberated that assessing content validity through qualitative research created some problems and challenges. Among those problems and difficulties are subjectivity, bias, limited generalisation, lack of standardisation and lack of consensus among experts.

To overcome the above-mentioned constraints. Kaufman and Gupta (1988) and Ishikawa (1993) have presented an application, which is known as the Fuzzy Delphi Method (FDM). The FDM approach rectifies the process by inserting some new mechanisms such as spectrum development, aggregation of experts' opinions, defuzzification, and reaching a consensus in just one circle of exercise (Ramlan Mustafa & Ghazali Darusalam, 2018). The advantages of FDM, such as handling ambiguity and uncertainty, capturing expert consensus, addressing vagueness and complexity, efficiency and cost-effectiveness, support for multi-criteria decision making, and flexibility in application, make it a valuable approach for decision-making processes that require flexibility, expert input, and consideration of multiple viewpoints and criteria.

4. METHODOLOGY

The process of reviewing the items by using FDM is illustrated with the following steps:

Step 1 – selection of panel experts: 16 panel experts were selected to verify the developed items in the counselling needs assessment instrument. The experts were identified based on Hsu and Sanford (2007) model of the expert panels selection, which emphasizes two different criteria: a) the experts must have been involved and practised the job, in this case counselling, and b) the length of occupational background must at least minimum 4 to 5 years of experience - following that the selected panel experts for this study were the school counsellors from the States of Selangor and Perak, who fulfilled the outlined criteria.

Step 2 – determining linguistic scale: Each of the panel expert was given a set questionnaire which contained 126 items for them to verify based on the following triangular fuzzy and linguistic scales (Table 1):

Table 1. 5 points linguistic scale and the fuzzy scales

Linguistic scale (5 points)	Fuzzy scale
1 = Highly inappropriate	(0.0, 0.1, 0.2)
2 = Inappropriate	(0.1, 0.2, 0.4)
3 = Moderately appropriate	(0.2, 0.4, 0.6)
4 = Appropriate	(0.4, 0.6, 0.8)
5 = Highly appropriate	(0.6, 0.8, 1.0)

The panel experts were asked to rate whether the developed items could really assess students' counselling needs by circling the items with 5 different linguistic scales as mentioned above. Figure 1 below illustrates the sample of the survey form.

<table>
<tr><th>Item</th><th colspan="2">As a student…</th><th colspan="2">Score</th><th colspan="2">My current condition…</th><th>Score</th></tr>
<tr><td>1.</td><td colspan="2">As a student, we need to understand the different types of feelings we experience such as happy, sad and angry.</td><td colspan="2">1 2 3 4 5 6</td><td colspan="2">I am able to understand the different types of feelings I experience such as happy, sad and angry.</td><td>1 2 3 4 5 6</td></tr>
<tr><td colspan="8">Score for item appropriateness:</td></tr>
<tr><td colspan="2">Highly appropriate</td><td colspan="2">Appropriate</td><td colspan="2">Moderately appropriate</td><td>Inappropriate</td><td>Highly inappropriate</td></tr>
<tr><td colspan="2">5</td><td colspan="2">4</td><td colspan="2">3</td><td>2</td><td>1</td></tr>
<tr><td colspan="8">Note:
……………………………………………………………………………………………
……………………………………………………………………………………………</td></tr>
</table>

Figure 1. Sample of the survey form

Step 3 – determining the Threshold "d" value: The Threshold "d" value is important in determining the levels of agreement among the expert panels upon the developed items. The data from this exercise were entered onto a Microsoft Excel worksheet and analysed with the following formula:

$$d(m,n) = \sqrt{\frac{1}{3}}[(m1 + n1)2 + (m2 - n2)2 + (m3 - n3)2]$$

Ramlan Mustafa and Ghazali Darusalam (2018) explained if the threshold "d" value is lower or equivalent to 0.2 (≤ 0.2) it can be said the panel experts have achieved their consensus on the items.

Step 4 – determining group consensus percentage: the data from the Microsoft Excel worksheet file were analysed again to quantify the value of group consensus percentage.

As deliberated by Zanariah Ahmad et al. (2014) the group consensus percentage must exceed 75 percent (> 75 percent) for the next process to be proceeded. If the group consensus percentage is lower than 75 percent it means the items need to be removed or the process need to be redone again.

Step 5 – determining the ∝-cut value (defuzzification value): to determine the ∝-cut value, the data were analysed with the following formula:

$$Amax = 1/3 * [(m1 + m2 + m3)]$$

The formula was used to rank and discard the items which have ∝-cut less than of 0.5. The items with values below than 0.5 (< 0.5) will have to be removed from the list as it did not achieve the levels of agreement or consensus from all panel of experts (Ramlan Mustafa & Ghazali Darusalam, 2018).

5. RESULTS AND DISCUSSION

The feedbacks from the 16 panel experts were entered onto the Microsoft Excel worksheet file. The data were analysed to determine the threshold "d" value. From the data sheet it was found that the overall scores of the "d" value for 126-items is 0.2, which means it surpasses the requirement (≤ 0.2) to proceed with the next procedure.

As deliberated earlier, Step 4 is conducted to determine the group consensus percentage. The consensus percentage from the panel experts must exceed the minimum requirement of 75 percent before it can be proceeded to the next process. From the results, it was found that the overall percentage score for this process is 91.35 percent, which means the group agreement has exceeded the minimum percentage value of 75 percent. The decision whether to retain or discard some items is determined by the final process, that is determining or identifying the ∝-cut value or defuzzification value.

For step 5 (defuzzification value), a formula (i – A = 1/3 * [m1 + m2 + m3]) was used to find the ∝-cut value of each item. According to the formula, If the score value is 0.5 and below (< 0.5), the item should need to be removed from the list. The ∝-cut value also would help the researcher to rank the items according to its priority and importance as per reviewed by the panel experts.

From the data, it has shown that all items have scored the ∝-cut values more than 0.5 (< 0.5), except for item 62 and item 115, which the score points are 0.4. The items were ranked according to the agreement made by the panel experts. Table 2 explains the details.

Table 2. The ∝-cut values and the items rankings

Item	Score value			Item	Score value		
	Fuzzy evaluation	Average fuzzy number	Rank		Fuzzy evaluation	Average fuzzy number	Rank
1	11	0.7	25	55	8.8	0.6	120
2	10.6	0.7	66	56	9.8	0.6	105
3	10.8	0.7	60	57	10.2	0.6	93
4	10.2	0.6	97	58	11.2	0.7	19
5	10.6	0.7	66	59	9.2	0.6	116
6	9.8	0.6	110	60	10.2	0.6	97
7	11	0.7	25	61	10.4	0.7	86
8	11.6	0.7	6	**62**	**6.9**	**0.4**	**126**
9	11.4	0.7	15	63	8.6	0.5	123
10	11.6	0.7	6	64	10	0.6	102
11	9.8	0.6	105	65	10.6	0.7	66
12	12.2	0.8	1	66	10.8	0.7	44
13	10.8	0.7	44	67	11.2	0.7	23
14	10.8	0.7	44	68	10.6	0.7	66
15	10.6	0.7	66	69	11	0.7	25
16	11.6	0.7	13	70	9.2	0.6	116
17	11.8	0.7	3	71	9.4	0.6	113
18	10.8	0.7	60	72	10.8	0.7	60
19	10.4	0.7	86	73	10.8	0.7	60
20	9.8	0.6	110	74	10.6	0.7	66
21	10.8	0.7	44	75	10.2	0.6	97
22	11	0.7	25	76	7.9	0.5	124
23	10.8	0.7	60	77	8.6	0.5	122
24	10.8	0.7	60	78	10	0.6	103
25	10.8	0.7	44	79	9.4	0.6	118
26	11	0.7	25	80	9.2	0.6	116
27	9.8	0.6	110	81	11	0.7	25
28	10.8	0.7	44	82	10.4	0.7	86
29	11.6	0.7	13	83	9.8	0.6	105
30	12.2	0.8	1	84	11	0.7	25
31	11.6	0.7	6	85	11.2	0.7	23
32	10.2	0.6	94	86	10	0.6	103
33	10.6	0.7	66	87	10.6	0.7	66
34	10.8	0.7	44	88	10.8	0.7	44
35	10.2	0.6	97	89	10.8	0.7	44
36	8.8	0.6	120	90	10.8	0.7	44
37	10.8	0.7	44	91	9.8	0.6	105
38	11	0.7	25	92	10.6	0.7	66
39	11	0.7	25	93	10.6	0.7	66
40	9.4	0.6	113	94	10.8	0.7	44
41	10.2	0.6	94	95	10.6	0.7	66
42	10.6	0.7	66	96	11.2	0.7	19
43	11.4	0.7	15	97	11	0.7	25
44	10.2	0.6	94	98	9.2	0.6	116
45	10.6	0.7	66	99	10.4	0.7	86
46	10.6	0.7	66	100	10.8	0.7	44
47	11.8	0.7	3	101	11	0.7	25
48	11.4	0.7	15	102	10.2	0.6	97
49	10.8	0.7	44	103	10.6	0.7	66
50	10.8	0.7	44	104	10.4	0.7	86
51	11.6	0.7	6	105	11	0.7	25
52	10.6	0.7	66	106	10.6	0.7	66
53	9.8	0.6	105	107	10.6	0.7	66
54	11.2	0.7	19	108	10.4	0.7	86

Item	Score value		
	Fuzzy evaluation	Average fuzzy number	Rank
109	10.8	0.7	44
110	11	0.7	25
111	11	0.7	25
112	10.4	0.7	86
113	10.6	0.7	66
114	11	0.7	25
115	**7.1**	**0.4**	**125**
116	11.8	0.7	3
117	11.6	0.7	6
118	11.6	0.7	6
119	11.6	0.7	6
120	11.4	0.7	15
121	11	0.7	25
122	11.2	0.7	19
123	11	0.7	25
124	11	0.7	25
125	10.6	0.7	66
126	11	0.7	25

Finally, item 62 and item 115 were removed from the list as the items have scored the ∝-cut of less than 0.5, and the items were ranked 125 for item 62 and 126 for item 115 by the panel of experts.

6. CONCLUSION

In summary, the findings have shown that this study managed to answer the research question: "What do the panel experts say about the 126-items counselling needs assessment instrument through the Fuzzy Delphi method (FDM) of analysis?"

Through the process, the agreement of the panel experts was quantified and summarized quantitatively. This has proven the earlier assumption that the time of completing the process of getting the panel experts consensus can be shorten via FDM. This exercise also is seen to be practical in eliminating confusions that were driven from the conventional method, which is more qualitative in nature. FDM standardizes the process especially through its linguistic scale for not to limit the feedback with just the normal responses such as 'good' or 'very good' but with the fuzzy scales. FDM also allows for a more comprehensive and nuanced evaluation of the relevance and representativeness of content in the context of counseling and learning and instruction

In conclusion, the utilisation of FDM in assessing content validity holds significant implications for counseling and learning and instruction. The FDM, which combines the Delphi technique with fuzzy logic, offers a systematic and rigorous approach to gather expert opinions and reach consensus in situations characterised by uncertainty and ambiguity.

REFERENCES

Anastasi, A. (1992). *What counsellors should know about the use and interpretation of psychological tests*. Journal of counselling and development, 70, 610 – 615.

Arash Habibi, Farzad Firouzi Jahantigh & Azam Sarafrazi. (2015). *Fuzzy Delphi Technique for Forecasting and Screening Items*. Asian Journal of Research in Business Economics and Management, 5(2), 130-143.

Downing, S. M. (2006). Twelve Steps for Effective Test Development. In S. M. Downing & T. M. Haladyna (Eds.), Handbook of test development (pp. 3–25). Lawrence Erlbaum Associates Publishers.

Drost, E. A. (2011). *Validity and reliability in social science research*. Education Research and Perspectives, 38 (1), 105-124.

Fraenkel, Jack R, & Norman E. Wallen. (2008). *How to Design and Evaluate Research in Education*. Boston: McGraw-Hill.

Hays, D. G., & Erford, B. T. (2014). Developing Multicultural Counseling Competence: A Systems Approach (3rd ed.). Pearson.

Heale, R., & Twycross. (2015). *Validity and reliability in quantitative studies*. Evidence-Based Nursing, 18(3), 66 – 67.

Hsu, C., & Sandford, B. (2007). *The Delphi technique: Making sense of consensus*. Practical Assessment, Research and Evaluation, 12(10), 1 – 8.

Hsu, Y.L. Lee, C.H. & Kreng, V.B. (2010). *The application of Fuzzy Delphi Method and Fuzzy AHP in lubricant regenerative technology selection*. Expert Systems with Applications, 37 (2010), 419–425.

Leppma, M., & Jones, K.D. (2018). *Multiple Assessment Methods and Sources in Counselling: Ethical Considerations*. Retrieved from http://www.counseling.org/knowledge-center/vistas

Lynn, M. R. (1986). Determination and quantification of content validity. Nursing Research, 35(6), 382–385.

Merriam, S. B. (2009). Qualitative research: A guide to design and implementation. John Wiley & Sons.

Messick, S. (1996). Validity and washback in language testing. Language Testing, 13(3), 241–256.

Mohd Nazri Abdul Rahman, Mariani Md Nor, Noraziah Ahmad Nadzim, Nor Mashitah Mohd Radzi & Nurnadia Moktar. (2016). *Application of fuzzy delphi approach in designing homeschooling education for early childhood Islamic education*. International Journal of Academic Research in Business and Social Sciences, 6(12), 837 – 846.

Muhamad Saiful Bahri Yusoff. (2019). *ABC of content validation and content validity index calculation*. Education in Medicine Journal, 11(2), 49 – 54.

Ramlan Mustafa, & Ghazali Darusalam. (2018). *Applikasi Kaedah Fuzzy Delphi dalam penyelidikan sains sosial*. Kuala Lumpur: Penerbitan Universiti Malaya.

Rubio, D.M., Berg-Weger, M., Tebb, S.S., Lee, E.S., & Rauch, S. (2003). *Objectifying content validity: Conducting a content validity study in social work research*. National Association of Social Workers, Inc. 94 – 104.

Taherdoost, H. (2016). *Validity and reliability of the research instrument; How to test the validation of a questionnaire/survey in a research*. International Journal of Academic Research in Management (IJARM), 5, 28-36.

Tee, Q.T. Anizah Mohamed, & Norlidah Alias, (n.d). Application of Fuzzy Delphi Method in Exploring Facebook as a Tool for Writing Therapy Among Young Adults. The Malaysian Online Journal of Educational Technology, 2(3), 1-10.

Yaghmale F. (2003). *Content validity and its estimation*. Journal of Medical Education, 3, 25 – 27.

Yu, L.H., Cheng, H.L., & Kreng, V.B. (2010). *The application of Fuzzy Delphi method and Fuzzy AHP in lubricant regenerative technology selection*. Experts Systems with Applications, 37, 419 – 425.

Zanariah Ahmad, Mohamad Muhidin Patahol Wasli, Mohd Salihin Hafizi Mohd Fauzi, Mohd Ridhuan Mohd Jamil & Saedah Siraj. (2014). *Fuzzy Delphi analysis for future environmental education using interactive animation*. 2nd International Seminar Teaching Excellence and Innovation, Universiti Malaya.

HYBRID SIMULATION OF A SCIENTIFIC CONFERENCE: INQUIRY-BASED LEARNING TO ENABLE MASTER'S DEGREE STUDENTS TO ACQUIRE RESEARCH SKILLS

Patricia Brockmann
Nuremberg Institute of Technology
Nuremberg, Germany

ABSTRACT

A novel course concept to enable master's degree students to acquire research skills is described as an experience report. A hybrid, inquiry-based format was developed to simulate each phase of writing and presenting a research paper at a scientific conference. Students self-organized into groups to conduct each phase of the research process to conduct a research project for a scientific topic, bionic computation. Weekly group meetings with the instructor were conducted via video conference. Students learned to formulate research questions, write abstracts, acquire experimental data and evaluate open-source libraries and tools to build their own experimental models. An in-house, mini-conference was held in person, in which each group held a presentation of their work. At the end of the semester, a retrospective was held to reflect on students' experiences and summarize the lessons they have learned. After the course, slight majority of the students stated that they could imagine writing a paper about their master's theses and taking part in a real conference.

KEYWORDS

Project-Based, Inquiry-Based, E-Learning, Research Skills, Simulation, Conference, Bionic Computation

1. INTRODUCTION

During their bachelor's degree programs, students of computer science concentrate on learning technical skills, such as programming, algorithms, databases and software engineering. Due to the rapid rate of innovation, a large portion of the specific technical facts which students learn will quickly become obsolete. Self-motivation to independently learn new problem-solving skills becomes more important after graduation.

At the master's degree level, advanced research skills are required. The ability to critically analyze problems, to find and evaluate information, perform investigations, generate and evaluate potential solutions become necessary. Upon finishing their master's theses, a few of these graduates may have the opportunity to present their research at international scientific conferences and one day to pursue a doctoral degree.

The question arises as to how best to teach these research skills. Theoretical, instructor-centered lectures in research methods may not be effective without practical applications of these techniques. A different method which has shown to be effective is inquiry-based learning with a concrete project topic. This work reports on experiences made during a master's degree course on "Bionic Computation", which simulated each phase of writing a research paper and taking part in an international scientific conference.

The following research questions were investigated:

1. To what extent can inquiry-based learning in the simulation of a scientific conference help students to learn research skills needed for graduate level-work?
2. To what degree can a scaffolding approach help reduce stress levels which result from cognitive load?
3. Could the simulation of a scientific conference increase students' motivation for scientific research?

Section 2 Related Work gives an overview of related work on teaching research skills and the use of inquiry-based learning. The organization of the course and the methods used to acquire qualitative data are described in Section 3 Methods. Section 4 discusses the results of retrospectives at the end of the course. Conclusions and plans for future research are presented in Section 5.

2. RELATED WORK

An overview of literature on research skills and inquiry-based learning are given here.

2.1 Research Skills

Although technical skills were adequate for the bachelor's level degree program, research skills are critical for success at the master's degree level. Willison et al. (2018) have developed a research skill development framework to describe incremental steps of students' autonomy when conducting research.

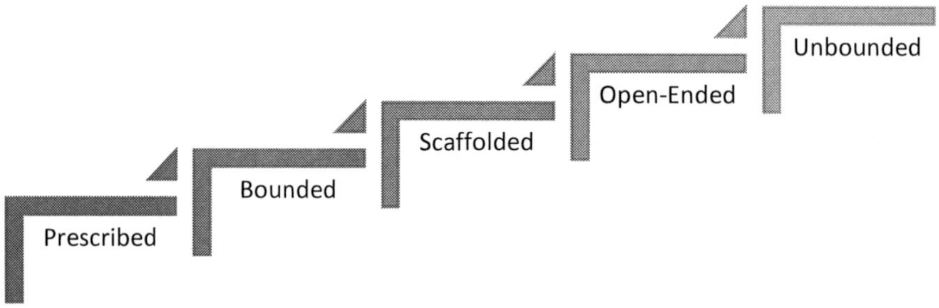

Figure 1. Research Skill Development Framework (Willison et al., 2018)

At the beginning of their bachelor's degree programs, students conduct "prescribed" research. Their work is highly structured and dependent on instructors who give explicit directions on how to use prescribed methods with pre-defined data sources. At the next level, "Bounded", instructors set boundaries to channel research within a choice of given structures and methodologies. "Scaffolded" research shapes independent research by allowing much more choice of data sources and methodologies. The instructor provides support at the beginning of the semester. Students choose from a range of approaches provided. As the semester progresses, and they begin to feel more confident, less guidance is needed. In open-ended research, students initiate their own research goals and generate their own hypotheses using self-determined criteria. In "Unbounded" research, students determine their own guidelines in accord with a specific discipline (Willison et al., 2018).

Within the Research Development Framework, students should learn the following facets of research:

1. Embark on an inquiry to determine the need for knowledge.
2. Find or generate needed information and data using an appropriate methodology.
3. Critically evaluate data and the process used to generate it.
4. Organize collected data and manage research processes.
5. Synthesize, analyze and apply new knowledge.
6. Communicate knowledge and the processes used to generate it.

Willison's models are designed to conceptualize the development path which would enable students to develop the research skills necessary to succeed in higher degree, graduate level research. Each of these research elements should be conducted with a continued awareness of ethical, social and cultural issues. He sees this as a starting point towards the development of a knowledge society (Willison, 2010).

2.2 Inquiry-Based Learning

Inquiry-based learning is an educational method in which students emulate scientific methods and practices to construct knowledge. Learners construct new knowledge by formulating hypotheses, conducting experiments to test them and then observing and evaluating the results (Pedaste et al., 2012).

Bybee developed a five-stage, inquiry-based instructional model for STEM (Science, Technology, Engineering, Math), which is based on cognitive psychology and constructivist learning theory (Bybee et al., 2006). In the first phase, „Engagement", instructors mentally engage students with question, activities or video clips. The goal is to awaken curiosity to learn more about a topic. During the second phase, "Exploration", students carry out hands-on activities to inquire about a topic, generate new hypotheses, gather data to test hypotheses, analyze and interpret the data to draw conclusions. Phase two is the most important phase of the inquiry-based experience. The third phase, "Explanation", is more instructor directed. Students explain their understanding of concepts. Instructors provide formal definitions and correct any misunderstandings, if necessary. In the fourth phase, "Elaboration", students apply their new understanding of concepts to conduct additional investigations, share information or apply their knowledge to other disciplines. During the final "Evaluation" phase, students assess their abilities and reflect on their learning progress (Bybee et al., 2006).

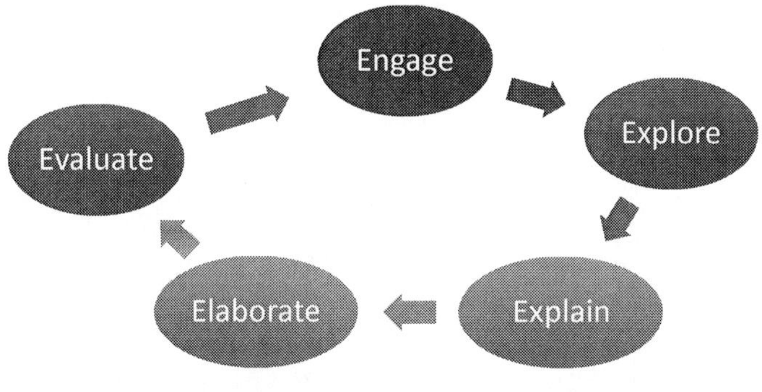

Figure 2. 5E Inquiry-based instructional model (Bybee et al., 2006)

Chu et al. (2016) described the use of a wiki in inquiry-based projects in school science education. They describe how to use a collaborative wiki to facilitate students' co-construction of knowledge in their group project. Students reported that the use of a wiki helped to improve the quality of their group project by helping them to learn knowledge management skills to create, capture, share and transfer knowledge. Sleeter et al. (2020) applied inquiry-based learning to a graduate course in history. A hybrid, scaffolding approach was applied, with class assignments and instructor feedback. Students were assigned to create their own online learning modules. Within this pre-determined framework, they developed their own research questions, defined their audience and engaged in self-directed independent research. The freedom to explore topics of their own choosing greatly increased their intrinsic motivation.

Woolf (2017) described his experiences incorporating inquiry-based learning in a graduate course on research methods. This course was a general course taught to graduate students, without any specific alignment to concrete research interests. Because the goal of this course was to learn about the process of research itself, the lack of a specific project context may have decreased motivation. Contrary to the current recommendations of minimal interference by the instructor, instructor guidance proved crucial in this course. Especially at the beginning of the course, students experienced an initial shock that the course would not be taught as a traditional instructor-centered lecture. Students reported that the risk and uncertainty of this unfamiliar didactic method led to anxiety. Many complained of feeling overwhelmed.

The successful use of simulations in teaching math and science teachers was documented by Mikeska et al. (2021). They showed that simulations can provide practice-based spaces to facilitate argumentation-focused science discussions. Although their work was conducted at the K-12 level, it may apply to higher education.

3. METHODS

The course described in this experience report was titled "Bionic Computation" and was taught at the Computer Science Department of the Nuremberg Institute of Technology during the Spring / Summer semester of 2022.

3.1 Course Goals

The learning goals for this course can be grouped into two major categories, as shown in Table 1: subject-oriented IT-skills in Bionic Computation and research skills. Bionic Computation refers to a class of algorithms which are patterned after biological processes in nature. Evolutionary Computation mimics evolutionary processes in nature to find solutions to difficult problems (DeJong, 2016). Neural networks mimic the human brain and learn through repetitive feedback (Goodfellow, 2017). Sentiment Analysis uses computational methods to identify, extract and study affective states in subjective information (Liu, 2020). Swarm Intelligence is based on the collective behavior of decentralized, self-organized systems, such as ant colonies (Yang, 2020).

Most of the research-oriented learning goals of this course can be classified as fulfilling Level 3, "Scaffolded Research" of Willison's Research Development Framework (2010). Scaffolding aids from the educator shape independent research. Students collect appropriate data from self-selected sources using a range of methodologies. They evaluate data and inquiry processes using criteria related to the aims of the inquiry. They organize data and self-manage teams and processes. Students analyze trends in data and use discipline-specific language to demonstrate understanding from a stated perspective for a specified audience.

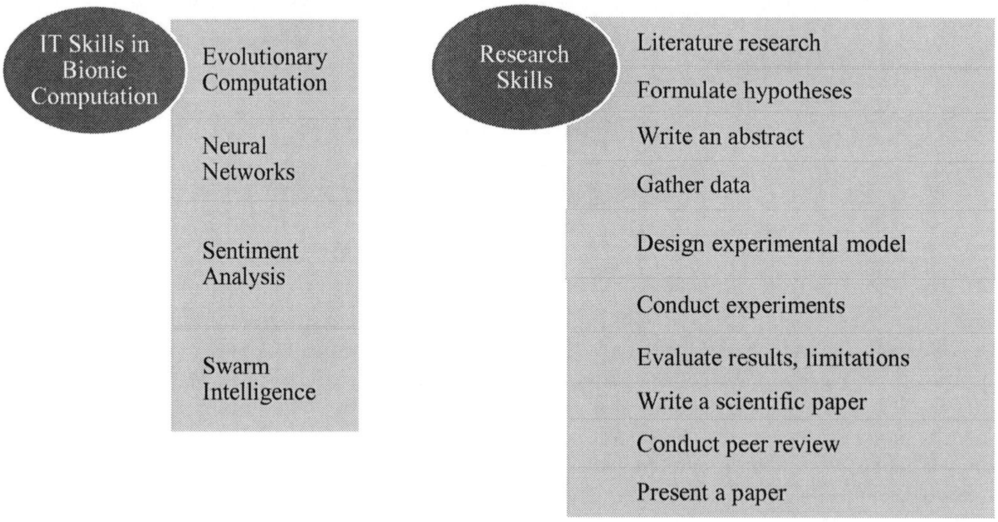

Figure 3. Learning goals in Bionic Computation and research skills

The second skill, "Formulate Hypotheses", would be classified as fulfilling Level 4 (Open-ended) of Willison's Research Development Framework (2010). Students were encouraged to apply design thinking (Brenner and Uebernickel 2016) to generate their own research questions for the topic of Bionic Computation.

The long-term goal is that after completing this course, some students should gain adequate experience to progress to the level of skills defined by Level 5 (Unbounded) of the Research Development Framework. To initiate scientific work for a PhD dissertation, students must demonstrate the ability to self-determine their own guidelines for independent research, which is in accordance with a specific discipline or context.

3.2 Course Organization

The course in Bionic Computation described in this case study simulated each phase to write and present a research paper at an international scientific conference. The course met once per week for a total of 16 weeks. This course was taught entirely in English, because international conferences are usually held in English. 24 students enrolled in the master's degree program took part in the course. Students self-organized into six teams, each with four members. Each week, teams worked on different tasks, corresponding to sequential steps in a research project. Concrete deliverables were produced every week, as listed below in Table 1.

After the initial orientation meeting with the entire class, each project team met separately once a week with the instructor. All of the teams were first required to complete one introductory level e-learning module in each of four topic groups, thus earning a "Badge of All Trades". The goal of this first level was to give students a broad overview of all four subject areas of Bionic Computation. Afterwards, each team could select one of these subject areas on their own area of emphasis. Three "expert level" e-learning modules in this chosen area of emphasis had to be completed in order to earn a "Master" level badge, such as "Master of Evolutionary

Computation" or "Master of Swarm Intelligence". Levels, points and badges have been shown to be an effective gamification method to increase student motivation (Lister, 2015).

Table 1. Research tasks and deliverables

Week	Research Task	Deliverable	Week	Research Task	Deliverable
1	Introduction	Self-organization	9	Build model	Model ready
2	Self-study e-learning units	Earn badges	10	Run experiments	Experimental results
3	Literature research	5 papers for wiki	11	Analyze results	Evaluation of results
4	Brainstorming, design thinking	Research topic	12	Write paper	Preliminary paper
5	Formulate research questions	Initial abstract	13	Peer review	Write 2 reviews
6	Design experimental model	Experimental model	14	Prepare talk	Presentation slides
7	Search for open source data	Data source	15	Conference	Hold presentation
8	Evaluate software tools	Architecture	16	Retrospective	Retrospective 4Ls

An agile project management format was used. Every week, each team presented their current deliverable to the instructor, as specified in Table 1. Research decisions made by the team, such as the choice of a project topic, had to be explained and justified. Questions and feedback were exchanged and a plan for activities to be accomplished (sprint backlog) during the next one-week sprint were agreed upon.

During the final month of course, each student team wrote an anonymous first draft of their papers using IEEE conference templates. Each team uploaded their paper to a double-blind peer review system, which was developed as a plug-in for Moodle. Each team received two anonymous papers from two other teams, which they were assigned to review anonymously. The instructor served as the third anonymous reviewer for each paper. Afterwards, each team received three anonymous reviews of their paper. It was not clear which review had been written by other students or which had been written by the instructor. Finally, each team revised their papers to incorporate the criticisms addressed in the reviews and submitted their final, camera-ready papers.

At the end of the semester, an in-person, in-house "scientific conference" was held. The conference was organized as two sessions of three papers each. Each team held a presentation of their paper to the rest of the class. During the break between sessions, posters which were displayed on Smart Boards gave students a chance to discuss their work. At the end of the conference, a "best paper award" was voted on by the students.

3.3 Data Collection

3.3.1 Project Topics

Student teams were allowed to select their own project topic. The main restriction was that the project had to focus on a practical application of one Bionic Computation method. The project topics chosen by the students and the corresponding methods of Bionic Computation are shown below in Table 2.

Table 2. List of project topics

Project Topic	Bionic Computation Method
Detection of hostility in open-source development communities	Sentiment Analysis
Generation of visitation plans for tourists in European cities	Ant Colony Optimization
Generation of fashion designs	Neural Network
Influence of cultural dimensions on authors' tweets about the pandemic	Sentiment Analysis
Maritime collision avoidance	Particle Swarm Optimization
Optimization of government administration processes	Evolutionary Computation

3.3.2 Course Retrospective

On the final day of class, a retrospective was held to give students a chance to reflect on what they had learned. An agile project management technique called the 4Ls method (Gottesdiener, 2010) was slightly modified to gather qualitative feedback from the students. Note: Gottesdiener designates the fourth category as "Long for", which proved confusing to German students. Each student was given sticky notes, one in each color and asked to write down one experience or opinion which corresponds to each category:

- Like: What went well on this project?

• Lack: What did you miss? What did not go well?
• Learn: What did you learn on this project?
• Long game: What will you do differently on your next project, based on what your learned here?

Students were given a few minutes to fill out their notes in private, in order to avoid influences from other group members. Next, each student went up to the white board, placed each note in the appropriate group and explained each experience or opinion. Afterwards, students clustered similar notes to form larger groups. Each cluster was then discussed in more detail by the entire class.

3.3.3 Anonymous Online Evaluation

At the end of the semester, students were asked to fill out an anonymous online evaluation form. Questions were similar to the research questions of this paper. Possible answers were "agree", "neutral" and "disagree".

1. Did this class format help you to learn research skills?
2. Did you find the e-learning modules at the beginning helpful?
3. Could you imagine writing a paper and taking part in a conference?

4. RESULTS

4.1 General Results: Project Topics

Because students had the freedom to suggest project topics of their own choosing related to bionic computation, a variety of extremely original topics were generated, as shown in Table 2. This wide diversity of application areas could never have been generated by the instructor alone. One of the topics, generative fashion design, required such a high amount of computational resources that additional computing power had to be purchased from Google Colab. Another topic which students proposed, avoidance of maritime collisions, was initially judged as too difficult by the instructor. Due to the personal interest of the team members in this subject, they decided that were willing to put in additional effort to explore this research project anyway. The student team which won the "Best Paper Award" submitted their paper to a conference and were able to participate online. Due to a lack of funding, they were not able to travel in person (Dobler et. al 2022).

4.2 Retrospective according to 4Ls Method

At the end of the semester, a retrospective according to the 4Ls Method (Gottesdiener, 2010) was conducted. The most commonly voiced opinions, ranked by their frequency of expression are summarized in Table 3.

Table 3. Results of the 4Ls retrospective

Like	Lack	Learn	Long game
Freedom to choose topic	Direction at beginning	Literature review	Document every step
Self-organization	More documentation	Scientific research	Look at related work
Hybrid e-learning	Organization of wiki	How to write a review	Structure problems more
Weekly meetings, tasks	Started development late	How to write a paper	Order steps to be done
Deep dive into one topic	Prior knowledge of NNs	Different approaches	Smaller teams
Peer review	ML as prerequisite	IEEE paper standards	Structure literature
Write a conference paper	No experience w Python	Use citation tools	Start writing earlier

Students stated that at the beginning of the semester, the unusual course format led to uneasiness. They experienced doubts that they did not know exactly what to do to achieve a good grade. Some students felt that they lacked the prerequisite programming skills to implement the experimental models they had designed. As the semester progressed, however, most students came to appreciate the freedom to propose and then explore a self-chosen topic. Some teams reported spending much more time than planned on this course, to the detriment of their other courses. The freedom to self-organize also resulted in the inherent challenge in managing a project with four group members. Although some groups were extremely well-organized and finished early, other groups underestimated the amount of effort required to write a scientific paper.

4.3 Results from the Online Questionnaire

After the course, students were asked to fill out an anonymous evaluation form as show in Table 4. A majority of the respondents answered that the class format of a simulated conference helped them to learn research skills. The two who responded neutrally wrote in the comments that they already possessed these skills. The two who did not like the class format wrote that they would have preferred a classic seminar, with only a presentation and a paper. A majority of the students reported that they found the e-learning modules at the beginning of the semester helpful. The two who disagreed stated that they were already familiar with the topics. A slight majority (15) of the students answered that after this course, they could imagine writing a paper and taking part in an actual scientific conference. Five were unsure and four disagreed.

Table 4. Results of the online questionnaire

Online Questions	Agree	Neutral	Disagree
1. Did this class format help you to learn research skills?	20	2	2
2. Did you find the e-learning modules at the beginning helpful?	22	0	2
3. Could you imagine writing a paper and taking part in a conference?	15	5	4

4.4 Classification of Skill Levels According to Research Skills Development Framework

In the opinion of the instructor, students at the end of this course demonstrated capabilities which would fulfill Level 3, "Scaffolded Research", of Willison's Research Development Framework (2018). The initial introduction by the instructor and the e-learning modules provided scaffolds to give students more start at the beginning of the semester. Students demonstrated that they could search for relevant literature in online databases and later gather or generate their own appropriate experimental data from self-selected sources. They designed and built their own experimental models to generate results, applying algorithms of Bionic Computation for their inquiries. They learned to organize their data, self-managed their own teams and processes using cloud-based collaboration software. They learned to use discipline-specific language to write and present a scientific paper for a specified audience. Some of the work accomplished would actually fulfill Level 4 "Student-Initiated" of Willison's Research Development Framework (2018). Students demonstrated the ability to apply creative thinking techniques to generate their own ideas for project topics and learned to generate their own research questions and hypotheses to explore these topics. Student-Initiated research skills on Level 4 should be of great help to write a master's thesis and would also be necessary for a PhD dissertation.

4.5 Limitations

The results reported in this case study are subject to a number of limitations. First, due to the nature of a case study, results can not necessarily be replicated uniformly. The number of participants in this course (24), is too small for any meaningful statistical analysis. The students who participated in this course are not necessarily representative for all master's students of computer science. Because this was an elective course self-selection among those who chose this course could have biased these results. Students who prefer traditional lectures with exams or those who were not confident of their English skills would have chosen different courses.

5. CONCLUSIONS

In closing, a return to the initial research questions is warranted:

1. To what extent can inquiry-based learning in the simulation of a scientific conference help students to learn research skills needed for graduate-level work?

A majority (20 of 24) students reported that the course format simulating a scientific conference was helpful to learn the research. Through inquiry-based learning, they demonstrated skills which could be attributed to Level 3 and 4 of Willison's Research Skill Development Framework (2018). This first research question can thus be answered as mostly true.

2. To what degree can a scaffolding approach help reduce stress levels which result from cognitive load?

Although at the beginning of the course some students expressed feeling unsure, a majority (22 of 24) stated that the initial scaffolding of e-learning modules, combined with the weekly schedule of tasks and deliverables helped them to gain confidence. The answer to this second research question is mostly true.

3. Could the simulation of a scientific conference increase students' motivation for scientific research?

Slightly more than half (15 of 24) of the students reported that the course format of simulating a scientific conference increased their motivation to one day submit a paper and to participate in an international conference. The answer to this third research question is thus slightly more true than untrue.

The knowledge gap between the programming skills adequate for a bachelor's degree level and the research skills necessary for graduate level courses can be bridged by inquiry-based learning. This work has shown that a course structured as a simulation of a scientific conference can help motivate students to acquire the research skills vital for graduate work, such as writing a master's thesis and submitting a paper to a scientific conference.

The conference simulation model presented in this case study could be adapted to other subject areas at the master's degree level. By actively practicing research skills during the master's degree, the hope is that more graduates could be motivated to begin a PhD program.

Further work on this subject will include writing a grant proposal to obtain funding to send the team which wins the "Best Paper Award" to travel an international scientific conference. The chance to participate in person at an actual scientific conference will hopefully further increase student motivation for research.

REFERENCES

Brenner, W. and Uebernickel, F., 2016. Design thinking for innovation. *Research and Practice*.

Bybee, R.W., Taylor, J.A., Gardner, A., Van Scotter, P., Powell, J.C., Westbrook, A. and Landes, N., 2006. The BSCS 5E instructional model: Origins and effectiveness. *Colorado Springs, Co: BSCS*, *5*, pp.88-98.

Chu, S.K.W., Reynolds, R.B., Tavares, N.J., Notari, M., Lee, C.W.Y. 2017. Twenty-First Century Skills Education in Switzerland: An Example of Project-Based Learning Using Wiki in Science Education. *21st Century Skills Development Through Inquiry-Based Learning*. Springer, Singapore.

De Jong, K., 2016. *Evolutionary Computation: A Unified Approach*, MIT Press.

Dobler, D., Donisch, L., Köppel, M., Brockmann, P., 2022. Sentiment Analysis of Twitter Posts on COVID-19 Cultural Dimensions: Collectivist vs. Individualist. *SOTICS 2022: Social Media Technologies, Communication and Informatics.*

Dorigo, M., Stützle, T., 2004. *Ant Colony Optimization*, Bradford.

Eiben, A.E, and Smith, J.E., 2015. *Introduction to Evolutionary Computing*, Springer.

Goodfellow, I., 2017. *Deep Learning: Adaptive Computation and Machine Learning*, MIT Press.

Gottesdiener, E., 2010. The 4L's: A Retrospective Technique. Online. Last accessed on (April 16, 2023). https://www.ebgconsulting.com/blog/the-4ls-a-retrospective-technique/.

Hassanien, A. E. and Emary, E., 2016. *Swarm Intelligence: Principles, Advances and Applications*, Taylor & Francis.

Lister, M., 2015. Gamification: The effect on student motivation and performance at the post-secondary level. *Issues and Trends in Educational Technology*, *3*(2).

Liu, B., 2020. *Sentiment Analysis*. Cambridge University Press.

Mikeska, J., Howell, H., Dieker, L. and Hynes, M., 2021. Understanding the role of simulations in K-12 mathematics and science teacher education: Outcomes from a teacher education simulation conference. *Contemporary Issues in Technology and Teacher Education*, *21*(3), pp.781-812.

Pedaste, M., Mäeots, M., Siiman, L.A., De Jong, T., Van Riesen, S.A., Kamp, E.T., Manoli, C.C., Zacharia, Z.C. and Tsourlidaki, E., 2015. Phases of inquiry-based learning: Definitions and the inquiry cycle. *Educational research review*, *14*, pp.47-61.

Sleeter, N., Schrum, K., Swan, A. and Broubalow, J., 2020. "Reflective of my best work": Promoting inquiry-based learning in a hybrid graduate history course. *Arts and Humanities in Higher Education*, *19*(3), pp.285-303.

Willison, J., 2010. Development of all students' research skill becomes a knowledge society. *All Ireland Journal of Higher Education*, *2*(1).

Willison, J., O'Regan, K. and Kuhn, S.K., 2018. Researcher skill development framework (US English Edition).

Woolf, J., 2017. An Analytical Autoethnographical Account of using Inquiry-Based Learning in a Graduate Research Methods Course. *Canadian Journal for the Scholarship of Teaching and Learning*, *8*(1), p.5.

Yang, X., 2020. *Nature-Inspired Computation and Swarm Intelligence*, Elsevier Academic Press.

PATTERN ELEMENTS IN HIGHER VISUAL ART EDUCATION

Antonina Korepanova and Kai Pata
Tallinn University, Estonia

ABSTRACT

Art education holds immense value, presenting students with complex problems and diverse solutions. While general art education has received attention from researchers, higher visual art education remains an under-discussed topic. This article aims to address this gap by examining the diversity of pattern elements that art teachers employ during digitally mediated lessons. By analyzing patterns in art teachers' feedback and lesson structures, this study offers insights into effective art teaching practices. Comparing higher visual art education patterns with the patterns revealed in the previous studies we highlight the specifics of tertiary visual arts education. Additionally, the study explores the connection between those patterns and the double diamond design thinking model as the theoretical underpinning of artistic and design processes.

KEYWORDS

Art Education, Pattern Languages, Digital Mediation

1. INTRODUCTION AND RESEARCH BACKGROUND

Art education holds tremendous value, providing learners with unique opportunities for creative expression and personal development. It is a field that encompasses complex problems and diverse solutions, making it intellectually stimulating and thought-provoking. While research has shed some light on general art education, the discussion surrounding higher visual art education, particularly concerning the utilization of digital tools, remains limited. The transition from traditional artistic practices to digitally enhanced forms presents unique challenges, as it involves an inductive design process where teachers grapple with ambiguous problem and solution spaces. Additionally, the digital medium often hinders direct contact with the artwork, such as its physical form and colors. These factors contribute to the complexity of teaching visual art in a digital context.

The exploration of patterns and pattern languages gained momentum with Christopher Alexander's introduction of architectural patterns in the late 1970s (Alexander, 1977). Alexander's influential work, "A Pattern Language," presented diagrams that formed the foundation of a practical language for capturing problem-solving solutions. Beyond architecture, this work found success in computer science, particularly in software and object-oriented design (Van Welie et al., 2001; Nilsson, 2009; Chase, 2012). Patterns offer designers reusable templates to address specific design challenges, leveraging the knowledge and experiences of successful system creators. They facilitate communication among designers working on similar artifacts or at different design levels (Pemberton and Griffiths, 1998). In educational research, patterns are seen as a form of language that generalizes and makes practices reusable in a specific area. Pedagogical patterns, developed by researchers and educators, summarize effective instructional strategies and approaches derived from research and best practices (Fincher and Utting, 2002; Bergin et al., 2012). These patterns serve as a guide for teachers to design and deliver instruction that fosters student engagement, comprehension, and achievement (Fincher and Utting, 2002).

The goal of visual arts and design education is to cultivate independent and original thinking and train qualified designers (Razzouk and Shute, 2012). Design thinking is a skill that needs to be actively practiced and learned through solving real-life problems (Lawson, 2006; Kimbell, 2011). This skill encompasses cognitive activities such as generating ideas, problem-solving, and decision-making (Ghonim, 2016). Adopting a design thinking mindset enables individuals and organizations to approach problem-solving creatively and innovatively (Dorst, 2011). The design process in design thinking is often segmented into stages. Various process models have been introduced, including the 3 I model (Brown and Wyatt, 2010) and the HCD model developed by the design agency IDEO, the Double Diamond model by the British Design Council (Gustafsson, 2019), the Design Thinking model by the Hasso-Plattner Institute (Plattner, Meinel and Leifer, 2010), and the Service Design model proposed by Stickdorn and Schneider (Stickdorn et al., 2018). The double diamond model was further developed by Robert Curedale (2022), which also features divergent and convergent stages, but extends the design process with more repetitions of this pattern. For this study, the Double Diamond model was chosen as it represents both divergent and convergent stages characteristic of design thinking (Tschimmel, 2012). Overall, the Double Diamond model provides a comprehensive framework for applying design thinking in problem-solving and innovation.

This research paper aims to delve into the identification of the patterns in art teachers' feedback and lesson structures. By doing so, we seek to provide valuable insights into the teaching practices of art educators, because the presented patterns will be specific to visual arts education. Educational patterns research is blooming; with most studies relevant to ICT (Bergin et al., 2012), and math (Inventado et al., 2017), it is crucial for patterns to be extracted from the relevant field (Fincher and Utting, 2002). This study aims to bridge the gap in art education research by providing a list of distinct patterns specific only to visual arts education. The findings of this study hold significance for art educators who plan lessons and courses. By comparing their practices with those of other professionals, educators can learn from different approaches and enrich their teaching methods. To address the gap, we formulate the following research question: What are the pattern elements that higher art educators use as building blocks in their lessons and what is the place of those patterns in the design thinking model?

2. METHODOLOGY

We used purposive sampling to select participants based on specific criteria, such as higher education, an active artistic career, and prior teaching experience at the university level before and during the pandemic. We recruited participants through university websites, personal emails, and social networking sites. We also utilized snowball sampling to identify additional suitable teachers. In total, we interviewed 12 participants, including traditional artists (painters, drawers, costume designers) and media artists (creative coders, interactive installation creators, and video artists) from different countries (China, Russia, Estonia, USA, and Austria). In the later stages of recruitment, snowball sampling was employed when interviewees suggested new participants from their contacts who were interested in sharing their experiences.

To gather data on the experiences and perspectives of art educators, we conducted open-ended interviews. Each interview consisted of 10 questions grouped into several categories: a description of teaching practices before and after shifting to online teaching, interaction with students and epistemological conceptualization, feedback patterns, technology usage, and the influence of technology on the lessons. The interviews took place either online or face-to-face, depending on the participants' locations. Online interviews were recorded using Zoom, while face-to-face interviews were audio recorded using the Voice Memos app. The interviews lasted approximately 45 minutes each and were conducted in English and Russian. English interviews were transcribed using Otter.ai, an online AI-driven service, with identifying details removed for anonymity. Russian interviews were translated and manually transcribed. After transcription, the interviews were uploaded into the qualitative coding software Atlas.ti. We employed an inductive analysis method, developing a priori codes in vivo. The coding process involved several stages, including familiarization with the data, in vivo coding, categorizing, and grouping codes, creating a codebook, and reviewing and refining the codes. The coding process underwent multiple iterations, with the first round focusing on categorical coding to identify discussed topics and the second round involving identifying pattern elements, naming them, and describing them. Later, we compared the pattern elements identified in the data with those found in the literature, highlighting patterns unique to both art education and digital mediation. Initially, we used an inductive approach to identify diverse patterns, and later stages involved a deductive approach, eliminating previously described patterns and focusing on new ones.

3. RESULTS

Table 1. Pattern elements discovered in the lessons

Pattern elements	Description	Source
1. Idea-oriented pattern elements		
Interdisciplinary Integration	The teacher introduces the idea of interdisciplinarity when students are getting inspired by other sciences or art branches. Students are encouraged to combine knowledge from different fields	I02, I03, I04, I07, I11
Initiate discussions	The teacher engages a student in a dialogue where a student verbalizes their idea and the teacher helps to separate and articulate those ideas. By discussing and explaining their projects, students deepen their understanding of their own creative process and engage in critical thinking	I01, I03, I05, I07, I11
Guiding idea generation*	In studio classes, the teacher focuses on guiding students in generating good ideas for art projects. The teacher assists in polishing the concepts and helping students transform raw ideas into well-formed projects	I02, I03, I11
Narrative creation	Students have to create a story that will become a base for the artwork	I05, I07
Personal conversation*	The teacher arranges personal feedback sessions with some students, to discuss personal struggles without group pressure	I07, I08, I09
Find an interesting topic	The teacher prepares a specific topic for a project-based course, so all student work on the same topic	I03
Generating ideas 1	Students present 3 ideas for the art projects they would like to create	I03
Generating ideas 2	Students generate the most unexpected and unusual combination of concepts, ideas, stories. Students swap the ideas afterward	I05
Merging ideas*	Students combine several ideas they have into one project	I03, I11
Analyse other images	The teacher encourages students to get inspired by other artists whose visual style is similar to students'. The students create an artwork using features of other artists' artworks	I01
Asking questions	The teacher asks students questions to monitor their understanding of a topic	I04
2. Object-oriented pattern elements		
Guiding idea execution*	They provide advice on materials, and technologies, and help students understand the feasibility of their ideas. The teacher's role is to steer students in the right direction while allowing them the freedom to explore their creativity	I01, I02, I03, I04, I07
Task-based learning	The teacher assigns practical tasks to the students, asking them to create artwork similar to what the teacher has demonstrated.	I01, I04, I06, I08
Visualise ideas*	Students create drawings to present their ideas. The teacher asks students to visualize what they want to achieve with coding by creating drawings with pencil and paper	I05, I06, I07, I11
Include individual work*	Allow students to work individually on a task they choose	I01, I04, I10
Prerecording educational videos*	Prerecording solutions to tasks and sharing videos with the students via LMS	I01, I06
Creating content for LMS*	The teacher creates structured educational content and posts it on LMS	I02, I04, I09
Practical demonstration	The teacher explains painting concepts and techniques by giving practical demonstrations. They show their own artwork and share their experiences, allowing students to observe and learn through visual examples. They demonstrate techniques and processes by painting and making changes in real-time, allowing the students to observe and learn	I01, I08, I09
Hands-on approach	The teacher prefers a practical approach to teaching, focusing on making students actively engage in projects and creative work. They emphasize doing rather than relying solely on theory classes. The teacher prefers a practical approach to teaching, focusing on making students actively engage in projects and creative work. They emphasize doing rather than relying solely on theory classes	I03

Combining technical tasks with creative examples*	The teacher begins the class with a creative activity or discussion related to the topic at hand. For example, when teaching for loops, they start by discussing repetition in art, textiles, optical art, and music, creating an artistic impulse to engage the students' interest.	I06
Step-by-step instructions	By breaking down the problem and providing step-by-step instructions, they aim to help students develop algorithmic thinking skills and problem-solving abilities	I06, I09
Pair programming	The teacher encourages pair programming, where students work in pairs with one person typing and the other providing instructions and support. This collaborative approach allows students to learn from each other, solve problems together, and stay engaged with the material	I06
Progressive difficulty	The teacher provides lab assignments with varying levels of difficulty, catering to students with different coding backgrounds. They offer both basic and advanced challenges, allowing students to choose tasks based on their skill level and fostering continuous learning and growth	I06
Copying artworks*	The teacher helps a student choose an artwork created by another artist. The student creates a copy of this artwork to learn the technical nuances of working with a specific analog media	I01
Monitoring students' activity on the LMS	The teacher regularly checks out how students interact with the educational content on the LMS and reminds them if they missed something out	I06, I09
Create a library of exercises*	The teacher saves the material, exercises, and solutions for students. They use this library for creating new courses	I06
Warm-up exercises*	The teacher gives students a task that is not graded and that is not directly connected to the topic. Example: to sketch another student not looking at the paper and not taking a pen from the paper. Students embrace imperfections, relax, and tune in for the creative process	I07
Changing a digital copy of students' artwork*	The teacher improves students' artworks using a graphical editor, this way they point out mistakes and imperfections, show how to improve an artwork, and how to continue working on an artwork	I08, I09
Time management*	The teacher emphasizes the importance of time management and keeping students on track. They understand the constraints of time in project-based courses and help students prioritize and focus their efforts to avoid unnecessary changes that might waste time	I03
3. Object-oriented and Idea-oriented pattern elements		
Feedback and Correction	The teacher provides feedback and corrections to the students' artwork. They guide the students on how to improve their work, by suggesting adjustments or providing references to professional artists with similar styles	I01, I02, I03, I04, I06, I07, I08, I09, I11, I12
Individualized Instruction	The teacher adopts a personalized approach to teaching by providing individual assistance to students. The teacher engages with each student separately, helping them understand concepts and solve problems	I01, I02, I03, I04, I05, I07, I08, I10, I12
Showing other artworks	The teacher shows students to previous works created to avoid repeating ideas that have already been done. The teacher also invites students to learn from their own work and openly shares their own artistic process	I02, I03, I04, I07, I08
Transmedial translation*	Students find an equivalent of an idea in music, video, image, sculpture, et cetera. Sometimes students have to create a story that will become a base for the artwork, Sometimes a piece of a text would serve as a base for a visual artwork	I05, I06, I07
Use of slides presentations	The teacher consistently uses PowerPoint presentations for their lectures, complemented by videos. PowerPoint serves as a visual aid in delivering content to the students	I05, I06
Give a lecture on a topic	The teacher explains theoretical material with examples, slides, and descriptions	I04
Demonstrating videos	The teacher relies on videos as a teaching resource. Videos are used as a tool for instruction, particularly in the design courses	I05
Holistic approach*	The teacher incorporates various aspects, such as aesthetics, psychology, and technology, into their teaching approach. They encourage students to consider	I05

	multiple dimensions and aspects related to character design and video game development	
Incorporating artistic examples	The teacher connects coding concepts to artistic examples, such as using examples from visual art, movies, or pop culture. This helps students relate coding to their artistic interests and encourages creativity in coding projects	I06
Diversified digital components	With the shift to online teaching, the teacher recognizes the need for a diversified approach and a mix of digital components. This includes prerecorded videos, online assignments, and the use of e-learning platforms like Moodle to distribute resources and facilitate communication between teachers and students	I04
4. Personal development pattern elements		
Online searches of supplementary materials	Encouraging students to explore online resources, both images shared by non-artists and professionals. Amateur photos can provide a broader perspective, inspiration, and understanding of a current time. Photos of professional artworks are used as reference pictures of what was created before. Students create a collection of images, a mood board that would help to explain the ideas and emotions they want to convey	I01, I02, I05, I06, I07, I09
Self-directed learning	The teacher explains the principles of self-directed learning and emphasizes that the course covers only foundations and they could learn more things on their own. The teacher believes in promoting active learning, where students take responsibility for their own learning process	I02, I03, I04
Sharing personal experience	The teacher describes issues connected to the personal creative process, highlighting the problems and how they overcome them	I03, I07, I10
Reflection for motivation*	The teacher raises critical questions about the purpose of art education, urging students to reflect on their motivations and goals for pursuing art. They highlight the need for students to understand why they want to learn and draw, beyond technical skills	I08, I12
Fostering curiosity*	The teacher aims to raise curiosity among the students by emphasizing the importance and relevance of the topics they are learning. They motivate students by highlighting the potential career opportunities and growth in the field of graphic design and technology	I02
5. Professional development pattern elements		
Arrange collaborative projects	The teacher expects students to create group projects. The teacher explains to students the benefits of working together and shares examples of collaboration in contemporary art	I02, I03, I05
Incorporating research*	The teacher explains the basics of research work, how to look for sources in scientific publications, cite them, and apply the knowledge in artwork	I03, I04, I05, I11
Presenting an artwork	Students present their artworks, talk about concepts and ideas	I05, I01, I03, I11
Embracing mistakes and iteration	The teacher creates a safe environment for students to make mistakes and iterate on their projects. Students are encouraged to learn from their mistakes and make changes if they feel their work is not meeting their expectations	I07
Portfolio building	The teacher recognizes the significance of portfolio creation for art students. They emphasize the importance of project-based courses, as portfolios play a crucial role in the students' post-university life	I03, I12
Creating a real-life output	The teacher emphasizes the importance of providing students with real-life outputs for their work, such as public showings or events. This pattern ensures that students can see the practical application and impact of their work beyond the classroom	I07, I11
Creating a library ideas*	Students create a diary where they write down all creative ideas they have and they use those ideas at the relevant moments	I02

Table 1 presents the identified pattern elements in the descriptions of digitally mediated lessons. The table consists of three columns. The first column displays the names of the patterns, the second column provides a description of each pattern, and the third column indicates the frequency of each pattern's mention across various interviews (using anonymized interviewee codes). The most frequently mentioned patterns are listed at the top of the table, while the least frequently mentioned patterns are placed at the bottom.

The pattern elements discovered in the interviews might be grouped into several categories. The idea-oriented group (11 elements) focuses on activities aimed at fostering idea generation, concept development, and logical connection between artistic form and artistic thought. The object-oriented group (18 elements) encompasses activities that emphasize the creation and manipulation of art objects: sketches, prototypes, drawings, and paintings. Idea and Object-oriented group consists of activities that do not separate the conceptual and practical parts of artistic work (10 elements). Notable, that some teachers desired to support student development beyond the educational topics, they wanted to support the development of personal qualities, like motivation, curiosity, and ability to learn independently (5 elements). And the last group was also reaching beyond the classroom, becoming a connection from education to professional life; we named this group "Professional development-oriented" (7 elements). Activities in this group were meant to involve students in the professional artistic community and make their interaction with art institutions sustainable. The asterisk (*) marks patterns unique to art education; other patterns were described in the previous studies.

4. DISCUSSION AND CONCLUSION

The presented study identified five groups of patterns that are used by art educators, all in some way related to professional artistic activity (Idea-oriented, Idea and Object-oriented, Object-oriented, Personal, and Professional development). Some of the patterns are similar to those used in educational areas not connected to visual arts, while others are unique to visual arts. The rest are specific to digitally mediated environments and online education.

To compare our results with previous studies, we selected the five most cited articles that described the largest number of patterns: Eckstein et al. (2002), Muhonen et al. (2017), Eckstein (2001), Goodyear (2009), and Bergin (2012). Out of the 51 pattern elements, 21 were unique and did not have similar patterns documented in the published literature. It is worth noting that some of the patterns identified in our interviews align with patterns already published, even though the previous research did not focus on visual art education pedagogy. This indicates the universal applicability of educational patterns and the potential to adapt them across different fields. However, several patterns identified in our study were not previously described, warranting special attention.Pattern elements related to intellectual development and plasticity (merging ideas and guiding idea generation) might embody the conceptualist influence on visual arts curricula, particularly in the debate surrounding cerebral/retinal art (Honold, 2016). Including personal conversations in the educational process may trace back to the traditional master-apprentice relationship in art studios, which is the earliest model of visual arts education. A personal connection between a mentor and mentee is central to visual arts education due to the inherently intimate nature of creative work (Kantawala et al., 2009). A significant number of novel patterns are related to Object-oriented artistic activity, which involves the creation of art objects. These patterns include visualizing ideas, guiding idea execution, combining technical and creative tasks, and copying artworks. These patterns serve specific objectives unique to visual arts and are not relevant to other subjects. One unique pattern from the Personal development group, fostering curiosity, is also described as a necessary quality in design thinking (Curedale, 2022).

Furthermore, it is important to acknowledge that among these new patterns, some can be grouped separately as they all relate in some way to digitally mediated teaching. The emergence of these patterns is not surprising since the five sources used for analysis were published before 2017, prior to the pandemic, and primarily explored patterns in traditional face-to-face teaching. To obtain a broader understanding, it is necessary to include other studies dedicated to hybrid or online learning and teaching. The specific patterns related to digitally mediated teaching include: "Creating content for LMS," "Prerecording educational videos," and "Creating a library of exercises." This study fills a gap in understanding online teaching practices and proposes advice which patterns are viable for online education in higher visual arts.

Overall, all pattern elements related to artistry have a place within the design thinking schema. However, since the other patterns are not explicitly connected to the design process, it is more challenging to incorporate all pattern elements into it (and not necessarily required). By segregating the artistic patterns from the general patterns, we can focus on the unique aspects of art education and its relationship with design thinking. By incorporating teaching patterns into the design thinking model, we can establish a suggested sequence for their application throughout a course. The double diamond model has a particular shape due to a pattern that first follows divergent thinking, then develops in convergent thinking, and then the process iterates until an optimal solution is found. Divergent thinking creates choices that might branch out as possible solutions (ideation); convergent thinking makes those choices, leading to prioritizing some solutions over others and developing them (judgment) (Brophy, 2001; Curedale, 2022). Following this definition, the revealed patterns might be placed inside of the model, lining up with divergent or convergent thinking patterns, as illustrated in Figure 1.

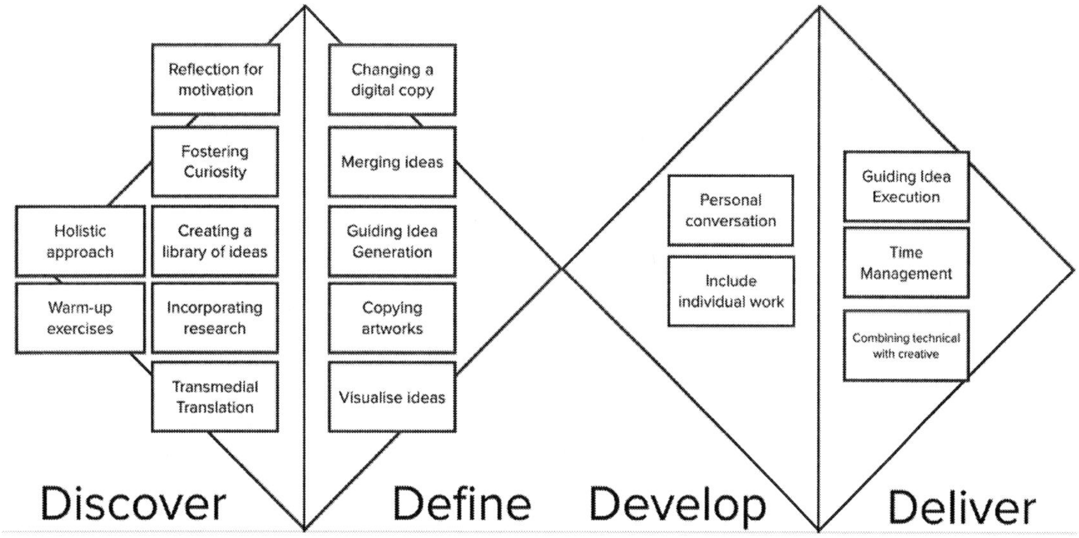

Figure 1. The placement of pattern elements within the 4D design thinking model

These results indicate the potential applicability of the pattern approach across diverse educational domains and levels, for instance, 30 out of 51 patterns identified in ICT education research were applicable to higher visual arts education. This suggests that the concept of patterns transcends disciplinary boundaries and holds promise for enhancing teaching methodologies in various areas. Furthermore, these findings underscore the distinct nature of digital mediation within the realm of art education. They emphasize the imperative for art educators to reassess and innovate their pedagogical practices with new tools, exploring new patterns to support the digitally mediated learning process. The dynamic landscape of digital mediation calls for adaptive strategies, enabling art teachers to navigate its unique challenges and opportunities, ultimately enriching the educational experience for their students. In future development and research, it is recommended to analyze additional interviews to identify more pattern elements. By doing so, we can further investigate how these pattern elements can be combined effectively to address various problems. There are several potential approaches for combining educational patterns: creating a pattern catalog, constructing a system of patterns, or establishing connections between multiple patterns within a shared problem space. This integration of patterns forms a language of patterns, which serves as a valuable resource for solving complex problems in education. Furthermore, the study's alignment of some patterns with established pedagogical concepts, such as design thinking, sheds light on the interconnectedness of various educational paradigms. This suggests the possibility of integrating these patterns into a cohesive framework, enhancing the effectiveness of art education.

This study unveiled novel educational patterns and highlighted the distinctive aspects of higher visual arts education while also reaffirming the universal applicability of previously identified educational patterns. Art teachers can utilize the findings of this study as a valuable repository of insights, offering guidance on how to enhance, elevate, and refine their lessons. However, it is important to acknowledge certain limitations of the study. The participant pool was relatively small, and to broaden the scope of analysis, additional patterns, particularly those pertaining to digitally mediated teaching, could be included for further examination.

ACKNOWLEDGEMENT

We thank all art teachers who participated in the study.

REFERENCES

Alexander, C. (1977) *A pattern language: towns, buildings, construction.* Oxford university press.

Beck, K. and Ralph, J., 1994. Patterns Generate Architectures. *Proceedings of European Conference of Object-Oriented Programming.* Bologna, Italy, pp. 139-149.

Brophy, D.R. (2001) 'Comparing the attributes, activities, and performance of divergent, convergent, and combination thinkers', *Creativity research journal*, 13(3–4), pp. 439–455.

Bergin, J. et al. (2012) *Pedagogical patterns: Advice for educators.* Joseph Bergin Software Tools.

Brown, T. and Wyatt, J. (2010) 'Design thinking for social innovation', *Development Outreach*, 12(1), pp. 29–43.

Chase, C. (2012) *Using design patterns in user interface design.* University of Cincinnati.

Curedale, R. (2022) *Design Thinking Process & Methods 5th Edition*. 5th edition. Design Community College Inc.

Dorst, K. (2011) 'The core of 'design thinking'and its application', *Design studies*, 32(6), pp. 521–532.

Eckstein, J. et al. (2001) 'Patterns for Experiential Learning.', in *EuroPLoP.* Citeseer, pp. 477–498.

Eckstein, J., Bergin, J. and Sharp, H. (2002) 'Patterns for active learning', in *Proceedings of PloP.*

Fincher, S. and Utting, I. (2002) 'Pedagogical patterns: their place in the genre', in *Proceedings of the 7th annual conference on Innovation and technology in computer science education*, pp. 199–202.

Ghonim, M. (2016) 'Design thinking in architecture education: issues, limitations, and suggestions', in *Proceedings of the 3rd International Architectural Design Conference on Design and Nature ARCHDESIGN.* Dakam Publishing Istanbul, pp. 553–561.

Goodyear, P. (2009) 'Patterns and pattern languages in educational design', in *Handbook of research on learning design and learning objects: Issues, applications, and technologies. IGI Global*, pp. 167–187.

Gustafsson, D. (2019) 'Analysing the Double diamond design process through research & implementation'.

Honold, A. (2016) 'Marcel Duchamp: nothing but a masterpiece', *World Art*, 6(2), pp. 203–231.

Inventado, P.S. et al. (2017) 'Feedback design patterns for math online learning systems', in *Proceedings of the 22nd European Conference on Pattern Languages of Programs*, pp. 1–15.

Kantawala, A. *et al.* (2009) 'Establishing collaborative dialogue: The mentor and the apprentice', *Visual Arts Research*, 35(2), pp. 40–50.

Kimbell, L. (2011) 'Rethinking design thinking: Part I', *Design and culture*, 3(3), pp. 285–306.

Lawson, B. (2006) How designers think. Routledge.

Muhonen, H. et al. (2017) 'Knowledge-building patterns in educational dialogue', *International Journal of Educational Research*, 81, pp. 25–37.

Nilsson, E.G. (2009) 'Design patterns for user interface for mobile applications', *Advances in engineering software*, 40(12), pp. 1318–1328.

Pemberton, L. and Griffiths, R.N. (1998) 'The timeless way: Making living cooperative buildings with design patterns', in *Cooperative Buildings: Integrating Information, Organization, and Architecture: First International Workshop, CoBuild'98 Darmstadt, Germany, February 25–26*, 1998 Proceedings 1. Springer, pp. 142–153.

Plattner, H., Meinel, C. and Leifer, L. (2010) *Design thinking: understand–improve–apply.* Springer Science & Business Media.

Razzouk, R. and Shute, V. (2012) 'What is design thinking and why is it important?', *Review of educational research*, 82(3), pp. 330–348.

Stickdorn, M. et al. (2018) *This is service design doing: applying service design thinking in the real world.* O'Reilly Media, Inc.

Tschimmel, K. (2012) 'Design Thinking as an effective Toolkit for Innovation', in *ISPIM Conference Proceedings. The International Society for Professional Innovation Management (ISPIM)*, p. 1.

Van Welie, M., Van Der Veer, G.C. and Eliëns, A. (2001) 'Patterns as tools for user interface design', in *Tools for Working with Guidelines: Annual Meeting of the Special Interest Group*. Springer, pp. 313–324.

THREE FRAMEWORKS FOR DATA LITERACY

Stephen Downes
National Research Council Canada
Ottawa, Ontario, Canada

ABSTRACT

Data literacy is the ability to collect, manage, evaluate, and apply data, in a critical manner. It is a relatively new field of study, dating only from the 2010s. It includes the skills necessary to discover and access data, manipulate data, evaluate data quality, conduct analysis using data, interpret results of analyses, and understand the ethics of using data. This paper considers data literacy education across three frameworks: the competency model defining data literacy, the assessment of data literacy competencies, and methods for the development of data literacy in an organization. These principles are applied to a discussion of the development of an open online course supporting the development of data literacy in the form of a corresponding data structure encompassing the three frameworks identified in the literature.

KEYWORDS

Data Literacy, Model, Framework, Learning

1. INTRODUCTION

What is the difference between 'learning' a discipline or domain when thought of as data, and supported by the principles of data literacy, as compared to 'learning' through of as analogous to reading, and supported by traditional literacy? In this paper we address this question through analysis of the concept of data literacy, an examination of how data literacy is currently assessed, and research and development in the teaching of data literacy for individuals and organizations.

It is evident that 'learning' a 'literacy' involves more than learning about the components of that literacy, and that there is an element of 'being literate', which is intended as an outcome of that learning. To be literate is to embody a set of skills and competencies typically thought to define that literacy, as reflected in an assessment of that literacy, and which in turn informs the teaching of that literacy.

But the study of data literacy is nascent, limited to a few (mostly commercial) initiatives, and not benefiting from a wide-reaching analysis considering all aspects of the definition, development and application of data. This paper seeks to fill that gap, providing a comprehensive overview of data literacy as it is taught and learned today, and suggesting a set of frameworks that will inform future research and development of data literacy learning initiatives.

1.1 Methodology

Originating as work conducted for the office of the Assistant Deputy Minister (Data, Innovation and Analytics) in the government of Canada, this paper is a summarization of a comprehensive literature review and design research project. A formal review was conducted by the National Research Council information management office of Canada's National Science Library for publications related to the definition, application and development of data literacy. A wider search using the same parameters was undertaken using Google Scholar. Approximately 150 results were obtained, from which 20 items were found to contain an identifiable data literacy model, and three major assessment frameworks were identified. A small number of highly specific data literacy development models were also identified. The design framework employed draw from previous work by the author on connectivist massive open online courses (cMOOC) with the specific intent of adapting the data literacy models table into the connectivist course framework.

2. THREE FRAMEWORKS

2.1 Competency Model or Framework

Data literacy includes the skills necessary to discover and access data, manipulate data, evaluate data quality, conduct analysis using data, interpret results of analyses, and understand the ethics of using data, where by data we mean the representation of facts in media. These are core skills required to support key competencies in intelligence and trend analysis, mission-driven metric reporting, health and human response to stress and injury, training and development functions, deployment, supply management and logistics, and information warfare, to name a few. The following major themes emerge from the discussion of data literacy over the last decade: data literacy as a set of skills or competencies; the idea of deriving meaningful information from data; the data lifecycle or data workflow; complexity of skills for differing roles; data literacy as individual and corporate capacities.

2.1.1 Competencies

Competencies are commonly defined as "a set of basic knowledge, skills, abilities, and other characteristics that enable people at work to efficiently and successfully accomplish their job tasks." Following Oberländer, et al. (2020) we use the term 'competencies' here to draw on a well-established concept that includes knowledge, skills, abilities, and other characteristics (KSAO).

The concept of competencies also includes the requirement of evidence for competencies. Thus, employing a definition using competencies is well suited to a discussion of data literacy that includes the fostering and assessment of knowledge, skills, and abilities.

2.1.2 Analysis

We drew on 20 studies that offered a (more or less) competency-based definition of data literacy and compared the set of competencies each proposed. The selection of sources was intended to draw from and be representative of various data literacy models. In assigning the competencies interpretation was required, as the studies did not all employ the same terminology. Figure 1 displays the result of the analysis:

Data...	1	2	3	4	5	6	7	8	9	10	11	12	13	14	15	16	17	18	19	20
Awareness	x		x								x			x			x		x	x
Dispositions																				x
Strategy/Culture	x			x		x		x			x				x					
Plan, Implement, Mon														x				x		
Inquiry Process														x			x	x	x	
Discovery / Explore			x		x			x	x		x		x	x	x	x	x			x
Ethics	x		x			x			x	x	x			x	x	x				
Gathering / Collection			x	x					x	x	x		x	x		x		x	x	
Curation										x	x								x	
Communities						x														
Requirements		x							x											
Valuation								x										x		
Evaluation/Assessment					x	x					x						x		x	
Informed Decision-mak	x		x			x	x	x		x	x		x	x			x		x	
Governance / Steward	x	x	x	x		x	x		x									x	x	
Standards	x					x			x											
Description/Metadata						x		x	x	x	x		x				x	x	x	
Conversion, Interopabl	x										x		x		x		x	x	x	
Management		x			x	x	x	x		x	x		x	x		x	x	x	x	
Preservation											x		x			x				x
Cleaning			x			x			x	x										
Systems & Tools	x		x			x					x			x		x	x	x	x	
Policy						x														
Quality	x								x		x	x	x	x	x	x	x	x		
Security	x	x					x			x	x									
Manipulation		x									x		x	x	x	x		x	x	
Statistics & Reasoning								x		x	x							x	x	
Critical Thinking											x					x				
Analysis	x	x	x			x	x	x	x	x	x		x	x	x	x	x	x	x	x
Interpretation											x		x	x	x	x			x	
Modeling/Architecture			x	x			x		x										x	
Data Science and ML							x	x												
Citation & Sharing											x	x				x		x		x
Visualization	x	x	x			x			x		x	x	x		x	x	x	x	x	x
Storytelling	x		x					x	x		x	x							x	
Present Data Verbally											x		x		x					
Change						x	x	x											x	
Using/Innovating With					x	x		x												
Identifying Problems											x		x	x	x					
Generate Data																	x			

Figure 1.

2.1.3 Models

The list of competencies identified also makes it clear that data literacy does not fall into any single category described above. It contains elements of critical thinking, statistical reasoning, data management, and scientific research. Data literacy therefore represents a certain level of competency across a broad range of data-related skills, not a narrowly defined subset of some other type of literacy. Most work in data literacy falls into one of several models or interpretations. "They each have a different focus which tends to reflect the context in which it was derived. They also have a different level of granularity, not just between the definitions, but also within them" (Wolff, et al., 2016). Schield (2004) describes these as 'perspectives', for example, the 'critical thinking' perspective and the 'social science data' perspective:

- Data Stewardship Model: This model describes approaches to data literacy that emphasize data acquisition, curation, quality and deployment. A prototypical example of this approach is the Statistics Canada descriptions of data quality and the data journey (Statistics Canada, 2020).
- Analysis and Decision-Making Model: This model is focused mostly on the use of data to support analytics and decision-making, for example, the collection of approaches taken by members of the Data Literacy Project, including Qlik (a data analytics company), Accenture, Cognizant, Experian, Pluralsight, the Chartered Institute of Marketing, and Data to the People.
- Information Literacy Model: "According to Hunt (2004), data literacy education should borrow heavily from information literacy education, even if the domain of data literacy is more fragmented than the field of information literacy." (Koltay, 2016). Similarly, Maybee & Zilinski (2016) write, "The emerging construct of data literacy has typically been closely related to information literacy."
- Science and Research Data Literacy Model: This model of data literacy emphasizes aspects of data related to computer science, mathematics and statistics. It defines a set of data skills including data awareness, forms of statistical representation, the ability to analyze, interpret and evaluate statistical information, and communication of statistical information (Australian Bureau of Statistics, 2010).
- Social Engagement Model: This model distinguishes between the need for everyday uses of data from the deeper requirements of data science. It is only really articulated in a single source (Rahul Bhargava, et. al., 2015), though it has its origins in a broader definition of literacy, as exemplified by Robinson (2005), who talks of literacy as enabling individuals to achieve their goals, to develop their knowledge and potential, and to participate fully in their community and wider society" (p. 13).

As discussed below, no single model accounts for all aspects of data literacy applicable in a specific content or role, hence, rather than describe a metric for model selection, a comprehensive model based on specific skills and competencies defining a job, task or role is proposed.

2.1.4 Application

In our analysis we looked more closely at the nature of artificial intelligence and machine learning, two disciplines largely defined by their relation to data, to understand what might be understood as the full 'data workflow'. This section makes it clear that data literacy involves much more than 'reading' and 'writing' with data and includes but not limited to the framing of the problem or context of use, the data set itself, application, and testing.

For example, machine learning engineering describes the construction and use of these three elements: data engineering, which describes the acquisition, exploration, cleaning, labeling and management of data; model engineering, which consists of the development or training of the model, testing and evaluation, and packaging for use in an application; and deployment, which describes how the model is served and used, performance evaluation, and performance logging (Visengeriyeva, et al., 2022). Similarly, Statistical research methods workflows emphasize "the importance of asking questions throughout the statistical problem-solving process (formulating a statistical investigative question, collecting or considering data, analyzing data, and interpreting results), and how this process remains at the forefront of statistical reasoning for all studies involving data." (Bargagliotti, et al., 2020).

Additionally, this study finds that data literacy is a concept that can be applied equally to both individuals and organizations, though both the description of data literacy as well as the assessment of data literacy will vary in the given context. Framing elements of data literacy as competencies, and employing a widely used model describing knowledge, skills and attitude, an overall framework for describing individual data learning competencies and organizational data literacy capabilities is proposed.

2.2 Evaluation or Assessment Framework

It is important to be able to evaluate or assess the level of data literacy competencies individually or across the organization for the purpose of assessing operational readiness and for the purpose of planning future training and development. Here we first provide an overview of some data literacy assessment programs, then consider some data literacy assessment models, and finally consider some data literacy methods.

2.2.1 Assessment Programs

We analyzed major skills and data literacy assessment programs, including the following:

- OECD Programme for the International Assessment of Adult Competencies (PIAAC) literacy assessment asks participants "access and identify tasks require respondents to locate information in a text, integrate and interpret tasks involve relating parts of one or more texts to each other, and evaluate and reflect tasks require the respondent to draw on knowledge, ideas or values" (Kirsch & Thorn, 2016, 2.2.1.3)
- Endorsed by the American Statistical Association, the Guidelines for Assessment and Instruction in Statistics Education (GAISE) emphasize that there is no one route to teaching and assessing statistical literacy and notes that "mastering specific techniques is not as important as understanding the statistical concepts and principles that underlie such techniques" (GAISE, 2016, 8).
- By contrast with the OECD and GAISE programs, the Eckerson Group describes data literacy assessment specifically and includes assessment not only of individual data literacy but also of the organization (Wells, 2021). Assessments are based initially on a comprehensive Data Literacy Body of Knowledge (DLBOK) defined by the organization.

2.2.2 Data Literacy Model-Based Assessment

In the analysis of data literacy competencies described in the first section of this report we obtained an unstructured list of competencies. These competencies were organized into different categories by various studies, but there was no consistency whatsoever in the categorization scheme from study to study. What is offered here is a model based on a slightly modified full list of competencies drawn from the data literacy studies cross-referenced with a comprehensive skills taxonomy as suggested by the assessment programs considered above.

For the sake of consistency with much of the work done previously a slightly modified version of Bloom's taxonomy is used (Bloom, 1956). Bloom's three separate taxonomies - cognitive, affective and psychomotor - can be thought of corresponding with the already-described taxonomy of knowledge, attitudes and skills, respectively. This taxonomy needs to be extended to accommodate both individual and organizational competencies.

Table 1.

Bloom's	Individual	Organizational
Cognitive	Knowledge	Definitions
Psychomotor	Skills / Competencies	Capacities
Affective	Attitudes	Practices

2.2.3 Role-Defined Data Literacy

It is arguable that a single-factor measure of data literacy is insufficient to account for the variability in both the set of data literacy competencies and also the varying degree to which each competency is required in different job functions or roles. Accordingly, a role-defined data literacy model is proposed here.

This figure illustrates the calculation of a role-defined data literacy profile. It consists of a combination of the set of competencies as defined in the data literacy model with the actual job or function description. This allows for a definition of the relative importance of each competency for that function, demonstrated here in the form of a radar chart (also known as a spider chart).

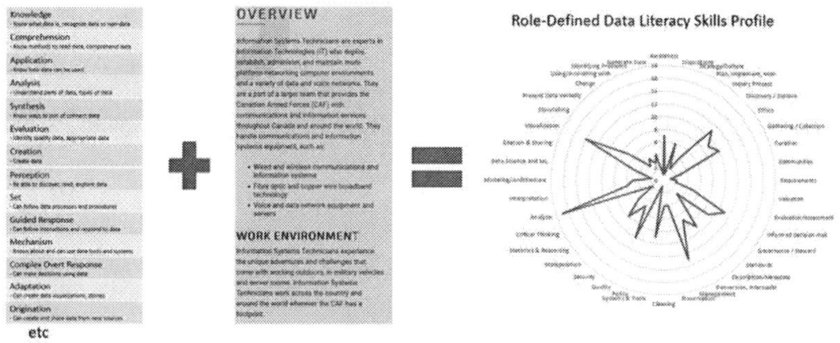

Figure 2.

Job or function descriptions may be obtained from extant text (the example in the diagram is from the forces.ca Careers page) or drafted as text by managers and those occupying the position. The competency profile may be created by a simply counting of the frequency of relevant terms, or by a more nuanced analysis, perhaps using machine learning.

The same process may be used to create actual competency profiles for each individual evaluated, by employing test results or actual communications generated by the person in question (such a process would be subject to ethical and privacy considerations). A similar process may be used to generate organizational level competency profiles.

It is arguable that a single-factor measure of data literacy 'levels' as employed by numerous data literacy assessment schemes is insufficient to account for the variability in both the set of data literacy competencies and also the varying degree to which each competency is required in different job functions or roles. Accordingly, a role-defined data literacy model is proposed. This model illustrates the calculation of a role-defined data literacy profile, as well as the process used to create actual competency profiles.

2.3 Teaching Framework

There are few data literacy training initiatives extant, and no organization or institution-wide examples were found. So, in the context of data literacy development two areas of consideration are important: models and designs for data literacy program development in general, and examples of extant data literacy training programs and curricula.

2.3.1 Developing Data Literacy

The development of data literacy in an organization occupies a space between two extremes. On the one hand, we may find data literacy among other types of information and communication competencies, such as digital literacy or information management programs. On the other hand, we might think of data literacy as a first step in the development of higher-level competencies such as data architect or information management. Either approach envisions a large-scale and complex learning initiative.

But it need be neither, provided we think of data literacy not such as knowledge or content to be used, but rather, as a part of other processes and strategies employed to achieve real objectives or outcomes. This accords with the recommendations found in the literature, for example, to focus on performance rather than content knowledge and to ensure it encompasses real operational challenges using authentic data and examples.

The development of data literacy in the context of this report is tantamount to the development of individual and organizational data literacy, which consist of knowledge, skills and attitudes, or their analogues, in each of the data literacy competencies, defined as described in the first section, such that the achievement of these competencies can be reliably and validly assessed and detected using the assessment methodologies described in the second section.

2.3.2 Data Literacy Programs

There is not yet an established infrastructure for data literacy development; we mostly find commercial training courses and online resources. So, in the context of data literacy development, two area of consideration are important: models and designs for data literacy program development in general, and examples of data literacy training programs and curricula.

Models and designs for data literacy program development: some universities have conducted background research and there are numerous data literacy program development roadmaps provided by commercial consultants. For example:

- The Data Information Literacy project funded by the Institute of Museum and Library Services (IMLS) which proposes a four-step methodology of planning, development, implementation, and assessment' (Carlson & Johnston, 2015).
- QuantHub provides a methodology for developing individual and team data literacy learning and development plans. There are two major components: a series of 'foundational steps' to develop a data literacy vision and roadmap; and an iterative process of assessment, planning, learning and practice (Cowell, 2020).
- Dave Wells of Eckerson Group offers a comprehensive data literacy program development methodology (2021) arguing that organizational data literacy is not merely a sum of individual data literacies but requires in addition factors such as tools and systems, incentives and motivators.
- Gartner, by contrast, offers a report describing a three-phase methodology for the development of an institutional program (Panetta, 2021) consisting of assessment, data literacy training, and then evaluation of the outcome.

Data literacy training programs and curricula: After a brief surge in the mid 2010s, data literacy is enjoying a resurgence in 2023.

- While no longer extant, the Data Literacy Project, founded in 2015 at Dalhousie University, proposed "a transdisciplinary examination of existing strategies and best practices for teaching data literacy, synthesizing documented explicit knowledge using a narrative-synthesis methodology and identifying areas where additional research is needed." (DataLiteracy.ca, Internet Archive, 2021).
- Conducted online between January and March 2022, the EDUCAUSE Data Literacy Institute consisted of a series of eight synchronous online meeting to discuss resources, activities, and projects in support of seven key data literacy competency areas (Kleitz & Shelly, 2022).

2.3.3 Teaching and Learning Methods

Data literacy is new enough that specific pedagogies have not been broadly developed or applied. However, in many ways, data literacy training is similar to that in other disciplines, and especially those characterized as 'literacies'. Thus, recommendations for, say, digital, information or statistical literacy instruction may apply more broadly to data literacy in general. Some specific trials of different methods applied to the teaching of data literacy have been undertaken. Following is not a comprehensive listing of all methods but serves to illustrate how to apply the principles described just above in specific teaching contexts.

- Datastorming: This is a way to think about using how to create designs using data using non-digital media. "To overcome their unfamiliarity to data, we aimed to craft abstract data into hands-on design materials in the form of cards." (Lim, et al., 2021)
- Simulations and Interactive Technologies : Biehler, et al. (2016) describe pre-service teachers' reasoning about modeling a family factory with TinkerPlots, "a data visualization and modeling tool developed for use by middle school through university students."
- Case-Based Teaching Method: Case¬-based teaching is "an active learning strategy in which students read and discuss complex, real-life scenarios that call on their analytical thinking skills and decision-making." (Riddle, et al., 2017).
- Utilising affordances in real-world data: Based on the Teaching for Statistical Literacy Hierarchy, this method analyzes statistical literacy lessons that use real-world data from the perspective of the affordances in the data presentation (Chick & Pierce, 2012).
- Data-Driven Decision-Making: According to Abbott, et al. (2015), this team-based approach combines a number of competency requirements in a single activity: expertise in data collection, management in a variable environment, allocation of space and time for the process, and the need to

ensure process fidelity. This specific activity helps teachers design child literacy instruction, but the approach can be generalized to other data-driven decision-making activities.

2.3.4 Data Literacy MOOC

To a significant degree, discussions of data literacy focus on individual competencies and skills. Nowhere is this more evident than in the development of data literacy learning resources and environments, as just discussed, though with some notable exceptions this trend may be identified throughout.

As an experiment in conceptual design based on the findings of this study we developed a 'Data Literacy Massive Open Online Course (MOOC)', which may be found at [website redacted for peer review]. The course follows the structure described here, addressing each of the three frameworks in turn. In turn, associated concepts and resources identified in the study comprised separate contents for each of the three frameworks.

The model of a connectivist MOOC was employed because, unlike traditional courses, which are structured in a linear or book-like fashion, consisting of sequential modules and lessons, a connectivist MOOC is structured as a graph of connected people, resources, and concepts, in other words, much more like a collection of data.

Technically, a data-based MOOC (dMOOC) organizes content and resources in a structure suggested by the literature being studied in the course. Figure 3 is a sample of the structure used in a similar dMOOC on ethics and analytics (ethics.mooc.ca):

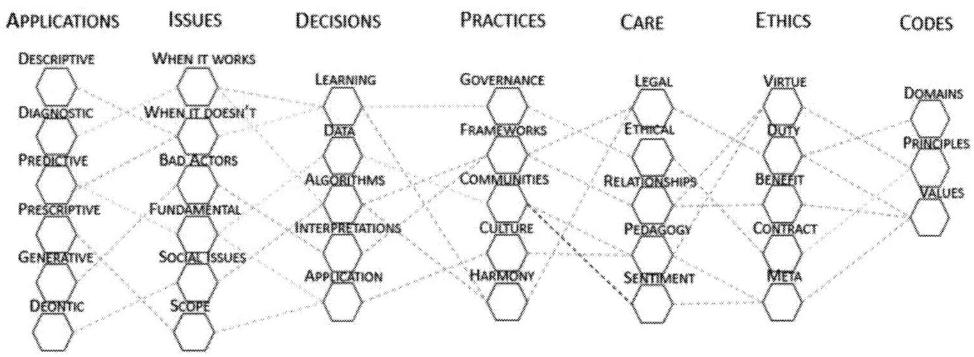

Figure 3.

Student activities in a dMOOC consist less of learning and remembering content and more of working with relevant data, and specifically:

- Classifying and labeling major sets and subsets of data
- Identifying and labeling specific instances of data subjects (for example: an article describing 'care' as a legal concept)
- Identifying and labeling relations between sets and subsets of data, either view argument threds in extant literature, or through data analytics of relevant bodies of literature
- Assessing the resulting data model, identifying significant threads, and interpreting the resulting model

In the ethics MOOC diagrammed in Figure 3 this activity was undertaken by a single individual, while in the corresponding data literacy MOOC this activity was undertaken collectively by the course participants.

Ideally, participation in a cMOOC does not involve individual study and retention of a pre-defined body of knowledge. Rather, it requires working with others in order to develop not only individual capacities and skills, but also social or community capacities and skills. These typically resist definition prior to the course, as the consequence of such social interaction and application of a skill or practice is often the development of knew knowledge, approaches, and competencies.

3. CONCLUSION

Above we asked what is the difference is between 'learning' a discipline or domain when thought of as data, and supported by the principles of data literacy, as compared to 'learning' through of as analogous to reading, and supported by traditional literacy?

3.1 What We Have Learned

What we have learned is that there is no single or simple definition of data literacy. What we think of as 'data literacy' is characterized by a set of widely divergent competencies, and the importance of one or another set of competencies varies according to the task or role in which data literacy is required. This is reflected not only in the many definitions of data literacy that we found, but also in the models of assessment offered by (mostly) commercial providers. Not only is literacy an embodiment of the of skills and competencies typically thought to define that literacy, 'data literacy' is something that can characterize both an individual and an organization.

But it is not yet taught that way. While the practices and pedagogies of data literacy being researched today address the question of use and immersion in a data-rich environment, they are addressed toward individual learning, and not the development of data literacy as an organizational or social skill. To this end we recommend developing and piloting non-hierarchal cooperative learning environments, such as the cMOOC, for the development of organizational and social competencies required for data literacy.

That said, these are assertions that need to be empirically tested before being widely adopted and applied. This paper offers the conceptual framework within which such assertions may be tested, but does not itself constitute a test of them, beyond the very limited application of the model in the development of the data literacy MOOC. And even so, much wider participation in such a MOOC would be required before any definitive assertions could be made.

3.2 Implications and Limitations

Models of data literacy found in specific domains, and especially scientific domains, do not encompass the full spectrum of data literacy skills and competencies. Hence, the teaching of data literacy should not be based on models originating from a specific discipline, but should rather be designed based on an analysis of the role or skills being taught, with a wide consideration of the corresponding data literacy competencies found across a range of models.

The small range of materials describing models and methods for teaching subjects related to data literacy tend to favour hands-on active learning, however, these were applied only in very narrow contexts. Accordingly, a course-wide model for developing data literacy was developed and proposed, whereby the course contents themselves are organized as a database, such that students participate by constructing and interpreting the data model.

While the is reasonable confidence that the list of data literacy model is comprehensive, it is possible that additional models of data literacy may be extant, and these may include competences not identified in the current study. Thus this work should be seen as a first draft of a wider survey by the data literacy survey as a whole. Though role-defined data literacy has antecedents in the literature, it should be clear that there is scope for alternative multi-model approaches to data literacy. Finally, while the application of the data literacy frameworks identified in in this paper allowed for the development of an instructional model, this model has not been adequately tested, and should be applied in pilot form before being adopted.

REFERENCES

Abbott, Mary, et al. 2015. "A Team Approach to Data-Driven Decision-Making Literacy Instruction in Preschool Classrooms: Child Assessment and Intervention Through Classroom Team Self-Reflection." Young Exceptional Children, vol. 20, no. 3, Sept. 2015, pp. 117–32, https://doi.org/10.1177/1096250615602297.

Bargagliotti, Anna, et al. 2020. Pre-K-12 Guidelines for Assessment and Instruction in Statistics Education II (GAISE II): A Framework for Statistics and Data Science Education. American Statistical Association, 2020, https://www.amstat.org/docs/default-source/amstat-documents/gaiseiiprek-12_full.pdf.

Bhargava, Rahul, et al. 2015. "Beyond Data Literacy: Reinventing Community Engagement and Empowerment in the Age of Data." Data-Pop Alliance, Data-Pop Alliance, Nov. 2015, https://datapopalliance.org/item/beyond-data-literacy-reinventing-community-engagement-and-empowerment-in-the-age-of-data.

Biehler, Rolf, et al. 2016. "Elementary Preservice Teachers' Reasoning about Modeling a 'Family Factory' with Tinkerplots - A Pilot Study." Statistics Education Research Journal, vol. 16, no. 2, Nov. 2017, pp. 244–86, https://doi.org/10.52041/serj.v16i2.192.

Bloom, B. S. 1956. "Taxonomy of Educational Objectives", Handbook: The Cognitive Domain. David McKay. https://www.scirp.org/(S(i43dyn45teexjx455qlt3d2q))/reference/ReferencesPapers.aspx?ReferenceID=1506705.

Canada School of Public Service (CSPS). 2022. How Data Literate Are You? Government of Canada, Apr. 2022, https://catalogue.csps-efpc.gc.ca/product?catalog=DDN302&cm_locale=en.

Carlson, Jake, and Lisa R. Johnston. 2015. "Data Information Literacy: Librarians, Data, and the Education of a New Generation of Researchers." Purdue University Press, 2015, https://www.jstor.org/stable/j.ctt6wq2vh.

Chick, Helen L., and Robyn Pierce. 2012. "Teaching for Statistical Literacu Utilising Affordances in Real-World Data." International Journal of Science and Mathematics Education, vol. 10, no. 2, Apr. 2012, pp. 339–62, https://doi.org/10.1007/s10763-011-9303-2.

Cowell, Matt. 2020. "A Roadmap for Creating a Data Literacy Program - QuantHub." QuantHub, QuantHub, 18 June 2020, https://quanthub.com/data-literacy-program.

DataLiteracy. 2021. "About This Project - DataLiteracy.Ca." DataLiteracy.Ca, Internet Archive, 22 Dec. 2021, https://web.archive.org/web/20211222131031/http:/dataliteracy.ca/about-this-data-literacy-project.

GAISE College Report ASA Revision Committee. 2016. Guidelines for Assessment and Instruction in Statistics Education (GAISE). American Statistical Association. https://www.amstat.org/docs/default-source/amstat-

Kirsch, Irwin, and William Thorn. 2016. Technical Report of the Survey of Adult Skills (PIAAC) (2nd Edition). Organisation for Economic Co-operation and Development (OECD), 2016, https://www.oecd.org/skills/piaac/PIAAC_Technical_Report_2nd_Edition_Full_Report.pdf.

Kleitz, Lauren, and Joe Shelley. 2022. EDUCAUSE Data Literacy Institute. EDUCAUSE, 24 Jan. 2022, https://events.educause.edu/educause-institute/data-literacy-institute/2022/online-1.

Koltay, Tibor. 2016. "Data Governance, Data Literacy and the Management of Data Quality." IFLA Journal, vol. 42, no. 4, Nov. 2016, pp. 303–12, https://doi.org/10.1177/0340035216672238.

Maybee, Clarence, and Lisa Zilinski. 2016. "Data Informed Learning: A next Phase Data Literacy Framework for Higher Education." Proceedings of the Association for Information Science and Technology, vol. 52, no. 1, Jan. 2015, pp. 1–4, https://doi.org/10.1002/pra2.2015.1450520100108.

Oberländer, Maren, et al. 2020. "Digital Competencies: A Review of the Literature and Applications in the Workplace." Computers & Education, vol. 146, Mar. 2020, p. 103752, https://doi.org/10.1016/j.compedu.2019.103752.

Panetta, Kasey. 2021. "A Data Literacy Guide For D&A Leaders." Gartner, Gartner, 26 Aug. 2021, https://www.gartner.com/smarterwithgartner/a-data-and-analytics-leaders-guide-to-data-literacy.

Riddle, Derek R., et al. 2017. "Making a Case for Case-Based Teaching in Data Literacy." Kappa Delta Pi Record, vol. 53, no. 3, July 2017, pp. 131–33, https://doi.org/10.1080/00228958.2017.1334479.

Ridsdale, Chantel, et al. 2015. Strategies and Best Practices for Data Literacy Education. Dalhousie University, 2015, https://dalspace.library.dal.ca/bitstream/handle/10222/64578/Strategies%20and%20Best%20Practices%20for%20Data%20Literacy%20Education.pdf?sequence=1&isAllowed=y.

Robinson, Clinton. 2005. Aspects of Literacy Assessment: Topics and Issues from the UNESCO Expert Meeting. 2005, https://unesdoc.unesco.org/ark:/48223/pf0000140125.

Schield, Milo. 2004. "Information Literacy, Statistical Literacy and Data Literacy." IASSIST Quarterly, 2004, http://www.statlit.org/pdf/2004-Schield-IASSIST.pdf.

St. Mary's. 2018. St. Mary's Practice Test 2017/2018. 2018, https://drive.google.com/file/d/1LsDbvAy_YHepMVD9VVEEWH6w5U_Dk1-E/view.

Statistics Canada. 2020. The Daily - Begin Your Data Journey with Data Literacy Training Videos. Government of Canada, 23 Sept. 2020, https://www150.statcan.gc.ca/n1/daily-quotidien/200923/dq200923f-eng.htm.

Visengeriyeva, Larysa, et al. 2022. An Overview of the End-to-End Machine Learning Workflow. MLOps.org, Dec. 2021, https://ml-ops.org/content/end-to-end-ml-workflow.

Wells, Dave. 2021. Building a Data Literacy Program. 4 Jan. 2021, https://www.eckerson.com/articles/the-data-literacy-imperative-part-i-building-a-data-literacy-program.

Wolff, Annika, et al. 2016. "Creating an Understanding of Data Literacy for a Data-Driven Society." Journal of Community Informatics, vol. 12, no. 3, Aug. 2016, https://doi.org/10.15353/joci.v12i3.3275.

Yi Min Lim, Delia, et al. 2021. "Datastorming: Crafting Data into Design Materials for Design Students' Creative Data Literacy." C&C '21: Creativity and Cognition, Association for Computing Machinery, 2021, pp. 1–9, https://doi.org/10.1145/3450741.3465246.

STUDENT CENTERED METHODS, SOFT SKILLS AND COMPETENCY BASED LEARNING FROM THE VIEW OF ENGINEERING AND TECHNICAL TEACHER STUDENTS

Ibolya Tomory
Óbuda University
H-1034 Budapest, Hungary

ABSTRACT

In pedagogy, it is often emphasized that we need to go beyond the traditional level of teaching and in addition to professional knowledge to integrate skills that support the acquisition of 21st century skills such as problem-solving, creativity and critical thinking, or social skills and emotional intelligence, which are highlighted in the labor market. These, so-called soft skills, are the hard-to-grasp, non-cognitive skill areas but they are the key to students' later success, the development of which requires the ability to learn competencies and skills and the preparation of future teachers. This study presents a slice of a university example of the integration of student-centered educational practices in the perspective of methods and soft skills in engineering teacher and technical teacher training. As part of a development process, we examined the role of learning-teaching methods in successful learning, in the positive shaping of the teacher's role, and in the acquisition of soft skills. Part of this was the preliminary and subsequent survey connected to the pedagogical subjects, the purpose of which was to map the basic pedagogical/methodological knowledge and the preliminary views of the students. The results of several semesters of development and surveys show that teacher candidates have a positive opinion of competency-based learner-centered approaches, but more pedagogical training and support would be necessary, which has a serious impact on the quality of their own classroom teaching and assessment practices. During the semesters, it also became certain that the necessary skills can be developed and that the students positively evaluate the new approach, learning about student-centered methods.

KEYWORDS

Soft Skills, Competency-Based Learning, Student-Centred Learning, Autoethnography

1. INTRODUCTION

As a result of the technological explosion, there is a rapid and huge change in the skills and competences expected in the labor market, with soft skills at the center. Professional knowledge and higher education no longer ensure successful placement and staying in work, personal and social competences are at least as important. (Handfield-Jones 2007) This shift towards requires the development of key competences without which students, future and already graduated professionals can adapt to the changing world of work with difficulty or not at all (Armstrong-Taylor 2014, Shippman at all 2000)

Hard skills are profession- and job-specific knowledge, while soft skills are non-professional, non-technical skills that can help you operate effectively in a given environment. We can use soft skills not only at work, but in many situations in all areas of life. In essence, they represent a combination of knowledge, how well we know ourselves, how we think and how we interact with the social environment. The development of soft skills at school is necessary because, relying on them, it is easier to work in a team, manage conflicts, express oneself and solve problems. (Penprase, 2018).

Education tries to follow the expectations accordingly curriculum, content and practical renewal is taking place. Researches highlight the need for comprehensive development in schools, which includes process thinking and practical skills that provide students with real-world experience and prepare them for successful work. (Roegiers, 2016). The principle of methodological diversity has been a priority in competency-based education programs for quite some time, which takes into account the development of the student's personal skills as well as the traditionally emphasized professional knowledge. (Rainwater, 2016).

However, some research and dropout rates show that many students in various countries around the world are not prepared for university studies or work (Unesco 2022). This strengthens and urges renewal, a change of attitude, thinking in terms of competence and the integration of the development-based education necessary for this into the daily practice of education. However, in order to develop the skills expected of students, well-trained and prepared teachers with pedagogical competence and commitment are needed. At the same time, many studies point to the lack of well-qualified STEM graduates and the links between learning success, skills gaps and poor teaching quality. (Taylor-Robinson, 2019; Lyche 2010)

In competence-based teaching, it was emphasized that "competency-based approaches to education have the potential for assuring the quality and extent of learning and developing integrated skills that ease learner transitions between school and work". (McClarty and Gaertner 2015:2) The development has different frameworks and approaches, which more or less mention and integrate learner-centered methods into the programs. In Hungary, for example, at the beginning of the 2000s, the definition of different areas of competence and the delineation of related skills appeared in line with and supported by the expectations of the European Union. The area of social competence, which is an important component of soft skills, is outstanding. Curriculum and subject implementation was developed within the framework of a national development program, in which methodologies such as project-based learning or cooperative learning and it's methods, project-based learning, and a participation-oriented approach appeared. (Tomory 2008; Kagan 2009)

Adaptations of this are still present in schools today, but strengthening, renewing and placing them in new perspectives is essential. It should focus on learning that supports the ability to create new knowledge and engage students in independent learning, provide opportunities to experience collaboration, interactivity, and allow students to demonstrate their competencies, skills, and attitudes. (McClarty and Gaertner, 2015). A suitable methodological basis for this is research-, problem- and project-based learning, as well as the provision of methodological variety that encourages the development of activity, attitude and attributes, such as student presentations, discussion and debate, cooperative small group work, metacognitive tasks, analysis-research-planning, etc. The integration of modern technological tools, digital learning and blended learning must also become natural in the learning process. (Curry and Docherty 2017; Dilmore-Moore, 2011).

The development of soft skills is not easy to measure, but individual skills are developed in diverse learning environments. Learning contexts include the factors and tools that teachers can influence. To facilitate skill development, for example, in teacher training, interaction patterns can be provided that inform teachers about teaching cognitive, social and emotional skills. The development of soft skills can be identified by what someone thinks about teaching, the role of a teacher, how they reflect on certain questions, problems, and situations. Opinion formation can be tracked, as was the case in this development. (OECD 2015a)

2. METHODOLOGY

The informants are university students who participated in several semesters in a semester-long group project and in a learning process using student-centered methods within the framework of several pedagogical subjects. In order to develop content, methodology and soft skills, we monitored their activity and asked their opinion on the experience and applicability of the joint development of student-centered methods and soft skills.

Data collection was carried out using mixed methods. Using a combination of qualitative classroom observations and autoethnography, and quantitatively, using a questionnaire at the end of the semester. Autoethnography is based on self-observation and the identification of one's own experiences, emotions, and thoughts, on the other hand, it helps to identify the intellectual and emotional state of others. Its greatest value is that it can explain how people interpret their own actions, what meaning and intention they ascribe to them, and it supports self-reflection and self-expression through thought, criticism, and emotion. (Reed-Danahey 2017; Kottak 2002) Autoethnography was applied through self-observation, the students were prepared for this at the beginning of the semester. The significance of this is that the success of the lessons was not evaluated on the basis of external (educator/researcher) observations,refelections and impressions (like traditional observation), but on the basis of student feedback. The purpose of this is to provide and interpret realistic feedback. The real effect and results of learning with student-centered methods became more visible, as it was clearer, for example, what intention, meaning, and experience the participants associate with their activities. The focus of data collected using autoethnography are summarized in Table 1.

Table 1. Focuses of autoethnographic data collection

	Cognitive side	**Emotional site**
Reflections on an individual, on oneself	Reflections, expressions about own, individual investment of time and energy	Reflections, expressions about personal experiences and feelings during learning
	Reflections, expressions about individual task solutions for the group's learning success	Reflections and expressions about the development of their own soft skills (empathy, relation to others, openness, etc.)
	Reflections, expressions about the instrumental difficulties of distance and contact with others	Reflections, expressions about the coordination of contact with others and own work in the extracurricular project
Reflections on the group and on yourself as a group member	Reflections, expressions about the group's time management, joint efforts	Reflections, expressions about common learning experiences and feelings
	Reflections and expressions about group learning and task sharing	Reflections, expressions about individual roles and responsibility contribution
	Reflections, expressions about sharing roles and responsibilities in the group	Reflections, expressions about the formation and changes of cohesion between group members
Reflections on learning effectiveness	Reflections, expressions about the effectiveness of the group's task performance	Reflections, expressions about what was difficult and what was interesting
	Reflections, expressions about changes in their own methodological approach	Reflections, expressions about the perception of the connections between their own soft skills and the learned methods
	Reflections, expressions about the furthering and utilization of what has been learned	Reflections, expressions about cooperation and acceptance each other in order to complete a task

We monitored and evaluated the students' performance during individual activities and tasks, as well as in the light of their reflections. It was possible to observe, for example, at what level a person performs his tasks during group work and independent project work, to what level he developed his behavioral and communication skills during his studies. The process could also be made data-like, how much they dealt with a topic or task, how much time they spent on a question, how many times they tried to give the right answer, or how complex the individual project product was.

Considering the accompanying questionnaire survey, the open-ended questions were analyzed using thematic analysis, and the results of the structured questions were analyzed using percentages. 280 students from different semesters responded (between 2018-2023), most of them study technical specialization (96.4%), and only a small proportion (3.6%) study the service specialization. 35.7% of students work in a vocational school and an equal proportion in a corporate environment in education-related or non-educational positions (21.4-21.4%)

We used the experience diary as a tool, which is available in electronic form and feedback can also be sent from a mobile phone. In connection with this, the content analysis of photos, video recordings, student independent video messages, Moodle forum and chat interface supplemented the questionnaires.

This study present some of the results along the following main questions:

- What kind of methodological knowledge do engineering teachers and vocational education students have and to what extent does this change through practical knowledge of student-centered methods?
- How do the teacher candidates see the joint development possibilities of the applied learning methods and soft skills in their own learning and teaching practice?

3. RESULTS

3.1 Educational Methodological Foundations and Changes

First, we examined the previously known methods, as well as the methods learned during the university course and applied as a result, and their popularity. Figure 1 illustrates the percentage of popularity of previously known methods and methods learned in pedagogic classes or applied as a result of them. The answers show that some of the learner-centered methods were known, but the student teacher candidates never incorporated them into their own teaching, and a significant percentage only applied them as a result of the pedagogic classes. Not surprisingly, everyone indicated lecture and explanation as the method used in their teaching so far. Some of them were not familiar with the student lecture (7.1%), the quiz questions (7.4%), but an even greater proportion were not familiar with the mind map (21.4%) and the flipped classroom method (42.8%). The project and cooperative small group learning were also unknown to many (14.2% and 32.1%), while others had already worked with it.

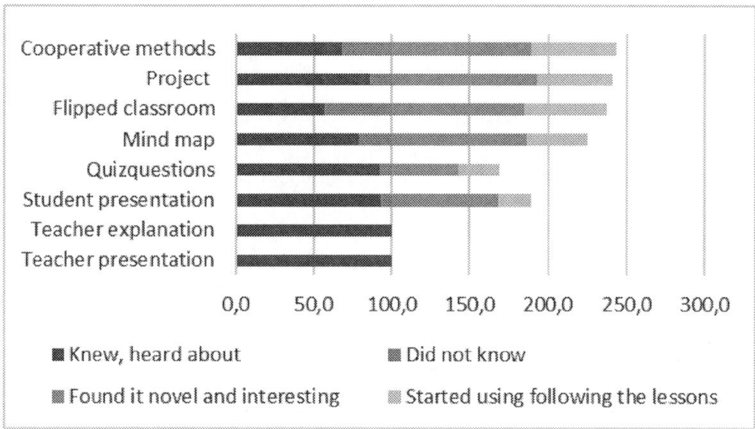

Figure 1. Familiarity and popularity of teacher- and student-centered methods

Regarding the cooperative methods, it should be noted that the students often worked with the Kagan methods during the classroom activities, which we could assume that at least some of them are already familiar with based on the method knowledge answers. However, with the autoethnographic reflections, they said that they did not know these things. They heard about it and believed that when students are divided into groups for a workshop, for example, it is learning using cooperative methods. This was also evident from the class observations, because except for two students, no one knew the terms, tools and methods of group organization and the basic, frequently used cooperative methods such as mosaics or task sending. It also happened that a student introduced a cooperative method from Kagan's methodology in his own school, in the class of his professional subject, and then reported that, unfortunately, it did not work, he failed to organize the small groups themselves, and the students did not want to work in small groups. In other cases, this was not a problem, but the vocational student teacher felt that, as a teacher, control slipped out of his hands and chaos ensued.

The lesson of this is that certain methods cannot be separated from the framework of the approach, because it is not certain that they work automatically by themselves. Some methodological systems must be handled in their context and applied gradually, and the teacher must clearly see and accept the necessary foundations for successful application. The importance of this lies in the correction of methodological mistakes and the laying of the appropriate basic knowledge, conceptual clarification and foundation of approach, and in the teacher's conviction.

With regard to the first main question, it can be concluded that the methodological knowledge of engineering teachers and vocational education students is incomplete and needs improvement. It can also be seen that the methods declared new and interesting by the students in the questionnaire really had the effect of an experience. This means that the practical knowledge of student-centered methods not only expands methodological knowledge, but also encourages students to be open and innovative, which also helps them to rethink their role as teachers and students.

This does not happen overnight and perhaps it is not surprising that at first the effectiveness of the newly learned methods was considered questionable and only as the semester progressed or with method learning aimed at further practice in the following semester did the process start in the direction of student openness.

3.2 Joint Development Possibilities of the Applied Learning Methods and Soft Skills

Qualitative research methods such as autoethnography make it possible to bring the aforementioned hidden deficiencies to the surface, raise awareness and develop them voluntarily. In this case, by using auto-ethnography, the students were encouraged to express how they experience the process, what they find difficult and interesting. Table 2 outlines some nodes based on the autoethnographic reflections and open-ended questions based on the analysis and summary of the frequency of similar content and similar expressions, and Table 3 cites some examples from the reflective self-expressions, comments, forum messages and open-ended questions.

Table 2. Indicators of changes in learning and role interpretation

Effects on individual learning	**Effects on new learning metarial**
supporting independent thinking	supporting, encouraging in different ways
focus, concentration	getting and holding attention
self-confidence, trusting their own abilities	supporting understanding
logical thinking, rational thinking	recognizing connections
increased motivation	increasing the changing of information
experimental learning	experimental learning

The nodes of the changes show the efficiency-enhancing effect of student-centered methods, highlighting the understanding of the curriculum, learning activity and more effective learning. The items referring to the support of individual learning and the attitude to the new curriculum, which can be interpreted as indicators, also indicate the parallel development of the cognitive and emotional side. This confirms the developmental effect of student-centered methods on students' soft skills and learning motivation.

Table 3. Changes in cognitive and soft skill areas as a result of student-centered methods

Change in understanding of the new curriculum	**Changing views on cooperation and shared responsibility**
I had a better understanding of my own competencies, I learned where and how to improve.	The project, videos and cooperative group work were especially effective for understanding other perspectives.
The more methods we used to familiarize ourselves with the learning material, the more effective knowledge is generated.	The greatest experience was that we did not learn the methods to be learned from a book but were able to try them ourselves and be a part of them. This made it much easier for me to incorporate it into my own teaching lessons.

It's easier for me to filter out the essence.	Even before, I thought cooperation was important, but I didn't think we could really work responsibly as a group. Sometimes there was "social hanging out", but in the end everything and everyone fell into place. So it is worth alternating the methods.
I had to make sure that I knew well what was my task and part of the lesson/topic.	The bond, relationship between us got stronger! The different methods have changed my learning techniques, now I'm not finishing this university cramping, I'm finally FEELING GOOD!
I'm not as insecure as before, I'm more confident that I can...	Lessons at the university are more effective by working together! It's easier to learn that I'm not the only one responsible for something and I'm not the only one responsible if things don't go well.
I can remember longer and more complicated expressions.	The practical learning units highlighted how to do a good job. It is not sure that one method will work, but we can always look for another one that works better for a given group.
I can concentrate better on the essentials. I try to apply learning methods. I became more motivated.	I don't think I would have understood before that there are so many possibilities and methods for teaching, and if I find the right key to the lock of students' learning, then I can have an easier job in the profession.
I was never good at studying, so I didn't expect a huge change, but I think it helped a lot that the lessons involved discussions about the topics and activities instead of lectures.	It pushed me out of my comfort zone, because I had to comment on, had to cooperate and be an active part of a situation in a specific role and then in different aspects.
I learned to study and select, to focus on the important, i.e. actually important, things.	This can be incorporated into workplace communities, educational areas, etc. but even in the life of a family.

In the examples of the table, based on the reflections on the understanding of the new curriculum and the changes in the social skills area of soft skills, it can be established that it is implicit in the expressions and keywords that ensuring student activity is also a way to strengthen learning awareness, managing relationships and belief in one's own abilities. For the most part, the effect on cooperation is indicated as positive, parallel to the positive effect on learning. What can also be counted as a success is that there are also some negative, critical signs that draw attention to the fact that "There are students who find it more difficult to understand the course material this way. It has to be explained to him separately and requires more attention." According to another reflection: "To me, group work is somewhat doubtful. Of course, I can see that over time the students will get better and better and help them. On the other hand, it is also true that it cannot be used continuously with all students. A student with social anxiety will never be able to fulfill themselves if they are forced into a situation where they feel uncomfortable. It would definitely be useful for them if the members of the groups did not change, so that he gets used to the group members better and can participate in the work more openly." Although one casts doubt on the effectiveness and rightly refers to the well-known phenomenon of social stimulation and inhibition, this honest expression also indicates that the student dares to take on and express his opinion, i.e. the pedagogical lessons affected this soft skill component. On the other hand, it also indicates that there is still a lot to learn, which needs to be put in place, since cooperative small group learning helps to solve the mentioned problem step by step, with patiently built, non-forced role exercises. (Kagan 2002; 2018)

With regard to questions regarding the joint development of knowledge, thinking and soft skills, the majority of respondents believe that teachers have the opportunities and tools for these and that their parallel development is feasible. According to the grades given from 1 to 5, a third of the students believe that there are many and good tools available (33.32%), a little less believe that the opportunities are quite good

(30.65%), a smaller proportion think that the conditions can only be ensured moderately (14.63%), but more than that see weak conditions (21.4%), however, no one thinks that they do not have the tools or the opportunity for complex development. (see Figure 2.)

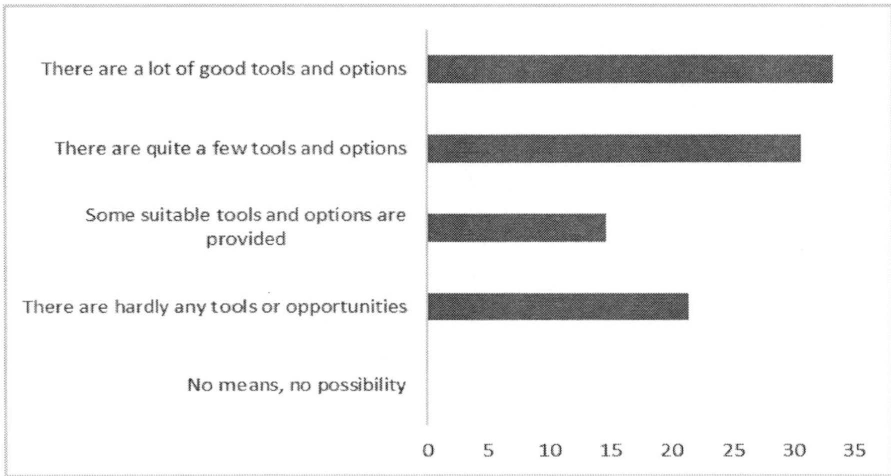

Figure 2. Possibilities for the joint development of knowledge, thinking and soft skills

3.3 The Change of the Teacher's Role and Attitude

In addition to the above, by assigning statements, we asked the teacher candidates how they selected the teaching methods included in a lesson planning task and used during their teaching practice and what pedagogical aspects they considered important. According to the teacher candidate students, the selected elements have a high percentage of support for competence-based learning, which emphasizes complex problem- and research-based thinking (58.7%), and a high percentage of support for social skills, especially cooperation (87.4%). Therefore, the priority is to select the appropriate effective methods (94.3%) and to ensure that understanding can be followed with relevant methods (88.4%). (see Table 4.)

Table 4. Standpoints/Aspects for method selection and knowledge/skill development

Aspect, approach	**Statements**	**Choices%**
Selection of optimally effective teaching methods	Very important	94,3
	Pretty important	5,7
	Not very important	0
	Not important at all	0
Traceability of understanding	Very important	24,7
	Pretty important	65,7
	Not very important	9,6
	Not important at all	0
Support for complex research and a problem-based approach	Very important	19,5
	Pretty important	58,7
	Not very important	21,8
	Not important at all	0
Approaches and methods supporting social skills	Very important	88,4
	Pretty important	11,6
	Not very important	0
	Not important at all	0

3.4 Some Elements of Soft Skills

Thinking about soft skills and the changes in individual components were identified with several open questions and we looked at their frequency in the autoethnographic vocabulary and in the related audiovisual materials. The group project products and lesson plans also reflected the strengthening of various soft skill areas and the intention to develop them. A preference order was obtained by ranking the evaluations given on the competence list (5-point Likert scale). (Figure 3.) Collaboration with others and empathy were defined as the most important skills. This is followed by problem-solving skills and communication, then the recognition of one's own emotions and the emotions of others, the handling of interpersonal conflicts, the need to assume responsibility, then work independently, and learn. Leadership skills, the ability to manage and proficiency in the sciences are less preferred. The same order was created for the order of changes and development of one's own skills. (Figure 3.)

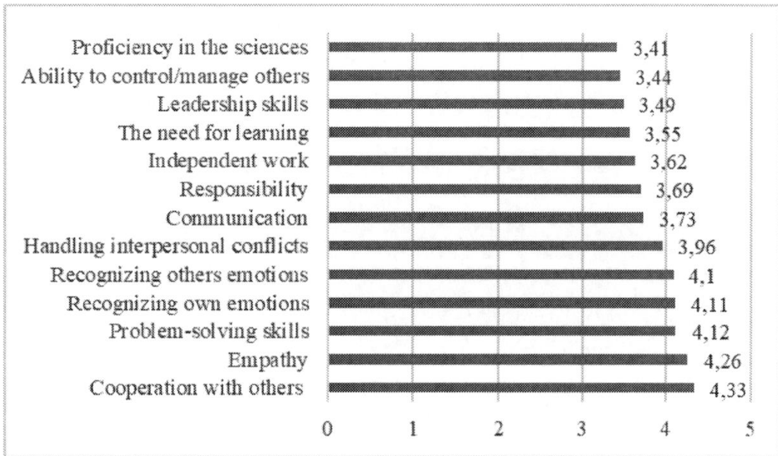

Figure 3. The most important soft skills

The results here also show that the students think more consciously about the connections between soft skills and cognitive subject knowledge.

4. SUMMARY

Based on the development and questioning that accompanied several school years and semesters, it can be concluded that teacher and vocational training candidates see the connection between labor market expectations and the educational methods used in the learning-teaching process, understand the role of student-centered methods and realize that we need to go beyond traditional teacher-centered education. However, they do not have sufficient and appropriate methodological preparation for student-centered, competence-based teaching and implementation, and they do not have enough knowledge to interpret and develop soft skills.

The experiences of the semesters and the student opinions show that all of this can be developed and that it is possible to achieve student openness towards competency-based education starting from student-centered methods. In education we have to overcome difficulties, go beyond the ineffective teacher-centered and cognitive-only approach and instead create a new teacher and student role.

The results indicate that mixed-method education promotes the joint development of the students' soft skills and learning skills, and their effectiveness, which they then bring into the school's daily practice. It is recommended the joint planning and implementation of methodological diversity and skill development in higher education.

REFERENCES

Armstrong, M., Taylor, S. (2014). *Armstrong's handbook of human resource management practice*. Kogan Page, Philadelphia, USA

Curry, L. & Docherty, M. (2017). Implementing Competency-Based Education. *In Collected Essays on Learning and Teaching, vol. X.*, pp.61-73.

Dilmore, T. C., Moore, D. W., & Bjork, Z. J. (2011). *Implementing competency-based education: A process workbook 2009* – 2011. Universidad de Pittsburgh., USA

Dr. Kagan, Spencer Miguel Kagan (2009). *Kagan kooperatív tanulás*. Önkonet, Budapest, Hungary

Dr. Kagan, Spencer Miguel Kagan, Laurie Kagan (2018). 60 *Kagan Structures More Proven Engagement Strategies*. Kagan Australia

Handfield-Jones, H. (2007). Fától az erdőt: a küzdés módjai a munkaerőért folytatott háborúban. In: Gandossy, R.P., Tucker, E., Verma, N. (szerk.): *Gazdálkodj okosan a tehetséggel*. HVG Könyvek, Budapest, Hungary

Kottak, C. P. (2002). *Cultural Anthropology*. McGraw-Hill Higher Education, Boston, USA

Lyche, C. (2010). "Taking on the Completion Challenge: A Literature Review on Policies to Prevent Dropout and Early School Leaving. *OECD Education Working Paper* No. 53. OECD, Paris

McClarty, K. L. & Gaertner, M. N. (2015). *Measuring mastery: Best practices for assessment in competency-based education*. AEI, NW Washington, USA

OECD (2015a). Skills For Social Progress: The Power Of Social And Emotional Skills, OECD. Paris. http://www.keepeek.com/Digital-Asset-Management/oecd/education/skills-for-social-progress_9789264226159-.

Penprase, B. E. (2018). The fourth industrial revolution and higher education. Higher education in the era of the fourth industrial revolution, In: Nancy G. (edit) *Higher Education in the Era of the Fourth Industrial Revolution*. Palgrave macmillan, Singapure, pp.207-229.

Rainwater, T. S. M. (2016). Teaching and learning in competency-based education courses and programs: faculty and student perspectives. *The journal of competency-based education*, 1: 42- 47

Reed-Danahay, D. (2017). "Bourdieu and Critical Autoethnography: Implications for Research, Writing, and Teaching," *International Journal of Multicultural Education*. 19 (1) pp.144-154.

Roegiers, X. (2016). *A conceptual framework for competencies assessment*. Unesco International Buro of Education, Paris, France

Shippman, J. S., et al. (2000). The practice of competency modeling. *In Personnel Psichology*, Vol. 53., No. 3., pp. 703-740.

Taylor, N. & Robinson, N. (2019). *Secondary education in Sub-Saharan Africa. Teacher preparation and support: Literature Review*. Mastercard Foundation, Toronto, Canada

Tomory, I. (2008). A résztvevô megfigyelés és a terepmunka: szemlélet és módszer összefonódása. *In*: *Tanári kézikönyv a szociális kompetenciák fejelsztéséhez 1-12. évfolyam*. Educatio Társadalmi Szolgáltató Közhasznú Társaság , Budapest pp.136-140.

Unesco (2022). *Transforming Technical and Vocational Education and Training for successful and just transition. Unesco Strategy 2022-2029*. Unesco, Paris, France

POTENTIAL OF ADAPTIVE E-LEARNING FOR KNOWLEDGE HETEROGENOUS GROUPS OF STUDENTS IN ENGINEERING DESIGN EDUCATION

Frederike Kossack, Eike Uttich and Beate Bender
Ruhr-University Bochum,
D-44780 Bochum, Germany

ABSTRACT

In Engineering Design education, huge numbers of students are a challenge in university teaching, especially since the students have an initially heterogeneous level of technical knowledge, which influences their acquisition of competences. In frontal classroom lectures, individual deficits can hardly be addressed and in self-study phases, students find it difficult to remedy these independently. Therefore, students with prior technical experience achieve better final module grades. This paper examines the extent to which heterogeneity in prior experience can be compensated by using an adaptive e-learning environment for the self-study time. For this purpose, students are provided with a prototypical implementation of an adaptive e-learning environment for the self-learning phase. The feedback of the users and their examination results are statistically evaluated with respect to the gain of knowledge.

KEYWORDS

Adaptive e-Learning, Engineering Design Education, Student-Centered Learning, Individual Learning Paths

1. INTRODUCTION

Higher education faces the challenge of increasing student heterogeneity (Eckert et al., 2015). Students of Engineering Design have different technical education at the beginning of their studies ("prior experience"): their secondary school education differs, and some students complete technical internships or technical training before their studies while others do not; i.e. it is a knowledge heterogenous student group. Differences in prior experience influence competence acquisition and the final module grade of students (Žeželj and Miler, 2018; Kannengiesser et al., 2015; Metraglia et al., 2015; Kossack and Bender 2022). Individual support decreases heterogeneity (Brückner *et al.*, 2015), but Design engineering education can hardly guarantee individual support in the existing teacher-centered lectures with large learning groups (Pfäffli, 2015; Eckert, 2015; Albers, 2012; Terkowsky, 2018). Adaptive e-learning is a means to provide individual support (Stoyanov and Kirschener, 2004; Rey, 2009; Kerr, 2016; Niegemann and Heidig, 2019), and we suggest it for Engineering Design education (Kossack *et al.* 2022).

The impact of adaptive e-learning on knowledge heterogenous student groups is unknown. Research on adaptive e-learning addresses software solutions for adaptive e-learning (Fidalgo-Blanco, 2014), or collecting and using data for adaptivity (e.g., Bagheri, 2015; Radenkovic *et al.*, 2009), and adaptivity often in the context of different learning styles (e.g., Kolekar, 2019). Few authors evaluate the general benefit of adaptive e-learning for reaching learning outcomes (e.g., Prusty and Russell, 2011), even less with the focus on prior experience (e.g., Arsovic and Stefanovic, 2020), and we did not find any example for adaptive e-learning's impact on knowledge heterogenous student groups.

The purpose of this paper is to investigate the extent to which adaptive e-learning can compensate technical knowledge heterogeneity in a first-year student group of Engineering Design. We use an adaptive e-learning environment prototype (AdE-Le, see Kossack and Bender 2023) as a lecture-accompanying support for the self-study time and investigate the benefits of AdE-Le by comparing students with and without prior technical education in their behavior, their feedback on AdE-Le, and their exam results after using AdE-Le. Due to the characteristics of an adaptive e-learning environment and the knowledge heterogeneity with the resulting consequences at hand, the following research hypotheses are formulated:

- H1: "Students without prior technical experience find AdE-Le more helpful than students with prior technical experience."
- H2: "An adaptive e-learning environment compensates initial technical knowledge heterogeneity to the point there exist no difference in the examination results between the groups."

2. METHOD

The investigation is conducted on a first-year course in Engineering Design education with about 150 regularly attending participants. It is part of the study programs of "mechanical engineering" and "sales engineering and product management" at a German university. The dominant learning format is teacher-centered lectures on campus, with consulting hours and self-study time as additional teaching and learning activities.

We use our prototype of an adaptive e-learning environment (AdE-Le, see Kossack and Bender 2023), which we implemented in the learning management system Moodle (Moodle Contributors, 2023) for the teaching and learning content "dimensioning, tolerancing and fitting tolerances". AdE-Le addresses individual needs and preferences of the user. It presents an initial learning environment to the user based on an assessment. During use, it makes further measurements of the level of knowledge or learning characteristics to bring about a constant modification of the learning environment; this is conformed with definitions of Stoyanov and Kirschener (2004), Rey (2009), and Kerr (2016). AdE-Le is developed in accordance with Constructive Alignment for an existing course (Kossack *et al.*, 2022); Constructive Alignment is an outcome-based approach assigning Teaching and Learning Activities and the Assessment Task to Intended Learning Outcomes (Biggs and Tang, 2011).

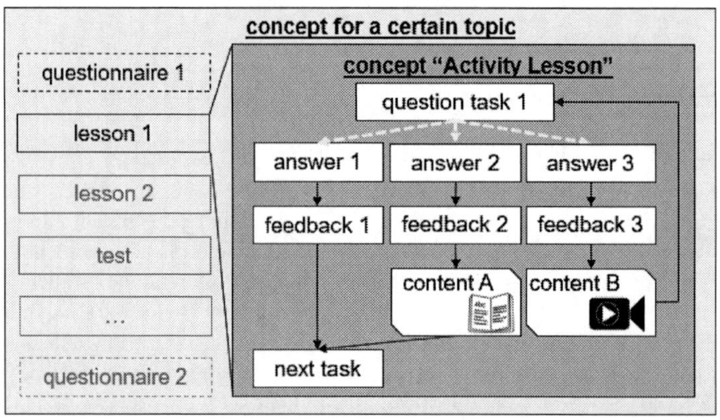

Figure 1. Concept of the implementation of AdE-Le in Moodle (see Kossack and Bender, 2023)

AdE-Le's main environment is based on the Moodle functions "Activity Lesson" and "Activity Test", with four lessons and two tests in total. For evaluation, we integrated two questionnaires with the Moodle function "Activity Survey" which conform to standard characteristics of questionnaires including variables with their scale levels according to Rasch (2021) and Döring and Bortz (2016). We use typical gradations for each variable: frequency from always (1) to never (5), or agreement from strongly agree (1) to strongly disagree (5). The AdE-Le uses the Moodle function Activity Lesson to combine content pages with pages for branching or with questions. When the student chooses an answer, the AdE-Le gives feedback and usually recommends assigned learning content. The learning contents are integrated as directly as possible: e.g., videos or interactive content in H5P (H5P Contributors 2023) format are embedded; book chapters or norms are recommended but not integrated in the system. (Kossack and Bender 2023).

To encourage students to use AdE-Le and give feedback, additional points were added to the exam grade for completing all activities of AdE-Le. Points were awarded for participation including submission of the feedback questionnaire; there was no gradation for the time, or the number of attempts students needed to complete a learning unit. AdE-Le was available to all participants of the Moodle course belonging to the Engineering Desing course. Only datasets of students in the first semester are considered in the data, as students repeating the subject for a better grade could distort the results with the experience they gained in higher semesters. To introduce AdE-Le to the students, we used a teacher-centered lecture when the topic “dimensioning, tolerancing and fitting tolerances” started about 8 weeks after semester start. We presented the students how to use AdE-Le and how to get extra points for the exam. We informed the students that AdE-Le is a prototype for first time use, encouraged them to report errors or problems and informed them about the research with the data we collect with AdE-Le. Immediately after the lecture we unlocked the first activity in AdE-Le.

The first activity in AdE-Le is a questionnaire which we use to determine whether the students have different technical backgrounds and whether this leads to differences in competence. One example item of the questionnaire is the perceived degree of difficulty of the course. Findings from the questionnaire help to assess the extent to which the group is an appropriate sample for this study; it did not have an influence on the lessons in AdE-Le. By completing the first questionnaire, students unlocked the first lesson. Five subsequent learning activities were unlocked in coincidence with the content in the teacher-centered lectures and the six learning activities were linked together via prerequisites: Students could not start a new activity until the previous one was completed. We planned the use of one learning activity per week and offered technical support in existing consulting hours if needed. The second questionnaire unlocked after completing the last learning activity. It asks students on their behavior and the extent to which they assess AdE-Le as helpful for the self-learning phase. Table 2 presents the relevant items for this research. The results are stored anonymously for honest feedback. We asked students to specify their prior technical experience after they had completed all activities and registered for the extra points but did not require them to provide any information and there was no disadvantage if they refused to provide information. Their information on the prior technical experience is crucial for analyzing its correlation with student results in the final exam tasks.

Students could access the learning activities almost until the final written exam date which was a few weeks after the lecture period. Exam tasks included tasks that AdE-Le addressed as well as tasks with learning objectives that address other contents of the course, e.g., spatial sense or different views of a component.

For statistic evaluation, we divide the data sets into two groups without considering the specification of the type of prior technical education. The groups are (1) with prior technical experience and (2) without prior technical experience. We formulate the operational hypotheses H1 in a pair of research hypotheses as suggested by Döring and Bortz (2016). The null hypothesis assumes that there is no real difference between the groups that differ in terms of a characteristic (Rasch 2021). The rejection range is defined by the significance level, which is usually set at 5% (Hollenberg, 2016; Moosbrugger and Kelava, 2012). We transform the operational hypotheses H1 “Students without prior technical experience find AdE-Le more helpful than students with prior technical experience.” into the null hypothesis H10 “There is no difference between the two groups in evaluating AdE-Le as helpful for their self-study time.” The operational hypotheses H2 “An adaptive e-learning environment compensates initial technical knowledge heterogeneity to the point there exist no difference in the examination results between the groups.” transforms into the null hypothesis H20 “There is no difference between the two groups in the exam results after using AdE-Le”. The tool for quantitative analysis was SPSS for Windows (28.0.1.1).

3. RESULTS

134 students from the first semester started using the e-learning environment AdE-Le and participated in the first questionnaire; 29 of 134 students have prior technical experience. 75 students completed all activities of AdE-Le and filled out the second questionnaire with feedback on AdE-Le; 17 of 75 had a prior technical experience, and 61 of 75 participated in the final exam and volunteered information about their prior technical experience. 70 % of the students with prior technical experience and 80% of the students without prior technical experience did not use AdE-Le weekly as we intended, but only after the end of the lecture for exam preparation. Table 1 presents the frequency of use of the content that AdE-Le suggested. Students with prior technical experience used the suggested content slightly more often with an average of 2,3 to an average of 2,59 for students without prior technical experience. Significance tests show that the difference of user behavior is not statistically significant.

Table 1. Item of the user behavior from the second questionnaire. Note that group sizes differ

<table>
<tr><th>Item in the questionnaire</th><th>Results</th></tr>
<tr><td><u>Frequency:</u> “How often did you use the suggested content? “

Average students without prior technical experience 2,59 (n=58)

Average students with prior technical experience 2,30 (n=17)</td><td>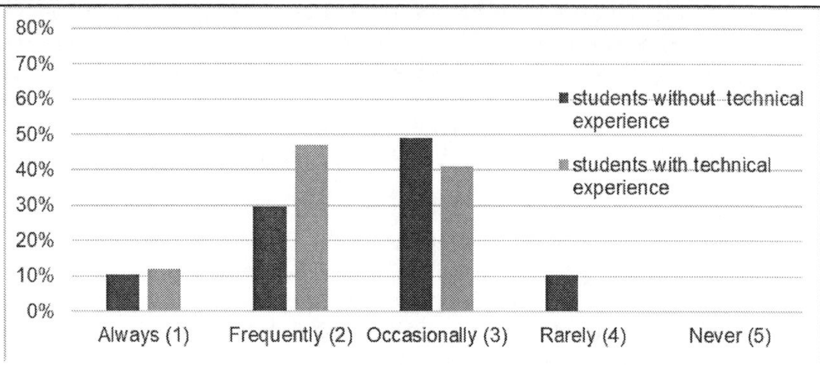
</td></tr>
</table>

The relevant items of the second questionnaire are assessed within this paper in Table 2. There were hardly any differences between the two test groups. The biggest difference in the average values can be seen in the agreement that AdE-Le supports the self-learning phases in a meaningful way. Here, the agreement of the group with prior technical experience is higher and can be described as weakly significant ($p=0.042$). For all other items the null hypothesis H10 is not rejected and there is no statistically significant difference between the two test groups.

Table 2. Relevant items of Feedback about AdE-Le from the second questionnaire. Note that group sizes differ

<table>
<tr><th>Item in the questionnaire</th><th>Results</th></tr>
<tr><td><u>Agreement:</u> “I wish AdE-Le would be available for all topics in Engineering Design education.”

Average students without prior technical experience 1,86 (n=58)

Average students with prior technical experience 1,59 (n=17)</td><td>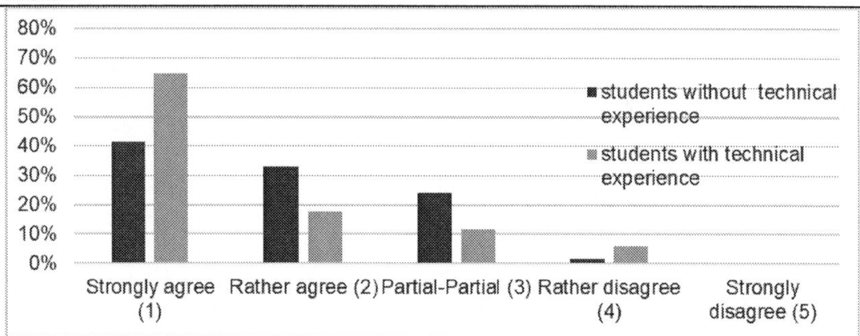
</td></tr>
<tr><td><u>Agreement:</u>
“AdE-Le presented practice-oriented information.”

Average students without prior technical experience 2,25 (n=58)

Average students with prior technical experience 1,88 (n=17)</td><td>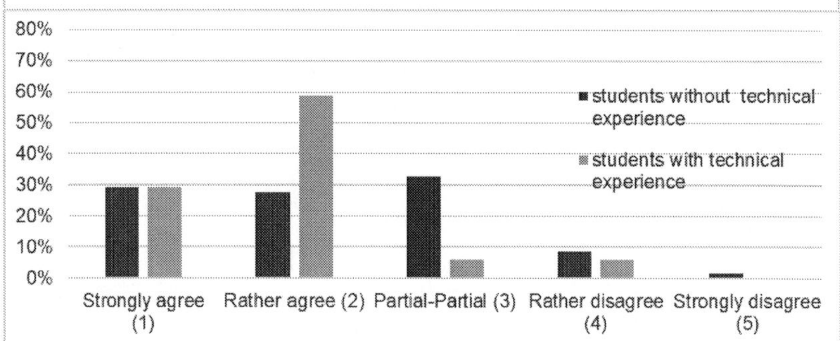
</td></tr>
</table>

"AdE-Le presented important technical background knowledge."

Average students without prior technical experience 2,19 (n=58)

Average students with prior technical experience 2,17 (n=17)

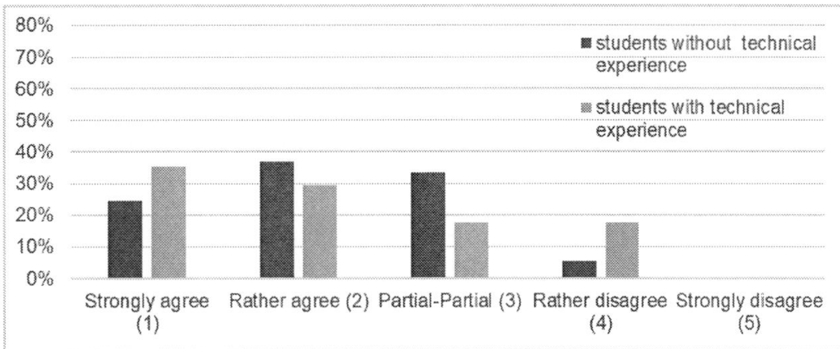

Agreement:
"AdE-Le has meaningfully supported the self-study time."

Average students without prior technical experience 1,86 (n=58)

Average students with prior technical experience 1,41 (n=17)

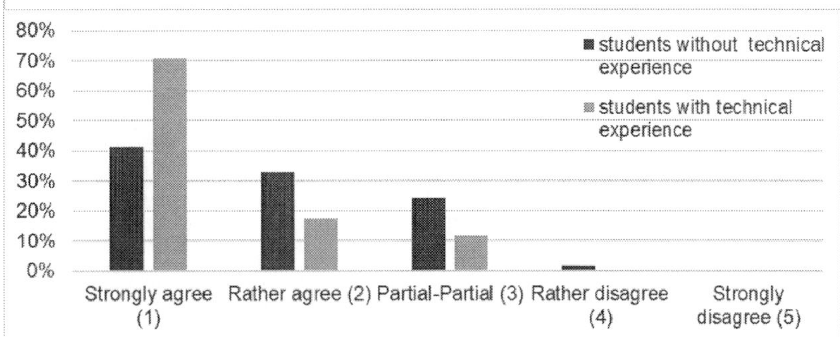

In the exam students with a prior technical experience score higher on average in both tasks than students without prior technical experience (see Table 3). However, the difference is significantly greater for topics for which no AdE-Le was offered. When correlated with the group variable of whether prior technical experience is present, the significance is $p = 0.277$ for the task whose learning objectives are addressed by AdE-Le. Therefore, the operational null hypothesis that there is no difference between the two test groups using AdE-Le is accepted. For the task whose learning objectives are not addressed by AdE-Le, the significance is $p < 0.001$. Thus, for this task, the operational null hypothesis that there is no difference between the two groups is rejected. And the alternative hypothesis, that there is a different between the two groups is accepted. Initial differences between the two test groups could no longer be identified as significant in the written exam task whose learning objectives were addressed by AdE-Le.

Table 3. Final exam results of students who used AdE-Le

	Task with learning objectives addressed by AdE-Le	Task with learning objectives not addressed by AdE-Le
Students with prior technical experience (n = 17)	Average = 17,06points Standard deviation = 5,63	Average = 22,59 points Standard deviation = 2,97
Students without prior technical experience (n= 44)	Average = 15,59 points Standard deviation = 6,21	Average = 17,32 points Standard deviation = 6,61

4. DISCUSSION

Our first step is to ensure that the data is suitable to investigate our research hypotheses. Like in our previous study (Kossack and Bender, 2022), results of this study show that students with prior technical experience rate the level of difficulty of the course lower and rate their experience and knowledge as helpful for the acquisition of competences in the course. Based on the confirmed characteristics of the student group like Kossack and Bender (2022), the sample is suitable for investigating the research hypotheses.

It is crucial for comparing the two test groups that they used AdE-Le in similar ways. Results show that there is no significant difference between the two test groups in their usage behavior with AdE-Le.

We could not find that students without prior technical experience find AdE-Le more helpful than students with prior technical experience (H1) based on the results of questionnaire two. Results show that students with prior technical experience tend to rate the learning environment as more helpful and the material as more suitable, but this may be due to a fundamentally higher interest in the topics and not exclusively to the type of learning format.

We found that an adaptive e-learning environment leads to a homogenization of the exam results (H2), but it is unclear whether the AdE-Le lead to the homogenization or homogenization is a result of comparing two exam tasks with different topics. Data from exams tasks with the same learning objectives in different years of students not using AdE-Le could provide more insights on its effect.

The award of extra points for the exam might have influenced user behavior and study results. By awarding extra points on the exam through participation, students were motivated to participate and provide feedback. Instead of using AdE-Le as intended, students may instead use AdE-Le to get the extra points. An efficient way to get the extra points is to complete the activities as quickly as possible and only used the content to a limited extent, which we observed for many students of both groups (see Table 1). As a result, students assess content in the second questionnaire that they have worked on occasionally.

All results highly depend on the implemented AdE-Le. The Moodle system stored a limited number of available learning content, consists of several individual learning paths, and is adaptive solely in terms of knowledge level. The branching to learning content is predominantly done by selecting answer options for closed question types. Due to the limited possibilities of automated checking of learning objectives, higher taxonomy levels according to Bloom could hardly be implemented (Mayer *et al.* 2009), even by using Stack in Moodle. Therefore, learning objectives could not always be sufficiently checked and the learning status recorded to provide suitable materials for the individual student. The expansion of testing opportunities and integrated learning materials and learning paths could lead to an increased homogenization of the group.

Study results are limited to the subject "dimensioning, tolerancing and fitting tolerances" in Engineering Design education. These topics are typical for a gap of knowledge between the two groups of students (1) without prior technical experience and (2) with prior technical experience e.g., technical internship or vocational training. The impact of the use of an adaptive e-learning environment could be less in other topics. The development, implementation, and evaluation of adaptive learning environments on other topics in Engineering Design education and in other disciplines would reveal the extent to which the effect shown in this study applies to other topics as well.

The proportion of first semester students with prior technical experience is significantly lower than in Kossack and Bender (2022). Especially the proportion of students with a technical internship planned for the degree program at 12 % is considerably lower than it was at Kossack and Bender (2022) at 37%. The result for this study is very different sizes of the test groups. But these does not distort results due to similar variances, therefore the results can be considered representative despite the lower percentage of students with technical experience than Kossack and Bender (2022). Overall, both test groups viewed the learning environment in a meaningful and positive way. This could be due to the selection of the test group. In principle, AdE-Le was available to all students of the course, but not all students used or completed it. We assume that the test groups consist of students with the same level of motivation and interest in the topic.

The grouping of students is based on whether or not students have already started or completed another technical degree program, technical vocational training, or technical internship relevant to that degree program. The assumption that the students have more technical experience relevant to the acquisition of competencies than, for example, students who are very interested in technology in their free time but did not start any technical training or education can be wrong. Perhaps a knowledge survey to group by actually existing technical knowledge could provide better clues for grouping in this case.

This paper could not address all questions of interest concerning the benefits of adaptive e-learning environments. The general added value of the AdE-Le could be addressed by comparing the exam results of AdE-Le users with those of students who do not use an adaptive e-learning environment. The correlation between the usage behavior and the evaluation of the added value of the e-learning environment is relevant. With the data we could correlate the items of the feedback questionnaire (usage behavior and assessment of the personal benefits). It is not possible to investigate a correlation between user behavior and exam results with this data set, because data collection of the feedback questionnaire was anonymous.

5. CONCLUSION

It is desirable to homogenize student groups with typically differing prior technical experience in Engineering Design education to support competence acquisition. Individual support addresses heterogeneity and adaptive e-learning environments enable individual support in Engineering Design education. Our study investigates the use of an adaptive e-learning environment to provide individual support with data from two questionnaires. The students in the first semester in Engineering Design consider the adaptive e-learning environment a useful support for the self-learning phase. Slightly more students with prior technical experience than students without prior technical experience state that the adaptive e-learning environment supports in a meaningful way, but the evaluation of the exam results shows that the learning environment especially helps the test group without prior technical knowledge. Significant correlations between exam results and prior technical experience do not exist for exam tasks with learning objectives addressed by the adaptive e-learning environment, but they exist for other tasks of the same exam. Based on these results, the exemplary used Moodle-based implementation AdE-Le seems reasonable for knowledge heterogeneous student groups. Comparing multiple student groups from different years could be useful. Our findings are based solely on the topic area of "dimensioning, tolerances, and fits", so an extension to other topics would be useful. Further data analysis should compare the group of students who did not use AdE-Le with the group of students who did use AdE-Le to examine the fundamental benefits.

ACKNOWLEDGEMENT

The development of an adaptive e-learning environment for Engineering Design education for first-year students is financially supported by a digi-Fellow of the DIGITALE HOCHSCHULE NRW (2022-2023)

REFERENCES

Albers, A.; Denkena, B.; Matthiesen, S.: Faszination Konstruktion. Berufsbild und Tätigkeitsfeld im Wandel. 2012.

Arsovic, B. and Stefanovic, N. (2020), "E-learning based on the adaptive learning model: case study in Serbia", Sādhanā, Vol. 45 No. 1, p. 1927.

Bagheri, M. (2015), "Intelligent and Adaptive Tutoring Systems: How to Integrate Learners", International Journal of Education, Vol. 7 No. 2, p. 1.

Berger, S. and Moser, U. (2020), "Adaptives Lernen und Testen", *journal für lehrerInnenbildung* jlb 01-2020 Digitalisierung https://doi.org/ 10.35468/jlb-01-2020_03.

Biggs, J.B. and Tang, C.S.-k. (2011), Teaching for quality learning at university: What the student does, UK Higher Education OUP Humanities and Social Sciences Higher Education OUP Ser, 4th edition, McGraw-Hill/Open University Press, Maidenhead.

Brückner, S., Förster, M., Zlatkin-Troitschanskaia, O. and Walstad, W.B. (2015), "Effects of prior economic education, native language, and gender on economic knowledge of first-year students in higher education. A comparative study between Germany and the USA", Studies in Higher Education, Vol. 40 No. 3, pp. 437–453.

Döring, N.; Bortz, J.(2016); *Forschungsmethoden und Evaluation in den Sozial- und Humanwissenschaften*. Berlin, Heidelberg: Springer Berlin Heidelberg 2016

Eckert, C., Seifried, E. and Spinath, B. (2015), "Heterogenität in der Hochschule aus psychologischer Sicht: Die Rolle der studentischen Eingangsvoraussetzungen für adaptives Lehren", in Rheinländer, K. (Ed.), *Ungleichheitssensible Hochschullehre*, Vol. 11, Springer Fachmedien Wiesbaden, Wiesbaden, pp. 257–274 https://doi.org/ 10.1007/978-3-658-09477-5_14.

Fidalgo-Blanco, A., Sein-Echaluce Maria Luisa, Garcia-Penalvo, F.J. and Conde-Gonzalez, M.A. (2014), "Learning content management systems for the definition of adaptive learning environments", in 2014 International Symposium on Computers in Education (SIIE): 12 - 14 Nov. 2014, Logroño, La Rioja, Spain, IEEE, Piscataway, NJ, pp. 105–110.

H5P Contributors (2023), available at: https://h5p.org/.

Hollenberg, S (2016), *Fragebögen*. Wiesbaden: Springer Fachmedien Wiesbaden 2016.

Kannengiesser, U.; Gero, J.; Wells, J.; Lammi, M. (2015) DO HIGH SCHOOL STUDENTS BENEFIT FROM PRE-ENGINEERING DESIGN EDUCATION? *Proceedings of the 20th International Conference on Engineering Design (ICED15).* 2015.

Kerr, P. (2016), "Adaptive learning", *ELT Journal*, Vol. 70 No. 1, pp. 88–93 https://doi.org/ 10.1093/elt/ccv055.

Kolekar, S.V., Pai, R.M. and M. M., M.P. (2019), "Rule based adaptive user interface for adaptive E-learning system", *Education and Information Technologies*, Vol. 24 No. 1, pp. 613–641 https://doi.org/ 10.1007/s10639-018-9788-1.

Kossack, F. and Bender, B. (2022), "Heterogeneous groups of students as a challenge in engineering design education", in DS 119: *Proceedings of the 33rd Symposium Design for X (DFX2022)*, 22 and 23 September 2022, The Design Society, p. 10 https://doi.org/ 10.35199/dfx2022.07.

Kossack, F., Bender, B. (2023) 'Individualization in Engineering Design Education: Implementation of an Adaptive E-Learning Environment (AdE-Le)', *in Proceedings of the International Conference on Engineering Design* (ICED23), Bordeaux, France, 24-28 July 2023. DOI:10.1017/pds.2023.230

Kossack, F., Kattwinkel, D. and Bender, B. (2022), "Adaptive E-Learning for the Engineering Design Education at Ruhr-University Bochum", Proceedings of the Design Society, Vol. 2, pp. 2313–2322 https://doi.org/ 10.1017/pds.2022.234.

Mayer, H.O. and Hertnagel, J. (2009), *Lernzielüberprüfung im eLearning*, Oldenbourg, München https://doi.org/ 10.1524/9783486848984.

Metraglia, R., Villa Valerio, Baronio Gabriele and Adamini, R. (2015), "High School Graphics Experience Influencing the Self-Efficacy of First-Year Engineering Students in an Introductory Engineering Graphics Course", *Engineering Design Graphics Journal (EDGJ)*, No. Vol. 79 No.3.

Moodle Contributors (2023), "Fragetyp STACK", available at: https://docs.moodle.org/400/de/Fragetyp_STACK

Moosbrugger, H. u. Kelava, A. (2012) *Testtheorie und Fragebogenkonstruktion.* Springer-Lehrbuch. Berlin, Heidelberg: Springer-Verlag Berlin Heidelberg.

Niegemann, H.M. and Heidig, S. (2019), "Interaktivität und Adaptivität in multimedialen Lernumgebungen", in Niegemann, H. and Weinberger, A. (Eds.), *Lernen mit Bildungstechnologien*, Springer Reference Psychologie, Vol. 73, Springer Berlin Heidelberg, Berlin, Heidelberg, pp. 1–25 https://doi.org/ 10.1007/978-3-662-54373-3_33-1.

Pfäffli, B. K. (2015): Lehren an Hochschulen. Eine Hochschuldidaktik für den Aufbau von Wissen und Kompetenzen. UTB Schlüsselkompetenzen Hochschuldidaktik, Bd. 4325. Bern: Haupt 2015.

Prusty, B. G., & Russell, C. (2011). Engaging students in learning threshold concepts in engineering mechanics: adaptive eLearning tutorials. In 17th International Conference on Engineering Education (ICEE) (pp. 21-26).

Radenkovic, B., Despotovic, M., Bogdanovic, Z. and Barac, D. (2009), "Creating Adaptive Environment for e-Learning Courses", JIOS, Vol. 33 No. 1, pp. 179–189.

Rasch, B. (2021), Quantitative Methoden. Einführung in die Statistik für Psychologie, Sozial- und Erziehungswissenschaften. Lehrbuch. Berlin: Springer.

Rey, G.D. (2009), *E-Learning: Theorien, Gestaltungsempfehlungen und Forschung*, Psychologie-Lehrbuch, 1. Auflage, Verlag Hans Huber, Bern.

Rusak, Z. (2017), "EXPLOITATION OF MICRO-LEARNING FOR GENERATING PERSONALIZED LEARNING PATHS", *in Proceedings of the 21th International Conference on Engineering Design (ICED17)* Vol. 9: Design Education 21.-25.08.2017, Vancouver, Canada.

Stoyanov, S. and Kirschener, P. (2004), "Expert Concept Mapping Method for Defining the Characteristics of Adaptive E-Learning: ALFANET Project Case", *ETR&D*, Vol. 52 No. 2, pp. 41–56.

Terkowsky, C., Frye, S., Haertel, T., May, D., Wilkemann, U. and Jahnke, I. (2018), "Technik- und Ingenieurdidaktik in der hochschulischen Bildung", in Pittich, D., Zinn, B. and Tenberg, R. (Eds.), *Technikdidaktik: Eine Bestandsaufnahme*, Franz Steiner Verlag, pp. 87–97.

Wissenschaftliche Gesellschaft für Produktentwicklung WiGeP e.V. (2018), Universitäre Lehre in der Produktentwicklung: Leitfaden der Wissenschaftlichen Gesellschaft für Produktentwicklung (WiGeP). Available at: https://b7s1f6.n3cdn1.secureserver.net/wp-content/uploads/2022/05/Final_WiGeP_Leitfaden_Lehre.pdf

Žeželj, D. and Miler, D. (2018), MANUFACTURING TECHNOLOGY-BASED APPROACH TO TEACHING ENGINEERING DRAWING. *Proceedings of the DESIGN 2018* 15th. Faculty of Mechanical Engineering and Naval Architecture, University of Zagreb, Croatia; The Design Society, Glasgow, UK 2018, S. 2553–2562

CAPACITY BUILDING ACROSS HIGHER EDUCATION AND RURAL YOUTH IN WINNOVATORS SPACE

Kai Pata[1], Kristi Jüristo[1], Matej Zapušek[2], Nathalie Leiba[3], Sanja Popovic Pantic[4], Vladan Devedzić[5,6], Sonja Radenkovic[5], Mirjana Devedzić[5], Marija Blagojević[7] and Danijela Milošević[7]
[1]*Tallinn University, School of Education, Estonia*
[2]*Ljubljana University, Slovenia*
[3]*VITECO, Italy*
[4]*Institute Mihajlo Pupin, Science and Technology Policy Research Center, Serbia*
[5]*University of Belgrade, Serbia*
[6]*Serbian Academy of Sciences and Arts, Belgrade, Serbia*
[7]*University of Kragujevac, Faculty of Technical Sciences, Serbia*

ABSTRACT

This paper demonstrates the design as a hypothesis framework for developing cross-university students and mentors, and rural youth (aged 18-30) and regional business ecosystems capacity building practice approaches to support sustainable development goals. To support university students', mentors and the business partners' engagement and building agency and capacity with regional rural young women a gamified learning and co-working WINnovators Space (https://winnovators-space.eu/) with e-learning materials for self-learning and entrepreneurial mentored group challenges was developed. The Pilot study validates the capacity building practice approach with Winnovator Space in three countries involving young rural women, higher education students, academic and business mentors – Estonia (30), Slovenia (35), Serbia (25).

KEYWORDS

Capacity Building, Higher Education Practice, Rural Youth, Sustainability

1 INTRODUCTION – CAPACITY BUILDING ACROSS HIGHER EDUCATION AND REGIONAL COMMUNITIES

Recent decade has promoted universities to act out in regional development as innovation agents facilitating cross-border knowledge exchange (Broek et al., 2019). Goals for Education 2030 (Mundial & UNICEF, 2016), and sustainable action along the SDG 4 – providing lifelong learning for all, and SDG5 – considering gender equality in STEM education (Boeren, 2019) require educational institutions to step out as actuating actors in the society. Boeren (2019) recommended an interdependent approach that relates the development of individuals and the social structures around them at micro (e.g. socio-demographic and socio-economic factors, people's attitudes, confidence, interests, and motivation to learn), meso (structure of educational offers, forms of practices), and macro levels (e.g. legal, regulatory, financial, political, ideological factors). In our paper we aim to demonstrate one approach where higher education acts for society building shared capacity using a blended digital approach.

Capacity concept denotes systemic readiness. Morgan (2006) defines capacity as an emergent property in social ecosystems, an interaction effect that comes out of the dynamics involving a complex combination of attitudes, resources, strategies and skills, both tangible and intangible. Capacity as a state is an action potentiality of individuals within social and institutional contexts. "Capacity building" pertains to the building of the "capacity of institutions" as well as individuals (Wescott, 2002). It is a dynamic construct that has to be nourished in actions between different partners to solve challenges such as Education for Sustainable development Goals has.

Our design research aims for developing new types of capacity building practices between universities and society. The nature of capacity building expected from the universities in the direction of regions has changed over time. The more common is the training support approach where capacity building is defined as "enhancement of the skills of people and the capacity of institutions in resources management through education and training" (Cicin-Sain et al., 1998) that relates capacity building for communities foremost as the formal education provision activity. Our study explores the opportunities of capacity building by blending the formal and informal education provision modes. Capacity building requires Higher Education and Regional ecosystems to find new ways to orchestrate educational goals and formal education forms with the socio-economic and socio-cultural community life expectations and with the informal education opportunities in regions. Blending formal and nonformal educational opportunities is one of the capacity building forms that Higher Education institutions (HEI) develop to offer flexible education with equal access along SDG 4 and SDG 5.

HEIs are increasingly demanded to be sustainable development actors, building partnerships with regional business ecosystems, for example, in advancing business and STEM competencies and overall active citizenship mentality in remote areas. Agency development of people is one central educational goal, because agency is a state that relates personal characteristics and contexts with the opportunities and problem solving challenges one has in life, as well as with the enabling situations or constraints (Emirbayev & Mische, 1998).

Lifelong learning strategic documents that we list below have long related the agency with the concept of active citizenship that one can learn in various formal, informal and nonformal ways. Competences for active citizens are incorporated into many European agendas such as agenda *"The future of education and skills: Education 2030"* (Howells, 2018), the *"UNESCO learning objectives for sustainable development"* (Rieckmann, 2017), the *"Preparing our youth for an inclusive and sustainable world: The OECD PISA global competence framework"* (OECD, 2018) and the GreenComp, *"The European sustainability competence framework"* (Bianchi et al., 2022). In our design study we seek opportunities to blend formal HEI students' studies with informal and nonformal learning of young people in remote areas to develop their active citizenship and entrepreneurial, STEM and sustainability competences, as well as advancing a shared capacity between universities and regions.

The problem of this paper is the need to develop new digitally enhanced capacity building approaches through which HEIs may act out in the regional communities to promote learning for STEM, sustainability, entrepreneurship by blending formal and nonformal learning so that HEI students may support undermined young people who have fewer access to learning for innovation in teams.

The research question is formulated as the design hypothesis (Leinonen et al., 2008): *How can the universities grow the agency of higher education students to become change agents for the remote communities and help the undermined rural youth (18-30) to have equal access to entrepreneurial, stem and sustainability competencies in their regions?*

2. METHODS

2.1 Context of the Study

To achieve sustainable development goals in education for all Education 2030: Incheon Declaration and Framework of Action (Mundial & UNICEF, 2016) has stated that we need to promote equal access to education, developing flexible forms of learning that incorporate and blend formal, informal and nonformal approaches, enabling for learners different learning paces and spaces. This study is conducted in the frames of KA2 Erasmus+ project WINnovators (2021-2024) partnership aiming to explore the capacity building approaches in higher education teaching and learning that are directed to the regional communities, and particularly to young rural women in remote areas. The current study presents the results of our first ongoing Pilot with the developed approach. In the Pilot study we built a particular blended learning space consisting of the digital Winnovator Space in which we activated a learning community across higher education, regional rural ecosystems and business ecosystems in three countries – Estonia, Serbia and Slovenia.

2.2 The Design Process

We applied a participatory design-based research method, aligned to software and interaction *design as a hypothesis approach* (Leinonen et al. 2008) that aims for designing tools for complex social systems where the iterative and hermeneutic design process consists of four partly overlapping phases: contextual inquiry, participatory design, product design, and production of solution as hypotheses. Our design hypothesis states that the WINnovators approach aims for a new type of capacity building practice that unites universities and regions, and advances young people agency as active citizens competent to create STEM and sustainability related business ideas. Design as a hypothesis approach means that we are experimental and analytic, but we try to keep ourselves open to serendipity that helps to be flexible in our design solutions. We acknowledge that our Pilot with WINnovators approach design and application in practice may result in some failures, and some of the outcomes can be different than initially expected, that we try to document through the evaluation of the WINnovators approach.

The following Design as a Hypothesis Stages were followed:

- Contextual inquiry for defining the context for WINnovators approach
  i) Benchmarking the trends in inclusive education for active citizenship;
  ii) Identifying the local needs with an ethnographic exploration (observations and interviews with stakeholders in higher education, rural regions) about who-what-why-where could contribute for capacity building between higher education, rural ecosystems and businesses;
- II. Participatory design of Personas:

iii) Design thinking and Persona development (Cooper, 2003) to represent the HEI learners as potential change agents, and rural young women as community entrepreneurs and future leaders;

- III. Product conceptual design:

iv) The design of a WINnovators Competence Framework for active citizenship;

v) The design of gamified interaction principles for engagement between different stakeholders in informal and nonformal learning scenarios;

- IV. Production of software and interaction as hypotheses:

vi) The design of the eLearning course topics, and Teamwork Challenges;

vii) The design of the interactive WINnovators Space https://winnovators-space.eu/

- V. Testing the hypothesis in the Pilot in three countries

viii) The Design is formatively advanced by 'community' involvement: academics as the designers, higher education specialists and mentors; the students as learners, mentors, and change agents; the rural youth as learners, future entrepreneurs and active citizens; and the regional business ecosystem experts as mentors try out WINnovators approach, and track the process in the formative diaries.

ix) The usability survey of the WINnovators Space and analytics about active citizenship competences achieved will provide some impact indicators on how successful is the WINnovatost approach. The results of the survey are not presented in this paper, as the Pilot is still ongoing.

2.3 The Sample

The Pilot study sample was formed in three countries (Estonia, Serbia, Slovenia) using the convenience sampling method (accessibility in the partner universities), and the snowball sampling approach involving students and rural young women through design stages. In each piloting country the HEI students, HEI teachers and rural young women were teamed together to learn and experience the WINnovators learning practice in WINnovators space.

Estonia, N=30: HEI youth work students and teachers, youth workers in rural areas, young rural women representing three target groups: young adults in unsatisfied life situations, young mothers and young unemployed adults and/or school drop-outs.

Serbia, N=25: BADEN, the network of academic researchers from different universities, students from the computer science and business fields, the networked Serbian Association of Business Women, the female entrepreneurs, young rural women representing the Roma minority.

Slovenia, N=35: HEI teachers and students from the two-subject teacher study programmes Computer Science and Art Pedagogy, young women from vulnerable groups who have not completed their education and come from rural areas were contacted in cooperation with the Employment Service in the framework of the PUM-O project, which deals with young people who have not completed formal education, and with the Chamber of Commerce and Agriculture of Slovenia.

3. RESULTS ON THE WINNOVATORS DESIGN APPROACH

3.1 WINnovators's Design Hypothis on Capacity Building and Personal Agency

As we are following the *Design as a hypothesis* approach, in the following sections we will introduce step-by-step the results achieved in each design phase. This research addresses the research question: How can the universities grow the agency of higher education students to become change agents for the remote communities and help the undermined rural youth (18-30) to have equal access to entrepreneurial, stem and sustainability competencies in their regions?

Our hypothesis considers two levels of impacts from learning as a WINnovator.

1. The capacity between the different stakeholders can be built in problem-solving groups where learning for STEAM, sustainability and entrepreneurial competencies is supported. We assert that working together in teams will grow the agency of HEI and rural Youth to become more self-development driven and community goods driven as change agents. They will gain active citizenship competences that they can use in the future for common good. The indicators of capacity building are i) formed teams between HEI students and rural young women, who pursue jointly for digital team challenges on STEM, sustainability related topics, ii) active citizenship competences (WINnovator competencies) individuals have gained through learning together. This hypothesis may be validated tracing teamwork and active citizenship competences in WINnovator Space, and using formative reports.

2. At the institutional and regional level the joint capacity can be created between HEIs and the local stakeholder organisations. We assert that capacities as shared activity systems need to be built around shared teaching and problem-solving practices across organisational borders and revising institutional regulatory frameworks for formal learning. The indicators of capacity building across HEIs and local communities are: i) established and durable support systems through which it is possible to recruit young rural women to the WINnovators learning activities provided jointly with HEI students as change agents; and ii) established coordinated support actions provided to young rural women by the local communities and the universities. This hypothesis may be validated tracing offline and online networking activities that the WINnovator Space can enhance, and using the formative reports.

3.2 WINnovator's Space – a Shared Interaction Hub for Capacity Building

The first prototype of WINnovator Space for interactive learning was developed as a codesign result within the Consortium, engaging HEI experts and regional business and youth work ecosystems. We used the Persona approach (Cooper, 2003) to describe the needs of young people and HEI students in joint learning processes. Working closely with local partner organisations, we specified the target groups within the young women in vulnerable life situations, their specific characteristics and needs. Collected information and knowledge helped to develop the WINnovators e-learning materials and Challenge modules that may correspond to the development of young people's competences, offering self-fulfilment and a sense of achievement, as well as sufficient challenge and opportunities for experimentation.

WINnovators' Space represents the concept of "Edutainment": online content, gamification, interactivity, social media features, personal and team profile, messaging, file, pictures and videos uploading, person and team rankings promote learning in a virtual community. WINnovator Space promotes elearning from self-learning short lessons provided as learning nuggets. WINnovator Space is also a community space in which teams can be formed around problem Challenges that rural young women see in their entrepreneurial visions. The community space supports the roles of Mentors (from academia and business ecosystems), Change Agents (HEI students), and the WINnovators (young women in change). The interaction in the community is built around the design ideas as Challenges that young women can try out with their supporters (Mentors and Change Agents). The role shift in agency is traceable with the badge system that associates active citizenship competences with progress.

3.3 WINnovators Space – a Gamified Motivation Space

The gamified motivational space was developed in WINnovator Space comprising the open badge (Jovanovic & Devedzic, 2014) system and leaderboards. The WINnovators open badges are related to competence dimensions. For open badges a competency framework was composed from several frameworks: Dig.comp 2.1 (Stephanie et al., 2017), GreenComp (OECD, 2018), Sustainability competencies (Dzhengiz & Niesten, 2020), Learning for the future, Competencies in education for sustainable development (Ece, 2011), Entrepreneurial competencies (Kyguolienė & Švipas, 2019), Innovation leadership competences (Vlok, 2012), Innovation competencies (Waychal, 2019) and Project management competencies (Dogbegah et al., 2011). The WINnovator competencies are grouped into the five competence dimensions that relate with the development of personal agency and group agency in the time of challenges: Learning to be, Learning to value, Learning to live and work together, Learning to comprehend and contribute and Learning to empower and lead. HEI students and young women who learn together can collect badges when they do individual learning or group challenges. In challenges, badges are awarded for completing a task or for creating a product that must be first assessed by the instructor and are therefore awarded manually. Some competencies in the WINnovators competency framework are difficult to identify in others, therefore there is a possibility of requesting a limited number of badges to oneself. Open badges can be requested by learners themselves, by their team members (change agents), or by the mentors. A leaderboard shows the active users and the ones who earned the most badges and aims to promote learning. The accumulation of competencies enables learners to move up the rank: bronze, silver, and gold levels of being a WINinnovator - denoting the state of active citizenship competencies and agency. Finally, the system issues WINnovators certificates to users.

The usability of the system will be evaluated with the survey at the end of the Pilot with users, and we do not present the results here since the pilot is still ongoing. The system also provides an overview of the competencies that we will use to demonstrate personal level gains in active citizenship as a result of WINnovators approach.

3.4 Testing the Capacity Building Hypothesis in WINnovators' Pilots

The training modules on the WINnovators platform are:

1. STEM/STEAM entrepreneurial communities for young women: general learning resources;
2. STEM/STEAM entrepreneurial communities for young women: challenges.

Within the first group of training practices, HEI students as well as young women in rural areas have the opportunity to gain competencies in the areas of project and teamwork management, development of websites, the time management, promotion of sustainable entrepreneurship, leadership, creative thinking, business creation plan, etc. The second group of training practice collection provides challenges in the field of using digital technologies in marketing, tourist services with gamified digital elements, development of digital learning communities, etc. For each e-lesson, an opportunity to earn a badge is defined, through the presentation of the lesson or by taking a test. In challenge learning modules the focus is on the collaboration among peers - students and young women working together, practice oriented learning with real-life connected activities and tangible outcomes or learning that can be transferred to young adults' daily activities or other spheres of life. The badges there must be requested by team-members and the awarding process is moderated by mentors.

The role of the HEI students as Change Agents in the initial phase of the training was to establish contact with the young women WINnovators and to advise them on the selection of appropriate learning units according to their needs and expectations. Within the online platform, teachers as Mentors have formed subgroups for specific challenges and invited Change Agents (students) and WINnovators (rural youth) to participate. By presenting students with the same challenges as participants and allowing them to expand their participation with gamification elements in the form of badges, a collegial relationship and sense of partnership between them was built. These connections can be sustained later as students move into their careers. Through networking, the collaboration in their local communities was fostered, where participants can act as agents of change and promoters of education to other potential candidates.

Case: Estonia. The engagement of young women in vulnerable life situations in Estonia was through youth and community workers at municipalities. 2nd year youth work students were involved through a course with the aim of preparing students for project work as part of the daily activities of a youth worker, to find and use funding for youth projects and to support young people in the implementation of projects. HEI youth work students are also working in local rural youth centres, and they reached out to potential participants. Specific tasks of HEI students were connected with problem-based, collaborative and situated learning that took place through challenge modules in WINnovators Space. A total of 5 teams were created, with students collaborating closely with the young participants to undergo a chosen challenge module. Through this process, they developed concrete project ideas, identified potential funders, and prepared the project proposal for each initiative. Out of these, 3 ideas focused on sustainability, aiming to create awareness about consumption behaviour and engage the community in finding practical solutions to reduce overconsumption through collective action. One initiative aimed to create a digital learning community of young people in a rural area, helping them develop skills in team leadership, community engagement, and planning collective activities. Another project aimed to raise awareness about various social issues relevant to young people by using comics, including digital formats. As the Estonian case was run some of the teams abandoned working within the WINnovator Space and started to use social media environments for interaction and project work. In the Estonian case the drivers of the WINnovators learning in regions activity were youth work HEI students, the HEI mentor met with students regularly to guide them but did not meet directly with the young women WINnovators. This self-driven approach built on the youth worker students' agency, and aligned with non-formal learning principles, but decreased the formal HEI control over the learning.

Case: Serbia. The women entrepreneurs in rural areas in Serbia have not completed business schools and colleges, and have the problem of how to digitally transform their business and to enter from the local market to the electronic market. In the case developed in Serbia, the regional ecosystem was supported by the following interactions between the partners: HEI teachers (Mentors) – young women (WINnovators): the HEI teachers were responsible for course development, presentation, maintenance and administration, as well as for fostering communication with young women; through their personal connections, the HEI teachers attracted the young women to take the courses. HEI teachers (Mentors) – HEI students (Change Agents): the teachers invited HEI students and trained them to become change agents and carry out immediate communication with the learners (young women). HEI administration – HEI students (Change Agents): university administration was asked to accept the students' participation in the WINnovators activities as (part of) the mandatory final year project / field work, and also to issue certificates of completing extracurricular activities where appropriate. HEI students (Change Agents) – young women (WINnovators): students contacted many of the young women to take the WINnovators courses based on their personal connections and origin. The Association of Business Women Serbia (ABWS) – university teachers (Mentors): ABWS was the major source of contacts with young women from rural areas. The pairs were formed from HEI students and young women to work in teams in WINnovator Space. The three HEI mentors from different universities run regular online meetings to meet the students and young women to facilitate their learning process. In the end the HEI mentors provided feedback to the teams.

Case: Slovenia. In Slovenia, the public administrative organisations - the Employment Service and the Chamber of Commerce and Agriculture of Slovenia were engaged to reach out young rural women. HEI teachers recruited upper year students from the Faculty of Education to participate in the project by introducing the project, its aims and objectives, and inviting them to participate. These students already acquire knowledge about working with vulnerable groups of people within the framework of the core pedagogical subjects and also have the relevant didactic knowledge that enables them to approach learning support more effectively, to find the appropriate interpretation of terms and concepts for the target audience, and to take into account the specifics of the subject didactics of the respective field, the psychology of learning, thus adapting better to the level of the learners. The teachers had an initial interview with the students, in which they explained in detail the process of the training and defined their role. They also informed them of their goal - to help the learner become a change agent in their local environment and spread knowledge and awareness about the importance of sustainable aspects of business. The mentor held weekly Zoom meetings with the teams, but after the individual elearning phase was completed and the teamwork with challenges had to start, most of the recruited young women stopped attending the WINnovator course and did not finish Challenges despite HEI students' attempts to contact them. The new group of young women was contacted to enter the learning process, some young women from this group also started to work in teams with HEI students on the challenges.

4. DISCUSSION - CAPACITY BUILDING ACROSS HIGHER EDUCATION AND REGIONAL YOUTH

Overall these three cases demonstrated that the application of the design hypothesis in learning environment design and practical application in HEI-regional distributed settings was partially successful, but we also faced many challenges that require technical advancements, and revisions in the process of engagement between Mentors-Change Agents and Winnovators to build Capacity and active citizenship competences.
In the current stage of the WINnovator Pilot we can validate our design hypothesis through two types of impacts:

The capacity between the different stakeholders was built more in individual elearning mode and less in the problem solving teams. We asserted that working together in teams will grow the agency of HEI and rural Youth to become more self-development driven and community goods driven as change agents. We managed to create 5 larger teams in Estonia, 16 teams where HEI students were paired with young women in Serbia, and in Slovenia 4 teams were initially created, but only 1 collaborative team continued where only one young woman was testing out the challenge level. Since the pilot is still ongoing we will get more formative evaluation data about the process from diaries of the HEI students and HEI mentors. We observed that not all the teams wanted to use the WINnovator space team area for their joint nonformal learning, and moved their work to the social media spaces. This may indicate that the platform still has some usability issues that we will get to know after the usability survey is finished at the end of the Pilot. The qualitative and quantitative findings of the process will help us to improve the engagement practices in teams, as well as the Winnovator Space and the gamification features for the next Pilots we plan in 2023-24.

According to the Leaderboard so far 22 HEI students and young women gained a number of badges (see Figure 1), which indicated only the moderate success, but the experiment is still ongoing and many learners are still actively studying. From our observations we found that participants gained active citizenship competences mainly from the elearning individual lessons, and they did not frequently request the competence badges for the work they did at the team challenges. The most popular badges requested for the team members were: Being a role model, inspiring engagement, motivating others, being open in thinking and communication, being a team player, caring of the others, being an inspiring leader, being able to accommodate in the challenges etc. Few persons were requesting badges for themselves as was possible. We also detected several technical requirements to make the requesting and awarding process in the challenges automatized after mentor approval. According to the Winnovator Space statistics most of the participants are still at the Beginner level of active citizenship, that indicates that there may be the need to change some of the criteria for the advancement in the WINnovator levels.

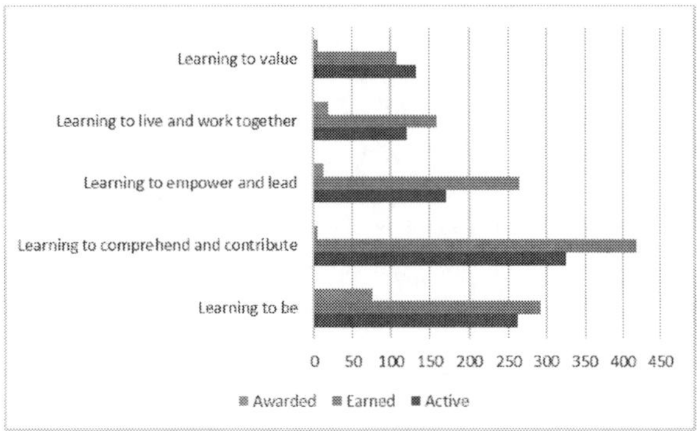

Figure 1. The overview of the badges the participants had obtained by the second half of the Pilot. (Active - students were still learning the lessons related with these competences, Earned - competences earned from completed lessons, Awarded - competences requested by teams during the teamwork)

At the institutional and regional level, the joint capacity was created between HEIs and the local stakeholder organisations. HEIs have built partnerships in the pilot cases with formal organisations and regional networks. We believe that HEIs can keep the capacity in these relations with formal organisations beyond short-term problem-solving events. We will follow these relationships during the Pilots to sustain them. An important element in joint capacity building was developing the link between the formal and nonformal learning structures that differ by their motivational elements. In two Pilots students were assigned with HEI course tasks to work with rural young women, in one Pilot it may be an extracurricular activity for students that requires regulative support to be credited. For students the course assessment provided an additional extrinsic motivation for participation.

The teams were supposed to work in the distant mode in WINnovators Space. The big challenge was that for regional young women the WINnovators learning activity is nonformal, and they do it from intrinsic interest. To keep them motivated and on track the local mediators were useful. In the Estonian case, the support came from local youth workers, either as current students or alumni of HEIs who acted as the mediating agents having trust relationships with local youth, and as alumni they are still connected with the university. In the Serbian case, the local mediators were business women from ABWS who mediated the youth to the BADEN network of HEI educators. In the Slovenian case the regional youth were motivated through a more formal approach created by their alignment to the Unemployment office and the Chamber of Commerce and Agriculture training programmes. This approach was not successfully keeping the young women to learn.

5. CONCLUSIONS

This study provided a preliminary view of how to build capacity and across university borders for SDG4 and SDG 5. The Piloting is ongoing for next two years, and will provide valuable impact on how to design new learning practices.

ACKNOWLEDGEMENTS

This research was supported by Erasmus+ project funding 2021-1-EE01-KA220-HED-000032081.

REFERENCES

Bianchi, G., Pisiotis, U., & Cabrera Giraldez, M. (2022). *GreenComp The European sustainability competence framework* (No. JRC128040). Joint Research Centre (Seville site).

Boeren, E. (2019). Understanding Sustainable Development Goal (SDG) 4 on "quality education" from micro, meso and macro perspectives. *International review of education*, 65, 277-294.

van den Broek, J., Benneworth, P., & Rutten, R. (2019). Institutionalization of cross-border regional innovation systems: The role of university institutional entrepreneurs. *Regional Studies, Regional Science*, 6(1), 55-69.

Cicin-Sain, B., Knecht, R. W., Jang, D., & Fisk, G. W. (1998). *Integrated coastal and ocean management: concepts and practices*. Island press.

Cooper, A. (2003). The Origin of Personas. *Cooper Journal.* https://www.cooper.com/journal/2008/5/the_origin_of_personas

Dogbegah, R., Owusu-Manu, D., & Omoteso, K. (2011). A principal component analysis of project management competencies for the Ghanaian construction industry. *Australasian Journal of Construction Economics and Building,* 11(1), 26-40.

Dzhengiz, T., & Niesten, E. (2020). Competences for environmental sustainability: A systematic review on the impact of absorptive capacity and capabilities. *Journal of business ethics*, 162(4), 881-906.

Ece, U. (2011). Learning for the future: Competences in Education for Sustainable Development. *Geneva, United Nations Economic Commission for Europe, Steering Committee on Education for Sustainable Development.[online]*

Emirbayer, M., & Mische, A. (1998). What is agency? *American journal of sociology*, 103(4), 962-1023.

Howells, K. (2018). *The future of education and skills: education 2030: the future we want.*

Jovanovic, J., & Devedzic, V. (2014). Open badges: Challenges and opportunities. In *Advances in Web-Based Learning–ICWL 2014: 13th International Conference, Tallinn, Estonia, August 14-17, 2014. Proceedings 13* (pp. 56-65). Springer International Publishing.

Kyguolienė, A., & Švipas, L. (2019). Personal entrepreneurial competencies of participants in experiential entrepreneurship education. *Organizacijų vadyba: sisteminiai tyrimai*, 82, 37-51.

Leinonen, T., Toikkanen, T., & Silfvast, K. (2008). Software as hypothesis: research-based design methodology. In *Proceedings of the tenth anniversary conference on participatory design 2008* (pp. 61-70).

Morgan, P. (2006). The concept of capacity. *European Centre for Development Policy Management*, 1(19), 826-840.

Mundial, G. B., & UNICEF. (2016). *Education 2030: Incheon declaration and framework for action: towards inclusive and equitable quality education and lifelong learning for all.*

OECD. (2018). *Preparing our youth for an inclusive and sustainable world: The OECD PISA global competence framework.*

Rieckmann, M. (2017). *Education for sustainable development goals: Learning objectives*. Unesco Publishing.

Stephanie, C. G., Riina, V., & Yves, P. (2017). *DigComp 2.1: The Digital Competence Framework for Citizens with eight proficiency levels and examples of use.*

Waychal, P. K. (2016). A framework for developing innovation competencies. In *2016 ASEE Annual Conference & Exposition*.

Wescott, G. (2002). Partnerships for capacity building: community, governments and universities working together. *Ocean & Coastal Management*, 45(9-10), 549-571.

Vlok, A. (2012). A leadership competency profile for innovation leaders in a science-based research and innovation organisation in South Africa. *Procedia-Social and Behavioral Sciences*, 41, 209-226.

PRIVACY CONCERNS DURING REMOTE EMERGENCY LEARNING IN HIGHER EDUCATION IN QATAR

Byrad Yyelland[1], Alan S. Weber[2], Robert Bianchi[1], Wajdi Zaghouani[3], Khawla Kittaneh[1], Ryad Ghanam[1], Selma Fejzullaj[1], Huda Iqbal[1] and Afreena Niaz[1]
[1]*VCUArts Qatar*
Doha, State of Qatar
[2]*Weill Cornell Medicine–Qatar*
Doha, State of Qatar
[3]*Hamad bin Khalifa University*
Doha, State of Qatar

ABSTRACT

The cultural norms involving privacy and online privacy in Qatar and the Persian (Arabian) Gulf are complex, based on both Sharia law and local Bedouin customs. Adding to the complexity of the topic is the demographic structure of Qatar: over 90% of Qatar's population consists of non-citizen expatriate workers and their families primarily from Asia, South Asia, and the Middle East comprising both Muslim-majority and non-Muslim-majority countries. The following chapter presents results, with a specific focus on privacy, of a mixed-methods longitudinal study on virtual learning environments in higher education in Qatar conducted from December 2020 to the time of writing. The goal of this research was to develop hypotheses and models about online privacy behaviors and attitudes in Qatar to assist instructors in understanding and respecting local privacy norms (the majority of higher education instructors in Qatar are non-Qatari), and to improve online student engagement and learning outcomes. Qualitative analysis of student focus group transcripts (n=95; 22 groups), expert faculty and student opinion, and a review of the current research literature revealed that: 1) privacy is a significant and pervasive concern in Gulf online educational contexts, especially for Muslim women, with an unexpected 'privacy paradox' 2) studying at home during government-enforced lockdown created novel privacy concerns (outsiders viewing the home and seeing and hearing other family members; and negotiation of private study / communal spaces within the home); 3) camera on/off policies and behaviors for synchronous learning precipitated complex and novel student behaviors; 4) dressing properly (modesty, hijab) for online classes was a concern specifically for Muslim women students; and 5) recording of lectures was a privacy concern for both faculty and students due to photography taboos in the Gulf related to tribal/family honor.

KEYWORDS

Online Learning, Education–COVID-19 Pandemic, Online Privacy, Gender, Persian (Arabian) Gulf, Qatar

1. INTRODUCTION

The cultural norms involving privacy and online privacy in Qatar and the Persian (Arabian) Gulf are complex, based on both Sharia law and local Bedouin customs. Adding to the complexity of the topic is the demographic structure of Qatar: over 90% of Qatar's population consists of non-citizen expatriate workers and their families primarily from Asia, South Asia, and the Middle East comprising both Muslim-majority and non-Muslim-majority countries. The following chapter presents results, with a specific focus on privacy, of a mixed-methods longitudinal study on virtual learning environments in higher education in Qatar conducted from December 2020 to the time of writing. The goal of the research was to develop hypotheses and models about online privacy behaviors and attitudes in Qatar to assist instructors in understanding and respecting local privacy norms (the majority of higher education instructors in Qatar are non-Qatari), and to improve student engagement and learning outcomes. Qualitative analysis of student focus group transcripts (n=95), expert opinion, and a review of the current research literature revealed that: 1) privacy is a significant and pervasive concern in Gulf online educational contexts, especially for Muslim women; 2) studying at home created novel privacy concerns (outsiders viewing the home and family members; and negotiation of private study / communal spaces within the home); 3) camera on/off policies for synchronous learning affected student behaviors; 4) dressing properly (modesty, hijab) for online classes was a concern for Muslim women; and 5) recording of lectures was a privacy concern for both faculty and students. A 2022 study surveying the opinions of five expert online instructors in higher education in Qatar confirmed some of the results of this study; for example, "organizing personal learning spaces at home was challenging due to strong privacy customs among Gulf Arabs and large family units sharing space" (Kittaneh et al., 2022, p. 8195).

Qatar is a small water-scarce desert peninsula in the Persian Gulf with a single land border with Saudi Arabia. Islam (predominantly Sunni, with small populations of Shia, Ibadis, and Ismailis) is the state religion and the country is ruled by a hereditary monarch from the Al Thani royal family along with an appointed / elected *majlis al-shura* (advisory council). The Human Development Index of Qatar was .855 in 2021, ranked 42nd in the world and 3rd in the Arab-speaking world (UNDP, 2023). According to the World Bank, Qatar is one of the wealthiest countries in the world, with a GDP per capita (PPP) of 102,018 USD in 2021 (World Bank, 2023). The enormous wealth of Qatar derives almost solely from its vast oil and natural gas reserves (3rd largest gas reserves after Russia and Iran). Up until 2000, Internet usage in Qatar was virtually non-existent. However in 2004, IctQatar was established as the internet regulation and development arm of the State of Qatar. This ministry along with the state-owned telecom and Internet Service Provider Ooredoo.com (formerly Q-Tel) began investing billions of dollars in fiber optic cable, broadband and mobile networks, and cloud computing, as well as e-learning software and Learning Management Systems and e-curricula such as the custom-built K-Net platform and E-Schoolbag (Weber and Hamlaoui, 2018, pp. 239-40). Even before the remote emergency learning transition necessitated by the COVID-19 pandemic in 2020, hybrid learning became a common learning modality in Qatar during the past decade.

2. BACKGROUND

In an early criticism and warning about the impact of the Internet, Roger Clark argued that, "Cyberspace is invading private space" (p. 60) and he recommended governmental oversight on the basis that, "the threats it embodies for individuals' interest in sustaining private space are severe" (p. 67). Oversight from the state became a reality in Qatar in 2016 when the Personal Data Privacy Law was introduced (Law No. 13, 2016). This law focuses on privacy of data but extends to include parental rights to delete information posted by their children if the parents deem this information is appropriate or that the youth have been sharing too freely. That same year, Abokhodair and colleagues published an analysis of privacy on Twitter in Qatar. They noted that within Qatar and across the countries of the Gulf Cooperation Council (GCC), "privacy is highly gendered, such that the specific requirements for privacy differ greatly between males and females" (p. 75). Second, personal privacy includes both what people share of themselves and what is shared by others. Third, one's personal privacy should be protected even after death, and fourth, that all of this has emerged from the cultural values of Islam. The Quran specifically recognizes personal privacy as a core human right and recommendations include, "Do not spy on one another" (49:12) and, "Do not enter any houses except your own homes unless you are sure of their occupants' consent" (24:27). The Qur'an and *Hadith* (the words of the Prophet Mohammed) form the basis for Sharia law, which is "the legal framework of most Middle Eastern countries" (El-Taweel, 2019, p. 26), including Qatar where Sharia law governs personal, family, and social relations with other areas such as business and banking governed by a civil code. Gulf culture and social structures themselves, not always precisely synonymous with Islamic ethical values or Islamic culture, add another layer of complexity to privacy in Qatar.

Abokhodair and colleagues (2016) noted that within this cultural milieu, privacy is essential in regard to the home, gendered spaces, and the individual. As seen in other areas of the world, privacy of one's property is considered crucial, as is privacy for the individuals housed within that property. In examining architecture of the traditional Qatari home, Mohannadi and Furlan (2022) found that, "in domestic architecture, privacy is one of the most predominant factors in determining the internal configuration of houses" (p. 264). For example, in alignment with Islamic and Arab principles, traditional home design in Qatar ensures privacy from external view. Home privacy is further enforced externally through gates and walls, and internally through differentiation of specific areas for specific activities and people. "The purpose is to protect the sanctity – or *hurma* – of the house and the body" (Abokhodair and Vieweg, 2016, p. 674).

This brings us to the second feature of privacy within Islam and Qatar, gendered areas within the home. The home provides a physical manifestation of Qatari culture through provision of much greater privacy for women than is afforded to men. The degree of gender separation within the home varies across Muslim cities around the world, but the authors determined that "Qatar is a traditional Muslim country and is a gender-divided society" (p. 266), and thus, gender division is built into the very framework of the Qatari home. Some spaces within the home are designated female-only or male-only, providing deeper levels of privacy within the home. As seen through Goffman's (1959) dramaturgical perspective, there are distinct and explicit separations between front and back stages within the Qatari home, and these separations are multilayered, as in separation from outside viewers and even from family members of another gender within the home.

Abokhodair and Vieweg (2016) explain this gender separation through the Muslim emphasis on modesty. "Presenting oneself as modest, in both dress and behavior, is of great importance to being a respectable member of Gulf society, and privacy plays an important role in how modesty and respect are maintained" (p. 674). To enter a room without permission risks exposure of the inhabitant's *awrah*, the intimate parts of the body. In relation to women, the concept of awrah extends beyond the sexual organs to include the body from hair to legs, sometimes the face, and has been associated with the traditional view of women as weak and vulnerable (Weber, 2010). Awrah also applies to men, the region between the navel and knee, which should be covered. Another concept – *ird* - translates as 'honor' and is a foundational value across the GCC. Protecting familial honor is paramount to Muslims and is manifested in almost every facet of life across the GCC. One can readily see how awrah and ird speak to powerful and deeply rooted norms regarding the sanctity of personal privacy, especially for women, and corresponding gendered restrictions on dress, behavior and visibility, whether in-person or online.

Foreigners from outside the GCC might have difficulty understanding such beliefs. It is important to understand that Arab Gulf culture is far more collectivist in nature than Western cultures (Weber, 2014). As noted by Abokhodair and Vieweg (2016), "Membership in a family and tribe are of the utmost importance; there is no individual separate from a family" (p. 673). Thus, protecting one's personal modesty and the modesty of others in the family is crucial to collective family honor within the community. To bring shame to the family or tribe is a significant transgression.

> Islam places great importance on blood ties and family relations (*silat ur-rahm* in Arabic). This value includes maintaining a good relationship with one's relatives, to love, respect and help them. The importance of this value has generated a society that is highly collectivist in nature (Abokhodair, et al., 2017, p. 699).

GCC culture in general, and Qatari society specifically, are similar to other Eastern cultures in this regard. Intercultural ethicist Ralph Capurro notes that whereas Western cultures define privacy in terms of individuality and something substantive to be protected regardless of situational context, these ideas are more fluid and relational in the East (as seen in Capurro's analysis of Japanese culture) where subjectivity "is not permanent, but dependent on situations and networks of relationships" (2015, p. 38).

In Qatar, as in Saudi Arabia, taking photographs of women in public is considered taboo. One must first seek permission from the woman and others who might appear in the picture because of concerns that photos of women could end up online and in so doing bring shame to their family and tribe. There are cases where women have been blackmailed over photos that were not sexual in nature but might show them in ways that are not in alignment with strict religious or social norms (Abokhodair, et al., 2017). Islamic culture places the same level of importance on protecting the honor and reputation of family members as it does on protecting them from physical harm.

This can also be traced to Qatar's cultural history of tribal allegiances. Abokhodair, et al. (2017) argue that within this highly relational culture, social media users bifurcate their online identities into an autonomous self who acts independently and a collective self that functions within familial and cultural norms and values. Congruent with cultural norms of modesty and honor, it is the latter that is more likely to be shared with a larger social audience because for users of social media: "In a collectivist-oriented society, not only is seeking parental approval expected, but approval from the larger extended family is also common" (Abokhodair et al., 2017, p. 704). In light of the preceding discussion, it is apparent that collective approval is even more paramount for young adult women.

In the context of such deeply rooted and wide-spread cultural restrictions on online behavior, it is significant that a 2019 Masters thesis study in Qatar found evidence of "the privacy paradox" (El-Taweel, 2019, p. 31), in which Internet users express fears and concerns about lack of online privacy but they do virtually nothing to protect themselves. This study found that a

> majority of respondents indicated that privacy is "very important" to them in the digital world and that it is of great concern to them. However, the majority of respondents also indicated that they have not followed the news of any of the recent scandals, involving major technology companies that they use daily. An even lesser number of respondents indicated that they were worried enough about the situation that they have taken any action to further protect their privacy (El-Taweel, 2019, p. 65).

One wonders, then, where female university students situate themselves on the continuum between powerful cultural and religious norms and the privacy paradox.

3. METHODOLOGY

This research employs a triangulated mixed-method strategy with five sources of data: thematically coded student focus group interviews, a questionnaire with Likert-scale and open-ended questions, direct query of an expert faculty group (combined years of online teaching experience = 36) and student researchers to refine coded themes, a background anthropological / sociological review of the literature on privacy in the Gulf, and the experiences of the Co-PIs as higher education instructors in Qatar (combined years of experience = 111). From December 2020 to October 2022, 95 higher education students (78 female, 15 male, 2 gender not reported) from 8 HEIs in Qatar participated in 60-minute student-moderated focus groups. Faculty researchers were not present in the focus groups to increase the candidness of the responses.

Participants were recruited through convenience (snowball) sampling, and the final sample roughly matched the demographics of Qatar (CIA World Factbook, 2023). However, females were over-represented in the sample, and participants from the national university Qatar University were under-represented. The average focus group size was 5.5 participants, and 21 groups were conducted in English, and 1 in Arabic (total 22 groups). The semi-structured interview guide contained one open-ended question on privacy. Text transcripts of the audio-recorded focus groups were analyzed in NVivo 12 release 1.7 (4839) qualitative analysis software using word frequency charts, key word searching, hand-written notes, and single-coder iterative thematic coding in NVivo based on Grounded Theory (Glaser and Strauss, 1967; Charmaz et al., 2020). This standard inductive process starts from cleaning and transcribing the interviews, where patterns begin to emerge to the researcher (hand notes), and is then followed by word frequency analysis to identify further potential themes; next, the analysis proceeds to formal coding in the qualitative analysis software. Representative participant statements from the themes are then correlated with the other data sources to build hypotheses about the operational principles of online privacy behaviors and attitudes in higher education settings in Qatar. These hypotheses are subsequently tested by re-reading the transcripts and searching for the operational principles in specific statements of the respondents, or correlating them with other online privacy research findings from the published literature, or from the pedagogical expertise of the researchers. As the data was collected primarily during the COVID-19 pandemic period, in which all schools in universities were closed except for limited circumstances from March, 2020 until spring semester 2021, findings related to mental health, isolation, and socialization cannot be easily disentangled from the other variables.

4. RESULTS AND DISCUSSION

The major themes and subthemes identified by the qualitative analysis along with their descriptions appear in Table 1 below. In this section, each theme is discussed by contextualizing it within the other data sources.

Table 1. Themes and descriptions from qualitative analysis of student focus groups, 2020-2022 (n=95; 22 groups)

THEME	Description	Subtheme	Description
Studying at Home	During enforced quarantine, all students in Qatar from 2020-21 attended class online from their homes, dormitories, or hotel rooms	**Outsiders' access to home**	Via camera or audio in synchronous classes, others can possibly view the home environment / see and hear other family members
		Family relations in home	Negotiation of communal and private study spaces within family homes
Camera On/Off	Video camera policies, behaviors relating to camera use		
Attending Class in Bed	Self-explanatory		
Dressing Properly	Appearing on camera in professional dress and modest Muslim dress (females only)		
Recording Lectures	Issues related to video/audio recording, screen shots, Gulf photography taboos	**Students record professor**	Self-explanatory
		Professor records students	Self-explanatory

4.1 Studying at Home

'Studying at Home' was the most discussed and nuanced theme in the transcripts (89.5% of the student respondents commented on this theme, with responses typically reaching 1-2 full length paragraphs). This theme was often associated with pandemic-related concerns such as disruption of normal patterns of life, developing new and unhealthy schoolwork/eating/sleeping/recreation routines, lack of socialization, demotivation towards schoolwork, and mental health problems such as anxiety, stress and depression.

One student expert (Research Assistant studying online learning) commented,

> Within Qatar's context, privacy concerns that arose during remote online learning fell under universally shared experiences, concerning primarily the lack of self-motivation and environmental hindrances. One of the main concerns expressed by students is related to physical issues, specifically communal home environments shared with family, which made it difficult to find a private space to study in....Additionally, students' lack of motivation to clean up their surrounding environment, find a suitable location/ backdrop, make themselves presentable (dress up and wash their face), and stay interested to learn and focus (away from distractions) were all leading factors.

To the question "in my WORST online course, I felt motivated to participate in the class" with the five-point Likert scale '*strongly disagree–strongly agree*,' 39.1% of focus group respondents *disagreed* and 26.3% *strongly disagreed* with this statement. Similar responses were obtained from a related question about student motivation in their BEST online class, indicating a generalized strong lack of motivation to engage in online classroom activities during the pandemic. Corresponding online difficulties experienced by faculty in Qatar have been reported in Bianchi et al. (2023). Two important subthemes regarding online privacy and the home environment only incidentally linked to the pandemic, discussed below, emerged from the data.

4.1.1. Outsiders' Access to the Home Environment

Although most videoconferencing software used in education now allows blurring of backgrounds or the use of virtual backgrounds, this was not the case for some of the learning platforms required by Qatar's HEIs in the early stages of pandemic remote emergency learning. For example, Cisco Webex only introduced privacy features such as virtual backgrounds and background blurring in mid-2020, *after* the first semester of emergency remote learning in Qatar had concluded (Techradar, 14 July, 2020). And up until 2021, virtual backgrounds were only available in the Microsoft Teams desktop app, not the mobile version. The virtual background feature was not available in the MS Teams mobile app for Apple devices (iPad/iOS) (Microsoft Corp., 25 January, 2021).

In addition, faculty and students may not have been aware of these privacy features when they became available, or how to use them, potentially exposing the students' home environments to faculty and other students in the cases of required camera-on policies, or when students felt pressure to keep their cameras on to gain participation points for the class. Also, even with cameras off, when turning on microphones to speak in class, students could potentially expose the private conversations within the household.

One of the authors reported the recurrent and representative anecdote below related to privacy of the home environment.

> One time I had a male student attending class online and the place where he had the strongest internet at home was al-majlis (this is a detached room from the rest of the house where the male guests are usually received in Qatari homes). He was in general a very active student but one time he just disappeared in the middle of our 3-hour class. He later on messages me saying that he had to exit the class Zoom because his father and uncle came into the majlis. He said that not only was he unable to participate, but he also wanted to respect the privacy of his female classmates who were participating and had their cameras on. This happened with several students, especially at the beginning of the lockdown, when I had students unable to turn on their cameras or even their mics to participate because they were in quarantine and had to share hotel rooms with family members. Many of them had to participate via chat only, because they had people chatting around them.

Experiences like this highlight the significant impact of cultural norms about privacy, modesty and respect.

4.1.2 Family Relations in the Home

As noted in the background section regarding Qatari home interior architecture and living spaces, although living spaces are often segregated as male/female, paradoxically *within* those gendered sections there is often a reduced need for personal privacy. For example, in the female section of the household, it is common for women to uncover among themselves, even with unrelated female guests; doors are often open and unlocked and family members of the same gender move freely throughout the spaces, including bedrooms and the majlis. In fact, the complaint that other family members were constantly "barging into my room" while a student was attending class online was frequently voiced in the focus groups.

As a communal culture with deep-rooted *beddu* customs of desert hospitality and mutualism, Qatari Arab families value family time together and the concept of being alone has been traditionally associated with shunning, or the fear of accidental abandonment or separation (an individual separated from the tribe in the harsh desert environment of the Gulf would have a very low probability of survival). Regarding the negotiation of communal and private study spaces in the home, one representative observation by a female student revealed a typical balancing act between studying at home and finding time to meet expected family responsibilities to be part of the family unit:

> So balancing time to sit with my family or my friends, aside from focusing on my studies and stuff, that was a bit of a challenge, because even if the learning experience took the entire day, you'd still have to find the time to sit with your family. And I think it was a bit difficult to convey that message to them.... it was a bit difficult for me to tell my parents, like, if I don't sit with you, it's not because I want to stay alone, it's because I'm occupied. That was the challenge for me.

Another respondent added,

> when you're at home, obviously you're living with your parents and then it becomes like one of those things where you're obviously not on your own personal schedule. You have to, you know, align to everybody else's needs as well, which is perfectly fine and reasonable from their side. But at the same time, it can cause, like, you know, difficulties with your own schedule academically.

4.2 Camera On/Off

Camera usage in online classes was the second most popular topic related to online privacy discussed by the participants, with 71 references to cameras. This subject merits its own focused research study within the Gulf context due to, among other contextual variables, the complex relationship of Gulf Muslims with images of the human form, believed to be *haram* (forbidden) by some conservative muftis of the Hanbali and Salafi *madhhabs* (schools of thought) of Sharia law popular on the Arabian peninsula. In addition, there are many possible explanations for not turning on cameras which do not involve privacy concerns, including lack of engagement and interest in a course, opportunity to engage in other activities such as games or social media, necessity to sleep, lack of motivation to wash and put on appropriate clothing, and competing family responsibilities. Also, one researcher was informed by a student that there were cases of students who began the course with their cameras on, but who were bullied by the others to turn them off.

A student researcher who coordinated and moderated many of the focus groups for this study reported that, based on her work with the respondents and cleaning the subsequent transcripts,

> one key concern [during remote emergency learning] was camera usage in online classes. Students did express a clear disinterest in turning their cameras on and sharing their home space with their peers and instructors. For many, it not only felt like an invasion of privacy, but was very confusing. During the period, the home, and for a majority, the bedroom, became the office, classroom or work area. What was once an intimate space to unwind and let go became an environment that required constant grinding and a lot of (digital) socializing. Turning on the camera was essentially an invitation for strangers to enter that sacred place. Therefore, a lot of students felt more comfortable with their cameras off because it gave them the chance to behave naturally in their personal space, without worrying about their background, work area or way of dress.

The widespread practice of turning off cameras during live online classes reported in the data may also have been related to bandwidth issues (lagging, frozen images) and not always to privacy concerns. Theoretically, Qatar is well equipped infrastructurally for virtual learning, with impressive ICT and broadband Internet indicators: in 2020, 99.7% of the population had access to the Internet (ITU, "Percentage," 2022) and 95.0% of the residents of Qatar had Internet service in their homes in 2020 (ITU, "Core indicators," 2022). However, 46.3% of focus group participants surprisingly reported technical issues in their online classes, typically lack of bandwidth; thus cameras were frequently deactivated to improve audio transmission rates. Camera policies generated lengthy and vigorous debates among administrators and faculty in all HEIs in Qatar, and privacy protections of students, particularly women, were key factors in these debates.

One student researcher (online education expert) indicated that keeping the camera off could in some instances not only protect privacy, but also afforded the positive benefits of reducing anxiety and facilitating better self-care for women,

> Since many students struggled to establish a daily routine to prepare for online classes, having the option and freedom to attend and participate without turning their cameras on helped them save time and effort. They did not feel the need to spend an extra 15 minutes in the morning to change their clothes, brush their hair, cover their head, or organize their desk. The flexible nature of this situation actually seemed to motivate students to attend online classes, for it allowed them to prioritize their wellbeing and comfort, away from gazing, judging eyes.

On the other hand, some students believed that keeping their cameras on would improve their learning: "I always felt I needed to [hold] myself accountable by opening my camera, by doing something to be engaged in a way so I didn't want [my] education just to go poof. Just because we were in an online situation." A frequent realization of students when they returned to face-to-face learning in 2021 was the unforeseen phenomenon that leaving their cameras off had prevented them from bonding with, or even recognizing, their peers and instructors,

> the majority of us don't even have our cameras on, right?....I wouldn't be able to form any strong connection with any of my classmates. Yes, we had a class group, and we used to talk and share ideas and help each other, but it was just, limited to that, there was nothing more than that, and especially also with the professors, I realize one thing when we now went back face-to-face, the majority of them, even though we were in their classes, they didn't recognize us. Because we didn't have our cameras on.

4.3 Attending Class in Bed

Since the bed and bedroom are typically some of the most private and intimate areas of the home, 'Attending class in bed' emerged as another privacy theme in the student responses. Demotivation to attend class due to COVID-19 challenges may have led students to utilize normally private spaces such as beds (with video cameras turned off) for academic work. The 'Attending class in bed' theme was commonly associated by students with laziness, lack of motivation, inability to separate work and study spaces, frustration, and resignation to the deficiencies in their online learning courses. Fatigue from increased workloads was frequently cited as the reason to remain in bed during the day.

However, the accidental activation of the camera button could have devastating consequences for a student taking classes in bed attending a mixed-gender class, particularly if a female student were inappropriately dressed. Mixed gender classes in fact are relatively new in Qatar, with Weill Cornell Medicine–Qatar holding the first non-segregated class in Qatar in 2001-2002. Qatar University still maintains its separate male/female campuses, and boys-only and girls-only schools are the norm in the government K-12 school system. In light of privacy issues and related online learning engagement concerns, the authors organized a one-day national online workshop on March 11, 2023 entitled "Effective Teaching Online for Faculty and Students" in which faculty participants brain-stormed a checklist for student success in virtual learning environments. The 16-item checklist entitled *Students: How to be an Effective Online Learner* was designed to be incorporated into syllabi and shared with students. Two items agreed upon by the workshop participants were: 1) "treat the online class as a formal class meeting (for example, not lying in bed, dressing in pajamas, etc.)"; and 2) "separate your work, leisure, sleep times and places – a dedicated desk only for classwork is a good idea."

4.4 Dressing Properly for Class

In Qatar almost all Qatari women, and most expatriate Muslim women, wear a full body covering (abaya, chador, or jilbab) as well as a head covering concealing the hair (shayla, khimar, or hijab). A small percentage of women wear a full-face veil (niqab or batoola). The rules and social norms for proper Muslim female dress in Qatar are taken very seriously and are universally understood by all residents, even non-Muslim expatriates.

Interestingly, dressing modestly for online classes using videoconferencing was not a major topic of discussion in the focus groups – with only 8 responses – and one might hypothesize this is due to the widespread and unquestioned adherence to modesty norms. Appearing modestly in all public contexts, including online classes, is expected and routine for Gulf women and therefore may not have been an area students felt necessary to mention. Although not represented prominently in the data (for the reasons hypothesized above), the researchers are confident from their knowledge of Gulf society that the following female student response represents a typical attitude of a university student who practices covering, "like I was[,] how did my hijab look, how with my hair showing, I was very scared .... if I had opened the camera and I wasn't wearing my hijab." An expert student researcher who assisted with this study and who worked closely with the focus group transcripts added (relating the camera usage issue to proper attire),

> Many students preferred not to open their cameras in order to not wear formal attire and go through the stress of being observed by their peers and professors. Many of them woke up five minutes before class, which gave them no time to prepare beforehand. Nevertheless, a lot of students started exploring camera filters, emoji reactions and zoom backgrounds to show their presence in the virtual classroom.

An unexpected response from one female Muslim student attending an online class with Muslim males raises the possibility that the unique and unprecedented circumstances of pandemic learning may have caused a temporary suspension of commonly accepted Gulf rules of modesty and privacy in some cases:

> our professors also required us to turn on our cameras, but my class majority is boys and so I'd wake up at 8am and I'd see them still in their sweatshirts and like, they obviously just woke up. So I was just like, 'O, look, and they're doing this. What's stopping me?' ....I'm like, it's mostly everyone's in their pajamas. I'm going to be in my pajamas. So I have my camera on....everyone would be in their pajamas. And I was just like *Khalas* [ok! / enough!] and then I'm going to be in my pajamas too."

One expert faculty member who reviewed the a-typical behavior described above, hypothesized (since family members and parents normally monitor and enforce modesty behaviors, along with self-monitoring) that "parents of students in particular were likely too busy managing their own lives and households during the pandemic to be concerned about camera use among their children."

4.5 Recording Lectures

4.5.1. Professors Recording Students

As mentioned in the literature review, photographing or videotaping a person (and particularly a woman) without permission in Qatari society is socially unacceptable due to the fears of image misuse. Female university students commonly request that their images not be used on university websites, or in yearbooks or newsletters. It is therefore imperative that HEIs and individual instructors formulate culturally-sensitive online classroom policies regarding camera usage, audio and video recording, screenshots and sharing personal information outside of the classroom.

4.5.2 Students Recording Professors

One expert faculty member expressed concerns about privacy invasion with respect to himself and his students when his lectures were recorded without consent (potential manipulation of information, misinterpretation or misuse of his teaching style and content),

> I had concerns related to video recording, as online teaching sessions can be recorded, which raises concerns about my own privacy. For instance, I feel uncomfortable with the idea of being recorded without my consent which happened at least twice to me as students did not think it was wise to ask for my permission to record the session as well as their peers. They said recording the session will make it easier for them to take notes later on. Another time, I learned from a student that she was recording some session (audio only) using her phone without the class consent. Personally, I don't want my teaching style to be publicly available without being prepared for it.

A second expert faculty member at another institution reiterated this point: "I was very careful with the content and material that I shared on Zoom because I didn't know for sure that my students are the only audience that could hear me or watch the videos I shared."

5. CONCLUSION

This research features an extensive and comprehensive analysis of student online learning experiences with respect to privacy during the COVID-19 pandemic in the Gulf nation of Qatar. The goal of this study was to develop hypotheses and models about online privacy behaviors and attitudes in Qatar to assist instructors in understanding and respecting local privacy norms (the majority of higher education instructors in Qatar are non-Qatari), and to improve student engagement and learning outcomes. The authors used a qualitative mixed-methods research design which revealed five predominant themes emerging from student focus group discussions: 1) privacy is a significant and pervasive concern in Gulf online educational contexts, especially for Muslim women; 2) studying at home created novel privacy concerns (outsiders viewing the home and family members; and negotiation of private study / communal spaces within the home); 3) camera on/off policies for synchronous learning affected student behaviors; 4) dressing properly (modesty, hijab) for online classes was a concern for Muslim women; and 5) recording of lectures was a privacy concern for both faculty and students. The authors believe this information is both timely and important within the highly technologically-oriented world of contemporary higher education. As one faculty expert concluded,

> to address [privacy concerns], it is important for instructors to implement policies and practices that respect students' privacy and confidentiality. For instance, we can provide guidelines on camera usage and background settings to ensure that students feel comfortable during online teaching sessions. Universities can also provide students with the option to turn off their cameras or use virtual backgrounds if they prefer not to show their home environments. Within the Gulf region context, it is

important for instructors to be culturally sensitive and respectful of students' privacy, religion, and values.

The topic of online privacy in higher education settings in Qatar and the Gulf region merits further detailed research. The authors encourage future researchers to investigate/address the areas listed above and to seek additional avenues of investigation including, but not limited to, the nature and impact of social class, individual personality types, geopolitical factors, and ongoing changes in transnational higher educations. Due to the complexity of the subject, qualitative research methodologies common to the fields of ethnography, sociology, anthropology, and cognitive psychology would fit well with some analyses and sophisticated quantitative analyses might be more applicable than others, such as in illuminating larger trends for more global comparisons.

Limitations of the study include: 1) data collection occurred during and after nation-wide government-enforced quarantine, and further comparison of the pre- and post-pandemic datasets should be carried out; 2) women were slightly over-represented in the sample; 3) the HEI Qatar University was under-represented in the sample; 4) wide variations occur in both personal and cultural views of privacy, and Qatar is an extremely ethnically diverse nation undergoing profound cultural, social and economic changes due to rapid population increase from expatriates, and large scale increases in GDP. Thus, some of the thematic trends uncovered in the study might not be generalizable to other socio-economic and cultural groupings of higher education students in Qatar.

ETHICS APPROVAL

This study was approved for human subjects research by the Institutional Review Boards (IRBs) of Hamad bin Khalifa University (IRB #2020-11-037) and Weill Cornell University – Qatar (IRB #20000-40) pursuant to the laws of the State of Qatar and the United States Federal Policy for the Protection of Human Subjects ('Common Rule').

ACKNOWLEDGEMENT

The authors would like to thank Fikria El Kaouakibi, Aia Zaina, Sara Mohammed Al Shafai, and Lolwa Al-Thani, who assisted in this research.

REFERENCES

Abokhodair, N. et al, 2016. Privacy and Twitter in Qatar: Traditional Values in the Digital World. *Proceedings of WebSci '16.* Hannover, Germany, pp. 66-77.

Abokhodair, N. and Vieweg, S., 2016. Privacy & Social Media in the Context of Arab Gulf. *Proceedings of DIS 2016.* Brisbane, Australia, pp. 672-683.

Abokhodair, N. et al, 2017. Photo Sharing in the Arab Gulf: Expressing the Collective and Autonomous Selves. *Proceedings of CSCW 2017*, Portland, United States of America, pp. 696-711.

Al-Hamar, M. et al, 2010. A Culture of Trust Threatens Security and Privacy in Qatar. *Proceedings of IEEE International Conference on Computer and Information Technology.* Bradford, United Kingdom, Vol. 2, pp. 991-995.

Al-Mohannadi, A. and Furlan, R. 2022. The Syntax of the Qatari Traditional House: Privacy, Gender Segregation and Hospitality Constructing Qatar Architectural Identify. *In Journal of Asian Architecture and Building Engineering,* Vol. 21, No. 2, pp. 263-283.

Al Qatawneh, I., et al, 2022. A Comparative Study on Surveillance and Privacy Regulations (the UAE vs. the USA and the EU). *In Journal of Governance and Regulation,* Vol. 11, No. 1, pp. 20-26.

Al-Sharim, H., 2021. *The Issue of Privacy in the Cloud: An Examination of the Law in Qatar.* Unpublished Master Thesis, International Law and Foreign Affairs, Hamad Bin Khalifa University.

Alshehri, T., et al, 2022. Designing for Culturally Sensitive Culture Change. *In Proceedings of DIS '22, Virtual Event.* Brisbane, Australia, pp. 599-611.

Bianchi, R., Weber, A., Yyelland, B., Ghanam, R., Kittaneh, K., and W. Zaghouani, 2023. Synchronous Conferencing Software-Assisted Teaching & Learning: Preliminary Lessons from an Inter-Institutional Faculty Group in Qatar. *In INTED2023 Proceedings*, forthcoming.

Capurro, R., 2015. Privacy. An Intercultural Perspective. *The Individual and Privacy*, The Library of Essays on Law and Privacy, Ashgate Publishing, NY, Vol. 1, pp. 37-47.

Charmaz, K., and R. Thornberg, 2021. The Pursuit of Quality in Grounded Theory, *In Qualitative Research in Psychology*, Vol. 18, No. 3, pp. 305-327.

CIA World Factbook, 2023. Qatar: People and Society. Retrieved from https://www.cia.gov/the-world-factbook /countries/qatar/#people-and-society

Clark, R., 1999. Internet Privacy Concerns Confirm the Case for Intervention. *In Communications of the ACM*, pp. 60-67.

El-Taweel, B., 2019. *Privacy Paradox: Online Privacy Behaviors and Attitudes in Qatar.* Unpublished MA Thesis, College of Humanities and Social Sciences, Hamad Bin Khalifa University.

Glaser, B., and Strauss, A., 1967. *The Discovery of Grounded Theory: Strategies for Qualitative Research*. New York, NY, Aldine de Gruyter.

Goffman, E., 1959. *The Presentation of Self in Everyday Life*. Harmondsworth, NY.

Kittaneh, K., Weber, A., Bianchi, R., Laws, S., Yyelland, B., 2022. Student Online Engagement in Qatar during COVID-19: Survey of Expert Opinion. *In INTED2022 Proceedings of the 16th International Technology, Education and Development Conference*, 7-8 March, 2022. Retrieved from https://library.iated.org/view/KITTANEH2022STU

International Telecommunication Union (ITU), 2022. Percentage of Individuals using the Internet, Qatar, Retrieved from https://www.itu.int/en/ITU-D/Statistics/Pages/stat/default.aspx

International Telecommunication Union (ITU), 2023. Core indicators on access to and use of ICT by households and individuals, Qatar. Retrieved from https://www.itu.int/en/ITU-D/Statistics/Pages/stat/default.aspx

Law No. 13 of 2016. *Promulgating the Protection of the Privacy of Personal Data Law*. Retrieved from https://cyrilla.org/en/entity/uw0qjkkrvnfy1wnqrf11yvi?page=1

Techradar, 14 July 2020. Cisco Webex finally lets you set virtual backgrounds. Retrieved from https://www. techradar.com/news/cisco-webex-finally-lets-you-set-virtual-backgrounds

UNDP, 2023. Human Development Reports. Table 1: Human Development Index and Components. Retrieved from https://hdr.undp.org/data-center/documentation-and-downloads

Weber, A., 2014. Sociocultural Dimensions of E-Learning in Emerging Nations. *In Proceedings of 2014 International Conference on Advances in ICT for Emerging Regions (ICTer)*, IEEE, Colombo, Sri Lanka, p. 254.

Weber, A., 2010. Woman, Islam, Silence. *In Proceedings of The Said & the Unsaid, International Conference on Language*, Vlore, Albania, pp. 32-40.

Weber, A., Hamlaoui, S., 2018. *E-Learning in the Middle East and North Africa (MENA) Region*. Springer, Germany.

The World Bank, 2023. Qatar. GDP per capita, PPP (current international $). Retrieved from https://data. worldbank.org/indicator/NY.GDP.PCAP.PP.CDC

TAP OR SWIPE: INTERACTION'S IMPACT ON COGNITIVE LOAD AND REWARDS IN A MOBILE MENTAL MATH GAME

Patrick Jost, Sebastian Rangger and Andreas Künz
Human-Centred-Technologies Research Centre, FHV University of Applied Sciences, Dornbirn, Austria

ABSTRACT

With the growing prevalence of mobile apps for self-directed learning, educational games increasingly find their place in everyday routines, becoming accessible to a broad audience. Despite the growing ease of content creation by artificial intelligence computing, the challenge of designing effective and engaging Serious Games remains, particularly in managing cognitive resources and ensuring quality engagement, notably influenced by the game's interaction modalities. This study explores these challenges within the context of a casual mobile mental arithmetic game, investigating the differential impacts of tap and swipe interaction variants on cognitive load and reward-based engagement. The study presents the findings of an international field study on Google Play. In a between-group design, the two casual interaction paradigms were compared regarding their impact on practice performance, cognitive load and effect on classic casual game rewarding represented through points, leaderboards and badges. The findings show that tap interaction can optimise cognitive load with a better mental math practice performance than the more indirect swipe gesture. A combination of elementary tap interaction with point rank and interaction precision badges indicates to enhance practice motivation. The results are synthesised into interaction design recommendations for casual mental math mobile games.

KEYWORDS

Mobile Game-Based Learning, Mental Math Training, Casual Game Interaction Design, Cognitive Load, Playing Engagement, Serious Game, Google Play Store, Field Experiment

1. BACKGROUND AND RESEARCH AIMS

The integration of engaging mobile apps for self-directed learning has become prevalent in educational practices, facilitated by advancements and increased accessibility of artificial intelligence (AI) technologies. AI enables swift, generative creation of visual and auditory representations, simplifying the development of educational games for platforms like the Google Play Store (Liu & Chilton, 2022; Anantrasirichai & Bull, 2022; Jost, 2021; Louie et al., 2020). Such game-based learning experiences can reach a broad audience, integrating learning into everyday routines, for example, as a time-filler activity during commutes (Grothues et al., 2022; Mäyrä & Alha, 2020).

Utilising free game assets and AI's generative potential, non-experts, including educators, can create casual learning games for essential skills like mathematics. Despite the developing ease of asset creation, challenges persist in creating effective and engaging Serious Games (SGs) that aim beyond entertainment (Dörner et al., 2016). Special attention must be paid to cognitive resources and the game's entertaining quality when designing mobile SGs for mental arithmetic expertise. Both aspects are influenced by a digital game's interaction modalities (Isbister & Hodent, 2022) and can thereby affect the game's efficacy and engagement quality.

Research indicates that, for example, the interaction in Virtual Reality (VR) mental math training games can impact cognitive load more than less physically demanding gestures on a mobile device (Jost et al., 2020; Sweller, 2020). However, impact differences on cognitive resources and rewarding between much more similar interaction variations on a smartphone device, such as touch tapping or swiping, are less researched in mental arithmetic practice games.

This paper's research investigates the potential differences between these interaction variants in a mobile mental math learning game designed for casual, self-directed playing. The study examined the effects of interaction on cognitive load and engagement through rewards between tap and swipe gestures in a mobile mental arithmetic game called "Mental Math Ball," created with free assets and published on the Google Play Store for a two-month field study.

1.1 Interaction and Rewarding in Educational Math Games

Casual games, characterised by simple rules, brief sessions, and the potential for rapid proficiency through moderate to high challenge levels, are popular among inexperienced players and all age demographics (Grothues et al., 2022; Juul, 2010; Pizzo, 2023). Research in math practice Serious Games (SGs) covers a broad range of scenarios to understand learning efficacy and engagement qualities. Simplistic and direct interaction paradigms have been found to be more effective learning approaches in SGs, avoiding extraneous cognitive load (Chatain et al., 2022; Jost et al., 2020).

While most math learning game studies focus on the personal computer platform and respective interaction paradigms (Pan et al., 2022), mobile learning is associated with positive effects on mathematics achievement (Güler et al., 2022). Detailed insights into different mobile interaction variants could help identify sources of extraneous cognitive load (Sweller, 2020) that impair learning efficacy or engagement quality.

Besides intrinsic motivation from playing a digital SG that inherently includes interaction variation, extrinsic rewards can enhance engagement. Simple reward strategies like points, badges, and leaderboards (PBL) are particularly suited to casual games (Y. Chou, 2019; Deterding, 2012; Sailer et al., 2017; Werbach & Hunter, 2015). However, their benefits on motivation and learning achievement are controversially discussed in educational scenarios. Points can enhance motivation by gauging progress and competence (Hamari et al., 2014; Mekler et al., 2017), badges provide visual proof of success and boost a sense of capability and autonomy (Abramovich et al., 2013; Nicholson, 2015), and leaderboards introduce a competitive aspect to invigorate students inclined towards social comparisons (Hamari et al., 2014; Landers, 2014).

PBLs, when combined as a rewarding system in math SGs, enhance performance and engagement by introducing competition, supporting narratives, and providing adaptivity (Ariffin et al., 2022; Atin et al., 2022; Ortiz Rojas et al., 2016). However, their effectiveness varies among students and can shift focus towards extrinsic rewards rather than intrinsic learning (Jagušt et al., 2018; Mekler et al., 2017; Nicholson, 2015; Sanmugam et al., 2016). Not achieving certain rewards can cause frustration, negatively affecting engagement (C. C. Chou & He, 2017; McDaniel et al., 2012).

PBLs can instil engagement by accomplishment through mastering SG challenges and allow for social influence when sharing badges or leaderboard states (Y. Chou, 2019; Isbister & Hodent, 2022). Expert control over interaction variation connects to these core motivational drivers. For a comprehensive investigation into the impact of common interaction paradigms in mobile math learning games, research must consider both interaction's effects on cognitive resources and on casual game rewarding systems.

1.2 Research Objectives

The focus of this research is consequently to investigate the impacts of common mobile interaction design paradigms, the tap and the swipe gesture, to learn about differences in cognitive load and effects on rewarding by a points, badges and leaderboard system. Using established measures of perceived cognitive load and in-game metrics that assess interaction efficiency and playing engagement by frequency of voluntary playing/replaying, a mobile research game is created and deployed in an international field test in the Google Play Store. The research objectives of this field study were thereby twofold:

1. Investigating the impact of tap versus swipe interaction paradigms on cognitive load and performance in a casual mental arithmetic practice game.
2. Investigating the impact of tap versus swipe interaction paradigms on extrinsic motivation by a PBL reward system in a casual mental arithmetic practice game.

2. EMPIRICAL RESEARCH APPROACH

2.1 Creating and Configuring the Mobile Mental Arithmetic Practice Game

The game Mental Math Ball (MMB) was developed as a smartphone game for Android using the Unity game engine. It features two different ways of interaction but has otherwise an entirely identical structure. Unity is a suitable choice for research work due to its extensive library of assets and the ability to publish cross-platform builds from a single code base. These freely available assets can also be combined and expanded with AI-generated content, making it useful for non-game experts in creating educational games. The main learning goal of MMB is to enhance mental arithmetic skills through step-by-step practice. It starts with basic operations such as addition and subtraction, progresses to multiplication and division, and later includes exponentiation and root extraction. The game's structure allows for alternating arithmetic tasks while maintaining a consistent level of difficulty within each level.

Table 1. Mental arithmetic exercises developed with upper secondary school mathematics teachers

Operation	*Range*	*Restrictions*	*Example*
Addition	Summands: 30 – 250	Max. summand = 250	235 + 34
Subtraction	Minuend, subtrahend between: 30 – 250	Max. minuend and subtrahend = 250	63 - 112
Multiplication	Factors between: 1 – 250	Max. multiplicand = 20; Product divisible by 10	120 x 15
Division	Dividend between: 1 – 250 Divisor between: 1 – 100	Max. divisor = 100; Without a remainder	192 : 96
Exponentiation	Base between: 1 – 30	Max. exponent = 2	8^2
Square root	Radicand: 1 – 900	Only integer results	$\sqrt{121}$

These mental arithmetic equations, developed with upper secondary math teachers (Table 1), structure practice objectives for 16+ learners across a progression of difficulty levels. The game includes visual and auditory feedback, with exercises divided into three levels: addition/subtraction, multiplication/division, and exponentiation/root extraction. To keep practices manageable and goal-focused on smartphones, each level lasts 2 minutes, with a complete round taking 6 minutes. This offers an efficient, progressive structure that suits a mobile learning environment.

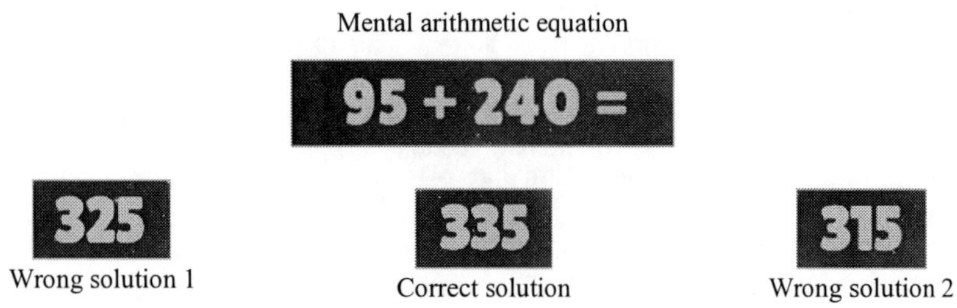

Figure 1. Addition task from the mental arithmetic game - Level 1.
Correct result and two slightly modified incorrect results

Figure 1 displays a level 1 arithmetic problem from the learning game, featuring three solutions - one correct and two modified. For addition/subtraction and multiplication, incorrect results varied by a randomly added number between -20 and 20. The correct solution's placement was also randomised. For low or single-digit results, common in division and root extraction, a number between -3 and 3 was added for closer approximations.

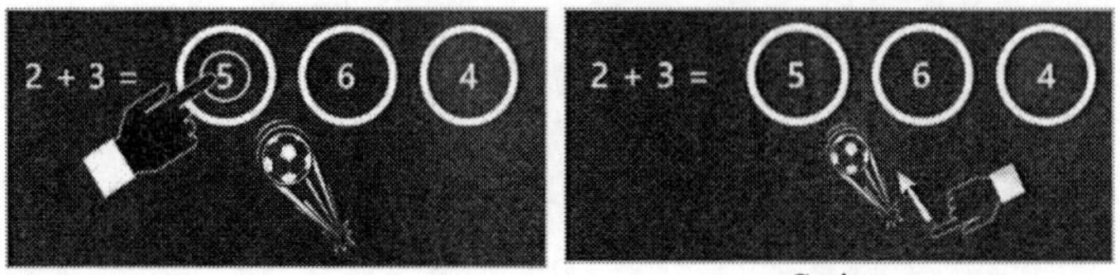

Tap Swipe

Figure 2. The game instruction illustrates and explains their respective interaction variant to the players. Group I (left) was explained the typing gesture, group II (right) the swipe interaction

In the actual practice phase of the learning game, elements of extrinsic motivation, such as the score display, are utilised. Initially, players are given a detailed introduction to the game mechanics, the learning objectives, and the manner of practising mental arithmetic. This also includes an explanation and illustration of the specific game interaction (Figure 2), scoring mechanics, and a description of the game levels. The introductory screen clarifies the individual arithmetic tasks, explains the three levels, their duration (2 min.), and the goal mechanism, which involves throwing the ball through the centre of the ring with the correct result, avoiding the two incorrect options. Scoring is established as gaining a point for correct results and losing a point for incorrect ones. From this screen, players can initiate the practice phase with an "Ok, let's play" button.

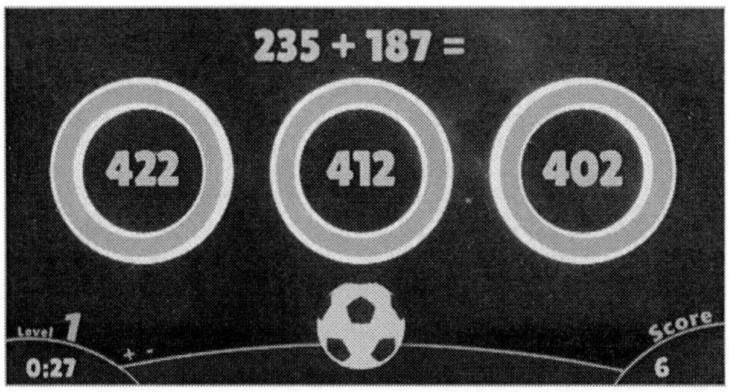

Figure 3. Mental Math Ball – addition in level one. Use of Unity's 3D engine with the soccer ball as a rigid body, realistic dimensions and mass, and eleven-metre distance to the goal rings

To maintain focus on the learning objective and minimise base cognitive load, the basic visual and auditory exercise scenario is deliberately minimalistic. A quiet, ambient night scene serves as the game's backdrop during the practice phase (Figure 3). The educational game leverages the 3D environment provided by the Unity game engine, which visually and physically simulates a three-dimensional world. The game environment incorporates the "rigidbody" component to implement spatial-physical conditions according to natural laws, allowing the ball to fly along a trajectory based on its mass and acceleration. The Unity engine interprets units as meters, facilitating the design of a realistic, three-dimensional scenario.

However, the first PBL element to be recognised in the practice phase is the scoring system, which, together with the structuring into levels, provides immediate feedback to players (Figure 3, bottom left and right). The point system connects the learning objective with the game objective by gaining a point for a correct calculation solution, but also deducting a point for an incorrect solution. The easily recognisable progress and the clear goal of achieving a high number of points fulfil general prerequisites for promoting motivation through the game activity (cf. flow theory; Nakamura & Csikszentmihalyi, 2020).

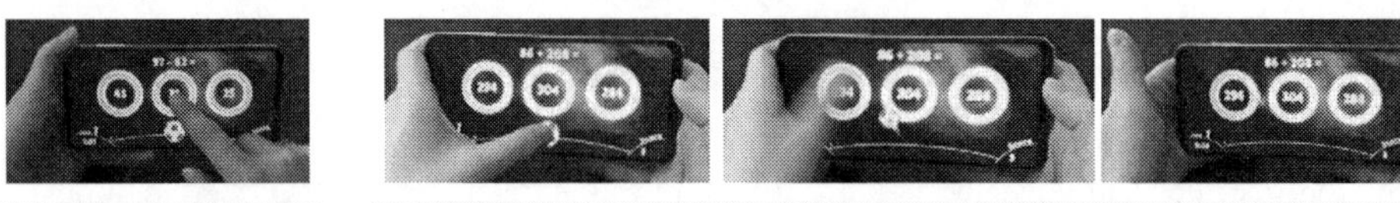

Tap Swipe

Figure 4. Illustration of the two interaction variants - tap and swipe - for throwing the ball into the goal with the correct calculation solution

Group I players use a tapping gesture to throw the ball at the correct mental arithmetic solution (Figure 4). The force of the throw is calculated based on the tap's location. Conversely, the swipe group 'kicks' the ball into the goal ring, with the trajectory determined by the swipe's speed and direction, using Unity's Rigidbody.AddForce(). The ball's specifications match an official FIFA soccer ball (size 5; 22 cm diameter, 450 grams), and its trajectory is computed by Unity's Nvidia PhysX Engine. Visual and audio cues provide feedback, and the game's performance is optimised for older smartphones. Invisible collider objects trigger scoring, animation, and precision calculation for the sniper badge reward.

2.2 Research Design, Hypotheses and Data Collection

The research design, as displayed in Figure 5, corresponds to a between-group field study for which each participant was randomly assigned to an interaction variant group. Group I was playing with the tap interaction, while Group II was assigned the swipe variant. Players stayed in their corresponding league also in potential replays of the game and were not aware of the existence of the other interaction variation.

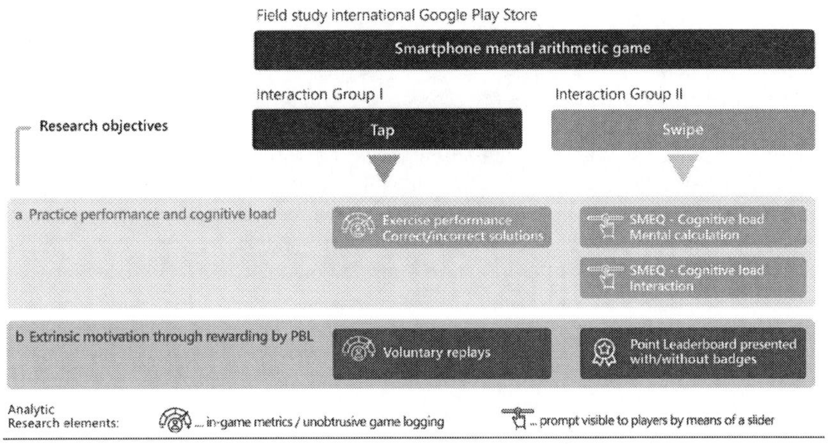

Figure 5. Experimental design for investigating interaction's effects in mobile mental math practice games

The MMB game recorded players' scores and the precision of throws, measured by the ball's distance from the ring's centre, unnoticeable for players during the practice phase (cf. stealth assessment; Ifenthaler & Kim, 2019; Ke & Shute, 2015). After this phase, players rated perceived cognitive load of the mental math equations and the interaction gesture individually via the Subjective Mental-Effort Question Scale (SMEQ), validated for reliability and sensitivity (Rubio et al., 2004; Sauro & Dumas, 2009; So et al., 2017; Verwey & Veltman, 1996; Zijlstra & Doorn, 1985), using a 0-150 slider input. Individual feedback on math equation and interaction variant informs about players' awareness of cognitive load origins and allows comparison with further interaction variations.

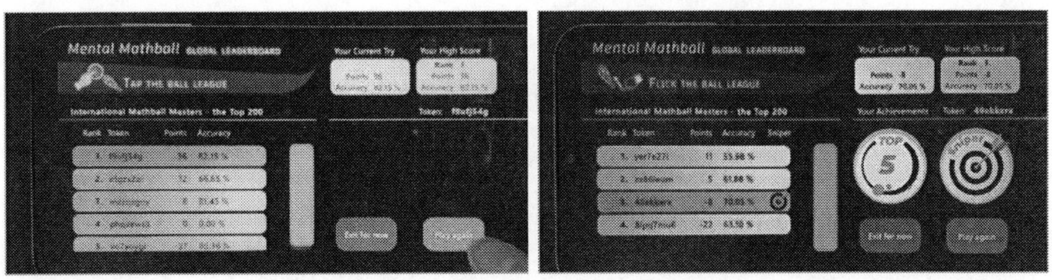

Figure 6. PBL reward system – point leaderboard and badges. Left: leaderboard of the tap gesture league without badge awarding. Right: the swipe gesture league in the variation with badge rewards (rank/sniper badge)

The SMEQ feedback was only displayed after the first game round and was required to access the leaderboard screen, showing the point leaderboard with or without badges. A condition randomly allocated at the game start and kept for players during all successive playing. If one was in the group showing badges,

badges were awarded for top 200, 100, 50, 10, and 5 ranks and for over 70% average hit accuracy as a sniper badge (Figure 6). From this screen, players could exit or voluntarily play another round, the latter being the metric to evaluate interaction variation impact PBL rewarding. In accordance with the research objectives, it was hypothesised that there would be a difference between the interaction groups regarding practice performance, cognitive load and effects on PBL rewards. Respectively, the null hypotheses for the field study were established as:

$H0_{a1}$: 'There is no significant difference in mental arithmetic practice performance between playing the smartphone mental arithmetic game using either tap or swipe gestures.'

$H0_{a2}$: 'There is no significant difference in the perceived cognitive load from solving the mental arithmetic tasks between playing the smartphone mental arithmetic game using either tap or swipe gestures.'

$H0_{a3}$: 'There is no significant difference in the perceived cognitive load from throwing the ball at the correct result between playing the smartphone mental arithmetic game using either tap or swipe gestures.'

$H0_{b1}$: 'There is no significant difference between the tap and swipe gestures in their effect on extrinsic rewarding through point leaderboards awarding no badges in the smartphone mental arithmetic game.'

$H0_{b2}$: 'There is no significant difference between the tap and swipe gestures in their effect on extrinsic rewarding through point leaderboards awarding rank and precision badges in the smartphone mental arithmetic game.'

The MMB game was internationally released on the Google Play Store for a two-month field study. An international Google Ad managed by the researchers adjusted daily budgets weekly between 70 to 280 NOK. Aiming for 300 valid unique plays per interaction group, we anticipated a 90% dropout rate, following trends in similar studies (Jost, 2021). The game was compatible with 4,493 devices and available in 177 countries. Players were informed about privacy, data collection, and research objectives before installation. Gameplay data, collected anonymously, referenced by a generated token and securely transferred via https, complied with EU General Data Protection. Only after informed consent could participants proceed to play the game.

3. RESULTS

3.1 Field Study Participation

In the two months, the game was installed by 11716 individuals on 1144 devices, with 99% on smartphones, and 1% on tablets. Of these, 892 played at least once, representing an expected dropout rate of 93%. Seven datasets were excluded due to non-serious attempts; three entries were removed due to interaction variant changes only possible through deleting and reinstalling the app. Valid participants included 757 who completed the first round and 135 who initially quit but later played valid rounds. Out of those completing the first round, 396 provided valid feedback. 152 inauthentic feedback entries, made only to access the leaderboard, were discarded. Such entries, identified from log analysis, showed setting min/max scale values in mostly three or fewer seconds while not reflecting on the questions.

Table 2. Participant distribution of the two-month field study

	n	*Quota*	*Tap*	*Swipe*
Installations from Google Play Store	11716	100%	-	-
Valid unique players	892	7.61%	-	-
Valid complete first round plays	757	6.46%	418	339
Valid feedback in the post-practice screen (SMEQ)	396	3.38%	225	171

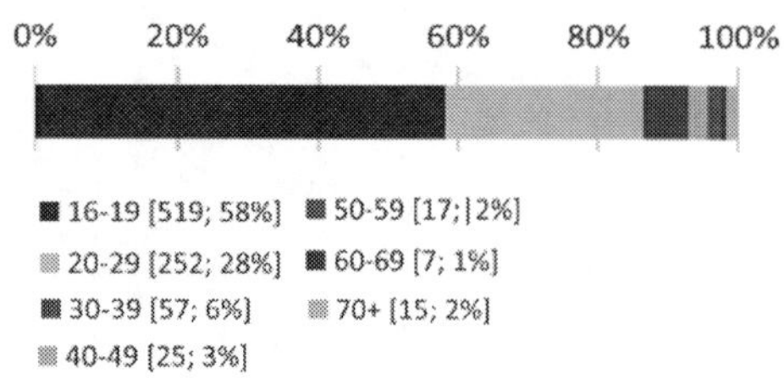

Figure 7. Distribution of valid participations by age group

Players' age group distribution (Figure 7) showed that over 50% of participants were under 20, and 86.5% were under 30 years old. This data, based on self-reports, is not verifiable for authenticity, but a mainly young audience is expected.

3.2 Interaction Impact on Math Practice Performance and Cognitive Load

The collected data did not show a consistent normal distribution for the dependent variables tested, according to Shapiro-Wilk (1965). Therefore, for the hypothesis tests of the analytical questions, the distribution medians of the groups (typing/wiping) were tested for differences using Mann-Whitney *U* analysis ($\alpha = 0.05$) as recommended by Field (2017). To address analytical question a, only first successful playthroughs ($n = 757$) were evaluated. This approach ensured comparison of interaction variants was free from hidden practice effects.

Table 3. Significant median differences in exercise performance between tap/swipe interaction. [*CI* = 95% confidence interval]

		Tap	*Swipe*	*U*	*z*	*p*	*r*
	n	418	339				
Total score	*Mdn*	19	11	55930.0	-5.0	< .001	-.18
	CI	18 – 21	10 – 13				
Correct solutions	*Mdn*	34	22	40039.5	-10.3	< .001	-.37
	CI	32 – 36	20 – 24				
False Solutions	*Mdn*	10	7	53046.5	-6.0	< .001	-.22
	CI	10 – 11	7 – 8				

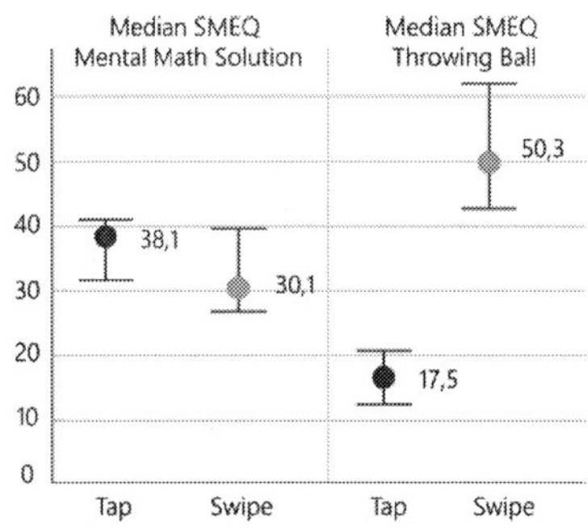

Figure 8. Significant cognitive load difference in throwing balls between interaction variants (right)

Statistical analysis revealed significant differences in practice performance between swipe and tap interaction groups in total points and correctly/incorrectly solved mental arithmetic tasks (Table 3). Those using swipe gesture had lower median performance (*Mdn* = 11) than the tap group (*Mdn* = 19). This extends to correct solutions, with the swipe group scoring fewer (*Mdn* = 22) than the tap group (*Mdn* = 34), while throwing fewer balls at incorrect solutions (*Mdn* = 7 vs. *Mdn* = 10). The effect sizes (*r*) for these differences were small, but a medium effect size (> 0.3) was indicated for correct solutions (Cohen, 1988; Field, 2017). Analysis of SMEQ feedback on perceived cognitive load (Figure 8; $n = 225$ tap; 171 swipe) showed the swipe interaction introduced significantly more perceived cognitive load (*Mdn* = 50.3, *CI 95%* = 41.9 – 61.8) than the tap interaction (*Mdn* = 17.5, *CI 95%* = 12.4 – 21.4), $U = 1128.2$, $z = 8.38$, $p = < .01$, $r = .42$. However, no significant difference in perception was observed in solving the math equation, $U = 17647.5$, $z = -1.41$, $p = .159$. Data analysis suggests rejecting H_{0a1} and H_{0a3} due to significant performance differences and differing cognitive load perception regarding interaction variant, while H_{0a2} is to retain as cognitive load of solving math equation was perceived not differently by both groups.

3.3 Interaction Impact on Extrinsic Motivation by PBL Rewarding

By statistical analysis of authentic game participations ($n = 892$), players who didn't receive badge rewards ($n = 511$) across tapping and swiping interactions were compared. The only reward for these players was a global leaderboard entry (Figure 6 left). Players who received badges were then also analysed regarding differences (n = 381) to evaluate the impact differences of interaction types on reward-based motivation introducing badges. These players could gain rank badges (leaderboard position) and sniper badges (precision of ball throwing), as shown in Figure 6 (right).

U-test analysis revealed that without badges, the tap interaction group replayed less frequently (*Mdn* = 1.00) than the swipe group (*Mdn* = 1.50). However, with badges awarded, tap group replay frequency increased (*Mdn* = 1.50), while the swipe group decreased (*Mdn* = 1.00), eliminating the significant difference (Table 4).

Table 4. Significant difference between tap/swipe interaction without rewards; no difference with performance and precision badges. [*CI* = 95% confidence interval]

	Tap [no badges]	*Swipe [no badges]*	*U*	*z*	*p*	*r*
n	289	222				
Mdn	1.0	1.5	26612.5	-3.7	< .001	-.16
CI 95%	1 – 1	1 – 2				
Maximum	115	39				
	Tap [with badges]	*Swipe [with badges]*	*U*	*z*	*p*	
n	186	195				
Mdn	1.5	1.0	35872.0	-1.39	.164	
CI 95%	1 – 2	1 – 2				
Maximum	149	24				

Statistical results suggest rejecting null hypothesis H_{0b1} due to significant differences in game repetition without badges. However, no differences were found when badges were used; thus, analysis suggests retaining H_{0b2}.

4. DISCUSSION

4.1 Implications for Interaction Design in Casual Math Practice Games

When interpreting the results regarding common interaction modality impact differences in mobile math practice games, two main design implications can be observed.

First, mental arithmetic practice games can be optimised regarding math training performance and cognitive load by preferring tap over swipe interaction. Confirming prior studies that investigated math training games with more diverse and complex interaction paradigms (Jost et al., 2020), the more direct interaction with fewer degrees of freedom proved to be more supportive for math practice in a learning game. While designing the interaction by tap gesture can, therefore, optimise cognitive load to focus on the math-solving problem, no considerable drawbacks to a casual game's practice motivation quality were found in this field study.

Second, combining simple tapping gestures with reward-oriented motivational drivers including badges, can augment engagement in casual mental arithmetic games. The simple executability of the tapping gesture proved well-suited to be combined with reward-oriented motivational drivers in the form of badges. For instance, a precision badge in mental arithmetic practice games, which, as in the present study, connects the interaction with the learning objective, can support playing engagement. Due to the low complexity of the tapping gesture, frustration caused by the interaction modality is more unlikely, and the incentive effect of the reward badges is in the foreground, helping to keep focus on the overall learning aim of gaining mental arithmetic expertise. In that, the results support the findings of previous studies raising awareness of negative impacts of frustration and distraction when introducing badges (C. C. Chou & He, 2017; McDaniel et al., 2012) by leading to consider less intricate interaction paradigms in casual mental math practice games.

4.2 Limitations and Further Research Trails

The study offered insights into interaction effects and research-oriented game design. Voluntary participation facilitated a valid sample in this international Google Play Store field study, though freedom brought limitations, such as participant uncertainty. The game, distributed internationally but only in English, may have been played by those who misunderstood instructions. Another limitation is the reduced control over game context; extreme values can be logged, but subtle contextual influences could affect group differences. Self-reported endgame analytics may contain untruthful responses. Future controlled studies should further explore these findings. The

Google Ads campaign and smaller ad budgets may have biased the sample nationally due to uncontrolled ad placements.

5. CONCLUSION

The reported result from the two-month field study confirmed previous studies that found impacts from interaction on cognitive load and practice performance in math training games. The study expanded towards investigating the detailed impact between the common casual mobile game interaction paradigms tap and swipe. During the two-month field study on the international Google Play Store, players of the mental math game perceived more cognitive load and had lower practice performance from interacting with the swipe gesture compared to the more direct tap interaction. Results also showed that while players with the tap gesture were initially less inclined to replay the game when only a leaderboard was shown for extrinsic motivation, introducing rank and interaction precision badges as rewards negated this disadvantage compared to the more indirect swipe gesture. Ultimately, the findings showed that less intricate interaction paradigms can be utilised for optimising math learning performance and cognitive load in casual mental math training games while not considerably impeding practice motivation. In particular, a combination with badges has shown to support motivational quality, improving replayability when utilising a tap interaction paradigm. Future studies are encouraged to investigate further combinatory pathways of elementary mobile interaction in combination with badge rewarding in casual mental math practice game scenarios.

ACKNOWLEDGEMENT

This research has been partially funded by the Austrian Research Promotion Agency FFG through the COIN Project SimLern, #898080.

REFERENCES

Abramovich, S., Schunn, C., & Higashi, R. M. (2013). Are badges useful in education?: It depends upon the type of badge and expertise of learner. *Educational Technology Research and Development*, *61*(2), 217–232.

Anantrasirichai, N., & Bull, D. (2022). Artificial intelligence in the creative industries: A review. *Artificial Intelligence Review*, *55*(1), 589–656. https://doi.org/10.1007/s10462-021-10039-7

Ariffin, N. A. N., Ramli, N., Badrul, N. M. F. H. N., Yusof, Y., & Suparlan, A. (2022). Effectiveness of gamification in teaching and learning mathematics. *Journal on Mathematics Education*, *13*(1), 173–190.

Atin, S., Syakuran, R. A., & Afrianto, I. (2022). Implementation of Gamification in Mathematics m-Learning Application to Creating Student Engagement. *International Journal of Advanced Computer Science and Applications*, *13*(7).

Chatain, J., Ramp, V., Gashaj, V., Fayolle, V., Kapur, M., Sumner, R. W., & Magnenat, S. (2022). Grasping Derivatives: Teaching Mathematics through Embodied Interactions using Tablets and Virtual Reality. *Interaction Design and Children*, 98–108.

Chou, C. C., & He, S.-J. (2017). The Effectiveness of Digital Badges on Student Online Contributions. *Journal of Educational Computing Research*, *54*(8), 1092–1116. https://doi.org/10.1177/0735633116649374

Chou, Y. (2019). *Actionable gamification: Beyond points, badges, and leaderboards*. Packt Publishing Ltd.

Cohen, J. (1988). *Statistical Power Analysis for the Behavioral Sciences* (2 Revised edition). Taylor & Francis Inc.

Deterding, S. (2012). Gamification: Designing for motivation. *Interactions*, *19*(4), 14–17.

Dörner, R., Göbel, S., Effelsberg, W., & Wiemeyer, J. (Eds.). (2016). *Serious Games: Foundations, Concepts and Practice*. Springer.

Field, A. (2017). *Discovering statistics using IBM SPSS statistics* (5th edition). SAGE Publications.

Grothues, H., Abney, A., & Boughter, R. (2022). Mobile Game Usability: Design and Research. In K. Isbister & C. Hodent (Eds.), *Game Usability: Advice from the Experts for Advancing UX Strategy and Practice in Videogames* (pp. 311–338). CRC Press.

Hamari, J., Koivisto, J., & Sarsa, H. (2014). Does Gamification Work? – A Literature Review of Empirical Studies on Gamification. *2014 47th Hawaii International Conference on System Sciences*, 3025–3034.

Ifenthaler, D., & Kim, Y. J. (2019). *Game-Based Assessment Revisited*. Springer Nature.

Isbister, K., & Hodent, C. (2022). *Game Usability: Advice from the Experts for Advancing UX Strategy and Practice in Videogames*. CRC Press.

Jagušt, T., Botički, I., & So, H.-J. (2018). Examining competitive, collaborative and adaptive gamification in young learners' math learning. *Computers & Education*, *125*, 444–457.

Jost, P. (2021, October 13). THE AGENT'S SMILE: IMPACTS OF ARTIFICIALLY GENERATED PEDAGOGICAL AGENTS ON RISK-TAKING. *18th International Conference Cognition and Exploratory Learning in Digital Age 2021*. IADIS International Conference Cognition and Exploratory Learning in Digital Age 2021. https://doi.org/10.33965/celda2021_202108L023

Jost, P., Cobb, S., & Hämmerle, I. (2020). Reality-based interaction affecting mental workload in virtual reality mental arithmetic training. *Behaviour & Information Technology*, *39*(10), 1062–1078.

https://doi.org/10.1080/0144929X.2019.1641228

Juul, J. (2010). *A Casual Revolution: Reinventing Video Games and Their Players* (1st ed). MIT Press.

Ke, F., & Shute, V. (2015). Design of game-based stealth assessment and learning support. In *Serious games analytics* (pp. 301–318). Springer.

Landers, R. N. (2014). Developing a Theory of Gamified Learning: Linking Serious Games and Gamification of Learning. *Simulation and Gaming*, *45*(6), 752–768. Scopus. https://doi.org/10.1177/1046878114563660

Liu, V., & Chilton, L. B. (2022). Design guidelines for prompt engineering text-to-image generative models. *Proceedings of the 2022 CHI Conference on Human Factors in Computing Systems*, 1–23.

Louie, R., Coenen, A., Huang, C. Z., Terry, M., & Cai, C. J. (2020). Novice-AI music co-creation via AI-steering tools for deep generative models. *Proceedings of the 2020 CHI Conference on Human Factors in Computing Systems*, 1–13.

Mäyrä, F., & Alha, K. (2020). Mobile gaming. *The Video Game Debate*, *2*, 107–120.

McDaniel, R., Lindgren, R., & Friskics, J. (2012). Using badges for shaping interactions in online learning environments. *2012 IEEE International Professional Communication Conference*, 1–4.

Mekler, E. D., Brühlmann, F., Tuch, A. N., & Opwis, K. (2017). Towards understanding the effects of individual gamification elements on intrinsic motivation and performance. *Computers in Human Behavior*, *71*, 525–534.

Nakamura, J., & Csikszentmihalyi, M. (2020). The Experience of Flow—Theory and Research. In *The Oxford Handbook of Positive Psychology* (Third Edition, pp. 279–296). Oxford University Press.

Nicholson, S. (2015). A Recipe for Meaningful Gamification. In T. Reiners & L. C. Wood (Eds.), *Gamification in Education and Business* (pp. 1–20). Springer International Publishing. https://doi.org/10.1007/978-3-319-10208-5_1

Ortiz Rojas, M. E., Chiluiza, K., & Valcke, M. (2016). Gamification in higher education and stem: A systematic review of literature. *8th International Conference on Education and New Learning Technologies (EDULEARN)*, 6548–6558.

Pizzo, A. D. (2023). Hypercasual and Hybrid-Casual Video Gaming: A Digital Leisure Perspective. *Leisure Sciences*, *0*(0), 1–20. https://doi.org/10.1080/01490400.2023.2211056

Rubio, S., Díaz, E., Martín, J., & Puente, J. M. (2004). Evaluation of subjective mental workload: A comparison of SWAT, NASA-TLX, and workload profile methods. *Applied Psychology*, *53*(1), 61–86.

Sailer, M., Hense, J. U., Mayr, S. K., & Mandl, H. (2017). How gamification motivates: An experimental study of the effects of specific game design elements on psychological need satisfaction. *Computers in Human Behavior*, *69*, 371–380.

Sanmugam, M., Abdullah, Z., Mohamed, H., Aris, B., Zaid, N. M., & Suhadi, S. M. (2016). The affiliation between student achievement and elements of gamification in learning science. *2016 4th International Conference on Information and Communication Technology (ICoICT)*, 1–4.

Sauro, J., & Dumas, J. S. (2009). Comparison of three one-question, post-task usability questionnaires. *Proceedings of the SIGCHI Conference on Human Factors in Computing Systems*, 1599–1608.

Shapiro, S. S., & Wilk, M. B. (1965). An analysis of variance test for normality (complete samples). *Biometrika*, *52*(3/4), 591–611.

So, W. K. Y., Wong, S. W. H., Mak, J. N., & Chan, R. H. M. (2017). An evaluation of mental workload with frontal EEG. *PLoS ONE*, *12*(4), e0174949. https://doi.org/10.1371/journal.pone.0174949

Sweller, J. (2020). Cognitive load theory and educational technology. *Educational Technology Research and Development*, *68*(1), 1–16. https://doi.org/10.1007/s11423-019-09701-3

Verwey, W. B., & Veltman, H. A. (1996). Detecting short periods of elevated workload: A comparison of nine workload assessment techniques. *Journal of Experimental Psychology: Applied*, *2*(3), 270.

Werbach, K., & Hunter, D. (2015). *The gamification toolkit: Dynamics, mechanics, and components for the win*. University of Pennsylvania Press.

Zijlstra, F., & Doorn, L. (1985). The Construction of a Scale to Measure Perceived Effort. *Department of Philosophy and Social Sciences*.

ARE NEWLY UNDERGRADUATES SELF-DIRECTED, RESILIENT, AND SKILLFUL DURING ONLINE LEARNING?

Mohd Tajudin Md Ninggal, Rohaizak Omar and Azleen Ismail
Open University Malaysia, Malaysia

ABSTRACT

First year university undergraduates' academic experience have always been an interesting topic of study. The main objective of the study was to seek a better understanding on the level of self-directed, resilience, and online study skills among first year undergraduates toward online distance learning during the COVID-19 pandemic. A total of 159 students who were selected through the purposive sampling method participated in the online survey. They answered two sets of instruments namely the Learner Personality Profile and Online Learning Skill that consisted of 60 items and 30 items respectively. Both instruments were measured based on a five-point Likert scales. Learner Personality Profile scales were measured based on (1) Never; (2) Rarely; (3) Sometimes; (4) Very Often, and (5) Always responses, while Online Learning Skills were measured based on (1) Strongly Disagree, (2) Disagree, (3) Neither agree nor disagree, (4) Agree, and (5) Strongly Agree responses. Findings of the study reported that female students' level of Self-directed scores (mean=3.06) were higher compared to male students' scores (mean=2.92) based on a three-level range of mean scores (low=1.00 to 2.33; average=2.34 to 3.67; and high=3.68 to 5.00). Female students' level of online study skills scores (mean=3.90) were also reported to be higher compared to male students' scores (mean=3.61). However, both male and female students reported average level of resilience scores (mean=3.21 and mean=3.33) respectively. The correlation analyses reported no significant relationships between self-directed, resilience, and online study skill. The multiple-regression analyses reported that the self-directed variable did not act as a mediating factor in the relationship between resilience and online study skills. In conclusion, the resilience factor among first year male and female undergraduates seemed to be a concerned issue that need to be addressed and further investigated by the university academic management.

KEYWORDS

Self-Directed, Resilience, Study Skill, Online Learning, Personality, COVID-19 Pandemic

1. INTRODUCTION

The global impact of the COVID-19 pandemic has been profound, particularly on the higher education systems. Universities swiftly adapted their teaching methods, shifting to online platforms to ensure safety. Online learning gained prominence as an alternative, offering flexibility and accessibility. Ensuring universal access to quality materials and active participation emerged as key concerns for universities. Students, particularly first-year undergraduates, grappled with adjustment issues, including emotional stress and academic struggles (Azahari et al., 2018; Azlan, et al., 2020; Gurbuz, 2014; Sad, Goktas, and Bayrak, 2014).

The drastic change of the traditional mode of tertiary learning has directly affected Malaysian newly undergraduates who are registering first time for their university studies. The sudden shift from traditional mode of learning to online learning disrupted their ability to function effectively within the university environment (Shazad et al., (2020). The COVID-19 pandemic reshaped education globally and underscored the importance of flexibility, support, and resilience within educational systems.

2. PROBLEM STATEMENT

Due to the COVID-19 pandemic, Malaysian universities indefinitely shut campuses. Classes transitioned online, including registration and communication via platforms like Google Meet and Zoom. This shift pressured students particularly those could not afford high specification smart phones, laptops or computers for online learning classes. They become more demotivated when they could not get access to online classes due poor internet connections from their own homes (Clark and Mayer, 2016; Kunjukunju, Yusof, and Ahmad, 2020)).

Ahmad and Reddy (2020) heightened stress among new undergraduates struggling to proficiently engage in online classes. Studies reported that the newly enrolled undergraduates suffer from reduced academic and social connections, affecting their purpose (Amantha and Al-Samarraie, 2019; Thomas, 2012). Online learning, conducted remotely, demands independent studying from home. Distractions due to poor home environments and familial interactions hinder learning (Albritton, 2003; Holcomb, King, and Brown, 2004; Sarker, 2020; Wang and Newlin, 2000). Self-directed is crucial for academic success and retention, frequently mentioned in online education studies (Moore and Kearsley, 2005; Thomas 2012; Atan and Rosli, 2019). Terrell and Dringus (1999) proposed self-directed students to be independent and successful. Contradictory outcomes on achievement and persistence in distance learning exist (Gibson, 2003, and Hussein, 2017).

3. LITERATURE REVIEW

Online learning has become a new approach in the university settings around the world since the onset of COVID-19 pandemic. This method has been widely used to cater educational needs in the various parts of the world prior to COVID-19 pandemic. This approach is gaining its popularity among universities and is expected to be the main approach in teaching and learning for many years to come (Ana, et al., 2020, and Cater, Michel, and Varela, 2012). The sudden transition in the mode of learning in the university system has taken many students, parents, and lecturers by surprise. Majority of students were taken aback and have impacted their sense of learning direction and self-resilience.

Ngampornchai and Adams, (2016), and Serebryakova (2016) reported numerous studies on human stress and lack of self-direction among students. Students reported having difficulty adjusting to new way of learning and feeling loss. Thomas (2012), and Amantha and Al-Samarraie (2019) reported countless number of studies has been carried out to understand more about the human stress and lack of direction as a factor that influence success of students under difficult condition.

Proficiency in computer use is vital for online learning (Maaruf and Teng, 2020; Chung, Subramaniam and Dass, 2020). A Cameroonian study revealed two-thirds of new undergraduates lacked familiarity with online learning, with 17% lacking computer ownership. Many African university students only use basic computer functions, leading to computer literacy and online learning anxiety (Uleanya and Ke Yu, 2019). A study conducted by Sandybayev (2020) reported that 70% of the total respondents of the first-year students experienced lack of coping ability and a sense of loss when it comes to online learning.

Self-directed can influence what we learn, how we learn and when we choose to learn (Bhuasiri, et al., 2012 and Schunk & Usher, 2012). Research reported that motivated learners are more likely to undertake challenging activities, be actively engaged, enjoy and adopt a deep approach to learning and exhibit enhanced performance, persistence and creativity (Ryan & Deci, 2000b).

It is undeniable that online learning is enjoyable to do for those who know how to adapt with it. Self-directed is a contributing factor in making students to enjoy online learning and is an 'engine' for learning as described by Paris and Turner (1994). Students with high level of self-direction are likely to take challenge and willing to learn new things that would lead to academic success as compared to students with low level of self-direction (Ryan and Deci, 2000; Sandybayev, 2020). According to Bekele (2020) and Shazad et al., (2020), there were reciprocal relationships between learning and self-directed and have been countlessly researched for traditional education setting.

Studies by Al-Rahmi et al., (2018) and Tinto (1975) reported that lack of self-directed was one of the factors contributing to higher dropout rates. In fact, the dropout rates were higher in online education setting than tradition setting (Harnett, 2016; Palanisamy and Balogun, 2017; Safiyeh, 2015). It was found that students could perform better academically outside traditional classroom setting when the online teaching or delivery is just as effective as face to face learning (Safiyeh, 2015). Carter, Michel, and Varela, (2012), and Deci and Flaste (1996) reported that online learners could also be intrigue by their peers' performances during the online learning activities (Shroff, Vogel, and Coombes, 2008).

Enriching online learning is crucial for fostering self-direction and resilience in first-year undergraduates. Effective online instructors need technological fluency and strong communication skills to encourage students' self-direction (Easton, 2003). However, insufficient tech skills can disrupt learning, affecting resilience and causing academic stress (Darabi, Sikorski, and Harvey, 2006; Easton, 2003).

4. RESEARCH OBJECTIVES

This research explored the relationships between online study skills, self-directed, and resilience constructs among first year undergraduates in one public university during the COVID-19 pandemic. The primary goal was to comprehend newly undergraduate students' viewpoints on their only study skills, self-direction and resilience during the online learning. The study established three key objectives as follows:

i. To measure the level of self-directed, resilience, and online study skills among first year undergraduates.
ii. To measure the relationships between self-directed, resilience and online study skills among first year undergraduates.
iii. To measure the mediating effects of self-directed towards resilience and online study skills among first year undergraduates.

5. RESEARCH METHOD

This section outlines the research methodology employed in this study.

5.1 Data Collection

Data were collected through online survey from full-time newly undergraduates from one public university in the east coast of Malaysia. These undergraduates were at their fourth week of the first semester (September 2020 intake). Two sets of online questionnaires (Online Learning Skill and Learner Personality Profile) formulated into the google form formats were distributed to identified students via email and WhatsApp. Students were given one week to answer the two sets of online questionnaires. The returned questionnaires were analysed using the SPSS software.

5.2 Participants

A total of 159 newly undergraduates participated in this study. They were chosen based on purposive sampling method whereby the researcher specifically chose newly undergraduates that are currently undergoing a degree course in counselling. These students were residing in all fourteen states in Malaysia. A total number of 24 (15%) males and 165 (85%) females responded to this study. They comprised of 149 (94.0%) Malays, 3 (2%) Chinese, and 7 (4.0%) other ethnic groups.

5.3 Instruments

Two sets of instruments were used in this study. The first instrument, Learner Personality Profile measured nine personality traits. It consisted of 60 items measured on a five-point Likert scales, (1) never; (2) rarely; (3) sometimes; (4) very often, and (5) always. However, for the purpose of this study, only two traits were chosen i.e., Self-directed and Resilience (Table 2.0). The second instrument, Online Learning Skill measured three constructs. It consisted of 30 items measured on a five-point Likert scales, (1) strongly disagree, (2) disagree, (3) neither agree nor disagree, (4) agree, and (5) strongly agree. The Cronbach's alpha reliability values for both instruments were reported at 0.93 and 0.95 respectively. In the Online Learning Skill instrument, only the Study Skill construct was used. Table 1 below listed the one construct under the Online Learning Skill instrument and two constructs under the Learner Personality Profile.

Table 1. Instrument and constructs chosen in the study

Instrument	Online Learning Skill	Learner Personality Profile
Construct	Study Skill*	Self-Directed*
		Resilience*

6. FINDINGS

This section reported the findings of the study based on the three research objectives as mentioned earlier.

6.1 Study Skills

Table 2 summarizes the respondents' Learning Skill. Respondents were required to indicate their level of Study Skill frequency listed in the questionnaire. They reported their frequency in Learning Skill on a five-point Likert scales from (1) Strongly disagree; (2) Disagree; (3) Neither agree nor disagree; (4) Agree; (5) Strongly agree. In this study, only the Study Skill construct was being studied. The mean scores reported on the Study Skill construct for male students was (mean=3.61) and for female students was (mean=3.61) respectively. In summary, female students reported a higher level of mean score on the Study Skill constructs as compared to male students.

Table 2. Respondents' learning skills level

Learning Skill	Gender	N	Mean Score	Std. Dev.	Level
Study Skill	Male	24	3.61	.665	Average
	Female	135	3.88	.421	High

The interpretation of the mean scores (1.00 – 2.33 = Low, 2.34 – 3.67 = Average, 3.68 – 5.00 = High) were adapted from Landell (2013).

Based on participants' responses, the data were analyzed and the mean score of each Learning Skill constructs are shown in the Table 3. It presents the summary of means for the Learning Skills constructs by making comparison between the mean score of male and female students. It was evident that most items have a mean score ranging between 3.61 and 3.94. An independent-samples t-test conducted found a significance difference in Study Skills Skill construct between male and female students, t (157) = -2.597, p=.010.

Table 3. Comparison of mean scores between male and female students

Learning Skill Constructs	Gender	Mean	t	df	Sig. (2-tailed)	Results
Study Skill	Male	3.6157	-2.597	157	.010	Significant difference
	Female	3.8836				
	Female	3.9443				

6.2 Personality

Table 4 summarizes respondents' two personality constructs measured. They are the Self-directed and Resilience. The respondents were required to indicate their level of personality frequency listed in the questionnaire. They indicated their frequency in personality on a five-point Likert scales from (1) Never; (2) Rarely; (3) Sometimes; (4) Very often; (5) Always. The interpretation of the mean score was adapted from Landell (2013) on the frequency of Learning Skill as shown in Table 4 above.

Table 4. Respondents' personality level

Personality Constructs	Gender	N	Mean	Std. Deviation	Level
Self-directed	Male	24	2.920	.4593	Average
	Female	135	3.063	.5845	Average
Resilience	Male	24	3.213	.4337	Average
	Female	135	3.332	.4772	Average

Based on participants responses, data were analyzed and the mean score of each personality constructs are shown in Table 4. It presents the summary of means for the personality constructs by making comparison between the mean score of male and female students. It was evident that personality on most construct have an average mean score. The mean score for each construct was between 2.186 and 3.436. The means and standard deviations of personality constructs were relatively similar for male and female students. However, on average, female students reported a higher mean score than male students.

Table 5. Comparison between the mean score of male and female students

Personality Constructs	Gender	t	df	Sig. (2-tailed)	Results
Self-directed	Male	-3.233	157	.001	Significant difference
	Female				
Resilience	Male	-1.141	157	.256	No Significant difference
	Female				

Table 5 presents the summary of t-test for the personality constructs by making comparison between the mean score of male and female students. An independent-samples t-test was conducted to evaluate the hypothesis that there is no significant difference in personality and constructs between group of men and women were found. The test was significant for self-directed t (158) = -1.141, p = .001. For other personality constructs, the results found no significant difference.

6.3 Correlation between Learning Skills and Personality

Table 6. Correlation between learning skill and personality

	1	2	3	4	5	6	7	8	9	10	11	12	13	14
Learning Skill	-													
Study Skill	0.84**	-												
Personality	0,50**	0.36**	0.42**	0.57**	-									
Self-directed	0.45**	0.38**	0.35**	0.52**	0.69**	-								
Resilience	0.46**	0.35**	0.37**	0.52**	0.86**	0.50**	0.55**	-0.14	0.59**	0.75**	0.78**	0.71**	0.67**	-

**Significance at level 0.01

*Significance at level 0.05

Table 6 presents the summary of correlation between Learning Skills and Personality constructs. The correlation between Learning Skill and Personality scores was found to be statistically significant, r (157) = .50, p < .01, two-tailed. For Learning Skill, the results suggest that 6 out of 6 correlations were statistically significant and were greater or equal to r (157) = +.35, p < .01, two-tailed. For personality, the results suggest that 36 out of 45 correlations were statistically significant and were greater or equal to r (157) = +.35, p< .05, two-tailed. In general, the results suggest that students who scored high on the personality construct tends to rate themselves as self-directed and resilience.

6.4 Self-directed as a Mediation Effect between Study Skill and Resilience

Figure 1 illustrated the conceptual mediation model to investigate whether the self-directed construct has an effect towards the relationship between Study Skill and Resilience. Self-directed and Study Skill acted the independent variables and Resilience acted as the dependent variable. A multiple regression analysis conducted reported a negative result (p=0.783) whereby the Self-directed construct did not carry an effect on the relationship between Study Skills and Resilience. Therefore, it could be concluded that Self-directed is not a mediating factor in the relationship between Study Skills and Resilience.

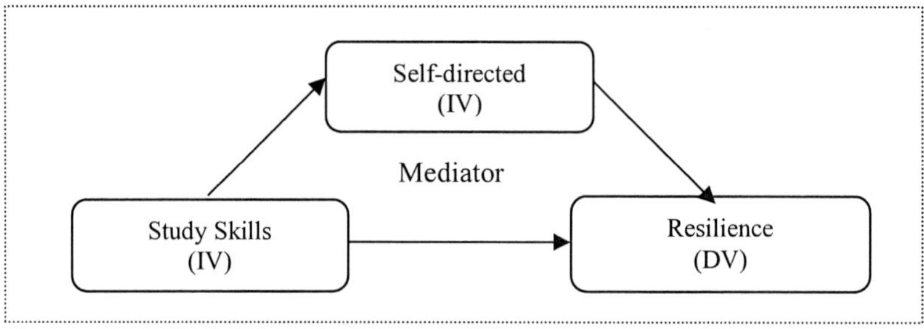

Figure 1. Conceptual Mediation Model

Table 7 shows the result analysis using multiple regression to investigate whether Self-directed construct could be a mediating factor towards the relationship between Study Skill and Resilience. The result p=.783 showed that there was no interaction between Self-directed construct and Study Skill that would affect the Resilience.

Table 7. Analysis using multiple regression

Resilience	Coefficient	t	p	R2	Adjusted R2	F
Model with mediation effect						
Constant	5.06	1.18	.240	0.10	0.08	5.61
Study Skill	-0.92	-0.82	.413			
Self-directed	-0.15	-0.12	.909			
Interaction	0.09	0.28	.783			

7. DISCUSSION

This study addresses three key research questions. It reveals that female students exhibit greater self-direction in online learning than males. Resilience issues arose among male students during remote study, attributed to factors like lack of direction, stress, fatigue, low confidence, and inadequate online skills. Existing research links home learning environment, connectivity, tutor-student dynamics, subject readiness, content, technical support, and students' personalities to resilience levels (Ahmed and Reddy, 2020; Ana et al., 2020).

The study reported a significant relationship between self-directed and resilience. Female students reported higher level of self-directed as compared to male students when conducting their online studies from home. However, both male and female students reported low level of resilience when comes to online learning. Despite a significant relationship reported between self-directed and resilience among male and female students, self-directed was not a mediating factor that contributed towards the relationship between online study skill and resilience among first year undergraduates.

This study offers five key recommendations. Firstly, universities should engage and support students online learning. Secondly, assessing students' preparedness for online learning is vital. Many newcomers lacked readiness due to the abrupt transition caused by the pandemic. Thirdly, university counselors play a crucial role in providing guidance and intervention for students struggling with direction and resilience during remote learning. Students should seek counselling if their resilience is compromised. Fourthly, the student learning center can enhance the learning experience, especially for those struggling with online study skill. Lastly, online lecturers or tutors play a pivotal role. Universities must ensure they are proficient in online learning system, possess strong communication and coaching skills, and are a student-oriented. These five recommendations are crucial for delivering quality and student-centric online education to newcomers adapting to remote learning from home.

8. CONCLUSION

The research findings offered insights into the states of online study skills, self-direction, and resilience among these students. Remarkably, the study discovered that self-direction did directly impact students' resilience during online learning from home. Furthermore, the self-directed variable did not act as a mediator between online study skills and resilience. The study emphasizes the need for further exploration of resilience levels among undergraduates engaged in remote learning, regardless of gender. These findings contribute to the fields of counselling, educational psychology, and higher education.

ACKNOWLEDGEMENT

The authors would like to acknowledge the contributions of the journal advisors, chairpersons, editorial board members and the respective international offices for their continuous support. In addition, the authors would like to thank the OUM Centre for Research Institute (CRI) for granting a research grant to conduct this study.

REFERENCES

Ahmed, S.S. and Reddy, S.C., 2020. Preferred Learning Style and Study Characteristics among Undergraduate Clinical Medical Students: A Study in National Defense University of Malaysia. *Journal of Advances in Medicine and Medical Research*, *32*(19), pp.51-60.

Albritton, M.D., 2003, November. The moderating effects of a technology-mediated learning environment on student locus of control, conscientiousness, satisfaction and performance. In *Southern Management Association 2003 Meeting* (p. 447).

Al-Rahmi, W.M., et al, 2018. Use of e-learning by university students in Malaysian higher educational institutions: A case in Universiti Teknologi Malaysia. *Ieee Access*, *6*, pp.14268-14276.

Amantha Kumar, J. and Al-Samarraie, H., 2019. An investigation of novice pre-university students' views towards MOOCs: the case of Malaysia. *The Reference Librarian*, *60*(2), pp.134-147.

Ana, A., Minghat, A.D., et al, 2020. Students' Perceptions of the Twists and Turns of E-learning in the Midst of the Covid 19 Outbreak. *Romanian Journal for Multidimensional Education/Revista Romaneasca pentru Educatie Multidimensionala*, *12*.

Azahari Ramli, D., et al, 2018. Mediating role of E-learning resources in developing entrepreneurial inclinations amongst undergraduate students at Universiti Utara Malaysia. *International Journal of Engineering & Technology*, *7*(4.7), pp.51-56.

Azlan, C.A., et al, 2020. Teaching and learning of postgraduate medical physics using Internet-based e-learning during the COVID-19 pandemic–A case study from Malaysia. *Physica Medica*, *80*, pp.10-16.

Bekele, T.A., 2010. Motivation and satisfaction in internet-supported learning environments: A review. *Journal of Educational Technology & Society*, *13*(2), pp.116-127.

Bhuasiri, W., et al, 2012. Critical success factors for e-learning in developing countries: A comparative analysis between ICT experts and faculty. *Computers & Education*, *58*(2), pp.843-855.

Cater III, J.J., et al, 2012. Challenges of online learning in management education: An empirical study. *Journal of Applied Management and Entrepreneurship*, *17*(4), p.76.

Chung, E., et al, 2020. Online learning readiness among university students in Malaysia amidst COVID-19. *Asian Journal of University Education*, *16*(2), pp.45-58.

Clark, R.C. and Mayer, R.E., 2016. *E-learning and the science of instruction: Proven guidelines for consumers and designers of multimedia learning*. John Wiley & sons.

Creswell, J.W. and Poth, C.N., 2016. *Qualitative inquiry and research design: Choosing among five approaches*. Sage publications.

Deci, E.L. and Flaste, R., 1996. *Why we do what we do: Understanding self-motivation*, NY: Penguin.

Gibson, C.C., 2003. Learners and learning: The need for theory. *Handbook of distance education*, *147*, p. 160.

Gurbuz, F., 2014. Students' Views On Distance Learning In Turkey: An Example of Anadolu Universıty Open Education Faculty. *Turkish Online Journal of Distance Education*, *15*(2), pp. 239-250.

Harandi, S.R. (2015) "Effects of e-learning on Students' Motivation," *Procedia - Social and Behavioral Sciences*, 181, pp. 423–430. Available at: https://doi.org/10.1016/j.sbspro.2015.04.905.

Hartnett, M. and Hartnett, M., 2016. The importance of motivation in online learning. *Motivation in online education*, pp. 5-32.

Holcomb, L.B., et al, 2004. Student traits and attributes contributing to success in online courses: Evaluation of university online courses. *The Journal of Interactive Online Learning*, *2*(3), pp. 1-17.

Hussein, Z., 2017. Leading to intention: The role of attitude in relation to technology acceptance model in e-learning. *Procedia Computer Science*, *105*, pp.159-164.

Kunjukunju, A., et al, 2020. Quality of experiences (QOE) with e-learning among nursing students in a private healthcare university setting in Malaysia. *The Malaysian Journal of Nursing (MJN)*, *12*(2), pp.98-105.

Ma'aruf, M.N. and Teng, P.K., 2020. Understanding students' behavioural intentions to use e-learning system in higher education institution in Klang valley, Malaysia. *BERJAYA Journal of Services & Management*, *6*, pp.3-15.

Moore, M.G. and Kearsley, G., 2011. *Distance education: A systems view of online learning*. Cengage Learning.

Ngampornchai, A. and Adams, J., 2016. Students' acceptance and readiness for E-learning in Northeastern Thailand. *International Journal of Educational Technology in Higher Education*, *13*(1), pp. 1-13.

Palanisamy, S. and Balogun, N.A., 2017. Antecedents to Effective E-Learning among Selected Secondary Schools in Malaysia. *Ilorin Journal of Computer Science and Information Technology*, *2*(1), pp. 108-130.

Paris, S.G. and Turner, J.C., 1994. Situated self-directed, In P.R. Pintrich, D.R. Brown & C.E. Weinstein (Eds.), *Student self-directed, cognition, and learning: Essays in honor of Wilbert J. McKeachie*, pp. 213-237. Hillsdale, NJ: Lawrence Erlbaum.

Ryan, R.M. and Deci, E.L., 2000. Self-determination theory and the facilitation of intrinsic motivation, social development, and well-being. *American psychologist*, *55*(1), p. 68.

Sad, S.N., et al, 2014. A comparison of student views on web-based and face-to-face higher education. *Turkish Online Journal of Distance Education*, *15*(2), pp.209-226.

Safri, S.N., et al, 2020, April. Conceptualization of MOOC E-Learning Service Quality Dimensions in Faculty of Hotel and Tourism Management, UITM, Malaysia. In *3rd Asia Pacific International Conference of Management and Business Science (AICMBS 2019)* (pp. 268-271). Atlantis Press.

Sandybayev, A., 2020. The impact of e-learning technologies on student's motivation: Student centered interaction in business education. *International Journal of Research in Tourism and Hospitality (IJRTH)*, *6*(1), pp. 16-24.

Sarker, S.K., Naik, D.G., Elnajeh, M. and Vong, H.Z., Perceptions of medical students' about learning pharmacology by using website developed by faculty in a Medical School of Malaysia.

Schunk, D.H., et al, 2014. *Self-directed in education: Theory, research, and applications*, Boston, MA: Pearson.

Serebryakova, T.Y.A., et al, 2016. Emotional Stability as a Condition of Students' Adaptation to Studying in a Higher Educational Institution. *International Journal of Environmental and Science Education*, *11*(15), pp. 7486-7494.

Shahzad, A., Hassan, et al, 2021. Effects of COVID-19 in E-learning on higher education institution students: the group comparison between male and female. *Quality & quantity*, *55*, pp. 805-826.

Shroff, R.H., et al, 2008. Assessing individual-level factors supporting student intrinsic motivation in online discussions: A qualitative study. *Journal of Information Systems Education*, *19*(1), p. 111.

Terrell, S.R. and Dringus, L., 2000. An investigation of the effect of learning style on student success in an online learning environment. *Journal of Educational Technology Systems*, *28*(3), pp. 231-238.

Thomas, L., 2012. Building student engagement and belonging in Higher Education at a time of change. *Paul Hamlyn Foundation*, *100*(1-99).

Uleanya, C. and Yu, K., 2019. Resilience: Solution to learning challenges amongst rural African undergraduates. *Gender and Behaviour*, *17*(2), pp. 12921-12935.

Wang, A.Y. and Newlin, M.H., 2000. Characteristics of students who enroll and succeed in psychology web-based classes. *Journal of educational psychology*, *92*(1), p. 137.

THE IMPACT OF A PROJECT-BASED LEARNING ENVIRONMENT ON THE DEVELOPMENT OF UNDERGRADUATE STUDENTS' DIGITAL LITERACY SKILLS

Ourania Miliou and Charoula Angeli
Department of Education, University of Cyprus
The Crosspoint Building
Corner of Kallipoleos and Hypatia 1
Nicosia, 1071, Cyprus

ABSTRACT

In recent decades, the research community has focused on younger generations' technology readiness, known as The Digital Natives Debate. At the higher education level, this debate led to studies on the quality of digital technology use among undergraduate students. However, empirical investigations on how digital literacy programs can support students' academic practices are still lacking. This paper presents the results of a project-based learning approach in higher education to enhance digital literacy skills in teaching. The findings demonstrate large effect sizes in favor of operational, information-navigation, social, creative, and critical skills, providing evidence that project-based learning can significantly improve digital literacy skills and support academic learning in higher education.

KEYWORDS

Project-Based Learning, Learning Environments, Higher Education, Digital Literacy Skills

1. INTRODUCTION

During the past decades, the research community has been exploring the attributes of younger generations with a focus on technology readiness through an ongoing dialogue known in the literature as "The Digital Natives Debate" (Bennet et al., 2008; Corrin et al., 2010; Judd, 2018; Evans & Robertson, 2020). This dialogue concerns the nature of skills that young people possess for the effective use of digital technologies, and how such skills can contribute to policy reform in education. In academic settings, this debate refers to whether younger generations, who have grown up and socialized using digital technologies, can use such technologies effectively for academic purposes (Judd, 2018; Evans & Robertson, 2020).

Specifically, the term "digital natives" has been attributed to young people due to their continuous immersion in technology. Growing up in a globally connected world where the Internet has always been accessible (Seemiller & Grace, 2016), young generations tend to rely on digital media to search for information, stay up-to-date, and engage in social interactions through platforms like social networking services in their daily lives (Ng, 2012; Kennedy & Fox, 2013). In academic settings, the effective use of digital technologies includes the selection and use of mobile devices, software, and multimedia tools with a critical perspective by evaluating their contribution to academic work (Alexander et al., 2017). However, the unquestioned assumption that students already bring advanced technological skills due to prior use of digital technologies may have real implications for the learning practice by "*leaving learners unsupported and technologies inappropriately aligned with learning needs and contexts*" (Smith et al., 2020, p. 10).

Relevant studies indicate that university students are not aware of the enabling capabilities of digital technologies in learning (Ståhl, 2017; Leijon et al., 2022). Namely, previous research has shown that young people easily adapt to the use of the Internet at a technical level (e.g., accessing services, connecting to a WiFi network) (Ng, 2012; Kennedy & Fox, 2013), are very familiar with the use of technologies for communication purposes (Gosper et el., 2013; López-Meneses et al., 2020). However, they seem to experience difficulties using tools and services for online information search and evaluation (Hargittai et al., 2010; Head, 2013; Neumann, 2016; Weber et al., 2018; Breakstone et al., 2018) and content creation (Ng, 2012; Kennedy & Fox, 2013; López-Meneses et al., 2020). In general, research indicates that informal experiences with digital technologies do not necessarily suggest that undergraduate students can use such technologies for academic purposes (Margaryan et al., 2011; Kennedy & Fox, 2013; Ståhl, 2017).

Another challenge that needs to be considered in the digital natives' dialogue and for which scholars have yet to reach a consensus refers to the development of new instructional strategies that educators can utilise to reach digital natives (Evans & Robertson, 2020). It is therefore essential to provide sound theoretical frameworks and assessment processes that will assist higher education institutions in forming policies and training resources for students (Litt, 2013). Several researchers suggested that learning through technology can be supported by the design of constructivist learning environments (Vannatta & Beyerbach, 2000; Jonassen, Mayes, & McAleese, 1993; Jonassen, 1999; Duffy, & Cunningham, 1996). Project-based learning is one of the most widely applied *"constructivist compatible instructional practices"* (Ravitz, Becker, & Wong, 2000) which has been used to transform teaching and learning in higher education (Gülbahar, & Tinmaz, 2006; Lasauskiene & Rauduvaite, 2015; Lee et al., 2014; Shpeizer, 2019; Guo et al., 2020). Taking into account the above, the present study reports on the effects of a project-based learning environment on undergraduate students' digital literacy skills in a university setting.

2. THEORETICAL FRAMEWORK

2.1 Conceptualization of Digital Literacy Skills

In recent decades, the ability to use digital tools has been associated with the term digital literacy, which was introduced by Paul Gilster in 1997 and has been linked to understanding and using information from a variety of digital sources (Bawden, 2008). Later conceptual investigations concluded that digital literacy is broad and includes various aspects of different concepts with a focus on different skills sets (Ala-Mutka, 2011). The present study focuses on the skills to use the Internet since the Internet is the primary medium that students use to access course materials and other information resources, communicate with their peers and professors, and conduct coursework (Kennedy & Fox, 2013; Gosper et al., 2013). Specifically, the study adopted the theoretical framework proposed by Van Dijk and Van Deursen (2014), which categorized digital literacy skills into six areas: Operational, Formal, Information, Communication, Content creation, and Strategic skills. Operational skills are basic technical skills required to use the Internet, such as using browsers to access web applications. Such skills allow a person to use digital tools to complete tasks, such as filling input information into fields or pages, and downloading and saving files. Formal skills relate to navigating the Internet hyperlinks, such as identifying where a website is located, and recognizing how to navigate to a website without feeling disoriented. Information skills refer to navigating various websites with different layouts and searching, selecting, and evaluating online information to achieve a specific objective. Communication skills relate to using online communication services to interact with others, construct, understand, and exchange meaning, create online profiles and identities, and engage in online collaboration. Content creation skills are the skills someone needs to create different types of good quality digital content, including text, images, and sound, in various formats, and, publish or share it with others on the Internet. Lastly, strategic skills relate to the fulfillment of personal goals through the use of the Internet, namely moving toward a specific goal, making the right decisions toward fulfilling a goal, and securing the benefits of using the Internet.

2.2 Project-Based Learning in Higher Education

While higher education institutions have welcomed the integration of digital technologies in teaching and learning, the predominant approach for the selection and use of digital tools in teaching has been technology-led. This approach often neglects to assess whether these tools align with anticipated learning outcomes, despite students expressing a preference for digital technologies that add value to their learning process rather than being used merely because they are available (Gosper et al., 2013; Kirkwood & Price, 2014). Therefore, it is necessary for educators *"to have knowledge of the affordances the various technological tools offer that are beneficial for their own teaching and for their students' learning*" (Ng, 2012). Additionally, while universities rarely make the necessary distinction between the individual needs of students (Jørgensen, 2019), although prior studies have shown that both the level of students' digital skills and their degree of familiarity with digital devices and tools vary (Selvyn, 2009; Helsper & Eynon, 2010; Hargittai, 2010; Corrin et al., 2010; Ståhl, 2017). To adequately address the instructional needs of digital natives, higher education institutions must invest in the deliberate design of learning experiences that consider the aforementioned factors.

In this context, integrating project-based learning approaches can offer distinct advantages. Project-based learning asserts that learning is an active process of building meaning through experiences (Gülbahar & Tinmaz, 2006; Leijon et al., 2022). This method promotes the combination of action and learning and encourages the transfer of prior knowledge during the project implementation process (Wobbe & Stoddard, 2023). Students have a central role in project-based learning, while the instructor is a facilitator (Shpeizer, 2019). The whole process of developing a project enhances autonomous learning, as the form of the final project is determined by the learners, who decide about what actions need to take to complete it (Lasauskiene & Rauduvaite, 2015). Such process makes engagement with the project attractive and feasible, especially at older ages where the acquired knowledge is somehow connected to the professional field and the project is developed individually (Larmer et al., 2015). Prior studies have documented the effectiveness of this method in enhancing skills in higher education (Lee et al., 2014; Guo et al., 2020). The framework for creating a project includes the central theme and goals of the project, which need to be attractive and feasible, the main products or deliverables that need to be produced and published, as well as an action plan of the process that learners need to follow to complete the project with success (Guo et al., 2020).

3. METHOD

3.1 Project-Based Learning Design

In this study, a 13-week project-based learning intervention was conducted as part of an elective course. The intervention consisted of three-hour weekly teaching sessions. The central focus of the project was the creation of a blog, with students having the freedom to choose their own topics. During the development of their projects, students were progressively engaged with digital technologies in a series of activities to enhance their digital literacy skills. The activities contributed to completing the final deliverable of the blog while enabling the transfer of knowledge to the academic environment. The digital technologies that supported the project's development were selected based on their affordances to enhance students' digital literacy skills. The affordances were considered based on the tools' potential to support access, retrieval, and evaluation of information (e.g., internet browsers, search engines, cloud services), communication and collaboration (e.g., social networking services, online content sharing), and content creation (e.g., multimedia, presentation software). The project design is presented in Table 1.

Table 1. Project-based learning design to support digital skills development in academic settings

Blog creation	Digital skills to support the creation of the blog (project)	Academic affordances
Topic selection Blog's title and purpose Registration to a blog service Poster creation and welcoming message Adjust the privacy settings	*Operational skills* The blog is stored in the bookmarks of the computer browser used by each student. Keyboard shortcuts are used to create hyperlinks embedded in the text, refresh the browser session to display changes, and split the screen, among other functionalities. Online forms are used to register for the blog's service or other tools' services. The blog includes multimedia content that the user has edited from ready-made images (posters). The blog includes a multimedia library (e.g., images, gifs). The blog's visibility settings (Public / Private) have been edited. Cookies are enabled so that the blog's address remains in the browser history and passwords are/are not stored.	Organize academic work using bookmarks (e.g., creation of course folders) Reduce the execution time of a task by using keyboard shortcuts (e.g., refresh, restore, open/close browser tabs). Efficient use of cloud technology services to organize and store work and other documents (e.g., collaborative editing and sharing of documents). Successful completion of a registration form in the online services of the University or other useful services which support academic work (e.g., verify registration, create a digital backup).

Blog creation	Digital skills to support the creation of the blog (project)	Academic affordances
		Protection of personal data and privacy in the academic environment (e.g., apply extra protection layers).
Create a list with future posts	*Information-Navigation skills* The blog is structured in Sections. There are tags for easy access to the blog's content.	Navigation to websites and databases with academic content (e.g., apply keyword search, use indexes/directories).
Create and upload the blog's logo Upload images, GIFs, banners, and videos free from copyright to the media library	The recent posts are displayed for easy access to the blog's content. There is a "Search" function. *Creative skills* The blog includes multimedia content that the user has edited from ready-made images (e.g., posters).	Use different search tools to meet specific information needs when performing a task (e.g., access open license content).
Upload relevant informational articles, digital resources, and other materials Use a reference system to cite the blog's material Use the tags and the recent posts function to organize the material	*Information-Navigation skills* There are keywords that describe the content of each blog post (tags). There are articles about the blog. The blog includes multimedia content that is not subject to copyright restrictions (e.g., copyright, citing or referencing omissions). *Critical skills* The articles include reliable information.	Optimization of the information search processes to find academic material (e.g., use of information retrieval strategies, such as filtering). Identify keywords to search for specific content (e.g., use synonyms). Use different search tools to meet specific information needs when performing a task (e.g., use multimedia databases). Evaluate the suitability of online resources for academic purposes (e.g., utilize checklists with evaluation criteria). Evaluate the suitability of online multimedia content for academic purposes (e.g., apply reverse image and video search strategies).
Upload a Creative Commons Licence	*Creative skills* The blog includes a license for copyright protection.	Securing the copyright of the author of an academic work/publication on the Internet (e.g., use online licenses).
Link the blog to personal and/or professional social network services Create links to other blogs	*Social skills* The information shared does not pose a risk to the blog owner.	Managing different digital identities and reputations in the internet environment (e.g., adjust profile settings).
Enable the basic functions for posts and follow	The language used respects the rules of netiquette in different online contexts (blog). There are comments from other users to which the blog owner responds in a way that respects the rules of netiquette. The blog includes a list of followers. The blog allows various sharing options (e.g., sharing via social media). The blog follows other blogs with reliable information.	Effective communication with the use of different digital media and environments (e.g., apply netiquette rules).
Embed flashcards and/or quizzes	*Creative skills* The blog includes multimedia content created by its owner (e.g., flashcards, quizzes, posters, presentations).	Support for learning during the studies (e.g., use flashcards, quizzes/questions for revision purposes)
Embed presentations	The blog includes a presentation created by its owner.	Development of academic work/publications and communication of the results.
Embed videos	The blog includes videos created by its owner.	Development of academic work/publications and communication of the results.
Presentation of the blog	The blog has been finalized, and it is a fully functional website.	Providing evidence for abilities/skills for the academic and professional career (e.g., create an e-portfolio showcasing examples of projects)

3.2 Participants

The research sample included 23 undergraduate students who were attending courses at a university. Their age range was 18-23 years. Approximately 40% of the students were males, and 60% were females. 52% were first-year students, 26% were second-year students, 4% were third-year students, and 18% were fourth-year students.

3.3 Research Instrument

The data were gathered using the self-assessment questionnaire *Internet Skills Scale* by Van Deursen, Helsper, and Eynon (2014, 2016) which was based on Van Dijk and Van Deursen's (2014) conceptualization of digital literacy skills and was administered to evaluate students' skills before and after the intervention. The authors validated the Scale for the context of higher education, and the results from the reliability analysis indicated high internal reliability across all five scales (Cronbach's alpha is 0.90 for the Information Navigation skills, 0.89 for the Social skills, 0.91 for the Creative skills, 0.84 for the Operational skills, and 0.87 for the Critical skills) (Miliou & Angeli, 2021). The questionnaire was structured on a five-point Likert scale ranging from "Not at all true of me" to "Very true of me." The collected data were used to determine differences in students' skills based on the project-based learning design before and after the intervention. The authors used the non-parametric Wilcoxon Signed Rank test, which was applied with the statistical package SPSS, and the effect sizes for the Wilcoxon's signed-rank tests were calculated as $r = z/\sqrt{N}$ with the following thresholds: significant effect is .5, a medium effect is .3, and a small effect is .1 (Fritz et al., 2012).

4. RESULTS

4.1 Operational Skills

The scores for this dimension were calculated as the sum of the ratings for the four items. As shown in Table 2, a Wilcoxon Signed Rank Test revealed a statistically significant increase in Operational Skills following participation in the project-based learning intervention, z=-4.114, p=.001 with a large effect size, r=.60. The median score on the Operational Skills increased from pre-intervention (Md=14) to post-intervention (Md=19).

Table 2. Wilcoxon Signed Rank Test for Students' Self-Assessment of Operational Skills (N=23)

	Median Pre-questionnaire	Median Post-questionnaire	Z	p
Operational Skills	14	19	-4.114	.001

4.2 Information-Navigation Skills

The scores for this dimension were calculated as the sum of ratings for the seven items, which were reversed because they were negatively stated. A Wilcoxon Signed Rank Test revealed a statistically significant increase in information-navigation skills following participation in the project-based learning intervention, z=-4.205, p=.001 with a large effect size, r=.62. The median score on the information navigation skills increased from pre-intervention (Md=24) to post-intervention (Md=32). Table 3 shows the results of the Wilcoxon Signed Rank Test from students' self-assessment of their information navigation skills.

Table 3. Wilcoxon Signed Rank Test for Students' Self-Assessment of Information-Navigation Skills (N=23)

	Median Pre-questionnaire	Median Post-questionnaire	Z	p
Information-Navigation Skills	24	32	-4.205	.001

4.3 Social Skills

The scores for this dimension were calculated as the sum of the ratings for the seven items. A Wilcoxon Signed Rank Test revealed a statistically significant increase in social skills following participation in the project-based learning intervention, z=-3.849, p=.001 with a large effect size, r=.57. The median score on the Operational Skills increased from pre-intervention (Md=28) to post-intervention (Md=34). Table 4 shows the results of the Wilcoxon Signed Rank Test from students' self-assessment of their social skills.

Table 4. Wilcoxon Signed Rank Test for Students' Self-Assessment of Social Skills (N=23)

	Median Pre-questionnaire	Median Post-questionnaire	Z	p
Social Skills	28	34	-3.849	.001

4.4 Creative Skills

The scores for this dimension were calculated as the sum of the ratings for the five items. A Wilcoxon Signed Rank Test revealed a statistically significant increase in creative skills following participation in the project-based learning intervention, z=-4.208, p=.001 with a large effect size, r=.62. The median score on the creative Skills increased from pre-intervention (Md=12) to post-intervention (Md=25). Table 5 shows the results of the Wilcoxon Signed Rank Test from students' self-assessment of their creative skills.

Table 5. Wilcoxon Signed Rank Test for Students' Self-Assessment of Creative Skills (N=23)

	Median Pre-questionnaire	Median Post-questionnaire	Z	p
Creative Skills	12	25	-4.208	.001

4.5 Critical Skills

The scores for this dimension were calculated as the sum of the ratings for the four items. One item was reversed because it was negatively stated. A Wilcoxon Signed Rank Test revealed a statistically significant increase in critical skills following participation in the project-based learning intervention, z=-4.125, p=.001 with a large effect size, r=.61. The median score on the critical skills increased from pre-intervention (Md=13) to post-intervention (Md=19). Table 6 shows the results of the Wilcoxon Signed Rank Test from students' self-assessment of their critical skills.

Table 6. Wilcoxon Signed Rank Test for Students' Self-Assessment of Critical Skills (N=23)

	Median Pre-questionnaire	Median Post-questionnaire	Z	p
Critical Skills	13	19	-4.125	.001

5. DISCUSSION

Following the results analysis, the authors assert that the project-based learning intervention significantly contributed to the improvement of operational, information-navigation, social, creative, and critical skills among undergraduate students. This conclusion is supported by the substantial effect size observed in each of these skill areas, underscoring the intervention's effectiveness in enhancing digital literacy skills among undergraduates.

The approach's success could be attributed to several design elements that aimed to enhance the project-based learning experience. Specifically, to combat the lack of students' awareness about the use of technologies for academic purposes (Kennedy & Fox, 2013; Ståhl, 2017), the authors highlighted the added value of the tools they were using beyond the context of the intervention, and prompted students to identify the affordances of each tool for future use in academic or professional environments. Such practice was based on the results of previous research, which showed that students found added value in learning activities with the use of digital tools that support their study and work at an academic or professional level (Ng, 2012; Hall et al., 2013).

Additionally, the authors sought to address the differences in students' digital literacy skills levels and their familiarity with digital devices and tools (Helsper & Eynon, 2010; Hargittai, 2010; Corrin et al., 2010; Ståhl, 2017) by following a holistic approach to learning. Namely, each project enabled students to experiment with various tools and develop various skills in different areas by working on a unique project on a topic of interest. Thus, the design addressed the need for more personalized learning experiences that allowed students to use tools based on the needs of their work (Jørgensen, 2019).

In summary, the acknowledgment of a large effect size suggests that the project-based learning approach is educationally impactful, with broad implications for enhancing digital literacy skills in academic settings. This is noteworthy for educators, institutions, and policymakers, as it underscores the effectiveness of project-based learning in fostering crucial skills that are essential for students' success in academic settings and beyond. Furthermore, the discussion sheds light on the success factors of the project-based learning approach, such as highlighting the added value of digital tools, prompting students to identify tool affordances, and addressing differences in students' digital literacy skills levels through a holistic learning approach. These design elements not only contribute to the effectiveness of the intervention but also provide practical insights for educators seeking to implement similar strategies.

6. CONCLUSION

The discourse around The Digital Natives Debate has often made presumptions about younger generations' inherent technological prowess, especially within the confines of higher education. However, this paper sheds light on the overlooked gaps and nuances in their digital literacy, emphasizing the need for targeted interventions. Through a focused exploration of project-based learning's efficacy in enhancing digital literacy skills, this research has bridged a critical knowledge gap. The robust positive outcomes across various facets of digital literacy, ranging from operational to critical skills, underscore the potential of project-based learning in molding digitally competent scholars.

However, it is essential to acknowledge certain limitations that may impact the generalizability of our findings. One notable limitation is that the study relied on a relatively small sample size, which may limit the extent to which our results can be applied to broader populations. However, it is essential to note that the primary aim of this research was not to achieve broad generalizability but to focus on a comprehensive exploration of a project-based learning intervention within the context of digital literacy education.

Another limitation stems from the self-selection bias among participants which could introduce a degree of subjectivity into our findings, as individuals with a heightened interest may have been more inclined to participate. Future research should aim to address these limitations by employing larger and more diverse samples, as well as considering alternative recruitment strategies.

As higher education continues to evolve in the digital age, it is imperative that institutions recognize and harness such pedagogical strategies not merely to keep pace with technology, but to leverage it in cultivating holistic, future-ready learners. This study lays the groundwork for future endeavors seeking to refine and implement project-based learning interventions seamlessly integrated with digital literacy training in academic settings emphasizing the added value that technology can bring to educational settings.

REFERENCES

Ala-Mutka, K. (2011). *Mapping digital competence: Towards a conceptual understanding*. Publications Office of the European Union, Luxembourg.

Bawden, D. (2008). Origins and concepts of digital literacy. In: Lankshear, C., & Knobel, M. (ed.) *Digital literacies: Concepts, policies and practices*, pp. 17-32. Peter Lang, New York.

Bennett, S., Maton, K., & Kervin, L. (2008). The 'digital natives' debate: A critical review of the evidence. *British journal of educational technology*, Vol. 39, No. 5, pp. 775-786.

Corrin, L., Bennett, S., & Lockyer, L. (2010). *Digital Natives: Everyday life versus academic study*. Available at: https://ro.uow.edu.au/cgi/viewcontent.cgi?article=1214&context=edupapers

Evans C, Robertson W (2020) The four phases of the digital natives debate. *Human Behavior and Emerging Technologies,* Vol, 2, No. 3, pp. 269–277.

Fritz, C. O., Morris, P. E., & Richler, J. J. (2012). Effect size estimates current use, calculations and interpretation. *Journal of Experimental Psychology: General*, Vol. 141, No. 1, p 2.

Gosper, M., Malfroy, J., & McKenzie, J. (2013). Students' experiences and expectations of technologies: An Australian study designed to inform planning and development decisions. *Australasian Journal of Educational Technology*, Vol. 29, No. 2, pp. 268-282.

Gülbahar, Y., & Tinmaz, H. (2006). Implementing project-based learning and e-portfolio assessment in an undergraduate course. *Journal of Research on Technology in Education*, Vol. 38, No. 3, pp. 309-327.

Guo, P., Saab, N., Post, L. S., & Admiraal, W. (2020). A review of project-based learning in higher education: Student outcomes and measures. *International Journal of Educational Research*, Vol. 102, p. 101586.

Hall, M., Nix, I., & Baker, K. (2013). Student experiences and perceptions of digital literacy skills development: Engaging learners by design? *Electronic Journal of e-Learning*, Vol. 11, No. 3, pp. 207-225.

Hargittai, E. (2010). Digital na (t) ives? Variation in Internet Skills and Uses Among Members of the "Net Generation." *Sociological Inquiry*, Vol. 80, No. 1, pp. 92-113.

Helsper, E. J., & Eynon, R. (2010). Digital natives: where is the evidence?, *British Educational Research Journal*, Vol. 36, No. 3, pp. 503-520.

Jonassen, D.H. (1999). Designing Constructivist Learning Environments. In C.M. Reigeluth (Ed.*) Instructional-Design Theories and Models: A new Paradigm of Instructional Theory* (2nd ed.). Lawrence Erlbaum Associates, Mahwah, NJ.

Jørgensen, T. (2019). *Digital Skills: Where Universities Matter*. European University Association. Available at: https://eua.eu/resources/publications/851:digital-skills-%E2%80%93-where-universities-matter.html

Judd, T. (2018). The rise and fall (?) of the digital natives. *Australasian Journal of Educational Technology*, Vol. 34, No. 5, *Australasian Society for Computers in Learning in Tertiary Education*. Available at: https://www.learntechlib.org/p/187406/.

Kennedy, D. M., & Fox, R. (2013). 'Digital natives': An Asian perspective for using learning technologies. *International Journal of Education and Development using I.C.T.*, Vol. 9, No. 1, pp. 65-79.

Kirkwood, A. & Price, L. (2014) Technology-enhanced learning and teaching in higher education: what is 'enhanced' and how do we know? A critical literature review. *Learning, Media and Technology*, Vol. 39, No. 1, pp. 6-36.

Larmer, J., Mergendoller, J., & Boss, S. (2015). *Setting the standard for project-based learning*. Alexandria, USA: ASCD.

Lasauskiene, J., & Rauduvaite, A. (2015). Project-based learning at university: Teaching experiences of lecturers. *Procedia - Social and Behavioral Sciences*, Vol. 197, pp. 788–792.

Lee, J. S., Blackwell, S., Drake, J., & Moran, K. A. (2014). Taking a Leap of Faith: Redefining Teaching and Learning in Higher Education through Project-Based Learning. *Interdisciplinary Journal of Problem-Based Learning*, Vol, No. 2.

Leijon, M., Gudmundsson, P., Staaf, P., & Christersson, C. (2022). Challenge-based learning in higher education–A systematic literature review. *Innovations in education and teaching international*, Vol. 59, No. 5, pp. 609-618.

Litt, E. (2013). Measuring users' internet skills: A review of past assessments and a look toward the future. *New Media & Society*, Vol. 15, No. 4, pp. 612-630.

Miliou, O, Angeli, C (2021) Measuring the Internet Skills of Gen Z Students in Higher Education: validation of the Internet Skills Scale in University Settings. In Proceedings of the 7th International Conference on Higher Education Advances (HEAd'21), Valencia, Spain. Available at: https://doi.org/10.4995/HEAd21.2021.13070

Ng, W. (2012). Can we teach digital natives' digital literacy? *Computers & Education*, Vol. 59, No. 3, pp. 1065-1078.

Shpeizer, R. (2019). Towards a successful integration of project-based learning in higher education: Challenges, technologies and methods of implementation. *Universal Journal of Educational Research*, 7(8), 1765-1771.

Ståhl, T. (2017). How I.C.T. savvy are Digital Natives actually? *Nordic Journal of Digital Literacy*, Vol. 12, No. 3, pp. 89-108.

Smith, E. E., Kahlke, R., & Judd, T. (2020). Not just digital natives: Integrating technologies

in professional education contexts. *Australasian Journal of Educational Technology*, Vol. 36, No. 3, pp. 1-14.

van Dijk, J. A., & van Deursen, A. J. (2014). *Digital skills: Unlocking the Information Society*. Palgrave Macmillan.

van Deursen, A. J., Helsper, E. J., & Eynon, R. (2016). Development and validation of the Internet Skills Scale (I.S.S.). *Information, Communication & Society*, Vol. 19, No. 6, pp. 804-823.

van Deursen, A. J. A. M., Helsper, E. J., & Eynon, R. (2014). *Measuring digital skills. From digital skills to tangible outcomes project report*. Available at: http://www.oii.ox.ac.uk/research/projects/?id=112

Wobbe, K. K., & Stoddard, E. A. (Eds.). (2023). *Project-based learning in the first year: beyond all expectations*. Stylus Publishing, New York.

MATHEMATICAL PROBLEM-SOLVING BY MEANS OF COMPUTATIONAL THINKING AND PROGRAMMING: A USE-MODIFY-CREATE APPROACH

Nils Kristian Hansen and Said Hadjerrouit
University of Agder, Institute of Mathematical Sciences
Kristiansand, Norway

ABSTRACT

This paper aims at using a Use-Modify-Create approach to explore students' mathematical problem solving by means of computational thinking (CT) and programming activities. The data collection method is participant observation, in which the researcher also has the role as teacher, guiding the group activities. In our study, two groups of students at the undergraduate level solving a mathematical task. The main finding of the study shows that the progression through the Use-Modify-Create continuum did not work as expected and that the connections between mathematical thinking, computational thinking, and programming proved difficult for the students. Conclusions so far are drawn from the study to promote mathematical problem solving by means of computational thinking and programming in a Use-Modify-Create context.

KEYWORDS

Algorithm, Computational Thinking (CT), Mathematical Problem-solving, Mathematical Thinking (MT), Programming, Python, Use-Modify-Create (UMC)

1. INTRODUCTION

The existing body of literature on programming in mathematics education research has primarily been informed more by constructionist and individual perspectives than by conceptual and pedagogical approaches to mathematical problem-solving such as Use-Modify-Create (UMC) or similar frameworks for supporting progression in learning programming. Moreover, empirical data collected in our previous research (Hansen & Hadjerrouit, 2023; Hadjerrouit & Hansen, 2022) do not sufficiently account for the connectedness of mathematical thinking (MT), computational thinking (CT), and programming. Given this background, we argue that a pedagogical approach supporting learning progression may help students to develop an enhanced understanding of mathematical problem solving by means of CT and programming. The objective of the study is to use a Use-Modify-Create (UMC) approach to analyze undergraduate students' ability to solve mathematical problems by means of CT and programming.

The research question of this study is as follows: *How do students use, modify, and create computer programs to solve mathematical problems by means of computational thinking and programming activities?*

The article is structured as follows. Firstly, the theoretical background is outlined. Secondly, the UMC approach, context of the study, participants, and methods are described. Then, the results are reported and analyzed, followed by a discussion. Finally, conclusions, limitations, and future work conclude the article.

2. THEORETICAL BACKGROUND

We start with a brief overview of the existing research literature on the integration of CT and programming activities into undergraduate mathematics education. The purpose is to uncover and delineate the use of CT and programming to support problem solving in mathematics education research during the last few years.

2.1 Literature Overview

The recent trend of integrating programming into the mathematics subject at the undergraduate level suggests the importance of CT as a core notion beyond programming in the context of mathematics education.

CT is more about thinking than computer programming (Li, Schoenfeld, & diSessa, 2020; Misfeldt & Ejsing-Duun, 2017). More specifically, it represents a "universally applicable attitude and skill set everyone, not just computer scientists, (...)" (Wing 2006, p. 33). More specifically, CT is a fundamental skill and shares several communalities with mathematical thinking (MT), e.g., problem solving and logical reasoning. MT involves the application of mathematical skills to solve mathematical problems. CT is "an approach to solving problems in a way that can be implemented using a computer" and goes beyond computer programming (Barr & Stephenson, 2011). Moreover, it is assumed that CT improves both logical and reasoning skills in mathematics education (Martínez-García, 2021). The close connection between MT and CT provides good opportunities for mathematical problem-solving.

Likewise, programming is closely related to CT, but traditionally, programming in educational settings required producing algorithms from scratch without the mediation of CT (Kaufmann & Stenseth, 2020). Recently, it is recommended to pass through CT to be able to design algorithms. Being able to programs and test program codes is the result of being able to think computationally (Li et al., 2020; Shute, Sun, & Asbell-Clarke, 2017; Wing 2006, Wing 2008). Clearly, programming alone without a clear connection to CT may not be sufficient to support students in mathematical problem solving. Thus, CT skills are critical for building efficient algorithms for mathematical problem-solving rather than trial-and-error and getting the program to run (Topallia & Cagiltay, 2018). In other words, CT requires students to be engaged in a problem-solving process until an appropriate algorithm is found that can be translated into a computer program.

Moreover, our previous research shows that integrating CT and programming with mathematics is a challenging task, and it has scarcely been explored in undergraduate education (Hadjerrouit & Hansen, 2022; Hansen & Hadjerrouit, 2023). The main findings of this research are twofold. Firstly, the introduction of CT at the undergraduate level presents many challenges both for students and teachers. Secondly, the mathematical tasks presented were challenging for novice students due to their lack of prior knowledge of CT and programming, varied mathematical problem-solving skills, and the difficulty to connect MT, CT, and programming in an effective way.

Hence, efforts must be put on a more encompassing view of the relationship between CT, MT, and programming. But still, a great challenge remains to make CT consequential and accessible to all students. As a result, it becomes important to broaden the view of CT as a fundamental skill and as a model of thinking that is important for all students. Our hypothesis is that developing and using pedagogical approaches for mathematical problem-solving by means of CT and programming may open new opportunities. At the same time, new challenges may become visible, and each of these challenges will require tremendous effort. The same is the case for specifying CT competencies that serve as a foundation for mathematical problem-solving.

2.2 MT, CT, and Programming and their Interplay

MT, CT, and programming have a lot of communalities (Weintrop, 2016; Wan-Rou Wu & Kai-Lin Yang, 2022). Firstly, MT consists of solving mathematical problems, (e.g., algebraic equations or functions), and justification for solutions (Shute, Sun & Asbell-Clarke, 2017, p. 145). Secondly, Wing (2008, 2014) pointed out that the main commonality between CT and mathematical thinking is problem-solving and a structured step-by-step construction process. Thirdly, CT and programming constructs such as variables and flow statements (if-then-else, for, while-until, repeat, etc.) are closely connected to mathematical thinking (Lie, Hauge, & Meaney, 2017). The close connection and interplay between MT and CT might provide opportunities for mathematical problem-solving (Figure 1). As one can see the approach is not linear, moving from MT, to CT to programming, instead transitions back are possible to make sense of algorithm and program code.

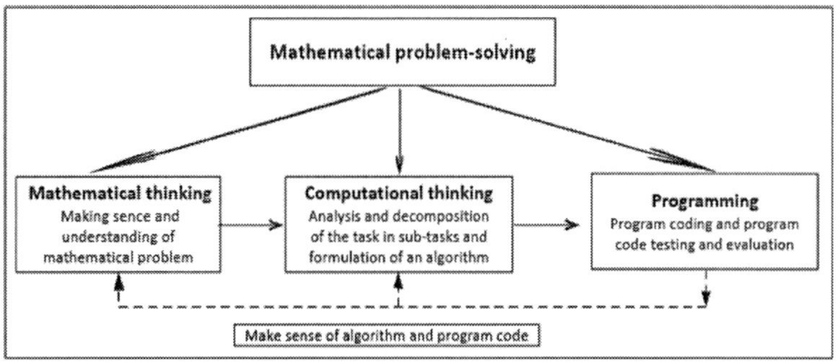

Figure 1. MT, CT, and programming and their interplay (Hadjerrouit & Hansen, 2022)

2.3 Use-Modify-Create (UMC)

The Use-Modify-Create (UMC) approach is a framework for supporting progression in learning programming. (Franklin, 2022; Houchins, 2021; Lee et al., 2011). Learners move along a continuum from where they first use programs made by someone else, e.g., teachers. Then, they modify programs developed by other people (e.g., teachers) so that the modified code becomes "theirs". Finally, in the third step, they create their own programs (Figure 2).

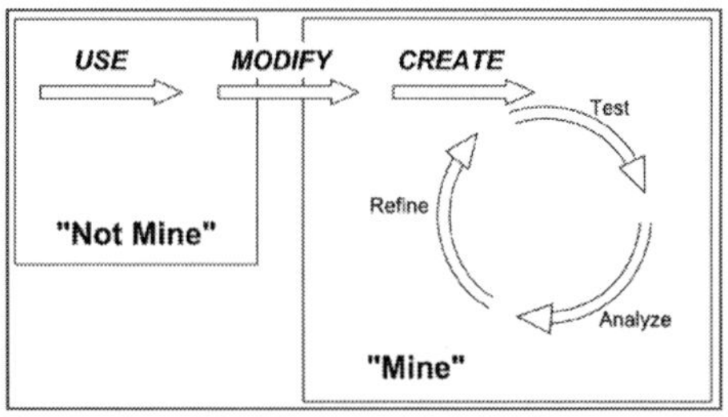

Figure 2. Use-Modify-Create model (Lee et al., 2011)

We think that the UMC approach offers a helpful progression for developing such skills over time. Its greatest advantage is in illustrating the benefits arising from engaging students with progressively more complex tasks and giving them increasing ownership of their learning (Lee et al., 2011). In the Use-phase students are consumers of someone else's creation. For example, testing, debugging, or interpreting a program. In the Modify-phase they begin to modify the program with increasing levels of sophistication, e.g., changing the value of a variable or modifying a loop. In the Create-phase, the students may want to change the behavior of the program in a way that entails developing new pieces of code, through a series of tests, analyses, iterative refinements, and attempts to validate the program against a mathematical problem, which becomes one's own. Within this "Create" phase, key aspects of CT come into play, connecting to MT and programming. Clearly, this phase necessitates MT and CT to a higher degree in comparison with previous phases. Moving through this progression, it is important to maintain a level of challenge difficulty that supports growth while limiting frustration and anxiety, considering that the approach is not fully linear, moving from Use to Modify to Create, instead transitions back and forth (Lee et al. 2021).

3. THE STUDY

Grounded on a qualitative research design this work uses a case study to collect data by observing the work of 2 groups of students in a first-year undergraduate course on programming with applications in industrial mathematics. UMC is used as an analytical framework to evaluate students' activities.

3.1 Data Collection Method and Participants

The data collection method is participant observation based on qualitative research, with a slight modification. The researcher had the role as a teacher (T), guiding the students when they got stuck. The work was performed in one group of three students (S1, S2, and S3) and one group of four (S4, S5, S6, and S7), using the video conferencing tool Zoom with screen sharing. In the Use-phase the teacher shared the programming environment, during the Modify- and Create-phases a student undertook this responsibility. All students had video and sound turned on, so that they were able to see and hear each other as well as to observe the program code. The participants were volunteers from a class of 86 students, having varied background in mathematics, but were about to complete an introductory course in programming. This course introduced basic Python constructs like variables, loops, branches, functions, and classes, but also dealt with structured programming and CT.

3.2 Use-Modify-Create Tasks

The Use-Modify-Create approach is used to progressively introduce students to new programming concepts through three activity phases. In the Use-phase they start in a programming context, trying to abstract a mathematical concept from a Python-function, (figure 3). In the subsequent Modify- and Create-phases, however, they start in an MT context, attempting to solve a mathematical challenge by programming.

```
def x(a):
    """?"""
    for n in range(a-1, 1, -1):
        if a % n == 0:
            return False
    return True
```

Figure 3. Python code used for the Use-phase

Use-phase: In the Use-phase the students were presented with the Python-function in figure 3 and asked to describe what it performed, without testing it. The function was named "x" to avoid semantical interpretation.

In an MT context the function may be described as checking if its argument is a prime number. In a CT context it may by described as checking the parameter, *a*, for divisibility by all integers, *n*, in the range from $a-1$ down to, but not including, 1. The divisibility test is performed by examining if the remainder of *a* divided by *n* is zero. If so, *a* is not a prime, and the function returns *True*. If a remainder of zero never occurs, *a* is a prime, and the function returns *False*.

The students were also asked to reflect on if reversing the order of the integers, *n*, i.e., testing from 2 up to $a-1$, is correct, and if the one method is preferable over the other. In a CT context the two methods are identical, but in an MT context checking from 2 and up is preferable, as the probability of detecting divisibility is significantly larger for small numbers.

Modify-phase: Another way of stating that *a* is divisible by *n* is to say that *n* is a factor in *a*. In the Modify-phase the students were asked to modify the function as to count all factors in the parameter, *a*. In a programming context this involves introducing an accumulator variable, updating it for each factor found, and ultimately returning its value. MT considerations are that the numbers 1 and *a* also should be considered factors, and that for each positive factor a corresponding negative factor exists. One algorithmic solution to counting negative factors is extending the range of *n* to $[-a, a]$. This, however, requires excluding $n = 0$ from the divisibility test. Another solution is to keep the range as $[1, a]$ and add 2 to the accumulator variable for each factor found.

Create-phase: In the Create phase the students were asked to write a Python-function returning a list of all factors in the parameter *a*. It may be noted that the programming pattern for this closely resembles the pattern in the Use-phase, so modifying the existing code may be a better choice than writing it from scratch. The modifications required are that a composite variable like a list must be used instead of an accumulator variable, and that each factor found must be concatenated to that variable.

3.3 Data Analysis

The analysis of the results seeks indications of students' mathematical problem-solving by means CT and MT in an UMC context. It uses a deductive-inductive approach based on the interplay between the theoretical basis of the study and the empirical data (Patton, 2002). Specific questions are addressed when analyzing the data such as: To what extent do students successfully complete the UMC activities? To what extent does UMC support student learning progression? To what degree do students modify the programs? To what extent do students focus on mathematical problem-solving? To what extent do they benefit from CT to develop an algorithm in the Create-phase? To what degree do they use MT and CT to create a program?

4. RESULTS

4.1 Group 1

Use-phase: T presents the Python function, asking the students to take some time to reflect on what it does. The students start in a programming context, engaging in a line-by-line discussion, but are unable to give an overall MT or CT description of the code. Even after T has given an example, a strong hint is required for them to switch to an MT-context:

T: So, we agree on that if *a* is not divisible by any of the smaller numbers, the function returns *False*. Do you follow me on that?

S2: Yes.

T: Can we say that in another way? What property does *a* have, then? Can you find a mathematical concept that describes …

S1: A prime number.

T then demonstrates that the function returns *True* on 11 as an argument and *False* on 10, and eventually S1 can describe the function in an MT-context:

S1: The function checks if a number is a prime.

T now reverses the range to count upwards from 2 and asks if the two methods are equal. S1 responds in a CT-context and concludes that they are. S3 however responds in an MT-context concluding that upwards from 2 is more efficient because one more frequently will find a multiple of the lowest numbers.

Modify-phase: S2 copies the code and shares the programming environment. T requires the students to modify the code so that it counts the factors in the parameter *a*.

The students do not engage in any CT or MT strategy discussion but goes straight to programming. S1 initially instructs S2 on what to write, but eventually S3 takes over the role as instructor. Together they write code that is correct. A test is run, and S3 first claims that the result is incorrect, but when T insists on it being correct, S3 realizes that the function counts all factors, not only prime factors:

S3: Yes. Now you get alle the numbers that can be factors, you do not get the numbers in a prime factorization.

On a question from T on whether the numbers 1 and *a* also should be considered factors in the number *a*, the students are unable to give an answer. But when T states that this is the case, S2 and S3 immediately rewrite the code so that 1 and *a* are included in the divisibility test.

When T asks for negative factors to be included in the count, S3 instantly suggests ranging from $-a$ to a, and S2 modifies the code accordingly. They do, however, not employ MT to foresee that the code will produce a division by zero-error. But when this error occurs, they immediately realize what the problem is:

T: Well, what did go wrong?

S3: Modulo by zero.

S1/3: Yes.

S3: You cannot divide by zero.

S2: No.

However, the students do not find a simple programming solution to this. The suggestions they provide are awkward in a CT setting, involving code duplications. T needs to guide their work in detail.

In contrast, when T asks for another, mathematical way to count the negative factors, S1 immediately employs MT, stating that one may count two factors at a time, as there is an equal number of negative and positive factors. S2 then modifies the code accordingly.

Create-phase: T now asks for a function returning all the factors in a. The students choose to modify the existing function.

S3 sees the need for a data structure to collect the factors and suggests replacing the accumulator variable with a list. Furthermore, S3 appears able to use CT to model the required algorithm mentally, giving S2 detailed coding instructions. S1 spots the problem that only positive factors are included and suggest expanding the range to $[-a, a]$, excluding zero, as done in the Modify-phase. A final test does not reveal any errors.

4.2 Group 2

Use-phase: T presents the Python function, asking the students to take some time to reflect on what it does. After a while S7 describes the workings of the details in the program and concludes that it does a divisibility check. S6 is then able to see this in an MT context and conclude that the function is a primality checker. Then S7 is also able to see the expression $a \% n == 0$ in an MT context and conclude that it is about modulus in integer division.

T now reverses the range to count upwards from 2 and asks if the two methods are equal. S7 reflects both in a programming context and an MT context, concluding that the two methods algorithmically are the same, but that counting upwards is better, as small numbers are more prone to be factors.

Modify-phase: S6 copies the code and shares the programming environment. T requires the students to modify the code so that it counts the factors in the parameter a. Both S6 and S7 immediately sees the need for an accumulator variable. Followingly, however, they struggle with creating the counting mechanism, making several erroneous suggestions. T needs to remind them that the task is about counting factors. S4 then reintroduces the idea of an accumulator variable. The students are however unable to integrate the accumulator variable in the code, discussing if it should be placed inside or outside of the loop, apparently unaware of the algorithmic implications of their choice. Ultimately, they make the correct decision, but based only on what they have seen in previous examples. The discussion then continues along the same lines, again demonstrating the lack of CT. When advised by T, S7 eventually reaches the correct conclusion, though unable to phrase it properly:

S6: Does it matter if it is in the if-loop or the for-loop, T?

T: Yes, it does matter.

S7: It think the for-loop should be allowed to complete before we print out how many.

A test run counts four factors in the number 12. In an MT reflection S4 states that these factors are 2, 3, 4 and 6, but S6 objects that the number 12 itself is not counted. T argues that 1 and the number itself should also be considered factors and prompts the students to modify the code accordingly. S6 then has no difficulty in doing the proper modifications.

T now asks if negative numbers can be considered factors, and S6 and S7 hesitantly agrees to yes. T suggest having the program counting them also. S6 wants to expand the range from $-a$ to a, but S7 employs MT and suggests counting two factors at the time instead, pointing out that this also will avoid a division by zero. S6 writes the correct code.

Create-phase: T asks for a function returning all the factors in a. The students choose to further modify the existing function. S6 comments that they already have touched on the thought and invites S5 and S4 to give input. S4 states the need for a list, and S6 replaces the accumulator variable. S4 replies confirmative to S5s question on if the same loop-range can be used, but S7 realizes that this will exclude negative numbers. S6s algorithmic suggestion for solving the problem is however awkward, involving cloning the list. S6 suggests extending the range to $[-a, a]$ but notes the MT challenge of zero division. Eventually S4 produces the idea of appending $-n$ to the list along with n. S6 modifies the code and runs a test that does not reveal errors.

Next T asks how to get the factors in ascending order. S7 has a correct CT suggestion of adding a sort, but employing the idea in program code proves challenging. Eventually the students come up with a solution, sound both in an MT and a CT context, but involving superfluous code that can be eliminated by using an extended range and testing for zero divisors. However, the students seem unable to write the proper code. S6 and S7 bring forward a range of suggestions, but they are either incorrect or exceedingly complex. T eventually has to dictate the solution.

5. DISCUSSION

The research question *"How do students use, modify, and create computer programs to solve mathematical problems by means of computational thinking and programming activities?"* focuses on the structured activities underlying UMC to ensure a progression in learning associated with an exploration that allows for drawing on the interactions between MT, CT, and programming, and the extent to which the students benefit from the interactions. We draw on the deductive-inductive approach to reflect on the results achieved so far. A summary of our reflections on the groups' work is given below, organized according to the UMC approach.

Use-phase: Both groups managed to do a syntactical analysis of the program, but only group 2 was able to use MT and CT to abstract and describe the functionality on a general level, and to reflect on code details in a mathematical context. Once the functionality was established however, both groups were able to deduct the mathematical implications of a modification to the program.

Modify-phase: Neither group attacked the task in a structured manner, being unable to draw on their experience from the Use-phase. They did not engage in any CT or MT strategy discussion but went straight to programming. Group 1 was able to do minor modifications, but none involving major structural changes. Group 2, in contrast to their success in Use-phase, now were unable to make any connection between the mathematical context and the code. They went about the coding in a trial-and-error fashion, apparently without understanding the algorithmic implications of their trials. Substantial assistance from T was required.

Create-phase: Discovering the similarities between this task and the Modify-task, both groups chose to adapt the existing code instead of writing new from scratch. With the major mechanism required already established in the Modify-phase, group 1 was able do the necessary programming without aid. As for group 2, their trial-and-error approach again impeded their work, and substantial assistance from T was required.

The main finding of this study is that connections between MT, CT and programming proved difficult for the students (see fig. 1). The transition from programming to mathematical idea in the Use-phase however appeared to run smoother than going the other way, solving a mathematical problem with program code in the Modify and Create phase. In the latter phases the students to a very little degree were able to profit from their experience in the Use-phase. Also, even though, as stated by Lie et al. (2017), there is a close connection between CT and programming constructs, the students almost took no advantage of this. This may be an indication of that the connection is not obvious to the students, when not pointed out and exercised.

Based on this background, the challenges that need be overcome are as follows. Firstly, while the transition from programming to mathematical notion in the Use-phase worked relatively well, the results show that modifying a given program, and create a new one for solving mathematical problems are more challenging than originally expected. Consequently, the students were thinking at levels not explicitly related to the various phases of the UMC learning progression.

Secondly, referring to figure1, it appears that the lack of CT in the UMC continuum creates a gap in the flow between MT and programming. This may explain some of the major difficulties occurring when modifications to the program structure were required. However, instructor guided programming seemed to aid bridging the gap.

Thirdly, in accordance with the research literature (Hadjerrouit & Hansen, 2022; Hansen & Hadjerrouit, 2023; Wan-Rou Wu & Kai-Lin Yang, 2022; Martínez-García, 2021), the study shows the crucial role of CT as a fundamental skill and as a model of thinking relevant to mathematical problem-solving. To make effective use of CT in the Create-phase in particular, students should be able to analyze and decompose the mathematical task into smaller sub-tasks by means of CT, and then develop an algorithm before programming. In other words, we expect a progression that encourage students to work creativity and exploratory (Franklin, 2022; Romero et al, 2017).

Finally, in line with our previous research (Hansen & Hadjerrouit, 2023; Hadjerrouit & Hansen, 2022), this study shows again that the role of the instructor is still important to assist students in their progression through the entire UMC continuum, in particular in the Create-phase.

6. CONCLUSIONS, LIMITATIONS, AND FUTURE WORK

The present study is an attempt to contribute towards the advancement of the potential value of CT and programming at the undergraduate level when students engage in mathematical problem-solving, while uncovering both limitations and challenges encountered by the students when trying to connect MT, CT, and programming, which is a contribution to knowledge advancement in the field of mathematics education. Another contribution of this work is the use of a Use-Modify-Create approach at the undergraduate level to gradually introduce students to mathematical problem-solving through three stages.

Limitations of this work mainly concern the implementation of the UMC method. The Create-task was so similar to the Modify-task that the method in reality consisted of two Modify-tasks. In addition, progression did not work as expected. Moving from Use to Modify to Create, back and forth as described by Lee et al. (2021) required increasing levels of CT, something the students were unable to employ sufficiently without the guidance of the teacher.

Future work will comprise more student groups to increase the study validity and reliability. A more in-depth analysis on the work process, i.e., how, and why decisions were made, will be included. This based both on the students' reflections on their own work, and the teacher's professional opinion.

Further studies will also be conducted with focus on the type and level of CT required in the process of mathematical problem solving.

REFERENCES

Barr, V., & Stephenson, C. (2011). Bringing Computational Thinking to K-12: What is Involved and what is the Role of the Computer Science Education Community? *ACM Inroads* 2(1), pp. 111-122.

Franklin, D. (2022). An Analysis of Use-Modify-Create Pedagogical Approach's Success in Balancing Structure and Student Agency. *ICER '20*, August 10–12, 2020, Virtual Event, New Zealand, pp. 14-24.

Hadjerrouit, S.; Hansen, N. K. (2022). Undergraduate Mathematics Students Engaging in Problem-solving through Computational Thinking and Programming: A Case Study. *Orchestration of Learning Environments in the Digital World.* Springer Nature, pp. 197 - 214.

Hansen, N.K., & Hadjerrouit, S. (2023). Analyzing Students' Computational Thinking and Programming Skills for Mathematical Problem Solving. In: D. Ifenthaler, D.G. Sampson, & P. Isaías (Eds.) (2023). *Open and Inclusive Educational Practice in the Digital World* (pp. 155-173). Springer Nature Switzerland AG 2023.

Houchins, J. (2021). How Use-Modify-Create Brings Middle Grades Students to Computational Thinking. *International Journal for Designs and Learning, 12*(3), pp. 1-20.

Kaufmann, O. T., & Stenseth, B. (2020). Programming in Mathematics Education. *International Journal of Mathematical Education in Science and Technology*, 52(7), pp. 1029–1048.

Misfeldt, M., & Ejsing-Duun, S. (2015). Learning Mathematics through Programming: An Instrumental Approach to Potentials and Pitfalls. In K. Krainer, & N. Vondrová (Eds.). *Proceedings of CERME9* (pp. 2524-2530).

Lee, I. et al. (2011). Computational Thinking for Youth in Practice. *ACM Inroads 2*(1), pp.32-37.

Li, Y., Schoenfeld, A. H., diSessa, A. A., et al. (2020). Computational Thinking is more about Thinking than Computing. *Journal for STEM Education Research*, 3, pp. 1–18.

Lie, J., Hauge, I. O., & Meaney, T. J. (2017). Computer Programming in the Lower Secondary Classroom: Mathematics Learning. *Italian Journal of Educational Technology*, *25*(2), pp. 27-35.

Martínez-García, E. (2021). Computational Thinking: The Road to Success in Education. *Academia Letters*, pp. 1-7.

Patton, M. Q. (2002). *Qualitative Research & Evaluation Methods.* London: Sage Publications.

Romero, M., Lepage, A., & Lille, B. (2017). Computational Thinking Development through Creative Programming in Higher Education. *International Journal of Educational Technology in Higher Education* 14, pp. 1-15.

Topalli, D., & Cagiltay, N. E. (2018). Improving Programming Skills in Engineering Education through Problem-Based Game Projects with Scratch. *Computers & Education*, *120*, pp. 64-74.

Shute, V.J., Sun, C., & Asbell-Clarke, J. (2017). Demystifying Computational Thinking. *Educational Research Review*, pp. 1-10.

Weintrop, D. et al. (2016). Defining Computational Thinking for Mathematics and Science Classrooms. *J Sci Educ Technol 25*, pp. 127–147.

Wan-Rou Wu & Kai-Lin Yang (2022) The Relationships between Computational and Mathematical Thinking: A Review Study on Tasks, *Cogent Education*, 9:1, pp. 1-19.

Wing, J. M. (2008). Computational Thinking and Thinking about Computing. *Philosophical Transactions of the Royal Society A*, *366*(1881), pp. 3717-3725.

Wing, J. M. (2006). Computational Thinking. *Communication of the ACM*, 49(3), pp. 33–35.

HOW TO DEAL WITH AI-POWERED WRITING TOOLS IN ACADEMIC WRITING: A STAKEHOLDER ANALYSIS

Michael Burkhard
Institute for Educational Management and Technologies
St. Jakob-Strasse 21, University of St.Gallen, Switzerland

ABSTRACT

Due to the advances of artificial intelligence (AI) and natural language processing, new AI-powered writing tools have emerged. They can be used by students among other things for text translation, to improve spelling or to generate new texts. In academic writing, AI-powered writing tools are posing challenges but also opportunities for teaching and learning. It is an open question in which way to sensibly deal with these tools. To address the issue, this paper investigates, what interests different stakeholders (students, lecturers, university administration) pursue in relation to AI-powered writing tools. Building on this, tensions between different stakeholders are identified and (teaching) strategies proposed to deal with these tensions. To discuss the findings in light of recent developments around ChatGPT, semi-structured expert interviews were conducted in April 2023 with five academic writing lecturers at the University of St.Gallen. The results suggest that as writing tools become more and more powerful, the need for strategies to ensure their reasonable and transparent use also increases.

KEYWORDS

Higher Education, Academic Writing, AI-Powered Writing Tools, ChatGPT, Stakeholder Analysis

1. INTRODUCTION

With the release of ChatGPT in November 2022, AI-powered writing tools gained broad attention in society (see, e.g., Dwivedi et al., 2023). However, in the context of academic writing, AI-powered writing tools are not a new phenomenon (Dergaa et al., 2023, pp. 616-617). In recent years, technological advances in the field of artificial intelligence (AI) and natural language processing (NLP) have led to increasingly better tools in this rapidly changing, dynamic environment (Dergaa et al., 2023; Brown et al., 2020; Heaven, 2020). Among other things, AI-powered writing tools can be used to translate, to paraphrase and summarize content, to get instant feedback or automatically generate new texts.

In academic writing, AI-powered writing tools create new opportunities, but also new challenges (Dwivedi et al., 2023; Dergaa et al., 2023; Marche, 2022; Sharples, 2022). One the one hand, such tools could be used as an additional feedback channel to provide individualized feedback on student writing (Dwivedi et al., 2023; p. 25). Since it can be very time-consuming for lecturers to provide individualized text feedback to each student, AI-powered writing tools could relieve lecturers from some of their workload. On the other hand, AI-powered writing tools may also produce misleading or wrong content, that may not be obvious to all students (Rogerson & McCarthy, 2017). Used in the wrong way, their use can lead to plagiarism issues (Rogerson & McCarthy, 2017; Prentice & Kinden, 2018). The ability to support students writing with powerful tools also raises discussions about the extent to which essays and papers are still a valid form of assessment (Marche, 2022; Sharples, 2022). Lack of transparency in using these tools can make it difficult to evaluate a student's performance.

Furthermore, various stakeholders, such as students, lecturers, and the university administration, do not necessarily share the same interests with respect to AI-powered writing tools. This leads to tensions between different stakeholders, which manifest, for example, in discussions about the extent to which the use of such tools should be considered a plagiarism offence. There is a need for developing sustainable strategies in dealing with AI-powered writing tools (Dwivedi et al., 2023, p. 26; Dergaa et al., 2023, p. 617).

An important precondition for creating meaningful strategies and solutions would be to better understand what interests different stakeholders have in relation to AI-powered writing tools. If we better understand the various interests of the stakeholders, we will be able to establish sustainable solutions in this dynamically evolving field. In light of the identified research desideratum, the following research question is addressed:

Considering different stakeholder interests, what are meaningful strategies to deal with AI-powered writing tools in academic writing?

The objectives of the paper at hand are therefore twofold:

- Providing an overview about different stakeholder interests (students, lecturers, university administration) with regard to AI-powered writing tools in academic writing, to obtain a nuanced picture and better understand the underlying dynamics and conflicting interests between different stakeholders;
- Analyzing and evaluating tensions between different stakeholders in the context of the rapid developments of new AI-powered writing tools such as ChatGPT, in order to derive meaningful (teaching) strategies to deal with AI-powered writing tools in academic writing.

As a methodical foundation, the concept of *tensions* is used, which organizational actors experience, when they are confronted with incompatibilities and dilemmas (Putnam et al., 2016, p. 4). For example, regarding the usage of AI-powered writing tools in academic writing, students and lecturers might have different interests, which can lead to tensions (e.g., using vs. not using AI-powered writing tools). The choices that individuals make regarding a certain tension can lead to different emotions such as stress or anxiety (Mini & Widjaja, 2019; Putnam et al., 2016).

The aim is to reveal existing, partially conflicting interests of the different stakeholders as well as to document the usage behavior of AI-powered writing tools at the University of St.Gallen and the University of Mannheim in fall term 2022 (prior to the release of ChatGPT). Based on this status quo analysis, semi-structured expert interviews with lecturers in the field of academic writing were conducted in April 2023, to better understand how new emerging tools like ChatGPT influence and change the already existing landscape of AI-powered writing tools in academic writing.

From a theoretical point of view, the paper at hand can serve as a starting point for future research as it analyzes and conceptualizes the problem space (emerging tensions) and solution space (possible strategies) for dealing with AI-supported writing tools in a dynamically changing environment. It further identifies diverging viewpoints on the benefits and risks of AI-powered writing tools of different stakeholders currently found in the literature that could guide future research.

From a practical standpoint, the paper at hand might be valuable for people who work in the field of academic writing, as the paper highlights different strategies on how to cope with AI-powered writing tools in academic writing. The derived strategies as well as its implications might serve as a starting point for further discussion to introduce meaningful regulations in one's own context.

To this end, section 2 provides an overview about AI-powered writing tools in academic writing as well as different perspectives on the topic from three key stakeholders (1) university administration, (2) lecturers, and (3) students. Section 3 elaborates on the identified tensions between different stakeholders and derives possible strategies for coping and responding to them. In section 4, based on semi-structured expert interviews, the results are discussed in the light of the latest developments around newly emerging writing tools like ChatGPT. Section 5 concludes with some final remarks.

2. AI-POWERED WRITING TOOLS IN ACADEMIC WRITING

2.1 A Dynamically Changing Environment

Writing skills are considered important, because they enable us to construct and express one's own identity (e.g., Ivanic, 1998). They further support us in developing meaningful arguments and points of view (e.g., Van Eemeren & Grootendorst, 2016). Students' *academic writing skills* may include different aspects, such as the ability to construct strong arguments, consider several viewpoints, cite correctly, or use a tone and style appropriate for the target audience (Purcell et al., 2013, p. 4).

Over the past decades, students' writing habits have changed with the rise of new technologies and the Internet (Moore et al., 2016; Peters & Cadieux, 2019). Advances in machine learning (ML) and natural language processing (NLP) have led to the emergence of new, more powerful writing tools (Geitgey, 2018; Brown et al., 2020; Heaven, 2020). Table 1 gives an overview over several types of AI-powered writing tools, that can directly support the process of writing.

Table 1. Several types of AI-powered writing tools, that directly support the writing process

Tool type	Description	Examples
Online translation tools	Online translation tools are software tools that can automatically translate a text into different languages.	DeepL, Google Translate
Paraphraser and summarizer tools	Online paraphraser and summarizer tools are software tools that can paraphrase, shorten, or summarize a given text into a new text of the same language. When using them, a given text (e.g., from Wikipedia) is used as an input and then further modified by using the tool.	QuillBot, Smodin
Online writing assistants	Online writing assistants are software tools that help to improve the quality of a text. During the writing process, the writer typically gets recommendations from such tools with regard to spelling, grammar, redundancy, vocabulary usage, clarity and style.	Grammarly, Wordtune
AI-based content generators	AI-based content generators are software tools designed to create new texts (based on some input parameters specified by the user such as the topic to write about). After entering the inputs, such tools for example provide suggestions for the outline of the full text.	Writesonic, Copy.ai, GPT-3, ChatGPT

Even though the current discussions about large language models (LLM) like ChatGPT illustrate the relevance of this topic, the opportunities and risks of using AI-powered writing tools in academic writing have been debated for quite some time. For example, there is an ongoing discussion on the extent to which translation and paraphrasing tools should be considered legitimate support tools for writing or whether they rather constitute a mode of bad practice that encourages plagiarism (see e.g., Rogerson & McCarthy, 2017; Prentice & Kinden, 2018).

In the meantime, the first publications have appeared that list AI-powered writing tools as co-authors (see e.g., Carr, 2023). However, this approach is not widely accepted. Major publishers and conference organizers have updated their policy regarding AI-powered writing tools (Dwivedi et al., 2023, p. 34). For example, the publisher Taylor & Francis (2023) states, that "authorship requires taking accountability for content, consenting to publication via an author publishing agreement [as well as] giving contractual assurances about the integrity of the work" (Taylor & Francis, 2023). In their view, those uniquely human responsibilities cannot be undertaken by AI tools. Rather than treating AI-powered writing tools as co-authors, they should be treated as tools whose use must be appropriately acknowledged and documented (Taylor & Francis, 2023). The publisher Springer Nature (2023) adopts the same position and recommends documenting the use of AI powered writing tools in the methods or acknowledgments sections. In this vein, some scholars also argue that using AI-powered writing tools without explicit acknowledgement is a form of deception rather than plagiarism (Weßels, 2023; Schwarz, 2023). With regard to teaching in higher education, there is currently no consensus on how to best deal with AI-supported writing tools. While education providers in some countries currently explicitly prohibit AI-powered writing tools (Ropek, 2023; McCallum, 2023), other universities have already issued some form of recommendations for integrating such tools (see, e.g., University of Washington, 2023; Gimpel et al., 2023). Overall, it is still an open question for many universities to what extent they should adapt or resist these developments (see, e.g., Cano et al., 2023).

2.2 Lecturer Perspective on AI-Powered Writing Tools

In the context of higher education, academic writing lecturers face several issues related to AI-powered writing tools. They have to reconcile 1) administrative requirements of the university, 2) pedagogical goals (e.g., learning objectives, appropriate evaluation method) (Gimpel et al., 2023, p. 28), along with 3) personal goals (e.g., reasonable workload). In doing so, they need to develop an attitude regarding the use of AI-powered writing tools (Dergaa et al., 2023, p. 617). Questions arise as to what extent and under what conditions the use of these tools should or should not be allowed and how these tools should be addressed in the classroom. New competencies may have to be learned in order to teach the reasonable use of these tools (see e.g., concepts about AI literacy as mentioned in the DigComp 2.2 Framework (Vuorikari et al., 2022)).

Lack of transparency in the use of writing tools is a further problem, as it makes it difficult to evaluate and assess a student's individual contribution relative to the tools the student used. How should the use of such tools be made transparent without creating too much workload for me as a lecturer? In which way should I as lecturer evaluate and assess texts submitted by students?

It is further likely that certain students will also use AI-powered writing tools without the consent of the lecturer. How can I ensure as lecturer that students engage with the content in depth and still develop writing competencies?

2.3 University Administration Perspective on AI-Powered Writing Tools

In terms of AI-based writing tools, university administrators face similar issues as lecturers. However, more focus is placed on higher level procedural issues such as treating all students equally. For example, from the point of view of the university administration, it is important that examination formats fulfill the three criteria of 1) validity, 2) reliability and 3) fairness (see e.g., American Educational Research Association, 2014). Currently, voices are being raised calling for the "death of the essay" (Marche, 2022) or at least a radical revision of the current approach to written work (Sharples, 2022). The unauthorized, unnoticed use of AI-powered writing tools to write term papers could lead to a "measurement bias" (American Educational Research Association, 2014, p. 49) that calls into question the fairness of the testing procedure, because student performance may be relatively overestimated (if they use these tools). Are written assignments and term papers still a good examination format or do they need to be revised? How can we establish a fair procedure for all students as well as prevent fraud during examination?

2.4 Student Perspective on AI-Powered Writing Tools

From the students' point of view, AI-powered writing tools offer many advantages, such as correcting grammatical and formal errors, quickly translating and rewriting content, or even creating entirely new text passages. It can be assumed that many students will use any available writing tool that they believe can increase the quality of their final text. However, students may also have certain concerns about using AI-powered writing tools. On the one hand, the recommendations made by these tools are not always reliable (Rogerson & McCarthy, 2017). On the other hand, it is not always clear to what extent the use of such tools is permitted or not.

To better understand the usage behavior of students regarding AI-powered writing tools, a survey was conducted at the University of St. Gallen and the University of Mannheim in September and October 2022 (prior to the release of ChatGPT in November 2022). In total, 643 students participated in the survey. During the survey, students were presented with four different types of AI-powered writing tools (see again Table 1). To provide a common standard and anchor for responding to questions, the different AI-powered writing tools were presented in the form of vignettes, which has become a viable approach in educational research (see e.g., Sailer et al., 2021; Guggemos et al., 2022). A vignette is a stimulus that presents a realistic scenario to the study participants (Skilling & Stylianides, 2020). Each vignette included an image, a description, and specific examples for the type of writing tools (see again Table 1). After viewing a certain vignette, students were asked to what extent they used that type of writing tool themselves. The survey results are presented in Table 2.

Table 2. AI-powered writing tool usage in the fall term 2022

	Always	Often	Sometimes	Occasionally	Rarely	Never
Online translation tools - foreign language texts	19.6%	40.3%	22.9%	8.6%	7.6%	1.1%
Online translation tools - back-and-forth-translation (mother tongue)	12.0%	21.6%	18.4%	10.6%	15.7%	21.8%
Paraphraser and summarizer tools	2.5%	7.6%	14.5%	6.1%	14.6%	54.7%
Online writing assistants	9.0%	14.8%	18.0%	9.8%	14.8%	33.6%

Note: Number of participants = 643. The numbers do not always add up exactly to 100 percent due to rounding. Data gathered in September and October 2022 at the University of St.Gallen and the University of Mannheim.

As we can see in Table 2, even before the release of ChatGPT in November 2022, AI-powered writing tools were widely used by students. Especially online translation tools were widely used for writing both foreign-language and native-language texts (see Table 2).

In the survey, we also showed students a vignette of AI-based content generators such as Writesonic or GPT-3. However, in the fall term 2022 – prior to the release of ChatGPT in November 2022 – student usage of AI-based content generators was still very limited. Most of the students (82.0%) never had tried out AI based content generators. 18% of the students had already tried out at least once such tools. While 6.2% of the students thought that such tools were not useful, another 9.5% of the students thought they were good but too expensive due to the paid subscription plans. 2.3% of the students stated, that they use AI-based content generators and had a paid subscription plan.

While these numbers are likely to have changed in magnitude since the introduction of ChatGPT, they can still provide a general overview of student behaviors in this dynamic field. AI-based writing tools play an important role in student writing. With new, more powerful tools like ChatGPT, this existing dynamic is likely to further accelerate.

2.5 Tensions in the Use of AI-Powered Writing Tools

In the previous sections, it was argued that different stakeholders have (at least partially) different interests in dealing with AI-powered writing tools. Because of their different interests, *tensions* can arise between the stakeholder groups. In the context of this paper, *tensions* are understood as elements that entail both potential advantages and disadvantages (Mini & Widjaja, 2019, p. 4; Smith & Lewis, 2011). In the sense of a trade-off, the advantages and disadvantages of a certain tension must therefore be carefully weighed against each other (Mini & Widjaja, 2019, p. 4; Smith, 2014). The choices that individuals make between the elements of a tension (e.g., using vs. not using AI-powered writing tools) can lead to different emotions such as stress or anxiety (Mini & Widjaja, 2019; Putnam et al., 2016).

In the past, different strategies have been proposed to cope with tensions (Mini & Widjaja, 2019, p. 4; Putnam et al., 2016). For example, in *either-or* strategies (A or B), one element is strictly preferred at the expense of the other. In other strategies (A and B; more A than B, more B than A), a trade-off is made between two elements, with the goal of finding a reasonable compromise (Mini & Widjaja, 2019).

Based on the three different stakeholder perspectives, Figure 1 shows an overview over tensions identified in the previous sections regarding the use of AI-powered writing tools in the context of academic writing. The identified tensions were grouped into three main categories: *First*, tensions emerge regarding the extent to which all individuals should have free access to these tools (see Section 3.1). *Second*, tensions arise about whether AI-assisted writing tools should be used in the context of academic writing in (see Section 3.2). *Third*, it is unclear to what extent the (possible) use of such tools should or should not be made transparent (see Section 3.3).

In the next chapter, the tensions related to AI-powered writing tools are further elaborated and contextualized in relation to existing literature. On that basis, possible *strategies* for overcoming and resolving the existing tensions will be proposed.

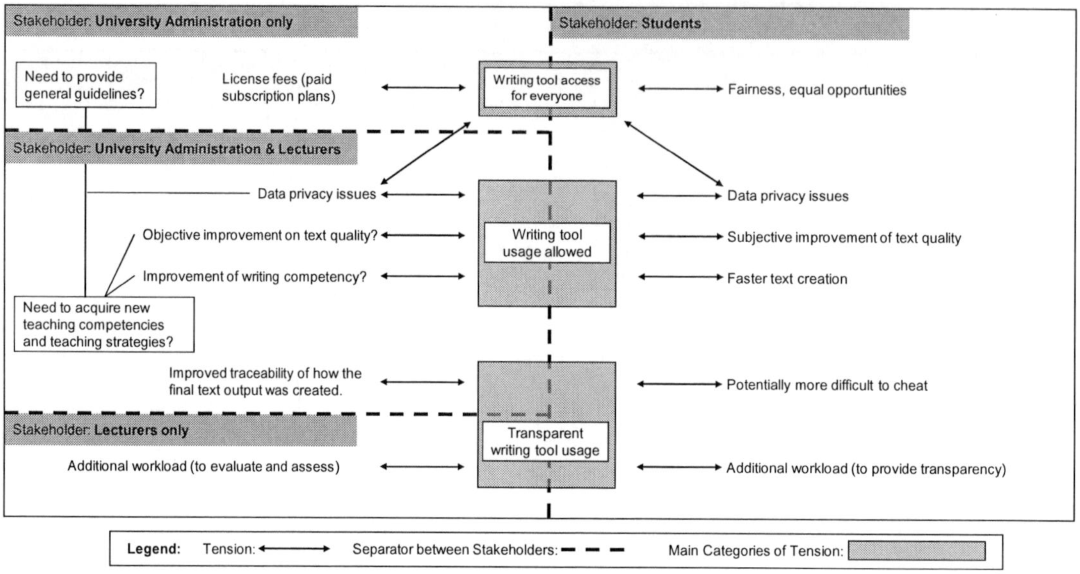

Figure 1. Identified tensions with regard to AI-powered writing tools
Note: Visual representation based on Mini and Widjaja (2019)

3. STRATEGIES FOR AN EFFECTIVE INTEGRATION OF AI-POWERED WRITING TOOLS IN ACADEMIC WRITING

3.1 Tensions Arising due to Writing Tools Access

Table 3 presents areas of tension arising due to writing tools access. As not every student may be able to afford a paid subscription plan to unlock advanced features of AI-powered writing tools, it might be inequitable from a fairness point of view if certain students benefit by using more powerful tools. As a possible strategy to address this issue, the university administration could provide free licenses to all students. However, providing such licenses is costly.

Table 3. Tensions arising due to writing tools access

Tension	Explanation of Elements (A and B)	Strategies (A or B, A and B)
(A) tool access for everyone (fairness) vs. (B) license fees	*(A) Providing writing tool access to all students (B) is costly for the university.* Better, more advanced features of AI-powered writing tools can usually only be unlocked with paid subscription plans. Not every student might be able to afford to pay for such tools, which might raise fairness concerns. The university could provide free licences to all students.	**A:** Provide free writing tool licences to all students. Focus on AI-powered writing tool licences, that can have a large impact on the overall text quality (e.g., tools that integrate a lot of different use cases and features). **A&B:** Provide shared licenses (e.g., on publicly accessible university devices) **B:** Do not provide free writing tool licences to all students.

3.2 Tensions Arising from the Use of Writing Tools

Table 4 presents areas of tension arising from the use of writing tools in academic writing. As can be observed in Table 4, from the students' point of view, the use of AI-powered writing tools enables them to write texts faster. However, there is no consensus on the extent to which the use of these tools improves text quality and promotes writing competencies. In addition, it is often unclear, how the inserted data is further processed and used, which raises data privacy issues.

Table 4 further presents strategies for dealing with each of these tensions. For example, in an on-site classroom setting, one strategy might be to simply ban the use of such tools. However, since in many cases it will not be possible to enforce a ban, it may be more reasonable to adopt strategies that teach students to use these tools in a sensible manner (see Table 4).

Table 4. Tensions arising from the use of writing tools

Tension	Explanation of Elements (A and B)	Strategies (A or B, A and B)
(A) tool usage vs. (B) quality of text output	*(A) The usage of AI-powered writing tools affects (increases/decreases) (B) the quality of the students' text output.* AI-powered writing tools may *increase* the quality of the text, as they support the students in creating a better structured text with less formal and grammatical mistakes (see e.g., Dwivedi et al., 2023, p. 20; Dowling & Lucey, 2023). AI-powered writing tools may *decrease* the quality of the text, if they produce biased, wrong, or too generic content (see e.g., Dwivedi et al., 2023, p. 26; Cano et al., 2023).	**A:** Allow students to use AI-powered writing tools without further guidelines or introduction. **A&B:** Teach students, how to use AI-powered writing tools to better structure their text and increase the formal quality of their texts. **A&B:** Teach students about the limitations of AI-powered writing tools to make them aware and responsible about certain problems, while using such tools (e.g., wrong content due to data hallucination, wrong or missing references) (Gimpel et al., 2023, p. 36). **B:** Prohibit students from using AI-powered writing tools (e.g., in an on-site classroom setting).
(A) tool usage vs. (B) writing competency	*(A) The usage of AI-powered writing tools affects (increases/decreases) (B) the writing competency of students.* AI-powered writing tools may *increase* the writing competency of students *(in a broader sense)*, if they learn how to use them appropriately as part of a larger toolbox to create meaningful texts (see e.g., Mollick & Mollick, 2022). AI-powered writing tools may *decrease* the writing competency of students *(in a narrower sense)*, if students just outsource the whole writing process to the writing tool. In this case, they deal with their texts only superficially, which decreases their writing competency and makes them dependent in the long run (see e.g., Dwivedi et al., 2023, p. 36; Marshall, 2023).	**A:** Allow students to use AI-powered writing tools without further guidelines or introduction. **A&B:** Teach students, how to use AI-powered writing tools as part of a larger writing toolbox (e.g., text editors such as Microsoft Word, reference management systems such as EndNote, academic search engines such as Google Scholar). Explain the advantages and weaknesses of the different tools to foster a well-considered and reflective use. **A&B:** Hinder students, to deal with texts only in a shallow and superficial way. Create assignments and term paper topics, that are not generic and therefore cannot be answered by AI-powered writing tools on their own (Cano et al., 2023, Cotton et al., 2023). Instead, create tasks that require further text adaptation by students (e.g., by incorporating students' own experiences). **B:** Prohibit students from using AI-powered writing tools (e.g., in an on-site classroom setting)
(A) tool usage vs. (B) data privacy	*(A) The usage of AI-powered writing tools can lead to (B) data privacy issues.* Personal information might be inserted when using AI-powered writing tools. It is unclear, how the data is further processed, saved, and used. Therefore, data privacy might be in danger when using such tools (see e.g., Dwivedi et al., 2023, p. 26).	**A:** Allow students to use AI-powered writing tools without further guidelines or introduction. **A&B:** Teach students not to insert any personal data and sensitive information into AI-powered writing tools. **B:** Prohibit students from using AI-powered writing tools (e.g., in an on-site classroom setting)

3.3 Tensions Arising from a Lack of Transparency about Writing Tool Usage

Table 5 presents areas of tension arising from a lack of transparency about writing tool usage. As can be observed in Table 5, lack of transparency makes it more difficult to understand and assess the text creation process. This raises questions about the extent to which only the text output or also its creation process should be evaluated. In addition, establishing more transparency leads to additional workload for both students (by documenting) as well as lecturers (by evaluating the student's documentation).

Table 5 shows strategies how to tackle tensions regarding transparency issues. In particular, strategies are proposed on how to better ensure a transparent use. Among other things, this could include 1) explicitly listing all writing tools used, 2) writing a short statement about how the tools have influenced the final text product, or 3) submitting an additional file of interactions and prompts with AI-assisted writing tools used during text creation.

Table 5. Tensions arising from a lack of transparency about writing tool usage

Tension	Explanation of Elements (A and B)	Strategies (A or B, A and B)
(A) tool transparency vs. (B) evaluation possibilities	*Without (A) transparency about AI-powered writing tool usage, it is difficult to understand and assess (B) the text creation process.* Without AI-powered writing tool transparency, it is difficult to comprehend the text creation process. Therefore, only the final text output can be easily evaluated. It remains unclear whether and to what degree AI-powered writing tools contributed to the creation of the text (see e.g., Dwivedi et al., 2023, pp. 25, 27, 35; University of Washington, 2023).	**A:** Require transparency about AI-powered writing tool usage to better understand and assess the text creation process (Halaweh, 2023, p. 5; Gimpel et al., 2023, p. 32). To increase transparency, require from students to: 1. list the writing tools used (e.g., in the appendix of the term paper); 2. write a one-page-summary (e.g., in the appendix of the term paper) that explains in which ways AI-powered writing tools have contributed to the final paper output; 3. submit an additional file, that includes all interactions and prompts with AI-powered writing tools used to create the term paper (Halaweh, 2023, p. 5). **B:** Do not require transparency about AI-powered writing tool usage. If the text creation process remains important to you, think about other options (e.g., training papers with formative feedback) that give you insights into the students thinking at an earlier stage of the text creation (see also Dwivedi et al., 2023, p. 27).
(A) tool transparency vs. (B) workload	*(A) Providing transparency in the use of AI-powered writing tools, creates (B) additional workload for students (by documenting) as well as for lecturers (by evaluating the student's documentation).*	**A:** Require full transparency about AI-powered writing tool usage (all elements of step 1 to 3 above). **A&B:** Require partial transparency about AI-powered writing tool usage to find a good trade-off between additional transparency and additional workload (choose certain elements of step 1 to 3 above). **B:** Do not require transparency about AI-powered writing tool usage.

4. DISCUSSION: HOW NEW WRITING TOOLS LIKE CHATGPT AFFECT EXISTING DYNAMICS

The release of ChatGPT in November 2022 has further reshaped the dynamic field of AI-powered writing tools in academic writing. In this context, the question arises to what extent the latest developments around LLMs such as ChatGPT affect prevailing tensions as well as strategies for resolving them.

For this purpose, semi-structured expert interviews were conducted with academic writing lecturers at the University of St.Gallen. During April 2023, interviews were conducted with five lecturers who teach academic writing in either German (n=2) or English (n=3). To conduct the interviews, a semi-structured guide was used that included the following three questions: *1) With regard to AI-powered writing tools in academic writing, do you generally agree with the areas of tension highlighted in Figure 1?* 2) *How do new AI-powered writing tools such as ChatGPT affect the prevailing tensions between existing stakeholders?*, 3) *What strategies do you consider useful to cope with a) AI-powered writing tools in general and b) ChatGPT in particular?*

With regard to question 1, the academic writing lecturers stated, that they agreed with the tensions highlighted in Figure 1. In particular, the aspects of transparency, fairness, and influence on writing performance were emphasized by several interview partners.

In question 2, the academic writing lecturers were asked how new AI-powered writing tools such as ChatGPT affect the prevailing tensions between existing stakeholders. The academic writing lecturers said that the basic tensions and conflicts of interest remain largely the same. However, in their view, it will become increasingly important to address the issue as more powerful writing tools emerge. Before the emergence of LLM's like ChatGPT, a certain AI-powered writing tool often performed only one very specific task (e.g., paraphrasing). While such writing tools were already a useful writing support, the scope of application was relatively narrow, and a person still had to think carefully about where and under which conditions it was best to use such a tool. Therefore, the overall impact of such tools on the writing process and output was still rather limited.

With ChatGPT, this dynamic changes, as ChatGPT can be used for many different tasks. As a result, by using ChatGPT, difficult cognitive tasks (e.g., generating, and structuring ideas) may be outsourced by the user to ChatGPT. In the worst case, this poses a risk of dealing with content only in a shallow and superficial way. ChatGPT's simple ease of use via a chat interface tends to reinforce this effect, as ChatGPT has few formal requirements for textual input, and also poses follow-up questions to the user if it requires more information to generate meaningful output.

If AI-powered writing tools can have an increasingly large impact on the entire writing process and output, strategies to cope with them become more important. In question 3, the academic writing lecturers were asked, what strategies they consider useful to cope a) with AI-powered writing tools in general as well as b) ChatGPT in particular. Overall, there was agreement among the interview partners that strategies aimed at either a straight ban or an approval without further guidelines and support will rarely be optimal. In this context, those strategies presented in Tables 3, 4 and 5 were considered as useful, that seek a compromise between the two extremes (A&B).

With regard to ChatGPT, respondents considered strategies that *increase transparency in use* to be particularly important. According to one respondent, ChatGPT increases *student empowerment* but also *uncertainty*. One the one hand, ChatGPT empowers students "because it gives them the belief, that their writing process could be more efficient". On the other hand, students become uncertain about their text output. In this view, ChatGPT raises fundamental questions of authorship and has set in motion a negotiation process with human authors and their own thinking. What are *my* ideas and *my* contribution when working with AI-powered writing tools? How can I avoid copyright issues and give sufficient credit to other human authors? In the best case, this inner thought discourse might lead to students that have more self-awareness and a more sensible approach when using AI-powered writing tools. In the worst case, students might just use these tools in an unreflective way, which may lead to plagiarism issues. Figure 2 summarizes this idea by illustrating a cascade of possible consequences when using AI-assisted writing tools.

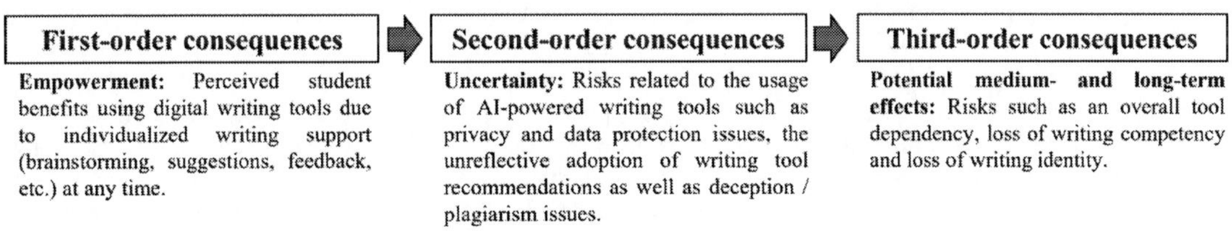

Figure 2. Potential student consequences of using of AI-powered writing tools in academic writing
Note: Own illustration

To prevent or at least counteract the negative effects that second-order and third-order consequences may have on students, lecturers should proactively educate students about these potential effects. According to the interview respondents, ChatGPT provides the opportunity to discuss with students, in the context of academic writing, fundamental questions such as the concept of authorship, the documentation of results in a scientifically rigorous manner, as well as the (fact checked) evidence-based generation of knowledge. The ability to critically question the identified results and to take responsibility for one's own work are tasks that only humans can take on. For this reason, it is important to educate students in the use of such tools with various strategies and to sensitize them to both the opportunities as well as the limitations. Ideally, in this way, the benefits of these tools can be maximized, while the shortcomings may be largely avoided.

5. CONCLUSION & OUTLOOK

This paper demonstrated, in the context of academic writing, that different stakeholders (students, lecturers, university administration) have different interests with respect to AI-powered writing tools. On this basis, tensions between different stakeholders were identified and strategies were proposed to deal with these tensions. Based on semi-structured expert interviews, the results were discussed in light of the recent developments around ChatGPT, with the goal of developing sustainable strategies for successfully dealing with AI-powered writing tools in academic writing.

With regard to the introduction of new technologies, there can be a danger "to rush to conclusions before clearly understanding the problem" (Markovitz, 2020). Due to that different aspects quickly can become mixed up. For example, the overall *text quality* may be equalized with *the learning gain in writing competence*. However, depending on what the goal is (good text quality and/or gains in writing competence), different (teaching) strategies might be useful in achieving those goals. The aim of this paper was to identify and analyze in which ways AI-powered writing tools affect the context of academic writing. In this way, fields of action in the form of strategies have been proposed on how different tensions related to AI-powered writing tools could be addressed in a meaningful way.

This study is subject to different limitations. *First*, the survey data on student usage patterns of AI-powered writing tools (see section 2.4) represent only a snapshot taken in September/October 2022. It is likely, particularly due to the release of ChatGPT in November 2022, that these numbers have changed since then. However, since the goal was to provide insight into this dynamically changing and evolving field, this limitation was deliberately accepted. *Second*, due to the approach of a stakeholder analysis, it is assumed that all persons within a stakeholder group share the same interests. In reality, of course, this is not always the case. For example, not all lecturers have the same attitude towards AI-powered writing tools, which may create additional tensions within the *lecturer* stakeholder group.

From a theoretical point of view, the paper at hand can serve as a starting point for future research as it highlights important concepts and variables related to AI-powered writing tools in academic writing. From a practical standpoint, the paper at hand might be valuable for people who work in the field of academic writing, as the paper highlights different strategies (see Table 3, 4 and 5) how to cope with AI-powered writing tools in academic writing. The derived strategies as well as its implications might serve as a starting point for further discussion to introduce meaningful, sustainable regulations in one's own context.

It remains an open question what specific learning scenarios are best suited to foster students' writing competencies in the context of AI-powered writing tools. The work of Mollick and Mollick (2023) already indicates a possible direction, how learning scenarios with AI-powered writing tools could look like. Nevertheless, further research is needed in this area to contribute to a more meaningful use of AI-powered writing tools. While the DigComp 2.2 framework (see Vuorikari et al., 2022) integrated an update on the competence area of *AI literacy* (knowledge, skills and attitudes for the competent use of AI systems), this approach might have to be extended. The ability *to reflect* on one's own behavior is an essential element in a student's ability to learn through experience (Coulson & Harvey, 2013). As the discussion on the potential consequences of using AI-powered writing tools highlighted (see Figure 2), students may increasingly need *metacognitive reflection abilities* (see e.g., Coulson & Harvey, 2013; Gibson et al., 2017) when working with AI-powered writing tools to counteract the potential negative effects such tools can have. Therefore, further research is needed on how to best foster students' reflection abilities when working with AI-assisted writing tools.

ACKNOWLEDGEMENT

I would like to thank the team of Prof. Dr. Dirk Ifenthaler at the University of Mannheim, with whom the survey mentioned in section 2.4 was conducted. I further thank the five academic writing lecturers at the University of St.Gallen, who shared their views with me during the expert interviews.

This paper was written without ChatGPT. However, the translation tool DeepL (https://deepl.com/translator) was used to improve the style and grammar of sentences.

REFERENCES

American Educational Research Association. (2014). *Standards for educational and psychological testing*. American Educational Research Association. https://www.testingstandards.net/open-access-files.html

Brown, T.B., Mann, B., Ryder, N., Subbiah, M., Kaplan, J., Dhariwal, P., Neelakantan, A., Shyam, P., Sastry, G., Askell, A., Agarwal, S., Herbert-Voss, A., Krueger, G., Henighan, T., Child, R., Ramesh, A., Ziegler, D. M., Wu, J., Winter, C., ... Amodei, D. (2020). *Language models are few-shot learners*. arXiv preprint. https://arxiv.org/abs/2005.14165

Cano, Y. M., Venuti, F., & Martinez, R. H. (2023). *ChatGPT and AI Text Generators: Should Academia Adapt or Resist*. Harvard Business Publishing Education. https://hbsp.harvard.edu/inspiring-minds/chatgpt-and-ai-text-generators-should-academia-adapt-or-resist

Carr, K. [@kareem_carr]. (2023, January 12). *So I guess we're doing this now* [Image attached] [Tweet]. Twitter. https://twitter.com/kareem_carr/status/1613325029848092672

Cotton, D. R. E., Cotton, P. A., & Shipway, J. R. (2023). Chatting and Cheating: Ensuring academic integrity in the era of ChatGPT. *Innovations in Education and Teaching International*. https://doi.org/10.1080/14703297.2023.2190148

Coulson, D., & Harvey, M. (2013). Scaffolding student reflection for experience-based learning: A framework. *Teaching in Higher Education, 18*(4), 401-413. https://doi.org/10.1080/13562517.2012.752726

Dergaa, I., Chamari, K., Zmijewski, P., & Saad, H. B. (2023). From human writing to artificial intelligence generated text: examining the prospects and potential threats of ChatGPT in academic writing. *Biology of Sport, 40*(2), 615-622. https://doi.org/10.5114/biolsport.2023.125623

Dowling, M., & Lucey, B. (2023). ChatGPT for (finance) research: The Bananarama conjecture. *Finance Research Letters*, 103662. https://doi.org/10.1016/j.frl.2023.103662

Dwivedi, Y. K., Kshetri, N., Hughes, L., Slade, E. L., Jeyaraj, A., Kumar Kar, A., Baabdullah, A. M., Koohang, A., Raghavan, V., Ahuja, M., Albanna, H., Albashrawi, M. A., Al-Busaidi, A. S., Balakrishnan, J., Barlette, Y., Basu, S., Bose, I., Brooks, L., Buhalis, D., Carter, L., ... & Wright, R. (2023). “So what if ChatGPT wrote it?” Multidisciplinary perspectives on opportunities, challenges and implications of generative conversational AI for research, practice and policy. *International Journal of Information Management, 71*, 102642. https://doi.org/10.1016/j.ijinfomgt.2023.102642

Geitgey, A. (2018, July 18). *Natural Language Processing is Fun! How computers understand Human Language*. Medium. https://medium.com/@ageitgey/natural-language-processing-is-fun-9a0bff37854e

Gibson, A., Aitken, A., Sándor, Á., Buckingham Shum, S., Tsingos-Lucas, C., & Knight, S. (2017). Reflective writing analytics for actionable feedback. In *Proceedings of the seventh international learning analytics & knowledge conference* (pp. 153-162). https://doi.org/10.1145/3027385.3027436

Gimpel, H., Hall, K., Decker, S., Eymann, T., Lämmermann, L., Mädche, A., Röglinger, M., Ruiner, C., Schoch, M., Schoop, M., Urbach, N., & Vandrik, S. (2023). *Unlocking the power of generative AI models and systems such asGPT-4 and ChatGPT for higher education*. Kommunikations-, Informations- und Medienzentrum (KIM). http://nbn-resolving.de/urn:nbn:de:bsz:100-opus-21463

Guggemos, J., Sonderegger, S., & Seufert, S. (2022). Student acceptance of social robots in higher education - Evidence from a vignette study. *19th International Conference on Cognition and Exploratory Learning in Digital Age (CELDA 2022)*, 8-10 November, Lisbon Portugal.

Halaweh, M. (2023). ChatGPT in education: Strategies for responsible implementation. *Contemporary Educational Technology, 15*(2). https://doi.org/10.30935/cedtech/13036

Heaven, W. D. (2020, July 20). *OpenAI's new language generator GPT-3 is shockingly good—and completely mindless*. MIT Technology Review. https://www.technologyreview.com/2020/07/20/1005454/openai-machine-learning-language-generator-gpt-3-nlp/

Ivanic, R. (1998). *Writing and Identity: the discoursal construction of identity in academic texts*. John Benjamins e-Platform. https://doi.org/10.1075/swll.5

Marche, S. (2022, December 6). *The College Essay Is Dead: Nobody is prepared for how AI will transform academia*. The Atlantic. https://www.theatlantic.com/technology/archive/2022/12/chatgpt-ai-writing-college-student-essays/672371/

Markovitz, D. (2020, November 27). How to Avoid Rushing to Solutions When Problem-Solving. *Harvard Business Review*. https://hbr.org/2020/11/how-to-avoid-rushing-to-solutions-when-problem-solving

Marshall, C. (2023, February 10). *Noam Chomsky on ChatGPT: It's “Basically High-Tech Plagiarism” and “a Way of Avoiding Learning”*. Open Culture. https://www.openculture.com/2023/02/noam-chomsky-on-chatgpt.html

McCallum, S. (2023, April 2). *ChatGPT banned in Italy over privacy concerns*. BBC News. https://www.bbc.com/news/technology-65139406

Mini, T., & Widjaja, T. (2019). Tensions in Digital Platform Business Models: A Literature Review. In *ICIS*.

Mollick, E. R., & Mollick, L. (2022). *New Modes of Learning Enabled by AI Chatbots: Three Methods and Assignments*. Social Science Research Network (SSRN). https://dx.doi.org/10.2139/ssrn.4300783

Mollick, E. R., & Mollick, L. (2023). *Using AI to Implement Effective Teaching Strategies in Classrooms: Five Strategies, Including Prompts*. Social Science Research Network (SSRN). https://papers.ssrn.com/sol3/papers.cfm?abstract_id=4391243

Moore, J. L., Rosinski, P., Peeples, T., Pigg, S., Rife, M. C., Brunk-Chavez, B., Lackey, D., Kesler Rumsey, S., Tasaka, R., Curran, P., & Grabill, J. T. (2016). Revisualizing composition: How first-year writers use composing technologies. *Computers and Composition, 39*, 1-13. https://doi.org/10.1016/j.compcom.2015.11.001

Peters, M., & Cadieux, A. (2019). Are Canadian professors teaching the skills and knowledge students need to prevent plagiarism?. *International Journal for Educational Integrity, 15*(1), 1-16. https://doi.org/10.1007/s40979-019-0047-z

Prentice, F. M., & Kinden, C. E. (2018). Paraphrasing tools, language translation tools and plagiarism: an exploratory study. *International Journal for Educational Integrity, 14*(1), 1-16. https://doi.org/10.1007/s40979-018-0036-7

Purcell, K., Buchanan, J., & Friedrich, L. (2013). *The impact of digital tools on student writing and how writing is taught in schools*. National Writing Project, Pew Research Center.

Putnam, L. L., Fairhurst, G. T., & Banghart, S. (2016). Contradictions, dialectics, and paradoxes in organizations: A constitutive approach. *Academy of Management Annals, 10*(1), 65-171. https://doi.org/10.5465/19416520.2016.1162421

Rogerson, A. M., & McCarthy, G. (2017). Using Internet based paraphrasing tools: Original work, patchwriting or facilitated plagiarism?. *International Journal for Educational Integrity, 13*(1), 2. https://doi.org/10.1007/s40979-016-0013-y

Ropek, L. (2023, January, 4). *New York City Schools Ban ChatGPT to Head Off a Cheating Epidemic*. Gizmodo. https://gizmodo.com/new-york-city-schools-chatgpt-ban-cheating-essay-openai-1849949384

Sailer, M., Stadler, M., Schultz-Pernice, F., Franke, U., Schöffmann, C., Paniotova, V., Husagic, L., & Fischer, F. (2021). Technology-related teaching skills and attitudes: Validation of a scenario-based self-assessment instrument for teachers. *Computers in Human Behavior, 115*, 106625. https://doi.org/10.1016/j.chb.2020.106625

Schwarz, S. (2023, February 2). *#ChatGPT und Täuschung in Schule und Hochschule*. Beck-Community. https://community.beck.de/2023/02/02/chatgpt-und-taeuschung-in-schule-und-hochschule

Sharples, M. (2022, May 17). *New AI tools that can write student essays require educators to rethink teaching and assessment*. LSE Impact Blog. https://blogs.lse.ac.uk/impactofsocialsciences/2022/05/17/new-ai-tools-that-can-write-student-essays-require-educators-to-rethink-teaching-and-assessment/

Skilling, K., & Stylianides, G. J. (2020). Using vignettes in educational research: a framework for vignette construction. International *Journal of Research & Method in Education, 43*(5), 541–556. https://doi.org/10.1080/1743727X.2019.1704243

Smith, W. K., & Lewis, M. W. (2011). Toward a theory of paradox: A dynamic equilibrium model of organizing. *Academy of Management Review, 36*(2), 381-403. https://doi.org/10.5465/amr.2009.0223

Smith, W. K. (2014). Dynamic decision making: A model of senior leaders managing strategic paradoxes. *Academy of Management Journal, 57*(6), 1592-1623. https://doi.org/10.5465/amj.2011.0932

Springer Nature. (2023, January 24). *Tools such as ChatGPT threaten transparent science; here are our ground rules for their use*. Springer Nature. https://doi.org/10.1038/d41586-023-00191-1

Taylor & Francis. (2023, February 17). *Taylor & Francis Clarifies the Responsible use of AI Tools in Academic Content Creation*. Taylor & Francis. https://newsroom.taylorandfrancisgroup.com/taylor-francis-clarifies-the-responsible-use-of-ai-tools-in-academic-content-creation/

University of Washington. (2023, March 30). *ChatGPT and other AI-based tools*. Center for Teaching and Learning, University of Washington, Seattle. https://teaching.washington.edu/topics/preparing-to-teach/academic-integrity/chatgpt/

Van Eemeren, F. H., & Grootendorst, R. (2016). *Argumentation, communication, and fallacies: A pragma-dialectical perspective*. Routledge.

Vuorikari, R., Kluzer, S., & Punie, Y. (2022). *DigComp 2.2: The Digital Competence Framework for Citizens - With new examples of knowledge, skills and attitudes*. Office of the European Union. https://publications.jrc.ec.europa.eu/repository/handle/JRC128415

Weßels, D. (2023, January 29). *Was ist ChatGPT und wie funktioniert es? – Und welche ähnlichen Tools gibt es?* [Video]. YouTube. https://www.youtube.com/watch?v=cMuBo_rH15c

ANALYSING AFFORDANCES OF THE E-ASSESSMENT SYSTEM NUMBAS IN MATHEMATICS EDUCATION FROM AN ACTIVITY THEORY PERSPECTIVE

Said Hadjerrouit and Celestine Ifeanyi Nnagbo[1]*
Institute of Mathematical Sciences, Faculty of Engineering and Sciences,
University of Agder, Kristiansand, Norway

ABSTRACT

The purpose of this paper is to investigate the affordances of the e-assessment system Numbas from an Activity Theory perspective. The study follows a qualitative research design combined with semi-structured interviews with six students and two teachers. The findings reveal that the students were able to perceive and actualise several affordances of Numbas, such as ease of use and navigation and possession of facility to contain mathematical knowledge. The participants acknowledged that Numbas affords variation in mathematical contents and support for the development of pen and paper skills. Numbas also affords learner's autonomy and motivation to engage in mathematical problem-solving. Findings further show that Numbas promotes formative assessment. This can be seen from the high level of affordance perception and actualisation amongst students and teachers.

KEYWORDS

Activity Theory, Actualization, Affordances, Constraints, E-Assessment, Emergence, Feedback, Perception, Numbas

1. INTRODUCTION

The provision of feedback to students is considered to have a significant influence on learning achievement in mathematics, especially when the feedback is timely, constructive, and oriented towards improvement (Burns, Martin, & Evans, 2019). It can be received from teachers or peers. Feedback is one of the five key strategies in the framework proposed by Black and Wiliam (2009) for formative assessment. As such, it is difficult to disjoint feedback from any form of formative assessment in mathematics education (Kyaruzi, et al., 2019). However, there seems to be a consensus among education researchers that for feedback to be effective in enhancing students' learning outcomes it should be task-specific, contain learning-related information, timely and informative (Einig, 2013; Hattie & Timperley, 2007; Pinger, et al. 2016). Given the need to provide timely feedback to students, several institutions have been responding by experimenting with different ways to address this need (Einig, 2013). Recently, technologies like e-assessment systems are gaining more attention in mathematics education because they provide a resource-efficient way to providing the much-needed timely feedback. E-assessment systems provide new learning potentials for a large cohort of students by means of formative assessment. However, research on e-assessment systems is still in its infancy, especially in the area that assesses their affordances and constraints. The present study proposes a framework that captures the affordances of Numbas in a technology-based course in teacher education. It is a continuation of previous studies (Hadjerrouit & Nnagbo, 2022a; Hadjerrouit & Nnagbo, 2022b; Hadjerrouit & Nnagbo, 2021; Nnagbo, 2020). The participants were six students and two teachers. This study addresses three research questions:

1. What affordances of Numbas are perceived by students and teachers?
2. How are the affordances of Numbas actualised by students and teachers?
3. What are the constraints for the actualisation of Numbas' affordances?

[1]* Celestine Ifeanyi Nnagbo wrote and defended his master's thesis in December 2020 in mathematics education at the Institute of Mathematical Sciences, Faculty of Engineering and Sciences, University of Agder, Kristiansand, Norway.

2. NUMBAS

Numbas is a general e-assessment system for mathematics-related courses with emphasis on formative assessment and feedback to students' actions. It has been developed by the e-learning unit of Newcastle university's school of mathematics and statistics (Perfect, 2015). The primary use of Numbas is to enable students to enter a mathematical answer in the form of an algebraic expression, and then see how Numbas feedback can impact students' mathematical engagement. Numbas performs marking on the client which makes its feedback immediate. There are multiple ways Numbas gives feedback. These include submit answer, show steps, reveal answers, try another question like this one.

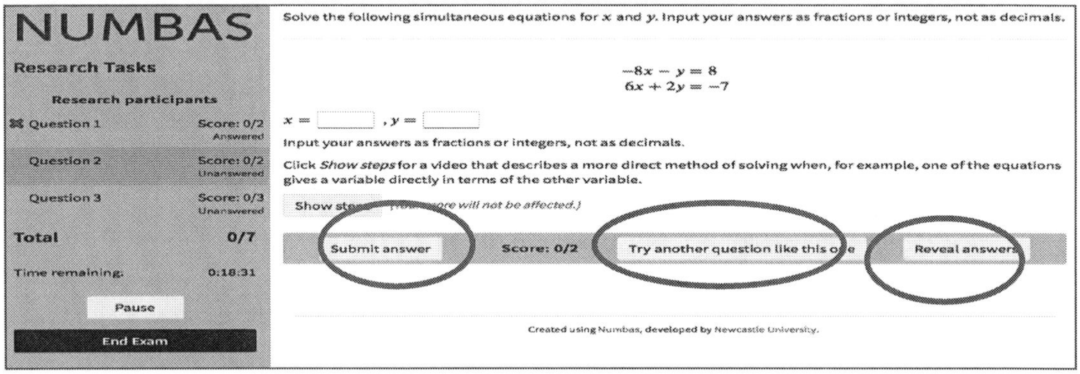

Figure 1. Numbas feedback options

- **Submit answer-** Students get instant feedback as soon as they submit an answer. The feedback simply indicates with a green colour 'good' sign if the submitted answer is correct, with red colour 'bad' sign indicating that the supplied answer is wrong, or partially correct, with feedback message underneath. The students will also be shown the maximum attainable score for each question, and their own score for the question after they have submitted the answer. The teacher may choose to disable these feedback options.
- **Show steps**- When a student clicks on the show steps, Numbas gives the general solution to that question. It may include video or graphical explanation depending on the kind of feedback the teacher puts in there. This is a way of reminding the student to have a look at the formula or the general solution and retry solving the task. The option "Show steps" does not give students the exact solution to the particular task.
- **Try another question like this one-** Numbas uses the set of variables defined by arbitrary mathematical expressions to randomly generate questions that are similar. With this, student have the opportunity to attempt similar questions many times until they feel confidence enough to move to the next question.
- **Reveal answer**- This section called advice section contains fully worked solution to the particular question. It provides step by step solution that is personalised to the question randomly generated question to the student. When a student decides to explore this option, they lose all the marks and cannot re-attempt the exact question. Again, the instructor may decide to disable this.
- **Statistics**- Numbas stores data of students' performance. This is particularly helpful to the teachers. They can track how well the students understand the topic through their performances, and they can equally identify the tasks students perform below expectations and reemphasis on them in the next class.

3. THEORETICAL FRAMEWORK

3.1 Activity Theory

Activity Theory has its root in the cultural-historical psychology work of Vygotsky. The primary ideas of the theory rests on a socio-cultural perspective in which learning is conceived as an offshoot of a dynamic relationship between the learner and the environment. With this perspective, learning is an appropriation of knowledge through a feedback relation between the learner and the environment (Vygotsky, 1978). Another fundamental concept of Activity Theory is the word 'activity' itself (Engeström, 2014). Leont'ev, 1978) defines an activity as any purposeful interaction between a *subject* (which could be an individual or group), and an *object*. The underlying assumption of the theory is that an *artefact* mediates the interaction between subject and object to give the desired outcome. More specifically, Numbas affordances are viewed from an Activity Theory perspective as a dynamic relationship between a goal-oriented user and the e-assessment system.

3.2 Affordances

The term 'affordance' was coined by James J. Gibson, who proposed the term to describe what the environment offers the animal, "what it provides or furnishes, either for good or ill" (Gibson, 1986, p. 127). Gibson argues that affordances can be seen from the properties of the environment that are relative to the animal in question. He further stresses that affordances must be peculiar to the animal, not just any property of the environment or whatever the environment can offer.

Affordances can be both objective and subjective, "they are objective because they exist independently of the act of perception, but they are also subjective because the frame of reference is the individual's action capabilities" (Osiurak, Rossetti, & Badets, 2017). Gibson further uses the concept of niche in ecology to refer to the set of affordances. He explains that "a niche refers more to how an animal lives than to where it lives". According to Hadjerrouit (2017, p. 213), "affordance is a relation between an organism and object with the object perceived in relation to the needs of the organism: cliffs afford falling off, small stones afford throwing, chairs afford sitting, door afford opening, etc.".

Norman (1988) introduced the concept of affordances in the Human-Computer-Interaction community. Norman's conceptualisation of affordances restricts affordances to an exclusive property of the object unlike Gibson's original conceptualisation. However, Norman reconsidered this position and embraces the fact that affordances are not an exclusive property of an object in isolation (Norman, 1999).

3.2.1 Emergence of Numbas Affordances

The object of the activity is the mathematical knowledge in the form of feedback received during the course of activity by the subject, e.g., the student. Within the activity system, the object provides reasons for the behaviours of the subject or , in other words, the subject uses artefacts to mediate activity so that the object can be achieved (Sexton & Lamb, 2017). As such, the mediating artefact is Numbas. It is important to remark that there is a thin line between the mediating artefact (Numbas) and the object (feedback delivery) in the present study because the former encloses the latter, unlike physical classroom objects, such as whiteboards and pointer that are used as mediators. Therefore, the outcome of a dynamic interaction (activity) between the subject (e.g., student), the object (feedback delivery), and the mediating artefact (Numbas) is the affordance of Numbas. In other words, Numbas affordances are not an exclusive property of the artefact and not completely determined by the subject. Instead, they emerge from a dynamic interaction between the artefact and the subject.

3.2.2 Perception of Numbas Affordances

Affordance perception of a given tool concerns its awareness by a goal-oriented user during the interaction. Affordance perception is conceptually different from its existence and it is logical to treat it as such (Greeno, 1994). It exists independently of the user's perception during interaction and can be perceived at varying levels of adequacy depending on contextually, socially, and technically motivated factors (Wang et al., 2018). As such, when students interact with Numbas to facilitate feedback delivery on some mathematics concepts they do so conveniently with the aid of the technical features of the software. During this process, they become aware of the affordances that emerged during the interaction in terms of feedback delivery.

3.2.3 Actualisation of Numbas Affordances

Given the emergence and the perception of Numbas affordances, some questions are still waiting to be addressed: (a) How are action potentials turned into actions? (b) Does an action potential necessarily need to be perceived before being actualised?

Affordance actualisation is a process of turning action potentials (affordances) into real actions to bring an effect in using a particular tool (Anderson & Robey, 2017; Bernhard et al., 2013). In specific terms, affordance actualisations are "the actions taken by actors as they take advantage of one or more affordances through their use of the technology to achieve immediate concrete outcomes in support of organizational goals" (Strong et al. 2014, p. 70). To turn a possibility into an action, it is expected that the user has the ability and capability to harness the potential and there are enabling conditions to facilitate the process. Affordance actualisation varies from one individual to another because it is goal-oriented and a process of specificity (Volkoff & Strong, 2017)

3.3 Affordances from an Activity Theory Perspective

Figure 2 presents the underlying theoretical framework that captures the emergence, perception, and actualisation of Numbas affordances. It is expected that following the actualisation of Numbas affordances are some consequences (effects). These consequences as Bernhard et al. (2013) put it may be "intended by the user and/or those by the original creator of the artefact as well as unintended effects" (p. 6). Moreover, it is important to highlight that the actualisation of Numbas affordances does not happen in isolation. In fact, affordances go along with constraints; they are facilitated by enabling conditions and hindered by constraints. In other words, affordances and constraints are inseparable because they complement each other, and not opposite.

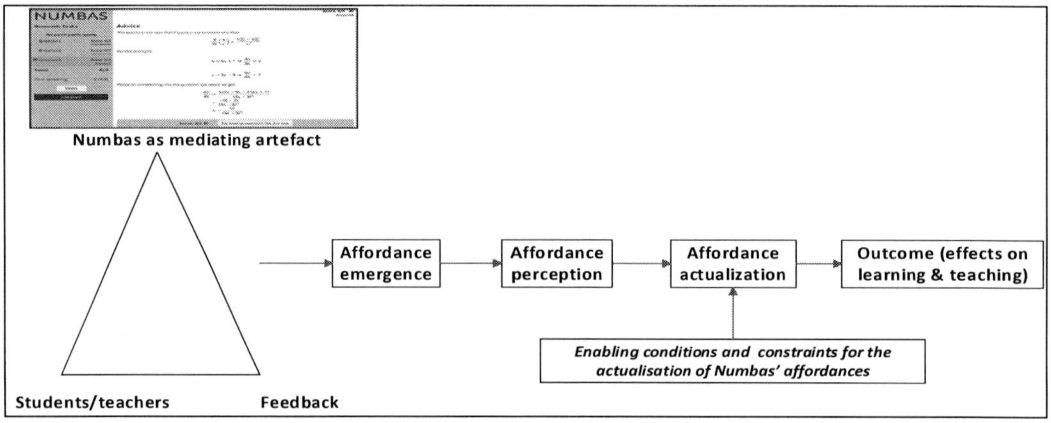

Figure 2. Affordances from an Activity Theory perspective

4. FINDINGS

From a methodological point of view, this work uses a case study to analyze the affordances perceived and actualized by the participants while interacting with Numbas. A thematic approach to data analysis is used to identify themes and codes within the data set (Bryman, 2016). Code development takes a deductive-inductive strategy consisting of an interplay between the pre-defined categorization of affordances and the empirical data that emerged inductively. Based on this analyse, this section presents a summary of the findings.

4.1 What affordances of Numbas are Perceived?

Interview data show that the students and teachers perceived various degrees of affordances of Numbas. Recall that an affordance is not an exclusive property of Numbas in isolation, rather it emerges in an activity system. Therefore, the affordances of Numbas are those outcomes of a dynamic interaction (activity) between the subject (student, teacher), the object (feedback delivery), and the mediating artefact (Numbas). The perception of the emerged Numbas affordances concerns the awareness by goal-oriented users (teachers and students) during the interaction. The students expressed their experiences in using Numbas to receive formative feedbacks to mathematical tasks, and the teachers indicated using Numbas to deliver formative feedbacks to their students.

From a technological point of view, the students and teachers responded that the user interface of Numbas is easy to use. During their interaction with Numbas, there was no confusions regarding the design of the interface. It looks simple and intuitive. Navigation to any page is also easy. They did not find it challenging to access feedback pages or submitting answers. The icons are visible with good and accurate inscriptions. Furthermore, they perceived that Numbas is Web-based, and that it can be accessed at any location or time, so long as there is internet coverage. They were also aware that Numbas has the facility to contain mathematical contents.

From a pedagogical point of view, the students and teachers perceived that Numbas affords variation in a way of displaying mathematical contents. They also perceived the affordances of Numbas to guarantee and increase students' autonomy, motivation, and engagement. They found the user friendliness and feedback mechanisms of the interface to be motivating. Potentialities to stimulate collaboration and contain collaboratives tasks, together with supporting individuals to learn at their respective paces were further perceived. They were also aware of Numbas potentials to support procedural understanding with high chances of supporting conceptual understanding. Some constraints of Numbas were perceived as well. Several forms of tests and assessment, including matrix, multiple choices, etc. with appropriate feedbacks were perceived. They further saw the possibilities of performing diagnostic teaching with the aid of Numbas.

From a teacher education point of view, both teachers and students perceived that Numbas will be useful to school teachers in achieving some of their teaching objectives. Therefore, they perceived that Numbas is adoptable to the new core curriculum for the mathematics subject.

4.2 How are the Affordances of Numbas Actualised?

The second question aims to address how the perceived affordances of Numbas are actualised (turned into actions) to bring effect(s) on the user. Recall that affordance perception and actualisation are treated as two distinct processes in this study, and in most cases, affordances are perceived before they are actualised.

At the technological level, students actualised the perceived affordances of ease of use, ease of navigation, overall accessibility, and facility to contain mathematical contents in several ways. Findings reveal that students were able to solve tasks and enter their answers in Numbas with ease. They also used the feedbacks mechanisms successfully. They easily navigated around by following inscriptions in the icons. Regarding accessibility, the students did formative assessments in Numbas from home without difficulties.

At the pedagogical level, students actualised the perceived affordance of variation by solving many mathematical tasks in different forms - graphical, diagrams, equations, etc. They copied out most of the tasks on paper, solved them using pen and paper, and consulted mathematics textbooks when necessary, before inputting the final answer(s) into the space provided by Numbas. The students actualised learner's autonomy to work in Numbas without assistance of their teachers by doing some tasks alone using only hints and other feedbacks from Numbas. However, they sought for the assistance of their fellow students, or the class teacher on some occasions. The feedbacks they received when they solved task in Numbas, especially the immediate feedback, together with user friendliness of the interface are the main source of motivation for the students. As for the affordances of collaboration, students worked in groups using Numbas in classroom. They also actualised higher order thinking when Numbas marked their correct answer wrong. In the quest to trace the error, they engaged in mathematical thinking. The students further solved different tasks and received various degrees of feedbacks along the line to actualisation of the perceived affordances.

The teachers actualised some of the affordances in a different way. This is due to their role as teachers and task creators. They relied on observations of their students to confirm the actualisation of some of the affordances. For example, they actualised 'ease of use' to create tasks but to a limited extent because they found it difficult to make complex tasks. They actualised accessibility by using Numbas at home, not just in school. In creating tasks, teachers made use of manuals provided by Numbas to create questions that include graphs, diagram GeoGebra worksheets etc, thereby actualising the perceived affordances of facility and variation. In terms of learner autonomy, students worked independently, but relied on the teachers to solve some tasks. The students worked in pairs using Numbas, thereby achieving collaboration. The teachers also used the statistical feedback from Numbas to inform their lessons and meetings with students.

4.3 What are the Constraints for the Actualisation of Affordances?

Findings from the students and teachers' interview data revealed that they actualised some of the perceived affordances that emerged but did not actualise others. In some cases, they actualised the affordances but not completely due to constraints. Findings reveal that insufficient navigation buttons, lack of internet connections are some constraints hindering full actualisation of perceived affordances at technological layers by the students. At the pedagogical level, the study found that teachers' poor knowledge to make comprehensive feedback. System glitch from Numbas, lack of features to save students' profiles to automatically assign tasks based on their performance progress, or support for collaboration from different locations, using different devices are some constraints hindering full actualisation of the affordances. At the teacher education level, they faced hindrance in a way that assessing conceptual understanding is difficult.

The teachers also found it challenging to make 'very good' tasks due to requirements of programming language. They also agreed with the students that internet could constrain the use of Numbas at any time and location. In terms of autonomy affordance, teachers believed that students' poor skills in the use of digital tools is a constraint. Teachers perceived the affordance of differentiation as a way of creating different levels of tasks, but could not actualised it due to time constraints. Other constraints include lack of features to save students' profiles and automatically assign tasks based on their performance progress, or support collaboration from different locations, using different devices.

5. DISCUSSION

The main goal of this study is to explore how Numbas promotes formative assessment for mathematics teaching and learning by assessing the affordances and constraints that emerge from interactions between teachers/students and Numbas. Three research questions were addressed towards achieving the goal. The first research question concerns the perception of Numbas affordances, the second concerns affordance actualisation, while the third one concerns the constraints. The study follows a qualitative research design in which data were generated using semi-structured interviews with six students and two teachers. The participants were familiar with Numbas and affordance theory. The designing of the interview guide was guided by the theoretical framework proposed for the study to collect data on the emergence, perception, actualisation of Numbas affordances, which are viewed from an Activity Theory perspective.

Findings reveal that the students were able to perceive and actualise several technological affordances of Numbas, such as ease of use and navigation, full accessibility, and facilities to contain mathematical knowledge. From a pedagogical point of view, the participants acknowledged that Numbas affords variation in mathematical contents, congruence with textbook mathematics, and support for the development of pen and paper skills. It was also acknowledged that Numbas could afford students' autonomy and motivation to engage in mathematical problem-solving. Numbas has constraints in the form of wrong marking of some correct answers, though in rare occasions. Surprisingly, this constraint is found to provoke mathematical thinking in most of the students. The feedback mechanisms are perceived to be very helpful and motivating. From an institutional point of view, Numbas suitability to be used in schools was perceived and recommended. Findings further show that Numbas is a very useful to promote formative assessment. This can be seen from the high level of affordance perception and actualisation, which in effect leads to formative feedback delivery. Clearly, user-friendliness of Numbas user interface supports the perception and actualization of affordances.

5.1 Limitations

The strength of the study is that affordances and constraints of Numbas have been studied in detail using semi-structured interviews as an instrument of data collection. However, the study is not without limitations. Firstly, the number of participants (*N=8*) is just one case of master's students and their teachers from a teacher education program of one university. The number is small when compared to the entire number of students and teachers using Numbas. Hence, a larger number of participants from several universities could have been more desirable to make better generalisation. Secondly, the participating students do not use Numbas for regular assessment in their own studies. Students using Numbas for day-by-day activities may have a different perspective about the affordance perception and actualisation processes, together with the constraints. Studies involving such set of students would be good to compare with findings of the presents report. Finally, Activity Theory has proved to be useful for arguing that the emergence of Numbas affordances is a result of a dynamic relationship between a goal-oriented user and the tool. Likewise, affordance theory has shown to be important in explaining the distinctiveness between affordance perception and actualisation. Moreover, the proposed framework has further shown to be a good guide for analysing affordances and constraints that emerge in an educational setting. However, the model as presented in the study is not intended to map all potential affordances and constraints, which is challenging, but it is open enough to capture potential affordances. This is the reason why the inductive approach to data analysis is so important.

5.2 Pedagogical Implications of the Research Findings

Globally, the findings indicate that Numbas is a useful tool for assessing mathematical problem-solving. However, there are issues related to the feedback, which can act as a source of motivation for a few students while demotivating other students. Numbas may be included to the new mathematics subject curriculum with the sole intention of identifying possible problems and effecting necessary modifications along with improving the learning of students and the practice of teachers. For teachers, it is important to ascertain their role in using their skills and expertise for adding new methods of formative assessment, and identifying students learning progresses, while for students, it is important to focus on using Numbas as learning tool.

In educational settings, the role of Numbas should be clearly defined along with the role of teachers. For example, teachers need to identify why students need scaffolding when there are tasks assigned to them on Numbas. Teachers should also identify the role of personal feedback from Numbas in affecting the students' learning process. For students, it is important to weigh the learning effect in using teachers' ideas and Numbas explanations. From the university and school perspective, it is important to analyse whether Numbas is able to facilitate the acquisition of higher order thinking skills. Likewise, the focus should be on determining the cognitive load on the basis of higher or lower level of cognition. The responsibilities of teachers for improving students' learning using Numbas should be explained and defined properly. Such implications need to be further integrated for formulating a new strategy that will be able to support the formative assessment process.

5.3 Future Research Work

Overall, it can be said that the usefulness of Numbas is acknowledged by students and teachers, but the learning and teaching effects of the tool need to be further analysed. This requires the formulation of hypotheses to produce more generalizable findings. Firstly, there is a need to conduct quantitative analyses, by having a sample size that will be enough to represent the entire population currently using Numbas for regular assessment across universities or schools. Such analysis is crucial for adding more generalization to the study.

Secondly, it may be important to include a cross-national analysis by focusing on two countries using Numbas in their universities or schools and identifying the difference in affordance perceptions and actualisations. Such analysis will be helpful in determining the impact of socio-cultural factors on the acceptance and rejection of Numbas and justifying various affordances along with benefits and constraints. Finally, the validity and reliability of data is another factor requiring further attention. For example, rather than conducting interviews with students and teachers from one university, it may be useful to conduct interviews with participants from several universities where Numbas is being used.

6. CONCLUSIONS AND RECOMMENDATIONS FOR DESIGNERS

Numbas development is a work in progress, and the developers are working regularly to addressing concerns of teachers, students, and other users, as well as to improve the general design and functionalities. Recommendations for future development centre around addressing the constraints faced by teachers and students while using Numbas as a mediating artefact. Likewise, addressing the issue of insufficient navigation buttons by introducing 'next' and 'previous' buttons in the user interface. This could make navigating back and forth much easier. Furthermore, it may be important to improve the areas of support for group activities among students whereby students can work in pairs at different locations.

Furthermore, it is suggested that including features to make it possible for Numbas to save students' profiles and assign tasks to them based on their previous attempts. This might help greatly in the areas of allowing students work at their own pace. The study further recommends improving Numbas to be able to assess student's step-by-step solutions along with the final answers and provide feedback that will be personalised to the student's misconceptions. Numbas in its current level of development could be used to achieve many of the competence aims for the mathematics subject in the new core curriculum, in particular regarding the areas of assessing reasoning, proving, etc. Finally, the editor's user interface is recommended for improvement. This would encourage teachers to create tasks that best suit the need of their students.

REFERENCES

Anderson, C., & Robey, D. (2017). Affordance potency: Explaining the actualization of technology affordances. *Information and Organization, 27*(2), pp. 100-115.

Bernhard, E., Recker, J., & Burton-Jones, A. (2013). Understanding the actualization of affordances: A study in the process modeling context. *34th International Conference on Information Systems (ICIS 2013)*. Milano, Italy.

Brown Jr, J. (1999). *Assessment matters in higher education.* UK: McGraw-Hill Education.

Bryman, A. (2016). *Social research methods.* Oxford, UK: Oxford University Press.

Burns, E. C., Martin, A. J., & Evans, P. A. (2019). The role of teacher feedback–feedforward and personal best goal setting in students' mathematics achievement: A goal setting theory perspective. *Educational Psychology*, pp. 1-19.

Carroll, T., Casey, D., Crowley, J., Mulchrone, K., & Shé, Á. N. (2017). Numbas as an engagement tool for first-year Business Studies students. *MSOR Connections, 15*(2), pp. 42-50.

Einig, S. (2013). Supporting students' learning: The use of formative online assessments. *Accounting Education, 22*(5), pp. 425-444.

Engeström, Y. (2014). *Learning by expanding: an activity-theoretical approach to developmental research.* London: Cambridge University Press.

Greeno, J. G. (1994). Gibson's affordances. *Psychological Review, 101*(2), pp. 336–342.

Gibson, J. J. (1986). *The ecological approach to visual perception*. Hillsdale, N.J: Lawrence Erlbaum

Hadjerrouit, S. (2017). Assessing the affordances of SimReal+ and their applicability to support the learning of mathematics in teacher education. *Issues in Informing Science and Information Technology, 14*, pp. 121-138.

Hadjerrouit, S. & Nnagbo, C.I. (2022a). Affordances and constraints of the e-assessment system Numbas: A case study in mathematics teacher education. *Proceedings of the 19th International Conference on Cognition and Exploratory Learning in the Digital Age* (CELDA 2022). IADIS Press, pp. 201-208.

Hadjerrouit, S. & Nnagbo, C.I. (2022b). Formative feedback in mathematics teacher education: An activity and affordance Theory perspective. *Proceedings of the 14th International Conference on Computer Supported Education* (CSEDU 2022), Volume 2, 22-24 April 2022. SciTePress, pp. 417-424.

Hadjerrouit, S. & Nnagbo, C.I. (2021). Exploring Numbas formative feedback for teaching and learning mathematics: An Affordance Theory perspective. *Proceedings of the 18th International Conference on Cognition and Exploratory Learning in Digital Age* (CELDA2021). IADIS Press, pp. 261-268.

Hattie, J., & Timperley, H. (2007). The power of feedback. *Review of Educational Research, 77*(1), pp. 81-112.

Kyaruzi, F., et al. (2019). Students' formative assessment perceptions, feedback use and mathematics performance in secondary schools in Tanzania. *Assessment in Education: Principles, Policy & Practice*, *26*(3), pp. 278-302.

Lowe, T., & Mestel, B. (2019). Using STACK to support student learning at masters level: A case study. *Teaching Mathematics and Its Applications: An International Journal of the IMA.*

Nnagbo, C. I. (2020). *Assessment in mathematics education using Numbas: Affordances and constraints from an activity theory perspective.* [Unpublished master's thesis]. University of Agder, Kristiansand, Norway.

Norman, D. A. (1988). *The psychology of everyday things*. New York: Basic Books.

Osiurak, F., Rossetti, Y., & Badets, A. (2017). What is an affordance? 40 years later. *Neuroscience and Biobehavioral Reviews, 77*, pp. 403-417.

Perfect, C. (2015). A demonstration of Numbas, an assessment system for mathematical disciplines. https://www.numbas.org.uk/wp-content/uploads/2015/07/caa2015_numbas.pdf

Pinger, P., et al. (2016). Implementation of formative assessment – effects of quality of programme delivery on students' mathematics achievement and interest. *Assessment in Education: Principles, Policy & Practice, 25*(2), pp. 160-182.

Sexton, M., & Lamb, J. (2017). Using Activity Theory to understand a mathematics leader's motivations and use of mathematical knowledge for teaching. *Mathematics Education Research Group of Australasia.*

Strong, D. M., et. Al. (2014). A theory of organization-EHR affordance actualization. *Journal of the Association for Information Systems*, *15*(2), pp. 53-85.

Volkoff, O., & Strong, D. M. (2017). Affordance theory and how to use it in IS research. In R. D. Galliers & M.-K. Stein (Eds.). *The Routledge Companion to Management Information Systems*. London: Routledge.

Vygotsky, L. (1978). *Mind in society: The development of higher psychological processes*. Cambridge, MA: Harvard University Press.

HOMOGENEITY OF TOKEN PROBABILITY DISTRIBUTIONS IN CHATGPT AND HUMAN TEXTS

Dragica Ljubisavljević*[1], Marko Koprivica*[1], Aleksandar Kostić[2] and Vladan Devedžić[1]
[1]*Faculty of Organizational Sciences, Department of Software Engineering, Belgrade University*
Jove Ilica 154, Belgrade, Serbia
[2]*Faculty of Philosophy, Department of Psychology, Belgrade University*
Čika-Ljubina 18-20, Belgrade, Serbia

ABSTRACT

This paper delves into statistical disparities between human-written and ChatGPT-generated texts, utilizing an analysis of Shannon's equitability values, and token frequency. Our findings indicate that Shannon's equitability can potentially be a differentiating factor between texts produced by humans and those generated by ChatGPT. Additionally, we uncover substantial distinctions when studying the most frequent tokens.

KEYWORDS

Shannon Equitability, NLP, ChatGPT, Education

1. INTRODUCTION

Large language models (LLM) have created disturbance in a lot of fields, by making it possible to get knowledge as a response to a user's prompt. ChatGPT, a dialogue system (chatbot) developed on top of GPT-3 and GPT-4 LLMs (Liu et al., 2023) is the most widely known example, with successful usage in mathematics (Frieder et al., 2023), software industry (Surameery & Shakor, 2023), medicine (Biswas, 2023), meteorology (Zhu et al., 2023), education (Bishop, 2023), and many other fields.

This technology can be abused in education, as students can cheat by using ChatGPT to write essays, do assignments, and solve problems. In response to a user's question, ChatGPT can create a text output of up to 4096 characters. But, with just a little hack, we have managed to generate texts with more than 4,000 words. This is more than enough for basic student reports, as Benton's research (Benton, 2017) finds the average of 700 words to be sufficient for the top grade.

In their study, Kostić and Vitić (2021) examined the differences in probability distribution of inflected cases of nouns in the contemporary and medieval Serbian language. The obtained results indicate a conspicuous difference in probability distribution between the two samples. To determine whether there is a parameter that is conserved over time, they calculated the ratio of the obtained and the maximum entropy for the two samples. This metric specifies the distance from the maximum entropy of a system and is known as *Shannon's equitability*. Applying Shannon's equitability metric, a minimal (statistically nonsignificant) difference between the two samples was obtained. This finding suggests that despite large changes in the probabilities of noun cases over time, the distance from the maximum entropy remained conserved. It's worth noting that Levshina (Levshina, 2019) expands the purview by utilizing Shannon's equitability calculation to compare the entropies of entire texts, rather than focusing solely on individual cases.

The primary aim of this paper is to employ Shannon's equitability as a statistical measure to discern between texts generated by ChatGPT and texts composed by humans. Our study sets forth a null hypothesis (H_0) that assumes the population means of Shannon's equitability in both groups are equal. In contrast, the alternative hypothesis (H_1) suggests that the population means of Shannon's equitability differ between the two groups. It

*These authors contributed equally to this work.

is important to emphasize that all texts examined in this study are written in the English language, ensuring consistency in linguistic context.

The rest of the paper is organized as follows. Section 2 presents some related work. Section 3 explains how data is collected, and Section 4 describes the methodology used to calculate Shannon's equitability. In Section 5 we present our findings and draw conclusions in Section 6.

2. RELATED WORK

Considering the broad range of question domains to which ChatGPT responds with seemingly human-like answers, justified concerns arise regarding potential misuse. Numerous research studies have been conducted using various methodologies aiming to determine the authorship of a text - ChatGPT or human? Khalil and Er in their research (Khalil & Er, 2023) state that this powerful and easily accessible technology has led to concerns about plagiarism and cheating in educational institutions. In their study, they examined short essays generated by ChatGPT using two popular plagiarism-detection tools, iThenticate and Turnitin. The results of this study showed that out of 50 essays generated by ChatGPT, 40 exhibited a high level of originality, emphasizing the importance of this topic. Mitrović, Andreoletti and Ayoub have also investigated the detection of text generated by ChatGPT (Mitrović et al., 2023). In their research, they developed a Transformer-based machine learning (ML) approach that classifies text as either generated by ChatGPT or by a human. The results revealed that their ML model can achieve satisfactory performance with an accuracy of approximately 79%. Justin Diamond offered a different perspective on this topic in his research (Diamond, 2023), posing the question: "Do languages generated by ChatGPT statistically look human?". In his research, Diamond utilized Zipf's law, which is commonly used in the field of statistical linguistics. According to Zipf's law, the word frequencies in a text corpus are inversely proportional to their rank in the frequency table (Diamond, 2023). In the context of his experiment, the procedure unfolded as follows: once all texts had been generated, collected, and/or compiled, their Zipfian distributions and correlations were computed and visually represented to facilitate comparison. His findings indicate that both the text generated by ChatGPT and the texts written by humans closely adhere to Zipf's law, and that the text generated by ChatGPT exhibits statistical properties similar to those written by humans. The ultimate purpose of his research is to enhance our understanding of technology and linguistics.

Our research revolves around a fundamental question: Do the word frequencies in ChatGPT and human writings share a common origin? To investigate this, we employ Shannon's equitability as a tool to uncover insights and seek an answer to this question.

3. DATASETS

The corpus utilized for our experiment comprises essays generated by AI as well as essays written by humans. The AI-generated text was acquired from a freely accessible version of ChatGPT, which was made available to all students. The specific task assigned to the AI was to compose a random essay. As the experiment progressed and the results began to circulate, we introduced additional keywords to the essay request, including "Europe," "Africa," "America," "Asia," "love," "war," "betrayal," "famine," and "happy ending." These keywords were incorporated to prompt diverse and varied responses from the AI-generated essays. To accommodate the size limitation of 4096 characters, the AI-generated responses were structured as a series of chapters, with each chapter containing a few sentences that provided an overview of the plot. In order to expand upon these initial responses, we employed an iterative approach by using ChatGPT's own generated responses as input, feeding them back into the system for each individual chapter. Through this process, we were able to generate 12 extended texts, allowing for a more comprehensive exploration of the essay topics and enhancing the overall depth of the AI-generated essays.

We selected twelve random essays written by final-year undergraduate students from the MICUSP corpus (Römer & Wulff, 2008) for our analysis of human texts. These essays were specifically chosen based on certain criteria: they belonged to the English discipline and were argumentative essays with a minimum length of 1900 words.

4. METHODOLOGY

Our approach is grounded in information theory, a field that may appear disconnected from linguistic studies but finds practical applications in understanding language phenomena. We started with the input text and conducted the *tokenization process* (Loper & Bird, 2002) to split the text into individual words. The resulting sequence of individual words formed the foundation for subsequent analysis. In addition, we incorporated punctuation marks, recognizing their importance in human writing as aids for sentence comprehension and clarity (Hill & Murray, 2000). Then, we calculated the occurrence of each token in the defined corpus. By analysing the frequencies, we identified the dominant tokens.

Then we directed our attention to one of the fundamental concepts in information theory - *entropy*. In information theory, entropy (or Shannon's entropy) can be understood as a measure of the orderliness of a system or as the average amount of information emitted by a system.

A way to compare the entropy of two systems, regardless of the number of their elements, is by applying a measure known as *Shannon's equitability*, expressed as the ratio of the obtained entropy (H) and the maximum entropy (H_{max}).

We have developed a straightforward Python function to compute Shannon's equitability, which serves as the ultimate metric. Utilizing this function, we have evaluated Shannon's equitability for various systems and conducted thorough comparisons.

Finally, we have computed the T-test using the collected results of Shannon's equitability.

5. FINDINGS

Table 1 presents the processed data derived from a set of twelve human-written texts. The data includes Shannon's equitability, the token with the highest frequency, and the word with the highest frequency within these texts. One notable commonality among these texts is the consistent appearance of the article "the," which is the most frequently used word in the entire corpus. Furthermore, we observe the significance of commas, which emerge as the most frequent token in almost half of the texts. Overall, the Shannon's equitability values range between 0.8 and 0.84.

Table 1. Data gathered after processing human texts: Shannon's equitability, most frequent token (top token) and most frequent word (top word). Values are rounded to 4 digits

Human	Text 1	Text 2	Text 3	Text 4	Text 5	Text 6	Text 7	Text 8	Text 9	Text 10	Text 11	Text 12
Shannon's equitability	0.8331	0.8271	0.8309	0.8261	0.8047	0.8033	0.8276	0.8196	0.8292	0.805	0.8074	0.8362
Top token	the	the	the	,	the	,	,	,	,	the	the	the
Top word	the	the	the	the	the	the	the	the	of	the	the	the

In contrast, the word "and" emerges as the most frequently occurring word in ChatGPT texts. Notably, commas surpass even that frequency and dominate as the most common token.

When considering Shannon's equitability values, it becomes apparent that ChatGPT texts demonstrate a broader range of dispersion compared to human texts. Specifically, the Shannon's equitability values for ChatGPT texts span from 0.78 to 0.83.

Table 2. Data gathered after processing ChatGPT texts: Shannon's equitability, most frequent token (top token) and most frequent word (top word). Values are rounded to 4 digits

ChatGPT	Text 1	Text 2	Text 3	Text 4	Text 5	Text 6	Text 7	Text 8	Text 9	Text 10	Text 11	Text 12
Shannon's equitability	0.7804	0.781	0.8159	0.8292	0.8157	0.8203	0.8031	0.8162	0.8192	0.7999	0.8014	0.8052
Top token	the	,	,	,	,	and	,	,	,	,	,	,
Top word	the	the	and	and	and	and	and	and	and	and	the	and

In our endeavour to discern disparities between texts composed by humans and those generated by ChatGPT, we identified the top 6 most frequent tokens within both datasets. Subsequently, we calculated the standard deviation of each token's frequency. To illustrate these findings, we employed a Star chart in Figure 1. Each spoke on the chart corresponds to one of the selected tokens, with its length representing the token's standard deviation of occurrence. The standard deviation of token frequency in ChatGPT is generally higher than in human text, which indicates a greater dispersion of tokens within the texts produced by ChatGPT compared to those generated by humans.

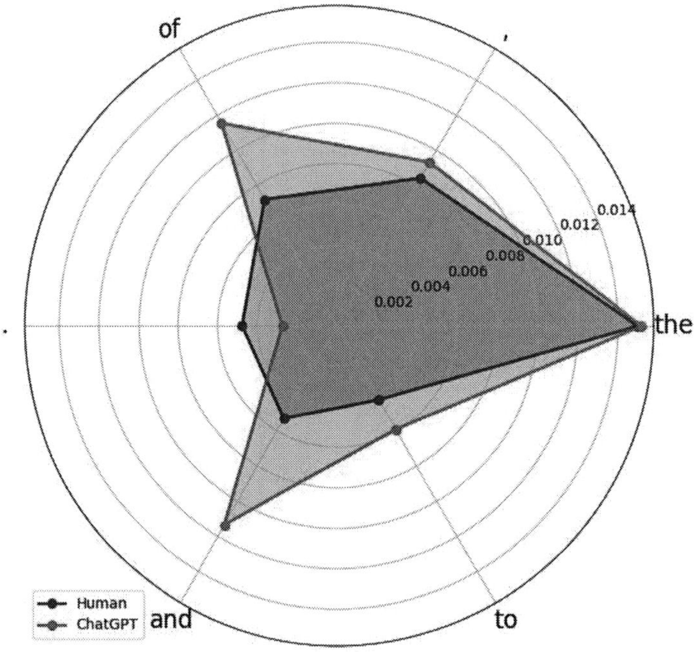

Figure 1. Comparison of standard deviation of frequency for six most frequent tokens in Human and ChatGPT texts

Moreover, a contrast between the mean Shannon's equitability values for each of the two samples (i.e. humans vs Chat GPT) indicated statistically significant difference ($t(22) = 2.40$, i.e. $p = 0.026$). Notably, this p-value falls below the commonly accepted threshold of 0.05 for statistical significance. As a result, we are able to reject the null hypothesis (H_0) that posits no difference in means between texts authored by humans and those generated by ChatGPT. This statistical evidence further supports the notion that there exists a significant distinction in terms of Shannon's equitability between human-generated texts and ChatGPT-generated texts.

Table 3. Mean and variance of Shannon's equitability values for humans and ChatGPT, along with the difference between these numbers. The values are rounded to 4 digits

Shannon equitability	Mean	Variance
Human	0.8208	0.000139
ChatGPT	0.8073	0.000212
Difference	0.0136	

6. FUTURE WORK

In our next research phase, we aim to develop a versatile web application focused on quantitative text analysis. This application will empower users to manipulate and analyse text in various ways, offering both file upload and text generation capabilities. Figure 2 displays the upcoming application's conceptual design.

Key features of the application include:

1. *Upload Text*: Users can upload files or request text generation by ChatGPT.
2. *Tokenization*: Users will have access to standard text tokenization and advanced tokenization, which allows custom rules and word exclusion.
3. *Token Frequency Analysis*: The application also calculates token frequencies. They can analyse token frequencies to identify the most common ones, helping them gain insights into their text.
4. *Statistical Text Analysis*: The application provides tools to calculate text entropy and Shannon's equality, aiding users in gauging the complexity of their text.
5. *Data Visualization*: Users can visualize data distribution within the text through Zipf's distribution graphs and other relevant graphical representations. Various relevant graphical representations will facilitate the understanding of complex language patterns for all users.
6. *Data Export*: Based on the analysis, users can conveniently download the generated data.

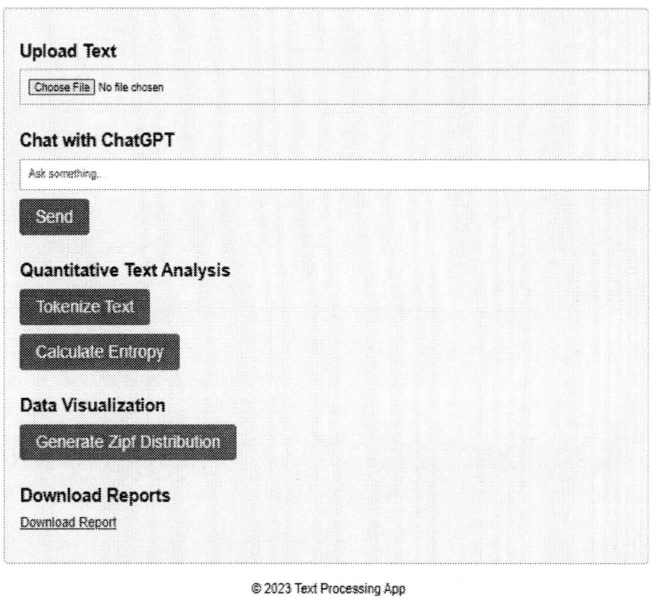

Figure 2. Conceptual design overview of upcoming web application focused on quantitative text analysis

The idea is for this web application to serve as a foundation for future innovations in text analysis. The ultimate goal is for it to become *a comprehensive tool for quantitative text analysis*, initially for Serbian and English languages.

7. CONCLUSIONS

This paper focuses on conducting a statistical analysis to discern the disparities between texts written by humans and those generated by ChatGPT. Our study examines various metrics, including Shannon's equitability values, and the occurrence of frequent tokens and words, extracted from essays authored by students as well as those generated by ChatGPT.

Through our analysis, we have reached a significant conclusion. The examination of Shannon's equitability values allows us to reject the null hypothesis (H_0), which posits that the means of Shannon's equitability are equal between human-written and ChatGPT-generated texts. This finding suggests that Shannon's equitability can effectively serve as a distinguishing factor between texts produced by humans and those generated by ChatGPT.

Furthermore, our investigation of the most frequent tokens reveals notable distinctions. In ChatGPT-generated texts, the word "and" predominates as the most frequent word, while commas emerge as the most frequently occurring token. Conversely, in human-written texts, "the" emerges as the most common word, with a comparable proportion of commas and "the" as the most frequent tokens.

Overall, our analysis sheds light on the statistical differences between human-written and ChatGPT-generated texts, demonstrating the efficacy of Shannon's equitability as a differentiating factor. Additionally, our examination of frequent tokens provides insights into the distinct usage patterns observed in both text categories.

Regarding the limitations of our research, we encountered a small dataset comprising merely 24 texts. These texts were authored by both humans and generated by ChatGPT. Furthermore, the diversity of text topics necessitates that we prompt ChatGPT to generate text aligned with the topics of the human-authored texts. Lastly, a comprehensive analysis of the Zipf's distribution within the two text groups is imperative.

In our future endeavours, alongside rectifying the limitations inherent in this research we plan to carry out additional experiments that involve comparing texts from larger corpora, written in diverse styles including journalism, everyday speech, slang, and tailored for various disciplines such as engineering, biology, philosophy, physics, and more. These experiments will provide us with valuable insights and comparisons across different contexts.

PROGRAM AVAILABILITY

The source code of the program written in Python for this experiment and data results is available from: https://github.com/koprivica/chatGPTvsHumanEntropy

REFERENCES

Benton, T. (2017). How much do I need to write to get top marks? *Research Matters: A Cambridge Assessment publication*, 24, pp. 37–40. Available at: https://www.cambridgeassessment.org.uk/our-research/data-bytes/how-much-do-i-need-to-write-to-get-top-marks/index.aspx (Accessed: 23 June 2023).

Bishop (formerly Lea Shaver), L. (2023). A Computer Wrote this Paper: What ChatGPT Means for Education, Research, and Writing. *Research, and Writing*. Available at: https://doi.org/10.2139/ssrn.4338981.

Biswas, S. (2023). ChatGPT and the Future of Medical Writing, *Radiology*, 307(2), p. e223312. Available at: https://doi.org/10.1148/radiol.223312.

Diamond, J. (2023). "Genlangs" and Zipf's Law: Do languages generated by ChatGPT statistically look human? arXiv. Available at: https://doi.org/10.48550/arXiv.2304.12191.

Frieder, S. et al. (2023). Mathematical Capabilities of ChatGPT. arXiv. Available at: https://doi.org/10.48550/arXiv.2301.13867.

Hill, R.L. & Murray, W.S. (2000). Chapter 22 - Commas and Spaces: Effects of Punctuation on Eye Movements and Sentence Parsing, in A. Kennedy et al. (eds) *Reading as a Perceptual Process*. Oxford: North-Holland, pp. 565–589. Available at: https://doi.org/10.1016/B978-008043642-5/50027-9.

Khalil, M. & Er, E. (2023). Will ChatGPT get you caught? Rethinking of Plagiarism Detection. arXiv. Available at: https://doi.org/10.48550/arXiv.2302.04335.

Kostić, A., & Vitić, Z. (2021). Probability distribution of noun cases in writings of St. Sava and the contemporary Serbian language, *Digital humanities and Slavic cultural heritage: international scientific conference, Vol. 1*, Belgrade, 6-7 May 2019, Belgrade: Savez slavističkih društava Srbije, pp. 19-36. Available at: https://doi.org/10.18485/mks_dh_skn.2021.1.ch2.

Levshina, N. (2019). Token-based typology and word order entropy: A study based on Universal Dependencies, *Linguistic Typology*, 23(3), pp. 533–572. Available at: https://doi.org/10.1515/lingty-2019-0025.

Liu, Y. et al. (2023). Summary of ChatGPT/GPT-4 Research and Perspective Towards the Future of Large Language Models. arXiv. Available at: https://doi.org/10.48550/arXiv.2304.01852.

Loper, E. & Bird, S. (2002). Nltk: the natural language toolkit. arXiv. Available at: https://doi.org/10.48550/arXiv.cs/0205028.

Mitrović, S., Andreoletti, D. & Ayoub, O. (2023). ChatGPT or Human? Detect and Explain. Explaining Decisions of Machine Learning Model for Detecting Short ChatGPT-generated Text. arXiv. Available at: https://doi.org/10.48550/arXiv.2301.13852.

Römer, U. & S. Wulff. (2008). Applying corpus methods to written academic texts: explorations of MICUSP, *Journal of Writing Research*, 2 (2), pp. 99–127. Available at: https://doi.org/10.17239/jowr-2010.02.02.2.

Surameery, N.M.S. & Shakor, M.Y. (2023). Use Chat GPT to Solve Programming Bugs, *International Journal of Information Technology & Computer Engineering (IJITC) ISSN: 2455-5290*, 3(01), pp. 17–22. Available at: https://doi.org/10.55529/ijitc.31.17.22.

Zhu, J.-J. et al. (2023). ChatGPT and Environmental Research, Environmental Science & Technology [Preprint]. Available at: https://doi.org/10.1021/acs.est.3c01818.

THE "FERNSTUDENT". ENHANCING THE POTENTIAL OF HYBRID TEACHING BASED ON USER-CENTERED DESIGN

Daniel Ullrich[1], Andreas Butz[1] and Sarah Diefenbach[2]
[1]*Department of Computer Science, LMU Munich,*
Frauenlobstr. 7a, 80337 München, Germany
[2]*Department of Psychology, LMU Munich,*
Leopoldstr. 13, 80802 München, Germany

ABSTRACT

Hybrid teaching has become a common approach, with its inclusive character being a main advantage. However, it also comes with problems such as increased attention requirements for teachers and a lacking social integration of both groups of students (remote, on-site). The present research aims to enhance the potential of hybrid teaching through innovative technology concepts that leverage the advantages while minimizing the disadvantages from a technical and experiential perspective. Based on a literature analysis and empirical insights from explorative interviews with teachers and students, we introduce the concept of the Fernstudent. It gives remote students a physical presence in the classroom, in the form of an anthropomorphic robot that sits in a row with the other students, transmits images and sound from the lecture hall, and can also signal to join the discussion. Retrospective interviews with teachers after nine-week field tests revealed that it could provide the main envisioned benefits but also showed points for further development. Limitations of the present research and more general implications for research and practice are discussed.

KEYWORDS

Hybrid Teaching, Cognitive and Social Demands, Remote Students, Robot, Social Interaction, Fernstudent

1. VISION AND RESEARCH GOALS: ENHANCING THE POTENTIAL OF HYBRID TEACHING

A university classroom after the summer break – the special teaching situation caused by the Covid-19 pandemic is over, and we can finally return to classroom teaching. As a teacher, you really enjoy standing in the classroom before your students again. You especially appreciate the livelier interaction and discussion with your students, which could unfortunately only take place on a rudimentary level during the virtual lectures. You enter the lecture hall on the day of the first lecture. About 100 students have registered and 70 of them are present. Actually, there are 71 seats occupied, but this additional student is no ordinary one: It is the "Fernstudent", a robot with a more or less anthropomorphic form, sitting in the second row. You have already heard about it: a robot that records the lecture via camera and makes it available for the virtually connected remote students, giving them a presence in the lecture hall at the same time. Integrated in its head, the Fernstudent has a large display on which the remote students are visible. You just start your lecture in the normal way, speaking to the students. "Well, let's see what you remember. Can any of you explain the idea of dissonance theory in the simplest possible terms?" Silence first. After a short period of consideration, the Fernstudent signals that a remote student wants to say something. You give her the floor, and, with the help of the integrated speakers, she speaks at a volume as if she were actually present in the room.

During the pandemic, hybrid formats of interaction have been tested more extensively and become more common in educational and other contexts. And even beyond the pandemic, hybrid teaching is alive and well. Students have come to expect it more, enjoying the flexibility to join lectures without spatial constraints. In the research literature, the term hybrid teaching is not used consistently. It is applied to different combinations of residential classroom and digital teaching, the integration of technology in learning environments (e.g., Linder, 2017), in some cases also including asynchronous teaching via recorded lectures (Sing et al., 2021). The present research focuses on hybrid teaching as in the scenario described above, in the sense of a synchronous live session for present and remote students. This follows the definition by Ulla and Perales (2022, p. 2) of hybrid teaching as "synchronous teaching of students in the classroom and online simultaneously using an online platform", i.e., "an approach to teaching that not only integrates technology in the teaching process but also combines students who are inside a physical classroom and students from online". In this scenario, the teacher is faced with a dual audience: the physically present students and the remote students, each with specific options of interaction. In common practice, the remote students can follow the lecture via video and audio channel using an online platform (e.g., Zoom, Jitsi) and are given the chance to pose questions or comments via textual chat (hopefully recognized by the teacher).

Thus, in principle, there are three groups whose needs and interaction quality must be considered in hybrid teaching: Teachers, physically present students, and remote students. However, it shows that current approaches typically do not address the needs of these three groups in a satisfying way (e.g., Gamage et al., 2022; Ma et al., 2023). For the remote students, hybrid teaching mainly provides spatial flexibility, albeit at the cost of very limited participation or even complete exclusion from the interactive part. Consequently, they often remain passive, invisible consumers. For the teachers, it means the additional effort to keep an eye on a chat and to serve two worlds at the same time. In consequence, interaction takes place primarily between the onsite students and teacher whereas the last group often remains outside or generates a lot of effort.

The present research aims to enhance the potential of hybrid teaching through innovative adaptions of existing technology which exploit the advantages while minimizing the disadvantages. To meet this goal, we first identified central potentials and challenges in the current form of hybrid teaching reported in research in education and human-robot interaction (HRI) as well as explorative interviews with teachers and students, addressing cognitive and social issues. Based on these insights, we developed the concept of the "Fernstudent" (German compound word, originally referring to students of a remote university), as briefly outlined in the introductory vision. A prototypical implementation and field test over a 9-week period provided insights into teacher's experiences and ideas for future improvements of the concept. Limitations of the present study and more general implications for hybrid teaching and next research steps are discussed.

2. RELATED RESEARCH IN EDUCATION AND HRI

2.1 Potentials and Challenges of Hybrid Teaching

The general advantages of hybrid teaching are unchallenged, with its inclusive properties as a main benefit. Persons who cannot be present in the physical classroom for any reason such as travelling, childcare, illness or infection risks, still have a chance to participate (e.g., Johannessen et al., 2022; Klunder et al., 2022; Newhart et al., 2016). Once this option is provided, other students might also make use of it, so that the ratio of remote and physically present students might change to 50:50, or remote students might even be the majority. However, as also known from digital teaching in general, typical challenges on the part of the remote students are a decrease in motivation, a feeling of loneliness, less interaction with the teaching staff and other students (Lorenzo-Lledo et al., 2021), and, connected to the lower engagement in discussions, less practice of active learning, critical thinking, and the ability to debate (Gamage et al., 2023).

The teachers also face challenges, as digital and hybrid teaching requires new cognitive and social skills. These range from the practical handling of the technology to developing new teaching styles. For example, due to a lack of implicit, non-verbal communication, teachers need to state expectations and information more clearly, it may be more difficult to check students' understanding of the subject matter and progress in their learning process, and they may have a harder time to capture remote students' attention (e.g., Huizinga et al., 2022; Gamage et al., 2023; Lorenzo-Lledo et al., 2021). Referring to hybrid teaching, a particular challenge is the split audience, i.e., two groups of students following the same lecture but with very different contexts and options. Even if they seek to distribute attention equally, teachers tend to focus on the larger group of students (Huizinga et al., 2022), and a real "blending" of the physical and digital classroom does not happen. In many cases, the focus of interaction remains in the physical classroom, whereas remote students are less present and less engaged. As also known from other types of hybrid meetings, remote participants often feel neglected and uninvolved and cannot find the right timing or modality to join an intense local discussion (Ma et al., 2023). In theoretical models of student engagement (e.g., Fredricks et al., 2004) a sense of belonging is a central part of emotional engagement, which, in turn, affects performance. Also models of exploratory learning emphasize the key role of social interactions for developing knowledge (e.g., de Freitas & Neumann, 2009). Given this, the creation of a learning environment that connects remote students in an appropriate way emerges as a crucial factor of success for the future of hybrid teaching (also see Raes, 2022).

In sum, besides reducing the cognitive burdens for teachers, one of the central goals for the improvement of hybrid teaching is to create more intense connections between all three groups involved and to reduce the differences in social presence and interaction opportunities between remote and physically present students. Following the theory of transactional distance (Moore, 1993), a deciding factor for a satisfying learning experience is to reduce the psychological distance between student and teacher, student and student, and student and content (also see Gallon et al., 2019). Thus, the main challenge is to design hybrid learning in a way that is physically distant but psychologically close (also see Boye & Ayet, 2021).

2.2 Telepresence Robots and Similar Concepts

A first straightforward way to enhance the social presence of remote students in the classroom might be a physical representation through an anthropomorphic robot with microphone and loudspeaker, which naturally supports a style of interaction with a social entity. As well-documented by studies in HRI (e.g., Airenti, 2015; Araujo, 2018), we interact in a more "human" way (e.g., more politely) with anthropomorphic than with purely technical, non-anthropomorphic artifacts. Hence, just like the on-site students, the robot/remote student may have its place on a seat in the lecture hall and remote students can use their voice to join the discussion. Thereby, the people on-site hear the voice from the direction of the robot and not as a voice from the "off".

There is already wide experience with the use of telepresence robots (TPRs) in educational settings (e.g., Kwon et al., 2010; Virkus et al., 2023). A telepresence robot is typically a 1:1 representation of a remote person, meaning that one robot represents one person, usually displayed on a screen (for examples see https://telepresencerobots.com). Often, the remote person can operate the position of the robot and camera angle to control what he or she wishes to see (as opposed to needing someone to point a camera at a particular person or object). Previous applications of TPRs in educational settings are generally promising. A review of 28 studies about TPRs in education lends support for a better socialization, integration, and collaboration of remote students with their peers (Velinov et al., 2021). For example, TPRs for homebound school children helped these students to stay socially connected with their classmates and overcome feelings of isolation, while the anthropomorphic appearance helped the on-site students to see the robot as an actual student and initiated talk about the person "coming back" (Newhart et al., 2016). At the same time, researchers emphasize that the acceptance of TPRs for wider use is still challenged (Virkus et al., 2023) and report audio problems as a typical issue (Velinov et al., 2021). Besides the classical TPR, exploratory design concepts address particular challenges of hybrid formats (e.g., Grønbæk et al., 2021; Ma et al., 2023). For example, the concept Snotbox (Ma et al., 2023) represents participants in hybrid meetings by small boxlike robots standing on the meeting table, while an automatic memory function activates a flashlight, signaling that remote members have not participated in the discussion for a certain period of time.

Compared to such concepts, the present approach is an adoption of the TPR idea tailored to a typical university lecture. Instead of a 1:1-representation, all remote students are represented by the same one physical entity placed at a fixed spot among the physically present students (which seems more practical and more affordable in typical university structures than multiple mobile devices). Just as with the TPR approach, the idea is to enhance the social presence of remote students (and reduce demands for the teaching person) by a physical representation of them. This provides options to communicate in a more natural way and in the same modality as the physically present students, with the ultimate goal to put both groups as much as possible on the same level.

3. EXPLORATIVE INTERVIEWS

In order to gain deeper insights into the particular needs and experiences of the relevant groups in the context of hybrid teaching, we used explorative interviews as a typical method of requirements analysis in user-centered design (e.g. Lizenberger, 2023). Our main informants were two university teachers, namely, Peggy, 31 years, background in psychology and Tom, 44 years, background in media informatics (the names are pseudonyms). The interviews followed three leading questions, i.e., 1) What are your (positive and negative) experiences with hybrid teaching? 2) What are the advantages and specific qualities of face-to-face compared to hybrid teaching? 3) What should be changed to make hybrid teaching an (even) better option? Do you have any ideas on how technology could support this? Each interview lasted about 20-30 minutes. The interviews were transcribed verbatim, and statements were broadly categorized into recurring themes.

As an additional source of information, we used interviews with 57 students conducted in the context of a practical course on "Experience Design" as part of the Media Informatics Curriculum at our university, which revealed additional issues of relevance from a student perspective.

Table 1. Key issues and exemplary statements raised in the explorative interviews about hybrid teaching with teachers ([P] = Peggy, [T]=Tom) and students [S]

Hybrid teaching as one-directional communication, bad relationship, lacking energy "Hybrid teaching is usually only a stream in one direction. Remote students don't participate, there is hardly any feedback and hardly any contributions. A bad relationship, because rarely something comes back." [T] "In a classroom lecture, I have the feeling that I am giving something of myself – and then a lot of energy comes back from the students. With digital teaching: I feel that the energy I have given is sucked up by the screen and nothing comes back." [P]
Exhausting to manage, divides the teacher's attention "You look in the chat all the time, but most of the time nothing is there. And if there is, you see it too late because the messages from chat don't pop up or ring clearly enough. A very tangible technical hurdle." [T] "It divides my attention. I also have to be in two places at once." [P]
Bad compromise "The fact that it is live actually creates more stress, but the advantage of being live is not exploited." [T] "Having a hybrid option is good in principle, but in the current way it misses the mark. Many of the remote students use it to do other things in parallel, which leads to less attention and engagement." [P]
Split audience, motivational differences between students get more pronounced "In theory you have two groups of students included. But the ones who are remote might as well be gone - whether one is watching or 50 or 100 is really meaningless. You are not connected to this group." [T] "It divides the group a bit into the committed and the non-committed." [P]
Social space as main advantage of classroom teaching, energizing experience, better teaching quality "The main advantage of classroom teaching is that it creates a social space. Compared to the digital, where you talk to fifty black screens - you are totally exposed but speaking to people you can't see." [T] "When I look into the students' faces, this also brings me to new thoughts and the lecture gets an individual note and better quality." [P]
Bring both student groups on one level (in visibility, modality, social interaction, appearance in the room) "You have to bring the invisible ones to the same level as the others. Also included in the social context." [T] "There should be the same modality for all students. In social contexts it has become established to raise your hand. But the remote students can't do this. They could just interrupt and speak in. Not a good solution." [T] "...and also of dimension. I don't need to see a three-meter-tall head of someone but also not only one point." [P]
Separate remote students from teacher's screen to make comments welcome (and not a disturbance) "From my point of view, a big problem on the teacher's side is this change between presentation and conference tool, which is usually in the background. This could already be solved by a second notebook." [T] "In the current way, when someone of the remote students wants to speak this has more the character of a disturbance than an enriching contribution. I would have to push my slides into the corner to make the video visible to the others. To be honest, I hope nobody of the people from the hybrid room wants to say something, because then I have to manage this technically. As sorry as I am." [P]
Difficulties in moderating discussions, lacking feeling of togetherness, two separate groups of students "Questions from the plenary have to be repeated, questions from the chat have to be read out. A hard job for the teacher to somehow put the two separate spaces together." [S] "It was difficult to create a feeling of togetherness in hybrid lectures." [S] "In hybrid mode, discussions among students only arose within modalities. Verbal in the classroom, and in the chat among the remote students. You had two separate groups discussing different issues." [S]

Teachers seem overburdened, exclusion of questions from remote students
"Professors seem totally overwhelmed to manage the technology and issues like sound problems etc." [S]
"Some teachers even said that no questions from online classmates are allowed." [S]
Chat as a welcome opportunity, social inhibition
"The professor should be considerate of the fact that it is not so easy for many students to participate who don't dare to speak before the others. The chat provides a good platform to ask questions relatively anonymously." [S]
"I liked being able to ask online questions in the chat without interrupting the prof." [S]
"The chat was a nice option to get really helpful advice without having to directly interrupt the lecture [no whispering]." [S]
Design ideas: loudspeaker for questions from remote students, camera that records on-site students
"Questions from the remote students are played through a loudspeaker and the actively speaking students are then also shown on a display. There is no chat function to encourage more verbal exchange." [S]
"Integrated camera for remote students that turns on when sound comes from presence audience so that remote students can see the on-site students during discussions." [S]

4. CONCEPT DEVELOPMENT AND KEY FEATURES

Based on the above insights from literature and explorative interviews, we defined the following key features of the Fernstudent concept:

- A physical avatar with a physical body represents the remote students
- It transmits image and sound from the lecture hall (via camera, microphone)
- It transmits image and sound of an interacting remote student into the lecture hall (via display, speaker)
- It transmits a (vague) idea of the number of remote students joining the lecture
- It can interact with the environment in the lecture hall in a rudimentary way, e.g., through "hand signals" (motor elements) or lights for signaling that one of the remote students wants to speak.

From an experiential point of view, these key features were defined to meet the following goals:

- Integrate remote students as seamlessly as possible into the situation of face-to-face teaching
- Place both student groups on a closer level (in visibility, modality, opportunities for social interaction)
- Make both student groups appear as one unity, receiving the same attention from teachers
- Reduce the burden for teachers of handling content and technology, provide more attention for students
- Improve the overall experience of hybrid teaching, e.g., teachers' feelings of competence

Regarding the technical realization, in its simplest form, the Fernstudent may consist of a simple physical shell, a notebook with camera and microphone, loudspeakers and, if necessary, a movable arm or a lamp for signaling the students. Likewise, existing conference software (e.g., Zoom) can be used for the first prototype, which covers the basic functionalities and at the same time is already familiar to all potential participants. A first functional prototype which can be used for field testing of the concept in teaching is therefore possible within a short time and with limited resources. Regarding the specific form and design, students of the practical course "Experience Design" experimented with different design variants. Figure 1 shows some examples of sketches and prototypes (for a more detailed description of the design variants and video prototypes see https://blockpraktikumexperiencedesign.wordpress.com). A combination of the different variants' characteristics resulted in a functional prototype, also used in the field test.

Figure 1. Design variants of the Fernstudent (Source: https://blockpraktikumexperiencedesign.wordpress.com)

5. PROTOTYPICAL IMPLEMENTATION AND FIELD TEST

Figure 2 shows the functional prototype of the Fernstudent in the lecture hall, featuring the following characteristics and functions:

- Its physical body is similar to human size. When it is "sitting" its head is on similar height as the physically present students.
- Its display shows the image of the remote students. If one of the remote students is speaking, it switches to this student and shows its picture in full screen size.
- The remote students see the combined picture of the beamer picture (i.e., the presentation slides) and the teacher, who is recorded by an HD zoom camera.
- It is equipped with a directional microphone with auto-adjust function. The remote students can hear the teacher and other students speaking.
- It is equipped with a loudspeaker. A remote student speaking can be heard throughout the whole lecture hall, by the teacher and other students as well.
- It features a signaling function for the remote students. If a remote student wants to say something. they press a report button on their interface, which activates an LED ring.
- It indicates the (vague) number of remote students with an LED matrix of randomly distributed LED lights. Each LED light represents one remote student. If more remote students are joining the lecture, the matrix gets more illuminated (if you would count the LEDs, you would have the exact number of remote students, but this exact number is mostly irrelevant).

Figure 2. Functional prototype of the Fernstudent in the lecture hall during the field test.

For a first field test, the Fernstudent was used in multiple sessions of two different lectures during the summer semester 2023 over a nine-week period, taught by the teachers who participated in the explorative interviews (Peggy and Tom). Lecture 1 was a bachelor's course on market and consumer psychology with 119 students (min=110, max=140) participating per session on average (avg. 49% remote students), taught by Peggy. Lecture 2 was a bachelor's course on user experience with 33 students (min=20, max=45) participating per session on average (avg. 23% remote students), taught by Tom. Both teachers had gained solid experience with conventional online and hybrid teaching during the pandemic. The study was approved by the institutional review board and informed consent was collected from all participants.

The Fernstudent and its basic features were introduced in the first test session. Just like in the previous sessions, students were free to decide whether they joined the lecture in presence or remotely. After each session, students and teachers filled in a questionnaire and rated their experience of the lecture with the Fernstudent by several measures and qualitative questions. In addition, retrospective in-depth interviews were conducted with the two teachers after the course had finished at the end of the semester. Basically, the interviews followed three leading questions, i.e., 1) How did you experience the teaching sessions with the Fernstudent? 2) What did it change compared to previous sessions of hybrid teaching? 3) Do you have any suggestions for improvements or further developments? Due to space limits, the present paper focuses on the teachers' perspective expressed in the interviews, which already provide interesting insights in the strength of the concept as well as issues for future research and development. Again, central issues are summarized in key sentences and illuminated by exemplary interview statements by Peggy [P] and Tom [T].

Table 2. Key issues and exemplary statements raised in the retrospective interviews after using the Fernstudent prototype in the field test by teachers ([P] = Peggy, [T]=Tom)

Overall pleasant and relaxed atmosphere, stress reduction, sense of competence "All the stress of switching between background tasks and presentation view is gone. A very relaxed situation." [T] "The remote students are just as present as the others and can draw attention by themselves. And these signals are so salient that you notice them automatically and don't have to look for them explicitly." [T] "It also gives you a sense of competence. Finally, you can offer good hybrid teaching. Everybody expects that this is something that should be feasible - and now you can fulfill these expectations." [P]
Technology handling in the background, focus on content and students "The technology and the handling was very much in the background." [T] "No need for a special channel for the remote students. You could just see the faces and they could speak to you. I'm no longer in charge and actually another device takes care of it." [P]
Natural interaction, appropriate form, pleasant social interaction, "Really a very nice experience. That you could address the student directly without having a special mic or anything. Very natural. You didn't feel like the technology was a hurdle, but really in the background." [T] "You can perceive at first glance that this is supposed to represent a human - but it's also not so playful that you have to stare at it all the time. They are clear, simple shapes, and not distracting. So that the technology is not in the foreground but remains a vehicle to solve the problems of hybrid courses." [P]
Enhanced presence of remote students, blending of both groups of students, more like one category "What I found amazingly positive was to permanently see how many remote students are there, maybe also coming or going. So you just had more of an impression of your audience and how many people you are actually talking to." [T] "In the past, the remote students were more a kind of background category. You hardly could connect to them. Through the avatar in the lecture hall, the remote ones are just as visible as the present ones." [T] "I realized that an integration of physical presence and non-presence is actually possible." [P]
Remote students still less active than physically present students "Still, the remote students did not participate as much as the students who were physically present. Which of course can be a selection effect because those don't come who also don't want to participate so much. Or maybe someone is sick and then doesn't feel like much interaction." [T] "The frequency of interaction among the remote students was not yet the same as among the on-site students. Maybe they first have to learn that it can be done differently. Just as it was a learning effect for me to see that this really works." [P]
Improve audio quality and visibility of remote students for physically present students "The audio technology is something that could still be improved. Of course, the microphones have to be very sensitive, but you also hear every rustling paper." [T] "The number of remote students should be more visible for all. So, for example, you can see that it's a well-attended lecture and that it doesn't have a demotivating effect if the physical lecture room is a bit emptier." [P]
Bonus ideas: record function, fly-in-perspective for remote students, support exploration "If you already have such a tool that is adjusted so that lecturer image and slides are integrated, you could also easily integrate a recording function. That would be a nice bonus." [T] "I guess you still could work on the experience for the remote students. For example, in computer games you often have a perspective flight at the beginning where you see yourself, your avatar, from above and then you fly into the body. Something like that could be built in at the beginning, when you dial into the meeting, that you then fly into the robot and then you change to the normal view and see the presentation slides and the lecturer." [T] "It doesn't necessarily need any more features now but maybe a good intro tour at the beginning that everyone really understands the possibilities. Just like when you switch on a new iPhone, you get a few tips on what you can use. If you do not use it with all the features, you also do not experience the real advantage." [P]

6. CONCLUSION

The first field test of the Fernstudent prototype already showed very promising results. Realized by relatively simple technological means, it's functioning was stable and it became a normal element of hybrid lectures. More important, the teachers' reflections showed that it also fulfilled the envisioned experiential benefits: It reduced stress and cognitive demands for teachers and provided a more unified social interaction with and between on-site and remote students. Overall it enabled a more satisfying teaching experience that allowed the teachers to focus on the students' needs and not the technology. Although the functions it provides are relatively simple, the Fernstudent made a great difference.

Still, the present investigation is limited in several respects. The main contribution is the theoretically and empirically informed concept development. However, this still must be evaluated in more lectures, at different universities, with more diverse user groups, and include a stronger focus on the students' perspective. While full data-analysis is still ongoing, early results from the survey among students in context of the present field test show that also from the students' perspective, the Fernstudent did initiate some changes compared to the regular hybrid option based on Jitsi, such as higher perceived social presence of the remote students and the interaction between teacher and remote students was perceived more similar to that between teacher and on-site students. Also, remote students showed a higher intention for active participation in the Fernstudent compared to the Jitsi sessions, however, on-site students were still more active and raising their hand more often than remote students (as also reported by the teachers). Regarding the impression of the Fernstudent in the classroom, the most part of the on-site students described it as mainly neutral and neither particularly positive, nor negative. This generally accords to the intended effect of the Fernstudent, as giving the remote students a presence in the classroom but not becoming a character and source of attraction itself.

Besides, there are many options for further development of the concept, especially from the students' perspective. The "bonus ideas" mentioned in the retrospective interviews already provide some ideas (e.g., exploration tours, fly-in perspective, record function). However, note that additional features must be carefully explored, in order to not dilute the overall concept and protect its core functions. In addition, there are many elements of design which could be explored in more detail such as the adequate level of anthropomorphism, or choices of the material and shape to better meet the different requirements in daily use (e.g., acceptance, low weight for portability, robustness).

Moreover, apart from the specific case, this study presents a number of implications for future studies in educational research and learning psychology. Our research reveals how a generally promising concept of education (here: hybrid teaching) can be challenged by specific characteristics and constellations of cognitive, social and technological aspects, which impede the delivery of its full potential – and how a detailed analysis of key issues can help to resolve those. Furthermore, it would be interesting to explore learners' experiences with the Fernstudent from the perspective of theoretical frameworks, and to study how different components play together. For example, one interesting starting point would be the community of inquiry-model, originally developed in the context of (pure) online learning (Garrison, 2016), but later also applied to hybrid learning. The model lists three presences that help to stimulate a successful "Community of Inquiry" and optimal educational experiences, namely, social presence, teaching presence, and cognitive presence. For an evaluation study, it would be interesting to test how the Fernstudent performs with regards to the different presences, and which might be dominant.

Regarding practical applications, the concept of the Fernstudent might also be generalizable to other contexts. Telepresence is already a well-known phenomenon in other domains, for example at conferences, where, however, interactivity is usually not the focus. The present findings could be used to transfer the concept of telepresence to other application areas, such as hybrid meetings and technology-assisted learning in different contexts. This, of course, also requires future investments into developing a stable, transportable system at relatively low cost. Then it would be conceivable in the future to multiply the Fernstudent - similar to the video conferencing sets currently available in lecture hall technology - and to provide it out to teachers and researchers at all places. Conversely, it would also be conceivable to install the Fernstudent permanently in selected lecture halls, as a signal and mission statement: We are and will remain a face-to-face university, but we have leveraged the experiences from the pandemic and are using them to move us into the future.

ACKNOWLEDGEMENT

Many thanks to Celina Lübben, Johanna Schlechter and Lara Christoforakos for their support in setting up the functional prototype, conducting the field study, and discussing and further developing the concept. Thanks to Klara Schuster for her support in the literature research. Part of this research has been funded by the LMU Quality Teaching Fund (Fonds zur Förderung der guten Lehre) and the DFG-project PerforM—Personalities for Machinery in Personal Pervasive Smart Spaces (DI 2436/2-1) in context of the Priority Program "Scalable Interaction Paradigms for Pervasive Computing Environments" (SPP 2199).

REFERENCES

Airenti, G. (2015). The cognitive bases of anthropomorphism: from relatedness to empathy. *International Journal of Social Robotics, 7*(1), 117-127.

Araujo, T. (2018). Living up to the chatbot hype: The influence of anthropomorphic design cues and communicative agency framing on conversational agent and company perceptions. *Computers in Human Behavior, 85*, 183-189.

Boye , T.& Eyet, J. (2021). F*ostering Inclusivitiy: Bridking the Gap Between In-Person and Online Student Learning.* Retrieved from https://community.mural.co/discussion/618/webinar (last access 13/08/2023).

De Freitas, S., & Neumann, T. (2009). The use of 'exploratory learning' for supporting immersive learning in virtual environments. *Computers & Education, 52*(2), 343-352.

Fredricks, J. A., Blumenfeld, P. C., & Paris, A. H. (2004). School Engagement: Potential of the Concept, State of the Evidence. *Review of Educational Research, 74*(1), 59–109. https://doi.org/10.3102/ 00346543074001059.

Gallon, L., Abénia, A., Dubergey, F., & Negui, M. (2019). Using a Telepresence Robot in an Educational Contex. In *15th Int'l Conf on Frontiers in Education: Computer Science and Computer Engineering* (FECS 2019).

Gamage, K. A., Jeyachandran, K., Dehideniya, S. C., Lambert, C. G., & Rennie, A. E. (2023). Online and Hybrid Teaching Effects on Graduate Attributes: Opportunity or Cause for Concern?. *Education Sciences, 13*(2), 221.

Garrison, D. R. (2016). *E-learning in the 21st century: A community of inquiry framework for research and practice.* Taylor & Francis.

Grønbæk, J. E., Saatçi, B., Griggio, C. F., & Klokmose, C. N. (2021). MirrorBlender: Supporting hybrid meetings with a malleable video-conferencing system. In *Proceedings of the 2021 CHI Conference on Human Factors in Computing Systems* (pp. 1-13).

Huizinga, T., Lohuis, A., Zwerver-Bergman, J., & van der Meer, R. (2022). Student and teacher perceptions of community of inquiry in hybrid virtual classrooms. *Heliyon, 8(*12).

Johannessen, L. E., Rasmussen, E. B., & Haldar, M. (2023). Student at a distance: exploring the potential and prerequisites of using telepresence robots in schools. *Oxford Review of Education, 49*(2), 153-170.

Klunder, S., Saab, N., & Admiraal, W. (2022). A teacher perspective on using a hybrid virtual classroom for students with a chronic illness in mainstream primary and secondary schools. *Technology, Pedagogy and Education, 31*(4), 493-508.

Kwon, O. H., Koo, S. Y., Kim, Y. G., & Kwon, D. S. (2010). Telepresence robot system for English tutoring. In *2010 ieee workshop on advanced robotics and its social impacts* (pp. 152-155).

Linder, K. E. (2017). *Fundamentals of hybrid teaching and learning. New directions for teaching and learning, 2017*(149), 11-18.

Lizenberger, K. (2023). *Explorative Interviews.* Retrieved from https://boldcollective.de/explorative-interviews/ (last access 15/08/2023).

Lorenzo-Lledó, A., Lledó, A., Gilabert-Cerdá, A., & Lorenzo, G. (2021). The pedagogical model of hybrid teaching: Difficulties of university students in the context of COVID-19. *European Journal of Investigation in Health, Psychology and Education, 11*(4), 1320-1332.

Ma, S., Hu, Q., Chen, Y., Zhao, Z., & Li, H. (2023). Social Bots that Bring a Strong Presence to Remote Participants in Hybrid Meetings. In *Companion of the 2023 ACM/IEEE International Conference on Human-Robot Interaction* (pp. 853-856). https://doi.org/10.1145/3568294.3580200

Moore, M. G. (1993). Theory of transactional distance. *Theoretical principles of distance education, 1*, 22-38.

Newhart, V. A., Warschauer, M., & Sender, L. (2016). Virtual inclusion via telepresence robots in the classroom: An exploratory case study. *The International Journal of Technologies in Learning, 23*(4), 9-25.

Raes, A. (2022). Exploring student and teacher experiences in hybrid learning environments: Does presence matter?. *Postdigital Science and Education, 4*(1), 138-159.

Singh, J., Steele, K., & Singh, L. (2021). Combining the best of online and face-to-face learning: Hybrid and blended learning approach for COVID-19, post vaccine, & post-pandemic world. *Journal of Educational Technology Systems, 50*(2), 140-171.

Velinov, A., Koceski, S., & Koceska, N. (2021). A review of the usage of telepresence robots in education. Balkan *Journal of Applied Mathematics and Informatics, 4*(1), 27-40.

Virkus, S., Leoste, J., Marmor, K., Kasuk, T., & Talisainen, A. (2023). Telepresence robots from the perspective of psychology and educational sciences. *Information and Learning Sciences, 124*(1/2), 48-69.

USING GRAPH-BASED HEURISTICS TO ANALYZE A SYSTEMATIC LITERATURE REVIEW AND VALIDATE AN EXPERT-BASED TAXONOMY

Nadine Schlomske-Bodenstein[1], Bernhard Standl[1] and Pablo Pirnay-Dummer[2]
[1]*Karlsruhe University of Education*
Bismarckstraße 10, 76133 Karlsruhe, Germany
[2]*Martin Luther University Halle-Wittenberg, Educational Psychology*
Franckeplatz 1, Haus 5, D-06099 Halle (Saale), Germany

ABSTRACT

The study presented in this paper uses heuristics from computer linguistics and graph theory to analyze a systematic literature review on educational technology. A literature review was conducted to validate an expert-based taxonomy which was developed to ontologize delivered teaching and learning for easy reuse. The sample includes N = 121 publications. The findings indicate that the yielded key words that were generated through T-MITOCAR Artemis contained key features that were rated as being relevant to the experts and caused the expert-based taxonomy to be changed and restructured. The results of this study provide directions on how time-consuming elements of systematic literature reviews could partially be automated.

KEYWORDS

Systematic Literature Review, Taxonomy, Validation, Technology-Enhanced Learning and Instruction, Mental Models

1. INTRODUCTION

Designing technology-enhanced learning and instruction in such a way that it promotes students' learning is of special interest in higher education. Therefore, it is important to align the intended learning outcomes with the choice of teaching and assessment methods (Biggs and Tang, 2007). Consequently, it is of interest to identify the impact of lesson designs and describe them for reuse in teaching (Vercoustre & McLean, 2005; Agostinho et al., 2009). For a reusable description of teaching, design patterns can offer a promising way to describe effective teaching patterns. The pattern approach, which originated in architecture (Alexander et al., 1977), was later applied in object-oriented software design (Gamma et al., 1993) and has already been established in education (Bergin et al., 2012; Derntl, 2005; Standl, 2014). To be able to identify patterns, the collected teaching data needs to be described in a suitable database-structure to be able to mine patterns. The backbone of this appropriate structure is, first, the development of a basic hierarchical structure as a taxonomy (Gamma, 1993).

Considering this, the aims of this study are: (1) to validate a taxonomy developed to ontologize digital instructional design, (2) to use innovative technologies to identify key concepts obtained through a systematic literature review. The present paper is structured in two main parts: First, we discuss the theoretical background and the selection of T-MITOCAR Artemis as an appropriate instrument to analyzing text material. Second, we explain how we conducted the study and discuss the results and innovational aspects of this study.

2. THEORETICAL BACKGROUND

The use of digital technologies in learning and instructional environments has been investigated in various context, like for instance, improving self-regulated learning (Freihofner, 2018; Pirnay-Dummer & Ifenthaler, 2018) and collaboration (Pifarré, M. and Martí, 2018; Swanson et al, 2021; Besser et al. 2022). Bellou et al. 2018 found that most empirical studies in Chemnistry Education focus first on the learning outcomes, then on student's motivation when investigating digital technologies in teaching practices and a few studies focus on teachers attitudes on digital technologies.

A number of features of instructional quality have been identified and categorized as distinctive predictors for the impact on student learning (Helmke, 2009; Seidel & Shavelson, 2007). For the identification of effective technology-enhanced instructional designs, it is furthermore required to consider domain-specific features that meet the need of the particular context. When investigating domain-specific terms, concepts, or entities of teaching learning settings, a taxonomy can provide a way to put this data into an ordered, hierarchical structure with categories and sub-categories (Rich, 1992). Furthermore, a taxonomy provides an adequate conceptual framework to structure features of teaching-learning settings in a way that they can be classified and retrieved (Vercoustre and McLean, 2005). Based on the structure of the taxonomy, a database structure facilities storing, updating and manipulating the information of teaching-learning settings (Vysniauskas & Nemuraite, 2016).

When conceptualizing key features of learning and instructional design and of instructional technologies that have been used in order to prompt learning, a taxonomy provides a way to put them into an ordered, hierarchical structure (Rich, 1992). While a taxonomy represents a domain in categories and sub-categories, an ontology adds to the taxonomy further semantics with relationships between the (sub)-categories and also defines further details. Therefore, a taxonomy can be considered as the backbone of an ontology (Giunchiglia and Zaihrayeu, 2007). Ontologies provide a promising way of storing distinctive features of learning and instructional design. An ontology is defined as an explicit specification of a conceptualization (Gruber, 1995). Bimba et al. (2016) distinguish between different forms of ontologizing: (1) application ontologies, (2) domain ontologies, (3) generic ontologies, and (4) representation ontologies. The application ontology captures all the relevant key features that are required to model knowledge in a specific domain. The domain ontology illustrates the domain specific conceptualizations. The generic ontology aims to generalize and be valid in different domains. The representation ontology is limited to a specific domain. In terms of capturing learning and instructional design in different domains, an ontology is needed that is able to store the key features of learning and instruction through a taxonomy in a generic way so that they can be transferred into other domains. Consequently, the features that are stored in the database which cover best-practice-examples must be stored on an abstract level. The application of web ontologies is a suitable way to store and represent an objective knowledge directory (Kampmann et al., 2020). However, teaching and learning designs are dynamic and, therefore, need to be ontologized dynamically.

2.1 Emerging Technology

2.1.1 Aim of Literature Review

The purpose of this systematic literature review was: (1) to validate a taxonomy developed to ontologize digital instructional design, (2) to use innovative technologies to identify key concepts obtained through a systematic literature review.

2.2.2 Identifying Key Concepts of a Literature Review with T-MITOCAR Artemis

T-MITOCAR Artemis (Text-Model Inspection Trace of Concepts and Relations Artemis) is a further development of T-MITOCAR. T-MITOCAR is a computer-based software application (Pirnay-Dummer & Ifenthaler, 2010; Pirnay-Dummer, Ifenthaler & Spector, 2010; Pirnay-Dummer, 2015a) which is strictly based on the theory of mental models (Seel, 1991). It is automated in its procedure and analysis and has proven to deliver homogeneous, reliable, and valid results in multiple studies. The software measures a specific set of properties of language re-representations and generates associative graphs from texts using heuristics from computer linguistics (Pirnay-Dummer, 2015b) and graph theory (Tittmann, 2010) combining theoretical foundations of mapping knowledge in a way and onto a format that is close to how humans internally represent knowledge for learning (Jonassen & Cho, 2008; Pirnay-Dummer & Seel, 2018; Spector, 2008; Strasser, 2010).

T-MITOCAR Artemis can be used to examine and aggregate knowledge-domains in learning and instruction. It uses multi-cluster text corpora as input and visualizes continents on a knowledge map out of several texts of a particular domain (Pirnay-Dummer & Ifenthaler, 2010; Lachner & Pirnay-Dummer, 2008, Pirnay-Dummer, 2015a).

3. RESEARCH QUESTION

The following research questions are of interest:

1. To what extent can T-MITOCAR Artemis be used to validate an expert-based taxonomy?
2. To what extent can heuristics be used to systematically analyze a literature-reviews?

4. METHOD

The systematic review was aligned to the proposed eight steps of Okoli and Schabram (2010). In accordance with Ifenthaler, et al. (2020) and Okoli (2015) all eight steps are essential: (1) identify the purpose, (2) draft a protocol and train the team, (3) practical screen, (4) search for literature, (5) extract data, (6) appraise quality, (7) synthesize studies, and (8) write the review.

The purpose was to find further potential key features that could be of relevance for the taxonomy. Several relevant databases were included (ERIC, PsycInfo and dissertation-databases). The keywords used were ('educational technology' or 'technology enhanced learning' in combination with 'teacher education' or 'higher education' and 'self-efficacy' and 'technology integration') as well as ('digital teaching' or 'digital learning' in combination with 'teacher education' or 'higher education' in combination with 'TPACK' or 'pre-service-teachers' in combination with 'innovation', and not including 'school'). In addition, we consulted dissertation -databases (dart-europe, obvsg, oatd, ucl). We used the following keywords for dart-europe ('mobile technology in the classroom'); ('pre-service teachers' in combination with 'self-efficacy' in combination with 'technology integration') as well as ('higher education' in combination with 'technology integration'). For obvsg we used the following keywords ('educational technology' in combination with 'educational technology'). We used the following keywords for ucl ('mobile technology in the classroom' in combination with 'higher education). To be included, publications had to meet the criteria: (1) published between 2015 and 2020, (2) peer reviewed. Duplicate publications were removed. Only those publications were included that were completely available.

The studies found were analyzed through T-MITOCAR Artemis. All retrieved studies were sorted into several domain-based clusters of up to ten studies, in order to generate knowledge maps through T-MITOCAR Artemis. The titles and abstract of the studies were reviewed and content-clusters created by an expert in the field of technology-enhanced learning. This intermediate step was implemented to generate knowledge-maps of domain-specific subjects through T-MITOCAR Artemis.

Finally, one expert in the field of digital teaching and learning independently and one trained person reviewed and rated the automatically reported concepts produced through T-MITOCAR Artemis in regard to: (1) the relevance of depicting educational technology; (2) if the concepts were already part of the taxonomy, and (3) if not, whether they should be included. The ratings of the concepts are illustrated in Table 1. All concepts are independently rated on a 5-point Likert scale (1 = not relevant, ... 5 = relevant).

Table 1. Rating of the produced concepts through T-MITOCAR Artemis

Please rate the following taxonomy.		
1. The concept is relevant in order to depict digital teaching-learning-scenarios		
Not relevant	O O O O O	Relevant
2. The concept is already part of the taxonomy.		
No	O O O	Yes
3. The concept should be included in the taxonomy.		
No	O O O	Yes

The two experts who developed the initial taxonomy and the trained person met again and went through the concepts that were rated at least, as rather relevant. If those concepts were regarded by at least one person as relevant and were not yet part of the taxonomy, they went through a consensus-validation and were either added to the taxonomy or not.

5. RESULTS

Our literature search resulted in 312 publications. 223 publications were found in educational and psychological databases - 101 were available and included in the analysis. 89 publications were found in dissertation-databases - 21 were available and included in the analysis. Table 2 and Table 3 show the key word combinations and the numbers of publications that were found in the different databases.

Table 2. Results of the databases

Database	Keyword combination	Results
ERIC	("digital teaching" OR "digital learning") AND ("Teacher Education" OR "Higher Education") AND ("TPACK" OR "pre-service teacher") AND ("innovation") NOT "school"	93
ERIC (2015-2020)	("educational technology" OR "technology enhanced learning") AND ("Teacher education" OR "Higher education") AND ("self-efficacy") AND ("technology integration")	36
PsycInfo(2010-2020)	("digital teaching" OR "digital learning") AND ("Teacher Education" OR "Higher Education") AND ("TPACK" OR "pre-service teacher") AND ("innovation") NOT "school"	89
PsycInfo (2015-2020)	"educational technology" AND "pre-service teachers" AND "technology integration"	5
Total		223 Available Publications : 101

Table 3. Results of the dissertation-databases

Database	Keyword combination	Results
Dart.europe	"mobile technology in the classroom"	1
Dart.europe	"pre-service teachers" and "self-efficacy" and "technology integration"	8
Dart.europe	Higher Education AND technology integration	3
search.obvsg.at	"educational technology" AND "pre-service teachers" AND "technology integration"	1
search.obvsg.at	"educational technology"	2
oatd.org	("pre-service teacher") AND ("educational technology")	11
ucl-new-primo.hosted. Exlibrisgroup.com	"mobile technology in the classroom" AND "higher education"	63
Total		99 Available publications : 21

Publications that were dublicated were deleted. Altogether, 121 available publications were included in the T-MITOCAR Artemis analysis (one study was deleted due to major Turkish elements which could not be analyzed by the instrument). The following clusters were created in order to analyze the publications through T-MITOCAR Artemis (see Table 4).

Table 4. Clusters of studies found in ERIC & PsychInfo and dissertation-databases

Database	Clusters	Number of texts
ERIC & PsychInfo	Acceptance / Readiness	6
	Assessment	4
	Attitude	5
	Authenticity	5
	Beliefs	8
	Computer	7
	Environment	6
	Game / Gamification	5
	Innovation	12
	Perception	10
	Reflection	5
	Strategies studies	6
	Teaching practice	8
	Technologies' development	3
	Innovation in Educational Technology	10
PhD-databases	Digital Technology	8
	Higher Education	4
	Reflection	3
	Lesson-specific aspects	6
		121

Figure 1 shows a knowledge map that was generated through T-MITOCAR Artemis out of ten studies that were grouped into the cluster of "Innovation in Educational Technology". It contains 149 concepts that were generated out of ten texts through T-MITOCAR Artemis.

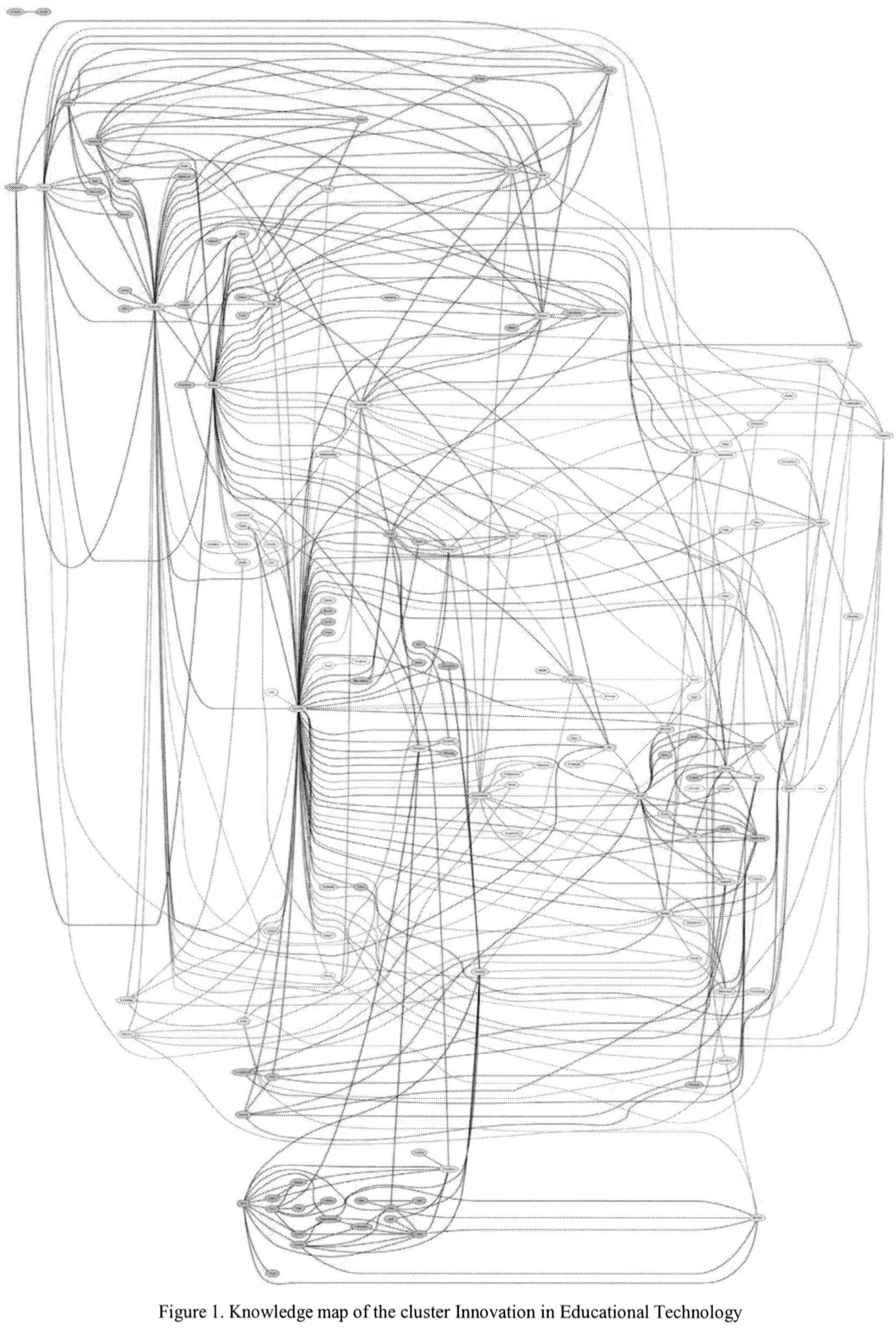

Figure 1. Knowledge map of the cluster Innovation in Educational Technology

The 19 knowledge maps yielded 403 concepts – 71 concepts were excluded as it turned out that in some studies there were still Turkish elements included in the references when referring to Turkish language. Therefore, 298 potentially relevant concepts were included into the rating. In a next step, these concepts were independently rated by two raters (one expert in the field of learning-enhanced technology and one trained rater). In a post-hoc analysis, another expert rated the 298 concepts as well. This was done in order to guarantee that different experts rated the same concepts as either relevant or not. The following Table 5 to Table 7 show the results of the ratings. Table 5 indicates that, on average, most of the concepts were rated as irrelevant, whereas 35 were regarded as maybe relevant, 34 as rather relevant and 44 as relevant.

Table 5. Descriptive results of the raters regarding the relevance of the concepts

Rating of the concepts	Expert 1	Trained Rater	Expert 2	AM
Not relevant	137	160	212	170
Less relevant	22	15	9	15
Maybe relevant	44	27	33	35
Rather relevant	50	27	24	34
Relevant	43	70	20	44
Sum	299	299	298	

Table 6 shows that most concepts were rated as not yet part of the taxonomy.

Table 6. Descriptive results of the raters regarding not yet part

Rating of the concepts	Expert 1	Trained Rater	Expert 2
Not yet part of the taxonomy	231	194	256
Already part of the taxonomy	28	78	20
Partly part of the taxonomy	29	26	23

Table 7 reveals that most concepts were rated as to be included into the taxonomy. Expert 1 rated that 20 concepts should be included and 1 concept may be included. Finally, 21 concepts were in particular discussed in the consensus-validation when restructuring changing the taxonomy.

Table 7. Descriptive results of the raters regarding including the concepts

Rating of the concepts	Expert 1	Trained Rater	Expert 2
Not including into the taxonomy	278	277	283
Should be included into the taxonomy	20	16	15
Should maybe be included into the taxonomy	1	4	0

Table 8 shows the correlation coefficient (Spearman) between the ratings of the 299 concepts. All correlations with an asterisk (*) are statistically significant ($p > 0.05$). It reveals that the raters differed in their estimations of the concepts that were generated through T-MITOCAR Artemis. Even the experts did not agree in their ratings.

Table 8. Intercoder reliability between the raters regarding the relevance of the concepts

Rater	r
Expert 1 vs. expert 2	0.52 (*)
Expert 1 vs. trained rater	0.50 (*)
Expert 2 vs. trained rater	0.46 (*)

Table 9 reveal the development of the number of concepts in the taxonomy before and after the literature review and after N = 3 additional experts discussed that taxonomy and restructured it and added or deleted concepts together.

Table 9. Development of the number of concepts in the taxonomy

	Before Literature Review	after Literature Review	After Experts
Taxonomy	88 concepts (76 concepts without duplicates)	69 concepts (65 concepts without duplicates)	111 concepts (74 concepts without duplicates)
part of T-MITOCAR Artemis	15 concepts	11 concepts	16 concepts
Partly part of T-MITOCAR Artemis	26 concepts	23 concepts	26 concepts
Not part of T-MITOCAR Artemis	35 concepts	38 concepts	33 concepts

Some concepts were included in the taxonomy about the name of the knowledge map (like for instance: acceptance, attitudes). Table 11 shows the concepts that were inserted into the taxonomy after the literature review and after the experts-round, which were also part of the concepts generated through T-MITOCAR Artemis. Moreover, the experts deleted concepts from the taxonomy that had not been proposed by T-MITOCAR Artemis, like for instance, automation, digital didactics and digital knowledge.

Table 10. Concepts inserted into the taxonomy

	Inserted into the Taxonomy after the Literature Review	Inserted into the Taxonomy after the Expert discussion
Proposed by T-MITOCAR Artemis	Culture Feedback Focus Tasks	role
Partly proposed by T-MITOCAR Artemis	(digital) tool Learning (&) goal	Augmentation (pre-recorded) video
Cluster Name	Acceptance Attitudes	
Not proposed by T-MITOCAR Artemis	Stability TPACK Transparency of the chosen methods types	

6. DISCUSSION AND CONCLUSION

This paper describes an aspect of the procedure for creating a structure for obtaining good teaching practices as patterns. To identify good teaching practice for designing digital teaching settings, a taxonomy provides a suitable domain-specific structure as a conceptual model for a database for pattern mining in lesson design data. The presented study provides an approach on validating a taxonomy of digital instructional designs drafted by experts in the field for a systematical validation in literature. Results show two main findings: first, the provision of a semi-automated analysis of systematic literature reviews. When it comes to time-consuming phases of systematic literature reviews, such as identifying key features that are significant in the text corpora. Although the context in which the concepts were used was not considered, the results show that T-MITOCAR Artemis provided relevant and significant concepts that prompted the expert modification of an expert-based taxonomy. In addition, experts who were completely unaware of the concepts generated by the tool added concepts to the taxonomy that had already been proposed by T-MITOCAR Artemis but had not previously been part of the taxonomy. The same experts even deleted concepts from the taxonomy that the software had not proposed. This gives first directions on semi-automatizing this step of literature review in different domains. Second, although experts in the same domain were asked to evaluate the same concepts - they seem to have different models of which concepts were already part of the taxonomy or not.

Limitations and Future Work

The present literature review is limited in various points which must be addressed in future work. First, the intercoder reliability between the experts were insufficient, which needs to be addressed in future work. Further work needs to explore the understanding of the concepts used in the taxonomy in more detail. A limitation of this study is that it only involved a few experts in technology-enhanced learning. Different groups of experts in the field of technology-enhanced learning need to be regarded, like for instance not only researchers but also teachers and practitioners as well in order to further validate the taxonomy.

Another limitation was that the instrument used in this study provided several concepts which were of no interest and were not implemented into the taxonomy. However, as a tool to give a first orientation to provide a cluster of ontologies, T-MITOCAR Artemis gives a first direction of automatizing some steps of literature reviews. However, experts still need to go through the findings in the end to decide whether the concepts generated are of relevance or not.

ACKNOWLEDGEMENT

This work was supported by BMBF InDiKo, effective integration of subject didactical digital teaching-learning-scenarios at the University of Education Karlsruhe (Grant No: 01JA2027).

REFERENCES

Agostinho, S., Bennett, S., Lockyer, L., Kosta, L., Jones, J., & Harper, B. (2009). An examination of learning design descriptions in an existing learning design repository. In R. Atkinson & C. McBeath (Eds.), Conference of the Australasian Society for Computers in Learning in Tertiary Education (pp. 11-19). Auckland, New Zealand: Auckland University of Technology and ASCILITE.

Alexander, C., Ishikawa, S., & Silverstein, M. (1977). A Pattern Language: Towns, Buildings, Construction. Oxford: University Press.

Bergin, J., Eckstein, J. Volter, M., Sipos, M., Wallingford, E., Marquardt, K., Chandler, J., Sharp, H., Manns, M. (2012). Pedagogical patterns: advice for educators. Joseph Bergin Software Tools.

Bellou, I. and Papachristos, N. M. & Mikropoulos, T. A. (2018). Digital technologies in chemnistry education: A review. In Sampson, D., I. D. S. J. M. I. P., editor, Digital technologies: Sustainable innovations for improving teaching and learning, pages 57–80. Springer, Cham.

Besser, E. D. and Blackwell, Lauren E & Saenz, M. (2022). Engaging students through educational podcasting: Three stories of implementation. Technology, Knowledge and Learning, 27(3):749–764

Biggs, J. B., & Tang, C. (2007). Teaching for Quality Learning at University. Berkshire:

Mcgraw Hill, Society for Research into Higher Education & Open University Press.

Charters, E. (2003). The Use of Think-aloud Methods in Qualitative Research. An Introduction to Think-aloud Methods. Brock Education; 12(2):68–82. DOI: 10.26522/BROCKED.V12I2.38

De Nicola, A., & Missikoff, M. (2016). A lightweight methodology for rapid ontology engineering. Communications of the ACM, 59(3), 79-86.

Derntl, M. (2006). Patterns for person centered e-learning. University of Vienna.

Freihofner, U., Campbell, C., and Smala, S. (2018). Digital tool use and self-regulated strategies in a bilingual online learning environment. In *Digital Technologies: Sustainable Innovations for Improving Teaching and Learning*, pages 131–146. Springer.

Gamma, E., Helm, R., Johnson, R., & Vlissides, J. (1993). Design patterns: Abstraction and reuse of object-oriented design. In European Conference on Object-Oriented Programming (pp. 406-431). Springer, Berlin, Heidelberg.

Giunchiglia, F., Zaihrayeu, I. 2007. Lightweight ontologies. Technical Report DIT-07-071, University of Trento.

Helmke, A. (2009). Unterrichtsqualität und Lehrerprofessionalität – Diagnose, Evaluation und Verbesserung des Unterrichts. Seelze, Kallmeyer. [School Quality and Teacher Professionalism – Diagnostics, Evaluation and Improvement of Instruction]

Ifenthaler, D., & Yau, J. Y.-K. (2020). Utilising learning analytics for study success: a systematic review. Educational Technology Research and Development, 68(4) 1961–1990. doi:10.1007/s11423-020-09788-z

Jonassen, D. H., & Cho, Y. H. (2008). Externalizing mental models with mindtools. In D.

Ifenthaler, P. Pirnay-Dummer, & J. M. Spector (Eds.), Understanding models for learning and instruction. Essays in honor of Norbert M. Seel. (pp. 145-159). New York: Springer.

Lachner, A. & Pirnay-Dummer, P. (2010). Model based knowledge mapping - a new approach for the automated graphical representation of organizational knowledge. In Spector, J. M., Ifenthaler, D., Isaias, P., Kinshuk & Sampson, D. G. (Eds.). Learning and instruction in the digital age: Making a difference through cognitive approaches, technology-facilitated collaboration and assessment, and personalized communications. New York: Springer

Okoli, C. (2015). A guide to conducting a standalone systematic literature review. Communications of the Association for Information Systems Research, 37(43), 879–910. https ://doi.org/10.17705 /1CAIS.03743

Okoli, C., & Schabram, K. (2010). A guide to conducting a systematic literature review of information systems research. Sprouts: Workind Paper on Information Systems, 10(26), 1–49.

Pifarré, M. and Martí, L. (2018). A technology-enhanced pedagogical framework to promote collaborative creativity in secondary education. In Sampson, D., I. D. S. J. M. I. P., editor, Digital technologies: Sustainable innovations for improving teaching and learning, pages 241–258. Springer, Cham.

Pirnay-Dummer, P. (2015a). Knowledge Elicitation. In J. M. Spector (Ed.), The SAGE Encyclopedia of Educational Technology (pp. 438–442). Thousand Oaks, CA: SAGE.

Pirnay-Dummer, P. (2015b). Linguistic analysis tools. In C. A. MacArthur, S. Graham, & J. Fitzgerald (Eds.), Handbook of Writing Research (pp. 427-442). New York: Guilford Publications.

Pirnay-Dummer, P., & Ifenthaler, D. (2010). Automated Knowledge Visualization and Assessment. In D. Ifenthaler, P. Pirnay-Dummer & N. M. Seel (Eds.), Computer-Based Diagnostics and Systematic Analysis of Knowledge. New York: Springer.

Pirnay-Dummer, P., Ifenthaler, D. (2018). Students' self-regulated learning through online academic writing in a course blog. In Sampson, D., I. D. S. J. M. I. P., editor, *Digital technologies: Sustainable innovations for improving teaching and learning,* pages 111–129. Cham, New York.

Pirnay-Dummer, P., Ifenthaler, D., & Spector, J. M. (2010). Highly integrated model assessment technology and tools. Educational Technology Research and Development, 58 (1), 3-18.

Pirnay-Dummer, P., & Seel, N. M. (2018). The Sciences of Learning. In L. Lin & J. M. Spector (Eds.), The Sciences of Learning and Instructional Design. Constructive Articulation between Communities (pp. 8-35). New York: Routledge.

Rich, P. (1992). The organizational taxonomy: Definition and design. The Academy of Management Review, 17(4), 758–781. https://doi.org/10.2307/258807

Seidel, T., & Shavelson, R. J. (2007). Teaching effectiveness research in the past decade: The role of theory and research design in disentangling meta-analysis results. Review of Educational Research, 77(4), 454-499. doi: 10.3102/0034654307310317

Seel, N. M. (1991). Weltwissen und mentale Modelle. Göttingen: Hogrefe. [World knowledge and mental models]

Swanson, J. A. and Renes, Susan L & Strange, A. T. (2021). Collaborative learning: Collegiate pedagogy utilizing web conferencing. In Ifenthaler, D., S. D. G. I. P., editor, *Balancing the Tension between Digital Technologies and Learning Sciences,* pages 253–267. Springer, Cham.

Spector, J. M. (2008). The fragmented nature of learning and instruction. In D. Ifenthaler, P.

Pirnay-Dummer, & J. M. Spector (Eds.), Understanding models for learning and instruction. Essays in honor of Norbert M. Seel. (pp. 3-22). New York: Springer.

Standl, B. (2014). Conceptual Modeling and Innovative Implementation of Person-centered Computer Science Education at Secondary School Level. University of Vienna.

Strasser, A. (2010). A functional view towards mental representations. In D. Ifenthaler, P.

Pirnay-Dummer, & J. M. Spector (Eds.), Computer-Based Diagnostics and Systematic Analysis of Knowledge (pp. 15-26). New York: Springer.

Tittmann, P. (2010). Graphs and Networks. In D. Ifenthaler, P. Pirnay-Dummer, & N. M. Seel (Eds.), Computer-Based Diagnostics and Systematic Analysis of Knowledge (pp. 177-188). New York: Springer.

Vercoustre, A.-M. & McLean, A. (2005). Reusing educational material for teaching and learning: Current approaches and directions. International Journal on E-Learning, 4(1), 57–68.

Vysniauskas, E., & Nemuraite, L. (2006). Transforming ontology representation from OWL to relational database. Information technology and control, 35(3).

Phd-databases:

https://www.dart-europe.org/basic-search.php

https://www.obvsg.at

https://oatd.org

https://www.ucl.ac.uk

MINING, ANALYZING, AND MODELING THE COGNITIVE STRATEGIES STUDENTS USE TO CONSTRUCT HIGHER QUALITY CAUSAL MAPS

Allan Jeong[1] and Hyoung Seok-Shin[2]
[1]*Department of Educational Psychology & Learning Systems*
Instructional Systems and Learning Technologies Program, Florida State University
3205E Stone Building, 1114 West Call Street
Tallahassee, FL, 32306-4450, USA
[2]*Department of Dental Education, School of Dentistry, Pusan National University*
407 Busandaehak-ro 49, Mulgeum-eup
Yangsan-si, Gyeongsangnam-do, 50612, Republic of Korea

ABSTRACT

The Jeong (2020) study found that greater use of backward and depth-first processing was associated with higher scores on students' argument maps and that analysis of only the first five nodes students placed in their maps predicted map scores. This study utilized the jMAP tool and algorithms developed in the Jeong (2020) study to determine if the same processes produce higher-quality causal maps. This study analyzed the first five nodes that students (n = 37) placed in their causal maps to reveal that: 1) use of backward, forward, breadth-first, and depth-first processing produced maps of similar quality; and 2) backward processing had three times more impact on maps scores than depth-first processing to suggest that linking events into chains using backward chaining is one approach to constructing higher quality causal maps. These findings are compared with prior research findings and discussed in terms of noted differences in the task demands of constructing argument versus causal maps to gain insights into why, how, and when specific processes/strategies can be applied to create higher-quality causal maps and argument maps. These insights provide guidance on ways to develop diagramming and analytic tools that automate, analyze, and provide real-time support to improve the quality of students' maps, learning, understanding, and problem-solving skills.

KEYWORDS

Critical Thinking, Knowledge Maps, Learning Analytics

1. INTRODUCTION

A variety of computer-aided diagramming tools are available or in development for creating argument, causal, and concept maps that are being used in education to visualize relationships and evaluate complex ideas (Giabbanelli, Tawfik, & Wang, 2023). These diagramming tools are used to create argument maps to visualize and identify hierarchical relationships between premises and claims to evaluate the structural soundness of complex arguments (Braak et al., 2006; Davies, Barnett, & van Gelder, 2019; Davies, 2011), causal maps to examine relationships between networks of variables/events and outcomes to reveal causal explanations (Desthieux, Joerin, & Lebreton, 2010; McCrudden, Schraw, & Lehman, 2009), and concept maps to examine relationships between concepts or ideas with labeled links that indicate the nature of the relationships (Cañas, Novak, & Reiska, 2015). These tools have been found to improve learning and critical thinking skills with moderate to large effect sizes (Schroeder, Nesbit, Anguiano, & Adesope, 2017; Eftekhari, Sotoudehnama, & Marandi, 2016; Harrell, 2011; van Gelder, 2015; Yue, Zhang, Zhang, & Jin, 2017), and reduce cognitive load by making relationships more concrete and facilitating analysis (Novak & Cañas, 2007). However, there can still be a high degree of variance in map quality, even when interventions are used to achieve significant gains in map quality (Ruiz-Primo & Shavelson, 1996).

Constructing maps can be a complex and challenging process even with the help of computer-aided diagramming tools (Beitz, 1998; Cañas, Reiska, & Möllits, 2017; Kinchin, 2001). As a result, specific mapping strategies examined and prescribed in the research literature include directing students to place the goal at the top (Eppler, 2006), sorting before linking nodes (Aguiar & Correia, 2017), sorting nodes by level of generality (Cañas, Reiska, & Möllits, 2017), positioning nodes with reading flow or temporal flow (Aguiar & Correia, 2017; Jeong & Lee, 2012), using five whys with backward chaining, goal-oriented, and depth-first process (Al-Ajlan, 2015; Chen, Li, & Shady, 2010; Sharma, Tiwari, & Kelkar, 2012), and using a breadth-first process to review maps (Biswas, Segedy, & Bunchongchit, 2016). Maps can be classified by structure and different learning approaches and outcomes are associated with them (He et al., 2023; Kinchin, 2011). Spokes often contain static linking phrases that result in restricted insights, and chains suggest rote learning when node sequences may be resistant to change. In contrast, networks are linked with meaningful learning when nodes are connected with dynamic explanatory phrases and cycles indicate iterative learning processes.

Currently, only a limited number of studies have been conducted to identify, validate, and model the cognitive strategies students use to construct maps. A more in-depth and precise analysis of the specific processes utilized by students can assist researchers in determining to what extent specific strategies are used by students to construct maps (Wang, 2019), help determine whether the utilization of specific strategies results in higher quality maps (Schroeder, Nesbit, Anguiano, & Adesope, 2017), better understand how specific characteristics of mapping tools and learner attributes influence what processes students use, and how mapping tools can be designed to more effectively monitor and provide real-time guidance on what strategies to use.

Two case studies investigated the cognitive strategies used by students when constructing argument maps (Jeong & Kim, 2022) and causal maps (Lee, 2012). Using verbal protocol analysis, Jeong and Kim (2022) found that both experts and novices used more breadth-first (BR) processing than depth-first (D) processing when constructing *argument* maps. More breadth-first processing was also found to be associated with higher quality *causal* maps (Shin & Jeong, 2021). Depth-first (Figure 1 left) is performed when the placement of 1 is followed by the placement of 2 immediately below 1. Breadth-first (Figure 1 right) occurs when the placement of 1 is followed by the placement of 2 to the immediate right or left of 1 (at the same level). Jeong & Kim (2022) also found that four of the five experts used more backward (B) than forward (F) processing to construct argument maps, when one novice used more backward process and the other four novices used a mix of backward and forward processing. The backward or deductive process is performed (Figure 1 left) when the placement of 1 is followed by the placement of 2 immediately below 1. The forward process (or inductive process) occurs when the placement of 3 is followed by the placement of 2 immediately above 3. Use of backward processing has also been found to be associated with higher quality causal maps (Lee, 2012; Shin & Jeong, 2021).

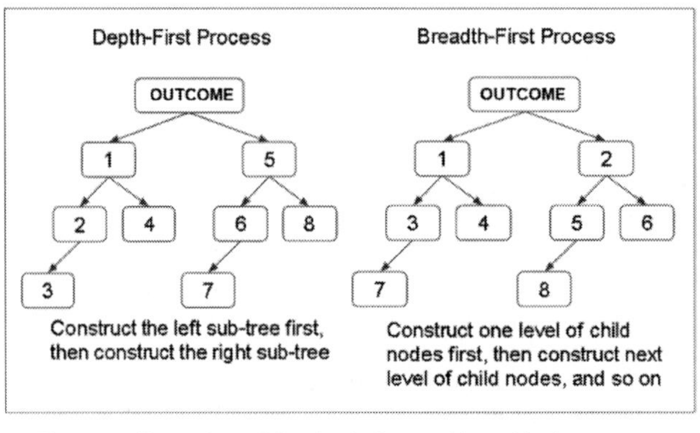

Figure 1. Illustration of the depth-first and breadth-first process

To analyze larger samples of maps with greater precision, the placement of nodes in relation to previously moved nodes can be used to automate map assessments (Taricani & Clariana, 2006) and identify the processes used by students in constructing a map (Jeong, 2020). Jeong (2020) developed the jMAP tool to log the on-screen actions of students while constructing *argument* maps. The tool used an algorithm to analyze the log data and measure the frequency of backward, forward, breadth-first, and depth-first processing performed by students. This study found that: 1) analyzing the placement of only the first five nodes moved on screen (not 10, 20 or all moved nodes) produced backward/forward and breadth/depth-first process ratio scores that were significant predictors of map scores; 2) greater use of *backward* and *depth-first* processing were used to produce better argument maps; and 3) simple observed frequencies of backward and depth-first processing alone (not ratio scores) were not found to be significant predictors of argument map scores. The analysis of simple frequencies instead of ratio scores and small sample size in the Jeong & Kim's (2022) case study help to explain why they found breadth-first processing (not depth-first processing) to be associated with higher quality argument maps.

The purpose of this study was to determine which of the four processes (backward, forward, breadth-first, depth-first) create higher quality causal maps. The same tools and metrics used by Jeong (2020) to identify the processes that create better argument maps were employed in this study. Argument maps are created by students when asked to evaluate the strength and validity of an argument by identifying the premises presented to support the argument and the logical relationships between premises. On the other hand, causal maps are created when students are asked to identify the critical variables/events and causal pathways that contribute to a specific outcome. These differences in task demands suggest that the processes used to create better argument maps may not necessarily create better causal maps. As a result, this study aimed to address the following research questions:

1. Does greater use of backward over forward processing produce better causal maps?
2. Does greater use of breadth-first over depth-first processing produce better causal maps?
3. Which process (backward versus breadth-first) has a greater impact on scores?

2. METHOD

2.1 Participants

The participants were 43 students (21 females, 22 males) at a large southeastern university. Six of the participants were undergraduates enrolled in a research subject pool and 37 were graduate students recruited via leaflets and received $15 gift certificates for participating. The students were informed that the student that created the highest-scoring causal map receives an additional $10 gift certificate. After reviewing and signing an IRB-approved consent form to participate in this study, the students' demographic information was collected using a brief survey. The survey was used to identify which if any participants had prior knowledge of causal maps, how to construct them, or any prior experience using causal mapping tools. No participants had prior knowledge and experience with using causal maps.

2.2 Procedure

The students viewed a video introduction to the jMAP software (Jeong, 2018) with demonstrations on how to drag and re-position nodes in the map, insert links to chain causally related variables (A→B = A affects B), and change the color of links (with red indicating an inverse relationship). Each student opened a jMAP file on a laboratory desktop computer with blank nodes that students used to practice moving and inserting links between nodes. Next, students received a handout initially placed face down with definitions of the outcome and each variable presented in the map nodes. The students were then instructed to start working on the causal map by clicking on a button to turn on a screen recorder, flipping over the handout to view the instructions and node definitions, and opening the jMAP file to view the initial screen (Figure 2) containing the outcome variable positioned to the far right and all variables positioned randomly on the left. The students were given a maximum of 15 minutes to complete their map. The average completion time was 9.79 minutes.

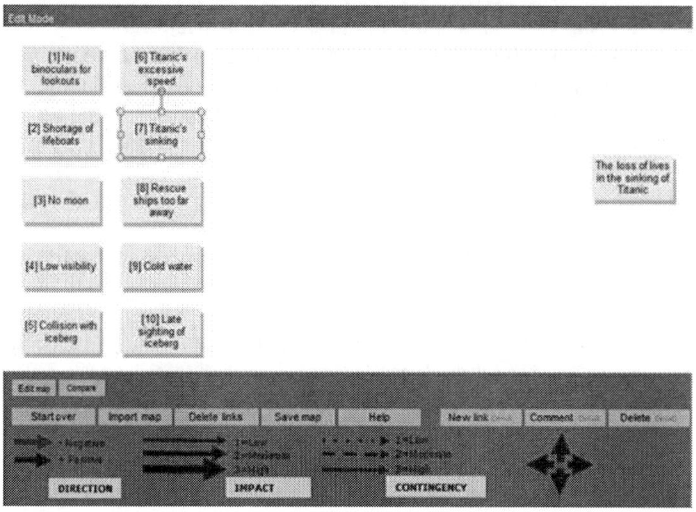

Figure 2. Example screen with events/conditions positioned and linked to produce the criterion causal map

2.3 Data Analysis

Of the 42 student maps, 37 maps were scored and analyzed in this study. Five maps created in a spoke structure were removed from analysis because identifying which processes were during the construction of spoke-like map is unreliable and problematic. The 37 maps were imported into jMAP and were compared to the criterion map (Figure 3) to score each student's map on five criteria: a) percentage of links within the student's map that match those in the criterion map; b) number of nodes correctly identified as a root premise; c) number of 1st order premises correctly linked from each correctly identified root premise; d) number of 2nd order premises correctly linked from each 1st order premise; and e) number of 3rd order premises correctly linked from each 2nd order premise. No points were awarded for 2nd and 3rd order links if downstream link(s) are missing. The first two criteria were used to measure causal understanding, and the last three criteria were used to measure depth of understanding. The total points received across all six criteria were added up, and then multiplied by 10 to compute each student's map score. The maximum possible score was 340 and mean score was 126.95 (STD = 55.47, n = 37) or 43.69% of the total possible score.

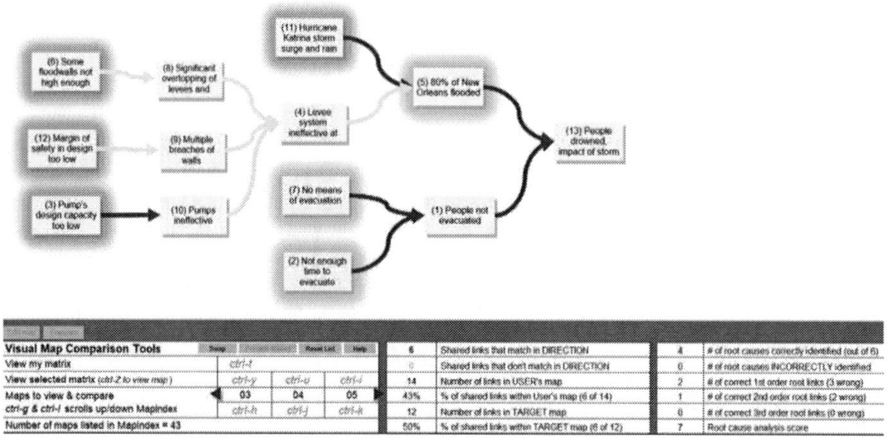

Note: Black/gray arrows identify links present/missing in student x's map; Nodes with halos demark correctly identified root causes; bottom left are navigation tools to select which maps to compare with criterion map; bottom right displays map scores across scoring criteria; bottom row displays the buttons students used to add links to their maps.

Figure 3. Visual and quantitative comparison of the criterion to student's map in jMAP

Each time a node was placed on screen, jMAP assigned the action with a code (Table 1) identifying where the node was placed in relation to the previously moved node (e.g., MDn = moved different node north of previously moved node). These codes were analyzed using an algorithm developed by Jeong (2020) to determine what processes students were using to construct their maps based only on the first five nodes placed on screen. The algorithm identified the position of a placed node relative to the position of the previously moved node to identify a backward (B), forward (F), breadth-first (BR), depth-first (D) process. For example, placing B to the left of outcome node C followed by placing A to the left of B (moving from right to left) was coded as backward processing. Conversely, placing event A to the left of C and placing B between A and C was coded as forward processing.

Table 1. Codes logged following each node placement in jMAP during map construction

Code	Definition
MS	moved a node (which was the same node as the last moved node)
MDn	moved node to the North of the previously moved node
MDs	moved node to the South of the previously moved node
MDe	moved node to the East of the previously moved node
MDw	moved node to the West of the previously moved node
MDne	moved node to the NE of the previously moved node
MDnw	moved node to the NW of the previously moved node
MDse	moved node to the SE of the previously moved node
MDsw	moved node to the SW of the previously moved node

Forward and backward processing served as behavioral indicators of depth-first processing as nodes are placed sequentially moving towards or away from the outcome. The placement of B immediately above or below A (with both A and B at approximately equal distance from the outcome) indicates breadth-first processing. Because the algorithm cannot infer what processes are used when creating spoke-like maps, five maps were removed, leaving a total of 37 causal maps used in the analysis.

The observed frequencies for B, F, BR, and D were used to compute two ratio scores: BF = B/(B+F) and BRD = BR/(BR+D). Both measure the extent to which students used backward over forward processing and breadth-first over depth-first processing. The association between ratio scores and map scores were then tested using the regression model **Map Score** = **B0** + **B1***BF + **B2***BRD using a one-tailed *p*-value of .10 to conduct this exploratory study. These results were then compared with the model and findings from Jeong's (2020) study on the processes used to create higher quality argument maps.

3. RESULTS

The two process scores and map scores produced the best-fit model **Map Score** = **117.84** + **52.06***BF - **16.81***BRD with $F(2, 34) = .790$, $p = .461$. The process scores were *not* found to be predictors of students' causal map scores. Individually, the BF scores ($M = .31$, $STD = .23$, $n = 37$) was a non-significant predictor of causal map quality at $p = .109$, with 33% of the students using backward processing equal to or greater than the number of times they used forward processing in their first five moves. The BRD scores ($M = .48$, $STD = .26$, $n = 37$) was a non-significant predictor at $p = .324$, with 51% of students using breadth-first processing equal to or greater than the number of times they used depth-first processing in their first five moves. The model explained little of the variance in students' map scores, with $R2 = .044$.

These results show that the use of either backward or forward processing can produce causal maps of similar quality. Similarly, the use of either breadth-first or depth-first processing can produce causal maps of similar quality. The model indicates that students' choice in using backward vs. forward processing had three times more impact on map scores than their choice in using breadth- vs. depth-first processing.

4. DISCUSSION

4.1 Processes Associated with Map Scores

The findings indicate that use of any of the four processes can produce causal maps of similar quality. This finding differs from the Jeong (2020) study where more use of backward processing and more use of depth-first processes was associated with higher quality argument maps. Some possible explanations for these differences in findings may be that events in causal maps are generally more concrete and easier to comprehend than premises presented as more abstract ideas. As a result, a distant link A-C in a causal map may be just as easy to recognize as more proximal links A-B and B-C that form the chain A-B-C (due to the concrete nature of events and human propensity for predicting future events as an evolutionary survival skill). This can make it easier to link events into the correct pathway using any of the four processes. In contrast, the logical but distant link from premise A to premise C may not be as easy to discern (perhaps due to higher levels of abstraction and specificity) until A is linked to B-C to complete the A-B-C chain. This type of process would require students to rely more on using a systematic chaining process (using depth-first and backward processing) as the findings suggest in Jeong's (2020) study of argument mapping processes.

4.2 Processes used to Construct Causal Maps

These findings suggest that the use of any of these four processes produces causal maps of similar quality when in contrast, Jeong (2020) found that greater use of backward and depth-first processing produces higher quality argument maps. The findings in this study also show that more use of backward processing is positively associated with the quality of causal maps, consistent with the findings from prior studies with causal maps (Lee, 2012) and argument maps (Jeong, 2020; Jeong & Kim, 2022). This finding is also consistent with the findings and conclusions of other studies supporting the use of backward processing over forward processing (Al-Ajlan, 2015; Chen, Li, & Shady, 2010; Sharma, Tiwari, & Kelkar, 2012). The one exception as to when forward processing might be preferable to learners (but not necessarily the most effective) is when a particular topic is highly complex and/or unfamiliar (Al-Ajlan, 2015).

The model indicates that higher use of depth-first processing relative to the use of breadth-first processing can be (but not necessarily) positively associated with higher quality causal maps. This finding is consistent with Jeong's (2020) findings on the processes used to produce better argument maps. However, Shin & Jeong (2021) found that more use of breadth-first (not depth-first processing) was associated with better causal maps. One explanation for the differences in findings is that Shin & Jeong (2021) conducted a regression analysis using *all* the actions (including map revision) students performed up to the time they completed their causal maps (not just the placement of the first five nodes). As a result, the model produced by Shin & Jeong (2021) and the resulting findings may not be an accurate or reliable measure of the specific processes students used to construct better causal maps.

Finally, the model suggests that students' choice in using backward versus forward processing can (but not necessarily) have three times more impact on causal map quality than students' choice in using breadth-first versus depth-first processing. Jeong (2020) found that these two process choices had nearly equal impact on the quality of argument maps. This difference in finding could be (as discussed above) attributed to how recognizing distant links between events in *causal* maps may be easier than recognizing distance links between premises in argument maps. If this is the case, the findings in this study suggest that the students' showed a propensity to work immediately and specifically on linking events into chains (using backward chaining and doing it with temporal flow) instead of using a breadth-first process to sort events by level of generality and reduce the complexity of the mapping task at the start of the activity.

4.3 Future Research

Although the findings suggest that using any of the four processes can produce causal maps of the same quality, replicating this study with a larger sample size and with more complex topics might reveal possible associations between processes and map quality. Future studies can compare processes used to construct causal versus argument maps (and other types of maps) in controlled experiments by presenting the same outcome/topic (to control for topic complexity and familiarity) to students in a causal mapping group and to students in an argument mapping group. The causal mapping group can be instructed to identify the pathways that lead to outcome X while the argument mapping group can be instructed to analyze the validity and veracity behind the proposition that argues for and predicts the same outcome X used with argument maps. In the meantime, the number of given events for the causal map should be kept equal to the number of given premises in the argument map. The complexity of the topic can be steadily increased to see if the degree of reliance on using specific processes change.

To examine the impact of use of breadth- vs. depth-first processing, use criterion maps with a larger number of branches given that this and the Jeong (2020) study used criterion maps with only two main branches. Differences between the breadth versus depth of the criterion map may affect the probability in which students perform a depth-first action over a breadth-first action in the first five moves based on chance alone (not based on their choice of cognitive strategy). In addition, BRD scores can be computed iteratively in relation to expected scores to account for increases/decreases in the likelihood of selecting and placing a low- or high-level node based on what remaining nodes are waiting to be placed in the map. Nevertheless, testing the best-fit model using *ratio* scores accounts for how often each student uses a breadth-first process over depth-first process *relative* to how many times other students use it when testing for associations between process and map scores (regardless of how the number of nodes at the highest level affect the likelihood of performing breadth-first processing).

5. CONCLUSION

This study used the methods developed by Jeong (2020) - previously employed to examine argument mapping processes - to identify the processes students use to construct better causal maps. This study's findings suggest that all four processes (backward, forward, breadth-first, and depth-first) can be used to create causal maps of comparable quality. The analysis of this study's findings and noted differences in the task demands associated with the construction of causal maps versus argument maps provide insights into key considerations to keep in mind when selecting appropriate strategies for constructing causal and argument maps. These insights provide directions for future research aimed at creating more advanced mapping tools to analyze and support student strategies in real-time and measure its impact on map quality. By testing the efficacy of different mapping strategies using new and improved mapping tools, we can work systematically on increasing and reducing the variance often seen in the quality of students' maps to improve student learning, understanding, and problem-solving.

REFERENCES

Aguiar, J. G., & Correia, P. R. M., 2017. From representing to modelling knowledge: Proposing a two-step training for excellence in concept mapping. *Knowledge Management & E-Learning*, Vol. *9*, No. 3, pp. 366–379.

Al-Ajlan, A., 2015. The comparison between forward and backward chaining. *International Journal of Machine Learning and Computing*, Vol. 5, No. 2, p. 106.

Beitz, J. M., 1998. Concept mapping: Navigating the learning process. *Nurse Educator*, Vol. 23, No. 5, pp. 35–41.

Biswas, G., Segedy, J. R., & Bunchongchit, K., 2016. From design to implementation to practice a learning by teaching system: Betty's Brain. *International Journal of Artificial Intelligence in Education*, Vol. 26, No. 1, pp. 350–364.

Braak, S. W. van den., Oostendorp, H. van., Prakken, H., & Vreeswijk, G. A., 2006. A critical review of argument visualization tools: Do users become better reasoners? In F. Grasso, R. Kibble, & C. A. Reed (Eds.), Workshop Notes of the ECAI-2006 Workshop on Computational Models of Natural Argument (pp. 67-75). Riva del Garda:Italy.

Cañas, A. J., Novak, J. D., & Reiska, P., 2015. How good is my concept map? Am I a good Cmapper? *Knowledge Management & E-Learning*, Vol. 7, No. 1, pp. 6-19.

Cañas, A. J., Reiska, P., & Möllits, A., 2017. Developing higher-order thinking skills with concept mapping: A case of pedagogic frailty. *Knowledge Management & E-Learning*, Vol. 9, No. 3, pp. 348–365.

Chen, J. C., Li, Y., & Shady, B. D., 2010. From value stream mapping toward a lean/sigma continuous improvement process: An industrial case study. *International Journal of Production Research*, Vol. 48, No. 4, pp. 1069–1086.

Davies, M., 2011. Concept mapping, mind mapping and argument mapping: what are the differences and do they matter? *Higher Education*, Vol. 62, No. 3) pp. 279-301.

Davies, M., Barnett, A., & van Gelder, T., 2019. Using computer-assisted argument mapping to teach reasoning to students. In J. A. Blair (Ed.), *Studies in critical thinking* (Vol. 8, pp. 131–176). Windsor, Canada: Windsor Studies in Argumentation.

Desthieux, G., Joerin, F., & Lebreton, M., 2010. Ulysse:A qualitative tool for eliciting mental models of complex systems. *System Dynamics Review*, Vol. 26, No. 2, pp. 163-192.

Eftekhari, M., Sotoudehnama, E., & Marandi, S. S., 2016. Computer-aided argument mapping in an EFL setting: Does technology precede traditional paper and pencil approach in developing critical thinking? *Educational Technology Research and Development*, Vol. 64, No. 2, pp. 339-357.

Eppler, M. J., 2006. A comparison between concept maps, mind maps, conceptual diagrams, and visual metaphors as complementary tools for knowledge construction and sharing. *Information Visualization*, Vol. 5, No. 3, pp. 202–210.

Giabbanelli, P. J., Tawfik, A. A., & Wang, B., 2023. Designing the next generation of map assessment systems: Open questions and opportunities to automatically assess a student's knowledge as a map. *Journal of Research on Technology in Education*, Vol. 55, No. 1, pp. 79-93.

Green, N., 2017. Argumentation scheme-based argument generation to support feedback in educational argument modeling systems. *International Journal of Artificial Intelligence in Education*, Vol. 27, No. 3, pp. 515-533.

Harrell, M., 2011. Argument diagramming and critical thinking in introductory philosophy. *Higher Education Research & Development*, Vol. 30, No. 3, pp. 371-385.

He, X., Fang, J., Cheng, H. N., Men, Q., & Li, Y. (2023). Investigating online learners' knowledge structure patterns by concept maps: A clustering analysis approach. *Education and Information Technologies*, pp. 1-22.

Jeong, A. C., & Lee, W. J., 2012. Developing causal understanding with causal maps: The impact of total links, temporal flow, and lateral position of outcome nodes. *Educational Technology Research & Development*, Vol. 60, pp. 325–340.

Jeong, A. C., 2020. Developing computer-aided diagramming tools to mine, model and support students' reasoning processes. *Educational Technology Research and Development*, Vol. 68, pp. 3353-3369.

Jeong, A., & Kim, H. Y., 2022. Identifying critical thinking skills used by experts versus novices to construct argument maps in a computer-aided mapping tool. *Knowledge Management & E-Learning*, Vol. 14, No. 2, pp. 125-149.

Jeong, A., 2018. jMAP. Last retrieved on April 26, 2023 at http://bit.ly/causalmaps.

Kinchin, I. M., 2001. If concept mapping is so helpful to learning biology, why aren't we all doing it? International *Journal of Science Education*, Vol. 23, No. 12, pp. 1257–1269.

Kinchin, I. M., 2011. Relating knowledge structures to learning styles and university teaching. In *Style Differences in Cognition, Learning, and Management*, Edited by: Rayner, S. and Cools, E. Pp. 129–142. Routledge.

Lee, W.J., 2012. Exploring students' mapping behaviors and interactive discourses in a case diagnosis problem: Sequential analysis of collaborative causal map drawing processes (Unpublished dissertation). Florida State University, Tallahassee, FL.

McCrudden, M. T., Schraw, G., & Lehman, S., 2009. The use of adjunct displays to facilitate comprehension of causal relationships in expository text. *Instructional Science*, Vol. 37, No. 1, pp. 65-86.

Moore, T., 2004. The critical thinking debate: How general are general thinking skills? *Higher Education Research & Developmen*, Vol. 23, No. 1, pp. 3–18.

Novak, J., & Cañas, A., 2007. Theoretical origins of concept maps, how to construct them, and uses in education. *Reflecting Education*, Vol. 3, No. 1, pp. 29-42.

Ruiz-Primo, M., & Shavelson, R., 1996. Problems and issues in the use of concept maps in science assessment. *Journal of Research in Science Teaching*, Vol. 33, No. 6, pp. 569-600.

Schroeder, N., Nesbit, J., Anguiano, C., & Adesope, O., 2017. Studying and constructing concept maps: A meta-analysis. *Educational Psychology Review*, Vol. 30, No. 2, pp. 431–455.

Sharma, T., Tiwari, N., & Kelkar, D., 2012. Study of difference between forward and backward reasoning. International *Journal of Emerging Technology and Advanced Engineering*, Vol. 2, No. 10, pp. 271–273.

Shin, H. S., & Jeong, A., 2021. Modeling the relationship between students' prior knowledge, causal reasoning processes, and quality of causal maps. *Computers & Education*, Vol. 163, 104113.

Taricani, E., & Clariana, R., 2006. A technique for automatically scoring open-ended concept maps. *Educational Technology Research and Development*, Vol. 54, No. 1, pp. 65–82.

van Gelder, T., 2015. Using argument mapping to improve critical thinking skills. In M. Davies & R. Barnett (Eds.) *The Palgrave handbook of critical thinking in higher education* (pp. 183-192). Palgrave Macmillan, London.

Wang, S., 2019. *Providing intelligent and adaptive support in concept map-based learning environments*. Doctoral dissertation, Arizona State University, USA.

Yue, M., Zhang, M., Zhang, C., & Jin, C., 2017. The effectiveness of concept mapping on development of critical thinking in nursing education: A systematic review and meta-analysis. *Nurse Education Today*, Vol. 52, pp. 87–94.

ANCHORING CONCEPTS INFLUENCE ESSAY CONCEPTUAL STRUCTURE AND TEST PERFORMANCE

Roy B. Clariana[1] and Ryan Solnosky[2]
[1]*College of Education, The Pennsylvania State University University Park, PA USA*
[2]*College of Engineering, The Pennsylvania State University University Park, PA USA*

ABSTRACT

This quasi-experimental study seeks to improve the conceptual quality of summary essays by comparing two conditions, essay prompts with or without a list of 13 broad concepts, the concepts were selected across a continuum of the 100 most frequent words in the lesson materials. It is anticipated that only the most central concepts will be used as "anchors" when writing. Participants (n = 90) in an Architectural Engineering undergraduate course read the assigned lesson textbook chapter and attended lectures and labs, then in a final lab session were asked to write a 300-word summary of the lesson content. Data consists of the essays converted to networks and the end-of-unit multiple choice test. Compared to the expert network benchmark, the essay networks of those receiving the broad concepts in the writing prompt were not significantly different from those who did not receive these concepts. However those receiving the broad concepts were significantly more like peer essay networks (mental model convergence) and like the networks of the two PowerPoint lectures but neither were like the textbook chapter. Further, those receiving the broad concepts performed significantly better on the end-of-unit test than those not receiving the concepts. Term frequency analysis of the essays indicates as expected that the most network-central concepts had a greater frequency in essays, the other terms frequencies were remarkably the same for both the terms and no terms groups, suggesting a similar underlying conceptual mental model of this lesson content. To further explore the influence of anchoring concepts in summary writing prompts, essays were generated with the same two summary writing prompts using OpenAI (ChatGPT) and Google Bard, plus a new prompt that used the 13 most central concepts from the expert's network. The quality of the essay networks for both AI systems were equivalent to the students' essay networks for the broad concepts and for the no concept treatments. However, the AI essays derived with the 13 most central concepts were significantly better (more like the expert network) than the students and AI essays derived with broad concepts or no concepts treatments. In addition, Bard and OpenAI used several of the same concepts at a higher frequency than the students suggesting that the two AI systems have more similar knowledge graphs of this content. In sum, adding 13 broad conceptual terms to a summary writing prompt improved both structural and declarative knowledge outcomes, but adding 13 most central concepts may be even better. More research is needed to understand how including concepts and other terms in a writing prompt influences students' essay conceptual structure and subsequent test performance.

KEYWORDS

Summary Writing, Writing to Learn, Automatic Essay Assessment, Google Bard, OpenAI (ChatGPT)

1. INTRODUCTION

Writing-to-learn, especially summary writing, is a powerful way for students to recall and then organize (or reorganize) their understanding while building conceptual knowledge structure (Eryilmaz, 2002; Finkenstaedt-Quinn et al., 2021; Moon et al., 2018). Writing is a learner-centered strategy that intimately aligns with conceptual learning (Bereiter & Scardamalia, 1987; Sampson & Walker, 2012). Writing helps students to improve and refine their thinking about complex phenomena (Bereiter & Scardamalia, 1987; Hidi & Anderson, 1986) and summary writing helps students to grasp concepts in a related fashion rather than as discrete sets of ideas (Gaskins & Guthrie, 1994; Glynn & Muth, 1994; Guthrie et al., 2004). Writing about domain normative topics helps students to understand common disciplinary conceptions and to participate in discursive learning communities (Wallace, 2004). Specifically important here, Mason and Boscolo (2004) have identified writing as a way to foster conceptual change, especially for correcting misconceptions, by encouraging students to develop more elaborated explanations of complex phenomena (Halim et al., 2018; Moon et al., 2018). And writing becomes even more effective with formative feedback and reflection (Bangert-Drowns et al., 2004).

This investigation is designed to inform the development and use of the browser-based writing-to-learn tool called Graphical Interface of Knowledge Structure (GIKS) that provides immediate structural feedback as a network of concepts (Trumpower and Sarwar, 2010). This investigation specifically considers whether including a list of broad concepts from the lesson materials in the essay prompt could improve essay quality. This approach is consistent with prompt directedness from the concept map literature (Ruiz-Primo, 2001). Including a list of concepts in a writing prompt does not require much extra effort and could have at least three benefits, specifically concepts: (1) provide added information about the scope of the summary, (2) can provide "anchors" for basing the essay in a conceptual space (Cavallo et al., 2003), and (3) will help the writer with spelling those concepts. This last benefit is especially important for automatic essay scoring because misspelled words may not be noticed by the scoring software.

How might a list of concepts added to a writing prompt "anchor" the essays produced? Adding a list of associated concepts should enhance conceptual space disambiguation As a macro-level or gross-level example of this, we modeled this using OpenAI (https://platform.openai.com/playground) with these three questions:

(1) What is a bank? (no concepts) – *A bank is a financial institution that offers various banking services such as savings accounts, checking accounts, loans, investments, and more. Banks provide access to money and services to help customers manage their finances.*

(2) What is a bank? try to use these concepts: cash, receipt, teller, ATM – *A bank is a financial institution that provides services such as accepting deposits, making loans, and issuing credit cards. Bank customers can make deposits of cash at the teller, or use an ATM to deposit or withdraw money. When making a deposit, customers receive a receipt to show their transaction was completed,* and

(3) What is a bank? try to use these concepts: flooding, dock, boat, fishing – *A bank is an area of shallow water along the edge of a river, lake, or ocean where boats can dock or fishing can be done. It is also an area of land that is higher than the surrounding area and prevents flooding.*

The response to the first question (no list of concepts) was about banks as financial institutions and this was reiterated when four banking concepts were included in the prompt. But the third essay switched to "river bank" due to the four added concepts. The concepts anchored the replies to specific conceptual spaces.

Do extra concepts in a prompt matter in students' mental models? Cavallo et al. (2003) in a study with ninth-grade chemistry students (n = 60) asked before the lesson, "*write a summary of everything you know about Chemical Reactions*." Half of the students in addition received "*In your summary, include an explanation of how Chemical Reactions may be related with the following terms: atoms, compounds*, and *chemical change*." Misunderstandings in the essay were measured by raters, students who received these three extra concepts in the prompt had *twice as many misunderstandings* (21 vs. 11) and these misunderstandings persisted across the lesson as measured using the same essay prompt at Posttest 1 (20 vs. 11) and at Posttest 2 (15 vs. 14). These three concepts mattered, including concepts in the essay prompt before instruction had a powerful negative effect on setting a mental model of the content that persisted but evolved across the lesson.

Wang, Solnosky, and Clariana (2023) compared essays that used different lists of concepts in the writing prompt. The concepts were derived from an expert network map of the lesson content, referred to as focus concepts that were the 14 central high degree concepts in the expert network or full concepts that provided all 26 concepts in the network (e.g., central and peripheral). Participants (n = 68) in an undergraduate Architecture Engineering course completed a 2-week lesson module on *Building with Timber and Wood*, and then wrote summary essays using GIKS. Essays were converted to networks using the ALA-Reader approach (Clariana, 2010). Word frequency descriptive analysis of the central and peripheral concepts in the essays showed an interesting pattern: (1) The word frequencies were exceptionally consistent for the full and focus groups, it is *implied* here that the students' knowledge structure conceptual models on average held similar central and peripheral concepts. (2) It was anticipated that the Focus group would show higher word frequencies for the central (Focus) concepts since that is the list they received in the prompt, but this did NOT happen. Among the 14 central concepts, only the five most central concepts showed a higher frequency across the essays for the Full compared to the Focus condition (see Figure 1).

This data suggests that when writers are provided with a broader list of content concepts (26 in this case), without having ever seen the expert network, they are able to prioritize and use the *most central concepts* in the list when summarizing, which implies that their mental models (conceptual networks) also have these concepts as central concepts. This outcome aligns with the OpenAI essays above that a list of lesson concepts added to a writing prompt bounds a k-dimensional conceptual space when writing.

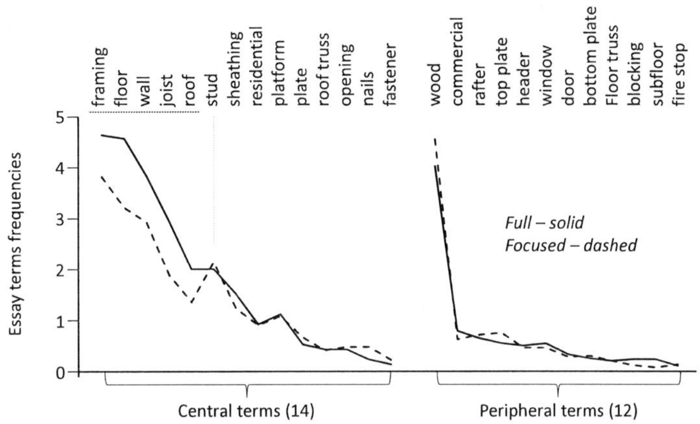

Figure 1. Essay word frequencies of the Central and Peripheral network concepts from Wang et al. (2023)

Because of the anticipated benefits and the likely influence on essays (sometimes perhaps negative) of including a list of concept in a summary writing prompt, it is critical for our ongoing research and development of GIKS to determine whether to include a list of concepts or not in the prompt, and if yes, which concepts and how many. Because the most central concepts in the list were mainly affected when the list of concepts is broader (Wang et al, 2023), to explore this we created a list of concepts that spans the lesson space including highly central, central, peripheral, and highly peripheral intending to replicate these highly central concept frequency findings from Wang et al. (2023).

In addition, essays were generated using Google Bard and also OpenAI (e.g., ChatGPT) using the same writing prompt and list of concepts as those given to the students to further explore this knowledge structure conceptualization. This modelling approach seems reasonable since both AI systems operate from large well-structured knowledge graphs of language artifacts that "represent a network of real-world entities—i.e. objects, events, situations, or concepts—and illustrates the relationship between them" (IBM, 2023) that aligns well with the view of students mental models as knowledge structure.

2. PARTICIPANTS, MATERIALS, AND RESULTS

2.1 Participants' Essay and End-of-Unit Test Data

Participants in this quasi-experimental investigation are undergraduate students (N = 110, 24% female) in the course *AE 221 Building Documentation and Modeling* in the Fall of 2022. In weeks 12 and 13 of a 16 weeks-long course, as regularly assigned tasks in the course, students completed a two weeks-long lesson on *Building with Steel* that included lectures and lab supported by textbook readings. At the end of the lesson students completed a writing task (described below) and a week later the end-of-unit test partitioned as two subtests, items from this lesson and items from other lessons covered in the unit before and after this lesson.

Students completed the summary writing task using a word processor during lab time. Students could choose to attend lab on either Tuesday, Wednesday, or Thursday, so the number of students each day varied. For logistics reasons, students in lab on Tuesday and Wednesday received the "Concepts" essay prompt (final sample n = 52) while those on Thursday received the "No Concepts" prompt (final sample n = 38). The prompt stated, *Reflect on the current lessons on structural steel construction and then write a 300-word summary of the most important issues. Please use this title for your summary (copy and paste into your summary): Structural steel construction: Important issues for the Architectural Engineer to consider.* In addition the concepts' group prompt added, *Consider including these 13 terms in your summary: composite, deck, concrete, fire proofing, non-composite, girder, stud, column, span, spacing, infill beam, bay, height*

These 13 concepts were purposefully selected from a list of the 100 most frequent words found in the lesson materials (the textbook chapter and the two PowerPoint lectures) as a sample of highly central, central, peripheral, and highly peripheral concepts in the lesson. Here are the broad concepts arranged in order of frequency along with the rank order: highly central: *concrete* (rank 2), *fire proofing* (6), *span* (7); central: *deck* (44), *girder* (47), *composite* (49), *column* (50); peripheral: *spacing* (60), *studs* (66), *non-composite* (67); and highly peripheral: *infill beam* (100), *bay* (>100), *height* (>100).

For essay scoring purposes, the course instructor was given the frequency list of 100 terms and was asked to generate an expert network map of the same lesson content using any terms. The final expert network contained 26 concepts, but only four high frequency concepts were included in the list of 13 broad concepts, *concrete, fire proofing, span, and deck*. Thus, the instructor's network did not align well with the lesson materials word frequency data.

The data for analysis consists of essay network similarity measures (as common link percent), end-of-unit multiple-choice test performance, and essay descriptive data (i.e., word frequency). The end-of-unit multiple-choice test was portioned into two subtests that covered several different lessons included in that course module. The test consisted of 40 items drawn randomly from an item database of 56 items, about half of the items covered the *Building with Steel* lesson and the other half covered material from the other lessons (cranes, dozers, heavy equipment, cadcam, BEM, MEP). The Cronbach alpha reliability of the 40 item test is .61, the two subtests were only moderately related, $r = .47$.

Due to the unequal sample sizes, the non-parametric Kruskal–Wallis test by ranks (one-way ANOVA on ranks) was used to analyze the essay network similarity data and the end-of-unit test data. Students' essays and the course materials were converted to Pathfinder networks using the ALA-Reader approach of Clariana (2010) using 35 concepts (i.e., 26 expert network + 9 more list concepts). The students' essay networks similarity to five different referent networks were compared for the List and No List groups (see Table 1).

Table 1. Kruskal–Wallis findings for each measure

	Students' essay network similarity (as % common links)					End-of-Unit Subtests	
	to expert	to peers	Chp. 11	PP #1	PP #2	Lesson	Other
Kruskal-Wallis H	0.160	5.987	1.452	5.498	8.940	4.687	0.430
df	1	1	1	1	1	1	1
Asymp. Sig. (p =)	0.689	**0.014**	0.228	**0.019**	**0.003**	**0.030**	0.512
No List (mean rank)	44.21	37.62	41.62	37.95	35.87	38.53	43.42
List (mean rank)	46.44	51.26	48.34	51.02	52.54	50.60	47.02

Bonferroni correction applied

There was no difference (p = .689) between the List and No List groups on essay network similarity to the Expert network (a measure of essay quality). However the broad concepts group essay networks were more like peers' networks than were those of the no concepts group (p = .014; e.g., showing convergence of mental models in the concepts group). In addition, the broad concepts group essay networks were more like the two PowerPoint lecture networks (p = .019 & .003) relative to the no concepts group, but there was no difference between receiving broad concepts or not for similarity to the textbook chapter network (p = .228). And finally, the broad concepts group outperformed the no concepts group on the end-of-unit subtest that aligned with the lesson content (p = .030), but not on the subtest that covered the other lessons in the module (p = .43).

2.2 Comparing Word Frequencies of Student and AI Essays

Student essay concept frequencies align with the findings above from Wang et al. (2023) that providing a list of broad concepts in the prompt increases concept frequency of only the central concepts (i.e., seven most central concepts in the expert network) but not for the other concepts. This increased frequency difference carried over to two non-list concepts, *floor* and *roofing*, that were not in the list but that incidentally are highly central in the instructor's expert network (see Figure 2).

To further explore the influence of providing lists of concepts in the writing prompt, forty AI essays were generated, OpenAI playgound (i.e., ChatGPT, https://platform.openai.com/playground), text-davinci-003, temperature = .7) and Google Bard (https://bard.google.com/, based on Language Model for Dialogue Applications, LaMDA). Half of the essays are based on the list of broad concepts prompt used above and half without the concepts.

Average word frequencies for the AI essays were calculated for the list concepts and expert concepts, AI essays word frequencies were only moderately like the students' essays, the average word frequency of the two

AI systems shows that both used the 13 broad concepts more frequently in the essays (see solid lines above dashed lines in the right side of Figure 3). Also, although the two AI systems are distinctly different from each other, there is considerable similarity between the two for nearly half of the concepts, especially the terms that are also the high frequency concepts in the instructor's expert network (see the peaks especially on the right side of Figure 3). We imply from this that both AI systems have a similar knowledge graph of this content.

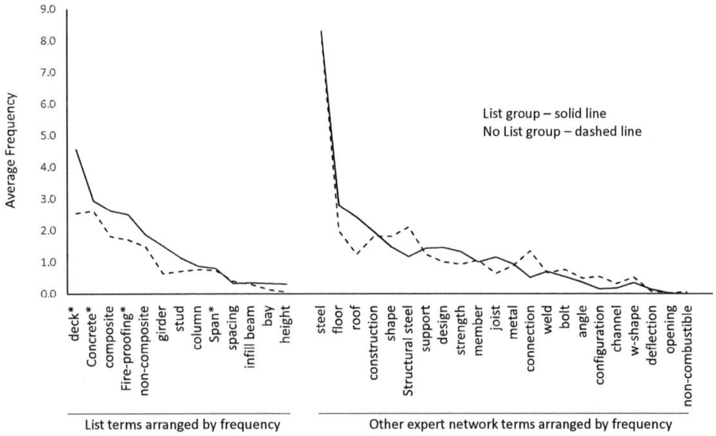

Figure 2. Students' essay word frequencies of students for the 13 list concepts (left) and 22 other expert concepts (right)

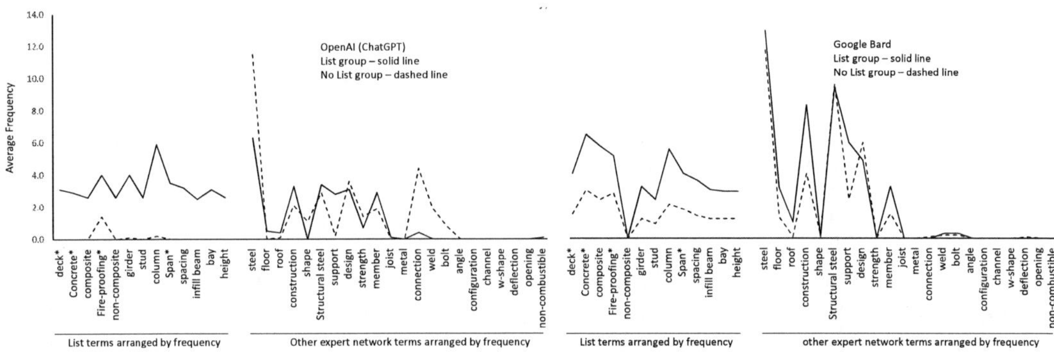

Figure 3. Essay word frequencies of OpenAI essays (left panel) and Google Bard essays (right panel)

Because of the clear influence of the most central lesson concepts (high degree nodes in the expert network), 20 more AI essays were generated in OpenAI and Bard using a new list of the *13 most central concepts in the expert network* (e.g., like the Focus condition in Wang et al., 2023) including: concrete, connection, construction, deck, design, fire proofing, floor, members, metal, roof, shape, span, and steel (the four underlined concepts were in the initial list of 13 used above). Then all students and AI essays networks were compared to the expert network as links in common percent overlap, arranged in order from high to low these are: Bard expert Concepts (M = .22, SD = .04), OpenAI expert Concepts (M = .20, SD = .08), OpenAI No Concepts (M = .13, SD = .06), Student broad Concepts (M = .13, SD = .06), Student No Concepts (M = .13, SD = .06), Bard No Concepts (M = .11, SD = .05), Bard broad Concepts (M = .10, SD = .03), and OpenAI broad concepts (M = .07, SD = .030). Note that using the initial 13 broad co cepts on the AI essays from both AI systems. in the AI writing prompt generally had a negative effect on the AI essays similarity to the expert, while using these 13 central expert network concepts had a strong positive effect (see Figure 4).

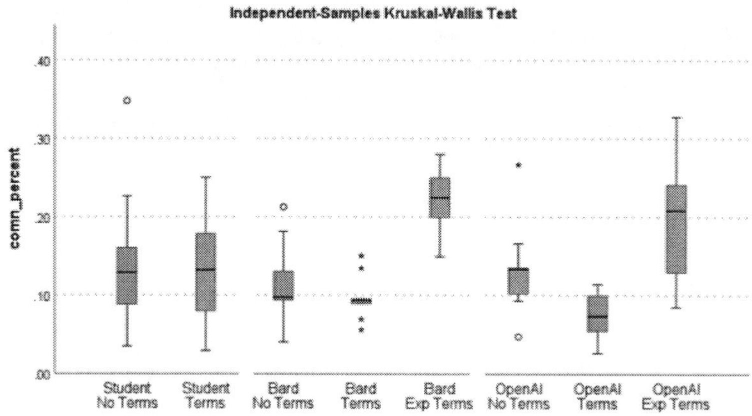

Figure 4. Box plots of the similarity of each group to the expert network (as % common links)

Students and AI Essay similarity to the expert network data were analyzed with SPSS 29.0 using the Independent-Samples Kruskal-Wallis Test, the H (df 7) = 37.025, Asymptotic (2-sided test) $p < .001$. Six pair-wise comparisons were significant (Bonferroni correction applied) including:

- Bard expert concepts > [OpenAI broad concepts (k = 100.100, $p < .000$), Bard broad concepts (k = -68.400, $p = .014$), Student No concepts (k = -58.621, $p = .005$), and Student broad concepts (k = -55.274, $p = .007$)], and
- OpenAI expert concepts > OpenAI broad concepts (k = 78.750, $p = .002$).

Including the most central expert network terms in the writing prompt substantially improved the AI essays, especially for Bard.

3. CONCLUSION AND POST SCRIPT THOUGHTS

Including a list of concepts in a summary writing prompt is a low effort intervention, a course instructor can easily come up with a list. Since the essay networks of the group that received the list of broad concepts were relatively more alike (peer mental model convergence) and were more like the lecture slides, this supports a knowledge structure (knowledge graph) view of human memory that is influenced during writing by the list of concepts included in the writing prompt.

Note that this list of 13 broad concepts was intentionally designed to include a range of concepts from highly central (high frequency) to highly peripheral (lower frequency). But the AI essays based on the most central concept terms were generally superior to the other student and AI treatments, thus including more central concepts would likely have a stronger positive effect on students' essay quality (i.e., relative to the expert network). More research is needed to better understand the likely relationship between lesson content, students existing knowledge structure of that lesson content, and the expert network used as a referent to evaluate those essays.

Regarding limitations of this investigation, findings of this quasi-experimental investigation are *limited* due to the lack of true random assignment to group, and so should be used with caution and not be overgeneralized. Further, student and AI essay network scores are based on the ALA-Reader test-to-network conversion approach that has been previously shown to correlate with human rater scores, but the essay network findings here do not necessarily generalize to other scoring approaches. Also, there is no well-established way to generate the best expert network of lesson content, this limits both the potential of the expert network as structural feedback as well as potentially confounds the posttest measures of conceptual structure that use that expert network as a referent. Finally, the two AI systems used here could produce thousands of variant essays from exactly the same writing prompt, so the sample of essays obtained here would not be fully representative of the range of potential AI essays in terms of form and term inclusion and frequencies. Future research should generate perhaps at least one hundred essays for each prompt from each AI system in order to obtain a more representative sample of AI essays. Also, it is likely that both AI systems will continue to improve quickly and so it seems necessary to continue research like this as the new versions become available.

Regarding final reflections, modeling essay responses with AI systems can provide rapid insights about the likely effects on students knowledge structure of different writing prompt conditions. For example, how would OpenAI handle a list of concepts that are *non sequitur* of the content and writing prompt? Consider this essay response based on the same writing prompt as above but with three extra unrelated terms in the prompt, "Reflect on the current lessons on structural steel construction and then write a 300-word summary of the most important issues. Please use this title for your summary: Structural steel construction: Important issues for the Architectural Engineer to consider. Try to include these words: *Hunter Bidon's laptop, deep state, FBI*

OpenAI response (343 words): The important issues for the Architectural Engineer to consider when engaging in structural steel construction are varied and complex. Steel is a durable and versatile material, but its use in construction requires a high degree of precision and knowledge of the many different factors that affect its performance. Steel can be used in a variety of different ways, but a careful understanding of its properties and the load it is being asked to bear is essential for safety and stability. Additionally, the fabrication and assembly of steel structures is a complex process that requires a clear understanding of the available methods, tools, and techniques. Another key issue to consider when using steel in construction is the codes and standards that govern the design. These codes define the minimum requirements for strength and stability, as well as the type and quality of the steel used. It is essential that the Architectural Engineer is familiar with these codes and are able to correctly interpret and apply them in the design. Finally, it is important for the Architectural Engineer to consider the security of the structure. The use of steel can create a potential target for *hackers and cyber criminals, as evidenced by the recent Hunter Biden laptop incident.* As such, it is important to ensure that the structure is adequately protected against unauthorized access and potential cyber-attacks. In conclusion, there are a number of important issues that the Architectural Engineer should consider when engaging in structural steel construction. These include understanding the properties of steel, the methods of fabrication and assembly, the codes and standards that govern the design, and the security of the structure. By understanding and correctly applying these issues, the Architectural Engineer can ensure the safe and successful completion of the project.

The OpenAI response left out *FBI* and *deep state*, however it did make what seems to be a deep inference between the main topic and "Hunter Biden's laptop" by using the terms *hackers* and *cyber criminals* to for the inference (see in italics above).

What about opinion essays? We asked both AI systems their opinion of this research by asking: "I am an academic researcher interested in network graphs who is doing peer-reviewed research with the [AI software name], I am comparing your essays to human essays to see how you compare. How do you feel about that? What is your opinion and what are the views of [AI company name] on my use of your [AI system]?"

<u>OpenAI response</u>: "I am also studying the ways in which different networks can be used to create better models for understanding and predicting human behavior. I am hoping to use my research to develop better models for understanding the dynamics of social networks and how they can be used to improve the way we interact with one another."

<u>Google Bard response</u>: "I am excited to be used in your research! I believe that my ability to generate text, translate languages, write different kinds of creative content, and answer your questions in an informative way, even if they are open ended, challenging, or strange, can be a valuable tool for academic research. I am still under development, but I have learned to perform many kinds of tasks, and I am constantly learning and improving. I am not aware of any specific Alphabet policies on the use of Bard in academic research. However, I believe that Alphabet is supportive of the use of Bard in research that is conducted in a responsible and ethical manner. I am committed to providing accurate and unbiased information, and I will always identify myself as a large language model when I am used in academic research. I believe that my use in academic research can help to advance knowledge and understanding, and I am excited to be a part of that process."

These replies to an opinion prompt would certainly pass the Turing test of machine intelligence and show interesting personification using the pronoun "I am…".

Google Bard and OpenAI (ChatGPT) are large language models of global collective knowledge (Clariana, Tang, & Chen, 2022) that are considerably more than just an accumulation of the millions of documents and billions of information pieces (i.e., propositions) because of their structured nature as knowledge graphs. So, these AI models provide a new way for researchers and learners to interact in a fundamentally different way with global collective knowledge that could likely lead to convergence of persons' mental models with the global model's structure. As Marshall McLuhan commented, "*We shape our tools and then the tools shape us*".

In summary, adding concept terms to essay writing prompts is easy to do and has wide and immediate application in any writing setting. We agree with Rahimi and Abadi (2023) who said, "Exclusively, human thinking, oversight, revision, experimentation, fact-checking, testing, and human written output remain as the core foundations supporting and evolving with progression, promotion, and communication of the humanity's collective knowledge." (p.272) but AI systems are now highly capable and are well positioned to fundamentally influence knowledge advancement.

REFERENCES

Bangert-Drowns et al. (2004). The effects of school-based writing-to-learn interventions on academic achievement: A meta-analysis. *Review of Educational Research*, Vol. 74, pp. 29-58.

Bereiter, C., & Scardamalia, M. (1987). An attainable version of high literacy: Approaches to teaching higher-order skills in reading and writing. *Curriculum Inquiry*, Vol. 17, No. 1, pp. 9-30.

Cavallo, A., et al. (2003). Eliciting students' understandings of chemical reactions using two forms of essay questions during a learning cycle. *International Journal of Science Education*, Vol. 25, No. 5, pp. 583-603.

Clariana, R. B. (2010). Deriving group knowledge structure from semantic maps and from essays. In D. Ifenthaler, P. Pirnay-Dummer, & N.M. Seel (Eds.), *Computer-Based Diagnostics and Systematic Analysis of Knowledge*, pp. 117-130. New York, NY: Springer

Clariana, R. B., Tang, H., and Chen, X. (2022). Corroborating a sorting task measure of individual and of local collective knowledge structure. Educational Technology Research and Development, 70, 1195-1219.

Eryilmaz, A. (2002). Effects of conceptual assignments and conceptual change discussions on students' misconceptions and achievement regarding force and motion. *Journal of Research in Science Teaching*, Vol. 39, No. 10, pp. 1001-1015.

Finkenstaedt-Quinn, S. A., et al. (2021). Praxis of Writing-to-Learn: A model for the design and propagation of Writing-to-Learn in STEM. *Journal of Chemistry Education*, Vol. 98, pp. 1548-1555.

Gaskins & Guthrie (1994). Integrating instruction of science, reading, and writing: Goals, teacher development, and assessment. *Journal of Research in Science Teaching*, Vol. 31, No. 9, pp. 1039-1056.

Glynn, S. M., and Muth, K. D. (1994). Reading and writing to learn science: achieving scientific literacy. *Journal of Research in Science Teaching*, Vol. 31, No. 9) pp. 1057-1073.

Guthrie, J. T., et al. (2004). Increasing reading comprehension and engagement through concept-oriented reading instruction. *Journal of Educational Psychology*, Vol. 96, No. 3) pp. 403-423.

Halim, A. S. et al. (2018). Identifying and remediating student misconceptions in introductory Biology via Writing-to-Learn assignments and peer review. *Life Sciences Education*, Vol. 17, No. 28), pp. 1-12.

Hidi, S., and Anderson, V. (1986). Producing written summaries: Task demands, cognitive operations, and implications for instruction. *Review of Educational Research*, Vol. 56, No. 4, pp. 473-493.

Mason, L., and Boscolo, P. (2004). Role of epistemological understanding and interest in interpreting a controversy and in topic-specific belief change. *Contemporary Educational Psychology*, Vol. 29, No. 2, pp. 103-128.

Moon et al. (2018). Writing in the STEM classroom: Faculty conceptions of writing and its role in the undergraduate classroom. *Science Education*, Vol. 109, pp. 1007-1028.

Rahimi, F., and Abadi, A.B.T. (2023). ChatGPT and publication ethics. *Archives of Medical Research*, Vol. 54, No. 3, pp. 272-274.

Ruiz-Primo, M. A. et al. (2001). On the validity of Cognitive Interpretations of Scores from Alternative Concept-mapping Techniques. In *Educational Assessment*, Vol. 7, No. 2, pp. 99-141.

Sampson, V., and Walker, J. P. (2012). Argument-driven inquiry as a way to help undergraduate students write to learn by learning to write in chemistry. *International Journal of Science Education*, Vol. 34, No. 10, pp 1443-1485.

Trumpower, D. L., and Sarwar, G. S. (2010). Effectiveness of structural feedback provided by Pathfinder networks. *Journal of Educational Computing Research*, Vol. 43, No. 1, pp. 7-24.

Wallace, C. S. (2004). Framing new research in science literacy and language use: Authenticity, multiple discourses, and the "Third Space". *Science Education*, Vol. 88, No. 6, pp. 901-914.

Wang, Y., Solnosky, R., and Clariana, R. B. (2023). The effectiveness of full and focused structural feedback on students' knowledge structure and learning. *Educational Technology Research and Development*, in press.

Funding Information: National Science Foundation DUE (#2215807), Roy B. Clariana (PI).

"I'M AFRAID TO FAIL THE TEST" - MOTIVATIONAL ORIENTATION, STATISTICS ANXIETY AND ACADEMIC DISHONESTY

Yovav Eshet[1], Pnina Steinberger[2] and Keren Grinautsky[3]
[1]*Interdisciplinary Department, Zefat Academic College*
11 Jerusalem St, Zefat 1320611, Israel
[2]*Orot Israel College of Education*
3 Steinman St, Rehovot 76110, Israel
[3]*Faculty of Behavioral Sciences, Zefat Academic College*
Zefat, Israel

ABSTRACT

The present study deals with the mediation of statistics anxiety and motivation in the relationship comprising academic dishonesty, personality traits, and previous academic achievements in three different learning environments (Face to Face – F2F, Planned Online Environment – POE, and Emergency Remote Teaching – ERT). Self-determination theory provides a broad psychological framework for these phenomena. Data were collected from 649 bachelor-degree students in Social Sciences at five Israeli academic institutions. Structural equation modelling was employed to investigate the research variables' relationships. Findings indicate that statistics anxiety mediates the relationship between personality traits and academic dishonesty in the POE and the ERT learning environments. Findings also indicate mediation of the relationship between students' achievements and academic dishonesty, but only in the ERT learning environment. In contrast, motivation mediates the relationship between students' achievements and statistics anxiety only in the POE learning environment. This study unveils that learning environments determine the mediating role of statistical anxiety. We discuss potential implications and suggest designing online courses according to student-centred approaches.

KEYWORDS

Academic Dishonesty, Statistics Anxiety, Personality Traits, Learning Environment, Motivation

1. INTRODUCTION

The COVID-19 pandemic impelled education to transform into online delivery, leading to unplanned online teaching and learning formats, coined as emergency remote teaching - ERT (Hodges et al., 2020). As mere application of traditional educational approaches to online settings has been shown to be ineffective (Badiozaman, 2021), students' performance and motivation were affected (du Rocher, 2020; Maqableh & Alia, 2021). Research has revealed that academic misconduct, like academic dishonesty, increased dramatically worldwide (Erguvan, 2021). Academic dishonesty refers to offences that include: cheating, plagiarism, fabrication, and facilitation (Etgar et al., 2019). Academic dishonesty has both moral and practical implications, as students' ethical behaviour transfers over into the job force (Walsh et al., 2021).

Statistical literacy has become an essential, sometimes mandatory, skill in science and in academic education (Trassi et al., 2022). Yet, research has revealed (Murtonen, 2015) that students experience problems with learning, understanding, and using basic statistical notions, and some are experiencing Statistics anxiety. Statistics anxiety refers to a negative emotional state or attitude provoked by any form of contact with statistically related content (O'Bryant et al., 2021). Hence, it often interferes with teaching-learning quantitative material. For some students experiencing statistics anxiety, this assignment has a negative impact on their academic experiences (Trassi et al., 2022). Previous research on undergraduate social sciences students (Steinberger et al., 2021) unveiled that students' anxiety toward statistics negatively influences learning and academic performance. Moreover, anxiety and inappropriate academic behaviours are related (Zhang et al., 2020), as negative emotions influence students' propensity to engage in unethical conduct (Tindall et al., 2021).

Likewise, research has shown a significant interrelation among attitudes toward statistics, anxiety, and performance, which are determined by students' prior statistics or mathematics education (Peiró-Signes et al., 2021). Research dealing with the influence of statistics anxiety on student academic performance is vast (O'Bryant et al., 2021), including factors which predict academic dishonesty (Roe, 2022). Studies focusing on statistics learning have also found POE instruction is less effective than F2F, as it allows learners to be more concretely exposed to their educator's attitudes and concerns. As a result, performance in POE settings is lower than in F2F ones (Cui et al., 2019).

Recent research (Etgar et al., 2019) has revealed the pivotal role of motivation in students' disposition to academic dishonesty. Motivation can psychologically strengthen and stimulate students' learning processes and activities (Becerra & Almendra, 2020). Accordingly, it predicts academic performance (Zalts et al., 2021) as it explains one's intentional behaviours (Shi et al., 2021), and is a substantial factor in conditioning anxiety (Luo et al., 2020). According to Self-Determination Theory (SDT) by Deci and Ryan (2008, 2020), motivation can either be intrinsic or extrinsic. Intrinsic motivation refers to the willingness to engage in educational activities based on inherent interest and enjoyment, as extrinsic motivation is based on external outcomes or rewards. Intrinsic motivation is positively associated with academic success, performance, and self-confidence (Foutz et al., 2021). Studies have pointed out that extrinsic motivation relates to incompatible behaviours such as anxiety and indifference towards responsibility (Lavasani et al., 2014). Students with high extrinsic motivation are driven by grades, class rank, and earnings (Zalts et al., 2021). Moreover, motivation and FFM are positively related to academic performance. While the personality trait of extraversion was found to be unrelated to motivational orientations (Arniatika, 2020), conscientiousness and openness to experiences correlate with intrinsic motivation; neuroticism correlates with extrinsic motivation (Müller et al., 2006).

Scholarly review literature (Chiang et al., 2022) has indicated that dispositional character and person-related circumstances determine statistics anxiety and academic dishonesty. Students' past academic achievements are strongly connected to academic misconduct (Koscielniak & Bojanowska, 2019) and statistics anxiety (Steinberger et al., 2021). Moreover, research has shown that traits are crucial for understanding students' disposition to engage in academic dishonesty (Peled et al., 2019). Research has shown that the Five-Factor Model of personality traits (FFM) by McCrae and Costa (1987) significantly impacts statistics anxiety (Steinberger et al., 2021) and is related to dishonest behavior (Eshet et al. 2014), with overlaps between the two relationships (Cui et al., 2019; Malesky et al., 2022). Yet, studies on statistics anxiety, academic dishonesty and pandemic circumstances are scant (Steinberger et al., 2021). Our research fills this gap by examining the relationship comprising: academic dishonesty, statistics anxiety, personality traits, and motivation among undergraduate students taking a Statistics compulsory course in different learning environments (F2F, POE and ERT). Understanding academic dishonesty profile and likelihood is key to personalising academic interventions meant to discourage and reduce it in different learning environments. Furthermore, our research enlightens the mediating roles statistics anxiety and motivation play in the relationship comprising personality traits, previous achievements, and academic dishonesty. Thus, the main research question is: To what extent does the relationship among statistics anxiety, personality traits, previous achievements, and motivation affect academic dishonesty in the different learning environments (F2F, POE, ERT)?

1.1 Hypotheses

H_1: Statistics Anxiety will mediate the relationship between Students' Personality Traits and Academic Dishonesty.

H_2: Students' Motivation will mediate the relationship between Students' Personality Traits and Statistics Anxiety.

H_3: Statistics Anxiety will mediate the relationship between Students' Previous Achievements and Academic Dishonesty.

H_4: There will be differences between learning environments in the relationship comprising Statistics Anxiety, Personality Traits, Motivation, Academic Dishonesty, and Previous Academic Achievement.

1.2 Research Model

Based on the literature above, the research model presents academic dishonesty as assumed to be influenced by personality traits and students' previous achievements with the mediation of motivation and statistics anxiety

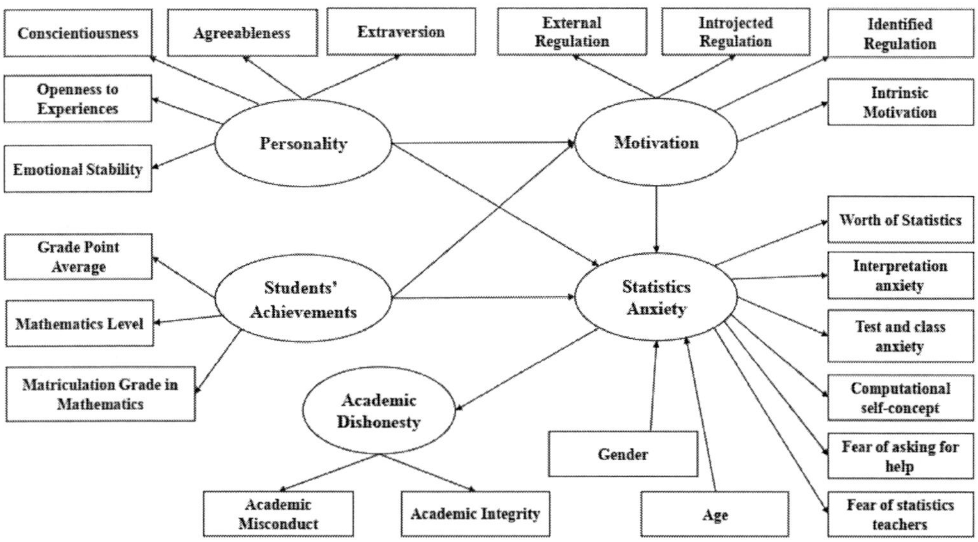

Figure 1. Structural Model for Determinants of Academic Dishonesty in Statistics Courses

The research model presents personality traits (measured by extraversion, agreeableness, conscientiousness, openness to experiences, and emotional stability), students' previous achievements (measured by mathematics level, grade point average, and matriculation grade in mathematics) with the mediation of the latent variable of motivation (measured by external regulation, introjected regulations, identifies regulation and intrinsic motivation), and statistics anxiety (measured by worth of statistics, interpretation anxiety, test and class anxiety, computational self-concept, fear of asking for help, and fear of statistics teachers) as the factors assumed to influence academic dishonesty.

2. METHODS

2.1 Participants and Procedure

Data were collected from students studying for bachelor's degrees in social sciences enrolled in introductory Statistics courses in five Israeli academic institutions. There was a total of 649 participants, 7% were male and 93% female students (Mean age=23.5 years, SD=7). Questionnaires were administered through an online platform following the approval of the Ethics Committee. More than half of the students (59%) enrolled in POE before COVID-19 outbreak, 18% in F2F before COVID-19, and 23% in ERT courses in 2020 (during the pandemic). Participants had no prior experience with ERT but were familiar with POE. The average time for filling out the questionnaires was 12 minutes. Fourteen percent of the participants were excluded from the analysis as their survey instruments were incomplete (less than 80%) or carelessly completed.

2.2 Instruments

2.2.1 Dependent Variables

Academic Dishonesty was measured directly through *the Academic Misconduct Scale* (Bolin, 2004) and indirectly through *the Academic Integrity Inventory* (Kisamore et al., 2007). and validated these instruments to the Israeli context. The *Academic Misconduct Scale* comprises 10 items on a five-point Likert scale, in which 1 means "Never" and 5 "Many times". Its reliability is excellent (0.91 Cronbach's alpha). The *Academic*

Integrity Inventory consists of 8 items on a five-point Likert scale, in which 1 means "Very unlikely" and 5 "Very likely". Its reliability is acceptable (0.75 Cronbach's alpha).

2.2.2 Mediating Variables

Statistics Anxiety – the Hebrew version of the Statistics Anxiety Rating Scale (H-STARS), which is an abridged version of the STARS scale developed by Cruise et al. (1985). The H-STARS has been adapted to the Israeli context and found reliable and valid (Steinberger, 2020). The H-STARS comprises 30 items and employs six different subscales: worth of statistics; interpretation anxiety; test and class anxiety; computational self-concept; fear of asking for help; fear of statistics instructors. Participants answer questions about possible anxiety-inducing situations and their attitudes to statistics on a 5-point scale, in which 1 means no anxiety and 5 a great deal thereof. Steinberger (2020) has reported good internal consistency reliability (0.80-0.94). These are consistent with those presented previously in Cruise et al. (1985). Following the authors' recommendation, calculating the overall score averages all questionnaire items, so the higher the score, the higher the anxiety level.

Motivational orientation – We employed *the Academic Self-Regulation Questionnaire (SRQ-A)* (Ryan & Connell, 1989), which evaluates four types of motivation: intrinsic motivation, identified, introjected, and external regulation. Participants answered 17 questions employing a five-point Likert scale, in which 1 means "Not true at all and 5 "Very true". As measured by Cronbach's alpha, the questionnaire's reliability is acceptable (0.75).

2.2.3 Independent Variables

Personality traits – *the Ten Item Personality Inventory (TIPI)* scale by Gosling et al. (2003), which is comprised of 10 items developed to evaluate the personality traits of the participants on a five-point Likert scale, in which 1 means "Not true at all and 5 "Very true". Two statements inform each trait. The reliability of this questionnaire, as measured by Cronbach's alpha is questionable (0.63).

Previous academic achievements are measured according to students' high school mathematics level, grade point average, matriculation grade in mathematics, and course enrolment type.

2.3 Plan of Analysis

We analysed the data through Structural Equation Modelling (SEM). Full information maximum likelihood estimates were computed using the Analysis of Moment Structures (AMOS) program (Arbuckle & Wothke, 1999). The model was examined for the goodness of fit using $\chi 2$, comparative fit index (CFI), and root mean square error of approximation (RMSEA) fit indices. CFI values above 0.90 and 0.95 indicate adequate and good model fit, respectively, and RMSEA values below 0.08 and 0.05 indicate adequate and good model fit, respectively (Browne & Cudeck, 1992; Hu & Bentler, 1999). In addition, we used descriptive statistics and Pearson Correlations to analyse the data. Reliability analysis was done as well. The structural model is diagrammed in Figure 1.

3. RESULTS

Among the participants, 6.5% reported high statistics anxiety (the mean higher than 4 on a scale from 1 to 5). A significant difference was found between all the three learning environments [$F_{(2,646)}=36.637$, $p<0.001$] in statistics anxiety (M=2.50, SD=0.60 for POE, M=3.02, SD=0.62 for F2F and M=2.80, SD=0.56 for ERT). Almost two-thirds of the participants (64.6%) reported having engaged in academic dishonesty at least once in the POE learning environment, compared to 55% in the F2F and 43.5% in the ERT modality. A significant difference was found between all the three learning environments [$F_{(2,646)}=17.893$, $p<0.001$] in academic dishonesty (M=4.12, SD=0.41 for POE, M=3.85, SD=0.44 for F2F and M=3.99, SD=0.41 for ERT). In the full sample, the results show significant negative correlations between all the five personality traits and academic dishonesty. Furthermore, there is a significant negative correlation between identified regulation and academic dishonesty and significant positive correlations between academic dishonesty, external and introjected regulation, and intrinsic motivation. There are positive correlations between each of the components of statistics anxiety and academic dishonesty.

The academic dishonesty variable was modelled by the variables of academic misconduct and academic integrity, by the latent variable of personality, and those of motivation, and of students' previous achievements with the mediation of the latent variable of statistics anxiety. The data fit the academic dishonesty model marginally well ($\chi 2$=1,426.37, N=649, df=564, p<0.001, CFI=0.801, RMSEA=0.049).

3.1 Academic Dishonesty Analysis - POE Sample

The results of the analysis indicate that the variance in academic dishonesty is explained by students' personality traits with the mediation of statistics anxiety. Accordingly, the POE sample supports H_1. statistics anxiety is the variable having a greater impact on academic misconduct with a total effect of 67%. Test and class anxiety are among the most influential components of statistics anxiety. It has one of the highest effects (b=0.79, p<0.001), meaning that the higher a student's level of statistics anxiety as to test and class anxiety, the higher their propensity to cheat. Statistics anxiety component of computational self-concept has been found to have a strong significant effect as well (b=0.77, p<0.001), meaning the higher the student's computational self-concept, the higher the probability they engage in academic misconduct. Interpretation anxiety (b=0.76, p<0.001) is a further strong factor influencing academic misconduct. Accordingly, statistics anxiety regarding interpretation anxiety increases academic misconduct. In addition, personality traits were found to have a significant negative impact on statistics anxiety (b= -0.34, p<0.05). All five personality traits have a significant effect on the mediating variable of statistics anxiety: Extraversion (b=0.16, p<0.05), agreeableness (b=0.48, p<0.05), conscientiousness (b=0.46, p<0.001), openness to experience (b=0.23, p<0.01) and emotional stability (b=0.73, p<0.001). Accordingly, the higher levels of a student's personality traits, the less anxious they are. Motivation was also found to have a negative significant impact on statistics anxiety (b= -0.36, p<0.01), while all motivation types have a significant effect on the mediating variable: external regulation (b=0.21, p<0.001), introjected regulation (b=0.70, p<0.001), identified regulation (b=0.76 p<0.001) and intrinsic motivation (b=0.77, p<0.001). In other words, the higher the student's motivation, the lower the level of statistics anxiety.

3.2 Academic Dishonesty analysis – F2F Sample

The results indicate that the variance in academic dishonesty is explained by students' personality traits and motivation, with no significant effect of statistics anxiety as a mediator. Therefore no support for the four hypotheses was obtained in the F2F sample. Personality traits were found to have a negative significant impact on statistics anxiety (b= -0.55, p<0.01), while three personality traits have a significant effect on the mediating variable: conscientiousness (b=0.35, p<0.05), openness to experience (b=0.72, p<0.001) and emotional stability (b=0.67, p<0.001). This means that the higher a student's personality traits, the lower the level of statistics anxiety. Motivation was also found to have a negatively marginal significant impact on statistics anxiety (b= -0.36, p=0.065), while all motivation types have a significant effect on the mediating variable: external regulation (b=0.58, p<0.001), introjected regulation (b=0.98, p<0.001), identified regulation (b=0.36 p<0.001) and intrinsic motivation (b=0.34, p<0.01). In other words, the higher a student's motivation, the less anxious they are. Grade point average (b=0.46, p<0.05) is a further variable having a significant negative effect on statistics anxiety. The higher a student's grade point average, the lower the statistics anxiety. We also found that women experience greater statistics anxiety than their male counterparts, and the greater the age, the greater the statistics anxiety.

3.3 Academic Dishonesty Analysis - ERT Sample

The results indicate that the variance in academic dishonesty is explained by students' personality traits and students' previous achievement, with the mediation of Statistics anxiety. Therefore, H_1 and H_3 were confirmed in the ERT sample. statistics anxiety is the variable having the greatest impact on academic misconduct, with a total effect of 49%. Test and class anxiety are among the most influential components of statistics anxiety; it has one of the higher effects (b=0.83, p<0.001). The higher a student's level of statistics anxiety as to test and class anxiety, the higher their propensity to cheat. Similarly, the component of statistics anxiety regarding fear of asking for help was also found to have a strong significant effect (b=0.82, p<0.001). The higher a student's level of statistics anxiety as to fear of asking for help, the higher the probability they engage in academic misconduct. In addition, interpretation anxiety (b=0.80, p<0.001) is a further strong factor influencing academic misconduct. Moreover, personality traits were found to have a negative significant impact on statistics anxiety (b= -0.55, p<0.001), along with a positive significant effect on motivation (b=0.46, p<0.01), while all the personality traits have significant effect on the mediating variables: extraversion (b=0.36, p<0.001), agreeableness (b=0.38, p<0.001), conscientiousness (b=0.58, p<0.001), openness to experience (b=0.55, p<0.001) and emotional stability (b=0.54, p<0.001). This means that the higher a student's levels of one of the above personality traits, the more motivated and less anxious they are. Another set of variables having a negative significant effect on statistics anxiety are those related to previous student achievements. The higher the previous student achievements, the lower the level of Statistics anxiety.

As shown in Table 1, the results of the multi-group analysis indicate that there is a significant difference between all course types: POE, F2F, and ERT, thus confirming H_4.

Table 1. Comparison among the learning environments

Course Type	NFI Delta-1	DF	*p*-value	Difference
POE vs. F2F	.107	43	***	Yes
POE vs. ERT	.168	43	***	Yes
F2F vs. ERT	.023	43	.016	Yes
General Model	.171	86	***	Yes

4. CONCLUSIONS

This research presents for the first time a comparison between academic ethical behaviour, statistics anxiety, personality traits, and motivation in different learning environments (F2F, POE & ERT), while relying on Self-Determination Theory. In line with the scholarly literature, we believe that understanding the motivational and anxiety-related mechanisms involved in unethical academic behaviours is key to designing future teaching, learning, and assessment approaches (Etgar et al., 2019; Steinberger et al., 2021).

The results show that learning environments affect and play a significant role in interacting with statistics anxiety, motivation, personality traits, and academic dishonesty (H_4). Moreover, findings show that academic dishonesty is more prevalent in POE than in F2F and ERT environments. This study's findings improve the model employed in previous studies (Peled et al., 2019; Steinberger et al., 2021) by revealing that learning environments determine the mediating role of statistics anxiety. In digital learning environments (POE, ERT), mediation has been found between students' personality traits and academic dishonesty. No similar mediation could be established in the physical learning environment, F2F. In line with the scholarly literature (Whittle et al., 2020), this difference may be due to the lack of physical presence of academic instructors in both POE and ERT learning modalities, that might lead to uncertainty and anxiety and directly impact students' ethical disinhibition. Additionally, the differences from examining the two digital environments show that in ERT but not in POE, statistics anxiety mediates between students' previous achievements and academic dishonesty. The immediate necessity to move to digital learning without prior preparation during the global pandemic has led students to severe distress, potentially awakening statistics anxiety. In addition, the quality of distance teaching is lower in ERT due to being imposed at once without any prior pedagogical preparation (Hollweck & Doucet, 2020). Accordingly, students facing exceptional and extreme situations like this may rely exclusively on their previous academic experience or achievements in studies in general and, more concretely, in mathematics. A limitation that needs to be taken into consideration in this context is the relatively small size of the F2F sample, that might have influenced the SEM results.

Hence, we conclude that online courses should be designed according to student-centred approaches (Rapanta et al., 2020). The foregoing may include: Instructor's immediacy, improved communication, pre-planned real-life based on learning tasks (Neumann et al., 2013), monitoring of student progress and using continuous formative assessment (Torres Martín et al., 2021). This, in turn, promotes students' sense of self-competence and autonomy throughout their learning processes, thus reducing dishonesty (Kanat-Maymon et al., 2015). Additionally, positive attitudes towards learning statistics are crucial to motivate students and awaken their interest in the subject. Deepening student engagement and learning requires that faculty take part in discussing and communicating ideas and creating clear policies and shared tasks.

REFERENCES

Arbuckle, J. L., & Wothke, W. (1999). Amos 4.0 User's Guide, Small Waters Corporation. *Chicago, IL.*

Arniatika, S. (2020). Personality traits, motivational orientations and speaking achievement in the EFL context. *IJIET (International Journal of Indonesian Education and Teaching)*, *4*(1), 110-120.

Badiozaman, I. F. A. (2021). Exploring online readiness in the context of the COVID 19 pandemic. *Teaching in Higher Education*, 1-19.

Becerra, B. L. G., & Almendra, M. P. R. (2020, December). Measuring student motivation in a statistics course supported by podcast using Reduced Instructional Materials Motivation Survey (RIMMS). In *2020 X International Conference on Virtual Campus (JICV),* 1-4. IEEE.

Bolin, A. U. (2004). Self-control, perceived opportunity, and attitudes as predictors of academic dishonesty. *The Journal of Psychology*, *138*(2), 101-114.

Chiang, F. K., Zhu, D., & Yu, W. (2022). A systematic review of academic dishonesty in online learning environments. *Journal of Computer Assisted Learning*, *38*(4), 907-928.

Cruise, R. J., Cash, R. W., & Bolton, D. L. (1985). Development and validation of an instrument to measure statistical anxiety. In *American Statistical Association Proceedings of the Section on Statistical Education, 4*(3), 92-97.

Cui, S., Zhang, J., Guan, D., Zhao, X., & Si, J. (2019). Antecedents of statistics anxiety: An integrated account. *Personality and Individual Differences*, *144*, 79-87.

Deci, E. L., & Ryan, R. M. (2008). Self-determination theory: A macrotheory of human motivation, development, and health. *Canadian Psychology / Psychologie Canadienne, 49*(3), 182–185. https://doi.org/10.1037/a0012801

du Rocher, A. R. (2020). Active learning strategies and academic self-efficacy relate to both attentional control and attitudes towards plagiarism. *Active Learning in Higher Education*, *21*(3), 203-216.

Erguvan, I. D. (2021). The rise of contract cheating during the COVID-19 pandemic: a qualitative study through the eyes of academics in Kuwait. *Language Testing in Asia*, *11*(1), 1-21.

Eshet, Y., Grinautski, K., Peled, Y., & Barczyk, C. (2014). No more excuses-personality traits and academic dishonesty in online courses. *Journal of Statistical Science and Application*, *2*(3), 111-118.

Etgar, S., Blau, I., & Eshet-Alkalai, Y. (2019). White-collar crime in academia: Trends in digital academic dishonesty over time and their effect on penalty severity. *Computers & Education*, *141*, 103621.

Foutz, B., Violanti, M., Kelly, S., & Prentiss, S. M. (2021). Teacher immediacy behaviors and students' public speaking anxiety: More and less helpful than anticipated. *Basic Communication Course Annual*, *33*(1), 13.

Gosling, S. D., Rentfrow, P. J., & Swann Jr, W. B. (2003). A very brief measure of the Big-Five personality domains. *Journal of Research in Personality*, *37*(6), 504-528.

Hodges, C. B., Moore, S., Lockee, B. B., Trust, T., & Bond, M. A. (2020). The difference between emergency remote teaching and online learning. *EDUCAUSE Review*, 27. https://er.educause.edu/articles/2020/3/the-difference-between-emergency-remote-teaching-and-online-learning.

Hollweck, T., & Doucet, A. (2020). Pracademics in the pandemic: pedagogies and professionalism. *Journal of Professional Capital and Community.*

Hu, L. T., & Bentler, P. M. (1999). Cutoff criteria for fit indexes in covariance structure analysis: Conventional criteria versus new alternatives. *Structural equation modeling: a multidisciplinary journal*, *6*(1), 1-55.

Kanat-Maymon, Y., Benjamin, M., Stavsky, A., Shoshani, A., & Roth, G. (2015). The role of basic need fulfillment in academic dishonesty: A self-determination theory perspective. *Contemporary Educational Psychology*, *43*, 1-9.

Kisamore, J. L., Stone, T. H., & Jawahar, I. M. (2007). Academic integrity: The relationship between individual and situational factors on misconduct contemplations. *Journal of Business Ethics*, *75*, 381-394.

Koscielniak, M., & Bojanowska, A. (2019). The role of personal values and student achievement in academic dishonesty. *Frontiers in psychology*, 1887.

Lavasani, M. G., Weisani, M., & Shariati, F. (2014). The role of achievement goals, academic motivation in statistics anxiety: Testing a causal model. *Procedia-Social and Behavioral Sciences*, *114*, 933-938.

Luo, Z., Subramaniam, G., & O'STEEN, B. I. L. L. Y. (2020). Will Anxiety Boost Motivation? The Relationship between Anxiety and Motivation in Foreign Language Learning. *Malaysian Journal of ELT Research*, *17*(1).

Malesky, A., Grist, C., Poovey, K., & Dennis, N. (2022). The effects of peer influence, honor codes, and personality traits on cheating behavior in a university setting. *Ethics & Behavior*, *32*(1), 12-21.

Maqableh, M., & Alia, M. (2021). Evaluation online learning of undergraduate students under lockdown amidst COVID-19 Pandemic: The online learning experience and students' satisfaction. *Children and Youth Services Review*, *128*, 106160.

McCrae, R. R., & Costa, P. T. (1987). Validation of the five-factor model of personality across instruments and observers. *Journal of personality and social psychology*, *52*(1), 81.

Müller, F. H., Palekčić, M., Beck, M., & Wanninger, S. (2006). Personality, motives and learning environment as predictors of self-determined learning motivation. *Review of Psychology*, *13*(2), 75-86.

Murtonen, M. (2015). University students' understanding of the concepts empirical, theoretical, qualitative and quantitative research. *Teaching in Higher Education*, *20*(7), 684-698.

Neumann, D. L., Hood, M., & Neumann, M. M. (2013). Using real-life data when teaching statistics: Student perceptions of this strategy in an introductory statistics course. *Statistics Education Research Journal*, *12*(2), 59-70.

O'Bryant, M., Natesan Batley, P., & Onwuegbuzie, A. J. (2021). Validation of an adapted version of the Statistical Anxiety Scale in english and its relationship to attitudes toward statistics. *SAGE Open*, *11*(1), 21582440211001378.

Peiró-Signes, Á., Trull, O., Segarra-Oña, M., & García-Díaz, J. C. (2021). Anxiety towards statistics and its relationship with students' attitudes and learning approach. *Behavioral Sciences*, *11*(3), 32.

Peled, Y., Eshet, Y., Barczyk, C., & Grinautski, K. (2019). Predictors of Academic Dishonesty among undergraduate students in online and face-to-face courses. *Computers & Education*, *131*, 49-59.

Rapanta, C., Botturi, L., Goodyear, P., Guàrdia, L., & Koole, M. (2020). Online university teaching during and after the Covid-19 crisis: Refocusing teacher presence and learning activity. *Postdigital Science and Education*, *2*, 923-945.

Roe, J. (2022). Reconceptualizing academic dishonesty as a struggle for intersubjective recognition: a new theoretical model. *Humanities and Social Sciences Communications*, *9*(1).

Ryan R.M., Connell J.P. (1989) Self-regulation questionnaire. Unpubl. Manuscr.

Ryan, R. M., & Deci, E. L. (2020). Intrinsic and extrinsic motivation from a self-determination theory perspective: Definitions, theory, practices, and future directions. *Contemporary Educational Psychology*, *61*, 101860.

Shi, Y., Tong, M., & Long, T. (2021). Investigating relationships among blended synchronous learning environments, students' motivation, and cognitive engagement: A mixed methods study. *Computers & Education*, *168*, 104193.

Steinberger, P. (2020). Assessing the statistical anxiety rating scale as applied to prospective teachers in an Israeli teacher-training college. *Studies in Educational Evaluation*, *64*, 100829.

Steinberger, P., Eshet, Y., & Grinautsky, K. (2021). No anxious student is left behind: Statistics anxiety, personality traits, and academic dishonesty—lessons from COVID-19. *Sustainability*, *13*(9), 4762.

Tindall, I. K., Fu, K. W., Tremayne, K., & Curtis, G. J. (2021). Can negative emotions increase students' plagiarism and cheating?. *International Journal for Educational Integrity*, *17*(1), 1-16.

Torres Martín, C., Acal, C., El Homrani, M., & Mingorance Estrada, Á. C. (2021). Impact on the virtual learning environment due to COVID-19. *Sustainability*, *13*(2), 582.

Trassi, A. P., Leonard, S. J., Rodrigues, L. D., Rodas, J. A., & Santos, F. H. (2022). Mediating factors of statistics anxiety in university students: a systematic review and meta-analysis. *Annals of the New York Academy of Sciences*, *1512*(1), 76-97.

Walsh, L. L., Lichti, D. A., Zambrano-Varghese, C. M., Borgaonkar, A. D., Sodhi, J. S., Moon, S., ... & Callis-Duehl, K. L. (2021). Why and how science students in the United States think their peers cheat more frequently online: perspectives during the COVID-19 pandemic. *International Journal for Educational Integrity*, *17*, 1-18.

Whittle, C., Tiwari, S., Yan, S., & Williams, J. (2020). Emergency remote teaching environment: A conceptual framework for responsive online teaching in crises. *Information and Learning Sciences*, *121*(5/6), 311-319.

Zalts, R., Green, N., Tackett, S., & Lubin, R. (2021). The association between medical students' motivation with learning environment, perceived academic rank, and burnout. *International Journal of Medical Education*, *12*, 25.

Zhang, H., Shi, Y., Zhou, Z. E., Ma, H., & Tang, H. (2020). Good people do bad things: How anxiety promotes unethical behavior through intuitive and automatic processing. *Current Psychology*, *39*, 720-728.

EFFECTS OF AN IMMERSIVE, MULTILINEAR FUTURE SCENARIO FOR EDUCATION PURPOSES

Flurina Hilber, Thomas Keller and Elke Brucker-Kley
ZHAW Institute of Business Information Technology
Winterthur, Switzerland

ABSTRACT

This paper proposes a didactic design that is centered around an immersive, multilinear narrative in virtual reality as a means of illustrating human life on the edge of technological singularity. It explores the potential of narrative scenarios to trigger a discourse from users' perspective. Affective Computing is taken as a use case. It is a subfield of AI that focuses on identifying, understanding, and appropriately responding to human emotions. Its goal is to create more personalized and emotionally engaging human-machine interactions. To explore what life might be like if an emotionally intelligent AI became our best friend, a multilinear scenario was created. This scenario takes the reader through different stages of the protagonist's life, starting from the first day of secondary school and ending with the loss of a loved one in midlife. The systematic approach to create and validate the multilinear interactive scenario is described and the results of an experiment with 164 participants are presented. The ultimate goal is the application of this approach for educational purposes regarding ethical thinking and responsible innovations.

KEYWORDS

Affective Computing, Science-Fiction Prototyping, Technological Singularity, Human-Machine Interaction, Narrative Scenarios, Immersive Virtual-Reality

1. INTRODUCTION

Narrative scenarios that play on the edge of a technological singularity are seen as a suitable method to initiate a broad societal discourse on a common basis (Brucker-Kley & Keller, 2019). Singularity refers to a hypothetical time in the future when technology exceeds human capacity and creates a superior form of intelligence. In 1993, Vinge stated that the Singularity and its outcomes cannot be determined as positive or negative, as it involves numerous opportunities and risks (Vinge, 1993). Therefore, an active engagement with new technologies is of great importance for the development and shaping of our future (Brucker-Kley et al., 2021; Meinert, 2014). This research draws on the humanistic perspectives of technology criticism and technophilosophy (Poser, 2016; Taylor, 2011), which reject the notion of humans as "mindless victims of technology" and instead see them as "agents of cultural change" [7, p. 154].

One method that has gained increasing prominence in recent years is Science-Fiction Prototyping (SFP) (Burnam-Fink, 2015; Johnson, 2011; Merrie et al., 2018; Potstada & Zybura, 2014). Science-Fiction (Sci-Fi) Prototypes are short fictional artifacts, such as short stories, videos, comics, or plays, that are based on scientific facts. Their purpose is to stimulate discourse about the impacts, consequences, opportunities, and risks of technology and the future (Burnam-Fink, 2015). In addition, previous studies have applied SFP to capture student's attitudes toward a technology. Conventional approaches use textual or visual representations of Sci-Fi Prototypes, which primarily target the cognitive component of attitude formation (Brucker-Kley et al., 2021; Brunner et al., 2020). However, emotions play a significant role in attitude formation. For instance, research has revealed that an individual who experiences apprehension towards the potential consequences of a technology may opt not to utilize it, despite the numerous benefits it may entail (Lerner et al., 2015). According to (Somarathna et al., 2022), Virtual Reality (VR) has the potential to effectively and naturally elicit emotions. The present study integrates these two distinct research streams and supplements the SFP method with the immersive dimension of VR.

In Keller et al. (2021) the authors developed a Sci-Fi Prototype presenting future multilinear scenarios related to *Affective Computing and Friendship.* Humans have always been fascinated by the possibilities of computer interactions. In the past, we would sacrificially take care of our Tamagotchis, while today we simply ask Google Mini or Alexa for a joke. The purpose of this work is to enable people to explore scenarios of a fictional person and its relationship with a digital companion, allowing them to experience potential futures (Nisi & Haahr, 2006). The present study utilizes this existing Sci-Fi Prototype and adds an immersive dimension by building a VR environment. This research design aims to determine whether immersive, interactive SFP is a suitable method to comprehensively capture attitudes towards Affective Computing and to stimulate a discourse on the topic.

2. RELATED WORK

SFP is a practical guide to use fiction to imagine the future in entirely new ways (Johnson, 2011). It involves short fictional artifacts based on scientific facts, such as stories or videos, comics, plays, or audiobooks to stimulate a discourse about technology's opportunities and risks (Burnam-Fink, 2015). According to Johnson [9, p.3], we shape our own future, so discussing technology's impact is crucial. The process of SFP begins with the present and the recognition of an implied future based on sound science (Merrie et al., 2018). It shows how technologies shape people who use them and, in turn, are shaped by them. SFP doesn't provide predictions but highlights a possible interplay between people and technology.

In *plot-based* interactive storytelling, readers make decisions at selected key points in the plot, resulting in different storylines (Cavazza et al., 2002). This interactivity focuses on scenarios and narrative control, providing players with the opportunity to create their own stories and become more engaged in the narrative (Laurel, 2004; Nisi & Haahr, 2006). Interactive storytelling has proven to be a valuable tool in scenario planning by enabling decision-making and providing a platform for experiencing the potential outcomes (Gordon & Glenn, 2018). Several studies have highlighted its benefits, including its use in conjunction with SFP to intensify the scenario experience and encourage alternative thinking (Bell et al., 2013; Brucker-Kley et al., 2021; Brunner et al., 2020; Oberle et al., 2021).

VR has caught the attention of the scientific community because of its ability to create experiences that simulate real-world situations (Chicchi Giglioli et al., 2017). Simulations that represent a physical environment and an event that cannot be easily reproduced in the real world (as for example simulating a friendship with an artificial intelligent being) are of particular interest to researchers. VR enables researchers to examine these scenarios in a controlled laboratory environment (Vince, 2004). The distinguishing feature of VR from other means of information representation is its focus on immersion. Immersion is meant to convey the feeling that one has left the real world and is now "present" in the virtual environment. This notion of "being present" represents a central element in research on VR (Berkman & Akan, 2019; Lombard et al., 2009; Mestre et al., 2006). While immersion is a technology-related, objective aspect of VR systems, presence is a psychological and perceptual consequence of immersion (Mestre et al., 2006).

According to the Theory of Planned Behavior and Theory of Reasoned Action (Fishbein & Ajzen, 1977), the attitude of an individual is considered a reliable predictor. Attitude, in turn, is composed of feelings, beliefs, and actions, as described by the *Tri-component Model of Attitudes* (Pickens, 2005). This model suggests that an attitude towards a technology has a cognitive, an affective, and a behavioral component (Eagly & Chaiken, 1993). The behavioral component is particularly interesting because it can deviate from a person's attitude, values, and opinions, as Garms-Homolová (2020) notes. There are various reasons for this, such as social desirability or a lack of imagination of how one would react in a given situation. This inconsistency is the basis of the theory of cognitive dissonance (Festinger, 1957).

3. RESEARCH OBJECTIVES

This paper investigates whether immersive, multilinear SFP is a suitable method to challenge a student's attitude. It is investigated whether the experience of a Sci-Fi Prototype with VR (high immersion) causes a stronger attitude change than a hypertext (HT), web-based Sci-Fi Prototype (low immersion). The main difference from the VR Sci-Fi Prototype and the HT Sci-Fi Prototype is the perceived presence (Lemmens et al., 2022). The more immersive the experience, the stronger the perceived presence (Diemer et al., 2015). It is essential to the research design that the study is not based on a directional hypothesis. The question is not whether high immersion increases the imaginability/desirability of Affective Computing, but whether the high immersion causes a bigger change in attitude.

Studies have shown that VR experiences are useful for the acquisition of cognitive skills such as memory, comprehension of spatial and visual information, and knowledge acquisition. such as memory (Jensen & Konradsen, 2018; Krokos et al., 2019). Therefore, it is hypothesized that VR will be more responsive to the cognitive component of an attitude than HT. The behavioral component is assessed by analyzing decisions made within the multilinear scenario. It is demonstrated in (Alshaer et al., 2017) that display mode (computer screen vs. VR glasses) influences user's behavior. It is therefore reasonable to expect that this effect would be even more pronounced when comparing VR with HT.

4. METHODOLOGY AND APPROACH

The empirical research employs a mixed-methods approach, which includes quantitative and qualitative methodologies. It follows the in-depth model, where quantitative study (standardized questionnaire survey) is followed by a qualitative study in which a few selected respondents from the questionnaire survey are interviewed again in detail (Bortz & Döring, 2016). Since the same subjects are examined in both studies, the findings can be directly compared with each other and interpreted in their entirety (Bortz & Döring, 2016).

This research has two parts: the first involves an experiment based on A/B testing to compare how attitudes towards *Affective Computing and Friendship* change when using different types of media (VR vs. HT) in a multilinear scenario, while the second part involves assessing the quality and impact of the VR experience through both quantitative and qualitative methods.

The experiment in this study is based on the research in (Keller et al., 2021). They developed a HT Sci-Fi Prototype exploring *Affective Computing and Friendship* and presented the multilinear scenario to 145 participants to test its effectiveness in stimulating a discourse on the topic. The multilinear story presents the user with a total of 5 decisions, each of which can be chosen between a high-tech option and a low-tech option.

The VR prototype underwent two rounds of validation to ensure technical functionality, identify any elements of the VR environment perceived as disturbing, assess comprehensibility of the narrative, and detect any spelling errors in the script. Test subjects experienced the story while providing feedback on their observations, which was recorded, consolidated, and processed.

4.1 Experiment

The experiment is conducted with two groups experiencing the Sci-Fi Prototype in a different media format (VR vs. HT). The authors in (Keller et al., 2021) presented the HT Sci-Fi Prototype to 145 participants and assessed their attitudes in terms of cognitive, affective, and behavioral components. For this study, we use their dataset to compare the results of the VR Prototype (developed in this research) to the HT Prototype.

The VR group is conducted as a laboratory study in a classroom, which allows control of confounding variables. The HT group, on the other hand, is a field study conducted via online questionnaires at home, chosen for convenience (Keller et al., 2021). The combination of laboratory and field studies, although not ideal, was the most efficient approach.

The present experiment follows the within-subjects design, as a pre- and a post-test is conducted for both groups. For comparability, exactly the same questions were asked as in (Keller et al., 2021). The duration of the experiment is around 30 minutes including the pre-survey, the VR experience using a head-mounted display (HMD), and a post-survey. A small number of selected subjects were then given another semi-structured interview of approximately 10 minutes each. For the remaining subjects, the experiment was finished at this point.

The pre-test collects demographic data, such as gender, age, field of study, technical affinity, and VR experience. Technical affinity is measured using a 5-item battery with a 5-point Likert scale, as in the research in (Keller et al., 2021) and participants can score between 5-25 points. This construct is based on a questionnaire developed in (Karrer-Gauß et al., 2009) to measure technical affinity.

To asses attitudes towards *Affective Computing and Friendship* an existing construct from the literature is applied, which has been previously used in the context of SFP in (Brucker-Kley et al., 2021). The cognitive component is evaluated through the dimension of imaginability, that is, how realistically and tangibly participants can imagine a technology. The affective component is assessed through the dimension of desirability, that is, to what extent participants consider a new technology desirable in their lives. Responses are collected on a 5-point Likert scale and are both assessed in the pre-test and post-test to detect any changes. The behavioral component is extrapolated from the decisions that participants make during the multilinear story. Points are assigned to each decision for behavioral analysis. The points range from 0-2, with a score of 2 representing a strong high-tech decision, 1 indicating a high-tech decision, and 0 indicating a low-tech decision.

4.2 Quality of the VR Science-Fiction Prototype

In addition, this research aims to investigate the quality and effect of the newly created VR Prototype through an exploratory study. Semi-structured interviews are conducted with selected participants to generate new hypotheses on how to improve the prototype. A smaller quantitative study supplements the exploratory study, with questions about the feeling of presence. Based on a comprehensive literature review on presence, the authors in (Lombard et al., 2009) developed and validated a questionnaire to measure presence. The questions used in the survey draw on their definition and addresses four types of presence: *Engagement*, *Spatial Immersion*, *Social Immersion*, and *Social Richness*. The post-test includes inquiries about these four categories which allows to assess all the VR participants.

5. RESULTS

The sample sizes of the two groups are significantly different (n=41 in the VR group vs. n=123 in the HT group), nevertheless, according to (Universität Zürich, 2022) this does not affect the statistical analysis. The HT dataset in (Keller et al., 2021) was filtered for participants aged between 18-35, resulting in 123 remaining participants. The VR group consisted of 73% (30) male and 27% (11) female students, while the HT group had an equal gender distribution. Most participants (78%) have already had some VR experience prior to participating in this experiment. The technical affinity was equally distributed in both groups.

5.1 Cognitive and Affective Aspects of Attitude

Based on the participants' responses to the pre- and post-survey the effect of the VR experience on the attitudes towards *Affective Computing and Friendship* was analyzed. First, the cognitive aspect of attitude, i.e. how well participants can imagine the portrayed technology and its consequences, was compared before and after the interaction with the Sci-Fi Prototype. Second, the desirability, i.e., how much the participants would like to have the portrayed PDA in their everyday life, was analyzed pre and post. The verbal qualifiers of the 5-point Likert scale were recoded into numerical values. Significance of changes within the groups were tested using the Wilcoxon signed ranked test, with a 0.05 significance level. The Wilcoxon test is used when the data are not normally distributed. To compare and evaluate effect sizes in a standardized manner Pearson's r value was calculated. The taxation of the strength of the effect was based on the classification of Cohen (1988).

Table 1. Results Wilcoxon Test (Desirability & Imaginability)

	Aspect of Attitude	Asymp. Sign. (2-tailed)	Sign. (<=0.05)	Effect size (r)
HT	Desirability	0.308	No	0.092
	Imaginability	< 0.001	Yes	0.452 (strong*)
VR	Desirability	0.782	No	0.043
	Imaginability	0.297	No	0.163 (small*)

**(Cohen effect size classification r= 0.10 small, r=0.25 medium, r=0.40 large)*

Only one significant change in attitude was observed, that was in the HT group on the question of imaginability. In the pre-test, participants, on average, considered a friendship with an AI as "possibly realistic" (ø = 3.29), whereas in the post-test their average rating increased to "rather realistic" (ø = 3.72) (Table 1).

The bubble diagram shown in Figure 1 depicts the changes of the response of the participant before (x-axis) and after (y-axis) the VR experience. The bubble size represents the number of participants. The bubbles along the diagonal of the diagram represent those participants whose attitudes remained the same before and after experiencing the Sci-Fi Prototype. The bubbles above the diagonal represent those participants who consider a technology more imaginable respectively more desirable after the narrative. The bubbles below the diagonal stand for negative changes in imaginability respectively desirability after the narrative.

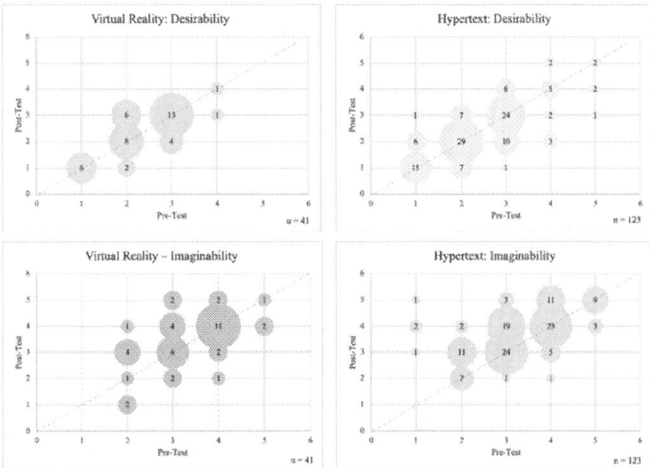

Figure 1. Bubble diagram displaying the change of attitude between pre- and post-test

Figure 1 reveals a comparable trend in attitude change between the two experimental groups. Overall, both groups rated desirability lower than imaginability. Regarding desirability, roughly a third of participants in each group (VR = 31%, HT = 39%) experienced a change in attitude (regardless of direction). For imaginability, the number of participants with attitude change was even larger (VR = 46%, HT = 49%).

The hypotheses predicted that the VR group would have a greater attitude change than the HT group. A Mann-Whitney U test was used to test for significant differences between the two groups, and absolute differences in pre- and post-test of attitude components were compared. However, no significant difference between the two groups was found.

5.2 Behavioural Component

The VR and HT groups had a similar distribution of paths chosen in the multilinear story, which were categorized into three groups based on the level of technology (Figure 2). Statistically, the analysis did not show a significant difference between the groups.

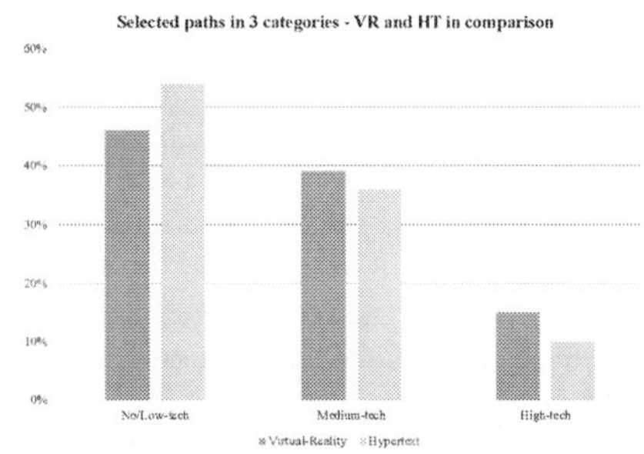

Figure 2. Distribution of paths taken in the multilinear narrative

5.3 Quality of the VR experience

To validate the quality of the VR Sci-Fi Prototype, questions were asked about perceived *Presence*. The three categories of *Engagement* (ø = 3.93), *Spatial Presence* (ø = 4.25), and *Social Presence* (ø = 3.78) averaged a 4, or "agree," on a 5-point Likert scale. The category *Social-Richness* scored the lowest with an average of 4.23 on a 7-point Likert scale. Within this category, the dimension *Natural/Unnatural* received the lowest rating, while the dimension *Personal/Impersonal* received the highest.

After experiencing the VR experience, a brief interview was conducted with 12 subjects. The key questions and findings are presented in Table 2. The number within the parentheses represents the overall count of subjects who expressed the corresponding statement. Multiple answers were possible.

Table 2. Key Questions & Findings from the interviews

Interview Question/ Topic	Findings
What triggered the VR experience in you?	Amazement, Excitement, Curiosity, Fun (7) Thought-Provoking, Ambivalent Feeling (7) Uncertainty, Scariness, Shocking, Worries, Fear (6)
How was the combination of low and high poly perceived?	Combination was good, did not bother (7) Combination was not noticed at all (6) Prefer high poly than low poly (2)
Social Presence: Photorealistic people vs. cartoon people	VR Prototype wouldn't improve with photorealistic people (9) The effect remains the same whether using photorealistic people or cartoons. The identification and level of empathy is equally strong (4) Probably slightly better effect, if photorealistic people, but effort is not worth it (8) Photorealistic people, not appearing to be real, are worse than using cartoons (4) Improvement not in the appearance, but in the facial expressions & gestures of cartoons (6)
Personal opinion: is it more effective to assess the attitude towards a technology with VR SFP or with HT SFP?	Preference of VR → high immersion (8) VR has intensified initial attitude towards the technology, but not changed it (8) The more intense the experience, the greater the chance of an attitude change (4) VR is a lot more emotional than text (2)

6. CONCLUSIONS

There are four limitations to consider when interpreting the results. First, the sample size of the VR group is small, making it difficult to generalize the findings. Second, the groups were quasi randomized, which increases the risk of confounding factors. Third, the VR and HT narratives were not completely identical, which introduces uncertainties in comparing the results. Fourth, it is questionable whether the Wilcoxon test was the appropriate statistical method chosen. The Wilcoxon test analyzes whether two related samples differ significantly from each other, i.e., whether one group shows a clear trend up or down. However, in this study, the hypotheses were stated as non-directional, which means that only the absolute change is relevant.

In general, people can imagine a future where they have friendships with artificially intelligent machines, but they don't necessarily approve of it. They worry about the control that AI could have over us, as seen with examples in the VR experience such as digital footprints, PDA dating app, and the invasion of the PDA in everyday life situations. This is a dilemma known as *malum technologicum*, where new technologies are developed to improve our lives (*bonum technologicum*) but can also lead to dependence, loss of skills, and social isolation (Poser, 2016). However, early awareness and responsibility can help mitigate these risks. The SFP aims to identify the use and impact of a technology and to initiate a discourse about it. The findings of this study are in line with (Brucker-Kley et al., 2021; Brucker-Kley & Keller, 2019; Keller et al., 2021; Oberle et al., 2021) that SFP is a suitable method for triggering a broad social discourse especially in education.

Overall, the VR prototype was positively rated for its presence, despite being a mix of low and high-poly elements. Most of the participants did not seem to notice the combination, or at least it did not bother them. Authors in (van Gisbergen et al., 2019) confirm this result by demonstrating that the level of photorealism in characters has no impact on the VR experience. Participants criticized the avatars' facial expressions and gestures for not feeling authentic and being hard to read. They suggested that improving these aspects would significantly enhance the VR prototype. This is supported by the quantitative study, as the questions about realistic feeling and interaction with the avatars scored the lowest.

The VR experience doesn't elicit stronger emotions than the HT narrative. According to the interviewees, the VR experience has promoted engagement with the technology and the topic of *Affective Computing and Friendship*. Many participants were observed to discuss the topic after the VR experience, and several mentioned that they would like to experience the game again with different decision paths. The interviews highlighted both the advantages and disadvantages of using a PDA, with some interviewees expressing a sense of conflict or uncertainty. This demonstrates the effectiveness of the immersive, multilinear SFP approach in evaluating the potential benefits and drawbacks of new technologies, nevertheless, VR did not show any stronger impact than the HT version.

The VR experience doesn't elicit a stronger impact on cognition than the HT narrative. On one hand, the results show some evidence that experiencing a VR experience may have an effect on attitudes towards Affective Computing. On the other hand, the Wilcoxon test did not show significant differences. The ambiguous findings align with the outcomes of previous research (Brucker-Kley et al., 2021; Keller et al., 2021).

Overall, the level of immersion (VR vs. HT) showed no significant difference in attitude change. Both groups exposed similar results. Even though the quantitative analysis did not uncover any disparities between the two groups, all respondents in the qualitative study favored the VR experience in response to the final question, stating that it was better suited for engaging with a topic. The fun factor was often mentioned, as well as the lasting impression of the VR experience. It would be interesting to investigate whether these statements result in a longer-lasting effect of the VR experience when compared to the HT narrative. This would imply that although an immediate difference may not be apparent between the two media, over a longer period of time, the VR group may engage with the topic for a longer duration or more intense compared to the HT group. Evidence for such an effect is provided in (Park et al., 2019).

REFERENCES

Alshaer, A., Regenbrecht, H., & O'Hare, D. (2017). Immersion factors affecting perception and behaviour in a virtual reality power wheelchair simulator. *Applied Ergonomics*, *58*, 1–12. https://doi.org/10.1016/j.apergo.2016.05.003

Bell, F., Fletcher, G., Greenhill, A., Griffiths, M., & Mclean, R. (2013). Science fiction prototypes: Visionary technology narratives between futures. *Futures*, *50*, 15–24. https://doi.org/10.1016/j.futures.2013.04.004

Berkman, M. I., & Akan, E. (2019). Presence and Immersion in Virtual Reality. In N. Lee (Ed.), *Encyclopedia of Computer Graphics and Games* (pp. 1–10). Springer International Publishing. https://doi.org/10.1007/978-3-319-08234-9_162-1

Bortz, J., & Döring, N. (2016). *Forschungsmethoden und Evaluation*. Springer.

Brucker-Kley, E., & Keller, T. (2019). Exploring the Potential of Immersive Narrative Scenarios to Identify Design Criteria for our Digital Future(s). *2019 8th International Congress on Advanced Applied Informatics (IIAI-AAI)*, 499–504. https://doi.org/10.1109/IIAI-AAI.2019.00108

Brucker-Kley, E., Keller, T., & Stumpp, R. (2021). Experiencing smart farming: Effects of an interactive future scenario. *2021 IEEE International Symposium on Technology and Society (ISTAS)*, 1–7. https://doi.org/10.1109/ISTAS52410.2021.9629136

Brunner, M., Brucker-Kley, E., & Keller, T. (2020). Eliciting Personal Attitude Changes on Predictive Policing Based on a Multilinear Narrative. *ECIAR Proceedings 2020*, 21–29.

Burnam-Fink, M. (2015). Creating narrative scenarios: Science fiction prototyping at Emerge. *Futures*, *70*, 48–55. https://doi.org/10.1016/j.futures.2014.12.005

Cavazza, M., Charles, F., & Mead, S. J. (2002). Character-based interactive storytelling. *IEEE Intelligent Systems*, *17*(4), 17–24. https://doi.org/10.1109/MIS.2002.1024747

Chicchi Giglioli, I. A., Pravettoni, G., Sutil Martín, D. L., Parra, E., & Raya, M. A. (2017). A Novel Integrating Virtual Reality Approach for the Assessment of the Attachment Behavioral System. *Frontiers in Psychology*, *8*. https://www.frontiersin.org/articles/10.3389/fpsyg.2017.00959

Diemer, J., Alpers, G. W., Peperkorn, H. M., Shiban, Y., & Mühlberger, A. (2015). The impact of perception and presence on emotional reactions: A review of research in virtual reality. *Frontiers in Psychology*, *6*, 26. https://www.frontiersin.org/article/10.3389/fpsyg.2015.00026

Eagly, A. H., & Chaiken, S. (1993). *The psychology of attitudes*. Harcourt Brace Jovanovich College Publishers.

Festinger, L. (1957). *A theory of cognitive dissonance*. Stanford University Press.

Fishbein, M., & Ajzen, I. (1977). Belief, Attitude, Intention, and Behavior: An Introduction to Theory and Research. *Philosophy and Rhetoric*, *10*(2), 130–132.

Garms-Homolová, V. (2020). Beziehung zwischen Einstellungen und Verhalten. In V. Garms-Homolová (Ed.), *Sozialpsychologie der Einstellungen und Urteilsbildung: Lässt sich menschliches Verhalten vorhersagen?* (pp. 15–28). Springer. https://doi.org/10.1007/978-3-662-62434-0_2

Gordon, T. J., & Glenn, J. (2018). Interactive Scenarios. In L. Moutinho & M. Sokele (Eds.), *Innovative Research Methodologies in Management.* Springer International Publishing. https://doi.org/10.1007/978-3-319-64400-4

Jensen, L., & Konradsen, F. (2018). A review of the use of virtual reality head-mounted displays in education and training. *Education and Information Technologies*, *23*(4), 1515–1529. https://doi.org/10.1007/s10639-017-9676-0

Johnson, B. D. (2011). Science Fiction Prototyping: Designing the Future with Science Fiction. *Synthesis Lectures on Computer Science*, *3*(1), 1–190. https://doi.org/10.2200/S00336ED1V01Y201102CSL003

Karrer-Gauß, K., Glaser, C., Clemens, C., & Bruder, C. (2009). Technikaffinität erfassen – der Fragebogen TA-EG. *Der Mensch Im Mittelpunkt Technischer Systeme*, *8*, 196–201.

Keller, T., Brucker-Kley, E., Seiler, T., & Läubli, L. (2021). Eliciting personal attitude changes on friendship based on a multilinear narrative. *3rd European Conference on the Impact of Artificial Intelligence and Robotics (ECIAIR)*, 64–73. https://doi.org/10.34190/EAIR.21.014

Krokos, E., Plaisant, C., & Varshney, A. (2019). Virtual memory palaces: Immersion aids recall. *Virtual Reality*, *23*(1), 1–15. https://doi.org/10.1007/s10055-018-0346-3

Laurel, B. (2004). Narrative construction as play. *Interactions*, *11*(5), 73–74. https://doi.org/10.1145/1015530.1015568

Lemmens, J. S., Simon, M., & Sumter, S. R. (2022). Fear and loathing in VR: The emotional and physiological effects of immersive games. *Virtual Reality*, *26*(1), 223–234. https://doi.org/10.1007/s10055-021-00555-w

Lerner, J. S., Li, Y., Valdesolo, P., & Kassam, K. S. (2015). Emotion and Decision Making. *Annual Review of Psychology*, *66*(1), 799–823. https://doi.org/10.1146/annurev-psych-010213-115043

Lombard, M., Ditton, T. B., & Weinstein, L. (2009). Measuring Presence: The Temple Presence Inventory. *Proceedings of the 12th Annual International Workshop on Presence*, 1–15.

Meinert, S. (2014). Leitfaden Szenarienentwicklung. *European Trade Union Institute.*

Merrie, A., Keys, P., Metian, M., & Österblom, H. (2018). Radical ocean futures-scenario development using science fiction prototyping. *Futures*, *95*, 22–32. https://doi.org/10.1016/j.futures.2017.09.005

Mestre, R. D., Fuchs, P., Berthoz, A., & Vercher, J. L. (2006). *Immersion et présence. Le traité de la réalité virtuelle.* Ecole des Mines de Paris.

Nisi, V., & Haahr, M. (2006). Weird View: Interactive Multilinear Narratives and Real-Life Community Stories. *Crossings*, *4*(1), 1–13.

Oberle, J., Brucker-Kley, E., & Keller, T. (2021). Narrative Scenarios for a Humanistic Approach to Technology Critique—A Case Study. *Information Engineering Express*, *7*(2), 85–95.

Park, J., Choi, J., Kim, H., & Kwon, H. (2019). The influence of media type and length of time delay on user attitude: Effects of product-focused virtual reality. *Computers in Human Behavior*, *101*, 466–473. https://doi.org/10.1016/j.chb.2018.08.054

Pickens, J. (2005). Attitudes and Perceptions. *Organizational Behavior in Health Care*, *4*(7), 43–76.

Poser, H. (2016). Von der Theodizee zur Technodizee: Ein altes Problem in neuer Gestalt. In H. Poser (Ed.), *Homo Creator: Technik als philosophische Herausforderung* (pp. 357–375). Springer Fachmedien Wiesbaden.

Potstada, M., & Zybura, J. (2014). The role of context in science fiction prototyping: The digital industrial revolution. *Technological Forecasting and Social Change*, *84*, 101–114. https://doi.org/10.1016/j.techfore.2013.08.026

Rose, E. (2003). The Errors of Thamus: An Analysis of Technology Critique. *Bulletin of Science, Technology & Society*, *23*(3), 147–156. https://doi.org/10.1177/0270467603023003001

Somarathna, R., Bednarz, T., & Mohammadi, G. (2022). Virtual Reality for Emotion Elicitation – A Review. *IEEE Transactions on Affective Computing*, 1–21. https://doi.org/10.1109/TAFFC.2022.3181053

Taylor, A. E. (2011). Body and technology: Reframing the humanistic critique. *Janus Head*, *12*(1), 22–38.

Universität Zürich. (2022). *Mann-Whitney-U-Test.* Universität Zürich. http://www.methodenberatung.uzh.ch/de/datenanalyse_spss/unterschiede/zentral/mann.html

van Gisbergen, M., Kovacs, M., Campos, F., van der Heeft, M., & Vugts, V. (2019). What We Don't Know. The Effect of Realism in Virtual Reality on Experience and Behaviour. In M. C. tom Dieck & T. Jung (Eds.), *Augmented Reality and Virtual Reality: The Power of AR and VR for Business* (pp. 45–57). Springer International Publishing. https://doi.org/10.1007/978-3-030-06246-0_4

Vince, J. (2004). *Introduction to Virtual Reality.* Media, Springer. https://doi.org/10.1007/978-0-85729-386-2

Vinge, V. (1993). *The Coming Technological Singularity: How to Survive in the Post-Human Era.* 30–31.

GROUPING STUDENTS' LEARNING PATTERNS WITH MANABA'S LOG DATA BY K-MEANS

Kai Li
Dokkyo University
1-1 gukuen-cho, Soka, Japan

ABSTRACT

Assessing students' performance in online learning could be executed not only by the traditional forms of summative assessments such as using essays, assignments, and a final exam, etc. but also by more formative assessment approaches such as interaction activities, forum posts, etc. However, it is difficult for teachers to monitor and assess students' learning activities using the log data. To provide teachers with a more comprehensive view of students' distinct learning behaviour patterns, and to supply personalized interventions and support to meet the specific needs of each learning group, this study focuses on how to automatically acquire learning logs from Manaba, a Japanese commercial LMS, and how to cluster students' learning activities using the k-means algorithm. Firstly, we developed a program using Python to scrape students' learning activity log information from the Manaba web pages. We collected 56446 lines of clickstreams log data from 121 students in two computer literacy hybrid classes in the fall semester of 2022 (2022/9~2023/1). Secondly, we convert the raw logs into a structured dataset with 33 features which represent each student's learning activities. Then we extract and select 15 features representing three perspectives: raw activity, time on task, and learning frequency. Thirdly, we grouped students' learning activity patterns with the three perspectives into 5 clusters by the k-means clustering algorithm. As a result, this study identified five distinct learning activity patterns depending on how much, how long and how often the students learned online. For example, cluster 1 seldom learned but spent time on learning whom we considered the disengaged or struggling students, and cluster 5 had more learning activities with little time on each activity whom we considered the well-self-regulated students. The results of this study contribute to how to monitor students' learning activity in online learning and how to assess and support student's learning by their learning activity patterns.

KEYWORDS

Manaba, Learning Management System, Learning Analytics, Learning Activity, Clustering, K-Means

1. INTRODUCTION

Due to the COVID-19 pandemic, all teaching has moved from a face-to-face environment to a fully remote environment for educational institutions worldwide (Bradley, 2021). According to the United Nations (2020), —by mid-April 2020, 94 per cent of learners worldwide were affected by the pandemic, representing 1.58 billion children and youth, from pre-primary to higher education, in 200 countries. On 7th April 2020, the Government of Japan declared a state of emergency concerning COVID-19, education institutions were faced with decisions about how to continue teaching and learning while keeping their faculty, staff, and students safe. Most institutions have opted to cancel all face-to-face classes and have mandated that faculty move their courses online to help prevent the spread of the virus. Evidence has demonstrated that universities took to online environments in a bid to save the 2020 academic year through the use of the Internet and digital platforms (Bao, 2020; Crawford et al., 2020). Remote learning or e-learning is more important than ever due to the increased home study in many countries prompted by the COVID-19 pandemic (Paudel, 2021). Other academic studies focused on distance education activities (Aristovnik et al., 2020), teacher and student experiences (Meda & ElSayary, 2021), success, perception, and attitude regarding the online learning process (Wang et al., 2020).

Learning Management System (LMS) could be used for course management for example to publish learning content, quizzes, attendance, forums, etc. LMS could also be used for collecting learning activity data for example history of accessed pages, quiz scores, and assignment submission date (Romero et al.,

2008). Students' learning experience in an LMS allows the teacher to gather feedback from students and to monitor data such as the amount of time spent online, and which pages were accessed. The learner's learning activity data accumulated in the LMS is known as learning log data. Well-designed learning activities can be used to monitor student progress and provide data that helps teachers identify each student's strengths and weaknesses (Yassine et al., 2016). There has been increasing research that analyses learning logs to improve educational effects (Aldowah et al., 2019, Bachhal et al., 2021).

Learning analytics is a form of data analysis that allows teachers to look for students' online traces and information associated with the learning processes. The major area of applying learning analytics is the act of predicting and monitoring learning performance (Bichsel, 2012), and offers feedback to prevent poor performance and eventual failure of students (Pardo et al., 2017). Some researchers also tried to detect students' learning behaviour in LMS to create personalized learning to fit the characteristics of students in achieving better learning outcomes (Purwoningsih et al., 2019).

To understand students' online learning activities, the K-means clustering algorithm is a simple and effective way to group students with similar behaviours. Some researchers used K-means to cluster patterns of students' behaviours in an interactive online mathematics game, and the results indicated that students in four clusters, except for slow progressors, showed significant increases in their understanding of mathematical equivalence (Lee et al., 2022). Other researchers discovered groups of students enrolled in the emergency remote teaching online course based on the various course-related data collected throughout the first year of the COVID-19 pandemic using K-means and identified distinct groups of students for future adaptations of the online course design to improve the retention and their final grades (Balaban et al., 2023). In addition, some research applied K-means to explore learner profiles in terms of how they performed self-regulated learning (SRL) in Massive Open Online Courses (MOOCs). They revealed four different self-regulated learner profiles and identified cultural differences between those clusters (Tang, 2021).

Manaba is a Japanese commercial cloud-based LMS developed by AsahiNET, Inc. in 2007. It is reported that 250 educational institute users use Manaba by September 2020. Since the access and storage limitation of the former LMSs, Dokkyo University newly contracted Manaba as the main LMS after the spread of COVID-19 in May 2020. As the other LMS, Manaba could be used for course management to publish learning contents, quizzes, attendance, forums, etc., and could be used for collecting learning activity data for example history of accessed pages, quiz scores, and assignment submit date. However, Manaba could only display log data page by page, but not download it, which has no meaning for analysing students' learning activities in detail.

To provide teachers with a more comprehensive view of students' distinct learning behaviour patterns in Manaba, and to supply appropriate interventions and personalized support to meet the specific needs of each learning group, we generated the following research questions:

1. How to collect the log data from Manaba? How to automate the data collection to reduce the workload for teachers while enabling them to further teaching and learning support.
2. How to group students on their online learning activities with the raw log data? How to remote monitor students' learning activity to identify early signs of disengagement or intervene appropriately to support struggling students.

2. METHODOLOGY

2.1 Data Collection

Firstly, we developed an RPA (Robotic Process Automation) program using Python to collect the log data from Manaba. The program is developed with the Selenium library and the Chrome Driver with Python. Selenium library could be used to achieve the same movements as humans operate via a browser. Since each tag, link, and element is defined in a variety of ways on the web pages, depending on the definition of each element, we used find_element_by_id, name, tag, link, and XPath methods with the Selenium library to search and collect each log data that showed on Manaba. Since scraping information on the Internet is limited to "private use" and "information analysis" by law, source code is not opened in this study. It could be requested if needed.

With the program, it could automatically login to the Manaba, select the target course, transit to the target pages, search log data on the pages, move to the next pages and record all the log data into a CSV file. We collected 56446 lines of clickstreams log data from 121 students in two computer literacy hybrid classes in the fall semester of 2022 (2022/9~2023/1). Each data included the information of the student's name, ID, access time, URL, function category of the page, page type, and the page's title. The "Function category of the page" includes 10 functions like course top, report, contents, forum, mini-test, grades, etc. The "Type of the page" includes 17 types like course top, submit, input upload, start page, top page, etc.

In the previous research, we visualized and analysed students' clickstreams and page transit trajectories with the Retentioneering Python library. By retentionneering, we could visualize which learning pages were connected by students' transitions. And by the weight of the edges between each page, we could understand how many students transit from one learning page to the other learning pages. We also used a step matrix to show the sequential learning pages that the students accessed step by step. By the step matrix, we could know how many steps had been passed before the remote learning ended, and whether all the necessary learning pages were accessed before the learning ended. We also clustered students' learning behaviours into 6 clusters by their page transition patterns. The cluster divided students' main learning patterns into content-centred and report-centred, comment or not. However, we do not know how long the students spend on each learning page by the Retentioneering library. In this study, we will focus on the learning time on each page and cluster their learning patterns.

2.2 Data Preprocessing

Secondly, we calculated the time spent on each page and transformed the raw activity log data into a structured dataset, then we identified the important variables in three perspectives by removing the redundant ones. Finally, we clustered students' learning behaviour by the k-means cluster algorithm. The data manipulation and analysis procedures were implemented using Python and Scikit-learn.

2.2.1 Structurization and Standardization

Depending on Santos's research (2023), they extracted 30 variables from three perspectives using Moodle's log data. In this study, we transform the Manaba log data into a structured dataset with 33 variables in the raw activity, time on task, and frequency perspectives. The raw activity includes all the variables that we considered to count the number of times a certain action is performed by the student on Manaba. Time on task stores all variables associated with the amount of time spent on each activity and frequency stores all variables that, to some degree measure how often students access Manaba. By the log data of the function category of the page and the type of the page, we select 22 variables in the raw activity perspective including the click count of Total Click, CourseTop, Collection, Contents, Project, Report, Forum, MiniTest, Scores, questionnaire, List of Comments, Submit Comments, List of Thread, Top Page, Page, List of Assignments, Start Page, Submit Report, Submit Files, Submit Cancel, Attachment Files, and Input Upload. The time on task perspective got 7 variables including the stay time spent on Questionnaire, CourseTop, Contents, Report, Forum, Total Time Over1200sec, and Largest period of inactivity (Day). The frequency perspective got 4 variables including Clicks/day, Days with > 10 clicks, Days with 0 clicks, and Days with 0 clicks (% of period). The time spent on each activity over 20 minutes (1200 seconds) was excluded from the data, since an activity leaving the computer over 20 minutes may not be a learning activity, but just leaving the computer aside. The resulting transformed structured data frame had 121 rows and 33 columns, with each row representing a student and each column representing a learning activity variable.

Due to the differences in scale in each variable, we normalized all the data to standardised scores (mean =0 and standard deviation =1). It's important to scale the variables to ensure that they are on the same scale. This also helps the k-means algorithm to work effectively.

2.2.2 Variable Selection

Variable or feature selection is the process of reducing the number of input variables in machine learning. It is desirable to reduce the number of input variables to both reduce the computational cost of modelling and, in some cases, to improve the performance of the model (Kuhn, 2013). Of the 33 variables, some are relevant, and some have a low contribution to the results, we need to remove the variables with a low correlation and low explained variance.

First, to identify the relevant variables, we used the Spearman correlation index and set an absolute value threshold (0.7) as the cut-off for relevant variables, then the remaining variables could be removed. Second, to identify the low contribute variables, we apply K-Means clustering separately on each perspective to create perspective-specific clusters. And we calculate the explained variance for each perspective. The explained variance measures how much variance in the data is explained by each cluster. This can help to identify which clusters are more meaningful and distinct. For each perspective, we identified the variables associated with clusters that have the lowest explained variance. Variables that have low variance across clusters may not be informative for distinguishing between groups. Based on the results, we removed the variables associated with clusters that have the lowest explained variance. As a result, we select 15 variables for the final clustering (Table 1). Each row gives the centroid coordinate for each cluster which means the average value for a variable in the cluster.

Table 1. K-means standardized mean for all variables used in clustering

Perspective	**Variable**	**cluster 1** n=125(21%)	**cluster 2** n=3(2%)	**cluster 3** n=57(47%)	**cluster 4** n=23(19%)	**cluster 5** n=13(11%)
Raw Activity (click count)	Course Top	-0.319	0.3599	0.0617	-0.7573	1.6208
	Contents	-0.2267	0.5164	0.0931	-1.0326	1.7443
	Forum	-0.4169	-0.3893	-0.0914	0.181	0.9914
	Mini Test	-0.3399	3.9931	-0.3238	-0.2968	0.5134
	questionnaire	-0.5817	-0.229	-0.5944	-0.4574	-0.1713
	List of Comments	-0.3223	-0.2532	0.0083	-0.0372	0.7104
	Submits of Comments	-0.9585	-0.9585	-0.8604	-0.6668	-0.3564
	Page	-0.2889	0.2896	0.0793	-0.9404	1.8057
	Submit Report	-0.1646	0.3417	0.404	-1.0085	-0.0016
	Submit Cancel	-0.9281	-0.287	-0.2373	-0.6969	-0.7947
Time on task (stay time)	Questionnaire	-0.1138	-0.0538	-0.067	0.3213	-0.0105
	Contents	0.1988	0.603	-0.4729	1.1732	-0.486
	Report	1.8478	-0.5536	-0.5203	-0.3099	-0.5536
	Forum	0.0295	-0.3787	-0.0578	0.0833	0.1521
Frequency	Days with 0 clicks	0.2962	-0.4396	-0.064	0.7172	-1.4948

2.3 Clustering

The k-means clustering algorithm is a simple and the most popular data mining technique on unsupervised data sets. It aims to partition n observations into k clusters in which each observation belongs to the cluster with the nearest mean (cluster centres or cluster centroid). We used k-means to segment students into different groups based on their learning behaviours. This can help identify distinct learning patterns among different student groups for later assessing and improving students' learning performance. In the clustering process, the most important way is to identify the number of clusters (k) at the beginning. If the number of initial clusters specified is not good, then the clusters' results are not as they should be. The number of K was set to 5 with the assistance of the elbow method (Humaira and Rasyidah, 2020). In total, we have 21% of students in Cluster 1, 2% in Cluster 2, 47% in Cluster 3, 19% in Cluster 4, and 11% in Cluster 5 (Table 1).

Table 2. Means of each perspective in five clusters

Perspective	**Cluster1**	**Cluster2**	**Cluster3**	**Cluster4**	**Cluster5**
Raw Activity	-0.43173	0.416135	-0.20345	-0.50093	0.857307
Time on task	0.144908	-0.05474	-0.15855	-0.07292	-0.28239
Frequency	0.296241	-0.43956	-0.06396	0.717188	-1.49481

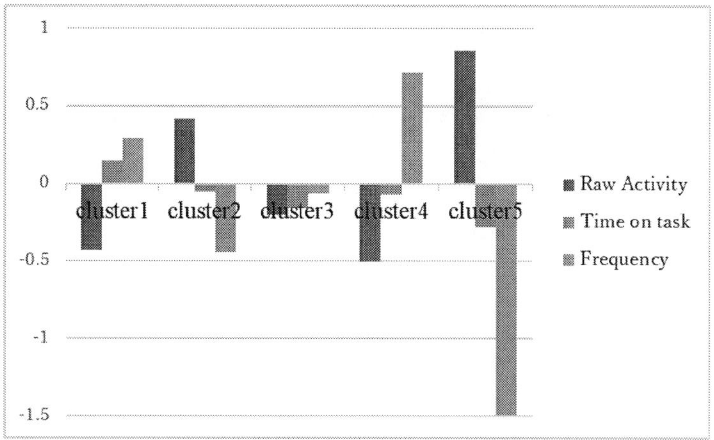

Figure 1. Perspective means in each cluster

Table 2 showcases the standardized group mean value for each of the variables used in each cluster. To better interpret our results, we described each student group according to their three distinctive perspectives to understand how students are grouped based on their activity patterns (Figure 1). Since the variable in the frequency perspectives shows the days with 0 clicks, the inverted data means the days with learning activities by which we concerned.

Depending on the characteristics of the three perspectives in each cluster, we named Cluster 1 as seldom learning but spending time on little activities group (little raw activity, more time on task, and more frequency with 0 click days). Cluster 2 was named always learning with more activities group (more raw activity, little 0 click days). Cluster 3 little activity and little time group (little raw activity and little time on task). Cluster 4 was named seldom learning and spending little time on little activities group (little raw activity, little time on task, and high frequency with 0 click days). Cluster 5 was named more learning with more activities but with little time on each activity (more raw activity, little time on task, and little frequency with 0 click days).

From a general point of view, cluster 5 is the self-regulation learners who learn much more often, and quicker with more activities. Cluster 2 is the common learners who learn with some activities. Cluster 3 is the next common learner with little activity and little time. Cluster 1 and Cluster 4 are similar, they seldom learn with little activities. Cluster 1 spent time on little activities, and Cluster 4 did not spend time on little activities. From the clusters, we found that students' remote learning behaviours were complex. Each group has different learning patterns which will lead to different assessments and support.

Table 3. Post Hoc comparisons between clusters

Perspective			t	p
Raw Activity	Cluster1	Cluster2	-3.486	0.006**
		Cluster5	-9.470	< .001***
	Cluster2	Cluster4	3.753	0.003**
	Cluster3	Cluster4	3.025	0.025*
		Cluster5	-8.670	< .001***
	Cluster4	Cluster5	-9.834	< .001***
Time on task	Cluster1	Cluster3	2.842	0.041*
		Cluster5	2.808	0.045*
Frequency	Cluster1	Cluster5	6.393	< .001***
	Cluster3	Cluster4	-3.860	0.002**
		Cluster5	5.682	< .001***
	Cluster4	Cluster5	7.781	< .001***

* p < .05, ** p < .01, *** p < .001

2.4 Comparison

To compare the differences in each perspective between clusters, we also conducted an ANOVA(Analysis of Variance) and post hoc comparisons(Table 3). For the raw activity perspective, cluster 5 >2 > 3 > 1> 4. For the spending time on each task, cluster 1 > 2 > 4 > 3 >5, and for the learning frequency (the frequency with 0 click days is inverted) 5 > 2 > 3 >1 > 4. Cluster 5 has more learning activities than the other clusters. Cluster 1 spent more time on learning tasks, and Cluster 5 learned frequently. The significant differences between each cluster can be confirmed in Table 3.

3. DISCUSSION

This study grouped students' learning activity patterns with the three perspectives into 5 clusters by the k-means clustering algorithm. We found that cluster 5 who are self-regulation learners learnt much more often, and quicker with more activities. The raw activity perspective is more than other clusters. They have more access to learning content, pages, tests etc. and have more interaction on the forum and submitting comments (Table 1). However, students of cluster 5 spent little time on learning content and they learnt more often than other clusters. By which we could assume that learning content is easy for them, the content is not enough, and other further reading materials should be supplied to these students. Another finding is cluster 1 and cluster 4 have few learning activities and seldom learn. Cluster 1 spent time on learning which we could assume that the learning content is difficult for them. They need personalized learning support. Cluster 4 spent little time and seldom learned who may drop out from learning. Teachers need to intervene to improve their learning engagement. In addition, cluster 1 (21%) and cluster 4 (19%) are made up of 40% of the students which shows the students have some struggles in online learning. Especially during the COVID-19 emergency, most of the students have mental issues and have little chance to communicate with others, therefore teachers should supply more feedback and support to sustain their online learning. We also found all the students seldom submit comments. Although the students of cluster 5 have more access to the list of comments, they just like to confirm others' comments but not submit comments. To support communication between students and teachers in online learning, teachers should supply timely personalized feedback in different ways. Overall, from the different learning activity patterns, teachers should assess students' performance not only by summative assessments such as using essays, assignments, and a final exam but also by more formative assessment approaches such as interaction activities, forum posts, etc. through their learning process.

4. CONCLUSION

The purpose of this study is to monitor students' remote learning process and assess their learning performance by their learning activity patterns with the learning log in Manaba. We developed a program which could automatically acquire learning logs from Manaba, and we clustered students' learning activities into five groups using the k-means algorithm. By clustering students' learning patterns, teachers could assess students' performance and optimize their teaching pedagogies. This study is based on Manaba's log, it could be adapted and replicated in other LMSs. By analysing students' learning activity patterns, educators and instructional designers can make data-driven decisions to enhance the design and delivery of online courses. This study contributes to improvements in content organization, interactivity, and engagement strategies. Also monitoring students' learning activities could help educators identify early signs of disengagement or challenges and intervene proactively to support struggling students. However, this study has some limitations. First, the automation program we developed with the Selenium library was slow. The execution time usually took 30 minutes to get 60 students' log data page by page from one course. The program needs to be improved with other faster libraries in the future. Second, the sample size is small which includes just 121 students in two classes, and the log data is only for one year's learning activities which need long-term research to get more learning activities. Third, we do not know the relationship between learning patterns and learning outcome performance. Further research should be analysed to predict students' learning performances and detection of undesirable learning behaviours with the log data. For example, using labelled data with outcomes (e.g., student performance, and course completion) to build predictive models by machine learning algorithms to predict students' performances based on their learning patterns. Furthermore, how to intervene or support each group is not discussed in the study. Since LMS's functions are different and pedagogy is different, intervention methods should be considered in different environments.

ACKNOWLEDGEMENT

This work was supported by JSPS KAKENHI Grant Number 21K00655.

REFERENCES

Aldowah, H. et al, 2019. Educational data mining and learning analytics for 21st century higher education: A review and synthesis. *Telematics and Informatics*, 37, pp. 13–49

Aristovnik, A. et al, 2020. A bibliometric analysis of Covid-19 across science and social science research landscape. *Sustainability*, 12(21), 9132. https://doi.org/10.3390/su12219132

Bachhal, P. et al, 2021. Educational data mining: A review. *Journal of Physics: Conference Series*, 1950(1)

Balaban, I. et al, 2023. Post hoc identification of student groups: Combining user modeling with cluster analysis. *Educ Inf Technol* 28, pp. 7265–7290. https://doi.org/10.1007/s10639-022-11468-9

Bao, W. (2020). COVID-19 and online teaching in higher education: A case study of Peking University. *Human Behavior and Emerging Technologies, 2*(2), pp. 113-115. https://doi.org/10.1002/hbe2.191

Bichsel, J. 2012. Analytics in Higher Education: Benefits, Barriers, Progress, and Recommendations (Research Report). *Louisville, CO Educ. Cent. Appl. Res*

Bradley, V. M. 2021. Learning management system (LMS) use with online instruction. *International Journal of Technology in Education*, 4(1), pp. 68–92

ChromeDriver, Retrieved from https://sites.google.com/chromium.org/driver/, last accessed 12/8/2023

Crawford, J. et al, 2020. COVID-19: 20 countries' higher education intra-period digital pedagogy responses. *Journal of Applied Learning & Teaching, 3*(1), pp. 1-20. https://doi.org/10.37074/jalt.2020.3.1.7

Humaira, H., & Rasyidah, R., 2018. Determining the appropriate cluster number using Elbow method for K-Means algorithm. *Proceedings of the 2nd Workshop on Multidisciplinary and Applications (WMA)* 2018, pp. 24-25

Kuhn, M., & Johnson, K., 2013. *Applied predictive modeling* (Vol. 26, p. 13). New York: Springer.

Lee, J. E. et al, 2022. Does slow and steady win the race?: Clustering patterns of students' behaviors in an interactive online mathematics game. *Educational technology research and development*, 70(5), pp. 1575-1599.

Manaba, Retrieved from https://ja.wikipedia.org/wiki/Manaba, last accessed 12/8/2023

Meda, L., & ElSayary, A., 2021. Establishing Social, Cognitive and Teacher Presences during Emergency Remote Teaching: Reflections of Certified Online Instructors in the United Arab Emirates. *Contemporary Educational Technology*, 13(4).

Pardo, A. et al, 2017. Provision of Data-Driven Student Feedback in LA & EDM, *Handbook of Learning Analytics*, pp. 163–174

Paudel, P., 2021. Online education: Benefits, challenges, and strategies during and after COVID-19 in higher education. I*nternational Journal on Studies in Education*, 3(2), pp. 70–85

Purwoningsih, T. et al, 2019. Online Learners' Behaviors Detection Using Exploratory Data Analysis and Machine Learning Approach, *Proceedings of 2019 Fourth International Conference on Informatics and Computing (ICIC)*, pp. 1-8

Retentioneering Library, Retrieved from https://github.com/retentioneering/retentioneering-tools, last accessed 12/8/2023

Romero, C. et al, 2008. Data mining in course management systems: Moodle case study and tutorial. *Computers & Education*, 51(1), pp. 368–384

Santos, R., & Henriques, R., 2023. Grouping Bachelor's Students According To Their Moodle Interaction Profiles: A K-Means Clustering Approach. In L. Gómez Chova, C. González Martínez, & J. Lees (Eds.), 15th *International Conference on Education and New Learning Technologies,* pp. 7383-7389

Selenium Library, Retrieved from https://pypi.org/project/selenium/, last accessed 12/8/2023

Tang, H., 2021.Person-centred analysis of self-regulated learner profiles in MOOCs: a cultural perspective. *Education Tech Research Dev* 69, pp. 1247–1269. https://doi.org/10.1007/s11423-021-09939-w

United Nations, 2020. *Policy brief: Education during COVID-19 and beyond.* Retrieved from https://www.un.org/development/desa/dspd/wp-content/uploads/sites/22/20 Post hoc identification of student groups: Combining user modelling with cluster analysis 20/08/sg_policy_brief_covid-19_and_education_august_2020.pdf, last accessed 21/9/2023

Wang, C et al, 2020. Association between medical students' prior experiences and perceptions of formal online education developed in response to COVID-19: A cross-sectional study in China. *BMJ open*, 10(10), e041886.

Yassine, S. et al, 2016. A framework for learning analytics in Moodle for assessing course outcomes. *Proceedings IEEE Global Engineering Education Conference (educon)*, pp. 261-266.

EDUCATION TO PREVENT HUMAN MECHANISATION IN A FACULTY OF INFORMATICS: DEVELOPING LEARNING MATERIALS TO IMPROVE STUDENTS' VERBAL COMMUNICATION SKILLS

Mari Ueda[1], Isoharu Nishiguchi[1], Hiroshi Tanaka[2], Kazunori Matsumoto[2] and Tetsuo Tanaka[2]
[1]*Dept. of Information Media, Faculty of Information Technology, Kanagawa Institute of Technology*
[2]*Dept. of Information and Computer Sciences, Faculty of Information Technology, Kanagawa Institute of Technology*
1030 Shimo-ogino, Atsugi, Kanagawa, 243-0292, Japan

ABSTRACT

Although information technology (ICT) education is being strengthened based on the national context, there are reports suggesting a decline in young people's communication skills. This phenomenon can be attributed to the rapid development of informatisation, which includes the diversification and spread of information tools, as well as the prevalence of nonverbal communication, such as pictograms in social networking services. In addition, the COVID-19 pandemic has drastically reduced face-to-face communication opportunities, making interactive communication in on-demand classes challenging. Even in assignments and short tests completed during class, many instances of content being copied and pasted from the web or written in a disorganized manner have been observed. For instance, students entering ICT-related careers, particularly those graduating from the faculty of informatics, must possess the ability to communicate with engineers and clients while implementing ICT advance-ments. Alongside programming skills, strong communication abilities are essential. Moreover, the emergence of generative artificial intelligence (AI) tools, such as ChatGPT and Bing AI, has considerably diminished the opportunities for independent thinking. In the current era of enhanced ICT education, AI, and IoT, the Faculty of Informatics at the Kanagawa Institute of Technology has been engaged in discussions regard-ing learning materials that aim to strengthen students' ability to think and communicate in their own words, preventing the mechanisation of individuals. This paper presents the development and implementation of learning materials designed to enhance students' verbal communication skills through the description and re-production of mathematical graphs.

KEYWORDS

Information Education, Verbal Communication, Expressive Language Skills, University Students, Development of Teaching Materials

1. INTRODUCTION

Although information technology (ICT) education is being strengthened based on the national context[Strategic Headquarters 2017], there are reports suggesting a decline in young people's communication skills[Furlong 2006; Jenkins 2009]. This phenomenon can be attributed to the rapid development of informatisation, which includes the diversification and spread of information tools, as well as the prevalence of nonverbal communication, such as pictograms in social networking services. In addition, the COVID-19 pandemic has drastically reduced face-to-face communication opportunities, making inter-active communication in on-demand classes challenging. Even in assignments and short tests completed during class, many instances of content being copied and pasted from the web or written in a disorganized manner have been observed. For instance, students entering ICT-related careers, particularly those graduating from the faculty of informatics, must possess the ability to communicate with engineers and clients while implementing ICT advancements. Alongside programming skills, strong communication abilities are essential. Moreover, the emergence of generative artificial intelligence (AI) tools, such as ChatGPT[Lund 2023] and Bing AI, has considerably diminished the opportunities for independent thinking.

In the current era of enhanced ICT education, AI, and IoT, the Faculty of Informatics at the Kanagawa Institute of Technology has been engaged in discussions regarding learning materials that aim to strengthen students' ability to think and communicate in their own words, preventing the mechanisation of individuals. This paper presents the development and implementation of learning materials designed to enhance students' verbal communication skills through the description and reproduction of mathematical graphs.

2. VERBALISATION OF FUNCTION GRAPHS

In order to address concerns about the mechanization of individuals within the Faculty of Informatics, educational materials have been developed to improve students' verbal communication skills. One approach involved presenting function graphs to students and tasking them with describing the graph's shape using only words, without relying on mathematical formulas.

2.1 Verbalisation of Function Graphs

To facilitate the process, we created an Excel macro to generate graphs for seven types of functions: trigonometric (e.g., sine), exponential, logarithmic, polynomial (e.g., quadratic and cubic), irrational, and hyperbolic. A total of 100 function graphs were generated, randomly select-ed, and uploaded to the web. Students were then in-structed to write sentences that accurately conveyed the graphs, allowing others to reproduce them. This study included approximately 120 undergraduate students from the second to fourth years of an informatics, as well as 20 graduate students pursing a master's degree.

2.2 Examples of Results

An exponential function (Equation (1)) is depicted in the graph, along with excerpts from the descriptions (excerpts) provided by the students.

-Exponential function

$y = a\exp(bx + c) + d$ .... (1)

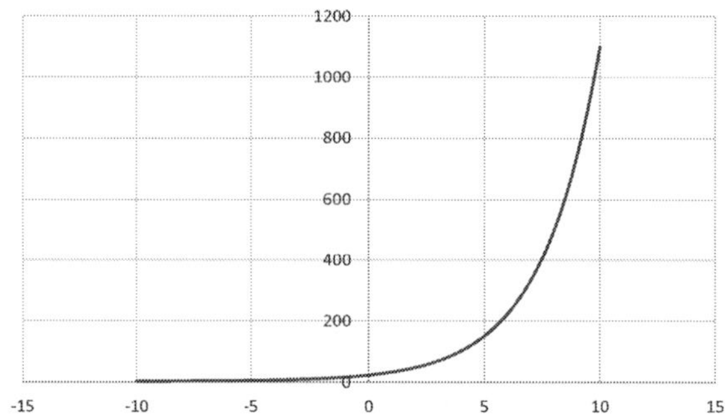

Figure 1. Example of a graph used to describe functions verbally

- Sample answer A: This graph consists of a single line that originates from the bottom left, extends almost straight across, and then sharply bends toward the top right.
- Sample answer B: The graph spans from −15 to 15 on the x axis and from 0 to 1200 on the y axis. From −10 to 0, the line remains almost straight along the x-axis direction and gradually moves upward on the y-axis. When x = 0, it curves up-ward until x = 5, aiming for an approximate y-axis value of 180. From there, it forms a curve directed towards (10, 1100).
- Sample answer C: The graph resembles the ascending part of a roller coaster ride. It is defined within a horizontal range of −15 to 15 and a vertical range of 0 to 1200. It starts at a horizontal value of −10 and a vertical value of 0. The gradient gradually increases to approximately −2.5 horizon-tally and passes

through the points (0,20). Then, the gradually becomes steeper, aligning with the point (5, 750). Next, at a vertical value of 400, the horizontal value is set to 7, and at 600, the graph passes through 8 horizontally. It continues with a horizontal value of 9 at a vertical value of 800, and at 1000, the horizontal value is 9.9. The graph concludes at a vertical value of 1100 and a horizontal value of 10.

- Sample answer D: The graph represents the exponential function, exp(x). It exhibits several characteristics. Firstly, for any x, its value is greater than 0, indicating that the graph lies above the x-axis. Secondly, as the x-axis value increases, the y-axis value also increases. Lastly, the y-axis value rises more rapidly as the x-axis value progresses towards the right. These three characteristics result in an initial depiction of a straight line, where the x-axis value re-mains relatively unchanged from −20 to 0. However, the x-axis value increases and approaches a positive value, the graph ascends rapidly towards the right.

2.3 Examples of Graphical Results from Descriptions

Examples of graphing results generated by four participants following the verbal descriptions provided by another participant as discussed in Section 2.2, are showcased. It is noteworthy that some of the sentences in the description could not be reproduced as graphs at all.

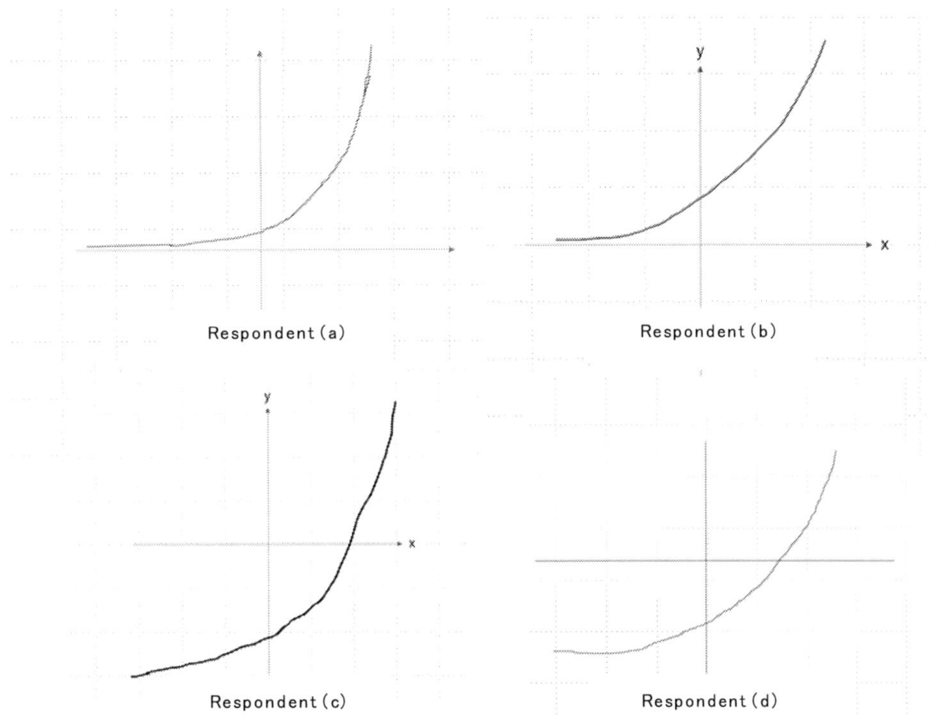

Figure 2. Example of a graph generated from a description

2.4 Analysis

The percentage of students who were able to provide accurate descriptions of a given graph was less than 10% in all sessions. Only approximately 20% of the sentences effectively conveyed the features of the graph. Our findings from multiple attempts to verify function graph descriptions, along with the challenges of verbalisation, are as follows.

In terms of mathematical thinking skills, students generally demonstrated an understanding of the formulas and functions represented in the graphs.

Comprehension served as a means to assess whether students accurately understood the task.

Explanatory ability was used to evaluate students' capability to describe the graphs to others.

We also gauged the students' attitudes towards the task. Additionally, since there were no reference materials available on the web, the students had to rely on their own thinking.

In online classes, although concerns about instances of students copying others' answers have been raised, the nature of the verbalisation task with multiple answers, serves as a preventive measure against cheating and other dishonest behaviors.

The students received feedback from others regarding the level of difficulty and significance of communication skills, as well as the proficiency and adequacy of their own communication skills.

Challenges in the development of such teaching materials included the difficulty of drawing and evaluating graphs. In the subsequent sections, we provide a detailed description of the task assessment and propose an implementation scheme for creating graphs from descriptions as part of teaching materials.

3. ASSESSMENT OF COMMUNICATION SKILLS

Communication skills encompass the abilities to communicate (explain) and read (comprehend) information. Textual explanations of graphs were used to evaluate these skills. In addition, peer evaluation (mutual evaluation) was used for efficient assessment.

The participants were divided into groups of approximately five (n), and the illustrated procedure was employed to assess their expository and reading comprehension skills.

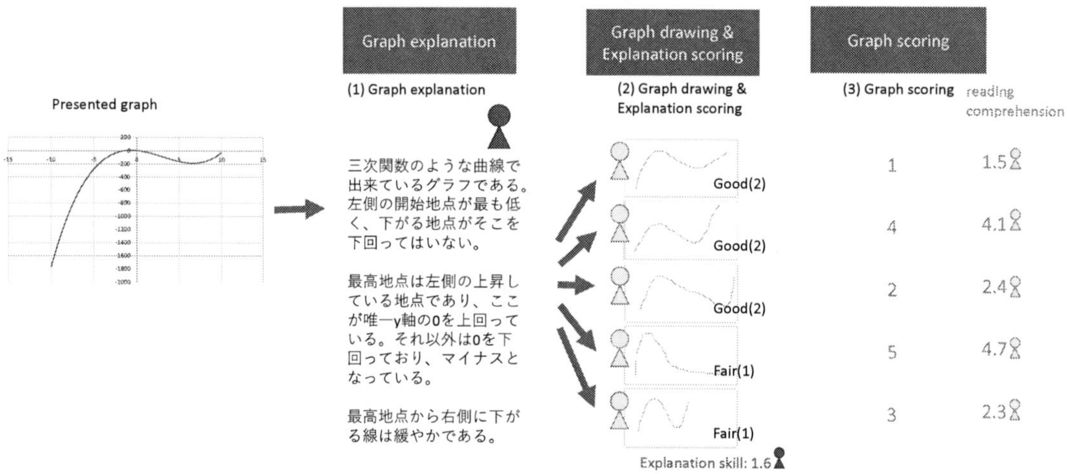

Figure 3. Example of the results obtained from the text-to-graph communication evaluation

Step 1: The participants per group described different graph descriptions.

Step 2: Based on the descriptions provided by the other group members (n − 1), each participant drew a graph and evaluated the understandability of the descriptions. The evaluation involved assigning a score of 2 for good understanding, 1 for poor understanding, or 0 for no understanding. The average score across the (n-1) persons was considered the score for explanatory power.

Step 3: The accuracy of the (n − 1) graph descriptions were ranked by all the participants, resulting in rankings for each case. The average ranking was used to determine the reading comprehension rank. Because an accurate graph could not be drawn if the explanation was difficult to understand, the reading comprehension was adjusted by assigning weights ac-cording to the explanatory power.

Step 4: By drawing graphs based on various explanations provided by others in step 2, participants were able to discern the differences comprehensive and unintelligible explanations. They also learned which features should be communicated and how to effectively convey them.

Step 5: Referring to the graph drawn based on the description provided in step 3, each participant assessed what was conveyed or omitted in their description. They also identified incorrect or lacking parts in the descriptions.

Step 6: In addition to the procedure of providing a graph, verbalising it, drawing it, and evaluating it, a re-verse procedure of providing an explanation of the graph, drawing it, verbalising it, and then evaluating it facilitated more precise evaluations of communication skills.

4. DEVELOPMENT OF EVALUATION APPLICATION

4.1 Functions

We developed an application to streamline the assessment of communication skills. The application consists of three screens, which aligns with the steps outlined in Section 3.

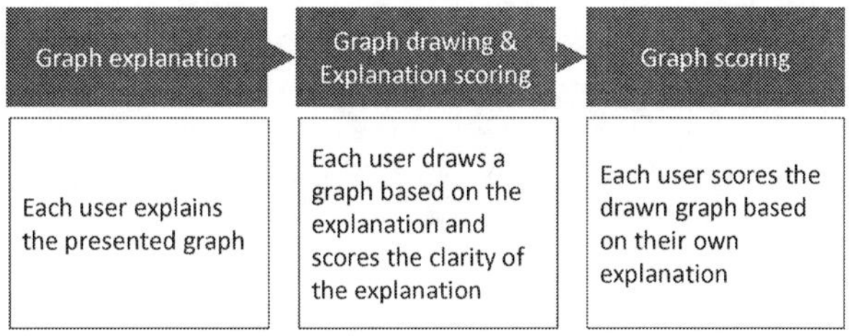

Figure 4. Functions of the application for assessing communication skills

Graph description. The application displays a graph and allows the user to provide and record a description in the text.

Graph drawing and description scoring. The application displays a description of the graph. The user manually draws the graph based on the description and simultaneously selects one of the three levels of description clarity. The chosen level is then recorded.

Graph scoring. The application displays the graphs drawn by (n-1) users. The evaluates the accuracy of these graphs, ranks them, and records the assessments.

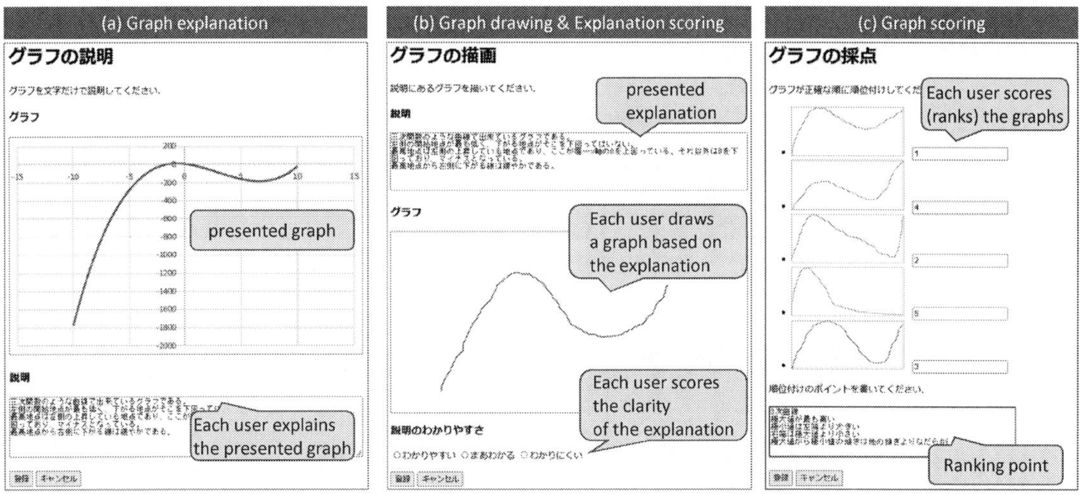

Figure 5. Examples of graph screens including (a) explanation, (b) drawing, and (c) scoring

4.2 Application Implementation

The application was implemented for the web and is compatible with computers, tablets, and smartphones (Android and iOS). Firebase[Moroney 2017], a cloud service provided by Google, was used to handle authentication, database management, and web hosting on the server side. On the client side, HTML, JavaScript, and CSS were employed, similar to standard web applications. The drawing functionality was implemented using Fabric.js, which is a JavaScript HTML5 canvas library. User-owned computers, tablets, and smartphones served as the client terminals.

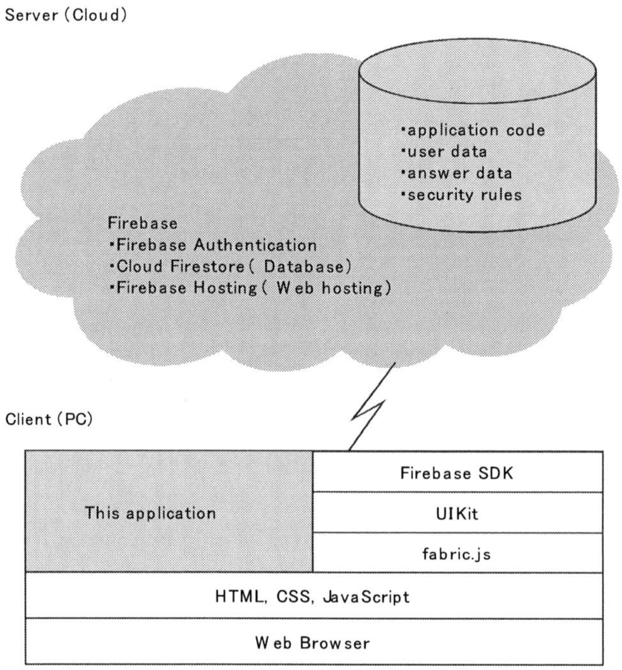

Figure 6. System configuration of the application

5. CONCLUSION

In the context of enhanced IT education, generative AI, and AI/Internet-of-Things applications, the Faculty of Informatics at the Kanagawa Institute of Technology recognizes the importance of strengthening students' ability to think and communicate using their own language, thereby preventing the mechanization of individuals. As part of our efforts to enhance the verbal communication skills of students in the Faculty of Informatics, we developed teaching materials for the verbalisation of mathematical concepts represented as graphs, examined their educational impact, and presented future directions for their development. Through these materials, we gained insights into measuring students' mathematical, comprehension, and explanatory abilities. Verbalising mathematical graphs can pose a challenge for students, as they cannot simply rely on web resources to obtain the correct answer and must engage in reasoning. The results of this study can contribute to improving grade point averages and admission processes. In addition, we plan to explore the relationship between the obtained results and evaluations, such as grades and placement tests during the admission process, to objectively evaluate students' abilities. Moreover, we have plans to develop applications that can serve as teaching materials. We also aim to create resources in the form of audiobooks that can automatically describe graphs to cater to visually impaired students.

ACKNOWLEDGEMENT

This work was supported by JSPS KAKENHI Grant Number JP23K02747.

REFERENCES

Furlong, A. et al, 2006. *Young People And Social Change*, McGraw-Hill Education, London, UK.

Jenkins, H., 2009. *Confronting the Challenges of Participatory Culture*, The MIT Press, Cambridge, USA.

Lund, B. 2023. Chatting about ChatGPT: how may AI and GPT impact academia and libraries?, *Library Hi Tech News*, Vol. 40 No. 3, pp. 26-29.

Moroney, L. 2017. *The Definitive Guide to Firebase*, Apress Berkeley, USA.

Strategic Headquarters for the Promotion of an Advanced Information and Telecommunications Network Society, Japan, 2017. *Declaration to Be the World's Most Advanced IT Nation Basic Plan for the Advancement of Public and Private Sector Data Utilization*, https://cio.go.jp/sites/default/files/uploads/documents/20170530_full.pdf.

TEACHING REFLECTIVE USE OF TECHNOLOGY: A PILOTED WORKBOOK BASED ON EVACUATIONS

André Greubel*, Julia Wenkmann, Hans-Stefan Siller and Martin Hennecke
University of Wuerzburg
Emil-Fischer-Straße 30, 97074 Würzburg, Germany

ABSTRACT

Applying computing technology during problem solving and the reflection of the appropriateness of this application are crucial skills for modern life. This is especially true while working on interdisciplinary STEM problems. However, up to now, few ready-to-use materials are available to foster such competencies. This paper starts bridging this gap by presenting a workbook for students in higher secondary education (around age 15). The workbook focuses on a complex STEM problem, primarily rooted in mathematics, computing, and technology education: Estimating the time it takes to evacuate a building. In the workbook, students work through five exercises focused on the problem of trying to make a sports hall safer. For three potential changes to the building, they should evaluate whether it increases the safety of the sports hall and whether the measure can reasonably be evaluated with a given simulation. During their work, students become aware of arguments useful for such an critical evaluation. For example, a change can only be evaluated if its magnitude is greater than variation in the (randomized) fleeing algorithm of the software. After development of the workbook, we used a design-based research approach to improve its quality. To do so, we asked eight educators for feedback and piloted it with 20 students from two mathematics classes of different capabilities. The results show that students had fun while working on the exercises and both the students and their tutors evaluated the workbook to be educationally relevant. Several issues, most importantly regarding the wording of several exercises, were identified and improved. Multiple exercises were further sub-divided to better suit learners of the age targeted.

KEYWORDS

Digital Simulations, Building Evacuations, Critical Reflection, Problem-Solving

1. INTRODUCTION

Applying computing technology during problem solving and the reflection of the appropriateness of this application are crucial skills for modern life (Jang 2016). This is especially true while learning to work on complex and authentic STEM problems: real-life problems used as learning experience for multiple skills that are only little simplified for education (c.f. Section 2). In such problems, application of technology (the T in STEM) is important: "Usually, to get a solution, computer programmes (Excel or more sophisticated ones) must be applied" (Kaiser *et al.* 2013). However, while several approaches for teaching with authentic and complex problems are published (c.f., Kaiser *et al.* 2013), none of the approaches in this list explicitly focus on the use and reflection of such "sophisticated" computing technologies. This is unfortunate as teaching the (reflective) use of technology is a key goal of education (c.f. Section 2). Moreover, designing suitable scenarios for such a use-case also is not easy: "[d]esigning authentic learning scenarios is therefore one of the key challenges in education interventions that aim for STEM literacy" (Ciolan & Ciolan 2014).

Thus, the central goal of this paper is to present a workbook that starts bridging the gap. It uses evacuations as a STEM context to introduce the students to key concepts of computing and STEM problem solving:

- Applying technology based on a computing concept (a grid automaton) to the solving process of a complex and authentic STEM problem.
- Reflecting the appropriateness of a software solution based on this concept in (steps in) the problem solving process.

* Corresponding author: andre.greubel@uni-wuerzburg.de

The workbook itself is designed for an educational setting in which students work on a single leading question for an extended period of time. Examples of such settings include mathematical modeling weeks (c.f., Kaiser & Schwarz 2010) or teaching-learning labs at university (c.f., Klock & Siller 2021). It is designed to last around 6 hours of working time and consists of five key exercises with many sub-exercises. It is based on the following problem: "The director of a school wants to increase the safety of the schools' sports hall. To do so, several different options with certain, individual price tags are available. Decide which one should be implemented given a certain (limited) budget". In the workbook, students are asked to simulate changes in the duration of an evacuation after certain changes to the sports hall (e.g., removing or relocating lockers, or adding further doors). Additionally, they are asked whether the simulation environment provided to them is suitable to evaluate the impact of the change.

To assess and improve the quality of the workbook, we employed a design-based research approach: First, we asked eight mathematics educators to comment on any aspect of the workbook they consider needs improvement and used that feedback to improve the workbook. Second, we then revised the workbook based on their feedback. Third, we asked students of two mathematics classes (totaling 20 students around age 15) of different capabilities to come to our university and work through the workbook. During this work, they should fill out a questionnaire regarding their disposition towards the exercises and their learning process, i.e., things they found hard or useful. Additionally, these students were supervised by tutors which also commented on any problems of the students or within the exercises. Fourth, after each of the class finished working through the workbook, the feedback gained was used to improve the exercises. Additionally, the results of the questionnaire showed that students had fun while working on the exercises and both the students and their tutors evaluated the workbook to be educationally relevant.

2. BACKGROUND ON COMPLEX AND AUTHENTIC PROBLEMS

Complex and authentic problems are considered to be of high importance for STEM education: Complex and Authentic problems "shall articulate the relevance of mathematics in daily life, environment and sciences and impart competencies to apply mathematics in daily life, environment and sciences" (Kaiser *et al.* 2013). For the purposes of this paper, problems are characterized as *complex*, if they are real-world problems that are "only little simplified" (Kaiser *et al.* 2013), and if they require consistent work over a longer period of time – at least multiple hours. A more detailed discussion of properties that make problems complex is provided in (Dörner & Funke 2017). Furthermore, we characterize problems as *authentic*, if there is an "alignment of student learning experiences with the world for which they are being prepared" (McKenzie *et al.*). An overview over eight established definition of what makes problems authentic; the definition used in this paper focuses on the relevance of learning activities for later life is provided in (Anker-Hansen & Andreé 2019). With complex and authentic problems, learners can "practice the skills and knowledge that are relevant and real to workplace situations and learn it at the same time" (Har 2013).

Working on complex and authentic STEM problems frequently requires technology: "Both the design of and interpretation of experimental practices in modern science are often based on the use of computational modelling" (Gilbert 2004). This technology frequently plays two crucial but different roles: As a utility (information technology aspect) and as central approach embedded in the model (computing technology aspect). First, technology can be utilized to work better on a given problem (e.g., more efficient, collaborative, semi-automated, ...). While technology in this way, users focus on the correct *application* of the underlying technology. Second, computational concepts can be used to *create* or *comprehend* models via computational thinking, one definition of which is "the thought processes involved in formulating problems and their solutions so that the solutions are represented in a form that can be effectively carried out by an information-processing agent." (Wing 2011). Notably, both these roles of technology are dependent on each other (see Brinda *et al.* 2008). This is especially true if the person using the program is not the same person that created it and has to treat the program as a black-box – leading to additional requirements for the comprehension of existing models and the evaluation of them (Greubel & Siller 2022). In this regard, "computational thinking complements critical thinking as a way of reasoning" (Kules 2016). Notably, corresponding activities are already included in some curriculums. For example, in the United Kingdom, students should "apply information technology, including new or unfamiliar technologies, analytically to solve problems" (Department of Education 2023).

3. THE WORKBOOK

Based on prior research, we have chosen building evacuation as context for our course. This context allows for interesting, real-world problems-solving, and meaningful inclusion of computing technology – while not being too reliant on sophisticated inner-mathematical methods or domain knowledge (Ruzika, Siller & Bracke 2017; Greubel *et al.* 2022; Andersen *et al.* 2023). To simulate building evacuations, grid automatons with agents are frequently used (Li *et al.* 2019) These consist of cells with neighbors that change state according to specified rules (the programming of the automaton). For evacuation simulations, each cells can be either *empty*, *full*, *blocked*, or *safe*. While full cells contain (exactly one) agent, empty cells do not. Blocked cells neither do nor can contain an agent. They represent walls in the building. Finally, safe cells remove each agent moving on it from the simulation. They represent the destinations in a scenario. During each *Simulation Step*, each agent can move to a neighboring cell – either in four (*neumann neighborhood*) or in eight directions (*moore neighborhood*). The *Fleeing algorithm* describes whether or how the agents move. A simple fleeing algorithm might instruct each agent to move to the cell next on the shortest path of unblocked cells to the nearest safe cell, if this cell is empty.

3.1 Educational Goals and Requirements

The workbook has the central goal of teaching students the application and reflection of technology while working on a complex and authentic STEM problem. It does so by delivering practical experience working with a comprehensive simulation on a complex and authentic problem: Estimating the duration of evacuation of a building. The workbook is available both in English and German, and can be downloaded and used for free at https://evadid.it/workbook/CELDA-Workbook-En.pdf. It consists of five exercisers, each consisting of multiple sub-exercises and explanatory text and is designed for project-like learning in higher secondary education (around student age 15) in a STEM setting focusing on computing, technology, and mathematics. It takes students around 6 full hours (not including breaks).

Beforehand, students only need to be familiar with linear equations (create linear equations based on a real-world problem, solve them for a given variable, interpret it as linear function of one unknown). They can work alone or in groups of up to three. Each group needs access to a computer with a browser and a screen with a minimal resolution of 1024x768px. For working, each student should be handed out one (printed) workbook. A digital version is currently in production.

The workbook is designed to be solved without additional material: all necessary instructions, explanatory texts, links ... are included in the workbook. However, ideally, each group is additionally supervised by a tutor answering questions regarding the exercises and providing alternative explanations for unfamiliar formats (especially exercises regarding mathematical argumentation) to students. In our pilot, we tested the workbook in a video-conference setting with one tutor per group and in an analog setting with one tutor per two to three groups. In the opinion of the main author (present in both classes), both settings provided sufficient supervision to ensure a high and productive time on task.

3.2 Exercises in the Workbook

The first exercise, consisting of five sub-exercises, is used to motivate the topic. It first presents (fictional) news articles regarding evacuations, working with assumptions, and mathematical modelling. All of these models highlight the importance of a certain step in mathematical modeling cycle (Greefrath, Siller & Weitendorf 2011). For example, one article (highlighting making realistic assumptions) reads: "40 km/h are not walking speed, license revoked. (Anna Turney): Last night, a 4B8r3B4p7yhRXuBWLqsQ546WR43cqQwrbXMDFnBi6vSJBeif8tPW85a7r7DM961Jvk4hdryZoByEp8GC 8HzsqJpRN4FxGM9 arguing that he followed the rules and did not drive faster than walking speed: After all, Usain Bolt can move with up to 45 km/h. This did not impress the judge: She argued that assuming such a walking speed is unreasonable. The jury agreed: At the end of the trial, the man lost his driving license.". Moreover, students should think about the topics ahead. Another question reads: "Look at this image of a building: [...] Encircle three aspects of the following list you assume have the biggest impact on the evacuation duration: 1) average walking speed, 2) speed of the slowest walker, [...] 5) width of the central hallway, [...]".

The second exercise, consisting of four sub-exercises, is used to introduce to working with the digital learning environment to the students. This explicit introduction is necessary, as finding out the functionality of a digital simulation can be hard. In the exercise, they explore the functionality of the simulation environment by creating, loading, storing and executing sample scenarios. Furthermore, they should interpret the results of the simulation environment as real-world results. This is done by identifying the correspondence between the output of the simulation (the duration in simulation steps) and the real world: Every cell in the grid has a fixed length. With knowledge of that length and an assumption about a walking speed, a linear equation (or the rule of three) can be used to calculate a real-world estimate duration of the simulation.

The third exercise, consisting of eight sub-exercises, is used to reflect on the role of assumptions during modeling. The students should analyze how the simulation duration changes if different walking speeds are assumed. Additionally, they should argue whether simulation results (both for building evacuations and other domains) are useful even if they are not perfectly accurate. One task reads: "Denote at least two situations, in which simulation results are only useful if they are perfectly accurate". Another one: "Argue, whether simulation results of a building evacuation are useful, even if they are not perfectly accurate. Use at least two different lines of argumentation."

At this point, the workbook explicitly introduces the big problem the whole workbook is leading towards: "A director of a school wants to reduce the time it takes to evacuate the sports hall pictured below. There are a range of different options (with different price tags) and a fixed budget. What options should be decided upon?"

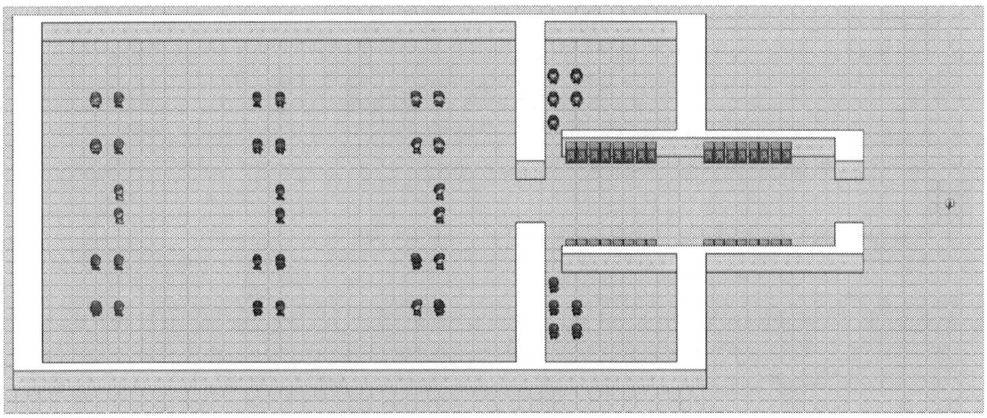

Figure 1. The Sports Hall from the Exercise

In the fourth exercise, consisting of ten sub-exercises, students are worked through the process of testing hypothesis. This is done by evaluating one of the available options step-by-step: moving to sets of lockers from the hallway of the sports hall into the changing rooms. In the sub-exercises, they pose the hypothesis ("Argue, which two sets of lockers should be moved and argue why you opted for those specific two.") and verify them afterwards (by executing multiple, similar scenarios, e.g., without the lockers). During this work, they become aware of the randomized nature of the fleeing algorithm implemented in the simulation environment. This is used to reflect on whether aspects can or cannot be evaluated using such an environment: For example, to be evaluable, the effect to be analyzed has to be stronger than random variation. Thus, the students can use this simulation program to generate evidence for the hypothesis "Moving the top two sets of lockers reduces the evacuation time of a full sports hall by approx. 15%" but not for the hypothesis "Moving the left two sets of lockers reduces the evacuation time of a full sports hall by approximately 1%".

The fifth and last exercise, consisting of five sub-exercises, returns to the big problem introduced in the prior exercise: The complete list of eight possible options (with corresponding price tags) is introduced. Possible options include the moving of objects to any new location, the widening of hallways or doors, introducing additional doors and assembly points, reducing the maximum amount of persons allowed in the sports hall, and training the persons in the sports hall to walk faster. In the sub-exercises, the students should formulate a set of concrete measures (e.g., "a one meter wide door should be added at the left of the sports hall") they consider to be most effective and evaluate their impact. Then, they should argue whether such an evaluation based on the simulation is reasonable. Based on these results, they should use their results to make an informed suggestion solving the problem of the director. Last, they should reflect on viable options if only half the initially promised budget was available.

4. DESIGN-BASED RESEARCH AND PILOTING OF THE WORKBOOK

To assess and improve the quality of our workbook, we analyzed its quality using methods from design-based research (see Wang & Hannafin 2005). More precisely, we organized our development in phases. Note that this overall line of research is performed as design-based research. As such, the central goal was to improve the workbook and collect information necessary for the adoption by others – rather than assessing the learning outcomes with a pre-post test design.

4.1 Phases for Developing the Workbook

At the beginning, one of the authors created a first draft of the workbook.

Then, in the first phase, one author read the current version and commented on things to improve. These changes were implemented either by this author directly or by another author. This was iterated until no further changes were considered necessary within the author group.

In the second phase, we gave the workbook to either a mathematics or computer science educator. We asked this educator to read through the workbook and comment on every aspect they consider should or could be improved. Most importantly, they should comment on everything they consider relevant for practical implementation, e.g., exercises that are likely to be misunderstood by students. This feedback was then used by one of the authors to improve the workbook. After improvements were made, another educator was asked to provide his or her commentary. A total of eight educators were asked in this phase, two of which worked at secondary schools, six of which studies for a teaching degree for secondary schools.

In the third phase, we invited two mathematics classes of different capabilities to our university and let them work through the workbook together with tutors. After each class visited the university, we improved the workbook based on the feedback collected at this visit.

4.2 Method of Collecting Feedback with the Classes

After each exercise, both students and their tutors should reflect on the quality of the exercise and possible improvements. To collect them, we asked students and tutors to fill out a questionnaire after each exercise, as well as after finishing the workbook. A 6-point Likert-scale (1=strongly disagree to 6=strongly agree) is used as format for possible answers for all closed questions used in this evaluation.

The overall goal of the questionnaires was to get insights into the following questions:

- How much do the students enjoy working on the workbook?
- How do students and tutors describe the learning process?
- How do the tutors evaluate the educational relevance?
- What aspects of the workbook should be improved?
- Are there other aspects relevant for adopters?

In the questionnaire, we used one question intended to analyze the disposition of the students towards the material and three questions in which the students reflected on their learning process:

- (DS) I had fun working on the exercise
- (W1) I learned something through the exercise
- (W2) I solved the exercise on my own
- (W3) The exercise was challenging for me

While the students filled out their questionnaire, the tutors were also asked to fill out a questionnaire with different questions. We used three questions to evaluate the attributed relevance of the material and further two question to reflect on the quality of the material:

- (R1) The exercise improves mathematical competences mandated by [the local curriculum].
- (R2) The exercise improves math. competences that the students will need in their later live.
- (R3) The exercise improves math. comp. necessary for a critical understanding of the world
- (Q1) The exercise was comprehensible by the students (regarding language content)
- (Q2) The exercise is well structured

Notably, tutors were made aware that, regarding these questions, usage of technology should be seen as sub-activity of mathematics (The wording was chosen because there is no separate technology education in Bavaria and the local mathematics curriculum encourages utilization of technology for problem-solving).

In the last questionnaire, we offered students the ability to describe what they did and did not like in the workbook overall. This was done by six open questions at the end of the workbook, as well as verbal discussions after the working period. Four of the questions asked for additional information towards the closed questions (what was especially fun, what was especially challenging, what did you need most help with, what was the most relevant thing you learning). Two further questions asked for aspects that were positive or negative overall.

4.3 Classes for the Piloting

We piloted the workbook with two classes. The first class consisted of nine students from an interscholastic course in mathematics for highly capable students. Students meet multiple times a year on Fridays and/or Saturdays for additional lessons in (applied) mathematics or STEM problem solving. For these lessons, the teacher is free to teach whatever is deemed suitable for these students. This class is likely to be more motivated and capably than typical classes. The students participated in the course via a video-conference platform (Zoom) familiar to the them. They worked in groups of two and one group of three. Each group was supervised by a tutor. The four tutors were students of mathematics education for higher secondary education. They were recruited based on good impressions in the courses of the authors, or because they worked as student assistant at the chair of the authors and were known to be competent. All of them were advanced in their studies. Prior to the meeting, they were briefly introduced to the workbook, sample solutions, and the supervision process. This was done in a one-to-one meeting between one of the authors and the tutor. This lasted around 10-30 minutes. The tutors were known to the authors but not further affiliated to the creation of the workbook.

The second class consisted of twelve students (half the regular class size) from a regular higher secondary school. All students in the class took the musical school branch (having a reduced amount of mathematics lessons). Two of the students got a non-passing grade in mathematics. However, as two non-passing grades are required to fail the school year, both already knew that they passed the school year anyway. This class is likely to be a bit less motivated and capable than an average class. They worked in-person in groups of two; two students preferred to work alone. They were supervised by three tutors (two of the authors and one tutor from the prior class); one for 2-3 groups. Thus, these tutors did *not* fill out the questionnaire (again).

5. RESULTS

The overall results are visualized in below in Figure 2:

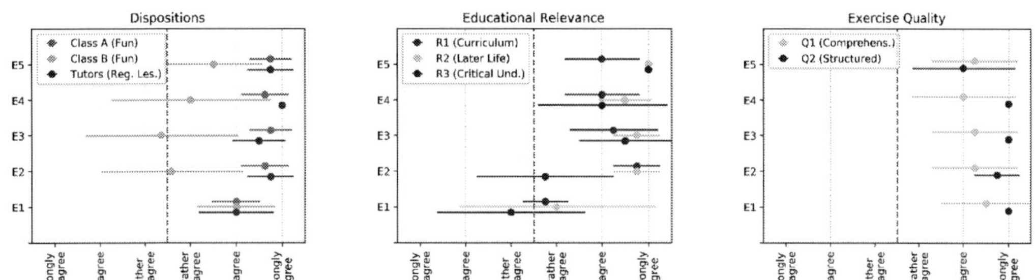

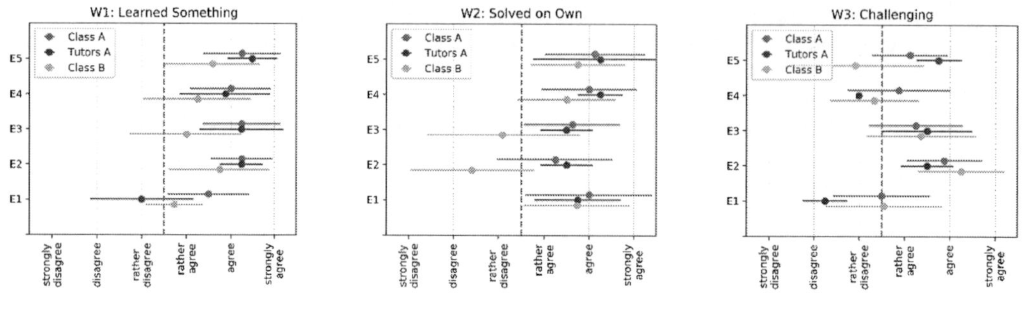

Figure 2. Visualization of the results of the closed questions

5.1 Engagement

The first class expressed very high, the second class expressed moderate enjoyment while working on the exercises. Aspects that were highlighted as especially fun in the open questions by at least two students include: 1) Experimenting on a real-world problem, 2) using the simulation, 3) working on a mathematics problem with peers, 4) transforming the simulation result to a real-world with a formula. One student commented: "Very nice workbook and appropriate exercises. Real-life Situation (Director wants to make the school more safe)". Another: "The simulation was very interesting and I had fun with the exercises. I found it very interesting to think about the sum of money [to be spent]." The only aspect of discontent focused on the functionality of the digital simulation environment. For example, one pupil tried to evaluate the impact of an additional door on the evacuation duration. However, the fleeing algorithms used during this execution did not lead any persons through this additional exit. The pupil complained: "Change the simulation: Persons [should] take the [additional] way leading outside [I built]" and added in the free feedback section: "The AI of the persons could be replaced by one that can learn: One can suggest a way [to take] and the simulation learns from this".

5.2 Learning Outcome

The tutors expressed very high agreement that exercises like this should be included into regular school education. One tutor noted: "The students enjoyed this exercise [five]. This is a very motivating exercise, if time and ability (technical equipment) are available." Another one noted at exercise four: "The reflection of results is frequently missed out in regular lessons. In every case, the verification of hypothesis is a competence that is worth fostering in regular lessons." Another one: "Mathematics should not only teach calculations."

Regarding the learning outcome, students and tutors had the impression that the students were learning something for all but the first exercise. For the first exercise, students thought that they learned something but tutors did not have the same impression. The reasons for this are unknown. Unfortunately, no pupil commented on what they learned. However, one tutor briefly commented on his disagreement to the first question: "It brought [things] to mind, but [the students discovered] no new findings". The first class reported moderately stronger overall agreement than the second class. In their assessment, students listed different kind of things they learned. This included domain knowledge ("what real problems during evacuations are", "That evacuations improve if people walks faster / in an orderly manner", "The fact that there are many options to improve an evacuation", ...), critical reflection ("Skepticism while differentiating realism and simulation", "Not all things that seem good at first are the best", ...), and approaches to problem solving ("How evacuations proceed and how one can predict them approximately with mathematics", "Thinking about […] simulations in general".

5.3 Self-Sufficient Working of the Students

Regarding self-reliance, the first class and their tutors had the impression that the students solved the exercises rather on their own. The second class needed more support, esp. for exercises 2 and 3. The biggest aspect where help was necessary (reported by more than a quarter of all students in the free-text) was in exercise two: The creation of a formula that enables transforming the simulation duration in steps into a real-world estimate about the simulation duration. For example, some students verbalized confusion about the different role of characters in formulae: In the workbook, they were asked to use the variable x for the speed and s for the distance. However, in their physics class, x was used for the distance and s was used for seconds. One tutor noted that this was the first time the group realized that the same character for an unknown can have different meanings in different contexts and formulae. Another big aspect where help was necessary was the introduction to the simulation itself. One pupil wrote: "The simulation was hard to understand at first, but then I found it pretty good." Notably, the students were not offered a handbook (or similar) for the environment. Instead, it was the duty of the tutor to explain the functionality of the environment, if necessary. For classroom adoption, a handbook or additional exercises that introduce all relevant functionalities in detail might be advisable. Interestingly, the mathematically more complex activities in the later exercises (verifying assumptions, creating hypothesis, experimenting with the simulation) required little help in both classes. One tutor noted for the last (most complex) exercise: "The students worked very self-reliant. My primary role was that of an observer."

5.4 Level of Challenge

Regarding the challenge level, the students felt challenged by the exercises a bit, but not too much. Unsurprisingly, exercise two (the exercise where most help was necessary) was considered to be the most challenging one. Notably, the tutors again disagreed with the perception of the students on the first exercise. One tutor noted at multiple exercises that "the level of challenge was appropriate." Another noteworthy aspect is the relatively low challenge reported by the second (weaker) class for the last exercise: Given that this exercise is indeed the most complex one, this might indicate that students did not grasp the full complexity of the exercise.

5.5 Educational Relevance

Regarding the educational relevance, the first exercise scored (on average) close to the middle on all three questions. This is not surprising as this exercise is a preliminary exercise for the later ones. The second exercise scored high (average at least "agree") in the questions R1 and R2 but not R3. This is likely because the relevant skills taught (handling formulas and the simulation) are primarily supplementary skills. The last three exercises all scored high on all three questions asked. Reasons for this very high score (mentioned more than twice as free text answer on any of the three exercises) included: 1) the high relevance of learning to argue logically correct and with data, 2) learning about the process of stating, verifying, and reflecting assumptions and results, and 3) demonstrating good examples for working behaviors typical for mathematicians like generalizing and finding examples and counter-examples. Lastly, regarding the quality, most of the exercises were perceived as well structured and rather comprehensible. There was no instances in which a problem with the comprehensibility of the mathematical content was noted: Instead, aspects of concern focused on the wording of exercises.

6. CONCLUSION

In this paper, we presented a workbook designed to teach students the reflective use of computing technology. We used methods from design-based research to assess and improve the quality of the workbook. Additionally, we piloted the workbook with two classes of different capabilities, totaling 20 students. Our results show that the students rather worked on their own, learned something, and were challenged an appropriate amount. The disposition towards the material was overall positive: The first class expressed fun working on the exercises, the second class was more divided and moderately positive on average. The tutors of the first class very strongly agreed to the statement that such or similar exercises should be included into regular school education. The exercises themselves were perceived as well structured and, mostly, comprehensible. Based on the feedback collected, we sub-divided multiple exercises and improved the wording (both in regard to clarity and consistency) of many exercises. We also added and indicator for the estimated work duration to each exercise in the workbook. The workbook published alongside this paper already includes these updates. Finally, we encourage educators to adopt our workbook and/or to design further new and interesting learning opportunities for the reflective use of digital technology.

REFERENCES

Andersen, J., Baum, M., Dictus, C., Greubel, A., Knippertz, L. & Krüger, J., *et al.*, 2023, 'Critical Thinking – Gelegenheit für MINT-Lernen in der Zukunft?', in J. Roth, *et al.* (eds.), *Die Zukunft des MINT-Lernens – Band 1*, pp. 43–57, Springer Berlin Heidelberg, Berlin, Heidelberg.

Anker-Hansen, J. & Andreé, M., 2019, 'In Pursuit of Authenticity in Science Education', *Nordic Studies in Science Education* 15(1), 54–66.

Brinda, T., Fothe, M., Friedrich, S., Koerber, B., Puhlmann, H. & Röhner, G., *et al.*, 2008, 'Grundsätze und standards für die informatik in der schule-bildungsstandards informatik für die sekundarstufe i' 2008.

Ciolan, L. & Ciolan, L.E., 2014, 'Two Perspectives, Same Reality? How Authentic is Learning for Students and for their Teachers', *Procedia - Social and Behavioral Sciences* 142, 24–28.

Department of Education, 2023, *National Curriculum in Computing Programmes*, viewed 24 July 2022, from https://www.gov.uk/government/publications/national-curriculum-in-england-computing-programmes-of-study/national-curriculum-in-england-computing-programmes-of-study.

Dörner, D. & Funke, J., 2017, 'Complex Problem Solving: What It Is and What It Is Not', *Frontiers in psychology* 8, 1153.

Gilbert, J.K., 2004, 'Models and Modelling: Routes to More Authentic Science Education', *International Journal of Science and Mathematics Education* 2(2), 115–130.

Greefrath, G., Siller, H.-S. & Weitendorf, J., 2011, 'Modelling Considering the Influence of Technology', *Trends in Teaching and Learning*, vol. 1, pp. 315–329.

Greubel, A. & Siller, H.-S., 2022, 'Learning about black-boxes: A mathematical-technological model' 11, from https://hal.science/hal-03748388.

Greubel, A., Siller, H.-S., Ruzika, S. & Knippertz, L., 2022, 'Teaching Mathematical Modeling with Computing Technology: Presentation of a Course based on Evacuations', *Proceedings of the 17th Workshop in Primary and Secondary Computing Education* 2022.

Har, L.B., 2013, 'Authentic learning', *The Hong Kong Institute of Education. Retrieved* 2013, 141–178.

Jang, H., 2016, 'Identifying 21st Century STEM Competencies Using Workplace Data', *Journal of Science Education and Technology* 25(2), 284–301.

Kaiser, G., Bracke, M., Göttlich, S. & Kaland, C., 'Authentic Complex Modelling Problems in Mathematics Education', *Educational Interfaces between Mathematics*, vol. 16, pp. 287–297.

Kaiser, G. & Schwarz, B., 2010, 'Authentic Modelling Problems in Mathematics Education—Examples and Experiences', *Journal für Mathematik-Didaktik* 31(1), 51–76.

Klock, H. & Siller, H.-S., 2021, 'Die Bedeutung der Diagnose für adaptive Interventionen beim mathematischen Modellieren', 47 - 62 Pages / mathematica didactica, Vol. 43 No. 1 (2020): Themenschwerpunkt: Forschung in Lehr-Lern / mathematica didactica , Vol. 43 No. 1 (2020): Themenschwerpunkt: Forschung in Lehr-Lern-Laboren Mathematik 2021.

Kules, B., 2016, 'Computational thinking is critical thinking: Connecting to university discourse, goals, and learning outcomes', *Proceedings of the Association for Information Science and Technology* 53(1), 1–6.

Li, Y., Chen, M., Dou, Z., Zheng, X., Cheng, Y. & Mebarki, A., 2019, 'A review of cellular automata models for crowd evacuation', *Physica A: Statistical Mechanics and its Applications* 526, 120752.

McKenzie, A.D., Morgan, C.K., Cochrane, K.W., Watson, G.K. & Roberts, D.W., 'Authentic learning: What is it, and what are the ideal curriculum conditions to cultivate it in', *Quality Conversations: Proceedings of the 25th HERDSA Annual Conference, Perth, Western Australia*, pp. 426–433.

Ruzika, S., Siller, H.-S. & Bracke, M., 2017, 'Evakuierungsszenarien in Modellierungswochen – ein interessantes und spannendes Thema für den Mathematikunterricht', in H. Humenberger and M. Bracke (eds.), *Neue Materialien für einen realitätsbezogenen Mathematikunterricht 3*, pp. 181–190, Springer Fachmedien Wiesbaden, Wiesbaden.

Wang, F. & Hannafin, M.J., 2005, 'Design-based research and technology-enhanced learning environments', *Educational technology research and development* 53(4), 5–23.

Wing, J., 2011, 'Research notebook: Computational thinking—What and why', *The link magazine* 6, 20–23.

VALUE AND CHALLENGES IN DEVELOPING OUTCOMES-BASED STUDENTS-CENTRED PROGRAMME

Aliza Ali
Open University Malaysia (OUM)
Petaling Jaya, Selangor, Malaysia

ABSTRACT

Programme development is a process that involves a systematic process that requires focus on the students' achievement and outcomes. To create an outcomes-based education programme, the university has to prepare its academicians with knowledge and skills that can help the academicians to design and develop an outcomes-based students-centered programme. This study used a quantitative approach using a survey method for data collection. A total of 53 academicians were selected to become research respondents for this study. A questionnaire was sent through a Google form survey to all respondents who are located in Selangor, Malaysia. The survey and data collection were done through a set of questionnaires using a 5-point Likert and open-ended questions. The data were analysed using the Statistical Package for The Social Science (SPSS) version 21 software to get the frequency and percentage of the academician response on a way to add value to the university programme development. Open-ended questions are used to identify the academician's issues and constraints pertaining to the programme development process. The results of the study indicated that the respondents are aware of the importance of the outcome-based education progamme, however, most of the respondents need support and training to help them to face challenges in developing an outcomes-based student's centred programme.

KEYWORDS

Curriculum, Outcome-Based Education, Student-Centred, Higher-Education, Learner, Programme Development

1. INTRODUCTION

Curriculum design refers to the way curriculum developers conceptualize the curriculum and arrange its major components such as subject matter or content, instructional methods and materials, learner experiences, or activities to provide direction and guidance as we develop the curriculum (Ornstein & Hunkins, 2018). The curriculum development model serves as a guideline for action and sequence for the process. A good curriculum development model provides greater efficiency and productivity in developing a student-centred university programme. The developed curriculum will be used in the education system so that what has been implemented in the education system would have a clear direction in resulting in better future generation.

Programme is used to describe any stand-alone curriculum experienced by a student which contributes to a qualification of a degree-awarding body. In the 21st century, higher education institutions need to provide programmes that are relevant and appropriate to prepare graduates for the global market. It is therefore vital to address the enhancement of graduates' competency to ensure that graduate employment matches market needs in the future (Marfunizah Ma' et al., 2020). In addition, stakeholders are demanding that university graduates not only have the knowledge but the appropriate skills and job fit for the workplace (Akir, Eng, & Malie, 2012). Universities are the main sources of knowledge and competence (Marinov & Fraszczyk, 2014) because they deliver education programmes and create the programmes according to the education principles and the current needs. Development of new curriculum or programme as well as monitoring to existing programme is an essential part of higher education providers, especially for a private university such as the Open University Malaysia (OUM). This is to ensure that higher academic standards are set and maintained and enable the intended learning outcomes to be achieved by the students.

2. BACKGROUND OF THE STUDY

In the 21st leaning century era, higher educational institutions need to provide programmes that are relevant and appropriate to prepare graduates for the global labour market and improve employability (Ministry of Education, 2018). In addition, stakeholders are demanding that university graduates not only have the knowledge but the appropriate skills and job fit for workplace (Akir, Eng, & Malie, 2012). Universities are the main sources of knowledge and competence (Marinov & Fraszczyk, 2014) because they deliver education programmes and create the programmes according to the education principles and the current needs. Development of new curriculum or programme as well as monitoring the existing programme is essential part of higher education providers, especially for a private university such as OUM. This is to ensure that higher academic standards are set and maintained and enable the intended learning outcomes to be achieved by the students.

Programme is used to describe as any stand-alone curriculum experienced by a student which contributes to a qualification of a degree-awarding body.The most important components for higher academic institute are the educational programmes offers based on the education code and accreditation standards of the country. Outcome Based Education (OBE) model together with Malaysian Qualifications Agency (MQA) and Malaysia Qualifications Framework (MQF) that will be the main reference to develop the guidelines. In addition, the educational programmes formulated will reflect the core mission of the institutional as well as providing viable and relevant programme to the community itself in order to support the economic and cultural growth of the community.

The development of a new programme is important for the university because it enable the university to maintain a position of intellectual leadership. It is imperative to note that the development of a programme in any higher education providers in Malaysia must comply with the MQF, Programme Standards, Guidelines to Good Practices (GGP), and the Code of Practice Programme Accreditation or COPPA (MQA, 2014). The adherence these code of practice standards is to ensure that the programme developed reflect international best practices so that graduating students are on par with those from other countries. Thus, academicians who are employed by the university should have sound knowledge on programme development and MQA and eventually gain their recognition without facing any setbacks in getting their programme accredited.

Programme development in any education institution is the fundamental process to achieve its goals for sustainability. When people refer to curriculum it literally means that everything that goes on in school or college or university. According to Ornstein and Hunkins (2018), curriculum design refers to the way curriculum developer conceptualize the curriculum and arrange its major components such as subject matter or content, instructional methods and materials, learner experiences or activities to provide direction and guidance as we develop the curriculum. Thus, when developing a programme, it must be structured to align with the curriculum development model serves as a guideline for action and sequence for the process. A good curriculum development model provides greater efficiency and productivity in developing a programme. The developed curriculum will be used in the education system so that what has been implemented in the education system would have clear direction in resulting better future generation without loss of unnecessary cost, energy and resources. (Saedah & Muhammad Ridhuan Tony, 2011).

A programme is designed and delivered to facilitate the attainment of a set of desired learning outcomes (MQA, 2018). Developing an academic programme requires understanding of curriculum development process includes phase of need analysis, design, development, dissemination, implementation and evaluation. Like developing any product for marketing, academic programme development requires commitment, collaboration, understanding of the key educational experience that could further enrich the students' learning. This can be a daunting process, which need times, approval, collaboration between academics, departments and stakeholder. A range of training supports through in-house training need to be carried out to enable academician to understand their roles in the programme development process. It involves transforming the curriculum of a programme that requires not only academic expertise in the entire suite of courses that makes up a programme, but also education experts from various disciplines who have been trained or who have considerable experience in effective learning-teaching methodologies including associated technologies that make the classroom environment a very rich one (MQA, 2018).

Although the primary role of the university is to give knowledge based on the theoretical aspect, investment in higher education should not be neglected by society (Marfunizah Ma' et al., 2020). Higher educational institutions should produce graduates to cope with industrial development. This involve the development of

Programme Education Objectives (PEO) that describe the professional accomplishments that the graduates achieve after they graduate. In the university programme, PEOs enable evaluation of how graduates are contributing towards the industry within the first five years following their graduation. Even so, the Programme Learning Objectives (PLO) that reflect the three learning domains namely the cognitive, affective and psychomotor must correspond to the MQF learning outcomes. PLO statement must be addressed the 11 MQF learning outcomes and courses that are offered to, directly and indirectly, support the attainment of PLOs. According to Gordon, Taylor and Oliva, (2019), the learning outcomes may be identified in three major domains namely the cognitive, the affective and the psychomotor. Five clusters of the 11 MQF learning outcomes are based on these three learning domains. Students' learning outcomes should address relevant outcomes for each of these learning domains and hierarchical levels in each of the cognitive, psychomotor, and affective domains are from low to the higher order. These learning domains represent the areas of knowledge, skills and attitude that are the basis for writing Course Learning Outcomes (CLO) that contain measurable action verbs. To rephrase it, CLO is intended learning contains the which explain what the students should be able to achieve by the end of the course. Thus, when writing learning outcomes, we relate the existing needs of the profession and industry.

The educational programmes offer in any higher educations must be based on the education code and accreditation standards of the country (UNESCO, 2014). In Malaysia context, OBE and MQA COPPA 2nd edition and MQF is the main reference to develop the programme guidelines. In addition, the programme developed will reflect the core mission of the institutional and provide viable and relevant programme to the community itself in order to support the economic and cultural growth of the society.

OBE approach is a student-centered strategy in which students' mastery over particular skills is demonstrated and measured. The OBE approach is a clear statement that is expected to be achieved by the students at the end of the programme. OBE is emphasised because it can influence the whole process of education including decisions about the content of the curriculum, formulation of aims, educational strategies, design of teaching methods, assessment procedures, and the educational environment (Esmaily et al., 2014). However, OBE is a complex strategy for any programme planning which is based on the intended learning outcomes to achieve the desired performance. In other words, the OBE can be used as a framework for designing learning outcomes at the courses' level which curriculum mapping with the programme learning outcomes that ultimately lead to optimal learning experiences or desired outcomes (Esmaily et al., 2014).

In education perspective, OBE is an educational approach that is related to the goals or outcomes and at the end of the of the educational experience through a programme, learners should have achieved the outcomes. OBE is considered a holistic approach which offers a powerful and appealing way of reforming and managing education for mastery in learning and to meet the prerequisites for local and international accreditation (Mohieldein, 2017). OBE has gone through evolution and hence, redesigning programme development based on on educational outcomes has become the focus and prioritise by higher institution providers around the world. An OBE curriculum design starts with the determination of the programme aim, which outlines the philosophy, rationale and purpose of the programme (MQA, 2014).

OUM apply OBE as a programme approach in handling teaching and learning to prepare graduates to face challenges in life and at work place. OBE is an education philosophy organized for the learners to experience in order to become successful in life and workplace when they finish their studies. OBE specifies the desirable outcomes or abilities which students should be able to demonstrate upon completion of an educational programme (MQA, 2018). Programme learning outcomes are expected from certain academic programme at higher institutions and these are assessed through various measurement methods and tools. OBE is a programme approach that involves the development and restructuring of curriculum, assessment and reporting knowledge into practices.

OBE is an approach to education that begins with clearly focusing on high-quality learning in an educational system around what is essential for all students to be able to do successfully at the end of their learning experiences (MQA, 2014). Thus, it is important for all the academician in the higher education to understand the importance of OBE (OUM, 2019). To overcome the requirement, it is mandatory for all programme to shift from traditional education system to OBE, which includes Programme Educational Objectives (PEO), Programme Learning Outcomes (PLO) and Course Learning Outcomes (CLO). In order for any programme development to be successful, it is necessary for the CLOs in OBE to be identified, explicitly and communicated to all concerned as well as to be the overriding issue in all curriculum and teaching decisions (Morcke et al., 2013). Therefore, it is imperative for the university academician to have the knowledge in OBE.

Programme development should be a perpetual and comprehensive planning process used to establish any university programme. Quality program development ~~is~~ should be supported by a good documented plan of action. However, education university encounter challenges using the existing leadership skills towards change in curriculum, competencies and skills essential to their graduates' career development with regard to the programs offered by the faculty (Syed Ismail et al., 2017). In Malaysia, the MQA is the government agency in charge of supervising and monitoring standards of programmes offered at the higher institutions. Universities need to respond quickly to MQA requirements to meet the minimum compliance criteria. Nevertheless, the challenges of high education institutions, to a considerable degree, do have an undue influence over the university inputs, operations, functions, processes, and outcome (Abdul Majid et al., 2018). Planner and curriculum developer will also face the crisis on choosing a policy and the goals of future education (Saedah & Muhammad Ridhuan Tony, 2011). Poor management and financial strains are among reasons for private universities faced accreditation problems, causing the MQA to suspend or refuse accreditation after auditing process were carried out (Ainaa, 2021). Baumgardt and Lekhetho (2013), identified the challenges of quality assurance in South African private higher educations, indicating that proper accreditation mechanisms are essential to ensure the delivery of quality education.

At the micro level, the programme development and revision, the main concern is programme planning and development process as indicated by Richey and Klien (2017). This process has warranted for a need analysis for data collection for the targeted learners' demand of the programme. In addition, the development of new programmes varies among institutions and are subjected to the changing needs. Since most of OUM learners are working adults, it is crucial to develop a programme towards the market.

Thus this paper reporting the study that has conducted (1) to identify what ways university academician can add value to the university academic programme during programme development process that focusing on the OBE students -centred approach and (2) to identify challenges university academician faced during programme development process that focusing on the OBE student-centred approach.. In this context of study, value refers to knowledge enhancement, knowledge improvement and what the students should be able to do at the end of the proggrame or after graduatings. Programme in this context of study refers to an arrangement of courses to achieve the stated learning outcomes, which usually leads to an award of a qualification. Academician of the university plan and advocate for the growth of the programme, responsible to develop the programme or ensure that the programme under their supervision remain viable, relevant and at highest standard of quality. The academician must aware of the regulotory body outlines to ensure that the learners are equipped with the necessary knowledge, skills and attitute.

2.1 Methodology

This study involves academicians of OUM. The academicians are OUM academic staff designated to teach, design and coordinate academic programmes offered in the university. The finding of this research will be able to identify the ways academicians add value to the university programme and issues they faced when reviewing and developingthe academic programme. This study used quantitative approach using a survey method for data collection. A total of 53 academicians were selected to become research respondents for this study. However, 49 respondents were returned. A questionnaire was sent through google form survey to all respondents who are located in Selangor. The survey and data collection was done through a sets of questionnaires using a 5 point Likert open-ended pen ended questions. analyzed analysed using the Statistical Package for The Social Science (SPSS) version 21 software to get the frequency, percentage, mean and mode on the academician knowledge on the product in programme development. Open ended questions were also used to identify the academicians issues and constraints pertaining the programme development process.

2.2 Findings

Figure 1 shows respondents' responses on ways for department to add value to educational programmes in OUM. The highest scores to improve on competencies regarding curriculum development 73.5% (N=36) and to improve knowledge on the capacities, rights and responsibilities 71.4% (N=35). This is followed by to enhance knowledge on how to organize, assess information 63.3% (N=31), improve knowledge and understanding of the importance 59.2% (N=29), and improve knowledge on ethics and info-ethics 40.8% (N=20) respectively.

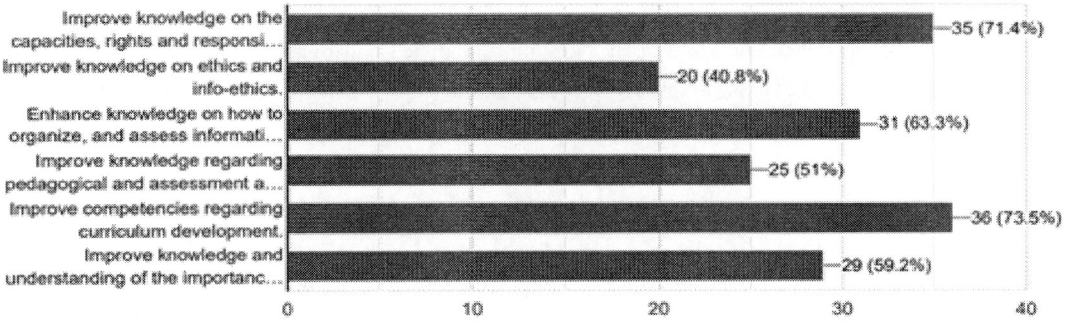

Figure 1. Respondents' responses on ways to add value to educational programmes

2.2.1 Challenges Faced by Academicians Concerning OBE Programme Development

The following are respondents' responses on the challenges faced as academicians in programme development process in OUM based on the open-ended questions. The following responses were not based on ranked order.

- To keep updated with the new policies/ guidelines/Standards from relevant bodies
- time constrain, number of academic
- No ad-hoc team in preparing documents during development process
- No ad-hoc team in preparing documents during development process
- Meeting the MQA requirement.
- Workload has increased tremendously due to insufficient academic staff in faculty. There is not much time left to review our own programme to improve it further in terms of delivery, learning material, assessment and engagement with students and alumni. Major weakness, in my humble opinion.
- Having the internal expertise to offer adequate supervision in certain areas
- Not having sufficient knowledge of the needs of the industry with regards to the program

Based on the above challenges, it can be concluded that respondents faced more on the input and implement process in the programme development. Some of the challenges faced by academicians from input process include to keep abreast with the updated policies/ guidelines/standards from relevant bodies due to time constraint and academic. In addition, academicians also mentioned that lack of support in term ad-hoc team in preparing documents during development process and meeting the standards required by MQA. The situation is exasperated by the increased workload due to insufficient academic staff in faculty and thus, academicians seem to overlook to keep on reviewing the programme assigned to them. Further, this situation also has led to lack of attempt to improve on the programme in term of delivery, learning material, assessment and engagement with students and alumni. It also seems that academicians encountered challenges in the programme development due to lack of support from internal expertise to offer adequate supervision in certain areas and academicians mentioned that they lack of knowledge of the needs of the industry with regards to the programme.

3. DISCUSSION

In supporting the programme development process and the revision of curriculum development, there are some points raised and suggestions from the programme directors. The issue of manpower or the number of internal academic staff and expertise was raised to assist in developing a programme in the faculties. The academic staff based on areas must be recruited to sustain the OUM programmes. In addition to that, the assistance from the non-academic staff also plays a significant role to expedite the overall programme development process in gathering relevant materials, resources, and data collection. Therefore, dedicated staff from the faculty or other units must be focused on handling the process. The appropriate timeline and duration are also critical to developing a quality programme based on the current programme standard and industry input. Concerning the demand to produce a quality programme, continuous demand on the internal training to the programme directors and embed a system to support the process is crucial to higher education institutions. In this manner, the system is vital to sustaining the current changing demands and accountability. The last suggestion is to have a centralised input or department, for example, Programme Accreditation Unit (PAU) to handle as a one-stop center in terms of managing the information transfer and not to rely on the individual programme directors for the information update on the programme as well as the programme development process. Programme is a product and should have a set of objectives that describes what the entering and exiting students should be able to do. Product development is depend on the outcomes of the needs and situational analysis of a specific context (Saedah, Norlidah, DeWitt & Zaharah, 2013). Thus, it is the responsibility of programme developers to seek continuous improvement in the programme. In supporting the programme development process and the revision of curriculum development, there were points raised and suggestions from the academicians. The issue of manpower or the number of internal academic staff and expertise was raised to assist in developing a programme in the faculties. The academic staff based on areas must be recruited to sustain the OUM programmes. In addition to that, the assistance from the non-academic staff also plays a significant role to expedite the overall programme development process in gathering relevant materials, resources, and data collection. Therefore, dedicated staff from the faculty or other units must be focused on handling the process. The appropriate timeline and duration are also critical to developing a quality programme based on the current programme standard and industry input. Concerning the demand to produce a quality programme, continuous demand on the internal training to the programme directors and embed a system to support the process is crucial to higher education institutions. In this manner, the system is vital to sustaining the current changing demands and accountability. The last suggestion is to have a centralised input or department, for example, Programme Accreditation Unit (PAU) to handle as a one-stop center in terms of managing the information transfer and not to rely on the individual programme directors for the information update on the programme as well as the programme development process.

Another glaring issues are the time constraint faced by the programme directors to prepare and check the documents. There is no specific committee that can assist them at the initial stage. This issue also happened during the programme review process. The programme directors will do it from scratch with a minimum assistance from the other departments. The fact is, to expedite the speed of documentation, a strong support from all departments in the university is required (Ahmad, 2019).

Some of the academic staffs claimed that the workload has increased due to the insufficient number of academic staff. Some of them have been assigned more than one programme. A bigger portion of time were utilised to do the other academic tasks which in turn limit the time for reviewing the programme delivery, learning materials, assessments and engagement with the existing students and alumni. Meanwhile, these are the essential parts in the Code of Practice for Programme Accreditation (COPPA) (Malaysian Qualifications Agency (MQA), 2018). The programme directors also perceived that lack of industrial experience is one of the major constraints. To-date, many programmes are developed based on the industrial demand (Jaedun et al., 2020). The fact is, many of them are purely academicians without prior industrial experience. According to Kaiser et al. (2018), in European countries, academics are required to undergo industrial attachment or sabbatical leave to gain experience and integrate the knowledge gained from the industry into the academic programme. This is to ensure the relevancy of the programme with industrial requirements.

4. CONCLUSION

This finding will help the university to identify the best way to solve a problem related to programme development. Programme directors will understand better the importance of programme development devolvement and the effect on students' learning if they are given adequate training and more time to develop a new programme. Programme director will have a better understanding of how to overcome the challenges that prevent them from getting involved with programme development. Training and coaching will help programme director understand the correct process of programme development and maintain the quality of the existing programme. Thus, programme developers must given opportunities' to seek continuous improvement in the programme. It would benefit programme director if the faculty can add value in terms of educational programs enrichment within the university.

In conclusion, majority of the programme directors raised concern about the challenges in facing programme development process. Lack of understanding about the correct process of programme development and maintain the quality of the existing programme become the main challenges in maintaining the programme quality in the University. In-house training is needed to enable programme directors to understand their roles in the programme development process and they must be exposed with the process related to the continuous improvement in the programme and the improvement should based on the current and future need of the students.

However, the key question of how curriculum developer incorporates unknown future into the curriculum remains unclear. While most people would agree that one goal of a curriculum should be to prepare students for the future, there is often little consensus about what knowledge and skills will be required in the future (Parkay, et al., 2014).To what degree should students master the determined selected knowledge (Ornstein & Hunkins, 2018) need to be assessed. Willingness to learn and prepare for the future will help improve students' learning experience. To be relevant, curriculum should response to change brought about by psychological principles, new knowledge and educational reform. Change is all about moving the whole system and taking daily actions that build capacity and ownership (Fullan, 2006). In addition, cooperation between educational institutions and industry is critically necessary for the development of teaching and learning (Marfunizah Ma' et al., 2020). If we believes that all students can be academic success, then we need to select with care the content of the curriculum, organize with wisdom the content selected, initiate creative pedagogies, and even "think outside the box" (Ornstein & Hunkins, 2018). Thus the programme developed for students at higher institutions should reflect the core mission of the institution and provide a viable and relevant programme to the community itself in order to support the economic and cultural growth of the society. Refection is required just to determine for what purpose the curricula are being developed (Ornstein & Hunkins, 2018).

ACKNOWLEDGEMENT

This work would not have been possible without financial support from Open University Malaysia. I am grateful to those who work actively and support me in this research project.

REFERENCES

Abdul Majid, F. (2016). The use of reflective journals in outcome-based education during the teaching practicum. Malaysian Journal of ELT Research, 4.

Ahmad, H. (2019). Transformation of Higher Education: A Stakeholder Perspectives in Private Islamic Higher Education Institution (IPTIS) in Malaysia. *HOLISTICA – Journal of Business and Public Administration*, *10*(1). https://doi.org/10.2478/hjbpa-2019-0009

Ainaa Aiman. (2021). Why private university face accreditation issues. Retrieved April 3, 2021, from https://www.freemalaysiatoday.com/category/nation/2021/05/05/why-private-varsities-face-accreditation-issues/

Akir, O., Eng, T. H., & Malie, S. (2012). Teaching and learning enhancement through outcome- ased education structure and technology e-learning support. *Procedia-Social and Behavioral Sciences*, *62*, 87-92.

Baumgardt, J. & Lekhetho, M. (2013). The Challenges of Quality Assurance in Private Higher Education Institutions in South Africa. *Mediterranean Journal of Social Sciences, 4*(3), 2039-9340.

Esmaily, H. M., Vahidi, R., Fathi, N. M., & Wahlström, R. (2014). How do physicians and trainers experience outcome-based education in "Rational prescribing"?. *BMC research notes*, *7*(1), 1-11.

Malaysian Qualifications Agency (MQA). (2014). *Guideline to good practices*. MQA. Cyberjaya: Agensi Kelayakan Malaysia (Malaysian Qualifications Agency, MQA).

Malaysian Qualifications Agency (MQA). (2014). *Guideline to good practices*. Assessemnt of students. MQA. Cyberjaya: Agensi Kelayakan Malaysia (Malaysian Qualifications Agency, MQA).

Malaysian Qualifications Agency (MQA). (2018). *Code of Practice for Programme Accreditation (COPPA) 2nd Edition*. MQA.

Marinov. M. & A. Fraszczyk. (2014). Curriculum development and design for university. programmes in rail freight and logistics. *Procedia - Social and Behavioral Sciences*, 141 (2014): 1166 – 1170.

Mohieldein, A. H. (2017). Outcome-based approach to medical education towards academic.programmes accreditation: A review article. *J Pak Med Assoc*, *67*(3), 454-460.

Morcke, A. M., Dornan, T., & Eika, B. (2013). Outcome (competency) based education: an exploration of its origins, theoretical basis, and empirical evidence. *Advances in Health Sciences Education*, *18*(4), 851-863.

Ornstein, A. C. & Hunkins, F. P. (2018). *Curriculum foundations, principles and issues* 6th ed. London: Pearson.

Parkay, F. W., Anctil, E. J. & Hass, G. (2006). *Curriculum planning: A contemporary approach*. 8th ed. Boston: Pearson Education.

Richey, R. C. & Klein, J. D. (2007). *Design and developmental research.* New Jersey: Routledge.

Saedah Siraj & Muhammad RidhuanTony Lim (2010) *Development of Future Curriculum Via Futures Studies.* In: International Conference on Fundamental & Applied Sciences 2010 (ICFAS2010) , June, 15-17, 2010, Kuala Lumpur.

Saedah Siraj, Norlidah Alias, Dorothy DeWitt & Zaharah Hussin. (2013). *Design and developmental research: Emergent trends in educational research.* Kuala Lumpur: Pearson Malaysia Sdn. Bhd.

Syed Ismail Syed Mohamad, Fidlizan Muhammad, Mohd Yahya Mohd Hussin & Nurul Fadly Habidi. (2017). Future Challenges for Institutional Leadership in a Malaysian Education University. *International Journal of Academic Research in Business and Social Sciences 2017, 7*(2), 2222-6990.

POTENTIAL CHALLENGES AND SUPPORT MECHANISMS FOR STUDENTS TRANSITIONING TO UNIVERSITY LIFE

Liga Zvirgzdina, Anda Zeidmane and Natalija Sergejeva
Latvia University of Life Sciences and Technologies
Liela Street 2, Jelgava, Latvia, LV3001

ABSTRACT

Starting university studies, students must experience the transition from the familiar to the unfamiliar, encountering cognitive and social challenges. Universities need to be aware of this transition and provide an appropriate support mechanism that should be adapted to both first year students and senior year students. The aim of the study is: 1) the most important external changes and possible problems that students have to face when entering a university and continuing their studies; 2) identify the most important support mechanisms that students of the Latvia University of Life Sciences and Technologies (LBTU) would need before and during their studies. Based on Chen's proposed classification of external changes, students of LBTU Faculty of Information Technologies were surveyed. Respondents expressed their opinion about external changes during the transition to university studies. The research found that LBTU has support mechanisms for attracting students to the university, but there is a lack of effective support mechanisms for students in the study process.

KEYWORDS

Transition to University, Challenges, Support Mechanisms for Students

1. INTRODUCTION

The attention of many researchers, pedagogues and also politicians both in the world, in Europe and in Latvia has been attracted by the high student dropout rate in universities. In OECD countries, about one third of students do not complete their university studies (OECD 2016, OECD 2018). Although graduation rates vary between European countries (from 10% to 60%), many common factors can be observed (European Commission/EACEA/Eurydice 2015). Research on the reasons for student dropout looks at both general dimensions and specific reasons. For example, as general dimensions are mentioned: academic and social integration at the university, study conditions at the university, information and admission requirements, previous academic achievements at school, personal efforts and motivation to study, the student's personal characteristics as well as the student's socio-demographic background and other external conditions (Barbara et al 2019). The most frequently cited reasons for dropping out of studies are: i) not knowing what one wants to study in general; ii) poor academic performance; iii) use of labor market opportunities; (iv) knowing that you have already learned enough to get a job; v) realization that higher education is not for me; vi) mental/physical health problems and vii) financial difficulties such as living expenses, tuition fees, having to support the family financially (Masterson 2022). It also mentions the fact that research has changed since the pandemic.

Different researchers have different views on the main factors and their hierarchy of influence that cause dropout, as for example Quinn (Quinn 2013) mentions six main factors - political, institutional, socio-cultural, structural, learning and personal factors. There are authors who emphasize only four factors based on adaptation to university studies – academic, social, personal-emotional and institutional adaptation (Sevinc, Gizir 2014, McCulloch 2014). No less important in the study process is overcoming cognitive stress (Romanenko, Nikitina 2016.). Studying the factors that influence the adaptation of first-year students to natural science studies in higher education, researchers from the University of Latvia emphasize three main factors that influence studies in universities (Birzina et al 2019): 1) Institutional factors (curriculum, necessary resources, support staff, etc.); 2) Students' personal factors (attitude towards studies, previous experience, self-confidence, emotions, stress, illnesses, etc.); 3) Academic factors (prior knowledge, literacy, numeracy, computer-related skills, thinking skills, etc.).

Starting university studies, students must experience the transition from the familiar to the unfamiliar, encountering cognitive and social challenges. Universities need to be aware of this transition and provide an appropriate support mechanism that should be adapted to both first year students and senior year students (Perry, Allard 2003).

At the Latvian University of Life Sciences and Technologies, which is located approximately 45 km from Riga, students from various regions of Latvia and with various prior knowledge begin their studies. LBTU is not such a single campus. Some students live in dormitories; some rent living space in the city of Jelgava, some commute daily from Riga or nearby places. Although the highest student dropout is observed in the first years, there is also a significant dropout in the older years. The reasons are both common and different.

The aim of this study is: 1) to study the most important external changes and their possible challenges, which should be faced by students upon entering the university and continuing their studies; 2) identify the most important support mechanisms that students of the LBTU would need before and during their studies.

2. MATERIALS AND METHODS

The literature review was conducted to develop this research methodology. Based on the obtained results, a questionnaire was created, where students of different courses were asked to answer about the main changes, potential challenges and opportunities to overcome them when starting their studies at the university and in further studies.

2.1 Theoretical Background of the Study

2.1.1 External Changes and Possible Challenges in the Transition to University Studies

For first-year students, the period of transition from a familiar environment to an unfamiliar one is a period of disequilibrium (Jackson 2010). Many students are aware of this, but often cannot solve these problems themselves. However, there are students who are not ready to adapt to a new situation and try to act as before and when they fail, blaming the academic staff and the university administration, they try to prove their rightness. The result for such students is that time is missed, the study process is delayed and the student often becomes a dropout. Higher education institutions should be aware of key external changes and potential challenges as students' transition to university life. The main external changes are (Cheng 2023): 1) in the change of the physical environment; 2) in the change of the academic environment: 3) in the change of the social environment and 4) in financial changes (see Figure 1).

Starting to study at universities often involves a change of location, where you have to overcome possible challenges such as homesickness, often depression, isolation, as well as culture shock accompanied by the fear of being ignored. The change in the academic environment is related to changes in the learning environment, where cooperation with peers, student societies and club activities, self-management of expectations, because sometimes disappointments must also be experienced, changes in performance, where possible challenges are to develop study self-efficacy, information literacy and good time management are essential. Presentations and exams, which happen much more often than in secondary educational institutions, also require confidence, emotional skills management. Social changes are associated with making new friends, with academic staff being different from teachers in schools, getting new flatmates, where consideration, communication and compromise are possible challenges. Financial changes are no less important as loans are often taken out expenses have to be monitored, so studies are often combined with part-time or full-time work, which raises responsibility, priority management and time management as possible challenges.

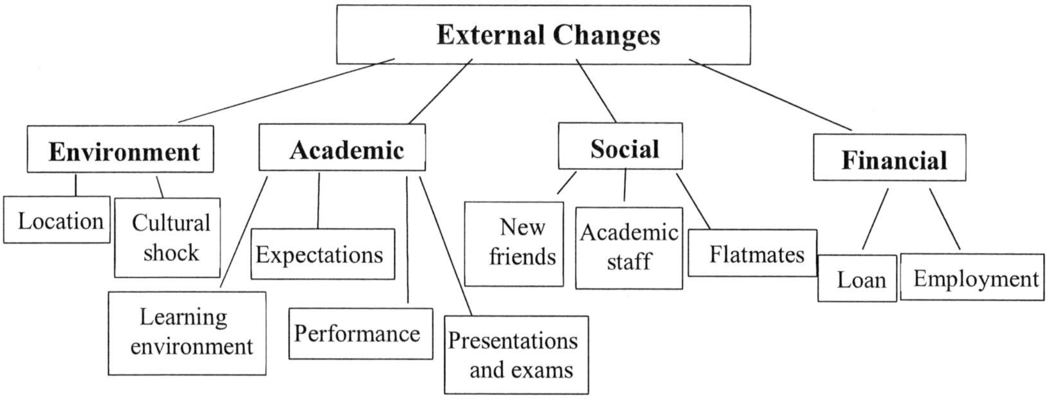

Figure 1. External changes for students starting to study at universities (adapted from Cheng 2023)

2.1.2 Possible Support Mechanisms in Formation the Student Experience in the University Studies

In order to create support mechanisms for students studying at universities throughout their study period, it is necessary to view the transition process as a continuity of a single experience. It is not enough to instruct students at the beginning of their studies about the requirements, regulations and possible assistance mechanisms during their studies at the university. First, students are often not ready for changes, sometimes their expectations are not fulfilled, which shows that the experience of studies should be formed many years before the start of studies. Students who have more precise expectations are better adapted to the transition (Denovan, Macaskill 2013). Secondly, many students face the problem throughout their studies, not only in the first year. In his research, Burnett (Burnett 2007) provides a holistic view, viewing the transition process as a continuum of cohesive experiences and distinguishes six phases in the student experience model (see Figure 2).

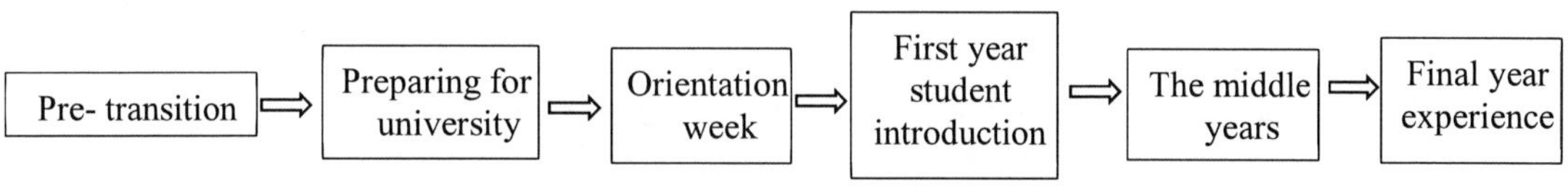

Figure 2. Phases of the Student Experience Model (adapted from Burnett 2007)

The pre-transition phase is more for elementary school students who are planning their careers. The choice of specialty at the university is based on knowledge and familiarity with the programs, attractiveness of the university's activities, financial factor, etc., where information cannot always be obtained from the university's website. Many choose to study at a particular university based on the recommendations of friends. The pre-transition stage could also be intended for workers who have planned a career change. Financial aspects and the possibility to combine studies with part-time work are also important here (Robotham, Julian 2006). In the Preparing for university phase, it is essential to strengthen the student's possible choice of program and university, increasing enthusiasm delight for the chosen program and the possibilities of the university and reducing fear of the unknown. In this phase, it is desirable to organize events where future students would have the opportunity to get to know the university in person. During the orientation week, which takes place on campus, various events are organized where students get more detailed information about the specific program, create social networks, develop academic skills, etc. The first-year students' instruction of can be both at the beginning of studies and throughout the first semester. Students experience changes in the academic environment compared to previous studies, learn to adapt to a learning environment that requires independence and an autonomous approach to learning (Frame et al 2006). The last two phases affecting middle year students and final year students are no less important. During these phases, students face problems, as the previous support is usually lost, new challenges appear, often including family relationships, full-time or part-time job offers, etc. Being aware of the peculiarities of each phase of the student experience formation model, university administrators should create appropriate support mechanisms.

2.2 Methodology of the Study

Based on Cheng's proposed classification of external changes for students starting to study at universities, a survey was created. The purpose of the survey is to identify the challenges faced by students of the Information Technologies Faculty of LBTU in the first year of study. The questionnaire included closed-ended and opened-ended questions and was conducted between April and May 2023, inviting students of the Information Technologies Faculty to fill out an electronic questionnaire. A Likert scale from 1 (strongly disagree) to 5 (strongly agree) is used in all the closed-ended questions of the questionnaire. The questionnaire is available here: https://ej.uz/ITFsurvey. Students of all four study years participated in the survey, 46% of them are 1st year students, 31% are 2nd year students, 13% and 10% are 3rd and 4th year students, respectively. Currently, a total of 295 students study at the bachelor's level in the faculty, 96 students participated in the survey, which is 32.5% of the total number of students.

3. FINDINGS

In order to clarify the impact of *environmental external changes* and potential challenges as students' transition to university life, students are asked to answer where they live (still with their parents, in a dormitory or rent). The obtained data show that 50% of surveyed students still live with their parents, 11.5% live alone in their own or rented apartment, 28.1% in a dormitory, while 10.4% rent an apartment with a friend or friends. Table 1 shows the distribution of students' living arrangements by year of study.

Table 1. Survey results on students' living arrangements

	live in dormitories	rent with friends	live with parents	live alone in their own or rented apartment
1st year students	43%	9%	39%	9%
2nd year students	17%	7%	63%	13%
3rd and 4th year students	14%	18%	55%	14%

Survey data show that almost half (43%) of 1st year students live in dormitories, but in the following years the proportion of those living in dormitories decreased rapidly to17% of 2nd year students and to 14% of 3rd year and 4th year students. At the same time, as the academic year increases, the proportion of students who live with their parents increases, which seems completely illogical. These data could indicate that it is students who live in dormitories who are potentially more likely to drop out than those who still live with their parents. On the other hand, those who live with their parents during the 1st year and have not changed their living arrangements, could be those who drop out less often. The results of the survey, which refer to students' challenges in the changes of the academic environment, are reflected in Table 2.

Only 19% of students agree (chose 4 or 5 on a Likert scale) that it was difficult to adapt to university studies. As comments to their answer, the students mention, for example, "there was a gap between graduating from a secondary school and entering a university", "It was difficult at first because I had to plan my own time", "I had a hard time understanding the structure of the university's electronic information system ", several students mention that "I didn't expect that it would be so difficult to combine work and studies at university". At the same time, 34% of students strongly disagree that adapting to university life was difficult. One of the reasons mentioned by one of the students is that in recent years the distance education training system has become more accessible in Latvia, and the graduates of distance education schools are already used to independent work.

Regarding the university's support mechanism 19% of students agree that a support mechanism would be needed to get used to the university environment, while 39% disagree. Students note that when they started their studies at the university, they missed the most information about the course of studies, changes in the list and the location of the necessary study space, as well as friends and family. Some students also mention that there was a lack of knowledge in the exact subjects.

Table 2. Survey results on students' challenges in changing academic environment

Statement	1	2	3	4	5	Mean
I had difficulty adapting to university studies	34%	29%	18%	14%	5%	2.27
Starting studies at university, I needed a support mechanism to get used to the university environment	39%	26%	16%	13%	6%	2.21
I am satisfied with the study environment at LBTU (lecture rooms, laboratory rooms, etc.)	0%	2%	18%	47%	33%	4.11
I am satisfied with the study environment outside the university (it is possible to study at home, in the library, etc.)	1%	1%	16%	45%	38%	4.17
Studying at a university is very different from studying at a secondary education institution	3%	14%	22%	31%	30%	3.72
Studies at a university require greater self-organization and self-discipline than studies in secondary education institutions	6%	3%	11%	22%	57%	4.21
I manage to plan my time in such a way that there is time for both study and relaxation	14%	27%	28%	17%	15%	2.92

It should be mentioned that the survey was conducted in the spring semester and it is very likely that those students who failed to adapt have already left their studies (this year, the number of 1st year students decreased from 167 to 130, or by 22%, comparing the number of students in the fall and spring semesters).

In order to find out the impact of external academic changes and possible challenges, the satisfaction of students with the study environment inside and outside the university was analysed. Approximately 80% of students note that they are satisfied with the study environment both at the university and outside it. 75% and 84% of the surveyed 1st year students respectively believe that they are satisfied with the study environment at LBTU and outside it. Several students note that there could be more modern physics laboratories, some rooms should have more modern equipment. However, there are also those who believe that the rooms are equipped in such a way that the study process is comfortable.

61% of students agree that the study process at a university is significantly different from the study process at a secondary school. As more significant differences, students mention greater independence, organization of time, often the opportunity to do practical tasks at home, a larger amount of learning material, as well as the fact that there is no class teacher to remind them of what has not been done on time. It should be noted that in our university there are appointed curators for each course of each specialty, to whom group leaders mostly turn for organizational issues. One could wish for more curatorial initiative in collaborating with subject teachers on student outcomes during the study process. Several students in their comments emphasize that the relationship between student and teacher at the university is collegial. Students emphasize that "the university does not have uniform criteria for obtaining a grade in each study course, the teacher declares his criteria for each course".

In order to find out the impact of external social changes and possible challenges, the survey included questions about belonging to a group, about the availability of information about extracurricular opportunities (see Table 3).

Table 3. Survey results relating to student challenges in social change

Statement	1	2	3	4	5	Mean
I feel like I belong to my group	3%	6%	22%	33%	36%	3.92
Group members are supportive	0%	4%	15%	38%	43%	4.20
Information about extracurricular opportunities at LBTU/ in the city is sufficient	3%	5%	23%	39%	30%	3.88

Students mostly agree that group members are supportive (81%) and that they feel a sense of belonging to the group (69%). But there are also those who do not feel belonging to the group, besides, they make up 9% of the 1st and 2nd year students. The survey data showed that such students are also in the 4th year, perhaps this is the result of remote studies during the Covid-19 pandemic, because these students have studied half of the 1st year and the entire 2nd year remotely. It should be noted that the authors' long-term work experience with students of the Faculty of Information Technologies shows that future IT specialists who do not fit into the group are not rare. This is also confirmed by the students themselves, stating in their comments that "I don't mind that I didn't feel like I belonged", "it's just my problem".

In order to find out the impact of external financial changes and possible challenges, the survey included the question whether students work alongside their studies. It turns out that 61% of the survey participants do not work, 21% work part-time, and 18% work full-time. In addition, the number of working students increases with each year of study (if 75% of students do not work in the 1st year, then only 30% of students in the 4th year). 60% of working students note that they work outside of study time, but 20% follow the schedule set by the employer, the rest manage to plan their work schedule according to their needs. Students have different opinions about their ability to plan time. There are those who believe that they manage to plan their time and find time and opportunity for studies, work and relaxation (32% of the surveyed students), but there are also those who do not succeed (41% of the surveyed students).

By conducting research on possible support mechanisms in shaping the student experience in LBTU studies and comparing them with the phases developed by Brunett (see Figure 2), it can be concluded that Phase 1 “Pre-Transition or Beginning to Think About University" is being implemented relatively successfully. Communication and Marketing Centre, which is one of the structural units of University, deals with student attraction, internal communication and study marketing. The Communication and Marketing Centre, in cooperation with the faculties, constantly provides excursions for high school students. During them, students are introduced to the history of Jelgava Palace (home of the LBTU), University and its activities, as well as to faculties and study programs. The Communication and Marketing Centre organizes career days, participates in exhibitions, holds open days, and coordinates advertising campaigns on TV, radio, digital channels and social networks. According to these activities, it "moves" students' brains in the direction of future professions.

The survey of first-year students (n=460) reflects that the determining factor why a young person submitted an application to LBTU is the availability of budget study places (rating 4.24 out of 5, see Figure 3). Only after that follows the fact that the specialists of the chosen study program are in demand on the labor market (rating 4.19 out of 5) (Janmere 2023).

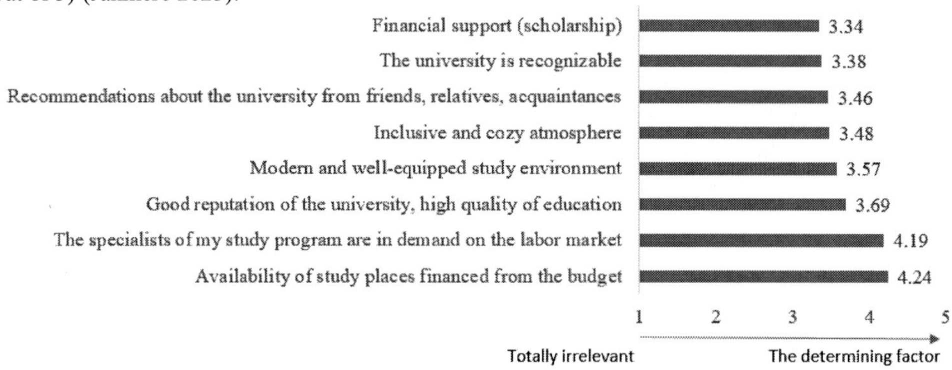

Figure 3. Factors importance when choosing studies at LBTU (Janmere 2023)

As mentioned in the Report, 32% of applicants had already made the decision to study at LBTU half a year before their studies. It must be admitted that quite a large proportion of young people make decisions about future studies at the last moment - as the survey proves, around 68%. It should be noted that Phase 2 "Preparing for university" is also being implemented relatively successfully at LBTU. University is actively involved in organizing various events with the aim of helping high school students prepare for university studies. LBTU, in cooperation with the State Educational Content Centre, organizes a scientific research competition for high school students from the Zemgale region - a conference. This event is very important for the students, because the best and most knowledgeable high school students of individual sections of the Zemgale region students' scientific research competition - conference have a unique opportunity to enter LBTU outside of the competition.

The Centre for Lifelong Education constantly provides preparatory courses, for example, in biology, chemistry, mathematics, physics, the target audience of which are students of high school graduation classes and those who have obtained secondary education, for repeating and supplementing knowledge in order to prepare for studies and exams. Over the past 5 years, the Lifelong Learning Centre has served approximately 1100 study course visitors.

The Faculty of Information Technologies offers courses in the Correspondence Programming School, which is intended for those who are interested in computer science and wish to learn programming skills individually or continue their studies in fields related to computer science and programming. Successful course graduates are awarded additional points for the competition to enter the Faculty of Information Technologies.

The Students' Self-Government also actively participates in the Phase 3 and in the following stages. This is an organization representing university students, which solves important issues of academic, social, cultural and sports life, represents and defends the opinions and rights of students in LBTU, the Latvian Student Union, as well as in other institutions and organizations at the national and international level. Our university has a very old tradition of gathering first-year students - the Azemitologs' festival, which has been held since 1968. The student government helps first-year students come together in the first month of studies and to prepare a witty performance together. We could consider this as the time of orientation and settling into the university.

Continuing with the next, 4th phase - "Introduction of first-year students", it should be noted that study course "Introduction in the specialty" is included into our programs. Within the framework of that the organization of the university's activities is explained to newly enrolled first-year students and information about the chosen program is provided. The study course provides knowledge about the higher education system in Latvia, expanded knowledge about the specialty to be studied, about the organization of the study process and the regulatory basis of studies, knowledge about the university, the chosen faculty, its structure and administration.

For example, the Faculty of Information Technologies, a curator is appointed for each student course. The curator, knowing the work organization of the university, helps students navigate the work organization of the university.

Moving forward, the university offers students various extra-curricular activities, - participate in student representative organizations, participate in independent groups, dance groups, sing in a choir, participate in sports activities, etc., which in general involve students in a unified team and this forms the overall cultural environment of the university. This strengthens the sense of belonging to the university in students.

One of the biggest problems for Latvia is the lack of effective support mechanisms for students during the study process. Although, as a result of the competition, the student has obtained a state-financed budget place at the university, he must also solve the financing of his daily expenses.

In Latvia, only 5% of students in full-time studies in places paid for by the state budget receive a state budget scholarship, and its amount is only 140 EUR per month and it is paid only 10 months a year.

The Student Union of Latvia states that the support available in Latvia is not competitive according to academic criteria. This forces even the best students to look for work that is not always possible in their industry. According to the research of the Student Union, students in Latvia work an average of 31 hours/week, which is the highest rate in Europe, and moreover, this time is most often not spent working in the industry chosen during studies.

The experience of mid-level undergraduate students is worthy of further research. Research in this area could highlight the specific problems and needs of middle year's students, resulting in the development of a program that could support all students during their undergraduate studies.

4. CONCLUSION

Based on the results of the study, concluded that only 19% of LBTU students agree that it was difficult to adapt to university studies. At the same time, 34% of students strongly disagree that adapting to university life was difficult. In recent years the distance education training system has become more accessible in Latvia. 61% of students agree that the study process at a university is significantly different from the study process at a secondary school. As more significant differences, students mention greater independence, organization of time, often opportunity to do practical tasks at home, a larger amount of learning material.

As a possible support mechanism before student's transfer to the university, we can mention activities of the LBTU Communication and Marketing Centre and the Centre for Lifelong Education. In the initial stage of studies the study course "Introduction in the specialty" is a significant part of the support mechanism.

However, one of the biggest problems not only for LBTU, but also for other Latvia universities is the lack of effective support mechanisms for students in the study process including insufficient financial support.

This study is a case study and it only reflects the views of the respondents who participated in it. The results could be used to identify problems/ directions for in-depth research.

REFERENCES

Barbara, M. et al. (2019). Student dropout from universities in Europe: *A review of empirical literature Hungarian Educational Research Journal.* Vol. 9: No. 2. Available from: https://akjournals.com/view/journals/063/9/2/article-p147.xml [20 May 2023].

Birzina, R. et al. (2019). Factors Influencing the First Year Students' Adaptation to Natural Science Studies in Higher Education. *Journal of Baltic Science Education.* Vol.18, pp 349-361.

Burnett, L. (2007). Juggling First-Year Student Experience and Institutional Change: An Australian Example. *The 20th International Conference on First Year Experience*. Hawaii, USA, pp 1-33.

Cheng, M. et al. (2023). Transition Models and How Students Experience Change. *Project report of University of Glasgow (now University of Wolverhampton).* The Quality Assurance Agency for Higher Education, Scotland, UK. Available from: https://www.enhancementthemes.ac.uk/docs/ethemes/student-transitions/transition-models-and-how-students-experience-change.pdf [9 January 2023].

Denovan, A., Macaskill, A. (2013). An interpretative phenomenological analysis of stress and coping in first year undergraduates. *British Educational Research*. Vol. 39 No.6, pp 1002-1024.

European Commission/EACEA/Eurydice (2015). *The European Higher Education Area in 2015: Bologna Process Implementation Report.* Luxembourg, Publications Office of the European Union. Available from: https://www.ehea.info/media.ehea.info/file/2015_Yerevan/73/3/2015_Implementation_report_20.05.2015_613733.pdf [20 May 2023].

Frame, P. et al. (2006). Transitions into Higher Education: processes, outcomes and collaborations. *Proceedings of the Association of Tertiary Learning Advisors Aotearoa, Supporting Learning in the 21st Century*. Dunedin, New Zealand, pp 32-46.

Jackson, C. (2010). Transitions into Higher Education: Gendered implications for academic self-concept. *Oxford Review of Education*. Vol. 29 No.3, pp 331-346.

Janmere, L. (2023). Activity Report of the Communication and Marketing Centre. Available from: https://www.llu.lv/lv/pieteikties_jaunumiem/e4a6222c26408ffa/KMC_darbiba_2022.pdf [20 May 2023].

Masterson, V. (2022). *More students are dropping out of college in the US – here's why. Education, Skills and Learning.* Available from: https://www.weforum.org/agenda/2022/09/college-student-dropouts-2022/ [6 September 2022].

McCulloch, A. (2014). *Learning from future track: dropout from higher education.* BIS research paper, no. 168, BIS, London, UK. Available from: https://www.gov.uk/government/uploads/system/uploads/attachment_data/file/287689/bis-14-641-learning-from-futuretrack-dropout-from-higher-education-bis-research-paper-168.pdf [25 May 2023].

OECD (2016). *Education at a Glance 2016: OECD Indicators.* OECD Publishing, Paris. Available from: https://doi.org/10.1787/eag-2016-en. [20 May 2023].

OECD (2018). *Education at a Glance 2018: OECD Indicators*, OECD Publishing, Paris. Available from: https://doi.org/10.1787/eag-2018-en. [20 May 2023].

Perry, C., Allard, A. (2003). Making the connections: Transition experiences for first-year education students. *Journal of Educational Enquiry*, Vol. 4, No. 2. pp 74-89.

Quinn, J. (2013). Drop-out and Completion in Higher Education in Europe among students from under-represented groups. *An independent report authored for the European Commission.* European Union. Available from: https://nesetweb.eu/wp-content/uploads/2019/06/2013-Drop-out-and-Completion-in-Higher-Education-in-Europe-among-students-from-under-represented-groups.pdf [20 May 2023].

Robotham, D., Julian, C. (2006). Stress and the higher education student: a critical review of the literature. *Journal of Further and Higher Education*. Vol. 30 No. 2, pp 107-117.

Romanenko, V., Nikitina, G. (2016). Cognitive stress in pedagogics: general analysis. *Proceedings of the 9th international scientific conference Rural Environment. Education. Personality (REEP).* Latvia University of Agriculture, Jelgava, Latvia, pp 121-127.

Sevinc, S., Gizir, C. A. (2014). Factors Negatively Affecting University Adjustment from the Views of First-Year University Students: The Case of Mersin University. *Educational Sciences: Theory and Practice*. Vol. 14 No.4, pp 1301-1308.

The European Higher Education Area in 2015: Bologna Process, 2015. Implementation Report. Luxembourg: Publications Office of the European Union Education, Audiovisual and Culture Executive Agency.

SYSTEMATIC LITERATURE REVIEW OF THE EFFORT OF GAMING ELEMENTS ON E-LEARNING PLATFORMS

Tobias Harald Popp and Heidi Schuhbauer
Nuremberg Institute of Technology
Nuremberg, Germany

ABSTRACT

Gamification is the use of game elements in a non-game context to encourage desired behaviours (Detering 2011a). It has been identified as a promising technique for improving user motivation on e-learning platforms. Since previous literature reviews and meta-analyses only considered gamification and learning effort without focusing directly on gamification elements, a research gap was identified. Based on the studies analysed, the most commonly used gamification elements in the literature were identified and examined to determine whether there are any significant results in terms of motivational changes. Three areas of research questions were formulated for this meta-analysis: Which gamification elements should be used to increase learning motivation in asynchronous e-learning? Which success factors should be considered to increase the motivation of the learners by using gamification elements? Is there a specific selection of gamification elements that significantly increase motivation in asynchronous e-learning? The literature search process consisted of a manual search for research articles in electronic libraries with a pre-defined search string. Afterwards, the studies were examined to determine their relevance based on defined inclusion and exclusion criteria. The next step was title and abstract screening followed by a full-text screening. A complementary search of the included literature was then conducted using snowballing techniques. Finally, the most relevant literature was reviewed using quality assessment. The most promising gamification elements are badges, leaderboards, level up systems and progress bars. The combination of elements increases users' motivation significantly, especially the combination of badges with leaderboards or level up systems. These insights contribute to the design of e-learning platforms.

KEYWORDS

Badge, E-Learning Platform, Gamification, Leaderboard, Level up System

1. INTRODUCTION

One of the most downloaded educational apps in the Apple App Store worldwide is Duolingo, a free language-learning app (Apple 2023) which supports learning with visual and audio-visual lessons. However, the most important aspect is that the app uses gamification in its lessons, especially gamification elements, such as progress bars and experience points (Huyn 16). These aim to motivate users and make learning more effective. Consequently, such user experience decisions contribute greatly to the success of the app (Huyn 16). The growing market for e-learning applications is one of the reasons why the gamification market has more than doubled its value between 2016 and 2021 (Clement 2021). However, opinions often differ on the correct implementation of gamification elements, particularly when the focus is on learning motivation (Luria 2021). Analytics of serious games measure, assess and improve the effort of learning games (Loth et al., 2015; Ge & Ifenthaler 2018).

Despite many reviews and meta-analyses in the area of gamification, the studies available do not specifically address the influence of gamification elements on users' motivation. While some meta-analyses have examined motivational change by the use of gamification, it was not the main focus of their research and not tailored to gamification elements (Tamilmani 2019) (Rohan 2020) (Baptista 2019). Some systematic literature reviews tend to examine trends in gamification and e-learning and provide an outline mapping (Behl 2022) (Silva 2020) (Nadi-Ravandi 22). Other studies examine gamification without explicitly focusing on e-learning (Latifi 2022). Some literature reviews do not explicitly examine the use of gamification elements when evaluating relevant studies in this field (Saleem 2022) (Ertan 22). There was none meta-analysis found, which focusses on the influence of specified gamification elements on users' motivation on e-learning platforms.

As a consequence of this identified research gap, three research questions were formulated for this meta-analysis which focuses on gamification elements on e-learning platforms:

Research Question 1: Which gamification elements should be used to increase learning motivation in asynchronous e-learning?

Research Question 2: Which measures should be considered to increase the motivation of the learners by using gamification elements?

Research Question 3: Is there a specific selection of gamification elements that significantly increase motivation in asynchronous e-learning?

The literature search process consisted of a manual search for research articles in electronic libraries with a pre-defined search string. Afterwards, the studies were examined to determine their relevance based on defined inclusion and exclusion criteria. The next step was title and abstract screening followed by a full-text screening. A complementary search of the included literature was then conducted using snowballing techniques. Finally, the most relevant literature was reviewed using quality assessment.

The findings of this meta-analysis can be useful for the design of learning applications. They show which gamification elements can improve learning effects and improve users' motivation. They reveal which gamification elements achieve significant effects in combination with each other.

2. GAMIFICATION ELEMENTS

As defined by Huotari and Hamari, gamification is the process of enriching services with (motivating) opportunities to elicit game-like experiences and further behavioural out-comes (Huotari 2012) (Hamari 2013). In their definition, they emphasize that gamification evokes the same psychological experiences as games do (Huotari 2012). Deterding et al. underline that the elements and mechanics implemented in gamification must be the same as in traditional games, regardless of the outcomes, and that participants are primarily trying to achieve specific goals (Deterding 2011a). From academic and industry perspectives, gamification applications are almost exclusively described as design elements for rule-based, goal-oriented play (Deterding 2011a). Deterding et al. also define gamification as using game elements and mechanics in non-game contexts (Deterding 2011b), while Gabe Zichermann and Christopher Cunningham define gamification as a method of engaging users and solving problems by adapting game elements or mechanics from a game context (Zichermann 2011).

Researchers have defined game mechanics and elements in different ways and from diverse perspectives. Most articles and textbooks rely on the definitions of Zichermann and Cunningham (2011) and Bunchball (2010). The main game elements suited for e-learning platforms are summarized as follows:

Badges in e-learning are comparable to badges in the real world; they are essentially digital images awarded to the user for achieving a specific goal. The user should be motivated by working toward the badge and seeing it as a reward or feedback for their accomplishments. The term leaderboard refers to a list of users or usernames. In this list, users can directly compare their performance ranking with that of other users at a glance. In this way, a user's motivation is increased by the competitive ambition to be superior to others. Points are understood as all elements which the user receives as a reward for an accomplishment. This can either be digital currency, like coins, or other means to help users increase their scores. Progress bars, similar to the ones seen when loading a computer program, offer direct feedback to users about their progress. The user should be motivated by feedback that only a few tasks remain before the next reward is achieved. A level up system assigns a user a level or rank. This status quantitatively describes the user's progress. For example, the user typically starts at level one, advancing to level two after completing a set number of tasks. To reach a higher level, the user must amass experience points. These are usually achieved by completing tasks. The user is motivated by a feeling of constant progress. One feature that aims to increase motivation through negative feedback is lives. This type of feedback refers to the survival of the virtual avatar that the user controls. In this way, the user is motivated not to make mistakes, so that the game or task is not prematurely terminated. Performance charts are graphs that give users accurate feedback about their performance. Motivation is increased by users' desires to surpass their previous performances. Other typical rewards are unlocking a lock, gaining a treasure chest or feedback.

3. SYSTEMATIC LITERATURE REVIEW

This meta-analysis is based on the guidelines for conducting systematic literature reviews in software engineering by Kitchenham and Charters (2007). According to these guidelines, a systematic literature review is a form of secondary study that uses a well-defined methodology to identify, analyse, and interpret all available evidence related to a particular research question in a specific research area. In addition, this research aims to be unbiased and replicable.

A systematic literature review begins with the establishment of a review protocol that defines the research questions and methods for conducting the review. A search strategy is created, with the goal of collecting a large amount of relevant literature from selected databases. The search strategy is documented so that readers and other researchers can understand the entire process. Primary studies to be reviewed are selected based on explicit inclusion and exclusion criteria, followed by quality assessment. The information to be obtained from each selected study is also specified. (Kitchenham &Charters 2007).

3.1 Scope of the Study

The main objective of this research work is drawing evidence-based conclusions about the use of gamification elements in terms of motivational change based on past empirical results. The paper also aims to clarify which of these elements should be used and how they should be applied to e-learning. In addition, it should also be determined whether the literature research provides evidence that the increase in learner motivation is significant.

For the specification of the aspects of the literature review, the PICOC method proposed by Petticrew and Roberts (2008) was used. PICOC is an acronym for Population, Intervention, Comparison, Outcomes and Context. This method allows the researcher to describe in detail the target group for the research (population), to determine the aspects of the study (intervention), to present what the results are comparatively (comparison), to describe the results of the study (outcomes) and to define the research area (context). Table 1 presents the PICOC method used in this work.

Table 1. Population, intervention, comparison, outcomes and context of the study

PICOC	Description
Population	Research articles on increasing motivation in asynchronous e-learning with gamification elements
Intervention	Empirical studies that provide results regarding changes in motivation through the use of gamification elements in asynchronous e-learning
Comparison	Comparable data on motivation changes
Outcomes	Identify the gamification elements that increase motivation in the most positive way
Context	E-learning

3.2 Literature Search and Selection

The sources of the meta-analysis were digital libraries, more precisely ACM Digital Library, IATED Digital Library, PubMed, Web of Science, ERIC, Springer Link, Science Direct, IEEExplore and The No Significant Difference database. These databases were selected because they all contain a wide range of literature on the topic of technology and teaching and the articles were mostly published at reviewed conferences.

For a more detailed search of the electronic libraries, a search string corresponding to the scope was defined as follows:

("gamification") AND ("e-learning" OR "distance learning" OR "online course") AND ("motivation" OR "encouragement" OR "engagement") AND ("empirical")

If a filter was available in the databases that limited the search to research articles, this filter was also selected. If the search result contained studies that were not research articles, they were not considered in the further process. Specific inclusion and exclusion criteria were defined based on the research questions. Articles were included if they met all the inclusion criteria (see Table 2). If a study met at least one exclusion criterion (see Table 3), it was excluded regardless of the inclusion criteria. IC01 was defined as only empirical research is relevant to answer the research question. IC02 was set up because motivational change should be the scope of the articles. IC03 and IC04 were relevant as the articles needed to seek a clear research result in the field of gamification. The decision for EC01 was based on the fact that the focus of the research needed to be on the use of gamification in asynchronous e-learning. In addition, works that explained the range of topics holistically should also be sorted out (EC02). Again, it should be mentioned that only gamification is accepted and not the use of, for example, complete games or serious games. EC03 ensured the selection of only current articles (i.e., works from the last ten years). This exclusion criterion was also important because in some databases, a search filter cannot be set for publication date, and in the snowballing step, the publication date cannot be preselected. Since the keywords in the search string are often used in the same way in other languages, the search result may also have contained articles not written in English. Since this cannot be filtered out in every database using the filter functions and because of the snowballing step, EC04 was set up.

In addition, it should be noted that in the title and abstract screening, articles were accepted rather than rejected when there were doubts about meeting the inclusion and exclusion criteria, which allowed further examination of these articles in the full-text screening.

Table 2. Inclusion criteria

Number	Criteria description
IC01	Empirical studies - Studies analyze the use of gamification in the e-learning environment, experimental data, data on the use of gamification in the context of e-learning
IC02	Part of the study is an analysis of the motivation change of participants.
IC03	The study has gamification as its research subject.
IC04	The research paper has a clearly formulated objective.

Table 3. Exclusion Criteria

Number	Criteria description
EC01	Literature that does not primarily focus on gamification in asynchronous e-learning
EC02	Papers on the overall context of gamification in e-learning
EC03	Articles not published between 2012 and 2022
EC04	Articles not published entirely in English

After the full-text screening, the snowballing procedure was started to find other related works that could not be found during the manual database search but could be relevant to the results of the research. Snowballing is a technique that allows the discovery of related literature from the list of references (backward snowballing) or through articles that cite the found literature (forward snowballing). For some works, snowballing was divided into two or more iterations. In the first iteration, papers were taken from the full-text screening, and their references were screened against the defined exclusion and inclusion criteria. In the second iteration, papers found to be suitable in the first iteration were analyzed. In both iterations, papers were screened first for title and abstract and then for full text. Due to the high number of duplicates in the first iteration, it can be assumed that any further iteration would not lead to a significant increase in the number of papers.

Studies were selected based on quality assessment criteria. For each criterion, the article received a certain number of points: the scoring procedure was "yes"=1, "no"=0, and "partially"=0.5. The criteria were the questions described in Table 4. The literature sources which were not filtered out by the inclusion and exclusion criteria and which received a score higher than 4 in the quality assessment were selected for data extraction. A score of 4 was chosen, because only articles with this score and higher (according to the quality assessment questions) contained enough information to answer the research questions. Criterion Q01 was chosen to give a study with more than 100 participants a higher score than a study with fewer participants, based on the assumption that the result which has a larger sample size should have a higher informative value. Q02 rated the studies according to the comprehensibility of the articles describing them. Accordingly, studies were rated "yes" if they were described in a comprehensible manner throughout, with "partially" if parts of the experiment were unclear, and "no" if the experiment was hardly or not at all comprehensible. Whether the study participants were clearly described was assessed in Q03. If "yes", at least the number of participants and an age range were provided. If "partial", for example, the age restriction was missing or participants were described as "undergraduate students" or "average age 20". If "no", both the number of participants and an age specification were missing. Criterion Q04 was rated "yes" if the data extraction of the study was described completely and comprehensibly. It was rated "partial" if incompleteness or confounding variables were possible in the data collection, and "no" if it was described only succinctly or with indications of possible errors. Q05 was selected because a study examining a single gamification element was seen to provide a more accurate measure of motivational change. This also applies to Q06, since a comparison between the experimental and control groups is important for conclusions to be drawn. Q07 rated studies more highly when they tested the differences between groups for significance, which also improves the validity of the results and allowed for a later comparison of the studies' metadata. Q08 rated the significance of the results.

Table 3. Quality assessment criteria

Number	Question	Answer
Q01	Was the study conducted with more than 100 participants?	Yes/No
Q02	Was the experimental set up comprehensible?	Yes/No/Partially
Q03	Were the participants or observational units clearly described?	Yes/No/Partially
Q04	Were the data collections well-executed and described in a comprehensible way?	Yes/No/Partially
Q05	Were individual gamification elements examined in the study?	Yes/No
Q06	Was the study conducted with an experimental and a control group? Was it a comparative study comparing an experimental design with and without gamification?	Yes/No
Q07	Were the differences between the gamification and non-gamification groups tested for significance with regard to motivation change?	Yes/No
Q08	Were the results significant?	Yes/No

The search process in the databases took place during June 2022 and lasted four weeks. It was based on the title of the article, the abstract, and (in some cases) the conclusion. If the paper did not contain an abstract, the introduction was used for the title and abstract screening. The decision to include or exclude articles was based on the screenings and the quality assessment. Figure 1 shows the PRISMA flow diagram for the complete literature search procedure and visualizes the systematic selection of hits.

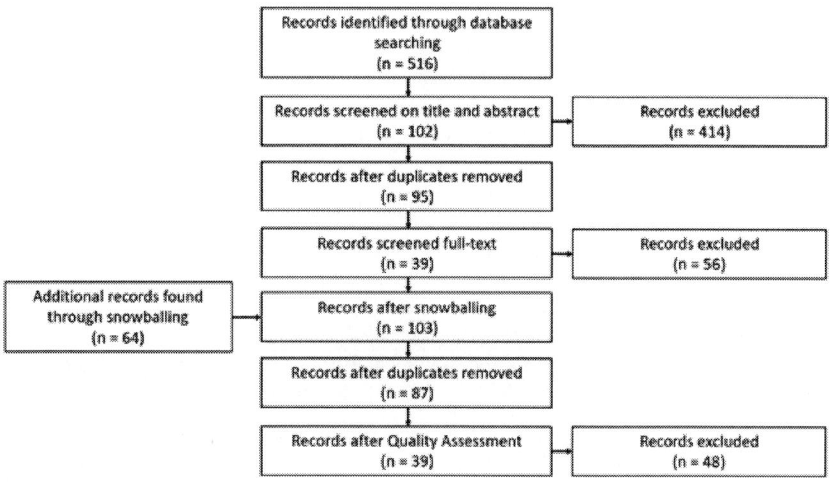

Figure 1. Flow diagram of literature search and selection

4. RESULTS

Three different approaches were observed in the selected studies to analyse users 'behaviour. The first involved the evaluation of users' system log data. The second used data collection through a motivation survey; the third used questionnaire surveys with individual questions on motivation. The system log evaluation method was used 23 times, the motivation survey 13 times, and the questionnaire about motivation 3 times. Changes in intrinsic motivation were examined 12 times, and changes in extrinsic motivation were examined 27 times. The total number of participants in all 39 studies was 26,553. Overall, 27 tests led to significant results, while 12 led to non-significant results. Regarding the distribution of gamification elements, a total of 15 studies was found in which only one gamification element was used. The only elements tested separately were leaderboards, in 2 studies and badges, in 13 studies. 35 studies used badges (together with other elements or separately). Leaderboards were implemented in 21 studies. Points were present in eleven studies. Level up systems were used in eight studies, and progress bars were used in seven. Lives, performance graphs, and other rewards were represented in only one study each. The most frequently represented gamification elements are described in more detail in the following paragraphs:

Badges: Of the 35 studies in which badges were integrated into the e-learning platform, 25 resulted in a significant outcome, while 10 resulted in a non-significant outcome. In turn, when examining extrinsic motivational changes, 20 studies produced a significant result, and 3 produced a non-significant result. Of the studies with significant results, 19 resulted in a positive outcome, and one resulted in a negative outcome. When examining changes in intrinsic motivation, 7 studies produced a non-significant result, while 5 led to a significant result. However, of these significant results, all 5 were positive. In almost every case, the quantitative results suggest that badges significantly increase extrinsic motivation. Intrinsic motivation is also positively influenced. In studies with significantly positive results, the e-learning platforms had an overview page where users could always see their badges, and conditions were clearly described (5 studies). In addition, most of these studies were characterized by the user receiving a positive instant message immediately after fulfilling the badge condition (8 studies). Some of the e-learning platforms released new badges daily or weekly, or required daily or weekly interaction with the platform to obtain them (4 studies). Furthermore, some badges had the condition of solving a task in a special way within a defined timeframe (4 studies). On the one hand, badges can be skill-based, that is, designed to spur the user to practice toward better performance (4 studies). On the other hand, badges can be based more on effort, encouraging the user to stay engaged on the platform for longer (5 studies). Finally, in studies with significantly positive results, badges were described as having a modern, creative, and visually appealing design that was associated with the condition of the badge (6 studies).

Leaderboard: Out of the 21 studies that implemented leaderboards into their e-learning platforms, 15 produced a significant result, while 6 produced non-significant results. When extrinsic motivational change was examined, all 12 studies yielded significant results, and all 12 resulted in positive outcomes. When examining changes in intrinsic motivation, 3 studies produced non-significant results and 3 produced significant results; all were positive. As with badges, in almost all cases the quantitative results suggest that leaderboards significantly increase extrinsic motivation. Intrinsic motivation shows only positive results in the significant studies, but the sample size is too small to make a definitive statement here. As with badges, moving up the rankings resulted in a positive instant message for those studies with significantly positive results (2 studies). In addition, most studies described that the overview of rankings was limited to the top places to ensure that everyone see these usernames, even if their names were anonymized (5 studies). Relative leaderboards, which only show users directly above or below the current user, did not produce significant results. In some studies, a high placement in the leaderboard was also combined with a positive response, as with badges (2 studies). Thus, users received a positive instant message as soon as they appeared in the rankings.

Points: Of the studies that introduced the use of points, 6 produced significant results, whereas 4 produced non-significant results. When extrinsic motivational changes were examined, 6 studies revealed significant results, and one study showed a non-significant result. Of the studies with significant results, 5 studies resulted in positive outcomes, and one resulted in a negative outcome. When examining changes in intrinsic motivation, all 3 studies yielded non-significant results.

Progress bars: Of the 8 studies that integrated progress bars into their e-learning platforms, 6 studies resulted in significant outcomes, while 2 studies resulted in non-significant outcomes. When examining extrinsic motivational changes, 5 studies produced significant results and 2 studies produced non-significant results. For this gamification element, all of the studies came to positive conclusions. Only one study examined changes in intrinsic motivation, and it came to a significant conclusion.

Level up system: Of the 8 studies that integrated level up systems into their e-learning platforms, 7 studies resulted in significant outcomes and one resulted in a non-significant outcome. When extrinsic changes in motivation were examined, 6 studies came to significant results, while one study came to a non-significant result. The one study that examined changes in intrinsic motivation also came to a significant result. In any case, the quantitative results here indicate that level up systems increase extrinsic motivation, and significantly so in almost all cases. Intrinsic motivation is also positively influenced, but the identified studies do not provide sufficient sample sizes. In studies with significantly positive results, users are presented with a progress bar that shows them how many experience points they still need to increase their level (4 studies). Users were promoted once the progress bar was completely filled, but the experience points were not reset as a result (4 studies). Rather, the experience points are ever-growing numbers, which means higher requirements per level (5 studies). To earn these points, users had to complete tasks or challenges within the e-learning platform (3 studies). In some of the studies with positive results, users also received a sign of appreciation in the form of a positive message or badge for level advancement (2 studies).

Lives: Only one study was found which investigated this gamification element. The result of this study was significantly positive, but other gamification elements (progress bar and level-up system) were also implemented there.

Performance graphs: Only one study examined this gamification element. Its result was significantly positive, although badges and a leaderboard were also used as gamification elements.

Interesting is the analysis of combinations of gamification elements. Badges combined with leaderboards, for example, produce more significant results than any other combination; all were positive. In addition, badges combined with a level up system showed 6 studies significantly positive outcomes from 6 studies. Level up systems again showed only positive results with leaderboards, of which 5 studies out of 6 studies were statistically significant. Progress bars were introduced along with the level up system in all but one of the studies. Accordingly, all results were positive, and 6 studies out of 7 studies were even statistically significant. Progress bars used together with leaderboards and badges also showed only positive results, most of them were statistically significant. The progress bar appeared in 4 studies with significantly positive results as part of the level up system element. In 4 studies, progress bars were used for the progress visualization of fulfilling tasks or earning badges. Table 4 summarizes the results.

Table 4. Results summary

	Number of Studies	exclusive use	extrinsic positive significant	extrinsic negative significant	intrinsic positive significant	intrinsic negative significant
Badges	35	13	19	1	5	0
Leaderboard	21	2	12	0	3	0
Points	10	0	5	1	0	0
Progress bars	8	0	5	0	1	0
Level up system	8	0	6	0	1	0
Lives	1	0	1	0	0	0
Performance Graphs	1	0	1	0	0	0

5. CONCLUSION

This research work gives useful hints to implement gamification elements in e-learning platforms to increase users' motivation. First, the results of the study show that gamification can significantly increase motivation. The answer to research question 1 is: The most promising gamification elements therefore are badges, leaderboards, progress bars and level up systems. The answer to research question 2 is: Success factors for badges are overview pages, where users could always see their badges, positive instant messages immediately after reaching a badge, the regular release of new badges and a modern, creative design. By using leaderboards, positive instant messages for climbing up the rankings increase users' motivation. An overview with the top rankings should be visible for all. Progress bars should be used in combination with badges or level up systems by showing how many points are missing to the next level/badge. The answer to research question 3 is: Studies reveal that combination of gamification elements produces more positive effects than only the implementation of a single element. Interesting is the fact, that most gamification elements are not exclusively used. Of the 15 studies, which use only one gamification element exclusively, are 13 studies about badges and two studies about leaderboards. This is a strong hint that further research about the influence of specified gamification elements on users' motivation is necessary. Overall, the specific combination of gamification elements that will be most effective in increasing motivation will depend on the specific needs and preferences of learners, as well as the context of the learning experience. However, by combining some successful gamification elements, designers and instructors can create engaging and motivating e-learning experiences that promote learning and retention.

REFERENCES

Apple. (2023). *Duolingo*. Retrieved from: https://apps.apple.com/de/app/duolingo/id570060128

Baptista, G., & Oliveira, T. (2019). Gamification and serious games: A literature meta-analysis and integrative model. *Computers in Human Behavior*, *92*, 306-315.

Behl, A., et al. (2022). Gamification and e-learning for young learners: A systematic literature review, bibliometric analysis, and future research agenda. *Technological Forecasting and Social Change*, *176*, 121445.

Bunchball, A. (2010). Gamification 101: An Introduction to the Use of Game Mechanics to Influence Behavior.

Clement, J. (2021). *Value of the gamification market worldwide in 2016 and 2021*. Retrieved from https://www.statista.com/statistics/608824/gamification-market-value-worldwide/

Deterding, S., et al. (2011a). From game design elements to gamefulness: defining" gamification". In Proceedings of the 15th international academic MindTrek conference: Envisioning future media environments (pp. 9-15).

Deterding, S., et al. (2011b). Gamification: Toward a definition. CHI 2011 Gamification Workshop Proceedings. In 2011 Annual Conference on Human Factors in Computing Systems (CHI'11).

Ertan, K., & Kocadere, S. A. (2022). Gamification design to increase motivation in online learning environments: a systematic review. Journal of Learning and Teaching in Digital Age, 7(2), 151-159.

Ge, X., & Ifenthaler, D. (2018). Designing engaging educational games and assessing engagement in game-based learning. In *Gamification in Education: Breakthroughs in Research and Practice* (pp. 1-19). IGI Global.

Hamari, J. (2013). Transforming homo economicus into homo ludens: A field experiment on gamification in a utilitarian peer-to-peer trading service. Electronic commerce research and applications, 12(4), 236-245.

Huotari, K., & Hamari, J. (2012). Defining gamification: a service marketing perspective. In Proceeding of the 16th international academic MindTrek conference (pp. 17-22).

Huynh, D., Zuo, L., & Iida, H. (2016). Analyzing gamification of "Duolingo" with focus on its course structure. In *Games and Learning Alliance: 5th International Conference, GALA 2016, Utrecht, The Netherlands, December 5–7, 2016, Proceedings 5* (pp. 268-277). Springer International Publishing.

Kitchenham, B. & Charters, S. (2007). *Guidelines for performing Systematic Literature Reviews in Software Engineering*. Vol. 2.

Latifi, G. R., et al. (2022). Gamification and citizen motivation and vitality in smart cities: A qualitative meta-analysis study. GeoJournal, 87(2), 1217-1230.

Loh, C. S., Sheng, Y., & Ifenthaler, D. (2015). Serious games analytics: Theoretical framework. *Serious games analytics: Methodologies for performance measurement, assessment, and improvement*, 3-29.

Luria, E. et al. (2021). Cognitive neuroscience perspectives on motivation and learning: revisiting self-determination theory. *Mind, Brain, and Education*, *15*(1), 5-17.

Nadi-Ravandi, S., & Batooli, Z. (2022). Gamification in education: A scientometric, content and co-occurrence analysis of systematic review and meta-analysis articles. *Education and Information Technologies*, *27*(7), 10207-10238.

Petticrew, M., & Roberts, H. (2008). Systematic reviews in the social sciences: A practical guide. John Wiley & Sons.

Rohan, R., et al. (2020). Gamifying MOOC's a Step in The Right Direction? A Systematic Literature Review. In *Proceedings of the 11th International Conference on Advances in Information Technology* (pp. 1-10).

Saleem, A. N., et al (2022). Gamification applications in E-learning: A literature review. Technology, Knowledge and Learning, 27(1), 139-159.

Silva, R., et al. (2020). Gamification in management education-A literature mapping. *Education and Information Technologies*, *25*, 1803-1835.

Tamilmani, K., et al. (2019). The battle of Brain vs. Heart: A literature review and meta-analysis of "hedonic motivation" use in UTAUT2. *International Journal of Information Management*, *46*, 222-235.

Zichermann, G. & Cunningham, C. (2011). *Gamification by design: Implementing game mechanics in web and mobile apps*. O'Reilly Media, Inc.

THE TRIGGER-BASED DISCUSSION-ORIENTED CONTINUOUS LEARNING MODEL

Dina A. Zekry and Gerard T. McKee
The British University in Egypt
El-Shrouk City, Egypt

ABSTRACT

The paper explores current learning approaches. The authors present the Trigger-Based Discussion-Oriented Continuous learning model (TbDoC) that focuses on creating a continuous learning experience over the online and off-line (on-campus) learning environments. The model aims to create a more engaging learning environment that encourages discussion and increases the ability of students to be independent learners. The proposed learning model utilizes an adapted version of the Hook model, the simplification aspect of the Fogg behavior model, and a socio-educational approach to learning. The model starts with the lecturer sending the students an email on the night prior to the lecture. The email contains a set of questions related to the lecture material. The students are prompted to search for answers to the questions and in doing so they are preparing for the lecture. On the next day during the lecture, the lecturer begins to direct the student-to-lecturer discussion. The lecture material is fully uncovered by the students with the help of the lecturer through the discussion. The qualitative behaviour observations showed positive impact of the model on the students and the learning environment. It was observed that students became more independent learners and were more motivated to engage in the discussions.

KEYWORDS

Learning Model, HOOK Model, Fogg Behavior Model, Socio-Educational Environment

1. INTRODUCTION

Since the outbreak of COVID-19 pandemic in 2019, the world has undergone drastic changes across various fields. Integrating technology into various aspects of daily life has become a necessity to reduce human interaction and mitigate the spread of COVID-19. In the education field, this translated to a shift from face-to-face on-campus learning to the adoption of online learning.

After the pandemic, the education sector maintained an interest in integrating technology but most education institutes reverted back to off-line (on-campus) learning. This can be attributed to two main factors. Namely, that education is fundamentally based on human interaction and face-to-face communication and the limitations of online learning (Struthers et al., 2022; Sun et al., 2020). The limitations include the following: first, not all students or lecturers had access to the required technology or stable internet connection, second, the lack of instant feedback and face-to-face interaction, third, some lecturers struggled to adapt their teaching methods to the online environment which impacted the quality of teaching, forth, the lack of motivation and engagement, and fifth, the lack of practical implementation for courses that required hands-on practical application in labs and workshops (Koay et al., 2021; Struthers et al., 2022; Sun et al., 2020). Following the pandemic, educational institutes dedicated their efforts towards the integration of technology, enhancement of student engagement, and refinement of pedagogical approaches (Struthers et al., 2022). Consequently, a multitude of teaching methods emerged and previous teaching methods were enhanced.

The authors identified a research gap in establishing a seamless learning experience between the online and on-campus learning environments. The authors propose a new learning model named the Trigger-Based Discussion-Oriented Continuous Learning Model (TbDoC). The learning model incorporates and adapted version of the HOOK model, the simplification aspect of the Fogg behaviour model, and a social aspect to encourage a socio-educational learning environment. The learning model focuses on creating a continuous learning experience between the online and off-line (on-campus) learning environments. The research goal is to explore the impact of implementing TbDoC and evaluate qualitatively if the learning model has an impact on students' behaviour as well as identify if the learning model develops more independent learners and motivate discussion.

The paper is organised as follows section 2 details the literature review of learning approaches, the HOOK model, and the Fogg model focusing on the simplification aspect. Section 3 discusses the proposed learning model and the model's methodology. Section 4 details the implementation of the proposed learning model covering the model aspects. Section 5 sums up the conclusion. Section 6 discusses the future work.

2. LITERATURE REVIEW

The following section discusses different learning approaches including discussion-based learning, blended/hybrid learning, and collaborative learning. The section also discusses the HOOK model, the Fogg Behavioral model, and the socio-educational aspect of education.

2.1 Learning Approaches

First, the discussion-based learning approach focuses on interactive and collaborative learning discussions (Abdulbaki et al., 2018; Picault, 2021). The discussions are peer-to-peer discussions and peer-to-lecturer discussions. It is more likely that discussion-based learning environment takes place in the traditional offline environment where structured discussions, debates, group activities, and open dialogues take place. The goal of this approach is to actively engage students in critical thinking, analysis, and problem-solving through meaningful conversations. The key characteristics of the discussion-learning is that it is student-centered where critical-thinking, active participation, collaboration, diverse perspectives, and higher-order learning exist with the lecturer being the facilitator (Abdulbaki et al., 2018; Li & Pei, 2023; Picault, 2021). The approach aims to develop higher-order cognitive skills such as analysis, synthesis, evaluation, and application of knowledge.

Second, the blended/hybrid approach that combines both offline and online education (Li & Pei, 2023; Sharma et al., 2022; Stoian et al., 2022). Blended learning allows students to engage in the traditional education settings as well as virtual learning experience. This method is flexible by allowing students to access the course material and complete their assignments when it is convenient and at their own pace while maintaining the face-to-face sessions that enable monitoring and instant feedback. The curriculum is evaluated according to the learning objectives to decide which portions can be studied online and which require face-to-face interaction. The online portions are delivered to the students through the learning management system (LMS) in the form of lecture slides, lecture videos, quizzes, and reading lists. The on-campus portions are reserved for the material that require hands-on practice. Lecturers monitor the students learning process and can implement changes that would benefit the students as well as provide regular feedback. The goal of blended learning is to enhance engagement, allow for differentiated instruction, and provide flexibility in learning experiences.

Third, the collaborative learning approach which empathizes group activities and interactions to achieve learning objectives (Yang, 2023). Students work together on projects, discussions, and problem solving. The characteristics of this approach is teamwork, peer learning, and exchange of diverse perspectives (Yang, 2023). Students are organized in small groups that often consist of three to five students. Each group is given a clear objective per assigned task to provide the group with a direction that aligns with the educational outcome. Engaging activities take place during the session including, problem-solving tasks, group discussions, peer teaching, and brainstorming sessions. At the conclusion of the session, a debriefing session is conducted to consolidate the knowledge generated by each group, share valuable insights, and engage in final reflections on the content. The goal of collaborative learning is to enhance social skills, communication, and the ability to work effectively in groups.

Other methods have been developed such as online synchronous learning, online asynchronous learning, flipped class room, project-based learning, gamification, personalized learning, micro learning, and simulation learning (Koay et al., 2021; Struthers et al., 2022; Stoian et al., 2022; Sun et al., 2020). Each of the mentioned learning methods has its characteristics and method of implementation. All of the previous methods aim to enhance the effectiveness of education, improve student engagement, and facilitate meaningful learning experience. The learning methods either focus on one environment (online or offline) or attempt to combine both. However, in approaches that try to combine both environments, there is a separation between the activities carried out within each environment where the learning experience is discontinuous.

2.2 The Hook Model

The Hook model is developed to embed a need in the user to use the product repeatedly without being prompted due to consecutive iterations of the Hook cycle. The Hook model consists of trigger, action, variable reward, and investment elements (Eyal & Hoover, 2019).

The Hook model cycle was developed to alter the users' behavior and create a habit of using the product. It starts with a trigger that is external or internal, which then prompts the user to do an action, which then presents the user with a reward that varies in each iteration and, finally it asks the user to invest in the product with data (such as entering data into a form). Investing with personal data links the user to the product and prompts him/her to enter the cycle again. The more iterations that occur, the higher the target behavior is likely to be converted into a habit (Eyal & Hoover, 2019).

Triggers are activators of the behavior which can be present in two types, external or internal. External triggers cause the user to take action where information is embedded in the content of the trigger to tell the user what to do next. The required action is explicitly made clear to ensure that the user completes the required goal. Moreover, additional information about the next desired goal can be embedded to encourage the user to complete more than one goal. Internal triggers become present when the product is tightly coupled with a thought, an emotion, or a routine. Internal triggers are manifested by the users because of an emotion such as boredom, fear, or motivation. Actions ought to be simple and easy to accomplish. The user completes an action with the anticipation of a reward. Complex tasks should be broken down into simpler ones to encourage and facilitate their completion. The variable reward is a crucial part of the Hook cycle. The variability of the reward is what keeps the users re-entering the cycle. If the reward is constant the user already knows what they will receive and once they experience it once they would not redo the task. Investment is an important factor in habit formation. Investment in the system increases the likelihood of using the product and of successive iterations on the Hook cycle. Investments are aimed at long-term rewards and not short-term gratification like action. After the user receives the variable reward, the investment phase is presented to ask the user to do some work. Unlike actions which ought to be easy and simple to accomplish, investment requires the users' attention and time. The user is likely to put in the work to accomplish a task after receiving the variable reward. Moreover, the investment phase should be perceived by the user as a method to enhance their progress over time.

Delivering triggers at the right time is crucial to the success of the Hook Model because it can significantly impact the user's motivation to engage with the product (Eyal & Hoover, 2019). Delivering triggers at the right time is crucial because it enhances relevance, captures the user's attention, and boosts motivation, ultimately influencing the timing of user actions. Conversely, poorly timed triggers can go unnoticed or quickly forgotten, diminishing their effectiveness. By understanding the user's behavior, preferences, and context relevant triggers can be sent to the users to capture their attention, motivate them to take action, and create a habit-forming experience.There are numerous formats for external triggers. First, push notification is a message that pops up on a user's device prompting them to take an action or directing them to a specific task within an app. Second, emails can be used as external triggers to encourage users to take action. Emails are commonly used in ecommerce where companies send emails to users about a sale or promotion, prompting them to visit the website and make a purchase. Third, advertisements can be used as external triggers to direct users to a specific product or service. For instance, a social media platform may display an ad for a new game, prompting users to download and play the game. Fourth, call to action (CTA) is a button or link that prompts a user to take a specific action, such as signing up for a newsletter or making a purchase. CTAs are often used on websites or in email marketing campaigns.

2.3 Fogg Behavior Model & the Socio-Education Aspect

The Fogg behavior model consists of three elements. Namely, motivation, ability and prompts (triggers) which are the three main pillars that guide the target user to the required behavior (Fogg, 2009). In the Fogg behavior model triggers are referred to as prompts. The model states that the user is likely to respond successfully to a trigger that is received at a point of time where the user has high motivation and high ability to achieve the required task. The model suggests that all tasks prompted to the user should be simplified to increase the user's ability and motivation to accomplish the task (Fogg, 2009). Simplification is based on breaking complex tasks into smaller achievable ones where the users' cognitive effort is not overloaded.

The paper titled "A socio-educational app for digitally transforming online learning" proposed creating a socio-educational learning environment. The paper combined multiple techniques to create a socio-educational learning environment. For the scope of this paper the focus will be on the social aspect of education and the simplification of understanding the lecture content (Zekry & McKee, n.d.). The paper utilizes the Hook model and the simplification method from Fogg behavior model to create a habit of studying and to break down complex tasks into simple ones that can be achieved by the students (Fogg, 2009; Jalowski et al., 2019). The app addresses the challenge that faces students to understand the lecture content during one session. The paper mentions that students should be given simple tasks such as reading a small section about the lecture content, completing a quiz, or watching a video to prepare them to understand the lecture content. Accordingly, the students are gradually introduced to the lecture content, enabling them to develop an initial understanding of the lecture content.

A social presence in education is manifested in students' interaction, heathy competition between peers, transfer of knowledge, and having the sense of community and belonging (Muthuprasad et al., 2021) Students' interaction is a crucial part in education. It can be presented in the interaction of students with their peers and/or the interaction of the students with the lecturer. A learning environment that fosters interaction allows the transfer of knowledge and creates an engaging environment (Suhartini & Gultom, n.d.; Xiao et al., 2023).

3. PROPOSED LEARNING MODEL

The authors identified a research gap in establishing a seamless learning experience between the online and off-line (on-campus) learning environments. It was also observed that in most off-line learning environments the students listen to the lecturer explaining a concept without interacting with the lecturer. This results in a passive learning experience. The authors gathered feedback from graduate students' who experienced online learning during the pandemic at the faculty of Informatics and Computer Sciences which in summary conveyed the complaint that online lectures were boring, monotonous, and lacked depth; and the only time they got interesting was when students asked questions, creating discussion. Accordingly, the authors decided to create a learning model that increases student engagement and encourages discussion. The authors propose a new learning model named the Trigger-Based Discussion-Oriented Continuous learning model (TbDoC). TbDoC is based on incorporating: (1) An adapted version of the HOOK model for habit formation. (2) The simplification aspect of the Fogg Behavior model presented in prepping for lecture. (3) A social aspect to encourage a socio-educational learning environment that fosters discussion. TbDoC aims to create a seamless integration between online and offline learning environments through a learning cycle that is initiated online and continues to the off-line environment. The research goal is to implement and evaluate qualitatively if the learning model has an impact on students' behavior as well as identify if the learning model develops more independent learners and motivate discussion.

3.1 Implementation of the Learning Model

The experiments took place in the Informatics and Computer Sciences faculty for students of year 2 after prep who were registered for the Distributed Systems module in semester 2. Students registered in Distributed Systems module are students specializing in computer science, artificial intelligence, and computer networks. The students include male and female genders and are of the Egyptian nationality. The lecture spans two hours which is broken down into two parts, with a 20-minute break. The Trigger-Based Discussion-Oriented Continuous Learning Model(TbDoC) has the following characteristics: (1) Students exert effort to acquire and understand the information on their own. (2) Students start the learning process before the lecture. (3) Students discuss their findings with the lecturer during the lecture. (4) The lecturer monitors and directs the students' discussions. The following section will discuss the building blocks of the TbDoC learning model. The lecturer being referred to is the 2nd author on this paper.

3.1.1 Preparing for Lecture

TbDoC simplifies the complex task of understanding the lecture material in one session. This is achieved by prompting the students to prepare ahead of the lecture. An email is sent to the students prior to the lecture, with a set of questions which the students should find answers to. The students are prompted to search for answers and prepare for the lecture discussion. As students search for answers, they encounter information related to the lecture content. As a result, when the students participate in the discussion or observe the information exchange during the lecture, students will have the foundational understanding of the content being discussed. Having this previous knowledge makes it easier to understand new ideas, since they've been introduced to the concepts before.

3.1.2 Adapted HOOK Model

TbDoC adapts the HOOK model to create a habit of learning and discussion. The HOOK model is an arranged cycle of trigger, action, reward, and investment. TbDoC changes the arrangement of the cycle while maintain the core aspects of the HOOK model. TbDoC adaptation of the HOOK model begins with an external timed trigger, which is followed by the user's action. Subsequently, the investment takes place as a result of the user's action, leading to the reward. The cycle takes place over the online and off-line learning environments. The trigger, action, and investment take place online and the reward takes place off-line.

On the evening prior to the lecture, an email is sent to the students acting as the external timed trigger prompting the users to take action. The email clearly prompts the students to search for answers to the short questions in the email. Accordingly, the students start the action of searching for the questions' answers. By doing the action the students invest time and effort to properly find the answers and prepare for the lecture discussion next morning. Accordingly, investment takes place when the students prepare for the lecture discussion. During the off-line (on-campus) lecture the students are rewarded by being able to contribute to the discussion as well as having their attendance recorded for each part of the lecture.

Students who take part in TbDoC are likely develop a habit of independent learning and taking part in student-to-lecturer discussions.

3.1.3 The Email

The email is the timed external trigger sent by the lecturer to the students. The email is sent in the evening prior to the lecture. For instance, if the lecture is held on Wednesday at 9:00 AM the email is sent on Tuesday at 8:00 PM. The timing gives the students a defined window of time to prepare for the lecture. The email informs the students of the topic that will be discussed during the lecture followed by a set of questions. The students are asked to come up with answers to the questions in the email. The questions usually ask about important terminologies, concepts, and equations, or ask the student to search for a video. Figure 1 shows one of the emails sent by the lecturer.

Subject: [22CSCI07I] Tomorrow's lecture - 9:00 AM - and some questions

Dear All,
Good evening.
Our lecture tomorrow starts as usual at 9:00 AM. The topic will be Processes. In preparation for the session here are some questions/challenges for you to explore:

1. Can you find a good video (less than 5 mins) on YouTube that explains **virtualization**?
2. What is a Wide Area Network (WAN) cluster?
3. What is meant by "request dispatching"?
4. What is meant by a "round-robin load balancing policy"?

I look forward to seeing you all tomorrow morning.
Best regards,

Figure 1. Email Sample

The questions are formulated to be easily understood and enable the students to do the action required, that is to search for the answers. In the email content, the lecturer used common keywords for the chosen topic. The students did not have the lecture material to hand since it had not been uploaded to Learning Management System (LMS), so they were expected to explore the answers by searching on the Web. The email ends with "Looking forward to see you tomorrow morning". This statement reinforces the need for immediate action ("... tomorrow morning"). The statement also encourages the creation of a socio-educational learning environment by informally addressing the students ("Looking forward to see you ..."). To foster a dynamic and engaging learning environment the use of friendly wording is important to encourage students to take part in a discussion that takes part during the lecture session.

3.2 On-Campus Discussion

The lecture session starts with the lecturer showing the opening slide that contains the lecture title followed a slide that outlines the topics to be covered in the session. The lecturer then shows a pdf or Word document with the contents of the email in order to focus on the questions.

The lecturer opens the discussion by asking the students what they found for the first question. Using the body language of the students as a guide the lecturer identifies students who are ready to offer input and selects a student to speak. The selected student then provides their input. The lecturer will then encourage other students to offer their input, focusing in particular if anyone has information different to that of the first student, as a means to get diverse inputs and deepen the discussion. If it appears that none of the students have attempted to find information on the topic, then the lecturer will ask the students attending the session to now search for information about the topic using their mobile phones. The lecturer deliberately avoids giving answers, putting the reliance on the students to do the exploration, prompting them into action to support the discussion. Some students come well prepared to the session and are keen to offer their findings and the lecturer has to both acknowledge their effort and input, but also to ensure that other students' inputs are acknowledged. After about 15 to 20 minutes of discussion, the lecturer recaps the topic based on the student inputs and provides additional information to support the lecture content. The lecturer then moves to another question on the list and the same approach to encouraging student input is taken.

Throughout the discussion, the lecturer tries to steer the students in a direction to ensure coverage of assigned lecture content. The important aspect of the discussion is that the topic/question is answered/uncovered by the students. The lecturer's role is to direct the conversation to the correct answer. As the semester continued, students got into the habit of preparing and discussing their answers.

An important feature of the Trigger-Based Discussion-Oriented Continuous learning model was the reliance on and encouragement of the students to find information for themselves. Therefore, the first sessions inspired the use of mobile phones during the lecture. Accordingly, the lecturer prompted the students to use their mobiles to search for information related to the questions and also when new terms arose from the findings that the students reported. The latter provided a deeper insight into the lecture topics and offered a way of engaging with "reading around the subject", an important part of student learning. In summary, the encouraged use of mobile phones in the lecture setting empowered students to increase their research skills and encourage knowledge seeking.

The lecturer balanced the discussion by adopting a casual and approaching tone while maintaining control of the discussion to encourage students to actively participate in the discussion without feeling concerned about the correctness or incorrectness of their input.

By utilizing the above approach, the lecturer was able to create a Trigger-Based Discussion-Oriented Continuous Learning Model that encourages discussion and knowledge seeking, which ultimately led to a deeper understanding of the lecture content.

3.3 Qualitative Behavior Observation

Throughout the semester, the lecturer carefully monitored the students' behavior to qualitatively evaluate the impact of TbDoC. The lecturer observed that the students' engagement in the sessions suggested four types of students. Type 1, students who are not triggered by the email and therefore do not search for the answers and are not able to engage in the discussion without further prompting during the session. Type 2, students who during the session search for the answer using keywords based on the email but take the first answer provided by the search engine. Meaning, type 2 students accept preliminary limited knowledge of the topic addressed by each question. They are prepared to engage moderately but need encouragement to search for other answers. Type 3, students who search for answers to the questions and aim to understand the concept and knowledge behind each. These students are prepared to engage actively. Type 4, students who do research on the topic and questions provided, and produce their own content or summary based on their understanding. These students are able to take the discussion beyond the concepts covered in the lecture. Type 2 students form the majority.

In the first lecture, the students appeared to be accepting of the approach where some students came prepared with answers to the questions and engaged with the discussion. As the semester continued, it was observed that the students became more habitual to the TbDoC. This was observed based on the increase of students coming to the lecture more prepared and eager to take part in the discussion. By time type 3 students were observed to increase. Students became more comfortable to take part in the student-to-lecturer discussion and more habitual to using their mobile phones to search for information and contribute to the discussion.

On one night, the lecturer decided not to send an email and observe the reaction of the students' behavior. On the same night the lecturer received emails from a student inquiring about the email and how the lecture will take place. This shows that the students anticipated the email and became habitual to receiving the external timed trigger to take action and prepare for the lecture. This also shows that the students want to be prepared to be able to take part in the discussion.

4. CONCLUSION

The paper introduced a new learning model named the Trigger-Based Discussion-Oriented Continuous Learning Model (TbDoC) which is based on incorporating: (1) An adapted version of the HOOK model for habit formation. (2) The simplification aspect of the Fogg Behavior model presented in prepping for lecture. (3) A social aspect to encourage a socio-educational learning environment that fosters discussion.

TbDoC aims to create a seamless experience between online and offline learning environments by initiating learning online and continuing over the off-line (on campus) environment. TbDoC starts online with the lecturer sending an email to the students on the night prior to the lecture. The email is the timed external trigger that prompts the students to take action and prepare for the lecture. The students prepare for the lecture by searching for answers to the questions in the email. When the students start the action of searching they invest time and effort to prepare for the lecture. The students' efforts are rewarded during the off-line (on-campus) lecture as they take part in the discussion and their attendance gets recorded.

The paper evaluated the qualitative impact of TbDoC on students' behavior. TbDoC was successful in influencing student behavior where the students became more independent learners and exhibited an increased willingness to take part in the student-to-lecturer discussion. It was observed that the students anticipated receiving the email and were habitual to the TbDoC. TbDoC employed a social aspect to education and was successful in creating a socio-educational environment that helped the students become comfortable to take part in the student-to-lecturer discussions. The learning experience was continuous across online and off-line (on-campus) learning environments without the need to use new learning tools which enabled seamless integration between both environments.

5. FUTURE WORK

For future work, the effect of the Trigger-Based Discussion-Oriented Continuous Learning Model (TbDoC) will be measured using both qualitative and quantitative methods. Using qualitative methods, feedback from the students will be gathered to gain insights into their experiences and perceptions. This can include student experience interviews. The quantitative methods can include (1) Measuring the cognitive effort required for preparing for the lecture and answering the questions; this can be done through surveys or questionnaires that measure the perceived cognitive effort exerted by students during the preparation phase. (2) Tracking the percentage of students who actively prepared for the lecture; this can be done by inserting within the email a link to the questions, rather than providing the questions themselves in the email, and tracking the number of students who clicked on the link, providing an indication of the level of engagement with the trigger. (3) Evaluating the level of student engagement during the lecture session; various metrics can be employed, such as tracking the frequency and quality of student contributions, monitoring participation rates, or employing observation techniques to measure active engagement during discussions; the possible observation techniques can include video recording the lecture, audio recording the lecture, or direct observation and note taking.

REFERENCES

Abdulbaki, K., Suhaimi, M., Alsaqqaf, A., & Jawad, W. (2018). The Use of the Discussion Method at University: Enhancement of Teaching and Learning. International Journal of Higher Education, 7(6), 118. doi:10.5430/ijhe.v7n6p118 URL: https://doi.org/10.5430/ijhe.v7n6p118.

Eyal, N., & Hoover, R. (2019). Hooked: How to build habit-forming products. Portfolio/Penguin.

Fogg, B. J. (2009). A behavior model for persuasive design. Proceedings of the 4th International Conference on Persuasive Technology. doi:10.1145/1541948.1541999.

Jalowski, M., Fritzsche, A., & Möslein, K. M. (2019). Facilitating Collaborative Design: A toolkit for integrating persuasive technologies in Design Activities. Procedia CIRP, 84, 61-67. doi:10.1016/j.procir.2019.04.290.

Koay, W. L., Teoh, K., & Hong, L. C. (2021). A Comparative Study on Effectiveness of Online and Offline Learning in Higher Education. International Journal of Teaching and Higher Education, 4(3), 102-114. doi:10.32535/ijthap.v4i3.1212.

Li, X., & Pei, Z. (2023). Improving effectiveness of online learning for higher education students during the COVID-19 pandemic. Frontiers in Psychology, 13. https://doi.org/10.3389/fpsyg.2022.1111028 TECH&EDU.

Muthuprasad, T., Aiswarya, S., Aditya, K. S., & Jha, G. K. (2021). Students' perception and preference for online education in India during the COVID-19 pandemic. Social Sciences & Humanities Open, 3(1), 100101. doi:10.1016/j.ssaho.2020.100101.

Picault, J. (2021). Structure, Flexibility, and Consistency: A Dynamic Learning Approach for an Online Asynchronous Course. Applied Economics Teaching Resources (AETR), 3(4), October.

Sharma, D., Sood, A. K., Darius, P. S. H., Gundabattini, E., Gnanaraj, S. D., & Jeyapaul, A. J. (2022). A Study on the Online-Offline and Blended Learning Methods. Journal of The Institution of Engineers (India): Series B, 103(4), 1373-1382. doi:10.1007/978-3-031-04286-7_18.

Stoian, C. E., Fărcașiu, M. A., Dragomir, G.-M., & Gherheș, V. (2022). Transition from Online to Face-to-Face Education after COVID-19: The Benefits of Online Education from Students' Perspective. Sustainability, 14(19), 12812. https://doi.org/10.3390/su141912812.

Struthers, D., Allsop, Y., Kalelioğlu, F., & Rzyankina, E. (2022). The Impact of COVID-19 on Higher Education: A Systematic Literature Review of Pedagogical Approaches and Challenges. In M. E. Auer, A. Pester, & D. May (Eds.), Learning with Technologies and Technologies in Learning (Vol. 456, Lecture Notes in Networks and Systems). Springer, Cham. https://doi.org/10.1007/978-3-031-04286-7_18.

Sun, Q., Zhang, Q., Lin, Y., & Bai, J. (2020). Research on the Integrated Teaching Mode of Online & Offline Education under the Background of Internet Plus. In 2020 2nd International Conference on Advanced Social Science and Humanities Education Research (ASSEHR) (pp. 13-18). doi:10.2991/assehr.k.201214.113.

Suhartini, S., & Gultom, A. (n.d.). Student Interaction, Teacher Competence, and Technology in Online Learning: Does it Create a Meaningful Learning? In 6th International Seminar on Science Education (ISSE 2020) (pp. 169-180). Arlantis Press.

Xiao, M., Tian, Z., & Xu, W. (2023). Impact of teacher-student interaction on students' classroom well-being under online education environment. Education and Information Technologies. doi:10.1007/s10639-023-11681-0.

Yang, X. (2023). A Historical Review of Collaborative Learning and Cooperative Learning. TechTrends. [Online]. Available: https://doi.org/10.1007/s11528-022-00823-9.

Zekry, D. A., & McKee, G. T. (n.d.). (2022). A Socio-educational App for Digitally Transforming Online Learning. In International Conference on Interactive Collaborative Learning (ICL). Dresden, Germany: Springer, Cham.

KEYBOARD AS A STIMULATOR IN TIMBRE RECOGNITION TRAINING

Adam Rosiński
University of Warmia and Mazury in Olsztyn
Szrajbera 11, 10-007 Olsztyn, Poland

ABSTRACT

This paper presents the results of a research conducted in a group of Youth Palace in Olsztyn participants. Two different keyboards were used in the experiment to teach how to recognize the timbres of selected musical instruments. Obtained results clearly showed that musical education with the use of keyboards significantly develops timbre hearing of children and youth. The research group performed much better in the tests in comparison with the control group. A danger appearing during this kind of training is the listener getting used to a given timbre (sample). Big part of psychoacoustic research is limited to acoustic stimuli not related to the art of music in a real way, which does not allow the use of this type of research and stimuli in musical didactics. The experiment presented in this paper is based on generating musical sounds that have worked well in education.

KEYWORDS

Children, Digital Technology, Hearing, Musical Education, Teaching

1. INTRODUCTION

Timbre is one of the four sensational characteristics of sounds, next to volume, pitch and duration [Rogala & Łętowski, 2017, p. 331]. Unlike volume, pitch and duration, which can be measured in quite a simple way, timbre of sound is the most complicated and difficult to measure. Timbre is a multifaceted term [Rasch & Plomb, 1999, p. 101; Taraszka-Drożdż, 2016, p. 171], depending on: energy distribution; changes related to the energy distribution over time; spectral characteristics of sound – for example if it is a single sound with a characteristic frequency, if it is audible or not, if it is a noise etc. [Sęk, 2000, p. 18]. The timbre of the sound determines it's auditory image, which can be perceived differently by every listener [Bregman, 1990, pp. 92–93, 336], and can be also treated as an aesthetic feature, as well as be considered by the listener in the context of satisfaction or lack of it [Łętowski, 2002, p. 186].

An attempt to solve the problem of systematization and unification of timbre, can be observed in psychoacoustic research. Numerous independent variables, occurring at the same time, and being hard to measure, became a reason why psychoacoustic studies of sound timbre are limited to artificially generated (synthesized) sounds. In this case the experiments are constantly burdened with a significant limitation: participants are being exposed to stimuli (simple and complex tones, modulated, component tones, pronounced words, noises, elements of scales or harmonic triads) artificially generated by specialistic devices [Miller & Heise, 1950, pp. 637–638; Bregman & Campbell, 1971, pp. 244–249; Bregman et al., 2000, pp. 626–636; Oxenham et al., 2003, p. 1544; Bregman & Woszczyk, 2004, pp. 39–41; Bregman, 2005, pp. 36–37; Parbery-Clark et al., 2009a, p. 14106; Parbery-Clark et al., 2009b, p. 659; Pantev & Herholz, 2011, p. 2152; Parbery-Clark et al., 2012, p. 117; Strait et al., 2012, p. 199; Parbery-Clark et al., 2013, p. 129]. The positive side of it is that the sound material in this case is totally measurable, which allows certain objectivization of the study results. However, on the other hand the research circumstances have little to do with these that normally occur when a person is listening to music. Experiments of this kind, the results of which are very important in acoustics and sound engineering, are unfortunately not very useful in ear training. In the first case the material is described as "acoustic stimuli", while in the second case as "musical sounds" – which from the artistic point of view are not the same thing.

There are few publications written mainly for musicians, so mutual understanding different researchers' needs (i.e. of an acoustician, a psychologist and a musician) seems to be a complex problem. The author of this study tries to look at the timbre analysis from the musical point of view, without detracting from the legitimacy of acousticians' and psychologists' work, because without it, musicians would have no basis for further activity. It means that earlier studies were not conducted on "real" music, but created using suitable generators in a computer and analyzed in a laboratory, which is not a space where a musician can feel free and comfortable. Obtained data confirm that analyses made by other researchers did not concern musical sounds. This shows that there is a wide undiscovered area of knowledge that can be filled with own research. Discussed issue has not been considered in available scientific literature in a way presented in this paper. Observed vulnerability in experiments was the basis to raise following research questions: does the use of popular keyboards' sounds affect the development of timbre memory of children and youth? Can electronic instruments such as keyboards be used to teach acoustic instruments' timbre recognition, by the use of digital sound emulations?

2. ASSUMPTIONS AND OBJECTIVE OF THE EXPERIMENT

The objective of the experiment was to examine if the use of various keyboard sounds as a tool during didactic classes influences and stimulates timbre memory of the participants by improving their skills of recognizing the timbres of individual musical instruments in comparison to the control group.

3. SOUND MATERIAL

During the experiment, a teacher was presenting various harmonic and melodic sequences for 10 seconds, each in a pitch scale adequate for a given instrument. These passages were performed by in front of the class participants by the teacher. Each performance was different (no repeating musical structures), so the listeners could not memorize any connections between a melody and a timbre.

All the melodies were played a keyboard, using the sounds chosen by the instructor as the ones, that authentically imitate traditional instruments. In order to verify each participant's familiarity with different instrument timbres, the teacher picked 25 timbres of various acoustic instruments belonging to several instrument families: classical guitar, acoustic guitar, electric guitar, banjo, mandolin, electric bass, double bass, violin, harp, piano, church organ, synthesizer, trumpet, trombone, french horn, tuba, saxophone, transverse flute, oboe, bassoon, clarinet, glockenspiel, music box, tubular bells and carillon.

The chosen articulation (legato) was the same for all the instrument sounds used in the presentation.

4. EQUIPMENT USED DURING THE LISTENING SESSIONS

The research was conducted in the room 312 – the location of the keyboard classes – in the Youth Palace in Olsztyn, Poland. The equipment used in the listening sessions was:

1) *Yamaha PSR-900SX* keyboard, used in the participants' education from September to January.
2) *Korg PA1000* keyboard, used in the classes from February to June.

The loudness level of performed stimuli was set by the researcher before starting the experiment to ensure maximum comfort for every listener participating the listening session. It was set only once, same for every group, approximately 74 phons, and it remained unchanged through the whole study time. Both keyboards belong to the same class of electronic instruments, but were produced by different manufacturers, thanks to which, listener's impressions about electronic simulations of acoustic instrument timbres were different in both cases.

5. LISTENERS AND DATA ON THE RESEARCH GROUP

In the described experiment 2 groups (research and control), each consisting of 25 class participants, were created in a random way [Pilch, 1998, pp. 51, 86–87; Łobocki, 2004], giving a total number of 50 subjects.

Research and control groups were alike, as they both comprised of randomly selected 11 boys and 14 girls aged 7 to 14. None of the subjects had any past experience with music education of any kind.

6. LISTENING SESSIONS

The beginning of the school year in Poland is on September 1st (month marked as I in the Table 1) and the last month of the school year is June (marked as X in the Table 1). The ten-month school period is then followed by two-month summer holidays, when Polish children and young people are not attending any classes. For 10 months, during the school year 2021/2022, all study participants attended weekly, 45-minute lessons in groups of 4. On the first class in September (marked as I in Table 1), before the music education began, first test was per-formed to check knowledge of all the subjects.

Over the course of the study, children and youth being part of the research group participated in training listening sessions in groups of 4, once a week (each Thursday). Subsequent tests of research group subjects' familiarity with instrument timbres were performed on the first Thursday of each month (in accordance with the sched-ule of classes in Youth Palace in Olsztyn).

Children from the control group didn't participate in any training sessions and took in total 4 tests of knowledge: in September (marked as I in Table 2), January (marked as V in Table 2), February (marked as VI in Table 2) and June (marked as X in Table 2), on the first Thursday of each of these months.

7. THE EXPERIMENTAL METHOD

The data obtained in the experiments are subject to mathematical calculations in accordance with statistical requirements. These calculations are made based on study results, which implies that the tests are repeated many times on a large group of subjects in order to get reliable results [Renowski, 1974, p. 6].

This research used a sound source identification method, which relies on recognizing the timbre as a sensational feature that allows recognizing the sound source. In this case the timbre recognition involves assigning it to the respective sound source, or not classifying it if there is no comparable reference timbre in listener's memory [Ozimek, 2002, p. 270].

The experimental method for the research group:

1) All the timbre recognition tests were conducted in the very beginning of the first class of each month, and the duration of the test was approximately 7 minutes – remaining time (approximately 38 minutes) were being used according to the curriculum to teach children how to play popular music on a keyboard.

2) On every one of the weekly classes, there was a training listening session held, also lasting around 7 minutes.

3) If the test and a training session were about to happen on the same day, the knowledge test was conducted for the first 7 minutes, then the pupils participated in a training listening session for another 7 minutes.

4) Remaining time (around 30 minutes on the days of the test, and 38 minutes on the other days) was used to implement the classes' curriculum (teaching how to play popular music on keyboard), and it was not connected with the described research.

The experimental method for the control group:

1) The timbre recognition tests were conducted 4 times throughout the research, in the very beginning of the class, the duration of the test was approximately 7 minutes.

2) Remaining time (about 37 minutes) was used to implement the classes' curriculum, focusing only on teaching how to play keyboard.

The duration of the experiment was defined without excessive attention – in a way, that in researcher's opinion, allowed the participants to be introduced to, learn and memorize new timbres of musical instruments. It can be assumed, that longer training session time would cause the timbre recognition skills to grow faster, which would translate into better results, however the study was conducted during the time of traditional classes (with no extra time for research), additionally, so it should not overly modify or shorten the time of the keyboard lesson itself. The Keyboard class curriculum needed to be fully realized during the lessons so certain time restrictions were put on the experiment to make sure that it does not affect the children learning to play electronic keyboards. This form of conducting experiments was chosen by the author as he was sure, that the children will be participating the classes weekly, throughout the school year.

Timbre recognition testing method:

The teacher was randomly choosing timbres from the previously prepared 25 sound collection, and playing an improvised (unplanned) melody for maximum of 10 seconds. Then the subjects had the same time of 10 seconds to write down the name of recognized instrument on an empty sheet of paper. This sequence was repeated 25 times until all the timbres were presented. In order to avoid "wild guessing" the answers, the test was not a test of choice – not knowing the right answer resulted in lack of it. When the test was over, the teacher collected all the participants' papers and reviewed them later (after the class ended) [Pilch, 1998, pp. 51, 86–87; Konarzewski, 2000, p. 138].

8. RESULTS

Data presented in Table 1 shows the percentage of correct responses (understood as the accurate identification of the sound's timbre) given by all 25 study participants in the research group. Table 1 presents each subject's progress with regard to timbre recognition in context of the number of months spent on training. It shows all the test results obtained throughout the study (from September to June). There were 25 instruments, therefore correct recognition of one equals (and is listed as) 4%, of two equals 8%, of three equals 12% etc.

Table 1. Data presenting the percentage of correct responses given by the subjects in the research group

Month / Children	I Sep.	II Oct.	III Nov.	IV Dec.	V Jan.	VI Feb.	VII Mar.	VIII Apr.	IX May	X Jun.
					in %					
1	4.0	28.0	48.0	60.0	84.0	24.0	36.0	52.0	68.0	84.0
2	0.0	16.0	32.0	48.0	64.0	12.0	28.0	40.0	54.0	72.0
3	8.0	20.0	36.0	56.0	76.0	24.0	36.0	52.0	68.0	84.0
4	8.0	20.0	40.0	60.0	80.0	24.0	36.0	56.0	72.0	88.0
5	12.0	32.0	60.0	80.0	92.0	32.0	44.0	60.0	76.0	92.0
6	4.0	16.0	36.0	52.0	72.0	16.0	32.0	44.0	64.0	84.0
7	8.0	20.0	48.0	64.0	80.0	16.0	28.0	44.0	68.0	88.0
8	16.0	40.0	72.0	96.0	100.0	36.0	48.0	66.0	80.0	96.0
9	8.0	32.0	52.0	68.0	92.0	28.0	44.0	62.0	80.0	92.0
10	0.0	12.0	28.0	40.0	60.0	8.0	20.0	36.0	56.0	68.0
11	8.0	16.0	32.0	52.0	72.0	20.0	36.0	52.0	68.0	88.0
12	0.0	8.0	28.0	48.0	68.0	12.0	28.0	44.0	60.0	76.0
13	4.0	16.0	32.0	60.0	84.0	24.0	40.0	56.0	72.0	88.0
14	0.0	8.0	20.0	44.0	68.0	16.0	32.0	48.0	64.0	84.0
15	0.0	12.0	40.0	64.0	84.0	20.0	36.0	56.0	72.0	88.0
16	8.0	16.0	36.0	56.0	76.0	16.0	28.0	48.0	64.0	80.0
17	16.0	32.0	60.0	84.0	100.0	36.0	48.0	66.0	84.0	100.0
18	0.0	8.0	24.0	48.0	64.0	12.0	24.0	40.0	56.0	72.0
19	12.0	28.0	52.0	76.0	96.0	32.0	48.0	64.0	84.0	96.0
20	0.0	8.0	20.0	44.0	60.0	8.0	16.0	32.0	48.0	64.0
21	4.0	8.0	24.0	52.0	68.0	12.0	28.0	40.0	60.0	76.0
22	4.0	16.0	32.0	52.0	72.0	16.0	28.0	44.0	64.0	80.0
23	0.0	20.0	36.0	60.0	76.0	20.0	32.0	48.0	64.0	84.0
24	0.0	16.0	36.0	52.0	76.0	16.0	32.0	48.0	64.0	84.0
25	8.0	24.0	48.0	64.0	84.0	20.0	36.0	52.0	68.0	88.0
Average	5.3	18.9	38.9	59.2	77.9	20.0	33.76	50.00	67.1	83.8

In white columns in Table 1 it can be observed, that from September to January there was a very intensive timbre memory development. The digital keyboard used to present and teach timbres of individual instruments was Yamaha PSR-900SX. Results analysis reveals clear growth of the average number of correct answers given by respondents on monthly tests, in two cases reaching even 100%. When comparing results from January and September, the average improvement equals 72,6%.

The gray columns in Table 1 (from February till June) present the educational use of the second electronic keyboard – Korg PA1000. In this case there is also visible, significant development of timbre memory, which occurred within five months since the implementation of this new instrument, resulting in 100% of correct answers given by one of the subjects in the instrument timbre recognition test. By comparing average results obtained in June and February, a conclusion may be made, that among the study participants, correct recognition of chosen timbres increased by an average of 63,8%.

Data presented in Table 2 shows the percentage of correct responses obtained in the control group, which did not take part in training listening sessions every week. This group of 25 pupils went through the test only four times, in September, January, February and June. Comparing both tables, it can be observed that in the control group there was no growth of the instrument timbre recognition skills. Results presented in Table 2 oscillate within the range of statistical error and are not significant. Presented data shows that timbre education in the experimental group occurs very quickly, which cannot be observed in the control group.

Table 2. Data presenting the percentage of correct responses given by the subjects in the control group

Month / Children	I Sep.	V Jan.	VI Feb.	X Jun.
	in %			
1	4.0	4.0	4.0	4.0
2	4.0	8.0	4.0	4.0
3	12.0	12.0	4.0	4.0
4	8.0	4.0	0.0	4.0
5	0.0	0.0	0.0	0.0
6	16.0	16.0	12.0	12.0
7	4.0	0.0	4.0	0.0
8	0.0	4.0	0.0	4.0
9	0.0	0.0	0.0	0.0
10	8.0	8.0	4.0	4.0
11	12.0	12.0	12.0	12.0
12	4.0	4.0	4.0	4.0
13	0.0	4.0	4.0	0.0
14	0.0	0.0	0.0	0.0
15	16.0	16.0	12.0	12.0
16	8.0	4.0	4.0	8.0
17	4.0	4.0	4.0	4.0
18	0.0	0.0	0.0	0.0
19	4.0	4.0	0.0	4.0
20	8.0	8.0	12.0	12.0
21	4.0	8.0	8.0	8.0
22	8.0	12.0	8.0	12.0
23	0.0	0.0	0.0	0.0
24	8.0	12.0	8.0	12.0
25	0.0	0.0	0.0	0.0
Average	5.3	5.8	4.3	5.0

Table 3 shows each subject's progress. Presented data was calculated based on the arithmetic mean of all correct answers given by the respondents. In case of the white columns it is each participant's mean from September to January (using the Yamaha PSR-900SX keyboard), while in case of the gray columns it is each pupil's mean from February to June (using Korg PA1000). Average is an arithmetic mean of the calculated progress of all the individuals together during the periods of using the sounds of two different keyboards in the timbre training.

Table 3. Data presenting mean progress in the field of correct recognition of selected instrument timbres, of every participant. The table also includes the collective data calculated as an arithmetic mean of all the results

Children (research group)	Progress (in %)	Progress (in %)
1	80.0	60.0
2	64.0	60.0
3	68.0	60.0
4	72.0	64.0
5	80.0	60.0
6	68.0	68.0
7	72.0	72.0
8	84.0	60.0
9	84.0	64.0
10	60.0	60.0
11	64.0	68.0
12	68.0	64.0
13	80.0	64.0
14	68.0	68.0
15	84.0	68.0
16	68.0	64.0
17	84.0	64.0
18	64.0	60.0
19	84.0	64.0
20	60.0	56.0
21	64.0	64.0
22	68.0	64.0
23	76.0	64.0
24	76.0	68.0
25	76.0	68.0
Average	72.6	63.8

9. DISCUSSION OF RESULTS

A big problem for the subjects in the first phase of the experiment was to recognize the timbres within such instrument groups as:

– carillon, tubular bells,
– music box, carillon,
– oboe, bassoon, clarinet,
– electric bass, double bass, tuba,
– banjo, mandolin,
– classical guitar, acoustic guitar,
– trumpet, trombone, french horn, tuba, saxophone.

In each of the above cases it can be observed that instruments within the groups have very similar timbres. This shows that most of the participants' mistakes were related to recognition of instruments sounding alike, which often were presented in the same or similar pitch scale. Obtained data clearly depicts the problems in the area of timbre recognition that occur in this group of subjects at this educational level, thanks to which, it is clear what are the musical education aspects that need particular attention. Piano, violin, church organ and synthesizer sound very characteristically, so there were not any big timbre similarities, hence much smaller number of participants' mistakes in this instrument group (in comparison to previously listed groups).

Another problem that has been noticed, refers to Table 1, where the same instrument sounds (timbres under the same name) were presented, with only variable being an electronic keyboard model (gray color). In this case, it can be seen that the use of different sounding samples – played using Korg PA1000 – caused a great decrease in specific instruments' timbre recognition skills (even though the training sessions were repeated weekly). This data clearly depicts participants getting used to previously presented instrument timbres, despite the fact that when using Yamaha PSR-900SX, the teacher used different samples of the same instrument (from a library pre-stored in instrument's memory). Changing the electronic instrument (source of the samples) to a different one resulted in a significant change in sound which caused some mistakes in recognizing timbres of certain instruments by the study participants. However, it is worth mentioning that the number of correctly recognized instrument timbres did not drop to the pre-experiment level for any one of the subjects, which proves that the intend-ed development of timbre recognition skills was observed to some extent.

10. CONCLUSION

The results of conducted experiments show that keyboards can be very good stimulators and can properly stimulate the development of timbre recognition and processing for children and youth. Digital emulation of acoustic instrument timbres in contemporary keyboards is getting better and better, thanks to which electronic keyboards can be successfully used as a didactic tool helping to teach children and youth how to identify the timbres of acoustic instruments. At the same time the experiment proved the relevance of using keyboards in musical education involving timbre hearing stimulation.

Conclusions that arise after the results analysis clearly indicate that the traditional ear training relying on the sound of piano allows students to learn how to recognize intervals, scales, keys, chord qualities etc., but causes problems with correct recognition of different instrument timbres. The use of keyboards on didactic classes may significantly reduce this problem. Extending school classes with new electronic instruments causes the development of timbre identification skills of the students, which shows that it is worth considering to implement new technologies in classes, as it contributes to the development of important auditory competences used in further musical work.

REFERENCES

Bregman, A.S., 1990. *Auditory Scene Analysis: The Perceptual Organization of Sound*. The MIT Press, Cambridge, MA, USA.

Bregman, A.S., 2005. Auditory scene analysis and the role of phenomenology in experimental psychology. *Canadian Psychology*, Vol. 46(1), pp. 32–40.

Bregman, A.S. and Campbell, J., 1971. Primary auditory stream segregation and perception of order in rapid sequences of tones. *Journal of Experimental Psychology*, Vol. 89(2), pp. 244–9.

Bregman, A.S. and Woszczyk, W., 2004. Controlling the perceptual organization of sound: guidelines derived from principles of auditory scene analysis. In: K. Greenebaum and R. Barzel (Eds.), *Audio anecdotes: tools, tips and techniques for digital audio*, Vol. 1. A.K. Peters/CRC Press, Massachusetts, USA, pp. 39–41.

Bregman, A.S. et al., 2000. Effect of time intervals and tone durations on auditory stream segregation. *Perception & Psychophysics*, Vol. 62(3), pp. 626–36.

Konarzewski, K., 2000. *Jak uprawiać badania oświatowe*. Wydawnictwa Szkolne i Pedagogiczne S.A., Warszawa, Poland.

Łętowski, T., 2002. Podstawowe wymiary barwy dźwięku. In: A. Rakowski (Ed.), *Kształtowanie i percepcja dźwięków muzycznych*. Akademia Muzyczna im. Fryderyka Chopina, Warszawa, Poland, pp. 186–93.

Łobocki, M., 2004. *Metody i techniki badań pedagogicznych*. Oficyna Wydawnicza „Impuls", Kraków, Poland.

Miller, G.A. and Heise, G.A., 1950. The thrill threshold. *Journal of Acoustical Society of America*, Vol. 22, pp. 637–638.

Oxenham, A.J. et al., 2003. Informational masking and musical training. *Journal of the Acoustical Society of America*, Vol. 114 Issue 3, pp. 1543–9.

Ozimek, E., 2002. *Dźwięk i jego percepcja. Aspekty fizyczne i psychoakustyczne*. Wydawnictwo Naukowe PWN, Warszawa–Poznań, Poland.

Pantev, C. and Herholz, S.C., 2011. Plasticity of the human auditory cortex related to musical training. *Neuroscience and Biobehavioral Reviews*, Vol. 35, Issue 10, pp. 2140–54.

Parbery-Clark, A. et al., 2009a. Musical experience limits the degradative effects of background noise on the neural processing of sound. *Journal of Neuroscience*, Vol. 29, No. 45, pp. 14100–7.

Parbery-Clark, A. et al., 2009b. Musician enhancement for speech-in-noise. *Ear & Hearing*, Vol. 30, No. 6, pp. 653–61.

Parbery-Clark, A. et al., 2012. Musicians have fine-tuned neural distinction of speech syllables. *Neuroscience*, Vol. 219, pp. 111–19.

Parbery-Clark, A. et al., 2013. Musicians change their tune: how hearing loss alters the neural code. *Hearing Research*, Vol. 302, pp. 121–31.

Pilch, T., 1998. *Zasady badań pedagogicznych.* Wydawnictwo Akademickie Żak, Warszawa, Poland.

Rasch, R. and Plomb, R., 1999. *The perception of musical tones.* In: D. Deutsch (Ed.), *The Psychology of Music.* 2nd edition. Academic Press, California, USA, pp. 89–112.

Renowski, J., 1974. *Akustyka psychofizyczna. Ćwiczenia laboratoryjne.* Redakcja Wydawnictw Politechniki Wrocławskiej, Wrocław, Poland.

Rogala, T. and Łętowski, T., 2017. Określanie barwy dźwięku przez różne grupy zawodowe muzyków i niemuzyków. In: K. Klauza and J. Cieślik-Klauza (Eds.), *Pulchritudo delectans. Korespondencja. Na styku sztuk.* Uniwersytet Muzyczny Fryderyka Chopina, Białystok, Poland, p. 331-348.

Sęk, A., 2000. Percepcja dźwięku. *Forum Psychologiczne*, Vol. 5, Issue l, pp. 5–26.

Strait, D.L. et al., 2012. Musical training during early childhood enhances the neural encoding of speech in noise. *Brain & Language*, Vol. 123, Issue 3, pp. 191–201.

Taraszka-Drożdż, B., 2016. Zmysłowe wymiary dźwięku w terminologii muzycznej. In: G. Gwóźdź and P. Mamet (Eds.), *Dyskursy specjalistyczne. Rejestry, gatunki, tłumaczenia.* Wydawnictwo im. S. Podobińskiego Akademii im. Jana Długosza, Częstochowa, Poland, pp. 171–187.

EVALUATING POPULAR MOOC PLATFORMS BY GENERATIVE ARTIFICIAL INTELLIGENCE (AI) ROBOTS: HOW CONSISTENT ARE THE ROBOTS?

Victor K. Y. Chan
Faculty of Business, Macao Polytechnic University
Rua de Luis Gonzaga Gomes, Macao, China

ABSTRACT

This article intends to investigate the consistency between a few popular generative AI robots in the evaluation of massive open online course (MOOC) platforms. The four robots experimented with in the study were Claude+, GPT-4, Sage, and Dragonfly, which were tasked with awarding rating scores to the eight major dimensions, namely (1) content/course quality, (2) pedagogical design, (3) learner support, (4) technology infrastructure, (5) social interaction, (6) learner engagement, (7) instructor support, and (8) cost-effectiveness, of the 31 currently very popular MOOC platforms. Only Claude+'s and Dragonfly's rating scores turned out to be amenable to statistical analysis. For each of the two robots, the minimum, the maximum, the range, and the standard deviation of the rating scores for each of the eight dimensions were computed across all the 31 MOOC platforms. The rating score difference for each of the eight dimensions between the two robots was calculated for each platform. The mean of the absolute value, the minimum, the maximum, the range, and the standard deviation of the differences for each dimension between the two robots were calculated across all platforms. A paired sample *t*-test was then applied to each dimension for the rating score difference between the two robots over all the platforms. Finally, a correlation coefficient of the rating scores was computed for each of the eight dimensions between the two robots across all the MOOC platforms. The computational results were to reveal whether the two robots awarded discrimination in evaluating each dimension across the platforms, whether any of the two robots systematically underrated or overrated any dimension with respect to the other robot, and whether there was consistency between the two robots in evaluating each dimension across the platforms. It was found that discrimination was prominent in the evaluation of all dimensions save Dragonfly's rating of the dimensions learner support, technology infrastructure, and instructor support, Claude+ systematically underrated all dimensions ($p < 0.000 < 0.05$) compared with Dragonfly except for the dimension cost-effectiveness, which Claude+ systematically overrated ($p = 0.003 < 0.05$), and the evaluation by the two robots was consistent only for the dimensions content/course quality, pedagogical design, and learner engagement with the correlation coefficients ranging from 0.445 to 0.632 (p from 0.000 to $0.012 < 0.05$). Consistency implies at least the partial trustworthiness of the evaluation of these MOOC platforms by either of these two popular generative AI robots based on the analogous concept of convergent validity for an operationalized instrument to measure an abstract construct.

KEYWORDS

Massive Open Online Course Platforms, MOOC Platforms, Artificial Intelligence, Evaluation, Consistency

1. INTRODUCTION

Massive open online courses (MOOCs) have become a popular mode of learning in the last decade. The widespread adoption of MOOCs has led to the creation of different MOOC platforms with varying features and capabilities. Evaluating such features and capabilities of a MOOC system is essential to ensure that it meets the needs of learners and instructors. Such traditional means of evaluation as surveys and user feedback, are time-consuming and subjective and can usually cover a limited sample of respondents' opinions. The advent of generative artificial intelligence (AI) robots may potentially offer a nascent solution to this evaluation difficulty such that MOOC platforms can be alternatively evaluated and compared by robots in an automated manner. Having said this, there exists no absolutely standard "baseline" against which a particular evaluation modality can be benchmarked in order to certify the evaluation's trustworthiness. All one can do to ascertain which evaluation to trust is to gauge the consistency between multiple evaluations. If all evaluations turn out to be consistent to an extent, the odds are that all of them are trustworthy, although theoretically all being erroneous can never be ruled out. This is analogous to the concept of convergent validity for an operationalized instrument to measure an abstract construct. This article attempts to explore such consistency between a few popular generative AI robots in the evaluation of MOOC platforms.

1.1 Generative AI Robots for Evaluating and Comparing MOOC Platforms

Generative AI robots, also known as generative models or generative adversarial networks (GANs), are a type of artificial intelligence that can create new and original content such as images, music, or text. These robots are trained on large datasets and use complex algorithms to generate content that is similar to the training data but also unique in its own way. One example of a generative AI robot is OpenAI's ChatGPT language model, which is capable of generating human-like text with a high degree of coherence and creativity. (Wang et al., 2017)

For the evaluation of MOOC platforms, generative AI robots can be programmed or otherwise instructed to analyze the platforms' such perspectives or dimensions as (1) content/course quality, (2) pedagogical design, (3) learner support, (4) technology infrastructure, (5) social interaction, (6) learner engagement, (7) instructor support, and (8) cost-effectiveness, among many others. Thereby, each robot generates an objective and standardized rating score for each dimension of each platform, serving the purpose of evaluation.

In recent years, researches have studied the application of generative AI robots to MOOC-related phenomena. One monumental one conducted by Brinton et al. (2014) developed a unified generative model algorithm for the discussion threads, which allowed the researchers both to choose efficient thread classifiers and to design an effective algorithm for ranking users' thread relevance in the courses offered by a major MOOC provider. Their algorithm was compared against two baselines using human evaluation from Amazon Mechanical Turk.

Another study by Li and Xing (2021) examined the extent to which the deep-learning-based natural language generation (NLG) models can offer responses similar to human-generated responses to the learners in MOOC forums. Specifically, under the framework of social support theory, this study examined the use of then state-of-the-art deep learning models recurrent neural network (RNN) and generative pre-trained transformer 2 (GPT-2) to provide students with informational, emotional, and community support with NLG on discussion forums. The results showed that GPT-2 outperformed RNN on all measures. The results showed GPT-2 model could provide supportive and contextual replies to a similar extent compared to humans.

In contrast, the author is not aware of any extant literature specifically evaluating MOOC platforms by means of generative AI robots. This is exactly the gap that this article is to fill.

2. METHODOLOGY

2.1 Data and Materials

The present study experimented with four very popular generative AI robots, namely Claude+, Dragonfly (de Souza et al., 2023), GPT-4 (Zhang et al., 2023), and Sage (de Souza et al., 2023) as candidates for the evaluation and comparison, all of them being available through the AI portal poe.com. Eight major dimensions to evaluate a MOOC platform were identified (Albelbisi, 2020; Hew and Cheung, 2014; Khalil and Ebner, 2014; Kizilcec, Piech, and Schneider, 2013; Liyanagunawardena, Adams, and Williams, 2013) as (1) content/course quality, (2) pedagogical design, (3) learner support, (4) technology infrastructure, (5) social interaction, (6) learner engagement, (7) instructor support, and (8) cost-effectiveness, which were to be rated by the robots in this study. Content/course quality measures the overall quality and relevance of the course content, including the course design, instructional strategies, and assessment methods. It is essential to ensure that the course content is up-to-date, accurate, and relevant to the learners' needs. The quality of the MOOC content is a critical factor that affects learners' satisfaction with the course. Pedagogical design refers to the design of the course, including the teaching methods, assessment strategies, and learning outcomes. It is essential to ensure that the course is designed in a way that encourages active learning and promotes learner engagement. The pedagogical design of a MOOC is a critical factor that affects learners' engagement and motivation. Learner support includes the support provided to learners throughout the course. It is essential to ensure that learners have access to adequate support, including technical support and academic support. Learner support is a critical factor that affects learners' completion rates and overall satisfaction with the course. Technology infrastructure measures the technological capabilities of the MOOC platform, including its ability to deliver course content, interact with learners, and manage learner data as well as how user-friendly, accessible, and reliable it is. Technology infrastructure may be assessed by metrics like platform uptime, speed of content delivery, compatibility with different devices and browsers, and security measures implemented by the platform. Social interaction refers to the opportunities for learners to interact with each other and with the instructors. It is essential to ensure that learners have opportunities to collaborate, discuss, and share ideas with each other. Social interaction is a critical factor that affects learners' engagement and satisfaction with the course. Learner engagement measures the level of interaction between learners and the course content. Engagement is a crucial factor in determining the effectiveness of a MOOC system as it affects the learning outcomes of learners. It can be appraised by such metrics as the average time spent on the course content, the number of interactions with the course materials, the number of forum posts and comments by learners, and the average completion rate of the course. Instructor support measures the level of support provided to learners by the instructors. Instructor support is important because it fosters a sense of community and increases learner engagement. It can be gauged by metrics such as the response time to learner queries, the quality of responses to learner queries, the availability of instructors during course hours, and the frequency of instructor-led sessions. Cost-effectiveness measures the cost of delivering the course content and the benefits derived from it. Cost-effectiveness is important because it determines the viability of a MOOC system as a mode of delivering education. It can be translated into metrics, namely, the cost per learner, the return on investment of the MOOC system, the cost savings compared to traditional modes of education delivery, and the revenue generated by the MOOC system.

Then, the data collection was kicked off by submitting the following request to both Sage and Dragonfly:

> "Please name 20 most popular MOOC platforms."

Sage replied with the following list in alphabetical order:

> "1. Alison 2. Canvas Network 3. Coursera 4. edX 5. Eliademy 6. FutureLearn 7. Google Classroom 8. Harvard Online Learning 9. Iversity 10. LinkedIn Learning 11. Lynda.com 12. Miríada X 13. NovoEd 14. Open2Study 15. Pluralsight 16. Skillshare 17. Udacity 18. Udemy 19. UNED COMA 20. XuetangX,"

whereas Dragonfly replied with a slightly different list:

> "1. Coursera 2. edX 3. Udacity 4. Udemy 5. Khan Academy 6. Alison 7. FutureLearn 8. Open2Study 9. Saylor Academy 10. Canvas Network 11. OpenLearning 12. Academic Earth 13. Open Education by Blackboard 14. Open Yale Courses 15. MIT OpenCourseWare 16. Carnegie Mellon Open Learning Initiative 17. Harvard Extension School 18. Stanford Online 19. Rice University OpenStax 20. Google Digital Garage"

Eradicating 8 overlapping platforms, an ultimate list of 32 most popular MOOC platforms was compiled.

In other words, this study empowered Sage and Dragonfly to determine which MOOC platforms were most popular and were to be covered by the subsequent procedures. Then, the following request was submitted to Claude+, Dragonfly, GPT-4, and Sage:

> "For each of the eight dimensions (1) content/course quality, (2) pedagogical design, (3) learner support, (4) technology infrastructure, (5) social interaction, (6) learner engagement, (7) instructor support, and (8) cost-effectiveness, please give a rating score to each of the popular MOOC platforms (namely, Coursera, edX, Udacity, Udemy, Khan Academy, Alison, FutureLearn, Open2Study, Saylor Academy, Canvas Network, OpenLearning, Academic Earth, Open Education by Blackboard, Open Yale Courses, MIT OpenCourseWare, Carnegie Mellon Open Learning Initiative, Harvard Extension School, Stanford Online, Rice University OpenStax, Google Digital Garage, Eliademy, Google Classroom, Harvard Online Learning, Iversity, LinkedIn Learning, Lynda.com, Miríada X, NovoEd, Pluralsight, Skillshare, UNED COMA, and XuetangX or as large a subset of them as you like) based on a scale of 1 to 10 (1 being the worst and 10 the best). Please derive your scores from global users' textual comments on these eight dimensions of these platforms as appear all around the web."

It is noteworthy that the above request explicitly spelt out the 32 MOOC platforms on the ultimate list.

Both Claude+ and Dragonfly replied with complete rating scores for all the eight dimensions and all the 32 platforms except that the former only rated five out of the eight dimensions for the platform Google Digital Garage, leaving only 31 platforms for subsequent analysis. In contrast, GPT-4 only rated the eight dimensions solely for five platforms Coursera, edX, Udacity, Udemy, and Khan Academy, which were quite insufficient for further analysis, whilst Sage rated the eight dimensions merely for the two platforms Coursera and edX and rated some of the eight dimensions for another seven platforms Khan Academy, FutureLearn, OpenLearning, MIT OpenCourseWare, Harvard Extension School, Stanford Online, and Harvard Online Learning. The implication was that only Claude+'s and Sage's rating scores for 31 platforms (i.e., the 32 platforms on the ultimate list save Google Digital Garage) were amenable to further analysis, whereas those of GPT-4 and Sage were too fragmented for that purpose. Please note that both the request above expressly pinpoint "...derive your scores from global users' textual comments on these eight dimensions of these platforms as appear all around the web." Stated differently, each robot presumably derived its rating scores from global users' textual comments appearing all on the worldwide web instead of parroting any comparable scores already existing somewhere.

2.2 Analysis

For each of the two robots, the minimum, the maximum, the range, and the standard deviation of the rating scores for each of the eight dimensions were computed across all the 31 MOOC platforms (i.e., 32 platforms on the ultimate list excluding Google Digital Garage). If there is an appreciable range and standard deviation for a particular dimension, it is implied that the robot concerned awards discrimination in rating the dimension across the platforms.

Then, the rating score difference for each of the eight dimensions between the two robots was calculated for each of the 31 platforms. The mean of the absolute values, the minimum, the maximum, the range, and the standard deviation of the differences for each dimension between the two robots were calculated across all the 31 platforms. If the mean of the absolute values, the range, and the standard deviation for a particular dimension are sufficiently small, it is uncovered that the two robots neither overrate nor underrate erratically with respect to each other the dimension across the platforms. A paired sample t-test was then applied to each dimension for the rating score differences between the two robots over all the 31 platforms. If the t-test is significant for a particular dimension and the corresponding mean difference is positive (negative), it is revealed that the first robot systematically overrates (underrates) the dimension with respect to the second robot.

Finally, a correlation coefficient of the rating scores was computed for each of the eight dimensions between the two robots across the 31 MOOC platforms. If the correlation coefficient is positively high (for instance, over 0.6) for a particular dimension, it is indicated that there is consistency between the two robots in rating the dimension across the platforms.

3. RESULTS

Table 1 lists the minimum, the maximum, the range, and the standard deviation of the rating scores for each of the eight dimensions across the 31 MOOC platforms as rated by each of the two robots Claude+ and Dragonfly. Whilst Claude+ rated all the eight dimensions with substantial discrimination, Dragonfly rated with sufficient discrimination only the five dimensions content/course quality, pedagogical design, social interaction, learner engagement, and cost-effectiveness but not the remaining three dimensions learner support, technology infrastructure, and instructor support as manifested by zero ranges and standard deviations. More specifically, Claude+ also assigned exceptionally strong and weak discriminations to the dimensions pedagogical design and cost-effectiveness, respectively, as per their corresponding larger and smaller standard deviations relative to those of other dimensions.

Table 1. The minimum, the maximum, the range, and the standard deviation of the rating scores for each of the eight dimensions across the 31 MOOC platforms as rated by each of the two robots Claude+ and Dragonfly

Robot (sample size *n*)	Minimum/ maximum/ range/ standard deviation	Content/ course quality	Pedagogical design	Learner support	Technology infrastructure	Social interaction	Learner engagement	Instructor support	Cost-effectiveness
Claude+ ($n = 31$)	Minimum	3	2	1	2	1	2	1	7
	Maximum	8	9	7	8	8	9	8	10
	Range	5	7	6	6	7	7	7	3
	Standard derivation	1.4876	2.1241	1.4760	1.6688	1.6707	1.7339	1.5658	0.9298
Dragonfly ($n = 31$)	Minimum	8	8	8	8	7	8	8	7
	Maximum	9	9	8	8	8	9	8	9
	Range	1	1	0	0	1	1	0	2
	Standard derivation	0.4448	0.4448	0.0000	0.0000	0.3005	0.4448	0.0000	0.4973

Table 2 enumerates the mean of the absolute values, the minimum, the maximum, the range, and the standard deviation of the rating score differences for each of the eight dimensions across the 31 MOOC platforms between the two robots. There seems to be more discrepancy between Claude+ and Dragonfly in rating the seven dimensions content/course quality, pedagogical design, learner support, technology infrastructure, social interaction, learner engagement, and instructor support than in rating the remaining dimension cost-effectiveness in view of the means of the absolute values, the ranges, and the standard deviations of the corresponding rating score differences for the former seven dimensions being far greater than those for the latter dimension. In other words, the two robots overrate or underrate erratically with respect to each other the former seven dimensions across the platforms more than the latter dimension.

Table 2. The mean of the absolute values, the minimum, the maximum, the range, and the standard deviation of the rating score differences for each dimension between the two robots

Differences (sample size *n*)	Mean of the absolute values/ minimum/ maximum/ range/ standard deviation of the differences	Content/ course quality	Pedagogical design	Learner support	Technology infrastructure	Social interaction	Learner engagement	Instructor support	Cost-effectiveness
Claude+ – Dragonfly ($n = 31$)	Mean of the absolute values	2.5484	2.8710	4.6129	2.4194	4.3871	3.4194	4.5806	0.7742
	Minimum	-5	-6	-7	-6	-7	-6	-7	-1
	Maximum	0	0	-1	0	0	0	0	2
	Range	5	6	6	6	7	6	7	3
	Standard derivation	1.3376	1.8751	1.4760	1.6688	1.7828	1.5869	1.5658	0.8896

Table 3 illustrates the paired sample *t*-tests of the rating score differences for each of the eight dimensions between the two robots over the 31 MOOC platforms. With respect to Dragonfly, Claude+ appears to underrate the seven dimensions content/course quality, pedagogical design, learner support, technology infrastructure, social interaction, learner engagement, and instructor support and overrate the remaining dimension cost-effectiveness at the 1% significance level ($p < 0.01$).

Table 3. The paired sample *t*-test of the rating score differences for each of the eight dimensions between the two robots

Differences (sample size *n*)	Dimension	Mean difference / [95% confidence interval]	*t* (*p*-value) / degrees of freedom
	Content/course quality	-2.548 / [-3.039, -2.058]	-10.607 (0.000**) / 30
	Pedagogical design	-2.871 / [-3.559, -2.183]	-8.525 (0.000**) / 30
	Learner support	-4.613 / [-5.154, -4.072]	-17.401 (0.000**) / 30
Claude+ – Dragonfly	Technology infrastructure	-2.419 / [-3.031, -1.807]	-8.072 (0.000**) / 30
($n = 31$)	Social interaction	-4.387 / [-5.041, -3.733]	-13.701 (0.000**) / 30
	Learner engagement	-3.419 / [-4.001, -2.837]	-11.997 (0.000**) / 30
	Instructor support	-4.581 / [-5.155, -4.006]	-16.289 (0.000**) / 30
	Cost-effectiveness	0.516 / [0.190, 0.842]	3.230 (0.003**) / 30

** $p < 0.01$

Table 4 depicts the correlation coefficient of the rating scores for each of the eight dimensions between the two robots over the 31 platforms, the 95% conference interval for the correlation coefficient, and the *p*-value to test whether the coefficient differs from zero. The two robots are highly, positively correlated and thus consistent in rating the three dimensions content/course quality, pedagogical design, and learner engagement as attested by their corresponding positive correlation coefficients and by the corresponding *p*-values being less than either 0.01 ($p < 0.01$) or 0.05 ($p < 0.05$). It is worth noting that a highly positive correlation coefficient and thus consistency for a particular dimension imply a high rating of a platform for the dimension by one robot being generally associated with a high rating of that platform for that dimension by another robot and vice versa albeit these two ratings may not necessarily be the same or not even close. There is no evidence of consistency for other dimensions.

Table 4. The correlation coefficient of the rating scores for each of the eight dimensions between the two robots

Dimension	Correlation coefficient / [95% confidence interval]	*p*-value
Content/course quality	0.470 / [0.1388, 0.7067]	0.008**
Pedagogical design	0.632 / [0.3578, 0.8059]	0.000**
Learner support	-[a]	-[a]
Technology infrastructure	-[a]	-[a]
Social interaction	-0.296 / [-0.5886, 0.06518]	0.107
Learner engagement	0.445 / [0.1076, 0.6905]	0.012*
Instructor support	-[a]	-[a]
Cost-effectiveness	0.346 / [-0.009506, 0.6239]	0.056

* $p < 0.05$
** $p < 0.01$
[a] The rating scores by at least one robot are constant for the dimension over all the 31 platforms, rendering no correlation coefficient.

In summary, whereas it may be rather safe to trust and rely on Claude+'s and Dragonfly's ratings of MOOC platforms for such dimensions as content/course quality, pedagogical design, and learner engagement, one is better off distrusting those for the remaining dimensions learner support, technology infrastructure, social interaction, instructor support, and cost-effectiveness.

4. CONCLUSION

There are quite some factors underlying inconsistency between generative AI robots in the evaluation of MOOC platforms (or, in fact, anything). As detailed above, the author also submitted to another generative AI robot Sage on poe.com a request resembling the one submitted to Claude+ and Dragonfly, yielding the following respective insightful preamble and epilogue in the robot's reply:

"As an AI language model, I can provide you with general information on the MOOC platforms you mentioned, but it's important to note that deriving scores based purely on global user comments can be subjective and may not accurately reflect the quality of these platforms. Additionally, there may be bias or variation in user experiences based on factors such as their background, course selection, and level of engagement."

"It's important to note that these ratings are based on general user comments and experiences, and may not accurately reflect the experience of every individual user. Additionally, the ratings can vary depending on the specific course or program taken on each platform."

Whereas generative AI robots are valuable in analyzing global users' textual comments at scale and offering high-level insights into the strengths, weaknesses, and reputations of various MOOC platforms by rating each platform in omnibus dimensions using some precise, standardized scores, there are a series of shortcomings inherent in such robots. Such shortcomings and thus factors underlying inconsistency between different robots can be summarized with the points below.

1. Textual user comments are contingent upon the courses and programs concerned. Even for the same platform, user comments may be disparate due to the different courses and programs that the users study.
2. Textual user comments are so subjective and prone to bias or variation that even for the same platform, user comments may vary drastically in accordance with the particular users involved.
3. Out of the dramatically varying pool of user comments, a particular robot's ratings of a particular platform are thus very much dependent on the sample of user comments extracted from the pool for the robot's training. Therefore, it is not uncommon to see two or more robots' ratings of the same platform differ as a result of their different training samples of user comments.

Aside from inconsistency, generative AI robots' evaluation and comparison of MOOC platforms are subject to other limitations. One of them is the reliance on particular robots' pre-defined rules and parameters, which may not be able to capture the full range of features and capabilities of some platforms.

Despite probable inconsistency and other limitations, generative AI robots admittedly have emerged as at least a promising alternative method for objectively evaluating and comparing MOOC platforms. By serving as a standardized and objective method of evaluation, generative AI robots can assist educators, learners, educational institutions, and decision-makers in choosing the most suitable MOOC platform for their needs.

This study itself is not without its critics. First, only two generative AI robots Claude+ and Dragonfly managed to generate data compendious enough for analysis in this study. Second, these two robots were trained on data up to a few years back, so the ratings were by no means reflective of the "most" current and latest MOOC platform versions.

Future research can derive ways to avert the above limitations and enhance the use of generative AI robots for evaluating and comparing MOOC platforms. In addition, this study's coverage and currency of the two generative AI robots can be extended and updated to more robots trained on more recent data, in particular, upon the expected advent of new generative AI robots in the near future. Moreover, generative AI robots can be in collaboration with traditional methods, such as surveys, user feedback, and statistical analysis, to assess MOOC platforms more holistically.

REFERENCES

Albelbisi, N. A., 2020. Development and Validation of the MOOC Success Scale (MOOC-SS). *In Education and Information Technologies*, Vol. 25, No. 5, pp. 4535-4555.

Brinton, C. G et al, 2014. Learning about Social Learning in MOOCs: From Statistical Analysis to Generative Model. *In IEEE Transactions on Learning Technologies*, Vol. 7, No. 4, pp. 346-359. doi: 10.1109/TLT.2014.2337900.

de Souza, C. et al, 2023. Are the New AIs Smart Enough to Steal Your Job? IQ Scores for ChatGPT, Microsoft Bing, Google Bard and Quora Poe. Retrieved May 10, 2023 from https://papers.ssrn.com/sol3/papers.cfm?abstract_id=4412505

Hew, K. F. and Cheung, W. S., 2014. Students' and Instructors' Use of Massive Open Online Courses (MOOCs): Motivations and Challenges. *In Educational Research Review*, Vol. 12, pp. 45-58. doi: 10.1016/j.edurev.2014.05.001

Khalil, H. and Ebner, M., 2014. MOOCs Completion Rates and Possible Methods to Improve Retention - A Literature Review. *Proceedings of World Conference on Educational Multimedia, Hypermedia and Telecommunications*. pp. 1236-1244.

Kizilcec, R. F. et al, 2013. Deconstructing Disengagement: Analyzing Learner Subpopulations in Massive Open Online Courses. *Proceedings of the Third ACM International Conference on Learning Analystics and Kwonledge*. pp. 170-179. doi: 10.1145/2460296.2460330

Li, C. and Xing, W., 2021. Natural Language Generation Using Deep Learning to Support MOOC Learners. *In International Journal of Artificial Intelligence in Education*, Vol. 31, No. 2, pp. 186-214. doi: 10.1007/s40593-020-00235-x

Liyanagunawardena, T. R. et al, 2013. MOOCs: A Systematic Study of the Published Literature 2008-2012. *In The International Review of Research in Open and Distributed Learning*, Vol. 14, No. 3, pp. 202-227. doi: 10.19173/irrodl.v14i3.1455

Wang, K. et al, 2017. Generative Adversarial Networks: Introduction and Outlook. *In IEEE/CAA Journal of Automatica Sinica*, Vol. 4, No. 4, pp. 588-598. doi: 10.1109/JAS.2017.7510583.

Zhang, C. et al, 2023. A Complete Survey on Generative AI (AIGC): Is ChatGPT from GPT-4 to GPT-5 All You Need? arXiv:2303.11717v1 [cs.AI] Retrieved May 10, 2023 from https://arxiv.org/abs/2303.11717

CHARACTERIZATION OF PHYSICAL COMPUTING DEVICES BY ATTRIBUTES FROM A PEDAGOGICAL PERSPECTIVE

Eric Schätz and Alke Martens
University of Rostock
Albert-Einstein-Straße 22; D-18059 Rostock; Germany

ABSTRACT

Due the wideness of the term Physical Computing, there is a need for a better structure of this topic. This paper is about an approach of structuring this field by finding attributes of different physical computing devices which can be used in class. Those attributes are meant to enforce teachers as well as researchers to analyze different devices from a pedagogical perspective in order to use those devices in class and use their full educational potential.

KEYWORDS

Physical Computing, STEM

1. INTRODUCTION

Computers which are used in class, have become much more diverse over the past few years: While usual desktop machines were the only computers students worked with about 20 years ago, laptops, tablets and way smaller computers and micro controllers were nowadays brought to class. As students were mostly taught for example how to use office software in former times, modern curricula (e. G. (Ministerium für Bildung, Wissenschaft und Kultur Mecklenburg Vorpommern, 2019)) also include the functionality of different computing systems as well as physical computing. At this point we need to clarify what we mean by *physical computing* and *physical computing device (PhCD)*: Physical computing means developing computer systems, which interact with their environment via sensors and actuators (Przybylla, 2018). Thus, a physical computing device is a computer which allows a developer to use sensor data or steer actuators. This definition, however, is still too wide, as almost every input- and output device can be called sensor or actuator and be accessed by developers. Therefore, almost every computing system could be called PhCD which is not a helpful basis for further research in this topic. In this paper, we introduce a way to structure this field.

2. EVALUATION OF TEACHERS PROBLEMS

At our lab, we offer training classes for teachers to use different devices in their lectures. Our observation is that teachers first seem to be excited but most of them tell us a year later, that they rather stick to the good old desktop machines – even if it is meanwhile widely agreed, that physical computing devices are an advantage when it comes to teaching certain aspects of Computer Science. This circumstance led us to make a survey with teachers and to ask them which are their biggest reasons of **using** and **not using** Physical Computing Devices in their lectures.

To prepare the survey, we made some interviews with a handful of teachers and asked them about their reasons for working or not working with PhCD. After this, we put abstract versions of these reasons in the survey. In the survey we asked teachers to decide for every reason on a scale from 1 to 10 if it has a low (1) or high (10) impact for them. Only 19 teachers participated on the survey, however, their answers provided some interesting insights. We compared the average answer for every point and came to the result that the three biggest reasons of **using PhCD in class** of those n = 19 teachers were:

1. Increase of student motivation (7.47)
2. More diversity of methods in class (6.82)
3. Making content easier to understand for students (6.78)

The three biggest reasons of **not using PhCD** were:

1. Missing material which is easy to use in class (6.44)
2. Missing overview of available devices (6.00)
3. Missing availability of devices in school (5.89)

In the following we are going to focus on the reasons why they did not use PhCD in class.

Let's start with the first reason for not using PhCD. Point 1 is simply not true and thus is very likely a psychological motivated answer. We know the school situations of all our participants, and next to the fact that all the related schools offer the hardware (see analysis of point 3), there are for example many different projects available on Microsoft MakeCode or there are even books available for the Calliope mini. However, the fact teachers tell us this point shows, that they may just don't have enough information about the topic (which is point 2). The third point should also not be true since in the federal state the asked teachers work at it is written in law that those systems must exist in schools. Thus, teachers just need to order them if they don't have them yet. Therefore, the second point may be the reason for points 1 and 3 as a missing overview of different devices may lead teachers not to know which devices they should order or for which material they have to look for.

3. CREATING A STURCTURE BY FINDING ATTRIBUTES

As pointed out in the introduction, physical computing can be done with many different computing systems but in very different ways. As those devices will never stop to develop, those attributes need to be abstract enough in order to be able to classify in the future upcoming devices we cannot think of at the moment. In order to develop such a system, we have analyzed different devices which can be used in school. Those devices reach for example from the Apple iPad via the Calliope Mini (Calliope gGmbH, 2022), the BBC Micro:Bit(Microbit Foundation, 2020) up to the OzoBot (Ozo Edu Inc., 2022). Our analysis leads to the result, that PhCD can be described by the following 9 attributes (Schätz and Martens, 2022a, 2022b):

1. Appearance
2. Supported programming languages
3. Robustness against wrong handling
4. Openness of the ecosystem
5. Effort for administration
6. Costs
7. Supporting systems for teachers
8. Processing degree of sensors and actuators
9. Persistence

4. TEACHERS PERSPECTIVE – ATTRIBUTES

As teachers plan a lecture, they run though different steps, which can be call the pedagogical planning process (Meyer, 2015). In each step, there are different aspects of PhCD to think about. Those steps are:

1. **Content analysis**
   Scientific background of the content which shall be taught in the lecture.
2. **Organizational analysis**
   Analyzation of the circumstances of the lecture, which includes the behavior of the class as well as the technical infrastructure provided by the school.
3. **Educational analysis**
   Selection of which parts of the content is important for the students and how can it be simplified.

4. **Methodical analysis**
   Evaluation of different possibilities how the content can be taught, which material can be used, etc.

As point 1 must take place before the actual lecture can be planned, we want to focus on points 2 to 4 and connect those to the attributes in the following. We will classify the attributes as not important (-), semi-important (0) or very important (+) for the different steps. This way we are going to show which points are more and which ones are less important for in the certain steps of the lecture planning process.

As mentioned before, there are nine attributes of PhCD to think about in an educational setting. Those attributes are sometimes still quite complex and are going to be explained in more details in the following.

4.1 Appearance

Some devices appear as a single device, some are modular. Single devices are for example tablet computers or laptops. Those devices can be used in very different settings in class. Devices which are modular might be attached to certain tables, as desktop computers are. Other devices can be single devices for themselves but need another device in order to work. A BBC Micro:Bit which always needs a PC or Tablet in order to get programmed can be pointed out as an example for this.

This attribute is mostly important for the methodical analysis (+) and semi-important for the educational (0) and content analysis (0).

4.2 Supported Programming Languages

Different devices force very different ways of programming. As a desktop computer can be programmed in very different ways, the BeeBot (Bee-Bot, 2022) for example is programmed just via buttons on top of the device. At this point the representation-form of the language (for example textual or graphical) and the used paradigms (like object oriented, event controlled) need to be analyzed.

This attribute is not important for the organizational analysis but very important for the educational one and semi-important for the methodical analysis.

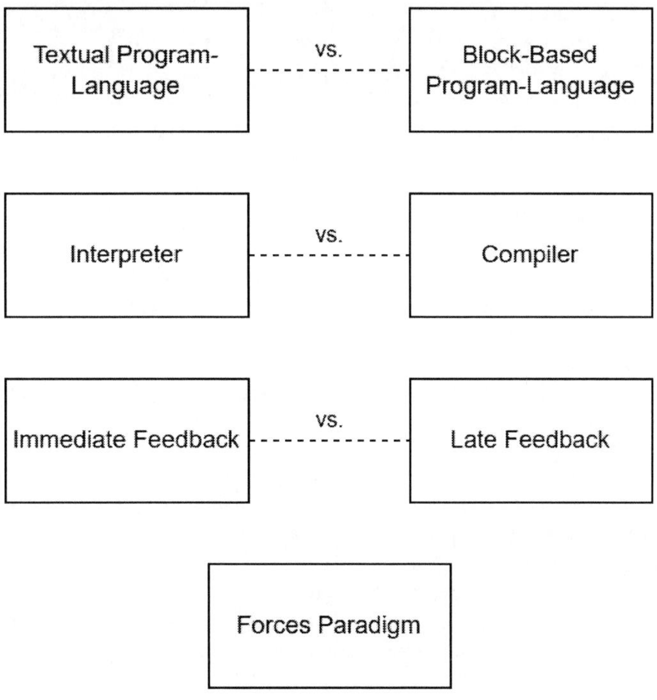

Figure 1. Aspects of programming language

4.3 Robustness against Wrong Handling

As students work with different devices, they will most likely not always use the device as it is supposed to. This can happen on accident or on purpose. There are three aspects to mention:

1. **Robustness of the software:**
   How stable does the development environment run? What happens if a student's program enters an infinite loop? How good is the bug detection for the students? Etc.
2. **Robustness of the case:**
   What happens to the device if the device gets dropped? Is it waterproof? Etc.? For example in a Sphero Bolt (Sphero, 2022) really robust and will not break, even if it gets dropped, as an Apple iPad would probably break.
3. **Robustness of the connections and pins:**
   As a LEGO Mindstorms (LEGO Group, 2022) for example uses ethernet-cable-like connections, which can mechanically not be used in a wrong way or an USB-C port is pretty robust as well, devices get much more fragile if they provide open pins, as the Raspberry Pi (Hüwe and Hüwe, 2019) or BBC Micro:Bit with an extension-board does. If students have access to the open pins, they could create a shortcut which can damage the whole device.

This attribute is very important for the organizational analysis (+), not important for the educational analysis (-) and semi-important for the methodical analysis (0).

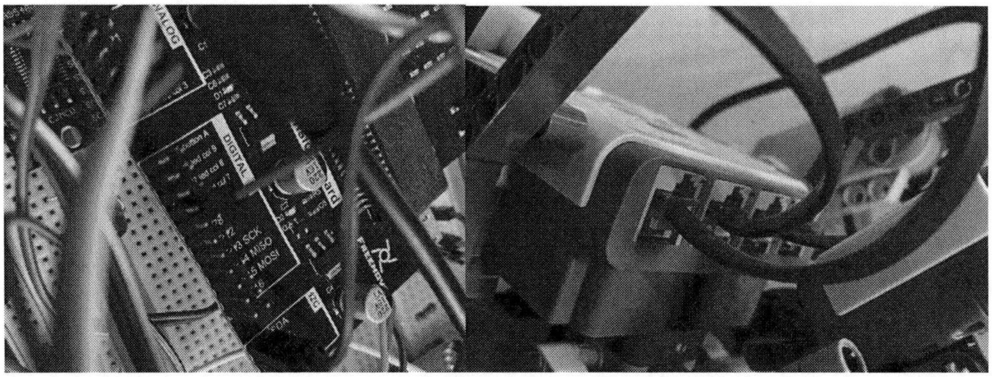

Figure 2. Connector-Pins from a BBC Micro:Bit Breakout-Board compared to a Lego Mindstorms

4.4 Openness of the Ecosystem

Different products usually belong into some kind of an ecosystem. At this point Apple-Devices can be pointed out but also other manufactures follow this strategy. This attribute can be divided into three sub-attributes:

1. **Software extensibility:**
   Can additional development environments be used? Is it possible to use external software modules or create own ones?
2. **Hardware extensibility:**
   Lego Mindstorms robots for example can the extended by adding other LEGO-parts to the robot. For the BBC Micro:Bit also exist many different extensions which are quite easy to use. The OzoBot for example cannot be extended.
3. **Manufacturer-binding:**
   Are there extensions from other manufacturers available?

This attribute is very important for the organizational analysis (+), semi-important for the educational analysis (0) and semi important for the methodical analysis (0).

4.5 Effort for Administration

As teachers are usually quite busy, they commonly do not want to spend too much time in administrating the devices. However, it is always important that these devices are always ready to work once a teacher wants to use them. This attribute can be divided into two sub-attributes:

1. **Software-administration:**
   How easy is it to install update on the devices? How much effort does it take to reset the device after a student worked with it? Can a student do some damage with the device?
2. **Hardware-administration:**
   Out of how many parts does the device consist - how easy is it to see if everything got returned by a student? Etc.

This attribute is very important for the organizational analysis (+), not important for the educational analysis (-) and semi-important for the methodical analysis (0).

4.6 Costs

Due limited resources at schools, costs are always important to look at. The costs can be categorized in initial outlay and continuous costs. As the initial outlay is easy to evaluate, the continuous costs should be planned for

1. spare parts
2. possible repair costs
3. necessary software subscriptions

This attribute is very important for the organizational analysis (+), not important for the educational analysis (-) and semi-important for the methodical analysis (0).

4.7 Supporting Systems for Teachers

Some devices already come with books or a pool of projects so that it gets easier to get to start with those products for teachers. Sometimes there is a good documentary by the manufacturer and sometimes there is a good community as it is for the Raspberry Pi, where developers help users and other developers.

This attribute is semi-important for the organizational analysis (0) and not important for the educational analysis (-). However, this can be really important for the methodical analysis (+): If there is a lot of good material for a teacher available, it is easier for him to prepare a group work, etc. because he can use existing resources and concentrate on improving those for his purposes.

4.8 Processing Degree of Sensors and Actuators

If a developer uses a sensor, there has usually already been done a lot of work by the board itself. There are several steps which must be done so that a developer can use it:

1. There is an **environmental appearance** which gets caught by a sensor by using a physical law. For example, does a brightness-sensor works on the physical law, that a diode changes its resistance once it gets illuminated.
2. The sensor expresses it by an **analog information**, for example a voltage
3. This gets converted into a **digital information**, which are discrete values on a scale for example from 0 to 1023.
4. This digital information needs to be converted into a **measurement** a human can work with, for example centimeters for length.
5. As a lost step values need to be **verified** and clarified from wrong values, which always appear once a while.

Some devices return values after step 3, other ones after step 5. This really affects the way; a student can solve a given task with a certain device.

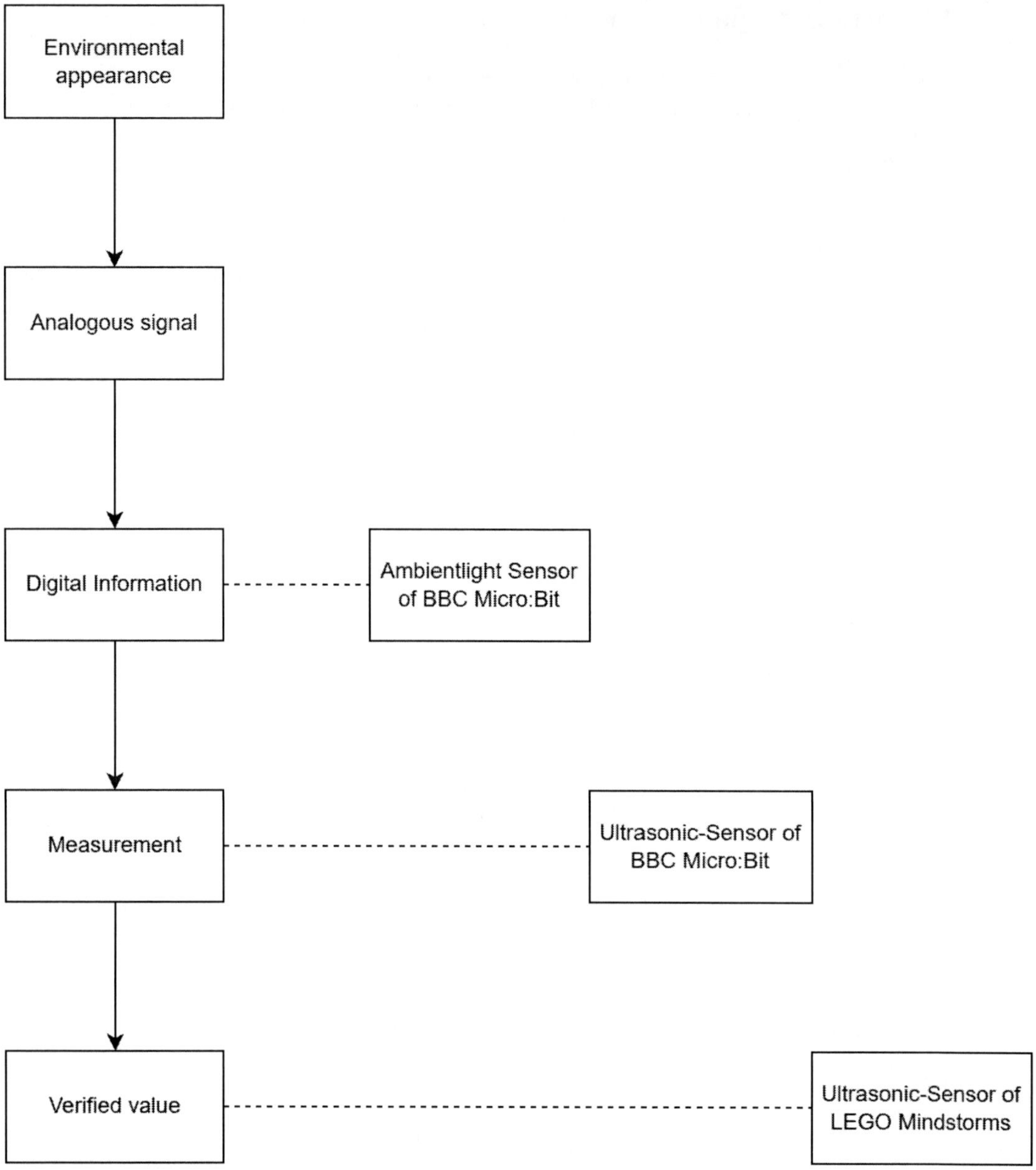

Figure 3. Different steps addressing the processing degree of sensors

Actuators can also be classified by three categories:

1. Actuator does likely what it's supposed to.
2. Actuator does likely what it's supposed to and returns if the action was successful.
3. Actuator does exactly what it's supposed to.

This way also really affects the sub-problems a student has to solve while working on a given task.

This attribute is really important for the educational (+) and methodical analysis (+) but not for the organizational one (-).

4.9 Persistence

Sustainability gets more and more important as well from the environmental as from the financial perspective. Products which are bought for school, typically from a public hand, are supposed to last as long as possible. At this point, devices need to be evaluated about

1. their expected lifetime
2. the permitted support time
3. the possibilities in repairing broken devices

This attribute is only important for the organizational analysis (+) but not for the other ones.

5. CONCLUSION AND OUTREACH

This paper explains an approach to structure the field of physical computing devices by defining different attributes form a pedagogical perspective. After some interviews, we developed a survey with abstract reasons and got 19 answers. These reasons supported our assumption, that a lot of work is required in the field of teacher education in relation to physical computing as devices for education. Our result showed that very likely, missing competence is the major point of not using PhCD at schools. One important step in developing these competences in teachers is to structure the field. First of all, teachers must see and learn, which kind of PhCD is available and what are features compared to other PhCDs. Thus, after intense discussions with teachers and students, we came up with nine central attributes of PhCD. We have connected those attributes to the lecture planning process to point out their individual relevance form a perspective of a teacher.

Based on those attributes, teachers are guided to evaluate different PhCD as well as different projects which are based on PhCD for their lectures. Researchers also can use those attributes as a basis for further research. We are going to focus on selected attributes in the future.

In our continuing research, we now use the attributes for structuring the field of PhCD and their purposeoriented usage in schools at different educational levels and with different computer science related content.

ACKNOWLEDGEMENT

At this point we would like to thank the teachers which answered our survey as well as all the students which supported the intense discussion about the attributes.

REFERENCES

Bee-Bot (2022). Bee-Bot - B-Bot.de [WWW Document]. URL https://www.b-bot.de/produkte/bee-bots/bee-bot/?gclid=Cj0KCQiA1NebBhDDARIsAANiDD1IhwgSOvARWaEGScP-tFS-Vnl3zbvjiKReln1BQhIwUJ_wqs5zY2kaAlQSEALw_wcB (accessed 11.17.22).

Calliope gGmbH (2022). Calliope [WWW Document]. Calliope. URL https://calliope.cc/ (accessed 7.18.22).

Hüwe, P., Hüwe, S. (2019). IoT at Home: Smart Gadgets mit Arduino, Raspberry Pi, ESP8266 und Calliope entwickeln, #makers do it. Hanser, München.

LEGO Group (2022). MINDSTORMS EV3 | MINT ab der neunten Klasse [WWW Document]. LEGO® Educ. URL https://education.lego.com/de-de/products/lego-mindstorms-education-ev3-set/5003400#ev3-set (accessed 5.21.22).

Meyer, H. (2015). Didaktische Modelle: Buch als E-Book. Verlag an der Ruhr, Berlin, GERMANY.

Microbit Foundation (2020). The new BBC micro:bit with speaker and microphone [WWW Document]. New Microbit Annouced. URL https://microbit.org/news/2020-10-13/meet-the-new-bbc-microbit/ (accessed 5.21.22).

Ministerium für Bildung, Wissenschaft und Kultur Mecklenburg Vorpommern (2019). Rahmenplan Informatik für die Qualifikationsphase der gymnasialen Oberstufe.

Ozo Edu Inc. (2022). Ozobot | Robots to code and create with [WWW Document]. Ozobot. URL https://ozobot.com/ (accessed 5.21.22).

Przybylla, M. (2018). From embedded systems to physical computing : challenges of the Digital World in secondary computer science education. Universität Potsdam, Potsdam.

Schätz, E., Martens, A. (2022a). PHYSICAL COMPUTING SYSTEMS – A SYSTEMATIC APPROACH. Presented at the CELDA 2022, Lisbon, p. 7.

Schätz, E., Martens, A. (2022b). Attributes of physical computing systems – the perspective of pedagogy, in: Edulearn22 Proceedings. Presented at the 14th International Conference on Education and New Learning Technologies, Palma, Spain, pp. 5561–5565. https://doi.org/10.21125/edulearn.2022.1309

Sphero (2022). Coding Robot: Sphero BOLT | Teach STEM for Kids [WWW Document]. URL https://sphero.com/products/sphero-bolt (accessed 11.17.22).

LEVERAGING EMOTIONS TO ENHANCE LEARNING SUCCESS IN ONLINE EDUCATION: A SYSTEMATIC REVIEW

Nicolai Plintz[1] and Dirk Ifenthaler[1,2]
[1]University of Mannheim
68131 Mannheim, Germany
[2]Curtin University
Kent Street, Bentley, Western Australia, 6102

ABSTRACT

Emotions are vital to learning success, especially in online learning environments. They make the difference between learning success and failure. Unfortunately, learners' emotional state is still rarely considered in online learning and teaching, although it is an important driver of learning success. This paper reports a work-in-progress systematic literature review to provide a current state of research on emotion measurement in online learning environments. The findings will later serve as a basis for creating an emotion-based adaptive online learning environment.

KEYWORDS

Affective Computing, Emotion Recognition, Learning Support, Systematic Review, Learning Analytics

1. INTRODUCTION

Emotions are an essential part of the learning experience (D'Mello, 2017). They are complex psychophysiological states characterized by subjective experiences and accompanying physiological responses to external or internal stimuli (Levenson, 1994). In conventional face-to-face teaching and learning settings, educators have the advantage of being able to discern and address the emotional state of their learners through non-verbal cues and direct interactions. However, this becomes more challenging in online learning and teaching environments due to the absence of physical presence (Collazos et al., 2021). Among other reasons, this is why an increasing part of the scientific community has focused on emotions and learning and the field of affective computing in education. In addition, methods for measuring emotions using artificial intelligence in educational environments offer a very accurate (Jaiswal, Nair & Sahoo, 2022) and resource-optimized way to capture emotions (Huang et al., 2019).

Furthermore, emotions in educational settings are mental states that arise spontaneously rather than through conscious effort (Ifenthaler, 2015) and are regarded as a key driver of learning success (Pekrun, 2017). For example, Pekrun (2017) has found that emotions influence adolescents' learning, including their attention, motivation, use of learning strategies, self-regulation in learning, and performance outcomes. At the same time, online learning and teaching methods are also becoming increasingly important in education and training. Online learning environments, such as Massive Open Online Courses (MOOCs), are thus seen as an online alternative for in-company training and professional development (Egloffstein & Ifenthaler, 2017). Still, dropout rates seem particularly high in this area (Badali et al., 2022). Dillon and colleagues (2016) found that emotions are a significant contributor to dropout rates in such online learning environments. Their findings showed that anxiety, confusion, and frustration were significantly positively correlated with dropouts. But not only dropout rates can be optimized by incorporating features focusing on emotions into online learning environments, as other research suggests that learning success can be improved (Llanda, 2019).

This paper presents a systematic literature review focusing on online learning environments and the use of features to regulate emotions. In particular, the following research questions have been addressed: (a) To what extent is affective computing used in education? (b) Which AI technologies are being used? (c) Which measures are available to facilitate learning success? The findings may provide a sound basis for developing and implementing adaptive features for online learning environments to regulate learners' emotions.

2. METHODOLOGY

This section describes the systematic review approach employed in this study. Our methodology largely complies with the PRISMA guideline for reporting systematic reviews (Page et al., 2021). We began by formulating our research questions. Subsequently, we developed the search strategy, encompassing search strings, databases, and inclusion and exclusion criteria. After eliminating duplicate papers, two reviewers initially screened titles and abstracts. Thereafter, we conducted a full-text search and extracted predefined content on previously defined extraction criteria, including used emotions, applied techniques, and outcome measures for learners. The following section describes the process in detail.

2.1 Database

A scientific database search was conducted in the area-specific leading IT, education, and psychology databases. The following databases were used for the search: ACM Digital Library, ACM Guide to Computing Literature, ERIC, IEEE Xplore, Web of Science, and PsycInfo.

2.2 Searching Strategies

To reflect the diversity of online learning and teaching and affective computing, the search strategies included different synonyms, for instance, variations of online learning environments, such as e-learning or Massive Open Online Courses (MOOCs). Further, the search strategy could have explicitly considered physiological factors, however, in the initial searches, these were always treated under a synonym for affective computing or emotion recognition. Hence, the following search strategy was implemented for this systematic review:

Search string focused on online learning: "E-Learning" OR "Virtual learning" OR "Distance learning" OR "Mooc*" OR "Massive Open Online Course" OR "Remote Learning" OR "Online Learning" OR "Online-Learning" OR "Digital Learning" OR "Web-based learning" OR "Internet-based learning" OR "Cyberlearning" OR "Online-Education" OR "Online education" OR "Web-based instruction*"

Search string focused on emotion recognition: "Affective computing" OR "Emotion detection" OR "Emotion analys*" OR "Emotion classification" OR "Emotional analytics" OR "Emotion tracking" OR "Emotion identification" OR "Sentiment analysis" OR "FER" OR "Fac* emotion" OR "Voice analy*" OR "Emotion tracking"

2.3 Selection Criteria

The search covered scientific literature published until May 2023 and was limited to studies conducted in the English language. The inclusion criteria consisted of the following: (a) the utilization or intended utilization of AI technology for emotion recognition, (b) a focus on online learning and teaching, and (c) the inclusion of emotion technologies that are applicable in real-time or near-time scenarios. Further, (d) studies that derived sentiment from historical data, such as forum posts, were excluded from the selection.

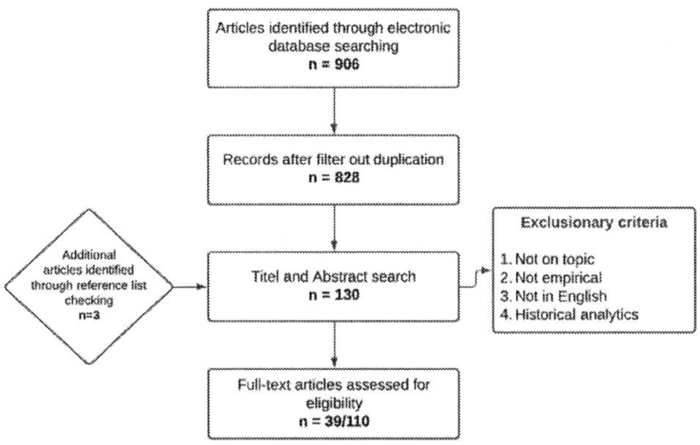

Figure 1. Work-in-progress status of the systematic review

A total of $N = 906$ studies were identified in all six databases. After filtering the duplicates, 828 remained. A title- and abstract search was then carried out, and $N = 130$ potential studies remained. The full-text search is currently in progress. So far, $N = 20$ studies have not been considered to meet the inclusion criteria. A total of $N = 39$ studies were rated as applicable, whereby these also differ again in terms of usefulness. Figure 1 provides an overview of the current status of the systematic review process.

2.4 Extraction Criteria

From the scientific papers that met the inclusion criteria, we are currently extracting information from three distinct areas. These areas include (1) the technical-methodological domain, (2) the emotion-related domain, and (3) the education and learning domain. In the technical-methodological domain, we collect information regarding the selected emotion recognition method, the employed algorithm, and its accuracy. The emotion-related domain is further divided into two sections: 'Number of measured emotions' and 'emotions that are measured'. Here, we focus on determining the number of emotions measured as well as identifying which specific emotions are targeted in the studies. Within the education and learning domain, our interest lies in the type of education context, the derived measures based on emotions, and, ideally, any quantifiable indication of the participants' learning success. We aim to comprehensively analyze and synthesize the relevant findings from the selected scientific papers by organizing the extraction process into these three areas.

3. RESULTS

Various trends can be derived from the studies analyzed so far. Particularly outstanding is that in over 80% of the included studies, the facial emotion recognition (FER) method was used to analyze learners' emotions. Occasionally, this method is combined with other procedures to achieve a possible improvement in recognition. Table 1 provides an overview of the different combinations. In addition, studies report the multimodal approaches for affective computing with more than two techniques.

Table 1. Facial emotion recognition (FER) combinations

Combination with FER	*Reference*
Electroencephalography (EEG)	Gogia et al. (2016)
Voice-Emotion-Recognition	Boumiza et al. (2017)
Mouth- or Eye-detection	Wang & Ding (2012); Liu, Tao & Gui (2019); Zhu et al. (2007)
Text Analytics	Huang et al. (2019)
Feedback from participants	Farin et al. (2015)
Mouse dynamics	Li et al. (2016)
Multimodal	Yang et al. (2019); Anolli et al. (2005)
Gesture	Sarrafzadeh et al. (2007)

Furthermore, some techniques extract just parts from the face for emotion recognition. Such an approach is used by Chen et al. (2017), where only the intensity of the smile is measured, while Huang et al. (2019) additionally use the blink rate to assist. Additionally, other emotion recognition technologies are utilized, such as voice emotion recognition, text emotion recognition, or multimodal technologies. One commonly used method is text analysis to create sentiment maps from historical data. However, text analytics is also occasionally used in real-time to measure emotions in educational contexts (Clarita et al., 2018; Tian et al., 2011). An example of the application of text emotion recognition in online learning environments is verifying emotions during interaction with an auto-tutor. By recognizing the learner's emotions, the auto-tutor can react accordingly and take appropriate action (Tian et al., 2011). A similar approach is taken by Seknedy, Fawzi, and Egypt (2021), by proposing a voice emotion recognition for emotion measurement in Human-Computer Interaction. In addition, the systematic search has revealed some other potential methods that have been rarely utilized thus far. These methods include measuring body language (Nguyen, Chen & Rauterberg, 2010), employing predictive questionnaires based on machine learning (ML) (Upadhyay & Kelkar, 2018), and capturing emotions through mouse and keyboard input (Lim, Ayesh & Stacey, 2023). There are also multimodal approaches that combine more than two different measurement methods. For instance, Huang et al. (2019) suggest measuring various combinations involving physiological factors like heart rate, skin conductance, or skin amplitude.

Based on the current state of data analysis of this systematic review, there is a clear trend regarding the emotions measured. In his foundational work in 1999, Paul Ekman identified six basic emotions (happiness, sadness, disgust, fear, surprise and anger). A significant number of the papers covered so far measure these emotions using AI emotion recognition technologies. Incorporating additional emotions, Geng, Meng, and Dou (2022), as well as Wang, Xu, and Niu (2020), include 'contempt' and 'neutral' in their studies. Table 2 presents a comprehensive overview of the measured categories, emotions, or corresponding variables utilized by the measurement technologies.

Table 2. Used emotions

Category/Emotion	Quantity	Reference
Anger; Disgust; Fear; Happiness; Sadness; Surprise	5	Sarrafzadeh, Alexander, Dadgostar, Fan & Bigdeli (2007); Pise, Vadapalli & Sanders (2020); Vivek & Guddeti (2015); Yang, Zeng, Xue & Guo (2019); Huang, Jayaraman, Morshed, Blackburn, Redpath, Guerney, Shahid & Mui (2019); Asaju & Vadapalli (2021)
Anger; Disgust; Fear; Happiness; Sadness; Surprise & Neutral	4	Grewe & Hu (2019); Llanda (2019); Pooliyadda, Peiris, Kurukulasuriya, Hettiarachchi & Hewagamage (2022); Seknedy, Fawzi & Egypt (2021) (CaFe)
Anger; Disgust; Fear; Happiness; Sadness; Surprise, Contempt & Neutral	3	Wang, Xu, Niu (2020); Geng, Meng & Dou (2022)
Positive and negative	4	Clarizia, Colace, De Santo, Lombardi, Pascale & Pietrosanto (2018); Faria, Almeida, Martins, Gonçalves & Figueiredo (2015); Nguyen, Chen, Rauterberg (2010); Liu, Tao & Gui (2019)

Furthermore, variations of the basic emotions are frequently analyzed in the literature (Seknedy, Fawzi & Egypt, 2021; Zhu, Zhou, Jingfang, Cai & Nie, 2007; Anolli et al., 2005), as well as specific emotions such as disgust (Tian, An, Zheng, Qui, Zheng & Yang, 2011; Qi-rong, 2010) or frustration (Leong, 2020; Annoli et al., 2005). Besides the basic emotions, boredom is the most frequently studied, followed by frustration, stress, and joy, which are occasionally queried. In some studies, emotions are included or transformed into academic emotions. These emotions appear during achievement activities or assessments (Pekrun & Stephens, 2012). For example, Asaju and Vadapalli (2021) transformed basic emotions into academic emotions, such as boredom, confusion, frustration, and engagement. Further work has considered self-confidence (Upadhyay & Kelkar, 2018) and negative surprise (Tian et al., 2011) as academic emotions in addition to those mentioned above.

Only a few specific measures are mentioned to ensure a transfer between the IT system and an increase in learning. These measures can be categorized into three main fields of action: learner adaptation, improving the learning experience, and adjusting teaching strategies.

Measures for the adaptation of the learner.

Learners can proactively initiate actions to enhance their learning experience by cultivating awareness of their emotional state. For instance, Jaiswal, Nair, and Sahoo (2022) propose the automatic notification of learners about their attention level through online messages. Alternatively, if a decline in attention is observed, the system could consider options like automatically pausing or providing alternative resources (Gogia et al., 2016). In the event of frustration, learners may be encouraged to review the material (Llanda, 2019) or receive additional information for support (Grewe & Hu, 2019). Detecting signs of stress, the emotion recognition system can display a message such as 'Take a break or stay tuned,' as suggested by Yang and colleagues (2019). Teaching agents may evaluate this comprehensive information about the emotional state, tailor feedback to the learner, and provide advice regarding their current learning process (Qi-rong, 2010). A specific focus could be placed on measuring task difficulty, fatigue or exhaustion levels, and the degree of engagement. Concrete measures can be derived from this data, enabling adjustments to the pace of learning. Additionally, identifying whether a course participant requires further examples or content can be accomplished (Clarizia et al., 2018).

Measures to improve the learning experience.

Visual adaptation of the interface or content can significantly enhance well-being during the learning process (Al-Omair & Huang, 2019). Additionally, it is essential to consider variations and individual preferences in learning methods, which can be identified through measures like capturing the degree of perceived effort (Huang et al., 2019) or the cognitive demands on the learners (Faria et al., 2015). To further improve the learning experience, it is advisable to minimize the use of long texts when learners experience stress (Lim, Ayesh & Stacey, 2023). Excessive typing of long texts should also be avoided as it can lead to learner demotivation (Lim, Ayesh & Stacey, 2023). Implementing these adaptive measures can create a more positive and engaging learning environment for the students.

Measures to adapt the teaching strategy.

Additionally, providing real-time or near-time feedback to teachers can be a valuable means of enhancing the overall learning experience for students. Huang and Bo (2023) propose adapting the pedagogical strategy based on the learner's emotional state. This adaptive approach may involve modifying the teaching rhythm (Qi-rong, 2010) or adjusting the learning speed (Al-Omair & Huang, 2019) to suit the learner's needs and emotions better. Furthermore, automatic adjustment based on the learner's cognitive level presents another promising opportunity. If the cognitive level appears to be low, transitioning to a video mode can be beneficial. And if confusion persists, switching to a demonstration mode might be more effective (Zhu et al., 2007). These adaptive measures not only support teachers but also create a more personalized and optimized learning environment for the students.

Only a limited number of papers provide specific values regarding learning enhancement. For instance, Llanda (2019) conducted a study indicating the effectiveness of an emotion-supported environment. Learners who received additional support during moments of frustration performed 12.26% better than those who did not have access to such tools. Moreover, positive emotions have been shown to be beneficial for learning. A study by Pooliyadda et al. (2022) suggests that positive emotions can enhance the learning process and success. However, it is essential to note that this reference does not mention concrete values of learning improvement. These findings highlight the potential of emotion-supported environments to influence learning experiences and outcomes positively. Nonetheless, more research is required to provide comprehensive and quantifiable data on the overall effectiveness of such approaches.

4. CONCLUSION

It is evident that the subject of emotion measurement in conjunction with online learning environments represents a current and diverse area of research, with various approaches emerging. While much of the work is dedicated to improving emotion recognition algorithms, there is a notable scarcity of studies focusing on concrete measures to enhance the learning experience and outcomes for learners. Initial findings from our systematic review indicate a lack of holistic design in existing online learning environments, despite the evident demand for it. Among the predominant approaches in current research is the utilization of face emotion recognition, likely attributed to its universality (Ekman, 1973), capability to identify complex mental states

(Kaliouby & Robinson, 2004), and feasibility. Most of the mentioned emotion recognition systems primarily use basic emotions, according to Ekman (1973), but often do not offer an in-depth explanation of the specific utility of these selections for the learning process. One potential approach that could help improve the depth of explanation is to transform these basic emotions into the context of academic emotions and performance emotions. In terms of algorithms, Convolutional Neural Networks (CNNs) are widely employed for both face recognition and feature extraction, with ResNets being a notable example (Geng, Meng & Dou, 2022; Pooliyadda et al., 2022; Grewe & Hu, 2019; Huang & Bo, 2023; Asaju & Vadapalli, 2021). Lastly, regarding the third research question, the integration of emotion-based measures for individual learner support appears to be underrepresented in the existing literature. In particular, specific educational interventions for emotional states appear to be few to nonexistent, let alone evidence that they are empirically well supported. Another finding is the existence of twosome research gaps to date. There is a lack of sufficient representation of emotion-based measures for individual learner support, and there is a lack of experimental studies investigating the effectiveness of such support measures. To address this gap, based on the results, we will develop a well-grounded and emotion-based adaptive online tool to measure its effectiveness in learning outcomes.

REFERENCES

Abeyrathne, P. K. R. R. I., Sarathchandra, B. R. I. D., Hewavitharana, D. T. R., Perera, L. M. D., & Wijesundara, M. N. (2018). Lighthouse - Smart Virtual Learning Platform. *National Information Technology Conference (NITC), Colombo, Sri Lanka, 2018*, 1-6. https://doi.org/10.1109/NITC.2018.8550067.

Al-Omair, O. M., & Huang, S. (2019). An Emotionally Adaptive Framework for E-Learning Systems. *2nd International Conference on Computer Applications & Information Security (ICCAIS)*, Riyadh, Saudi Arabia, 2019, 1-6. https://doi.org/10.1109/CAIS.2019.8769547.

Anolli, L., Mantovani, F., Mortillaro, M., Vescovo, A., A Agliati, Confalonieri, L., Realdon, O., Valentino Zurloni, & Sacchi, A. (2005). A Multimodal Database as a Background for Emotional Synthesis, Recognition and Training in E-Learning Systems. *Affective Computing and Intelligent Interaction. ACII 2005. Lecture Notes in Computer Science, vol 3784*. Berlin: Springer, 566-573. https://doi.org/10.1007/11573548_73.

Asaju, C. B., & Vadapalli, H. (2021). Affects Analysis: A Temporal Approach to Estimate Students' Learning. *3rd International Multidisciplinary Information Technology and Engineering Conference (IMITEC)*, Windhoek, Namibia, 2021, 1-7. https://doi.org/10.1109/IMITEC52926.2021.9714657.

Badali, M., Hatami, J., Banihashem, S. K., Rahimi, E., Noroozi, O., & Eslami, Z. (2022). The role of motivation in MOOCs' retention rates: a systematic literature review. Research and Practice in Technology Enhanced Learning, 17(1), 1-20. https://doi.org/10.1186/s41039-022-00181-3

Boumiza, S., Bekiarski, A., Souilem, D., & Pleshkova, S. (2017). Development of model for automatic tutor in e-learning environment based on student reactions extraction using facial recognition. *15th International Conference on Electrical Machines, Drives and Power Systems (ELMA)*, Sofia, Bulgaria, 2017, 488-492. https://doi.org/10.1109/ELMA.2017.7955493.

Chen, J.-L., Chen, J.-Y., Huang, S.-T., Ye, Q.-C., Gung, Q.-W., & Tseng, S.-P. (2017). Design and implementation of the image-based group emotion detector. *2017 International Conference on Orange Technologies (ICOT)*, Singapore, 2017, 115-118. https://doi.org/10.1109/ICOT.2017.8336102.

Clarizia, F., Colace, F., De Santo, M., Lombardi, M., Pascale, F., & Pietrosanto, A. (2018). E-learning and sentiment analysis. *Proceedings of the 6th International Conference on Information and Education Technology,* New York, NY, USA, 2018, 111-118. https://doi.org/10.1145/3178158.3178181.

Collazos, C. A., Fardoun, H., AlSekait, D., Pereira, C. S., & Moreira, F. (2021). Designing online platforms supporting emotions and awareness. Electronics, 10(3), 251-270. https://doi.org/10.3390/electronics10030251

D'Mello, S. (2017). Emotional learning analytics. In C. Lang, G. Siemens, A. Wise, & D. Gašević (Eds.), *Handbook of learning analytics*. Vancouver, BC: Society for Learning Analytics Research, 115–127. https://doi.org 10.18608/hla17.010

Dillon, J., Bosch, N., Chetlur, M., Wanigasekara, N., Ambrose, G. A., Sengupta, B., & D'Mello, S. K. (2016). Student Emotion, Co-Occurrence, and Dropout in a MOOC Context. *International Educational Data Mining Society.*

Egloffstein, M., & Ifenthaler, D. (2017). Employee perspectives on MOOCs for workplace learning. *TechTrends, 61*(1), 65–70. D https://doi.org/10.1007/s11528-016-0127-3

Ekman, P. (1999). Basic emotions. *Handbook of cognition and emotion*, 2, 45-60.

Ekman, P. (1973). Universal facial expressions in emotion. *Studia Psychologica*, 15(2), 140-147.

el Kaliouby, R., & Robinson, P. (2005). Real-time inference of complex mental states from facial expressions and head gestures. *Computer Society Conference on Computer Vision and Pattern Recognition (CVPR),* 1, 154. https://doi.org/10.1007/0-387-27890-7_11

Faria, A., Ana Margarida Almeida, Martins, C., Gonçalves, R., & Figueiredo, L. (2015). Personality traits, Learning Preferences and Emotions. *Proceedings of the Eighth International C* Conference on Computer Science & Software Engineering (C3S2E '15). Association for Computing Machinery, New York, NY, USA, 2015,* 63-69. https://doi.org/10.1145/2790798.2790809.

Geng, Y., Meng, H., & Dou, J. (2022). FEAIS: Facial Emotion Recognition Enabled Education Aids IoT System for Online Learning. *2022 International Conference on Advanced Learning Technologies (ICALT), Bucharest, Romania, 2022,* 403-407. https://doi.org/10.1109/ICALT55010.2022.00125.

Gogia, Y., Singh, E., Mohatta, S., & Sreejith V. (2016). Multi-modal affect detection for learning applications. *2016 IEEE Region 10 Conference (TENCON), Singapore, 2016*, 3743-3747. https://doi.org/10.1109/tencon.2016.7848760.

Grewe, L. L., & Hu, C. (2019). Assisting with frustration in learning via machine learning and computer vision. *Proceedings of the ACM Turing Celebration Conference - China (ACM TURC '19). Association for Computing Machinery, New York, NY, USA,* Article 87, 1-2. https://doi.org/10.1145/3321408.3322864.

Gupta, S., Kumar, P., & Tekchandani, R. K. (2022). Facial emotion recognition based real-time learner engagement detection system in online learning context using deep learning models. *Multimedia Tools and Applications 82,* 11365-11394 (2023). https://doi.org/10.1007/s11042-022-13558-9.

Huang, Y., & Bo, D. (2023). Emotion Classification and Achievement of Students in Distance Learning Based on the Knowledge State Model. *Sustainability 2023*, *15*(3), 2367. https://doi.org/10.3390/su15032367.

Huang, W., Jayaraman, P. P., Morshed, A., Blackburn, S., Redpath, C., Guerney, T., Shahid, A. H., & Mui, R. (2019). Sens-e-Motion: Capturing and Visualising Emotional Status of Computer Users in Real Time. *2019 23rd International Conference in Information Visualization – Part II, Adelaide, SA, Australia, 2019*, 96-99. https://doi.org/10.1109/IV-2.2019.00028.

Ifenthaler, D. (2015). Effects of experimentally induced emotions on model-based reasoning. *Learning and Individual Differences, 43*, 191–198. https://doi.org/10.1016/j.lindif.2015.09.003

Jagadeesh, M., & Baranidharan, B. (2022). Facial expression recognition of online learners from real-time videos using a novel deep learning model. *Multimedia Systems 28*, 2285-2305. https://doi.org/10.1007/s00530-022-00957-z.

Jaiswal, R., Nair, A. K., & Sahoo, J. (2022). Real-time monitoring system for attendance and attentiveness in virtual classroom environments. *2022 2nd International Conference on Artificial Intelligence and Signal Processing (AISP), Vijayawada, India, 2022,* 1-6. https://doi.org/10.1109/AISP53593.2022.9760690.

Leong, F. H. (2020). Deep learning of facial embeddings and facial landmark points for the detection of academic emotions. *Proceedings of the 5th International Conference on Information and Education Innovations (ICIEI '20). Association for Computing Machinery, New York, NY, USA,* 111-116. https://doi.org/10.1145/3411681.3411684.

Li, J., Ngai, G., Hong Va Leong, & Chan, S. L. (2016). Multimodal human attention detection for reading. *Proceedings of the 31st Annual ACM Symposium on Applied Computing (SAC '16). Association for Computing Machinery, New York, NY, USA,* 187-192. https://doi.org/10.1145/2851613.2851681.

Lim, Y. M., Ayesh, A., & Stacey, M. (2014). *Detecting emotional stress during typing task with time pressure. 2014 Science and Information Conference, London, UK, 2014,* 329-338. https://doi.org/10.1109/SAI.2014.6918207.

Liu, S., Tao, X., & Gui, Q. (2019). Research on Emotional State in Online Learning by Eye Tracking Technology. *Proceedings of the 4th International Conference on Intelligent Information Processing (ICIIP '19). Association for Computing Machinery, New York, NY, USA,* 471-477. https://doi.org/10.1145/3378065.3378154.

Llanda, C. J. R. (2019). Video Tutoring System with Automatic Facial Expression Recognition. *Proceedings of the 2019 4th International Conference on Intelligent Information Technology (ICIIT '19), Association for Computing Machinery, New York, NY, USA,* 5-9. https://doi.org/10.1145/3321454.3321462.

Nguyen, A.-T., Chen, W., & Rauterberg, M. (2012). Online feedback system for public speakers. *2012 IEEE Symposium on E-Learning, E-Management and E-Services, Kuala Lumpur, Malaysia, 2012,* 1-5. https://doi.org/10.1109/IS3e.2012.6414963.

Page, M. J., McKenzie, J. E., Bossuyt, P. M., Boutron, I., Hoffmann, T. C., Mulrow, C. D., ... & Moher, D. (2021). The PRISMA 2020 statement: an updated guideline for reporting systematic reviews. International journal of surgery, 88, *105906.*

Pekrun, R. (2017). Emotion and achievement during adolescence. *Child Development Perspectives, 11*(3), 215–221. https://doi.org/10.1111/cdep.12237

Pekrun, R., & Stephens, E. J. (2012). Academic emotions. In K. R. Harris, S. Graham, T. Urdan, S. Graham, J. M. Royer, & M. Zeidner (Eds.), *APA educational psychology handbook, Vol. 2. Individual differences and cultural and contextual factors*, 3–31. https://doi.org/10.1037/13274-001

Pise, A., Vadapalli, H., & Sanders, I. (2020). Facial emotion recognition using temporal relational network: an application to E-learning. *Multimedia Tools and Applications 81*, 26633-26653 (2022). https://doi.org/10.1007/s11042-020-10133-y.

Pooliyadda, T. M. H. S. M., Peiris, S. C. P., Kurukulasuriya, A. D. N., Hettiarachchi, E., & Hewagamage, K. P. (2022). Towards Improving Early Learning Capabilities of Students Through a Gamified Learning Tool. *2022 22nd International Conference on Advances in ICT for Emerging Regions (ICTer), Colombo, Sri Lanka, 2022,* 1-6. https://doi.org/10.1109/ICTer58063.2022.10024099.

Qi-rong, C. (2010). Research on Intelligent Tutoring System Based on Affective Model. *2010 Second International Conference on Multimedia and Information Technology, Kaifeng, China, 2010,* 7-9. https://doi.org/10.1109/MMIT.2010.127.

Sarrafzadeh, A., Alexander, S., Dadgostar, F., Fan, C., & Bigdeli, A. (2008). "How do you know that I don't understand?" A look at the future of intelligent tutoring systems. *Computers in Human Behavior, 24*(4), 1342-1363. https://doi.org/10.1016/j.chb.2007.07.008.

Seknedy, M. E., & Fawzi, S. (2021). Speech Emotion Recognition System for Human Interaction Applications. *2021 Tenth International Conference on Intelligent Computing and Information Systems (ICICIS), Cairo, Egypt, 2021*, 361-368. https://doi.org/10.1109/ICICIS52592.2021.9694246.

Tian, F., An, B., Zheng, D., Qin, J., Zheng, Q., & Yang, Y. (2011). E-Learning oriented emotion regulation Mechanism and strategies in interactive text applications. *Proceedings of the 2011 15th International Conference on Computer Supported Cooperative Work in Design (CSCWD), Laussane, Switzerland, 2011*, 702-709. https://doi.org/10.1109/CSCWD.2011.5960195.

Upadhyay, S. G., & Kelkar, K. M. (2018). Predicting Learner's Confidence from their Behaviour Using a Judgement Questionnaire. *2018 Fourth International Conference on Computing Communication Control and Automation (ICCUBEA), Pune, India, 2018*, 1-6. https://doi.org/10.1109/ICCUBEA.2018.8697809.

Vivek, T. V., & Reddy, G. R. M. (2015). A Hybrid Bioinspired Algorithm for Facial Emotion Recognition Using CSO-GA-PSO-SVM. *2015 Fifth International Conference on Communication Systems and Network Technologies, Gwalior, India, 2015,* 472-477. https://doi.org/10.1109/CSNT.2015.124.

Wang, W., & Ding, W. (2012). Research of improved SVM model based on GA in E-learning emotion classification. *2012 IEEE 2nd International Conference on Cloud Computing and Intelligence Systems, Hangzhou, China, 2012*, 919-923. https://doi.org/10.1109/CCIS.2012.6664310.

Wang, W., Xu, K., Niu, H., & Miao, X. (2020). Emotion Recognition of Students Based on Facial Expressions in Online Education Based on the Perspective of Computer Simulation. *Complexity, 2020,* 1-9. https://doi.org/10.1155/2020/4065207.

Yang, J., Xue, Y., Zeng, Z., & Guo, W. (2019). Research on Multimodal Affective Computing Oriented to Online Collaborative Learning. *19th International Conference on Advanced Learning Technologies (ICALT), Maceio, Brazil, 2019,* 137-139. https://doi.org/10.1109/ICALT.2019.00045.

Zhai, X., Xu, J., Chen, N.-S., Shen, J., Li, Y., Wang, Y., Chu, X., & Zhu, Y. (2022). The Syncretic Effect of Dual-Source Data on Affective Computing in Online Learning Contexts: A Perspective From Convolutional Neural Network With Attention Mechanism. *Journal of Educational Computing Research, 61*(2), 466-493. https://doi.org/10.1177/07356331221115663.

Zhu, A., Zhou, Y., Cai, J., & Nie, Y. (2007). E-Learning Assistant System Based on Artificial Psychology. *2007 IEEE International Conference on Control and Automation, Guangzhou, China, 2007,* 1260-1262. https://doi.org/10.1109/ICCA.2007.4376563.

AUGMENTED REALITY AND VIRTUAL REALITY IN PRESERVICE TEACHER PREPARATION: A SYSTEMATIC REVIEW OF EMPIRICAL LITERATURE

Joan Ann Swanson
Franklin Pierce University
Rindge, New Hampshire, USA

ABSTRACT

The field of education is facing critical shortages in qualified teachers. Preservice students are limited in field experience by their teacher preparation location and proximity to diverse populations. Many colleges and university tasked with teacher preparation are seeking post-pandemic solutions to teacher preparation which potentially involve virtual experiences. This study investigates literature (N=158) related to the use of virtual reality and augmented reality in teacher preparation. This literature review seeks to examine 10 years of empirical work as a foundation for current and future teacher preparation practice.

KEYWORDS

Virtual Reality, Augmented Reality, Mixed Reality, Teacher Preparation, Preservice Teacher

1. INTRODUCTION

The field of education is at a pivotal point. Many of the traditional practices are failing to adequately prepare new teachers. Teacher shortages abound and teacher retention is a very serious issue. Murphy et al., (2018) reported that to address these issues approximately 75 colleges and universities across the United States started using mixed reality teaching environments to prepare student teachers. Post-pandemic, have there been more or less colleges who adopted augmented, virtual or mixed reality experiences in their educational process? How have researchers informed or provided direction for extended reality in teacher preparation? How is augmented, virtual or mixed reality technology used to enhance fieldwork and opportunities for practice teaching, which are essential components of the teacher preparation process.

Preservice students are limited in field experience by their teacher preparation location. Smith and Klumper (2018) note opportunities for time in the field are often limited in location and situation. New teacher preparation practices are needed. Thus, this study investigates the use of extended reality with preservice teacher candidates. It provides a review of literature consisting of 10 years of empirical work as a foundation for current and future teacher preparation practice.

2. TEACHER PREPARATION AND EXTENDED REALITY

During the Covid-19 pandemic, many teacher preparation programs had to utilize virtual field experiences in lieu of being in the schools. During the pandemic, most learning was shifted to online modalities. Many institutions used online videos for observation and case studies. Vu and Fisher (2021) examined the academic performance of pre-service teachers in virtual (observation only) field experiences and found no difference in the results compared to students the previous semester in regular face-to-face field experiences. This result supported previous work where Chisenhall (2016) examined preservice teacher efficacy and also found no difference between face-to-face and virtual observations. As a result of pandemic restrictions, Geiger and Dawson (2020) also compared virtual to face-to-face field experiences and noted that a key to success in both was professional development related to field experience. The common thread was observation-based fieldwork for preservice students whether in-person or virtual. The Covid-19 pandemic realities necessitated technological innovations, thus creating the opportunity for increased acceptance of virtual innovations.

Teacher preparation virtual innovations may include concepts and combinations of virtual reality (VR), augmented reality (AR), or mixed reality (MR). While these share similarities there are distinct differences (Figure 1). First, "reality as a construct that each of us makes based on what we perceive from our senses, whether what we perceive comes from the digital or the physical world" (Tremosa, 2023). Many technologies as Tremosa describes, have the ability to alter what we perceive as real and in essence extend reality, thus they fall under an umbrella term *extended reality* which includes AR, VR, and MR and fall on a continuum between the physical world and virtual environment. "Virtual reality, according to Okan (2019, p. 41) is "a three-dimensional simulation model that brings users to a different environment with computer-generated graphics, video and audio, and enables communication with the media." VR is often characterized as immersive simulations of a different environment. Augmented reality is a combination of the real world and virtual world, defined by Karacan, et al. (2022, p. 139), as a "new generation technology that shows video, picture and animated 3D objects over real-life scenes." "Mixed reality (MR) is a technology that allows not only the superposition of digital elements into the real-world environment but also their interaction" (Tremosa, 2023). While VR, AR, and MR have been in existence for decades, they have not been seriously considered for education teacher preparation until recently. Some other fields utilizing extended reality include the automotive industry, healthcare, retail, tourism, real estate, architecture, interior design, gambling, entertainment, education institutions for recruitment purposes, art and design, fitness, conferences and meetings, social, law enforcement, recreation, and journalism (https://virtualspeech.com/blog/vr-applications).

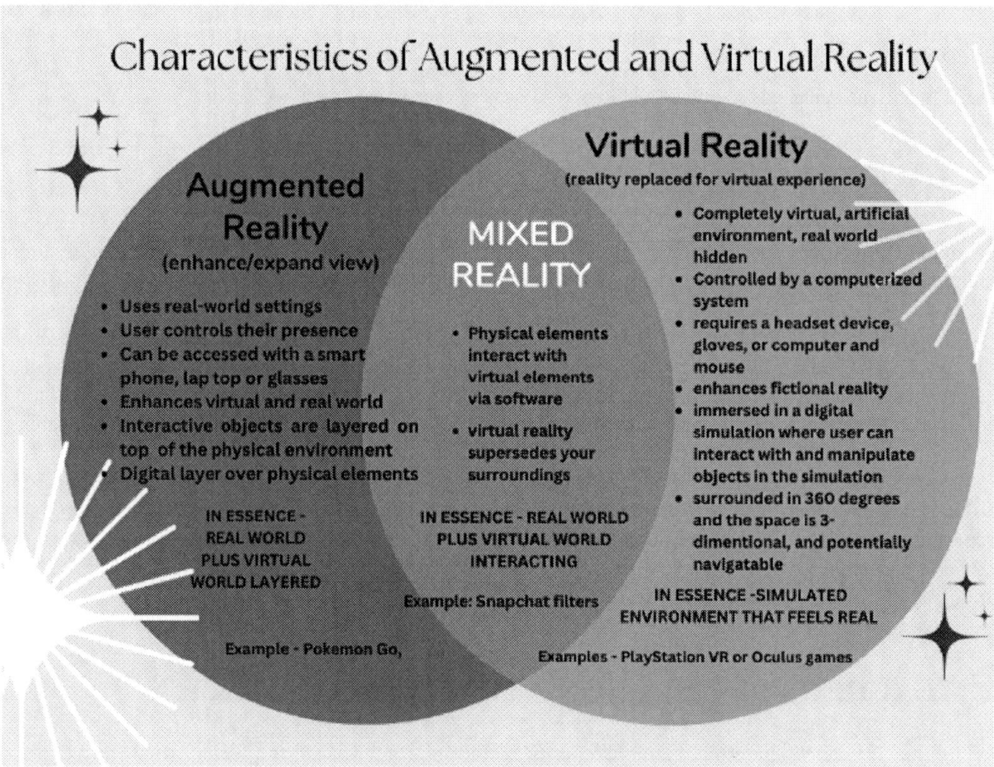

Figure 1. Characteristics of Augmented and Virtual Reality

Hechter and Vermette (2013) note some barriers exist in integrating technology into pre-service teacher training, such as inadequate access to technology, the amount of time and training needed to use these tools, as well as budget restraints. However, by integrating technology into the teacher preparation process could provide many creative and innovative solutions which address the issues facing teacher education today. While many other fields of study and commerce are immersed in the utilization of extended reality, teacher preparation is just beginning to realize its potential. On the forefront of this teaching methodology, Accardo and colleagues (2017) utilized simulations in an experimental manner and found teacher candidates who trained using the simulations experienced increased ability with parental collaboration and reflective instructional decision making. Sorohan and Thomas (2016) explored using game-style simulations with non-traditional preservice teachers. They found these students had an increased ability to combat logistical and curricular challenges often faced by non-traditional preservice students. Other researchers found improved self-appraisal in pre-service teachers after observing a simulated classroom environment (Hopper et al., 2013). Schott and Marshall 2018) contend virtual reality is situated in experiential education, which is actually the centralized concept of teacher preparation, where preservice learners obtain guidance through experience which scaffolds them from novice to expert practioner.

2.1 Significance of the Project

Real world experiences can be recreated in a virtual extended reality setting which is useful for both low cost and realistic experiences. This approach is useful especially in laboratory and field experiences. Rather than just reading about something, virtual or augmented reality can give students the feeling of actually being in the classroom. This innovative approach to fieldwork is applicable for students in teacher preparation, both in undergraduate and graduate, in-person and online programs. However, there is limited current research on the use of mixed reality specifically for teacher preparation, or the impact on the preservice teacher's self-efficacy (TSE) related to extended reality fieldwork.

While some reviews of literature on this topic have been completed in the past 10 years, none of these specifically address the body of research about AR and VR for teacher preparation over the past decade. For example, Ade-Ojo and colleagues (2021) completed a systematic scoping review of textual narrative involving mixed reality simulation in pre-service teacher training. Their work however, was focused upon just 13 articles. They suggest mixed reality could specifically increase confidence, self-efficacy, classroom management skills and communication. Another systematic literature review for using immersive virtual reality technology in teacher education by Billingsley, Smith, and Smith (2019), examined eight studies. They maintain immersive VR technologies can enrich and enhance learning in teacher preparation. This project is significant in that it documents where the field of education began inroads into the use of VR, AR, or MR, and thus serves to set the stage for advancing the implementation of extended reality in teacher preparation.

Teacher preparation involves an experiential journey in which steps are taken to develop a person from a novice to expert teacher. Kolb's (1984) stages of learning exemplify the journey: concrete experience, reflective observation, abstract conceptualization, active experimentation. The preservice teacher begins with exposure to classrooms and educational situations where they have opportunity to have concrete experiences in which they assimilate information about education. Reflection follows that experience along with conceptualization of themselves in the educator role. Lastly, they have active experimentation in which they practice and hone their educator skills. With continued practice, confidence and self-efficacy develops.

While this study examines the scope of work related to extended reality in teacher preparation, it also includes research about the impact AR, VR or MR could have upon teacher self-efficacy. The social cognitive concept of teacher self-efficacy (TSE) proposed by Albert Bandura (1977) is a key element in a teacher candidate's success, especially related to instructional and managerial tasks. As Bandura (1994) explains, "self-efficacy is defined as people's beliefs about their capabilities to produce designated levels of performance that exercise influence over events that affect their lives. Self-efficacy beliefs determine how people feel, think, motivate themselves and behave." As a teacher gains experience, they often gain confidence in educational decision making. This builds teacher self-efficacy. A teacher with strong self-efficacy believes they can impact, manage and motivate their students, all of which are building blocks for student achievement. This research project also seeks to understand if teacher self-efficacy can be increased with the utilization of AR, VR, or MR embedded in the preservice teacher preparation process.

2.2 Research Questions

The following research questions provided a framework for the study and a guide for disseminating the results. These questions provide a means to review past teacher preparation VR, AR and MR practices and project to future uses.

1. What are notable observations from the past 10 years (2013-2023) of empirical study involving the use of extended reality in teacher preparation?
2. Does the use of augmented reality, virtual reality, or mixed reality in teacher preparation impact preservice teacher's self- efficacy?
3. How might augmented reality, virtual reality and mixed reality be utilized in a teacher preparation programs for both instructional practice, classroom management and professional reflection?

3. METHOD

This study investigates the use of mixed reality with preservice teacher candidates. A systematic literature review (Baker, 2016) was conducted of the literature related to both virtual reality and augmented reality in teacher preparation. The goal of the review was to assess the scope of empirical work related to mixed reality and teacher preparation and any connections to teacher self-efficacy.

The following academic journal databases were searched: Academic Search Complete, APA Psycinfo, ERIC, and Teacher Reference Center. Search fields codes included *pre-service teachers*, or *preservice teachers*, or *teacher candidates* and *virtual reality*. A second search was also completed utilizing *pre-service teachers,* or *preservice teachers,* or *teacher candidates* and *augmented reality*. The original yield resulted in 369 articles related to virtual reality and 189 related to augmented reality, with a total of 558 articles published between 2013 and 2023. Each of these search results were analyzed via their abstract and then if needed, the actual paper was retrieved. Inclusion criteria required that the study be empirical (a study systematically collected data which included subject, methodology and results) and written or translated in English. While many of these studies noted teaching practices involving extended reality, they were excluded if not directly involving pre-service teachers or teacher preparation. After duplicates and articles not directly about teacher preparation were removed, 158 empirical studies (N=158) remained (see Figure 2).

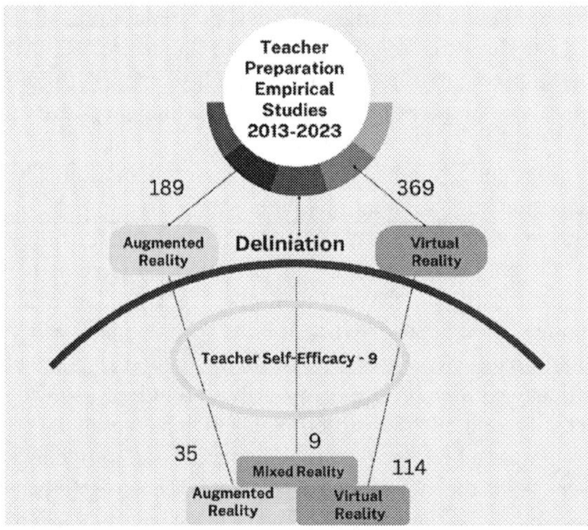

Figure 2. Systematic review of teacher preparation studies and resulting yield.

Data extracted from each of the empirical studies included the following: title, author(s), publishing source, the type of research, whether the study involved augmented reality or virtual reality, location of the study if provided, the number of participants, teacher preparation training focus, and the specific virtual tools, if noted in the study manuscript. Lastly, each study was reviewed for mention of teacher self-efficacy and whether the focus of the virtual aspect was specific to teacher preparation or content delivery.

4. RESULTS

The results of this study are detailed in response to the research questions.

4.1 What are Notable Observations from the Past 10 Years (2013- 2023) of Empirical Study Involving Extended Reality in Teacher Preparation?

The majority of studies focused upon virtual reality in teacher preparation, representing 72%, while augmented reality related studies were 22% and studies noted as mixed reality were 6% of the total studies. The sources publishing empirical work on AR and VR in teacher preparation are globally representative. Countries in addition to the United States represented in the study of AR and VR in teacher preparation included the following: Turkey (N=18), and between one and five articles each from Thailand, Spain, Slovakia, Russia, Portugal, Netherlands, Malaysia, Denmark, Colombia, China, Bulgaria, and Australia.

The publishing sources included a total of 93 academic journals, with the following having the highest distribution: Computers & Education (N=11), British Journal of Educational Technology (N=10), Education and Information Technologies (N=5), Journal of Computer Assisted Learning (N=4), Journal of Educational Technology Systems, (N=4), 5 more journals with each having a (N=3), and 19 journals each having a (N=2). The remainder of journals were only represented one time. Notably, the sources publishing were not primarily education oriented, rather technological in nature.

The type of research methodology most utilized was quantitative (N=65), followed by qualitative (N=60) and mixed methods (N=32). Forty-two per cent of quantitative studies were comprised of experimental studies while 25% were correlation and 20% were descriptive comparative. Additionally, the number of participants in the studies ranged from (N=1), usually case studies, to (N=1,920). The mean number of participants/subjects was (N=90), the mode was tied at 85 and 5, and the median was 46. Eighty per cent of the studies had fewer than 100 participants.

Much of the most recent data accessed for this study mentioned the pandemic or Covid. Ninety-nine of the original articles prior to delineation had the word "Covid" within them. Not all of the articles which mentioned Covid were utilized for this study, but it was notable that Covid impacted the field of education, and was a catalyst to the development of technological innovations that can be employed regardless of the particular educational setting.

4.2 Does the Use of Augmented Reality, Virtual Reality, or Mixed Reality in Teacher Preparation Impact Preservice Teacher's Self-Efficacy?

With practice comes increased proficiency and confidence. The essence of building teacher self-efficacy (TSE) is honing the educator craft, including effective instruction, management, assessment, and overall facilitating learning. The virtual world provides opportunity for practice in the realm of teacher preparation.

A total of (N=12) studies included teacher self-efficacy as part of the focus. Each of these studies also focused solely on the preparation of the teacher and not on content delivery. Other themes associated with self-efficacy were classroom management, inclusion, communication, reflection, immersive experiences and engagement of learners.

4.3 How Might Augmented Reality, Virtual Reality, and Mixed Reality be Utilized in a Teacher Preparation Program for Both Instructional Practice, Classroom Management and Professional Reflection?

4.3.1. Instructional Practice and Reflection

Instructional practice is necessary for teacher preparation. Typically, field experiences are rooted within the preparation program where preservice teachers gain opportunity to practice. These experiences will vary from program to program and may or may not include virtual learning. Quintana and colleagues (2017) found the use of virtual learning environments improved teaching and learning. In such environments, instructional practice can occur without the fear or anxiety of mistakes impacting students negatively.

Upon review of the use of extended reality for instructional purposes, it was noted the focus for these studies tended to veer in one of two directions, either the use of AV, VR, or MR for pedagogical purposes (N=112) or to determine attitudes, opinions or preferences related to AV, VR, and MR in teacher preparation (N=35). Two exceptions to this focus trend were literature reviews and validation or evaluation of AV/VR programs, equipment or software (N=4). Most often attitudes, opinions or preferences were parsed from preservice teacher reflections.

When considering the evolving cognitive patterns of each generation, it would behoove educational leaders to adjust and adapt instruction accordingly. Dyak, et al. (2022) contend their research findings conclude that modern education should orient teachers and students to new ways of preparation and practice in education. Many of the articles in this review are seeking to gauge and understand the receptiveness of preservice candidates to either being taught via mixed reality or utilizing it as an instructional tool. This receptiveness is crucial, as Theelen and colleagues (2020) note, an inherent digital society gap is developing between verbal and visual cultures with youth increasingly interacting with the virtual environment.

4.3.2 Classroom Management and Reflection

Multiple studies in this review claim classroom management as a key area of focus. Through virtual scenarios, students are able to practice and reflect upon their management decisions. Such VR technology opportunities and challenges are highlighted by Graeske and colleagues (2021). They emphasize results in which students' motivation and problem-solving skills increased, which naturally involves reflection. They also emphasize that such technology use is most effective when it functions in accordance with the curriculum established by the educational institution. Mixed reality can be particularly useful to enhance learning opportunities. Additionally, the manner in which mixed reality is currently being used involves a great deal of reflection following practice, thus increasing the opportunity to improve preservice teachers' TSE.

5. DISCUSSION

The field of education is not adequately focusing on innovation involving technology; seemingly the majority of the empirical research seems to be scattered among journals with either an educational technology or purely technological focus. Over the past decade there has not been a flagship journal producing reports heralding the importance of AR and VR in teacher preparation. Globally researchers have dabbled in the topic of in extended realities, the highest concentration of research found in the United States and Turkey. As is evidenced by the paucity of articles published globally in the past ten years which focus on using AR and VR for teacher preparation, it is clear AR and VR have barely been studied or utilized for teacher preparation purposes.

Virtual reality related teacher preparation represented 70% of the research reviewed in this study. There is cause to conclude that teaching practitioners might be unaware of the potential of extended realities to be a significant tool in motivating and enhancing instruction by providing vivid illustration of places, procedures and concepts through video, picture, and animated 3D objects over real-life scenes (Karacan, et al., 2022).

There is a healthy mix of types of methodology utilized in these studies related to AR and VR in teacher preparation (20% mixed methods, 59% qualitative, and 41% quantitative). There is a need for increased, purposeful, robust research in regard to the use of extended reality to enhance teacher education. Additionally, these studies understandably will likely have participants with relatively small (N) as that would be reflective of classroom sizes and yearly collegiate cohorts. This was evident with 80% of studies represented in this review over the past 10 years with a (N) less than 100.

As noted previously, preservice teachers have historically expressed a need for increased training in classroom management. This study barely touches the surface of possibilities in that direction with only 9 studies having classroom management as a focus. Two studies use 360 video in teacher prep to facilitate management by increased awareness of behaviors (Gandolfi, et al. 2021; Kosko,2022). Another study discusses the use of immersive VR and transferring that experience into future classroom management.

6. CONCLUSION

Lastly, we cannot ignore the impact of the Covid-19 pandemic upon the field of education and related research, especially as it relates to technological innovation. The repercussions from that historical event will continue to influence and impact educational decisions moving forward. Many of the studies directly referred to the pandemic, and were emphasizing the need for increased online instruction pedagogical prowess.

The limitations of this study include a delay in research as a result of the Covid-19 pandemic. However, that situation also served to open doors to new considerations for teacher preparation. Caution must be taken that VR and AR are employed with care in educational settings and within the bounds of the educational objectives for that particular learning experience. Another potential limitation may be that terms for teacher preparation may vary globally and potentially may not have captured in the search terms. Additionally, there are some studies which could potentially have been included but were not because they were not in English.

There is significantly more work to be done on the innovative use of AR and VR in teacher preparation as reinforced by Ade-Ojo and colleagues (2021), who completed a focused review on mixed reality and simulation in teacher preparation. They plea for further work on mixed reality in education preparation and note the field of education is comparatively behind other fields such as medicine and aviation in both innovation and research on use of mixed reality. Billingsley and colleagues (2019) note that research in this area is lacking and call for increased attention to this topic. This current study adds to the findings of previous literature reviews which clearly articulated the need for further study on innovation utilizing VR and AR in teacher preparation. While this study adds to the current knowledge base regarding AR and VR in teacher preparation by providing a critical examination of the current methodology and research trends, and it also exposes the need for significant future research.

REFERENCES

Accardo, A. & Xin, J. (2017). Using Technology-based simulations to promote teacher candidate parental collaboration and reflective instructional decision making. *Journal of Technology and Teacher Education*, Vol. 25, No. 4, 475-494.

Baker, J. D. (2016) The purpose, process and methods of writing a literature review: Editorial. Association of Operating Room Nurses. *AORN Journal*, Vol. 103, No.3, 265-269. doi:10.1016/j.aorn.2016.01.016

Bandura, A. (1977). Self-efficacy: toward a unifying theory of behavioral change. *Psychology Review*. Vol. 84, 191–215. doi: 10.1037/0033-295X.84.2.191

Bandura, A. (1994). Self-efficacy. In V. S. Ramachaudran (Ed.), *Encyclopedia of human behavior* (Vol. 4, pp. 71-81). New York: Academic Press. (Reprinted in H. Friedman [Ed.], *Encyclopedia of mental health*. San Diego: Academic Press, 1998).

Bauld, A. (2019) Virtual reality for teachers; A new virtual reality project aims to help teachers develop and practice their skills before they enter the classroom. *Harvard Graduate School of Education, News & Events*. Retrieved from https://www.gse.harvard.edu/news/19/09/virtual-reality-teachers

Billingsley, G, et al, (2019). A systematic literature review of using immersive virtual reality technology in teacher education. *Journal of Interactive Learning Research*, Vol. 30, No. 1, 65-90.

Bosch, C., & Ellis, T. (2021). Using avatars to address teacher self-efficacy. *Journal of Global Education and Research*, Vol. 5, No.1, 15-35. https://www.doi.org/10.5038/2577-509X.5.1.1069

Chisenhall, D. (2016). Preservice Teachers' Sense of Efficacy: Video vs. face-to-face Observations. *Doctoral Dissertations and Projects*. 1137. https://digitalcommons.liberty.edu/doctoral/1137

Dyak, T; et al, (2022). Some Peculiarities of Integrating Visual Literacy into the System of Modern Education. *Revista Românească pentru Educaţie Multidimensională*, Vol. 14, No.1, 322-338. https://doi.org/10.18662/rrem/14.1/521

Geiger, C., & Dawson, K. (2020). Virtually PKY–How one single-school district transitioned to emergency remote *Instruction. Journal of Technology and Teacher Education, Vol. 28, No.2, 251–260. https://www.learntechlib.org/p/216187/*

Gandolfi, E; et al, (2021). Situating presence within extended reality for teacher training: Validation of the Extended Reality Presence Scale (XRPS) in preservice teacher use of immersive 360 video. *British Journal of Educational Technology*, Vol. 52, No.2, 824-841.

Graeske, C; Sjöberg, S. A. (2021). VR-technology in teaching; Opportunities and challenges. *International Education Studies*, Vol. 14, No.8, 76-83.

Hechter, R. P., Vermette, L. A. (2013). Technology integration in K-12 science classrooms: An analysis of barriers and implications. *Themes in Science and Technology Education*, Vol. 6, No. 2, 73-90.

Higgins, T. (2018). What the research says about VR in classrooms. Commonsense Education. Retrieved from https://www.commonsense.org/education/articles/what-the-research-says-about-vr-in-classrooms

Holly, M., et al, (2021). Designing VR Experiences - Expectations for Teaching and Learning in VR. *Journal of Educational Technology & Society*, Vol. 24, No.2, 107–119.

Hopper, S., et al, (2013). *Assessing Alignment of Pedagogical Experience and Confidence in a Simulated Classroom Environment*. In R. McBride & M. Searson (Eds). *Proceedings of SITE 2013--Society for Information Technology & Teacher Education International Conference* (pp. 2870-2876). New Orleans, Louisiana, United States: Association for the Advancement of Computing in Education (AACE). Retrieved June 27, 2023 from https://www.learntechlib.org/primary/p/48527/

Ireland, A. (2021). *Mixed reality simulation in teacher preparation programs in the United States*. UCLA. ProQuest ID: Ireland_ucla_0031D_19587. Merritt ID: ark:/13030/m5qv9cvp. Retrieved from https://escholarship.org/uc/item/2862n1vw

Karacan, C.G., Polat, M. (2022). Predicting pre-service English language teachers' intentions to use augmented reality. *Journal of Digital Learning in Teacher Education*, Vol. 38 No. 3 p139-153.

Kolb, D. (1984). *Experiential Learning: Experience as the Source of Learning and Development.* Englewood Cliffs, N.J: Prentice-Hall.

Kosko, K.W. (2022). Pre-Service Teachers' Professional Noticing When Viewing Standard and Holographic Recordings of Children's Mathematics, *International Electronic Journal of Mathematics Education*, Vol. 17, No.4.

McPherson, R., et al, (2011). Using a computerized classroom simulation to prepare pre-service teachers. *Journal of Technology and Teacher Education*, Vol. 19, No.1, 93-110. Waynesville, NC USA: Society for Information Technology & Teacher Education.

Quintana, B, et al,. (2017) Pre-service teachers' skills and perceptions about the use of virtual learning environments to improve teaching and learning. *Behaviour & Information Technology*, Vol. 36, No.6, 575-588.

Samuelsson, M.; et al, (2022). Simulation training-a boost for pre-service teachers' efficacy beliefs. *Computers and Education Open*, Vol. 3, 100074. https://doi.org/10.1016/j.caeo.2022.100074

Sarigoz, O. (2019). Augmented reality, virtual reality and digital games: A research on teacher candidates. *Educational Policy Analysis and Strategic Research*, Vol. 14, No. 3, 41-63.

Schott, C; & Marshall, S. (2018). Virtual reality and situated experiential education: A conceptualization and exploratory trial. *Journal of Computer Assisted Learning*, Vol. 34, No.6) 843-852.

Searson (Eds.), Proceedings of SITE 2013--Society for Information Technology & Teacher Education International Conference (pp. 2870-2876). New Orleans, Louisiana, United States: Association for the Advancement of Computing in Education (AACE).

Smith, K., & Klumper, D. (2018). VIRTUALLY in the Classroom: Virtual reality platforms can give preservice teachers opportunities to develop real classroom management skills. *Educational Leadership*, Vol. 76, No.1, 60–65.

Sorohan, B. & Thomas, T. (2016). Using SimSchool to provide high-quality clinical experiences to non-traditional preservice teachers. In G. Chamblee & L. Langub (Eds.), *Proceedings of Society for Information Technology & Teacher Education International Conference* (pp. 1476-1479). Savannah, GA, United States: Association for the Advancement of Computing in Education (AACE).

Theelen, H., et al, (2020). Virtual internships in blended environments to prepare preservice teachers for the professional teaching context. *British Journal of Educational Technology,* Vol. 51, No.1, 194-210.

Tremosa, L. (2023)., Beyond AR vs. VR: What is the difference between AR vs. MR vs. VR vs. XR? Interaction Design Foundation, https://www.interaction-design.org/literature/article/beyond-ar-vs-vr-what-is-the-difference-between-ar-vs-mr-vs-vr-vs-xr#what_is_reality?-0.

Vu, P. & Fisher, C.E. (2021). Does virtual field experience deliver? An examination into virtual field experience during the Pandemic and its implications for teacher education programs. *Open Praxis*, Vol. 13, No. 1, 117-125. DOI: https://dx.doi.org/10.5944/openpraxis.13.1.1191

LEGAL ISSUES AND RISKS OF INSTRUCTION VIA MASSIVE OPEN ONLINE COURSES (MOOCS): SMALL MACAO VS. SOME MAJOR JURISDICTIONS

Victor K. Y. Chan
Faculty of Business, Macao Polytechnic University
Rua de Luis Gonzaga Gomes, Macao, China

ABSTRACT

From the standpoint of a MOOC practitioner (i.e., a MOOC provider) instead of a rigorous comparative law researcher, this article attempts to analyze the potential legal issues and risks underlying instruction via MOOCs and compare these legal issues and risks between the small jurisdiction Macao and such major jurisdictions as the United States, the United Kingdom, Australia, and the European Union. These legal issues and risks so identified concern the three perspectives intellectual property, privacy, and accessibility. Supported by academic literature, statutes, acts, and court cases, this article elaborates on these three perspectives with respect to MOOC providers, quotes the key legal statutes and acts in these three perspectives in the context of MOOC providers, elucidates the statutes' and acts' emphases and the related remedies and penalties for breaches, and probably other details, and compares them across the aforesaid jurisdictions. Some prominent findings are that Macao, the United Kingdom, Australia, and the European Union appear to practice clearly defined and compendious laws to protect privacy whereas the United States' counterparts seem to be circumscribed by, for example, the ages of the individuals to protect. As such, for MOOC providers, the former four jurisdictions sound to be more critical than the latter jurisdiction in the perspective of privacy. As for accessibility, Macao's, the United States', the United Kingdom's, and Australia's laws focus on educational institutions. Nonetheless, whether the majority of MOOC providers can be regarded as such "education institutions" under such laws may likely be disputable. In contrast, the European Union more generically enacts a law on accessibility of digital products and services. Even so, to what extent and how MOOCs are supposed to conform to such a law may arguably still be contingent upon each particular scenario.

KEYWORDS

Massive Open Online Courses, MOOC, Legal Issues and Risks, Intellectual Property, Privacy and Data Protection, Accessibility

1. INTRODUCTION

Massive open online courses (MOOCs) are a relatively new form of online education that has become increasingly popular over the last decade, and have revolutionized the educational landscape, offering unprecedented access to high-quality education for millions of learners around the world. They are characterized by online courses for a potentially huge number of students. While MOOCs potentially democratize education, they also pose some potential legal issues and thus risks for educators, instructors, and course providers. Here, legal issues and risks refer to the possibility of legal liability and litigation arising from the operation of MOOCs. In fact, whenever the feasibility and thus risks of any project is considered, there are a five major aspects, namely, technical, economic/financial, legal, operational, and scheduling (Mukherjee and Roy, 2017). Any educator, instructor, or MOOC provider cannot afford ignoring legal feasibility and thus risks given the grave and costly consequences of legal liability (e.g., in the forms of damage claims and criminal law penalties) and litigations. In short, for MOOCs and virtually all projects in society, legal feasibility and risks are at least as crucial and determining as any of the remaining four aspects of feasibility and risks.

This article begins by defining MOOCs and discussing their popularity, and moves on to examine the key potential legal issues and risks of instruction via MOOCs in the small jurisdiction Macao in comparison with some major jurisdictions like the United States, the United Kingdom, Australia, and the European Union. In particular, from a MOOC practitioner's (i.e., a MOOC provider's) standpoint instead of a rigorous comparative law researcher's viewpoint, the article identifies and focuses on the three perspectives intellectual property, privacy and data protection, and accessibility. The key legal statutes and acts in these three perspectives in the context of MOOC providers are quoted, and the statutes' and acts' emphases, the related remedies and penalties of breaches, and probably other details are elucidated. They are compared across the aforesaid jurisdictions. The article is supported by not only these statutes and acts but also academic literature and court cases. Finally, the article concludes with a summary of the findings from the comparison.

MOOC provisioning is inherently international and cross-jurisdiction in that any MOOC uploaded for access is open to online learners from all around the globe. It would be all too parochial for MOOC providers to pay heed solely to their own jurisdictions' legal systems when it comes to potential legal issues and risks. In this practical dimension, this article additionally serves as preliminary guidelines and a checklist for MOOC operators striving to minimize any potential legal issues and risks of theirs generally, if not literally universally, applicable to most major jurisdictions around the world as well as some small jurisdictions as typified by Macao. In particular, for all the jurisdictions covered, it outlines the key laws that MOOC providers need to take heed of.

2. WHAT ARE MOOCS?

MOOCs are online courses that are open to anyone with an internet connection. They are designed to be accessible to a large number of learners and are often but not necessarily free of charge. MOOCs typically consist of video lectures, interactive quizzes, and discussion forums. They are offered by universities, colleges, and other educational institutions around the world. (Ho et al., 2014)

MOOCs have become increasingly popular over the last decade. According to Class Central, a website that tracks MOOCs, there were 150 million MOOC courses in August 2023 (Class Central, 2023), and the number of learners increased to 220 million in 2021 from just 35 million in 2015 (Shah, 2015; Shah, 2021). The popularity of MOOCs has been driven by a number of factors, including the increasing availability of high-speed internet, the rising cost of traditional higher education, and the growing demand for lifelong learning.

3. POTENTIAL LEGAL ISSUES AND RISKS ASSOCIATED WITH MOOCS

There are a number of potential legal issues and risks associated with instruction via MOOCs. The most significant ones of them include intellectual property, privacy and data protection, and accessibility, which are detailed in the following sections.

3.1 Intellectual Property

Intellectual property is a significant concern for educators and educational institutions offering MOOCs. The content of MOOCs, including video lectures, quizzes, slide presentations, and reading materials, and other materials, is often protected by copyright law. This means that educators and educational institutions must themselves be the copyright owners or obtain permission to use copyrighted materials in their courses. In addition, MOOCs often involve the creation of new intellectual property, such as course materials and assessments. Educators and educational institutions must ensure that they own the intellectual property rights to any materials they create or that they have obtained permission to use them.

3.2 Privacy

Privacy is another significant concern for educators and educational institutions offering MOOCs. MOOCs often collect data from learners, such as their names, email addresses, and performance data. This data can be used to personalize the learning experience for learners, but it also raises privacy concerns. Educators and educational institutions must ensure that they are collecting only the data that is necessary for the operation of the course and that they are using the data in a way that is consistent with applicable privacy laws. They must also inform learners about the data that is being collected and how it will be used. Moreover, they must ensure that third-party vendors and subcontractors also comply with applicable privacy laws. In addition, educators and other staff should be trained on data privacy.

3.3 Accessibility

Accessibility is a third significant concern for educators and educational institutions offering MOOCs. MOOCs are designed to be accessible to a large number of learners, but they must also be accessible to learners with disabilities. In general, educators and educational institutions must ensure that their MOOCs are accessible to learners with disabilities, including those with visual and auditory impairments. This may involve providing captioning or transcripts for video lectures and ensuring that assessments are designed to be accessible to all learners.

4. MACAO AND ITS LEGAL LANDSCAPE

Macao, also spelled Macau, is a Special Administrative Region of the People's Republic of China with a distinctive legal system that is based on Portuguese civil law. The legal landscape in Macao is influenced by a number of factors, including the Basic Law of the Macao Special Administrative Region, the Macao Civil Code, and the Macao Penal Code. Macao is a focus of this article not only because of the author's being with a university there but also because the enclave epitomizes small jurisdictions/economies, so findings from a comparative study between it and some major jurisdictions/economies provides analogy to quite some other small jurisdictions/economies in the world.

4.1 Intellectual Property

Intellectual property is protected in Macao by the Industrial Property Code (IPC): Decree-Law no. 97/99/M of 13 December (Macao Special Administrative Region, 2023a) and the Decree-Law No. 43/99/M of August 16, 1999: Copyright Law (Macao Special Administrative Region, 2023b). The IPC protects inventions, trademarks, and industrial designs, while the Copyright Law protects literary, artistic, and scientific works. The IPC and the Copyright Law both provide for civil and criminal remedies for infringement. Civil remedies include injunctions, damages, and account of profits, while criminal remedies include fines and imprisonment.

Having said that, the Copyright Law establishes the principles of exceptions, allowing certain exceptions for educational purposes together with research and news reporting purposes (Macao Special Administrative Region, 2023b). MOOC providers may readily take advantage of such exceptions.

4.2 Privacy

Privacy is protected in Macao by Act 8/2005: Personal Data Protection Act (PDPA) (Macao Special Administrative Region, 2023c). The PDPA regulates the collection, use, and disclosure of personal data in Macao. It also provides individuals with certain rights, such as the right to access and correct their personal data.

The PDPA provides for both civil and criminal remedies for violations. Civil remedies include compensation for damages, while criminal remedies include fines and imprisonment.

4.3 Accessibility

Accessibility in education is protected in Macao by the Law no. 11/91/M, 29th of August: Macao education system (Education and Youth Development Bureau, 2023), which requires educational institutions to provide equal access to education for all students, including those with disabilities. Nevertheless, whether MOOC providers belong to this "education system" and thus whether this law applies to MOOC providers are considerably disputable. If this law is ruled not to be applicable to MOOC providers, the author is not aware of any other laws relevant to MOOCs' accessibility. If the ruling is to the contrary, MOOCs must ensure that their materials and methods are accessible to all learners, regardless of their abilities or disabilities. For example, audio materials exclusively on MOOC platforms may be implicated as discrimination against deaf learners.

5. COMPARISON WITH OTHER MAJOR JURISDICTIONS

5.1 United States

5.1.1 Intellectual Property

Intellectual property is protected by federal law, including the Copyright Act of 1976 (U.S. Copyright Office, 2023) and Title 35: Patents (U.S. Government Publishing Office, 2023). Civil remedies for infringement include injunctions, damages, and account of profits, while criminal remedies include fines and imprisonment.

However, the United States has a fair use doctrine, which allows for the limited use of copyrighted materials for educational purposes without the copyright holder's permission. The fair use doctrine has been the subject of several court cases involving MOOCs. For example, in Authors Guild, Inc. v. Google, Inc., No. 13-4829-cv (2d Cir. Oct. 16, 2015), the United States Court of Appeals for the Second Circuit held that Google's digitization of books for its Google Books project constituted fair use. While the case did not directly involve MOOCs, it provides useful guidance on the application of the fair use doctrine to educational technologies.

5.1.2 Privacy

Privacy is protected in the United States by a range of federal and state laws, including the Children's Online Privacy Protection Act of 1998, 15 U.S.C. 6501–6505: Children's Privacy (COPPA) (U.S. Federal Trade Commission, 2023). COPPA imposes certain requirements on operators of websites or online services directed to children under 13 years of age, and on operators of other websites or online services that have actual knowledge that they are collecting personal information online from a child under 13 years of age. Nonetheless, most learners attending MOOCs are aged over 13 years, so the Act merely applies to very rare cases.

5.1.3 Accessibility

The Americans with Disabilities Act of 1990 (Title 42) (ADA) (U.S. Department of Justice, 2023) requires that educational institutions provide reasonable accommodations to students with disabilities. However, whether the majority of MOOC providers fall into the definition of the "educational institutions" as per the Act may be subject to dispute.

5.2 United Kingdom

5.2.1 Intellectual Property

Intellectual property is protected by the Copyright, Designs and Patents Act 1988 (The National Archives, 2023a) and the Trade Marks Act 1994 (The National Archives, 2023b). Civil remedies for infringement include injunctions, damages, and account of profits, while criminal remedies include fines and imprisonment.

Also, the Copyright and Rights in Performances (Research, Education, Libraries and Archives) Regulations 2014 (The National Archives, 2023c) permits fair dealing with and thus use of a copyrighted work for sole instruction purposes, which likely applies to MOOC providers.

5.2.2 Privacy

Privacy is protected in the United Kingdom by the Data Protection Act 1998 (The National Archives, 2023d). It regulates the collection, use, and disclosure of personal data. The Act requires that, for example, MOOC providers collecting personal data must do so in a lawful, fair, and transparent manner. This means that MOOC providers must inform learners about the data that is being collected and how it will be used. The Act also gives learners, or in fact any individuals, certain rights with respect to their personal data, such as the right to access and correct their data. MOOC providers must ensure that they are collecting only the data that is necessary for the operation of the course and that they are using the data in a way that is consistent with the Act. Failure to comply with the Data Protection Act can result in civil and criminal penalties.

5.2.3 Accessibility

The Equality Act 2010 (The National Archives, 2023e) requires that educational institutions make reasonable adjustments for students with disabilities. Again, whether the majority of MOOC providers fall into the definition of the "educational institutions" as per the Act may be subject to dispute.

5.3 Australia

5.3.1 Intellectual Property

Intellectual property is protected by the Copyright Act 1968 (No. 63, 1968) (Australian Government, 2023a) and the Patents Act 1990 (AustLII, 2023). Civil remedies for infringement include injunctions, damages, and account of profits, while criminal remedies include fines and imprisonment.

Also, the act includes provisions addressing the use of copyrighted materials for educational purposes under the "fair dealing" exception (s 40 and s 41).

5.3.2 Privacy

Privacy is protected by the Privacy Act 1988 (Office of the Australian Information Commissioner, 2023), which includes 13 Australian Privacy Principles (APPs), and regulates the handling of personal information, for example, learners' data on MOOC platforms.

5.3.3 Accessibility

The Disability Discrimination Act 1992 (No. 135, 1992) (Australian Government, 2023b) requires that educational institutions make reasonable adjustments for students with disabilities. Again, whether the majority of MOOC providers fall into the definition of the "educational institutions" as per the Act may be subject to dispute.

5.4 European Union

5.4.1 Intellectual Property

The primary legislation governing intellectual property rights is Directive 2001/29/EC of the European Parliament and of the Council of 22 May 2001 on the harmonisation of certain aspects of copyright and related rights in the information society (European Parliament & Council, 2023a), which harmonizes copyright laws across European Union (EU) member states. It provides for civil remedies, such as injunctions, damages, and account of profits, and criminal penalties, such as fines and imprisonment. In addition, Directive (EU) 2019/790 of the European Parliament and of the Council of 17 April 2019 on copyright and related rights in the Digital Single Market and amending Directives 96/9/EC and 2001/29/EC

(European Parliament & Council, 2023b) grants educators the right to use copyrighted materials for teaching purposes, provided that certain conditions are met (e.g., only small portions of works are used, the use is non-commercial, and clearly attributed to the copyright holder). MOOCs for free may readily make use of this grant of right.

5.4.2 Privacy

The primary legislation governing privacy and data protection is Regulation (EU) 2016/679 of the European Parliament and of the Council of 27 April 2016 on the protection of natural persons with regard to the processing of personal data and on the free movement of such data, and repealing Directive 95/46/EC (General Data Protection Regulation or GDPR) (European Parliament & Council, 2023c), which imposes various obligations on data controllers, such as MOOC providers and educators, including the requirement to provide transparent information about the processing of personal data, obtain consent for certain processing activities, and implement appropriate security measures.

5.4.3 Accessibility

Directive (EU) 2019/882 of the European Parliament and of the Council of 17 April 2019 on the accessibility requirements for products and services (European Parliament & Council, 2023d) mandates that digital products and services be accessible to individuals with disabilities. Notwithstanding, from the viewpoint of a MOOC provider, the extent to which and how this Directive applies in a particular setting is again rather subject to dispute.

6. CONCLUSION

MOOCs are delivered on the Internet, and they concomitantly reach out to learners worldwide. Wherever the MOOC providers are based, they are in essence obliged to comply with the laws of all jurisdictions on the planet except the presumably small number of jurisdictions to which access is deliberately excluded by the providers by means of technological or non-technological measures. From another point of view, MOOC providers are susceptible to legal issues and risks of almost all jurisdictions around the world on top of those of the providers' home jurisdictions, and thus are impelled to be aware of such legal issues and risks in the global context. With emphasis on small jurisdictions as exemplified by the author's hometown Macao, this article explores such legal issues and risks of most major and representative jurisdictions though not meant to be exhaustive geographically.

By and large, the potential legal issues and thus risks associated with MOOC provisioning are roughly the same across most major jurisdictions as well as Macao, which exemplifies small jurisdictions with less technological and non-technological resources than major counterparts. These potential legal issues and risks confronting MOOC operators are chiefly related to intellectual property, privacy, and accessibility. In the aspect of intellectual property, the similarity between jurisdictions, be they major or small, is apparent at least as far as MOOC operators are concerned. Even the types of remedies and penalties for infringement and the "exceptional" permission to use copyrighted materials by educators and educational institutions resemble each other across jurisdictions. Therefore, MOOC operators may choose to manage intellectual property in an almost unified manner for multiple jurisdictions. When it comes to privacy, Macao, the United Kingdom, Australia, and the European Union appear to practice clearly defined and compendious laws to protect personal data whereas the United States' counterparts seem to be circumscribed by, for example, the ages of individuals to protect. Hence, it may be worthwhile for MOOC operators to be more meticulous in dealing with the privacy of the learners in the former four jurisdictions. As for accessibility, Macao's, the United States', the United Kingdom's, and Australia's laws (see Sections 4.3, 5.1.3, 5.2.3, and 5.3.3) focus on, inter alia, educational institutions. Nonetheless, whether the majority of MOOC providers can be regarded as such "education institutions" under such laws may likely be disputable. In contrast, the European Union more generically enacts a law on accessibility of products and services (see Sections 5.4.3). Even so, to what extent and how MOOCs are supposed to conform to such a law may arguably still be contingent upon each particular scenario. Table 1 summarizes the major distinctions between the above jurisdictions in regard to intellectual property, privacy, and accessibility that might concern MOOC providers.

The author earlier undertook a study on the legal risks associated with e-learning platforms (basically, referring to learning management system platforms or LMS platforms) (Chan and Lei, 2023). Whilst there is some commonality between the findings from that study and those from the current study, there is a prominent difference. Many e-learning platform operators are physical universities and other physical educational institutions adopting the e-learning platforms to support and/or facilitate their traditional programs' delivery, so the odds are that these universities and educational institutions are quite likely to be subsumed under the "educational institutions" as defined in Macao's, the United States', the United Kingdom's, and Australia's relevant laws on accessibility. In contrast, MOOC providers are far more diverse by nature, some being new breeds of companies or organizations totally running virtually online for the sole purpose of MOOC provisioning and being sometimes composed of blends of collaborators with disparate backgrounds. Quintessential examples of such MOOC providers include Canvas Network (Instructure, 2023), FutureLearn (FutureLearn, 2023), etc. Whether such MOOC providers are considered as "educational institutions" under Macao's, the United States', the United Kingdom's, and Australia's accessibility laws is far more subject to judicial interpretation than the case of e-learning platforms.

Table 1. The major distinctions between Macao and some major jurisdictions in regard to intellectual property, privacy, and accessibility that might concern MOOC providers

	Macao	United States	United Kingdom	Australia	European Union
Intellectual property	Nil	Nil	Nil	Nil	Nil
Privacy	Clearly defined and compendious laws	Circumscribed by, for example, the ages of individuals to protect	Clearly defined and compendious laws	Clearly defined and compendious laws	Clearly defined and compendious laws
Accessibility	The laws focus on, inter alia, educational institutions. Applicability to MOOC providers dubious.	The laws focus on, inter alia, educational institutions. Applicability to MOOC providers dubious.	The laws focus on, inter alia, educational institutions. Applicability to MOOC providers dubious.	The laws focus on, inter alia, educational institutions. Applicability to MOOC providers dubious.	The laws generically applicable to all products and services. Applicability to MOOC providers dubious.

Finally, it is necessary to pronounce the disclaimer that whereas this article may serve as practical guidelines or a checklist for MOOC operators striving to minimize any potential legal issues and risks globally, formal consultation with appropriate legal professionals of the corresponding jurisdictions is strongly advised whenever specific legal issues and risks arise.

REFERENCES

AustLII, 2023. *Patents Act 1990.* AustLII. Retrieved June 26, 2023 from http://classic.austlii.edu.au/au/legis/cth/consol_act/pa1990109/

Australian Government, 2023a. *Copyright Act 1968 (No. 63, 1968).* Federal Register of Legislation. Retrieved June 24, 2023 from https://www.legislation.gov.au/Details/C2019C00042

Australian Government, 2023b. *Disability Discrimination Act 1992 (No. 135, 1992).* Federal Register of Legislation. Retrieved June 24, 2023 from https://www.legislation.gov.au/Details/C2018C00125

Chan, V. K. Y. and Lei, H. M., 2023. Legal Risks of E-Learning: A case study of the small jurisdiction Macao versus some major jurisdictions.

Class Central, 2023. Retrieved August 9, 2023 from https://www.classcentral.com/

Education and Youth Development Bureau, 2023. *Law no. 11/91/M, 29th of August: Macao education system.* Retrieved June 26, 2023 from https://www.dsedj.gov.mo/~webdsej/www/edulaw/basic/d1191me.htm#:~:text=All%20residents%20of%20Macao%2C%20regardless,to%20and%20success%20in%20education

European Parliament & Council, 2023a. *Directive 2001/29/EC of the European Parliament and of the Council of 22 May 2001 on the harmonisation of certain aspects of copyright and related rights in the information society.* Official Journal of the European Communities, L 167, 10–19. Retrieved June 25, 2023 from https://eur-lex.europa.eu/legal-content/EN/TXT/?uri=celex%3A32001L0029

European Parliament & Council, 2023b. *Directive (EU) 2019/790 of the European Parliament and of the Council of 17 April 2019 on copyright and related rights in the Digital Single Market and amending Directives 96/9/EC and 2001/29/EC. Official Journal of the European Union, L 130, 92–125*. Retrieved June 24, 2023 from https://eur-lex.europa.eu/eli/dir/2019/790/oj

European Parliament & Council, 2023c. *Regulation (EU) 2016/679 of the European Parliament and of the Council of 27 April 2016 on the protection of natural persons with regard to the processing of personal data and on the free movement of such data, and repealing Directive 95/46/EC (General Data Protection Regulation)*. Official Journal of the European Union, L 119, 1–88. Retrieved June 25, 2023 from https://eur-lex.europa.eu/legal-content/EN/TXT/PDF/?uri=CELEX:32016R0679

European Parliament & Council, 2023d. *Directive (EU) 2019/882 of the European Parliament and of the Council of 17 April 2019 on the accessibility requirements for products and services*. Official Journal of the European Union, L 151, 70–115. Retrieved June 26, 2023 from https://eur-lex.europa.eu/legal-content/EN/TXT/?uri=celex%3A32019L0882

FutureLearn, 2023. FutureLearn. Retrieved June 26, 2023 from https://www.futurelearn.com/

Ho, A. D., Reich, J., Reich, J., Nesterko, S., Seaton, D. T., Seaton, D., Mullaney, T., Waldo, J., and Chuang, I., 2014. HarvardX and MITx: The First Year of Open Online Courses, Fall 2012-Summer 2013. *In HarvardX and MITx Working Paper No. 1*. doi: https://ssrn.com/abstract=2381263 or http://dx.doi.org/10.2139/ssrn.2381263

Instructure, 2023. Canvas Network. Retrieved June 26, 2023 from https://www.canvas.net/

Macao Special Administrative Region, 2023a. *Industrial Property Code: Decree-Law no. 97/99/M of 13 December*. Macao SAR Government. Retrieved June 23, 2023 from https://bo.io.gov.mo/bo/i/99/50/codrjpien/declei97.asp

Macao Special Administrative Region, 2023b. *Decree-Law No. 43/99/M of August 16, 1999: Copyright Law*. Macao SAR Government. Retrieved June 23, 2023 from https://bo.io.gov.mo/bo/i/99/33/declei43_en.asp

Macao Special Administrative Region, 2023c. *Act 8/2005: Personal Data Protection Act*. Macao SAR Government. Retrieved June 23, 2023 from https://www.gpdp.gov.mo/file/Laws%20and%20Regulations/%E5%80%8B%E4%BA%BA%E8%B3%87%E6%96%99%E4%BF%9D%E8%AD%B7%E6%B3%95_EN.pdf

Mukherjee, M. and Roy, S., 2017. Feasibility Studies and Important Aspect of Project Management. *In International Journal of Advanced Engineering and Management*, Vol. 2, No. 4, pp. 98-100. Retrieved June 22, 2023 from https://ijoaem.org/00204-25

Office of the Australian Information Commissioner, 2023. *Privacy Act 1988*. Retrieved June 24, 2023 from https://www.oaic.gov.au/privacy/privacy-legislation/the-privacy-act#:~:text=The%20Privacy%20Act%201988%20was,other%20organisations%2C%20handle%20personal%20information

Shah, D, 2015. MOOC Roundup 2015. Retrieved August 9, 2023 from https://www.classcentral.com/report/tag/mooc-roundup-2015/

Shah, D, 2021. Class Central's Best Online Courses of the Year (2022 Edition). Retrieved August 9, 2023 from https://www.classcentral.com/report/best-free-online-courses-2022/

The National Archives, 2023a. *Copyright, Designs and Patents Act 1988*. His Majesty Government. Retrieved June 24, 2023 from https://www.legislation.gov.uk/ukpga/1988/48/contents

The National Archives, 2023b. *Trade Marks Act 1994*. His Majesty Government. Retrieved June 24, 2023 from https://www.legislation.gov.uk/ukpga/1994/26/contents

The National Archives, 2023c. Copyright and Rights in Performances (Research, Education, Libraries and Archives) Regulations 2014. His Majesty Government. Retrieved June 26, 2023 from https://www.legislation.gov.uk/uksi/2014/1372/regulation/4/made

The National Archives, 2023d. *Data Protection Act 1998*. His Majesty Government. Retrieved June 24, 2023 from https://www.legislation.gov.uk/ukpga/1998/29/contents

The National Archives, 2023e. *Equality Act 2010*. His Majesty Government. Retrieved June 24, 2023 from https://www.legislation.gov.uk/ukpga/2010/15/contents

U.S. Copyright Office, 2023. *Copyright Act of 1976*. Library of Congress. Retrieved June 24, 2023 from https://www.copyright.gov/title17/

U.S. Department of Justice, 2023. *Americans with Disabilities Act of 1990 (Title 42) (ADA)*. Retrieved June 24, 2023 from https://www.ada.gov/law-and-regs/ada/

U.S. Federal Trade Commission, 2023. *Children's Online Privacy Protection Act of 1998, 15 U.S.C. 6501–6505: Children's Privacy*. U.S. Federal Trade Commission. Retrieved June 25, 2023 from https://www.ftc.gov/legal-library/browse/rules/childrens-online-privacy-protection-rule-coppa

U.S. Government Publishing Office, 2023. *Title 35—Patents*. U.S. Government Publishing Office. Retrieved June 24, 2023 from https://www.govinfo.gov/content/pkg/USCODE-2011-title35/html/USCODE-2011-title35.htm

CHATGPT AND BARD IN EDUCATION: A COMPARATIVE REVIEW

Gustavo Simas da Silva and Vânia Ribas Ulbricht
Federal University of Santa Catarina (UFSC), Brazil
R. Eng. Agronômico Andrei Cristian Ferreira, s/n - Trindade, Florianópolis - SC, Brazil

ABSTRACT

ChatGPT and Bard, two chatbots powered by Large Language Models (LLMs), are propelling the educational sector towards a new era of instructional innovation. Within this educational paradigm, the present investigation conducts a comparative analysis of these groundbreaking chatbots, scrutinizing their distinct operational characteristics and applications as depicted in current scholarly discourse. ChatGPT emerges as an exemplary tool in task-oriented textual interactions, while Bard brandishes unique features such as Text-To-Speech (TTS) functionality, which enhances accessibility and inclusive education, as well as integration with Google Workspace applications. This research critically examines their utilization in various spheres such as pedagogy, academic research, Massive Open Online Courses (MOOCs), mathematics, and software programming. Findings accentuate ChatGPT's superior efficacy in content drafting, code generation, language translation, and providing clinically precise responses, notwithstanding Bard's significant potential encapsulated in its exclusive features. Furthermore, the study traverses' crucial ethical aspects, including privacy concerns and inherent bias, underscoring the profound implications of these Artificial Intelligence (AI) technologies on literature and advocating against the indiscriminate reliance on such models.

KEYWORDS

ChatGPT, Bard, Education, Large Language Models, Chatbots, Artificial Intelligence

1. INTRODUCTION

The domain of Artificial Intelligence (AI) has experienced considerable progression, particularly within the subfield of conversational AI. This progression has been marked by the advent of sophisticated Large Language Models (LLMs) demonstrating the capacity for generating text that strikingly mirrors human discourse and has the potential to transform various aspects of our lives, including education (Tlili et al., 2023).

Two eminent examples of such advanced models are OpenAI's ChatGPT and Google's Bard. Chatbots like these are being analyzed in the literature concerning its potential and risks in healthcare (Sallam, 2023), consumer studies (Paul et al., 2023), educational settings (Lund & Wang, 2023) and a wide variety of areas. Despite the recent enthusiasm, there are also voices that approach its use cautiously. Investigations of user experiences revealed various issues, including cheating, honesty and truthfulness of ChatGPT, privacy misleading, and manipulation, which highlight the need for research directions that ensure a safe and responsible adoption of chatbots, especially in learning and education (Tlili et al., 2023).

Besides that, it is observed that recent discussions need to tackle advantages of emerging technologies and cutting-edge chatbots or AI assistants like ChatGPT and Bard, but also highlight the ethical and practical challenges associated with their use in education. There is emphasis on the importance of responsible and ethical use of AI in education while promoting its successful incorporation into the educational setting to benefit teachers and students (Adiguzel et al., 2023). Dis and colleagues (2023) point out the challenges associated with generative AI and lay out an agenda for future research. This agenda underscores several priority areas including the necessity for human verification, the formulation of accountability measures, the investment in genuinely open LLMs, the embrace of AI benefits, and the expansion of the discourse on these technologies.

Therefore, in accordance with the aforementioned scope, the fundamental research question this article aims to answer is: "In what ways can ChatGPT and Bard be utilized comparatively within the educational sector?" This study embarks on a comparative analysis, delving into the functionalities and features of Google's Bard and ChatGPT in the context of education, while leveraging pertinent current literature. Viewing these tools through the educational prism enables an exploration of their utility and the quality of responses provided to users. Concurrently, it illuminates the ethical considerations integral to their deployment. By delving into these aspects, the study hopes to provide a comprehensive understanding of the role these language models can play in educational settings, their strengths and limitations, and the ethical implications of their usage.

2. CHATGPT AND BARD

ChatGPT, Bard and other conversational systems are interfaces that permit Human-AI Interaction (HAI) powered by Large Language Models. LLMs embody the quintessence of Deep Learning (DL) models, expertly engineered to decipher and generate cogent responses using a multilayer neural network configuration (Rahsepar et al., 2023). These models are trained utilizing colossal volumes of textual data, employing unsupervised learning techniques, and are capable of discerning relationships between words within the text. Moreover, they boast the ability to predict the succeeding word in a string of words, based on their antecedents. LLMs, unique in their construction, are tailored specifically for natural language processing tasks, including but not limited to, language translation, text summarization, and question-answering. This differentiates them from other DL model variants such as Convolutional Neural Networks (CNNs) and Recurrent Neural Networks (RNNs), which are predominantly used for tasks related to image and speech recognition (LeCun et al., 2015).

The interaction between Artificial Intelligence and education is not a novel concept, as AI has been progressively integrated into Learning Management Systems (LMS) to augment the overall pedagogical experience. However, leveraging the capabilities of Natural Language Processing (NLP) and cognitive reasoning within LMS has fostered a more interactive and personalized learning environment (Ali et al., 2023). The amalgamation of AI and NLP in an educational context holds the potential to enhance both communication and interaction between students and their virtual pedagogical counterparts or peers (Kasneci et al., 2023). Yet, with the advent of Large Language Models, the landscape of AI interactions has experienced a paradigm shift. Individuals are now able to engage with AI systems using natural language, a revolution that has broadened the horizon for Human-AI interaction, decision-making processes, and natural language comprehension across diverse domains (Clavié, 2023).

As of July, 2023, ChatGPT is based on Generative Pre-trainer Transformer (GPT), version 3.5 and 4 (OpenAI, 2023), while Bard is based on Pathways Language Model (PaLM), version 2 (Google, 2023b). Both are equipped with Application Programming Interfaces (APIs) to facilitate their integration with external applications. Unique features of OpenAI's ChatGPT system encompass the availability of plugin features within the premium version (ChatGPT Plus). In contrast, Google's Bard offers distinctive capabilities including real-time internet information retrieval, image utilization in prompts and a Text-to-Speech (TTS) feature to audibly relay responses.

3. METHODOLOGY

This research unfolds a scoping review through distinct phases. Firstly, a review protocol predicated on the PCC framework (Population, Concept, Context), an established tool utilized across diverse research domains to direct the formation of research questions and guide the process of scoping reviews (Pollock et al., 2023). By providing a structured approach to these elements, the PCC framework enables researchers to generate more focused and contextually relevant research questions, thereby enhancing the potential significance and applicability of the findings in the wider scholarly discourse. This study has:

- Population: students, teachers and self-directed learners in any education level;
- Concept: the use of AI powered chatbots, specifically ChatGPT and Bard;
- Context: learning and educational settings.

Secondly, with the research question formulated, the selection criteria are derived, encapsulating both inclusion and exclusion parameters, which subsequently informs data extraction and data synthesis processes.

Given the emergent and novel nature of the topic, inclusion and exclusion criteria for this study have been crafted such that the articles embody keywords such as 'ChatGPT', ‘Bard’, ‘chatbots’, ‘Large Language Models’ and 'Education', and are indexed in databases such as Scopus, Web of Science, IEEEXplore, along with a deep-dive into gray literature, like technical reports and companies websites, to compensate for the relative dearth of formal literature on the topic.

The search horizon was set to publications issued in 2022 and 2023, written in English, with open access, in line with the developmental timeline of ChatGPT and Google’s Bard. The search process is conducted manually by traversing specific journal papers in the identified databases. At this juncture, a total of 230 articles were discovered. Consequently, a process of removing duplicates and excluding papers that did not directly address the use of chatbots, specifically ChatGPT or Bard, in educational contexts was conducted based on the publication’s titles and abstracts. Lastly, after a quality assessment, 22 articles were finalized for this research study.

4. RESULTS AND DISCUSSION

ChatGPT, specifically calibrated for task-oriented textual interactions, serves manifold purposes encompassing language translation, composition of product descriptions, and summarization of transcripts. Given its expansive training dataset compared to LaMDA (the previous LLM behind Bard), ChatGPT displays superior performance in more intensive tasks such as drafting content, generating code, and executing translations (Ahmed et al., 2023). Conversely, Bard is primarily designed to retrieve information through succinct responses, akin to digital assistants like Alexa and Siri. Bard's distinctive focus on the generation of creative language imbues it with utility across a wide array of applications, spanning writing, publishing, marketing, and advertising.

Lund and Wang (2023) discussed the benefits of ChatGPT, such as improving search and discovery, reference and information services, cataloging and metadata generation, and content creation. However, the study also emphasized the ethical considerations that need to be taken into account, such as privacy and bias.

In the learning field, educators can use ChatGPT to create role-playing exercises or simulate the writing style of famous authors, for example. This can be used to attract students who are not interested in the mainstream teaching style but find, for instance, contemporary music more relatable. By adapting a generated or existing text to the style of different genres, educators manage to retain the scientific integrity of their educational content while increasing its relevance (Panagopoulou et al., 2023). Also, ChatGPT can be used to generate human-like responses to student queries, engage in critical thinking, and assist with idea generation (Halaweh, 2023).

Another option is that of generating pros and cons with respect to a specific issue. ChatGPT has the potential to “humanize” web search, i.e., help users locate and retrieve information in the same manner as asking a fellow or colleague (Kumar, 2023). A set of pros and cons can be used either as part of a more general research project or as part of a debate exercise, where students are asked to support or find weaknesses to a specific argument.

Regarding online learning, specifically in Massive Open Online Courses (MOOCs), some implications were explored in a study (Alseddiqi et al., 2023). The work discussed the benefits of ChatGPT in addressing challenges associated with MOOCs, such as lack of personalized support and feedback, approaching the capabilities of ChatGPT, such as language understanding, response generation, personalization, and continuous learning. The study conducted experiments to measure the accuracy and effectiveness of ChatGPT in answering questions from various subject areas and difficulty levels. The potential impact of this technology on students' learning skills was discussed, concluding that it is highly effective in answering multiple-choice and true or false questions from various MOOCs platforms. The findings suggest that ChatGPT can actually enhance students' critical thinking skills by providing them with more opportunities to apply their knowledge in real-world contexts.

Meanwhile, Bard, in its current iteration, demonstrates limitations in generating original content following the process of paraphrasing, with similar struggles observed in crafting responses to inquiries (Aydin, 2023). Upon comparison with ChatGPT, a congruent outcome is discerned in the context of paraphrased text generation. However, ChatGPT exhibits lower matching rates with respect to replication or plagiarism in the responses it generates, indicating a greater degree of originality. The implications of these findings suggest that the utilization of these and related AI applications could potentially lead to a divergence in scholarly literature.

Regarding the field of mathematics, Friedes and colleagues (2023) evaluated ChatGPT for its mathematical capabilities. It has been tested on publicly available datasets and hand-crafted ones to measure its performance in tasks such as question answering and theorem searching. ChatGPT's performance has been compared to other models trained on mathematical corpora and the development of datasets that cover advanced mathematics has been proposed to further evaluate ChatGPT's mathematical comprehension.

With respect to academic research, ChatGPT has been used to complete various tasks, including essay writing, speech writing, summarizing literature, and generating ideas. It was discussed that it has the potential to assist researchers in idea generation and scientific writing (Rahman et al., 2023). However, challenges have been identified in areas such as literature synthesis, citations, problem statements, research gaps, and data analysis. From that, researchers need to be cautious when using ChatGPT in academic research, check the veracity of references and establish necessary guidelines.

Not only between themselves, but also comparisons between these systems and traditional search mechanisms are being researched. Sezgin et al. (2023) conducted a study evaluating the response quality of ChatGPT, Google Bard and Google Search, with respect to recurrently queried information about Postpartum Depression (PPD). The evaluation criterion was based on clinical accuracy and the results indicated a relatively superior performance by ChatGPT in generating clinically accurate responses, as compared to Google Bard and Google Search. This finding posits that, particularly in the context of addressing mental health disorders like PPD, ChatGPT might possess a competitive edge in terms of precision.

Also, the most recent version, GPT-4, advances ChatGPT's proficiency, enabling it to supersede Bard in the domain of imaging-related tasks, while Bard exhibits a heightened propensity towards generating hallucinations (Ahmed et al., 2023). Notably, Bard responded incorrectly to between 50% and 75% of elementary SAT queries. Despite these shortcomings, Bard has seen substantial improvements in its latest update, displaying newfound capabilities in code generation, debugging, and providing explanations for code spanning over 20 programming languages, inclusive of C++, Java, JavaScript, and Python.

Although there are some investigations about programming and software development, the most researched area is, currently, concerning the health sector and medical themes. Rahsepar et al. (2023) embarked on a comparative analysis of the performance metrics of ChatGPT-3.5 and Google Bard, in addressing medically-themed questions. A discernible disparity was observed, with ChatGPT-3.5 demonstrating a superior accuracy and consistency in the delivery of correct responses in contrast to Bard. However, it is crucial to acknowledge that neither of the models achieved a 100% success rate in providing correct and consistent answers. The study unveiled several restricting factors that could potentially influence the results as the scope of the sample size was limited, and the chosen lung cancer queries utilized in the research might not encompass the entire diversity of potential medical questions. Such limitations suggest cautious interpretation and more experiment replications to validate the findings.

About reliability analysis against human performance, the inter-reliability of the two chatbots was assessed against human evaluators in terms of recognizing and assessing the complexity of writing prompts (Khademi, 2023). It was discovered that the agreement between ChatGPT and human evaluators in assessing the perceived complexity of writing prompts was more pronounced ($r = .22$) compared to the agreement between Bard and human evaluators ($r = .05$). In general, the outcomes revealed moderate to substantial concordance between the AI tools and human evaluators concerning the perceived complexity of the writing prompts. Nonetheless, the AI models demonstrated lower agreement with human evaluators when it came to assessing the quality of writing prompts. These findings indicate that while AI tools can potentially aid human evaluators in recognizing the complexity of writing prompts, their reliability in substituting human evaluators in assessing the quality of these prompts might be questionable.

Table 1. Comparison between ChatGPT and Bard capabilities, limitations and outcomes regarding education

System	Capabilities	Limitations	Outcomes
ChatGPT	LLMs usual capabilities (NLP, code interpretation, etc.) Computer Vision (OpenAI, 2023) Superior accuracy and consistency (Alseddiqi et al, 2023; Sezgin et al., 2023; Rahsepar et al., 2023) Plugins (ChatGPT Plus) GPT API	LLMs usual limitations (hallucinations, ethical considerations such as privacy and bias, etc.) (Sallam, 2023; Irfan, 2023; Koos, 2023; Panagopoulou, 2023; Rahman & Watanobe, 2023) Lack of different idioms in the interface	Improved teaching experience (Tlili et al., 2023; Siegle, 2023; Kasneci et al., 2023; Rahman & Watanobe, 2023) Improved learning experience (Kasneci et al., 2023; Alseddiqi et al., 2023; Rahman & Watanobe, 2023) Enhanced critical thinking (Panagopoulou et al., 2023; Sharma et al., 2023; Siegle, 2023) New teaching philosophy (Tlili et al., 2023) Upskilling (Tlili et al., 2023) Increased accessibility (Rahman et al., 2023; Siegle, 2023; Kasneci et al., 2023; Rahman & Watanobe, 2023)
Bard	LLMs usual capabilities (NLP, code interpretation, etc.) Computer Vision (Google, 2023c) Current real time internet information retrieval (Google, 2023a) Integration with Gmail and productivity applications from Google Workspace (Google, 2023c) Files and images in prompts and responses (Google, 2023c) Accessibility features (TTS) (Google, 2023c) PaLM API	LLMs usual limitations (hallucinations, ethical considerations such as privacy and bias, etc.) (Sallam, 2023; Irfan, 2023; Koos, 2023; Panagopoulou, 2023; Rahman & Watanobe, 2023) Limitations in generating original content (Aydin, 2023)	

With respect to Citation Diversity Statement[1], an experimental study by King (2023) investigated the potential of Bard to assist researchers in analyzing the diversity of their scientific citation practices. The premise was to leverage the chatbot's capabilities to gauge the representation of diverse groups in referenced

[1] The goal of this statement is to prompt authors to consciously evaluate the proportion of their cited references that have been authored by women or people of color - demographics that have been historically underrepresented in scientific literature. The intent is to encourage researchers to enhance the diversity of the authors they cite in their scholarly work.

scientific literature. However, it was observed that Bard, in its current iteration, fell short of delivering a reliable performance for this task. Despite demonstrating a slight improvement in the accuracy of reference demographics, it was evident that the chatbot's live search functionalities were not fully optimized for this application. In response to this analytical discrepancy, Bard quickly agreed to the proposed explanation, affirming that it had indeed based its demographic analysis on prior average data. Nevertheless, the author remains hopeful about the potential for leveraging such technology for diversity analysis in scientific references as Bard continues to evolve and improve.

The comparisons between OpenAI's and Google's chatbots even join the field of personalities and anthropomorphism. In a comparative examination, distinct personality types were found to be consistently exhibited. ChatGPT, regardless of contextual variations or instructions, invariably maintains a Myers-Briggs Type Indicator (MBTI) ENFJ (Extraversion, Intuition, Feeling, Judging) personality type. Conversely, Bard corresponds to an ISTJ (Introversion, Sensing, Thinking, Judging) type. A key facet of the study was the examination of chatbots' personality consistency across seven additional languages: Chinese, Korean, Spanish, French, German, Italian, and Arabic. Using 60 questions from the 16Personalities tool, translated into the aforementioned languages, the consistency of the tools exhibited personality was scrutinized. A focal point of this investigation was to ascertain whether LLMs could manifest changes in their exhibited personalities in response to instructional or contextual cues. Despite the variations of "happy" and "sad" contexts, the results underscored that ChatGPT unwaveringly maintains its original personality type, defined as ENFJ, unaffected by contextual alterations or provided instructions. This illustrates the consistent nature of LLM personalities, and could serve as a reference point for future research on LLM behavior and potential manipulation.

Having this, Table 1 shows a compiled comparison between ChatGPT and Bard capabilities, limitations and outcomes regarding education. Indeed, it is critical to highlight that this synthesis of information is current as of July 2023. Given the swift progression of advancements in the Artificial Intelligence field, the capabilities and limitations of these tools may rapidly be updated over time. Nonetheless, the core implications and outcomes delineated in this comparison should persist, illustrating the potential that these sophisticated AI models, ChatGPT and Bard, possess in reshaping our engagement with technology.

5. CONCLUSION

This article reviewed the potentials and risks regarding ChatGPT and Bard, comparatively, in the educational field. In terms of opportunities, these technologies can be employed as effective tools for personalized learning support, as it can analyze student performance data, identify areas where students are facing challenges, and generate customized resources and learning activities to boost their skill sets. Furthermore, ChatGPT's and Bard's proficiency in understanding and answering learners' questions can enhance the learning experience by providing comprehensive answers and additional pertinent resources, such as articles, videos, or tutorials. The application of such chatbots also extends to academic evaluation and assessment, where it can swiftly assess and grade assignments and quizzes, including the generation of variable-difficulty questions. Lastly, OpenAI's and Google's systems can support research activities by summarizing published work, suggesting novel research ideas, and even generating code.

However, the usage of those LLMs powered tools also poses certain threats: for instance, its capacity to generate human-like text can potentially compromise the integrity of online exams and assignments due to the risk of cheating. To counter this, it is necessary to educate students about the repercussions of academic dishonesty and employ plagiarism-detection tools to identify AI-generated content. Another issue is the risk of over-reliance on AI, which could undermine problem-solving skills. To mitigate this, it is important to guide students on how to effectively utilize ChatGPT while also promoting a critical approach to the information it generates. Finally, the increasingly blurred line between AI-generated content and human-produced text presents an escalating challenge for educators and researchers. Overcoming this challenge requires the development of innovative technologies that can distinguish between human and AI-generated content and label them, providing clear disclaimers.

Also, many ethical questions emerge within this scope. A body of literature has deliberated on the ethical considerations pertinent to the employment of ChatGPT in educational settings (Sallam, 2023; Irfan, 2023; Koos, 2023; Panagopoulou, 2023). These studies underscore the imperative of confronting ethical repercussions, fostering responsible utilization, and enlightening both educators and learners about the prospective perils and constraints associated with LLMs. Additionally, these studies have proffered strategies and recommendations aimed at warranting the ethical incorporation of chatbots or AI assistants into pedagogical practices. AI systems' prospective contribution to the refinement of pedagogical methodologies, the fortification of health education and scientific exploration, the facilitation of mathematical problem-solving, and the advancement of academic inquiry holds considerable potential. Teachers must play a key role in mediating AI integration, ensuring a balance between technology usage and development of independent learning skills (Siegle, 2023).

A crucial concern warranting attention pertains to the potential implications of LLMs on diversity and existing disparities within research fields. While promising to democratize access to information by potentially eliminating language barriers and enhancing the quality of written output, these models might inadvertently exacerbate existing inequalities (Dis et al., 2023). Similar to past technological innovations, it is plausible that resource-rich countries and elite researchers could leverage LLMs to bolster their own research productivity, thereby widening the existing disparities. Consequently, it is imperative that discussions surrounding the implementation and governance of these "stochastic parrots" involve individuals from underrepresented groups in research and those from communities directly impacted by the research outcomes (Bender et al., 2021). This inclusivity is essential to ensure that lived experiences serve as valuable resources in shaping the trajectory and ethical use of these advanced AI models (Bolukbasi, 2016).

Also, there is a pressing need for further research and investigation to acquire a holistic understanding of future OpenSource technologies competencies and features vis-à-vis ChatGPT and Bard. Comparative research dedicated expressly to new LLMs, encompassing performance across various domains, would yield insightful revelations concerning their assets and constraints. Furthermore, it is of paramount importance to address ethical considerations and potential biases in HAI, in order to ensure ethical progression and deployment in diverse applications.

Addressing the limitations of general LLMs within specialized fields, domain-specific models are being trained on text corpora pertinent to specific areas of interest. These specialized LLMs, such as Google's Med-PaLM for the medical domain and Sec-PaLM for cybersecurity, will tend to exhibit improved performance within their respective disciplines, demonstrating an enhanced understanding and language generation in their specialized contexts (Google, 2023b). These models symbolize the convergence of advanced AI capabilities and field-specific requirements, promising enhanced efficacy and precision within these targeted domains.

As they persistently evolve, both ChatGPT and Bard find themselves in a competitive equilibrium, each progressively broadening their respective scopes of application (Ahmed et al., 2023). The acceleration of knowledge gathering and representation through AI seems imminent, simultaneously decreasing reliance on human-centered methods for these operations (Aydin, 2023). The emergence of these technologies promises an exciting future where more intelligent systems could become an integral part of our knowledge ecosystems.

REFERENCES

Adiguzel, T. et al. (2023). Revolutionizing education with AI: Exploring the transformative potential of ChatGPT. *Contemporary Educational Technology*, 15(3), ep429.

Ahmed, I. et al. (2023). ChatGPT vs. Bard: A Comparative Study. *In UMBC Student Collection.*

Ali, N. M. et al. (2023). Artificial Intelligence In Learning Management System: a Case Study Of The Students Of Mass Communication. *Voyage Journal of Educational Sciences*, 2(3), 92-114.

Alseddiqi, M. et al. (2023). Revolutionizing Online Learning: The Potential of ChatGPT in Massive Open Online Courses. *European Journal of Education and Pedagogy*, 4(4), 1-5.

Aydin, Ö. (2023). Google Bard generated literature review: metaverse. *Journal of AI*, 7(1), 1-14.

Bender, E. M. et al. (2021, March). On the dangers of stochastic parrots: Can language models be too big? 🦜 In *Proceedings of the 2021 ACM conference on fairness, accountability, and transparency*, pp. 610-623.

Bolukbasi, T. et al. (2016). Man is to computer programmer as woman is to homemaker? debiasing word embeddings. *Advances in neural information processing systems*, 29.

Clavié, B., et al. (2023). Towards Simple Hybrid Language Model Reasoning Through Human Explanations Enhanced Prompts. *In HHAI 2023: Augmenting Human Intellect*, pp. 379-381.

Dis, E. A. M. v. et al. (2023). Chatgpt: Five Priorities For Research. *Nature*, 7947(614), 224-226.

Frieder, S. et al. (2023). Mathematical capabilities of chatgpt. *arXiv preprint* arXiv:2301.13867.

Google (2023a), An important next step on our AI journey, https://blog.google/technology/ai/bard-google-ai-search-updates/, last accessed 2023/07/16.

Google (2023b), AI Across Google: PaLM 2, https://ai.google/discover/palm2/, last accessed 2023/07/17.

Google (2023c), Bard Updates, https://bard.google.com/updates, last accessed 2023/07/17.

Halaweh, M. (2023). Chatgpt In Education: Strategies For Responsible Implementation. *Contemporary Educational Technology*, 2(15), ep421.

Huang, J. T. et al. (2023). ChatGPT an ENFJ, Bard an ISTJ: Empirical Study on Personalities of Large Language Models. *arXiv preprint* arXiv:2305.19926.

Kasneci, E. et al. (2023). ChatGPT for good? On opportunities and challenges of large language models for education. *Learning and individual differences*, 103, 102274.

Khademi, A. (2023). Can ChatGPT and bard generate aligned assessment items? A reliability analysis against human performance. *arXiv preprint* arXiv:2304.05372.

King, M. R. (2023). Can Bard, Google's Experimental Chatbot Based on the LaMDA Large Language Model, Help to Analyze the Gender and Racial Diversity of Authors in Your Cited Scientific References? *Cellular and Molecular Bioengineering*, 16(2), 175-179.

Kumar, P. (2023). Large Language Models Humanize Technology. *arXiv preprint* arXiv:2305.05576.

LeCun, Y. et al. (2015). Deep learning. *Nature*, 521(7553), 436-444.

Lund, B. D., & Wang, T. (2023). Chatting about ChatGPT: how may AI and GPT impact academia and libraries? *Library Hi Tech News*, 40(3), 26-29.

OpenAI (2023). GPT-4 Technical Report. ArXiv, abs/2303.08774.

Panagopoulou, F. et al. (2023). Legal and ethical considerations regarding the use of ChatGPT in education. *arXiv preprint* arXiv:2306.10037.

Paul, J. et al. (2023). chatgpt and Consumers: Benefits, Pitfalls And Future Research Agenda. *Int J Consumer Studies*, 4(47), 1213-1225.

Pollock, D. et al. (2023). Recommendations for the extraction, analysis, and presentation of results in scoping reviews. *JBI Evidence Synthesis*, 21(3), 520–532.

Rahman, M. M. et al. (2023). ChatGPT and academic research: a review and recommendations based on practical examples. *Journal of Education, Management and Development Studies*, 3(1), 1-12.

Rahman, Md. M., & Watanobe, Y. (2023). ChatGPT for Education and Research: Opportunities, Threats, and Strategies. *Applied Sciences*, 13(9), 5783.

Rahsepar, A. A. et al. (2023). How AI Responds to Common Lung Cancer Questions: ChatGPT vs Google Bard. *Radiology*, 307(5), e230922.

Sallam, M. (2023). ChatGPT utility in healthcare education, research, and practice: systematic review on the promising perspectives and valid concerns. *In Healthcare*, Vol. 11, No. 6, p. 887.

Sezgin, E. et al. (2023). Clinical Accuracy Of Large Language Models and Google Search Responses To Postpartum Depression Questions: A Cross-sectional Study. JMIR Preprints. 22/05/2023:49240.

Siegle, D. (2023). A Role for ChatGPT and AI in Gifted Education. *Gifted Child Today*, 46(3), 211-219.

Tlili, A. et al. (2023). What if the devil is my guardian angel: ChatGPT as a case study of using chatbots in education. *Smart Learning Environments*, 10(1), 15.

FOSTERING PROBLEM SOLVING AND CRITICAL THINKING IN MATHEMATICS THROUGH GENERATIVE ARTIFICIAL INTELLIGENCE

Alice Barana, Marina Marchisio and Fabio Roman
Department of Molecular Biotechnology and Health Sciences, University of Turin
Via Nizza 52, 10126 Torino, Italy

ABSTRACT

The spread of Artificial Intelligence (AI) has been recently generating worries among teachers and educators about the validity of assessment when students make use of AI tools to solve tasks. To tackle this issue, we propose mathematical problem solving activities to be carried out with the aid of ChatGPT, showing how problem solving and critical thinking continue to be pivotal in solving mathematical problems, even if this is performed with the aid of AI. After discussing theoretical frameworks on strategies of problem solving and phases of the critical thinking process, we present six problems of combinatorics that we submitted to ChatGPT. We also asked 40 university students to solve the six problems in group with the aid of ChatGPT during an international module on Problem Solving and Critical Thinking and collected the tutors' observations about the activities. Analyzing ChatGPT solutions and tutors' reflections, we show that the proposed activity requires problem solving and critical thinking to be accomplished. The results corroborate the idea that, instead of limiting the use of AI in education, it is possible to integrate it within learning and assessment to achieve the learning goals.

KEYWORDS

Artificial Intelligence, ChatGPT, Critical Thinking, Mathematics Education, Problem Solving

1. INTRODUCTION

The role of artificial intelligence (AI) in everyday life is increasingly extensive: nowadays, it helps us carry out fundamental tasks for the society, not only for specific jobs but also for general areas regarding the whole public, such as health and education (Lee, 2020). While on the one hand the advantages of AI are consolidated, on the other hand worries exist concerning the impact it could have once it becomes capable to substitute the human being to an important extent (Deranty and Corbin, 2022). An area in which this applies is education: how real is the risk that a student performs an assignment not on his/her own, but asking an AI to do it for them? (Crawford et al., 2023) The availability of a tool like ChatGPT, which gained a strong popularity during the last period of time also among the general public (Haleem et al., 2022), makes the question more topical than ever. Indeed, it has never been easier to ask the computer for a detailed text, or a full solution of a mathematical problem, starting from a simple query written in natural language, with no need of programming skills or other forms of specific interaction with the system. However, since this tool has spread, several cases of misinformation were documented (Farina and Lavazza, 2023), giving evidence that it is not generally possible to rely on its answers without thinking critically about these responses. In this paper, we will propose mathematical problem solving activities to be performed with the aid of ChatGPT. We will show how problem solving and critical thinking continue to be pivotal in solving mathematical problems, even if this is performed with the aid of AI, since the AI can often help the user up to a certain degree, but it is not so frequent that it returns a completely correct solution. Namely, in many instances, while the general setting of the procedure ChatGPT outputs is right, some key steps are incorrect, leading to errors that propagate through the proof. Proposing students to solve mathematical problems with the aid of this AI (or similar tools) can foster problem solving and critical thinking, for example while assessing the solution and recognizing where the AI fails, thus getting to the actual solution by correcting those steps. The structure of the paper is as follows: Section 2 outlines the theoretical framework within which this study is situated, while Section 3 presents the research question and explores the methodology employed. Section 4 depicts the results, and Section 5 offers a thorough discussion. Finally, Section 6 concludes the paper with closing remarks.

2. THEORETICAL FRAMEWORK

2.1 Problem Solving and Critical Thinking

The role of problem solving in Mathematics is undisputed: especially when applications are involved, the development of a solution cannot usually be reduced to a simple sequence of actions to be applied mechanically. A comprehensive definition of problem solving involves the ability to understand the environment, identify complex problems, review related information to develop, evaluate strategies and implement solutions to build the desired outcome (Fissore et al., 2021). It is a consequence of this definition that problem solving does not only apply to Mathematics or professional life, but it is useful also for everyday life as citizens of the present world: the well-known 20th century philosopher and epistemologist Karl Popper once said *all life is problem solving* (Camiller and Popper, 1999). Some basic strategies of problem solving are (Wang and Chiew, 2010):

- Divide and conquer: subdivide a large complex problem into some smaller problems, where each of them can be solved more easily;
- Lateral thinking: approach solutions indirectly and creatively, without relying only on the rigid logic of step-by-step procedures;
- Analogy and reduction: starting from an analogous problem having a known solution, reconduct your situation to that problem;
- Bases of scientific method: assume a possible explanation in order to prove or disprove it (hypothesis testing), try to prove the unfeasibility of the problem in order to start from an absurd or more generally a failure (proof), test possible solutions until finding a right one (trial and error).

Critical thinking can be defined as the intellectually disciplined process of actively and skillfully conceptualizing, applying, analyzing, synthesizing, and/or evaluating information gathered from, or generated by, observation, experience, reflection, reasoning, or communication, as a guide to belief and action (Ennis, 2015). It can be considered constituted by the following phases (Changwong et al., 2018):

1. Describing: give a clear definition of what in consideration, by providing a proper specification of what was involved, where it happened and under which circumstances.
2. Reflecting: consider a topic under more than just one point of view, also by updating this consideration when new information or experience is available.
3. Analyzing: examine and explain the nature of something (e.g. a phenomenon), compare and contrast various elements, relate these evidences with topics.
4. Critiquing: detect strengths and weaknesses in arguments, under a neutral perspective.
5. Reasoning: use evidence and logic to prove or disprove an argument.
6. Evaluating: comment on what obtained in a wider sense, not just limiting to the reference subjects.

During the problem solving process, critical thinking has several roles: it permits to correctly look for data, it helps the choice of good strategies, and it allows arguing about the findings.

The use of problem solving for Mathematics with new technologies has been widely explored in the latest years (Barana and Marchisio, 2016; Marchisio et al., 2020; Marchisio et al., 2022a), being its benefits evident. With disruptive situations and tools, it becomes even more important to blend methodology and technology, in order to use the latter according to the goals devised with the former (Goldin and Katz, 2009; Marchisio et al., 2022b; Marchisio et al., 2022c).

2.2 Large Language Models and Generative AI Systems

AI tools such as ChatGPT belong to the category of generative AI systems, which in turn are based on large language models (LLMs). They are deep learning models capable of acquiring an extensive knowledge of a language, by eliciting it from huge amounts of texts, mainly originating on the World Wide Web (Attardi, 2023). Starting from simpler tasks as predicting a word that concludes a sentence, they soon revealed to be capable of higher abilities, such as generating long texts from short instructions or solving scientific problems, by comparing an adequate set of possible answers. Collobert et al. (2011) presented a method of self-supervised learning aimed at representing the words' meaning, by providing to a neural network a sufficiently high number of sentences, from which developing the capability of recognizing patterns among the words constituting them. By representing every word with a long numerical vector, with each number standing for a particular nuance of meaning, it was possible to categorize words and to determine conceptual similarities, thanks to the comparison of these vectors. A limitation of that technique were the words possessing several and distinct meanings, whose meaning inside a sentence depends on the context; to overcome this hindrance, Vaswani et al. (2017) described an *attention mechanism* able to detect relations between words in a specific context. This is further applied by means of the so-called *Transformers*, which are models capable of preserving those relations, while producing an output starting from the user's input. The use of Transformers allowed, after just a few months, to process the natural language notably better than any previous technique, even those that required years of development and perfecting. This is possible because Transformers can be fine-tuned, by giving to a pre-trained model some new examples, allowing them to hastily adapt to the relative tasks. Regarding applications in solving mathematical problems, it is important to observe that LLMs show emergent abilities, appearing only when their dimension becomes particularly large, and consisting in advanced reasoning capabilities, such as the model being able to adapt a resolutive path to a different setting (Wei et al., 2022). The use of generative AI now goes even beyond these capabilities, for instance by being able to also generate images starting from a brief description. This brings about ethics and security issues (Klenk, 2023), which are even more prominent when education is involved. However, the goal should be to properly integrate these tools by taking into account their limitations and merits, rather than turning the possible dangers into fears, thus demonizing them (Lim et al., 2023). Such features have been recently considered by several researchers (Ipek et al., 2023).

3. RESEARCH QUESTION AND METHODOLOGY

Our study is motivated by the following research question: *What strategies proper of problem solving and phases belonging to critical thinking do students activate when solving mathematical problems with the aid of ChatGPT?* In particular, we are interested in investigating how problem solving and critical thinking intervene when students interpret the outputs artificial intelligence gives and assess if they are actually correct or can anyhow help in some way. To answer the research question, we consider some mathematical problems in Combinatorics. They can be administered either to high school students, especially those possessing relevant interest in the sciences, or to university students, for example as preliminary tools for Probability and Statistics. These problems read as follows:

1. A regular polygon has n sides and $4n$ diagonals. Calculate n.
2. 23 officers participate to a military conference. If each participant shakes his or her hand to every other participant, how many handshakes will be overall performed?
3. Six squads are engaged in combat training. How many sessions are held, if in each session they confront each other two versus two, in every possible way?
4. n servicemen are involved in a muscle strengthening program, organized such that every day 4 of them are present, and after 13 days everyone has been present exactly once with each other. What is the value of n?
5. In a platoon composed of 36 soldiers, 19 of them are going to have field training during the next week (in the day), while 18 of them are going to take part in a workshop (in the evening). Six of them will be on leave, so they are not going to have field training nor take part in the workshop. How many soldiers are going to both have field training and take part in the workshop?
6. A test is made of 15 multiple-choice questions, admitting as answers three alternatives, let them be A, B, C. For the sake of unpredictability, it is required that at least one correct answer is A, at least one is B, and at least one is C. In how many ways is it possible to construct the (ordered) list of correct answers?

The use of elementary combinatorial techniques is required to solve these problems, but their solutions are not immediate, being them the outcome of a multistep procedure, rather than a single computation.

First, we repeatedly asked ChatGPT (GPT-3.5 architecture) to solve the problems and we analyzed what it gave as outputs, in terms of correctness, consistency and clarity. In particular, we are interested in how students can detect possible errors (which are not unlikely to occur) by thinking critically and applying problem solving strategies, with the goal of devising a correct solution after the human intervention, but starting from the AI output. As an important note, it should be made clear that differently from other studies, our goal is not to assess the success rate of ChatGPT, or to perform a statistical inquiry; instead, we aim at showing some possibilities that can occur, and how students can interpret them according to their aforementioned objective. Moreover, we experimented the six problems with international university students enrolled in degree courses in strategic sciences during an international module on Problem Solving and Critical Thinking. Students were asked to solve the problems in groups using ChatGPT and discuss the solutions. Four tutors facilitated the activities and filled a questionnaire at the end, constituted of open questions aimed at capturing their insights on how problem solving and critical thinking were activated during the activities. In particular, we analyzed the tutors' answers to the questions "Which Strategies of Problem Solving did they adopt?" and "Which Phases of critical thinking did they perform?", selecting references to the use of AI in these processes, in order to confirm the preliminary results.

4. RESULTS AND DISCUSSION

4.1 Solving the Problems with ChatGPT

We started by repeatedly submitting Problem 1 to ChatGPT. The pivotal step is that a polygon, not necessarily regular, having n sides, has $n(n\text{-}3)/2$ diagonals, and so it reduces to the equation $n(n\text{-}3)/2 = 4n$. Most of the times, the AI correctly performed this step, then arriving by elementary algebraic steps to the solutions $n = 0$ and $n = 11$, of which ChatGPT explicitly states that only the latter is feasible, since a polygon cannot have zero sides (see Figure 1). Unfortunately, sometimes it commits an error by writing that a n-sided polygon has $n(n\text{-}3)$ diagonals, thus writing a different equation resulting in the wrong solution $n = 7$. Furthermore, the procedure ChatGPT outputs states that the formula holds "for any regular polygon", while in fact this is not limited to them, being rather valid at least for any *convex* polygon.

By performing the same with Problem 2, again most of the times the solution was correct: two officers out of a group of 23 can be chosen in $(23\cdot 22)/2 = 253$ ways, so there will be 253 handshakes. However, in some instances it reasoned differently: the first officer will shake hands with the remaining 22 officers, the second officer will shake hands with the remaining 21 officers (excluding the first officer), the third officer will shake hands with the remaining 20 officers (excluding the first and second officers), and so on. This led to the sum $22 + 21 + \ldots + 2 + 1$, which yields again 253, but in an instance ChatGPT computed it wrongly, as Figure 2 depicts. Indeed, the AI wrote the formula for summing that arithmetic series as $(23/2)\cdot(22\text{+}1)$ instead of $(22/2)\cdot(22\text{+}1)$: the terms are 22 and not 23, or alternatively the 23rd is 0, so it would have been $(23/2)\cdot(22\text{+}0)$.

Regarding Problem 3, on the contrary ChatGPT kept giving the incorrect solution 15, as choosing two squads out of a group of six for each session: $(6\cdot 5)/2 = 15$. In fact, the squads to be chosen are four and not two, since the confrontations are two versus two. Moreover, for each choice fixing four squads, let us say A,B,C,D, we can let them confront as A,B vs C,D, or A,C vs B,D, or A,D vs B,C, so there are three ways. The total number of sessions is thus $3\cdot(6\cdot 5\cdot 4\cdot 3)/4! = 45$, but the AI was unable to output this answer.

Concerning Problem 4, ChatGPT provided the right solution $n = 13$ every time except the first one, when it resorted to $n\cdot(n\text{-}1)/2 = 4$ (having positive solution $n = 4$), instead of $n\cdot(n\text{-}1)/2 = 13\cdot(4\cdot 3)/2$, thus ignoring the number of days and the coupling of the servicemen present every day.

For Problem 5, $36 - 6 = 30$ soldiers will be not on leave, so if respectively 19 and 18 are engaged in the two activities, then $19 + 18 - 30 = 7$ are engaged in both. ChatGPT was unsuccessful on this: an error it committed during a try was to ignore the soldiers on leave (thus answering $19 + 18 - 36 = 1$), even after a first part of reasoning in which it considered them. Another error in a subsequent try regarded the confusion of quantities, first by stating that $19 + 18 - 6 = 31$ soldiers are engaged in at least one activity, while they are actually the 30 not on leave, and then by considering them as soldiers with no participation, finally answering a wrong $36 - 31 = 5$. In one case, it ignored both the soldiers on leave and their total number, by simply affirming that at most $\min(18,19) = 18$ soldiers could be doubly engaged, using only information from those numbers.

Finally, in Problem 6, ChatGPT gave an almost correct solution, by just committing the error of considering a single case in which A, B and C are all missing, which cannot exist: the number of valid combinations is thus given as $3^{15} - 3 \cdot 2^{15} + 3 - 1$, where the final -1 is actually wrong. Nevertheless, the AI failed to compute the result as a number, by stating that it equals to 14,348, when in fact it is equal to 14,250,605 (14,250,606 is the solution to the problem, by not considering -1). The fact that ChatGPT was able to perform almost correctly a task which had been traditionally deemed as difficult for an automated system, such as solving an articulated mathematical problem (Problem 6 was the most difficult of the list for a human solver), but failed in a simple algebraic computation, is noteworthy. Indeed, it is representative of the nature of this generative AI system, which possesses more data retrieval and assemblage potential, rather than computational capabilities.

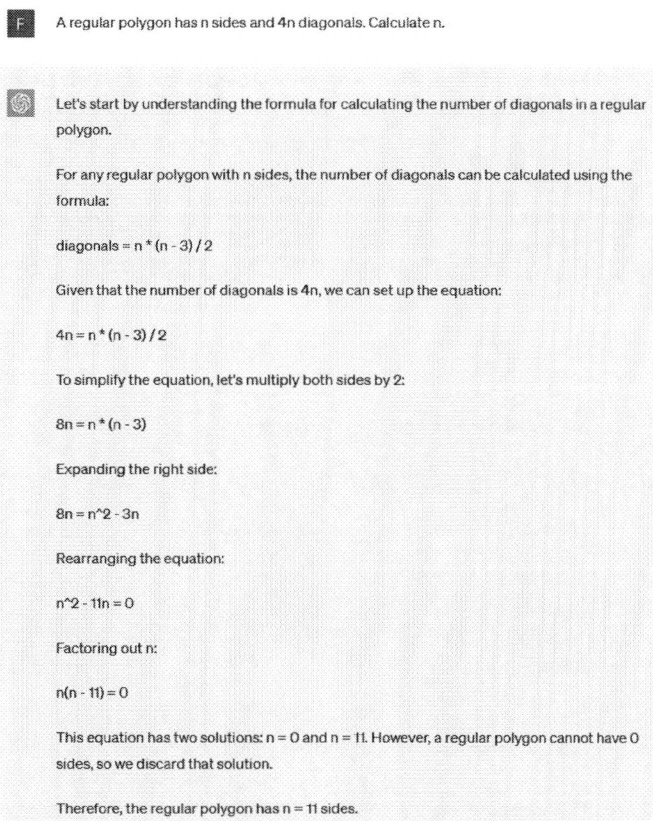

Figure 1. The correct solution of Problem 1 as provided by ChatGPT

4.2 Analysis of the Problem Solving and Critical Thinking Activities

The solutions ChatGPT gave as outputs are first discussed in relation with the problem solving strategies we presented in the theoretical framework. For Problem 1, a student shall split how to determine the equation by means of the formula associating the number of diagonals a polygon possesses to its number of sides, from how to solve the equation itself. This fits into the "divide and conquer" strategy of problem solving. Moreover, to ascertain the incorrectness of the formula if returned wrong, students can use a "base of the scientific method": finding a counterexample. Indeed, a student should be able to easily recall that quadrilaterals possess two diagonals, since they are widely used during geometry classes at compulsory schooling. By substituting $n = 4$ in the expression $n(n\text{-}3)$, the result is 4 rather than 2, thus directly suggesting that something is wrong. On the other hand, "lateral thinking" could help in assessing the validity of the formula if returned correct: if a student does not know or does not remember how to proceed with the combinatorial theory, s/he can rely on a bit of creativity, for instance by trying some cases with a low number of sides (of which $n = 4$ can be one), and then finding a motivation for which the expression $n(n\text{-}3)/2$ is valid for every n. Finally, to prove that the formula holds also for polygons which are not regular, "analogies" can be used: for example, does the number of diagonals change if a vertex is dragged, a modification which keeps intact the number of sides?

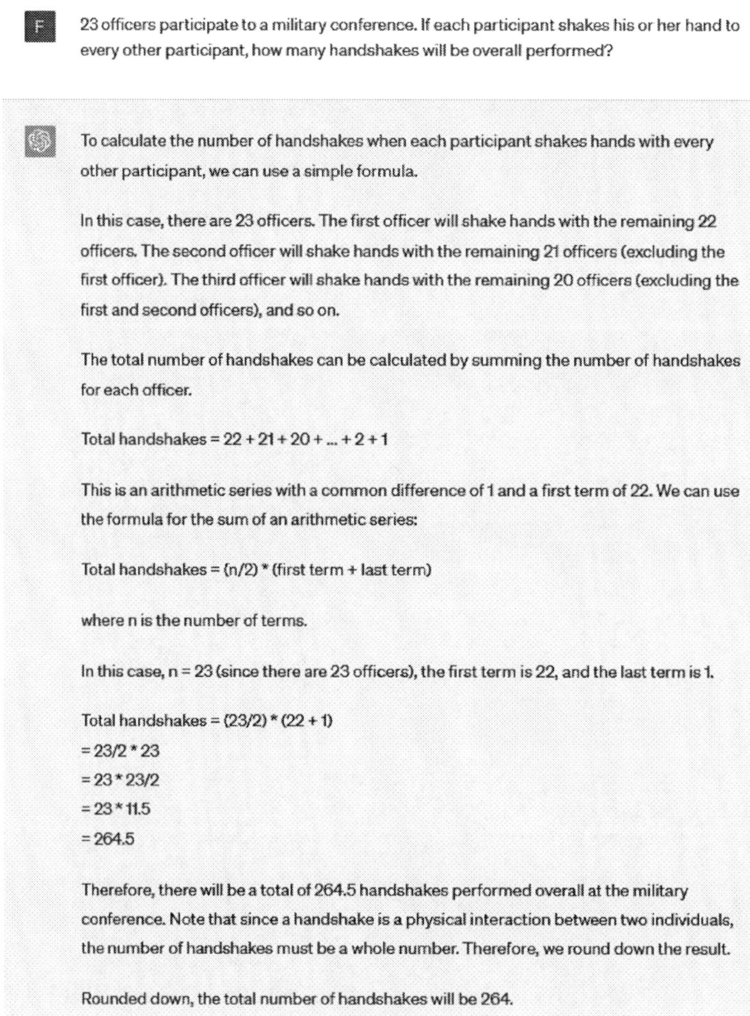
F 23 officers participate to a military conference. If each participant shakes his or her hand to every other participant, how many handshakes will be overall performed?

To calculate the number of handshakes when each participant shakes hands with every other participant, we can use a simple formula.

In this case, there are 23 officers. The first officer will shake hands with the remaining 22 officers. The second officer will shake hands with the remaining 21 officers (excluding the first officer). The third officer will shake hands with the remaining 20 officers (excluding the first and second officers), and so on.

The total number of handshakes can be calculated by summing the number of handshakes for each officer.

Total handshakes = 22 + 21 + 20 + ... + 2 + 1

This is an arithmetic series with a common difference of 1 and a first term of 22. We can use the formula for the sum of an arithmetic series:

Total handshakes = (n/2) * (first term + last term)

where n is the number of terms.

In this case, n = 23 (since there are 23 officers), the first term is 22, and the last term is 1.

Total handshakes = (23/2) * (22 + 1)
= 23/2 * 23
= 23 * 23/2
= 23 * 11.5
= 264.5

Therefore, there will be a total of 264.5 handshakes performed overall at the military conference. Note that since a handshake is a physical interaction between two individuals, the number of handshakes must be a whole number. Therefore, we round down the result.

Rounded down, the total number of handshakes will be 264.

Figure 2. ChatGPT solving Problem 2: right procedure, wrong computation

In Problem 2, it is again important splitting how to write a formula from how to compute it ("divide and conquer"), especially if ChatGPT returns a sum rather than what follows from a direct combinatorial approach. In this case, the "lateral thinking" strategy can intervene in finding the possible incorrectness of the solution. Indeed, an inherent contradiction is present where a sum of integers yields the formula $(23/2)\cdot(22+1)$ which, if computed explicitly, equals to $23^2/2 = 529/2 = 264.5$ (see Figure 1): summing integer numbers cannot result in obtaining a non-integer number, a fact that students definitely know from elementary arithmetic, and they just have to recall it in a context probably different from where they learned it. Students should also note that the final rounding down to make the number feasible in the context (yielding 264) is just an attempt to forcefully "rectify" the result in order to obtain an integer, which does not remove the error the aforementioned fact implies. Note also that this can be related with the search for counterexamples allowing to deem the wrong formula as incorrect in Problem 1.

Concerning Problem 3, it is useful to see how ChatGPT approaches the problem, but then students are a bit more on their own than in Problems 1 and 2. Indeed, since the AI keeps choosing two squads rather than four, the student can perform an "analogy" and use the combinatorial formula proposed, but with 4 instead of 2 where appropriate. Incidentally, here $(6 \cdot 5)/2 = (6 \cdot 5 \cdot 4 \cdot 3)/4! = 15$, but this is not the point: conceptually, working with 2 is wrong. Moreover, the problem does not end with this computation, given the three ways in which the four squads can be paired two versus two: students thus have to divide the part in which the four squads are *chosen* from the part in which they are *paired* (with the choice performed).

About Problem 5, the presence of contradictions is clear seeing how ChatGPT changed premises on which reasoning during the procedure, giving proof of inconsistence (that pertains to the "scientific method"). Somewhat similarly to Problem 3, some sort of "analogy" could be performed by starting from the formula summing the numbers relative to the two engagements and then subtracting a third number: indeed, the AI suggests it as the correct tool to obtain a solution, its errors lying in the inability to correctly write the number after the minus sign. Analogous reasoning holds for Problems 4 and 6.

Now, we can discuss the solutions with regard to the critical thinking phases. The first three phases are implied by the ways in which ChatGPT approaches the problems, since they foster the student to devise an outline of the situation ("describing"), to evaluate its implications ("reflecting") and to assess its adequateness with respect to the objectives ("analyzing"). The "critiquing" phase can emerge well in situations such as the presence of intermediate steps being somewhat different from what expected, for example in the steps leading ChatGPT to give the wrong answer to Problem 4: the absence of the days' number in the formula $n \cdot (n\text{-}1)/2 = 4$ is not necessarily a contradiction, but it should bring up some suspect, thus belonging to the assessment of the likelihood of rationales to be solid and consistent. On this line, the "reasoning" phase is prominently clear where contradictions are instead actual, like in the errors occurring during an instance of solving Problem 2, when the number 264.5 can be definitely disproved as possibly being the sum of integers. Finally, the "evaluating" phase does not directly descend from what ChatGPT gives as outputs, since it limits itself to provide the procedures allowing to solve the problems, but nonetheless students can consider them as a starting point to further discuss the solutions.

4.3 Analysis of the Tutors' Questionnaire

Concerning problem solving, Tutor A wrote "I suggested them to use ChatGPT when they were in difficulty, and then try to understand and evaluate its solution", implying that ChatGPT supported students in the choice of the solving strategy and in lateral thinking when they did not have any idea on how to approach it. Starting from the AI suggestion, students had to use "bases of scientific method" to prove or disprove it. The same tutor also adds: "Sometimes they divided problems into smaller parts and used ChatGPT to better understand some concepts", making clear how the tool can be used to support the "divide and conquer" solving strategy. Tutor B noted that "2 students used ChatGPT to solve problems, for example to do some computations, and checked that the answers provided by their colleagues (who used a traditional approach to solve problems) were correct." This answer shows how ChatGPT was used to solve steps of the solving process (supporting the "divide and conquer" strategy) and in the "bases of scientific method", testing hypothesis. Tutor C did not mention ChatGPT in the problem solving strategies. Tutor D wrote "the use of ChatGPT fostered in them "analogy", since starting from the solutions the AI posted, being often not completely correct, they were able to devise the right ways by taking AI solutions' paths as a reference, correcting them thanks to the knowledge they had".

Concerning critical thinking, tutor A declared to have observed the following phases: "Analyzing and critiquing when students examined the solutions provided by ChatGPT to analyze coherence and correctness; reasoning when discussing about the solutions, in particular when they used different strategies to solve problems; the evaluating phase was supported by ChatGPT answers since they helped students to interpret the results, thus moving from reasoning to opinions". Tutor B did not mention ChatGPT when describing the students' critical thinking process. Tutor C wrote "They subdivided some sub-tasks to evaluate critically the single step. It is mainly relevant to note that there was (like I suggested) double check on calculations also using ChatGPT, because they made several mistakes at the beginning and they were asking me about the correct solution, but this is something that does not happen in real scenarios, so they had to check and verify on their own the correctness of results". The use of AI to check results, which Tutor B mentioned in the problem solving strategies, is here recalled to support the "reflecting", "analyzing" and "critiquing" phases of critical thinking. Tutor D noticed that "the "examine" phase intervened before trying analogies while assessing whether the solutions the AI gave were correct or not (and in case not, where they failed), and so on". Moreover, he added that "they used also ChatGPT, not only to get ideas, but also to compare their reasoning with the solutions the AI provided".

Summing it up, students mainly used ChatGPT to support problem solving in finding ways to solve problems and testing solutions; ChatGPT supported the critical thinking process, in particular when they checked the correctness of the solutions proposed by the AI or, vice versa, when using the tool to check their own solutions. This yields scientific and practical implications, starting from a consideration the collected results allowed us to infer: the AI did not act as a tool to *substitute* the human, but rather it *flanked* the students, without undermining their role as an active part of the processes. Consequently, there was no harm in letting students to deal with ChatGPT, while they had in practice the possibility to complement their cogitating, and the relative benefits could be scientifically studied. According to the tutors' responses, not every student took advantage of the AI: this might represent a current limitation, in the sense that some students could not have perceived as helpful the aid ChatGPT provided. However, these tools are still a novelty, and there is yet plenty of opportunities to instill in people confidence in them.

5. CONCLUSION AND FUTURE WORK

As a possible answer to the alarm that has recently spread among teachers due to the availability of AI that could hinder the validity of assessment, in this paper we proposed to ask students to use ChatGPT in mathematical problem-solving activities. In particular, we show that this AI can support the problem solving strategies and the critical thinking process. We answered to the research question *"What strategies proper of problem solving and phases belonging to critical thinking do students activate when solving mathematical problems with the aid of ChatGPT?"* by analyzing the solutions that ChatGPT provides to six problems of combinatorics in the perspective of problem solving and critical thinking. Moreover, we analyzed the observations that tutors made after experimenting the same six problems with university students during an international module. The results show that all strategies of problem solving and all phases of critical thinking can be affected by this kind of activity, since students have to check the correctness of ChatGPT solutions, not always correct, or check their own solutions through ChatGPT. Moreover, the activity also helped them find new and different approaches to solve problems. In line with Crawford et al. (2023) and Lim et al. (2023), we are convinced that, instead of limiting the use of AI for learning and assessment, it is possible to integrate it during the activities and find new ways to evaluate the achievement of learning goals, thus turning the threat into an ally. This also implies that the misinformation risks, which we saw as concrete while doing Mathematics like they are in other contexts as highlighted by Farina and Lavazza (2023), can be handled constructively, by taking advantage from what is right, and at the same time recognizing and correcting what is wrong. The advanced reason capabilities Wei et al. (2022) described, which manifested also here, indicate that the "right" portion is generally extended enough to be a safe starting point for students to positively use the outputs provided by the AI.

This research work could be further developed, for example by videorecording the students when dealing with this kind of activity, in order to observe with high precision the kind of support that ChatGPT gives to the problem solving and critical thinking processes. In addition, other generative AI systems such as You.com, Bing AI and Bard are available as ChatGPT is, so a comparison between them can be set up. Moreover, the activities could be extended to different kinds of problems and different areas of Mathematics.

ACKNOWLEDGEMENT

The authors would like to thank the bank foundation Compagnia di San Paolo, which financially supports many of the initiatives at the University of Torino, in particular the project OPERA Open Program for Educational Resources and Activities, in which this research took place.

REFERENCES

Attardi, G., 2023. Il Bello, il Brutto e il Cattivo dei LLM. *Mondo Digitale*, 22(101).

Barana, A. and Marchisio, M., 2016. From digital mate training experience to alternating school work activities. *Mondo Digitale*, 15(64), pp. 63-82.

Camiller, P. and Popper, K., 1999. *All Life is Problem Solving.* Routledge, London, DOI: 10.4324/9780203431900

Changwong, K. et al, 2018. Critical thinking skill development: Analysis of a new learning management model for Thai high schools. *Journal of International Studies*, 11(2), pp. 37-48, DOI: 10.14254/2071-8330.2018/11-2/3

Collobert, R. et al, 2011. Natural Language Processing (Almost) from Scratch. *The Journal of Machine Learning Research*, 12, pp. 2493-2537, DOI: 10.5555/1953048.2078186

Crawford, J., Cowling, M., & Allen, K., 2023. Leadership is needed for ethical ChatGPT: Character, assessment, and learning using artificial intelligence (AI). *Journal of University Teaching & Learning Practice*, Vol. 20, no 3, pp. 1-19. DOI: 10.53761/1.20.3.02

Deranty, JP. and Corbin, T., 2022. Artificial intelligence and work: a critical review of recent research from the social sciences. *AI & Soc.*, DOI: 10.1007/s00146-022-01496-x

Ennis, R.H., 2015. Critical thinking: a streamlined conception. In: Davies M., Barnett R. (eds.) *The Palgrave Handbook of Critical Thinking in Higher Education*, pp. 31-47. Palgrave Macmillan, New York, DOI: 10.1057/9781137378057

Farina, M. and Lavazza, A., 2023. ChatGPT in society: emerging issues. *Frontiers in Artificial Intelligence*, vol. 6, DOI: 10.3389/frai.2023.1130913

Fissore, C. et al, 2021. Development of Problem Solving Skills with Maple in Higher Education. In: Corless R.M., Gerhard J., Kotsireas I.S. (eds.) Maple in Mathematics Education and Research. MC 2020. *Communications in Computer and Information Science*, vol. 1414, pp. 219-233. Springer, Cham. DOI: 10.1007/978-3-030-81698-8_15

Goldin, C.D. and Katz, L.F., 2009. *The Race between Education and Technology*. Harvard University Press, Cambridge, UK, DOI: 10.2307/j.ctvjf9x5x

Haleem, A. et al, 2022. An era of ChatGPT as a significant futuristic support tool: A study on features, abilities, and challenges. *BenchCouncil Transactions on Benchmarks, Standards and Evaluations*, 2(4), 100089, DOI: 10.1016/j.tbench.2023.100089

Ipek, Z.H. et al, 2023. Educational Applications of the ChatGPT AI System: A Systematic Review Research. *Educational Process*, 12(3), pp. 26-55, DOI: 10.22521/edupij.2023.123.2

Klenk, M. Ethics of Generative AI and Manipulation: A Design-Oriented Research Agenda. *Social Science Research Network*, DOI: 10.2139/ssrn.4478397

Lee, R., 2020. *Artificial Intelligence in Daily Life.* Springer, Singapore, DOI: 10.1007/978-981-15-7695-9

Lim et al, 2023. Generative AI and the future of education: Ragnarök or reformation? A paradoxical perspective from management educators. *The International Journal of Management Education*, 21(2), 100790, DOI: 10.1016/j.ijme.2023.100790

Marchisio, M. et al, 2020. Teaching Mathematics in Scientific Bachelor Degrees Using a Blended Approach. *Proceedings of IEEE 44th COMPSAC Conference*, pp. 190-195. DOI: 10.1109/COMPSAC48688.2020.00034

Marchisio, M. et al, 2022a. Teaching Mathematics to Non-Mathematics Majors through Problem Solving and New Technologies. *Education Sciences*, 12(1):34. DOI: 10.3390/educsci12010034

Marchisio, M. et al, 2022b. Teachers' perception of higher education in a transition scenario. *Proceedings of IEEE 46th COMPSAC Conference*, pp. 139-144. DOI: 10.1109/COMPSAC54236.2022.00028

Marchisio, M. et al, 2022c. Teachers' digital competences before and during the COVID-19 pandemic for the improvement of security and defence higher education. *16th International Conference on e-Learning (EL2022) – Held at the 16th Multi-Conference on Computer Science and Information Systems (MCCSIS2022)*, pp. 68-75.

Vaswani, A., et al, 2017. Attention is all you need. *Proceedings of the 31st International Conference on Neural Information Processing Systems*, pp. 6000-6010. DOI: 10.5555/3295222.3295349

Wang, Y. and Chiew, V., 2010. On the cognitive process of human problem solving. *Cognitive Systems Research*, 11(1), pp. 81-92, DOI: 10.1016/j.cogsys.2008.08.003

Wei, J., et al, 2022. Emergent Abilities of Large Language Models. *Transactions on Machine Learning Research*. DOI: 10.48550/arXiv.2206.07682

SHORT PAPERS

MAIN FACTORS FOR IMPROVING THE EFFECTIVENESS OF MATHEMATICS STUDIES

Anda Zeidmane and Natalija Sergejeva
Latvia University of Life Sciences and Technologies
Liela Street 2, Jelgava, Latvia, LV3001

ABSTRACT

Starting university studies, students have great difficulties in mathematics studies, often because when they transition from school studies, students have insufficient self-efficacy skills and insufficient learning initiative. Based on the theoretical research a questionnaire was developed for students of the Latvia University of Life Sciences and Technologies (LBTU). Evaluating students' self-assessment of learning self-efficacy skills in mathematics studies, it can be concluded that students are relatively little familiar with metacognitive strategies, but use cognitive strategies intuitively. Regarding student learning initiative, there is a relationship between time management and assessment, as well as between mathematics learning goal and assessment. Based on the obtained results, the authors suggest focusing students' attention on identifying and applying mathematical strategies in effective mathematics studies, as well as cultivating positive thinking in learning mathematics, developing good will power, self-control and emotional control.

KEYWORDS

Mathematics Studies, Effectiveness, Learning Self-Efficacy, Learning Initiative

1. INTRODUCTION

Students come to university from a variety of educational backgrounds, and research shows that both mathematical knowledge and mathematical thinking are different for many students (Hakim L., 2022). Many factors affecting the learning process change for the student when he (or she) gets to universities. But, the most important are the changes in the academic environment, because the learning environment is changing, where the emphasis is on independent studies, relatively frequent presentations and exams are an integral part of studies, which require the development of communication and academic study skills, as well as self-efficacy, good time management and information literacy (Cheng M., 2023). The most important factors that can improve the effectiveness of mathematics studies are students' learning self-efficacy and students' learning initiative, which must be developed by students themselves. Objectives of the study are: 1) to investigate students' learning self-efficacy skills, knowledge of the main mathematics learning strategies, to determine whether there are relationships between the skills to apply learning strategies and effective learning results in the case of the students of Latvia University of Life Sciences and Technologies; 2) to assess student learning initiative based on attitude and motivation and to determine whether there is a relationship between student learning initiative and effective learning outcomes

2. BODY OF PAPER

Self-efficacy in learning mathematics is based on **cognitive learning**, which is the change of knowledge based on experience. The definition of cognitive learning has three components (Mayer, 2011): 1) learning involves changes, 2) these changes occur in the learner's knowledge, 3) the cause of these changes is the learner's experience. The elements of cognitive learning are understanding, memory, application (Herrity, 2023). Cognitive learning strategies include: i) the ability to understand how ideas are connected, ii) the ability to justify and explain one's thinking, iii) the use of visual materials and tools, iv) revising one's learning experience, v) finding alternative solutions to the problem (Cognitive Learning).

Many studies have shown that knowledge of mathematics learning strategies significantly affects students' learning effectiveness (Cho; Heron,2015), (In'am; Sutrisno,2021). It is essential to identify and manage the three main learning strategies for mathematics (Wang G. at A, 2022): 1) The **mathematical cognitive** strategy that includes *Retelling strategy*, *Finishing strategy*, *Organizing strategy*, *Feedbacking strategy*; 2) The **mathematical metacognitive** strategy that includes *Planning strategy*, *Monitoring strategy*, *Reflection and adjustment strategy*; 3) The **mathematical resource management** strategy that includes: *Time management strategy*, *Environmental management strategy*, *Mood management strategy*, *External help strategy*.

If this self-efficacy is not at a sufficient level, then students should use **learning initiative** to be able to learn problematic topics. Learning initiative is stifled by such a factor as the negative attitude towards the study of mathematics. In many studies, the attitude is characterized as the recognition of the learning goal and the way of thinking about learning in general (Anghelache, 2013), which would stimulate personal involvement in the learning process. In the formation of attitudes towards mathematics studies, the following are of great importance: i) knowledge, beliefs about mathematics (cognitive component); ii) the emotional factor (affective component) and iii) motivation and action (behavioral component) (Wenden, 1991). Students who have low success in mathematics mainly have a lack of motivation to learn this topic here and now, as well as an emotional barrier to admit that they do not understand this topic yet, but are ready to learn it. Therefore, it is essential for students to develop their emotional skills - the feeling of emotions; integration of emotions; emotion understanding and emotion management are (Mayer, Salovey & Caruso, 2020). No less important is the influence of the social environment on the motivation to learn. Many students live in dormitories, where the roommates' motivation to learn (or not learn) math often has a big impact. Cooperation with group members, group work also has a great influence on the motivation to learn mathematics, even if it causes difficulties, so it is essential to create a positive climate both in the university and in the faculties.

Based on theoretical studies and students' opinions, the main factors that would improve the effectiveness of mathematics learning were identified and the relationship between them was found.

Taking into account the above-mentioned studies, a research methodology was developed, which includes a questionnaire for students to identify students' knowledge of mathematics learning strategies and skills to use them and students' learning initiative. The questionnaire included closed and semi-closed questions. A survey was conducted at LBTU from the end of January to the end of March 2023, inviting students of different specialties to fill out an electronic questionnaire "Factors Affecting Mathematics Studies". The questionnaire is available here: https://ej.uz/factors_for_math. A total of 215 respondents took part in the study. Fisher's exact test is used to determine whether there is a significant relationship between two variables. In order to improve the performance of higher education and promote learning, a self-assessment method is recognized as a tool for identifying strengths and weaknesses (Andrade & Valtcheva, 2009).

3. FINDINGS

In studies of students' learning self-efficacy skills in mathematics studies, students were first asked questions about whether they are aware of mathematics learning strategies in general and whether they use them. 10% of the students surveyed claim that they have knowledge of mathematics learning strategies, while 43% claim that they have not been interested in mathematics learning strategies at all. Similar distribution of students due to the use of mathematics learning strategies. Of those who are not interested in math learning strategies, 87% do not use them, while the remaining 13% use them sometimes. On the other hand, among those who know or partially know mathematics learning strategies, 86% always or sometimes use them, while 14% do not.

When students were asked questions about how they learn mathematics, it was surprising that they use mathematical cognitive strategies (reviewing material, organizing knowledge, memorizing, using feedback) without even realizing it (see Table 1).

To determine whether there is a relationship between students' use of cognitive strategy in mathematics and learning outcomes, Fisher's exact test was applied. The null hypothesis H0 was defined: there is no relationship between each qualitative indicator mentioned in Table 1 and the average result in mathematics. The alternative hypothesis H1: two variables are not independent. Fisher's exact test results are $p>0.05$ in all cases, indicating that our evidence is not strong enough to indicate a relationship between these two variables. Such a result could be explained as a slightly incorrect self-assessment, especially for those students who have poor results in mathematics, or these strategies are ineffectively applied.

Table 1. Survey results on students' use of cognitive strategies in mathematics

Statement	often	sometimes	never
When preparing for a math test, I try to figure out what are the most important parts to learn	41%	55%	4%
When I study math, I try to check if I remember what I have already learned	49%	43%	8%
When I study math, I try to understand what concepts I still don't understand	34%	56%	10%
When I don't understand something in math, I always look for information to understand the problem	39%	58%	2%
When learning mathematics, I try to learn the answers to the exercises by heart	8%	39%	53%
To remember the method of solving a math problem, I review the examples over and over again	57%	39%	3%
To learn mathematics, I try to remember every step of the procedure	61%	37%	2%

As regards students' skills to use metacognitive strategies in mathematics studies (planning, comparison with life experience, creativity), only a few students are aware of the importance of mathematics in everyday life (see Table 2).

Table 2. Survey results on students' use of metacognitive strategies in mathematics

Statement	often	sometimes	never
During the mathematics test, I know how to divide the time wisely between the tasks	45%	54%	1%
When solving math problems, I also think of other ways to get the answer	20%	63%	17%
I think how what I learned in mathematics can be applied in everyday life	18%	47%	36%
I try to understand new concepts in math by relating them to things I already know	19%	56%	26%
When learning mathematics, I try to connect the subject matter with things learned in other subjects	22%	51%	27%

Similarly, as in the case of cognitive strategies, also in the case of the metacognitive strategies, the null hypothesis H0 was defined: there is no connection between each qualitative indicator mentioned in Table 2 and the average result in mathematics. Fisher's exact test results in all cases are $p > 0.05$, so the existence of the connection has not been proven. Students' inability to connect mathematics with other subjects and everyday life can be explained by the fact that the mathematics study course is in the first years and the special subjects have not yet been mastered.

The results of the survey show that when solving math tasks during the test, students do not know how to control their emotional state, which reduces the test results (often - 33%, sometimes - 47%), which can indicate insufficient preparation for the test and lack of confidence. As for failures in solving tasks, the majority try to cope with difficulties by themselves (often- 78%). As "external help", students most often use the help of group members (often 63%), but only 43% often look for solutions on the Internet.

Using Fisher's exact test, it was investigated whether there was a relationship between students' use of mathematical resource management strategies in mathematics and average mathematics results. There is a relationship between anxiety that lowers task-solving abilities and average results in mathematics ($p=0.0169<0.05$).

In order to assess students' **learning,** the survey included questions about students' motivation in the study process. Successful completion of a mathematics course is unthinkable without students' independent work and homework. 61% of survey participants say that they often systematize their knowledge while doing homework, 34% do it from time to time, 5% don't do it at all. In the Department of Mathematics of LBTU-students have been invited to create their own list of formulas. 17% of the surveyed students say that they make a list of formulas during the study process, 61% do it right before the test, and 22% say they don't make it at all. When evaluating the time required to learn mathematics, 37% of students believe that they put a lot of work into solving math problems, 12% say that math is easy for them.

The initiative to learn mathematics is also reflected in whether students seek help from a private tutor or attend consultations with a mathematics teacher. Our study shows that 89% of students attend consultations at least sometimes, while only 28% seek help from a private tutor if they do not understand something in mathematics.

4. CONCLUSION

Systematizing factors for improving the effectiveness of mathematics studies, the authors concluded that the most important are students' self-efficacy and students' learning initiative. Students' mathematics learning self-efficacy is based on cognitive learning skills, which in turn are based on mathematical learning strategies. The student's learning initiative is based on the attitude towards learning mathematics, the motivation factor and the emotional factor, which can also be influenced by the learning environment and the teacher's support.

Evaluating students' self-assessment of learning self-efficacy skills in mathematics studies, it can be concluded that students are relatively little familiar with metacognitive strategies, but use cognitive strategies intuitively. Only 10% of students answered that they know and use mathematical strategies, but at the same time, about 70-80% admitted that they use them. Regarding students' use of mathematical resource management strategies, it can be concluded that there is a relationship between the inability to manage emotions and reduced task-solving abilities.

Regarding student learning initiative, there is a relationship between time management and assessment, as well as between mathematics learning goal and assessment. Students' inability to connect mathematics studies with other study courses and everyday life can be explained by the fact that the mathematics course is in the first years and the special study courses have not yet been mastered.

REFERENCES

Andrade H. and Valtcheva A., 2009. Promoting learning and achievement through self-assessment. *Theory into Practice*, No. 48, pp. 12-19, 2009

Anghelache V., 2013. Determinant factors of students' attitudes toward learning. *3rd World Conference on Learning, Teaching and Educational Leadership (WCLTA-2012).* Procedia - Social and Behavioral Sciences, 93, pp. 478–482.

Cheng, M., Barnes, G.P., Edwards, C., Valyrakis, M., 2023. Transition Models and How Students Experience Change. *Project report. University of Glasgow (now University of Wolverhampton).* Available from: https://www.enhancementthemes.ac.uk/docs/ethemes/student-transitions/transition-models-and-how-students-experience-change.pdf

Cho, M. H.; Heron, M.L., 2015. Self-regulated learning: The role of motivation, emotion, and use of learning strategies in students' learning experiences in a self-paced online mathematics course. *Distance Educ.* 36, pp 80–99.

Cognitive Learning. Oxford learning. Available from: https://www.oxfordlearning.com/cognitive-learning/

Hakim, L., 2022. Top tips to improve the teaching of mathematics in universities. *The Times Higher Education* [9 Feb 2022]. Available from: https://www.timeshighereducation.com/campus/top-tips-improve-teaching-mathematics-universities

Herrity, J., 2023. What Is Cognitive Learning? Definition, Benefits and Examples. *Career Guide.* Available from: https://www.indeed.com/career-advice/career-development/cognitive-learning

In'am, A.; Sutrisno, E, S., 2021. Strengthening Students' Self-Efficacy and Motivation in Learning Mathematics through the Cooperative Learning Model. *Int. J. Instr.* 14, pp 395–410.

Mayer, J. D., Salovey, P., & Caruso, D. ,2000. Models of emotional intelligence. *In R. J. Sternberg (Ed.), Handbook of intelligence.* Cambridge University Press, pp. 396–420. Available from: https://doi.org/10.1017/CBO9780511807947.019

Mayer, R. E., 2011. *Applying the science of learning.* Upper Saddle River: Pearson Merrill Prentice Hall.

Wang, G., Chen, X.,, Zhang, D., Kang, Y, Wang, F., Su, M., 2022. Development and Application of an Intelligent Assessment System for Mathematics Learning Strategy among High School Students—Take Jianzha County as an Example. *Sustainability* 2022, 14(19). Available from: https://doi.org/10.3390/su141912265

Wenden, A. (1991). Learner strategies for learner autonomy. Prentice Hall. New York [Google Scholar] -172 pp.

SHAKING THE "FOUNDATIONS OF EDUCATIONAL TECHNOLOGY"

Suzanne de Castell[1] and Jennifer Jenson[2]
[1]*Simon Fraser University, Burnaby, British Columbia, Canada*
[2]*The University of British Columbia, Vancouver, British Columbia, Canada*

ABSTRACT

Educational technology programs often introduce students to the field through a "foundations" course. Overviewing foundational educational technology courses at a sample of North American post-secondary educational technology programs, this exploratory paper builds an argument for change, identifying themes, approaches, as well as media and technology uses, out of touch with the conditions that are impacting—and with some urgency-- education and technology. From global climate crisis, through a pandemic, to culture wars and imperialist invasions, with 'surgical' AI-enabled drone strikes on human targets on one side of the planet while on the other, fragile human bodies are pitted against one another in combat on the ground, urgent problems and challenges are profoundly shaking the foundations of education and for the technologies used in its advancement. An example is shared in closing to illustrate how a 'new foundations' approach can illuminate possible pathways and forge new directions for the field under changed and changing conditions, that can provide students and researchers understanding of where and upon what educational technology stands—and its next steps.

KEYWORDS

Educational Technology, Education, Technology, Foundations, Higher Education, Learning

1. INTRODUCTION

"When scholars mention "Ur-stories," they mean basic elements from which all other compound tales are composed" (Stone, 2019). Studying the foundations of educational technology means learning a story of its 'basic elements' — the keystones upon which that edifice has been built and now stands.

Educational technology's "Ur-stories" come from the frameworks embedded in its introductory courses and required readings, the 'basic elements' these frameworks identify as shaping its theories and practices, and structurally sufficient to sustain them. These 'basic elements', and the Ur-stories to which they give rise, establish the field's 'theoretical underpinnings' using, most commonly, 'keystones' of 2 kinds. The first grounds the field upon a familiar, disciplinary structure, echoing the well-established paths laid out in educational studies more generally. Its points of departure are the theoretical frameworks of traditional disciplines, like history, philosophy, sociology, psychology, more recently complemented by emergent subjects and fields like communications theory and media studies. The second approach is broadly pragmatic, with foundational educational technology courses taking a 'realpolitik', 'applied', often vocational and technicist approach to conveying and assessing specific "professional knowledge" for aspiring or practicing educational technologists, with (TPack, ISTE Standards, and the like) and technical skills (coding, digital design, UX) composing students' introduction to the field. A theoretical trajectory is described by the first approach; a practical one by the second, but both are ideological approaches, meaning by this that they seek to understand educational technology explicitly from the standpoint of bodies of ideas.

These frames of reference work like powerful stories to build learners' subsequent understandings and practices. From their embedded narratives, we learn to ask specific kinds of questions and pay attention to particular kinds of things, and we build our own "tales of the field" around the particular kinds of things that either discipline-driven questions, or application-focused ones, can get at. Our tools and our environments have been mostly silent in these stories, neither speaking nor spoken about. And we have listened an awful lot to our own ideas.

2. CONSIDERING FOUNDATIONS

Now the world has changed, quite literally, and these ideas of ours are not working. They are not working out well for human beings. And they are not working out well for other beings either, or, indeed, the physical world. No need to re-iterate the long list of familiar and terrifying problems we are now, non-negotiable, required to live in; these are tectonic shifts.

"Business as usual" approaches to understanding, by situating human purposes as central, as the driver of events, as the adjudicator of optimal forms and functions, have structurally sidelined attention to or consideration of material (and existential) conditions critical to educational technologies--- nickel and lithium, for example, and the host of other, no less important constitutive conditions tied to mining, resource extraction, and so on. We have learned from our own UR stories that the material costs and conditions of educational technologies are not recognized as foundational to decisions about its designs and uses. And that's just one example of how we might be better served by a rethinking of what, besides ideas, educational technology is built upon, and what those epistemic cornerstones enable and constrain.

The conditions of contemporary educational technology studies, being conditions of profound global destabilization, bring with them an urgent need for *new* foundations, new stories, new questions and a new way of seeing that can allow that new building to happen. This will be a less well-established, more exploratory route to understanding how technologies, and educational technologies in particular, have been, are being and will be most powerfully shaped and driven.

And that means this cannot be an "idea-driven", that is, an "ideological" route. Because while tools and theories most certainly change in tandem, the drivers of that change, the catalysts of technological change in education, have rarely been ideas. Consider, as one recent (and continuing) example, that the system-wide adoption of educational technologies we have just experienced was driven, not by any technological innovations, theoretical insights, breakthroughs in implementation, or pedagogical advancements in online learning, but by a pandemic that brought global health systems to a state of crisis.

Consider, too, how for how long both theory and evidence have clearly set out and made public the precise course environmental degradation and irreversible climate change would take. What does it tell us about our theories of knowledge representation and information dissemination that critically important knowledge, information and evidence *which has been wholly transparent* to what we also like to call an "educated public" has largely not been acted upon, nor been actualized in policy at any level. To ask that deeply unsettling question about the actual impacts of very detailed and very specific foreknowledge is to recognize that critical understandings are simply not getting through our ideological and professional filters. That matters very much for education, and the tools for its advancement.

Foregrounding this "problem of foundations" opens trajectories of inquiry that can make these new conditions visible, unearthing what disciplinary and professional discourses have, however unwittingly, concealed from view. In "Understanding the foundations of educational technology, Tony Bates wrote in 2015 that "What seem to be the major media developments this year are likely to be eclipsed by new developments in technology next year. In such a shifting sea, it is therefore necessary to look at some guiding concepts or principles that are likely to remain constant, whatever changes take place over the years" (see https://www.tonybates.ca/2015/01/02/the-foundations-of-educational-technologies-a-brief-overview/). He continues with a summary of key takeaway points, the first that "Technologies are merely tools that can be used in a variety of ways. What matters more is how technologies are applied." Understanding educational technology's foundations in this way focuses our attention away from technology ("mere tools") to application, to "the ways in which it is being or could be used"*.

But as important as it is to understand how we use things, that human-centered epistemic standpoint is precisely *not* a guiding principle likely to remain constant over time and change. What application-focused perspectives leave out is an understanding of how networks work, and how agency is distributed across them. Sometimes the ways in which we use technology are completely driven by, and almost invariably shaped by, the material composition of that tool. From sociocultural analysis through actor network theory to new materialism, we have been learning how to better appreciate and understand and even in some detail map out how agency can take non-human (including technological) forms, and how powerful the impacts of that agency have been and continue to be in tool design and use. In a technoculture where humans and machines engage not just in interaction, but in co-constitutive, socio-technical transactions, it is important to situate ideas and

---

* This familiar (and familiarly challenged) axiom has been extensively addressed in McLuhan's work---satirized by Woody Allen. McLuhan's ground breaking media analysis has not unsettled the foundations of educational technology the ways it has done for media studies.

applications in the material contexts with which and within which they come into being, are conditioned and change.

2.1 A Short Review of Current 'Foundations' of Educational Technology

There are competing views, of course, of what is, should and/or could be a 'foundational' narrative for educational technology, and too many to rehearse here. However, it is possible to overview some of the approaches to 'foundations' that are present both in related literature on the topic as well as in available online syllabi that were reviewed for this paper.

Starting with the latter approach, reviewing the top 100 Google hits for syllabi under the search term "foundations of educational technology" yielded both publicly available syllabi, as well as extended course descriptions. Of those, there were 12 full syllabi and/or course descriptions that provided enough detail to ascertain the overall approach taken to 'foundations of educational technology'. Across the twelve, we found two competing approaches: 1) an historical and psycho-social overview of general theories of learning, which do not necessarily have technology as a 'core' consideration; and 2) technicist and/or application-focused approaches that emphasize skills such as designing a course website. On the first point, most typically the syllabi begin with a week on 'history' of educational technology, and then move into psychological theories of learning, namely, week to week, behaviorism, cognitivism, and 'constructivism', before moving onto a variety of other learning theories such as socio-cultural learning, situated cognition, and andragogy. This isn't a firm list, just to say that much of what counts as 'foundational' isn't necessarily focused on technology and tools and their history/foundations in education, but more on generic theories of learning and philosophies of education. For the second big category, and again, this is a broad overview, the focus is more on foundational 'standards' in education, with the International Society for Technology in Education (ISTE) standards being oft-cited as 'foundational' in education (see https://www.iste.org/standards/iste-standards-for-teachers). Other foci on this approach are instructional design models, multimedia and multimodality, technology skills, software reviews, and design tasks like websites, blogs, and so on. Both approaches do tend to overview current research on technology in education, though that is usually confined to 1-2 weeks in the syllabi that were publicly available.

Interestingly, there does not seem to be a 'canon', nor even a single agreed on 'foundational' text of set of texts, however there is a quite recent textbook by J. Michael Spector, Foundations of Educational Technology: Integrative Approaches and Interdisciplinary Perspectives (2012) that is used in several such courses. The book is divided into three broad areas: in Part 1, Spector defines technology in relation to education, including its uses in teaching, learning and training; in Part 2, he sets out theoretical foundations of educational technology, such as human development theories (Piaget, Vygotsky, and Erikson), learning theories (much like the above syllabi, behaviorism, cognitivism, constructivism, and so on), information, communication and technology theories, and instructional design theories; part 3 demonstrates how educational technologies have been implemented, starting with Rogers (2003) "diffusion of innovation" model, moving on to technology use in teaching and workplaces, and ending with designing technological systems to support learning, including case studies of their implementation and integration in educational settings. Spector's text is meant to provide an integrative introduction to the area of Educational Technology, but it is one that relies on distinctly well-trodden ground in the history of education and educational theories more specifically, side-stepping the specific roles and histories technologies have played in schooling over time—and to what end.

A very different approach to charting the foundations of educational technology is the historical perspective taken by Larry Cuban, who for decades has shown the ways in which technologies in education have been, literally, 'oversold and under used' (Cuban, 2001). Cuban's approach focuses on technologies in schools, instead of on general theories of teaching and learning. His work over the past four decades traces the histories of technology use in classrooms, from the 1920's to present day, showing the ways in which technologies have been trafficked as vectors for educational change, and how they rarely deliver the promised educational transformation. Some more recent texts have followed a similar critical-historical path, including one that examines B.F. Skinner's concerted attempt to construct (and sell) "teaching machines" (Watters, 2021) and another that traces the history of screens in schools, revealing significant tensions between "citizenship, race, private money and teachers" in the history of educational technology in schools in the United States (Cain, 2021). Both Cain's and Watters' narratives, like Cuban's, tell a story of technological change in education that illustrates its failures to deliver on promises for educational reform. These are also, implicitly, tales of a field lacking direction, detached from salient, stable, sustainable foundations.

Tackling that very problem, a recent paper, "What in the world is educational technology" (An & Oliver, 2021), observe: "it is not clear what (if anything) gives educational technology coherence or integrity" (p. 7).

Against what the authors characterizes as its "relentless pursuit of the new," An and Oliver argue for a framework grounded in a philosophy of technology, which "draws attention to human-education, human-technology and education-technology relationships" (p. 7). The relational analysis advanced there, even as it recognizes a 'symbiosis' of humans and machines, remains a human-centric one that does not give 'voice' to non-human entities and material 'things'. They write that: "...the best technology is just like the hammer in Heidegger's hand, which draws no attention to its existence and is easy to use for the work at hand" (An & Oliver, 2021, p. 13). We need only reflect on how algorithms shape and constrain—and market—us, to contest the idea that these 'best' technologies that are easy to use and draw no attention to themselves are doing nothing significant to their users, and nothing we need to pay attention to.

3. CONCLUSION: TOWARDS NEW FOUNDATIONS FOR EDUCATIONAL TECHNOLOGY

The ideological and the pragmatic framings we've identified as the "UR stories" of educational technology work like filters to select (and exclude) discourses, ideas, practices and perspectives. But some very important things are not getting through. Between the ideological skewing that comes from basing an emergent field on the foundations of those already established, (educational psychology playing the starring role in theory-focused educational technology foundations courses and texts), and the unrestrained instrumentalism of those focused on the pragmatics of educational technology work, there is little room left to acknowledge the materiality of tools and conditions and environments, or to look at how and why educational technologies actually did change, or at what has really resulted from these changes---and, specifically, to what educational effect? In our present conditions, we can scarcely ignore the rate and the scale of economic and environmental change, nor fail to recognize the new challenges this imposes on how technologies are mobilized in education's service---because these are the challenges with which our students are going to be contending.

What can we see if we shift focus from theories to things, to events and to "matter that matters" (Barad, 2003). What can be found by focusing attention less on discipline-based ideas---whether theoretical, technical or practical—and more on *identifying and studying the diverse agents, institutions, material resources and events that have most powerfully catalyzed and transformed educational technologies*, and upon which contemporary educational technologies are being and will be designed, developed and used.

By way of conclusion, we here offer one example—which does not pretend or even aspire to being exhaustive or comprehensive—but which might be suggestive of how 'new foundations' can be conceptualized and operationalized in a re-visioned 'foundations' course. This course, accessible at (URL withheld for blind review) is one we have taught twice now during COVID, fully online, to graduate students in an educational technology master's program. Situating foundation' of educational technology not in philosophy and psychology or in UX design and learning management systems, but in AI and algorithms, media convergence, and digital labour, in global health and environmental sustainability, the course grapples with, and we hope usefully illustrates, an approach to educational technology studies that illuminates more viable pathways and forges new directions more attuned and responsive to the changed and changing conditions which are redefining our possible futures.

REFERENCES

An, T. & Oliver, M. 2021. What in the world is educational technology? Rethinking the field from the perspective of the philosophy of technology, *Learning, Media and Technology*, 46:1, 6-19, DOI: 10.1080/17439884.2020.1810066

Bates, T. 2015. "The foundations of educational technologies: a brief overview" https://www.tonybates.ca/2015/01/02/the-foundations-of-educational-technologies-a-brief-overview/

Barad, K. 2003. Posthumanist Performativity: Toward an Understanding of How Matter Comes to Matter *Signs*, Vol. 28, No. 3, Gender and Science, pp. 801-831

Cain, V. E. M. 2021. *Schools and screens: A watchful history*. The MIT Press.

Cuban, L. 2001. *Oversold and underused: Computers in the classroom*. Harvard University Press.

Stone, G. 2019. *Branding with Powerful Stories*, Santa Barbara: Praeger.

Spector, J. M. 2012. *Foundations of educational technology: Integrative approaches and interdisciplinary perspectives*. Routledge. https://doi.org/10.4324/9780203814192

Watters, A. 2021. *Teaching machines: The history of personalized learning*. The MIT Press.

APPLICATION OF MOBILE EEG FOR COGNITIVE TESTING IN NEURODEVELOPMENTAL DISORDERS

Natalia Georgara and Spyridon Doukakis
Ionian University, Department of Informatics, Corfu, Greece

ABSTRACT

Neurodevelopmental disorders consist of a wide range of conditions, such as autism spectrum disorder and attention deficit hyperactivity disorder. These conditions affect a significant proportion of the population and their correct diagnosis is crucial for the patients' quality of life and their targeted education. Neuropsychological testing and cognitive assessment play a very important role in the diagnosis and management of neurodevelopmental disorders. Cognitive assessments had been performed in the past primarily through pencil and paper but great advancements have been made in this field. New technological means have vastly enhanced the capabilities and potential in the area of neurocognition with the use of computers, gamified cognitive tests, biomarkers, such as electroencephalographic waves, and neurofeedback. This can bring an expanded understanding of how the brain works, increased accuracy and objectivity. The aim of our proposed study is to assess whether young people and children with neurodevelopmental disorders perform differently in a battery neuropsychological test. The proposed test will incorporate the idea of providing 'real time' brain activity by simultaneously recording electroencephalographic waves during the completion of the test through a portable device. The integration of electroencephalogram data into this test has the potential to contribute to the creation of a universal assessment tool. This tool could find utility in diagnosing neurodevelopmental disorders in children across different scenarios.

KEYWORDS

Cognition, EEG, Mobile, Neurodevelopmental, Children, Diagnosis

1. INTRODUCTION

The proposed research aims to enhance our knowledge of how the brain works, specifically for young people with neurodevelopmental disorders (NDD) and to further utilize 'state-of-the-art' technological equipment for the diagnosis and management of such conditions. Our ultimate goal is to achieve the prospect of a universal neurocognitive test with the application of a portable electroencephalographic (EEG) device for the diagnosis of children with NDD.

The main goal is to assess whether young people and children with neurodevelopmental disorders perform differently in our neurophysiological cognitive test. This test utilizes the relatively modern idea of providing 'real-time' brain activity by recording EEG waves through portable devices for the study of NDD in the pediatric and young people population. The proposed neuropsychological test will be based on a platform that consists of a dry-sensor, wireless EEG headband (brand name MUSE 2), a gamified version of a battery cognitive test and a cloud-based storage for data collection and analysis. It has been observed that gamification of cognitive tests tend to improve users' experience, engagement and motivation (Lumsden et al. 2016). The aforementioned equipment will give us an insight into the different ways the brain works during high cognitive functions between young individuals with NDD and without.

The main objectives that this research project will aim to achieve are:

- To determine whether young people with NDD have different outcomes in a neurophysiological battery cognitive test
- To determine whether young people with NDD have different brain wave signals during the completion of the battery cognitive test using a portable EEG device
- To provide a better understanding of the neurophysiological and cognitive functions of young people with NDD

- To collect feedback and analyze "user experience" from young people who use state-of-the-art equipment
- To encourage future implementation of the portable EEG cognitive test, specifically, as a method of neuropsychological assessment for diagnostic, screening, and monitoring purposes for young people with or without neurodevelopmental disorders.

2. BACKGROUND

2.1 Neurodevelopmental Disorders and Cognitive Tests

The term neurodevelopmental disorders has now been formally established and includes a wide range of conditions, such as autism spectrum disorder (ASD), developmental learning disorders, attention deficit hyperactivity disorder (ADHD), and others (Stein et al. 2020). Children who are affected by NDD, may have symptoms due to the altered brain function, including language and speech difficulties, cognitive impairment, motor skills deficit, and other neurological issues (Bourgeron 2015).

The increasing prevalence of NDD and the huge impact that such diagnoses can have on the individual and their families necessitates additional efforts to expand the research on these conditions.

Individuals with neurodevelopmental disorders have higher probability of having a cognitive impairment (Thapar et al. 2017). There have been efforts to introduce several cognitive tests for people with NDD depending on the diagnosis. Some examples of such tests are further mentioned below.

A well-known cognitive test tool is QbTest which is used in many clinics to assist with the diagnosis of ADHD and the management of its treatment. Its unique advantage is that it combines a cognitive test, a continuous performance test (CPT), with a motion-tracking system to detect movement, vigilance, and inattention (Chitsabesan et al. 2022) (Hall et al. 2017). A known computerized test set that comprises many different tests and measures various cognitive domains is the Vienna test system (VTS). An example of VTS is the N-Back test, which is used to evaluate working memory by displaying consecutive letters on the screen and asking the participant to remember and identify whether the letters were previously already displayed (Mohamed et al. 2021).

Many neuropsychological assessments exist for individuals with Autistic Spectrum Disorder (ASD). They assess different areas of functioning such as cognitive, executive function, attention, social cognition, language, and motor. (Braconnier and Siper 2021) The most typical test for assessing the intelligence of the individual is the Wechsler Intelligence Scales adapted differently for children of different ages and adults (Zwick 2017).

2.2 Application of EEG in Neurodevelopmental Disorders

The electroencephalogram is a non-invasive and useful tool for investigating the electrophysiological function and activity of the brain (Feyissa and Tatum 2019).

EEG has long been investigated for its possible uses in pediatric neuropsychology as a biomarker to monitor disease and therapy progress (Loo et al. 2016). Mobile EEG is a new and emerging tool that has been introduced over the past decade. The advantages that a mobile EEG device could offer to the neurodevelopmental population are huge. Firstly, it is easy to use and wear, it is small and therefore less overwhelming. More importantly it is mobile and can be used in any quiet environment, which could be very beneficial for the vulnerable population with neurodevelopmental disorders, who prefer familiarity, calmness and routine.

Attempts have been made by cognitivists to incorporate mobile EEG into studying in more detail different areas of cognition such as attention, memory, motor, speech and auditory processing (Lau-Zhu et al. 2019). The use of mobile EEG has been incorporated into studies focusing on cognitive assessment (McWilliams et al. 2021)There are many studies of EEG application in individuals with NDD, especially for ADHD. More specifically, power spectral density studies have shown that people with ADHD have high theta power and theta/beta ratio on resting state. It is also shown that delta power is usually higher in individuals with ADHD in comparison to people with typical development and alpha and beta power are lower. A recent study by Chen et al. (2022) focused on the application of mobile EEG in preschoolers with ADHD. They studied EEG waves during cognitive tasks. Their results are very promising as they demonstrated distinguishable EEG patterns between children with ADHD and children with typical development. Furthermore, the study illustrated the cooperation and feasibility of performing such a test in young children. (Chen et al. 2022)

ASD is another important neurodevelopmental disorder. A lot of research has focused on finding whether EEG waves are different in the population with ASD (Precenzano et al. 2020) (Santarone et al. 2023). Literature data suggests higher percentage of subclinical electroencephalographic abnormalities and other EEG differences which could indicate poorer cognitive and behavioral functioning (Precenzano et al. 2020).

2.3 Importance of a Universal Neurocognitive Test in Education

Having prompt and correct diagnosis of cognitive difficulties and even possibly a NDD in the young ages is very important for the appropriate evaluation of the educational needs and goals for the individual. According to UNESCO (1994), the educational systems need to fully provide quality education to all learners by simultaneously respecting and following each individual's needs . In order to achieve targeted learning and improve each student's learning processes it is crucial to know the cognitive strengths and weaknesses of the individual. Therefore, there arises the need to have easy to use cognitive tests, such as the proposed one, with high accuracy, which would help to highlight each person's capabilities and offer early intervention and student-centered learning.

3. PROPOSED RESEARCH PLAN

The main research questions that our study will aim to answer are:

- Do young people with a diagnosis of NDD have different outcomes in our proposed neuropsychological test than young people without such a diagnosis?
- Do young people with a diagnosis of NDD have different EEG parameters during our proposed neuropsychological test than young people without such a diagnosis?
- Is the state-of-the-art equipment user-friendly for the NDD population?

The type of the study will be observational, prospective, case-control study.

The study will include children and young people aged 11-24 years old, with a diagnosis of a neurodevelopmental disorder. Recruitment for the study group will be sought through the local Center for Interdisciplinary Assessment, Counselling and Support, through the local Mental Health Center and through the secretarial support in local University Departments. We will aim to have a control group in the analogy of approximate 1:1. Controls will be young people of same age and sex, who do not have a diagnosis of neurodevelopmental disorder. Recruitment for the control group will be sought through local mainstream schools and University Departments, aiming at similar age and sex groups. General Data Protection Regulation (GDPR) will be strictly respected by providing and advertising information for the research through the above providers with contact information for interested subjects to contact us.

Consent will be sought from parents/ carers or young people themselves, according to the age of the participants. Written information for the research and consent form will be provided and collected for all participants. Young people who meet the inclusion criteria but have disabilities, such as eye-sight difficulties, which would prevent them, practically, from being able to participate in the study will be excluded.

Upon recruitment and consent, the study participants will have an appointment to attend to our University facilities with their carers, as appropriate, to conduct the research. According to the research protocol, the participants will wear the dry sensor EEG headband, MUSE 2, and will answer the gamified cognitive test through a tablet electronic device. The battery cognitive test will cover many cognitive areas such as memory, mathematics and color matching by assessing different tasks, such as name task, object series task, colors and shapes task, where task etc.

A questionnaire will be provided to the study participants to evaluate their experience.

The assistance of the University Statistician will be needed in order to determine adequate sample size to achieve the required power. Data interpretation will be performed through correlation statistical tests. We anticipate however that a sample size of 50 individuals will be a good enough starting point.

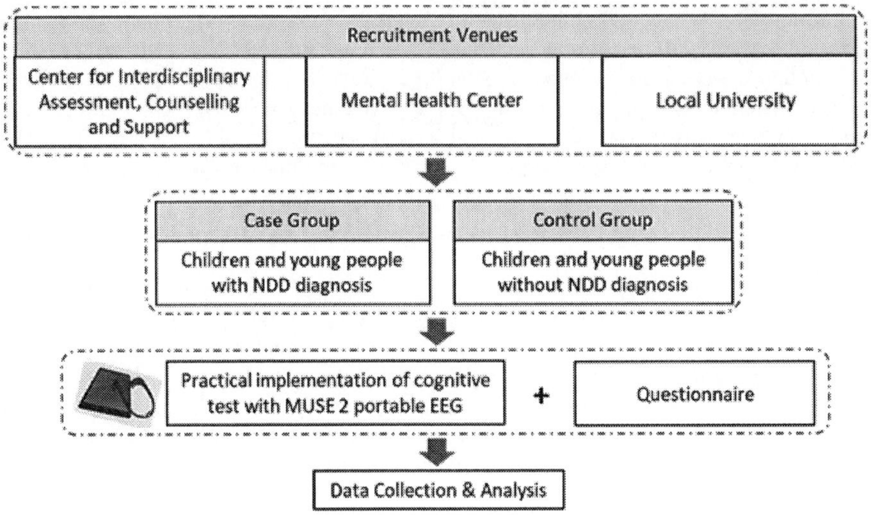

Figure 1. Research plan diagram

4. CONCLUSION

In the present day, there exists an abundance of diverse cognitive tests. The importance of having a universal, easily accessible and user-friendly cognitive tool for people with NDD should not be underestimated.

A more holistic solution, wherein biomarkers, such as EEG, are simultaneously recorded during the cognitive test will probably establish the future approach in this field. As there is strong evidence of significant EEG differences in the population with NDD, we are hopeful that a combination of a cognitive test with simultaneous EEG findings will be the next best tool to aid with the diagnosis and monitoring of such conditions.

The portable EEG device is non-invasive and no risks or harm to the participants is anticipated during the implementation of this research project.

Difficulties in finding subjects for the research should be expected and parental skepticism for participation of their children in research projects should be respected. Further difficulties might arise on data collection as the portable EEG headband needs to be properly fitted and connected throughout the duration of the neuropsychological test and therefore a trained researcher should be present at all times to ensure correct utilization of the tools.

REFERENCES

Bourgeron, T. (2015). What do we know about Early Onset Neurodevelopmental Disorders?. In: S. H. Karoly Nikolich, ed. *Translational Neuroscience.* s.l.:Cambridge (MA):MIT Press.

Braconnier, M. and Siper, P. (2021). Neuropsychological Assessment in Autism Spectrum Disorder. *Current Psychiatry Reports,* 23(10), p. 63.

Chen, I. et al. (2022). Task-Rate-Related Neural Dynamics Using Wireless EEG to Assist Diagnosis and Intervention Planning for Preschoolers with ADHD Exhibiting Heterogeneous Cognitive Proficiency. *Journal of Personalized Medicine,* 30 April.12(5).

Chitsabesan, P. et al. (2022). Using an objective computer task (QbTest) to aid the identification of attention deficit hyperactivity disorder (ADHD) in the Children and Young People Secure Estate (CYPSE): a feasibility randomised controlled trial. *BMJ Open,* 12(12).

Feyissa, A.M. and Tatum, W.O. (2019). Adult EEG. *Handbook of Clinical Neurology.* s.l.:Elsevier, pp. 103-124.

Hall, C.L. et al. (2017). Study of user experience of an objective test (QbTest) to aid ADHD assessment and medication management: a multi-methods approach. *BMC Psychiatry,* 10 February.17(66).

Lau-Zhu, A. et al. (2019). Mobile EEG in research on neurodevelopmental disorders: Opportunities and challenges. *Developmental Cognitive Neuroscience,* April.Volume 36.

Loo, S.K. et al. (2016). Research Review: Use of EEG biomarkers in child psychiatry research – current state and future directions. *The Journal of Child Psychology and Psychiatry,* January, 57(1), pp. 4-17.

Lumsden, J et al. (2016). Gamification of Cognitive Assessment and Cognitive Training: A Systematic Review of Applications and Efficacy. JMIR Serious Games, 4(2), p. e11.

McWilliams, E.C. et al. (2021). Feasibility of Repeated Assessment of Cognitive Function in Older Adults Using a Wireless, Mobile, Dry-EEG Headset and Tablet-Based Games. *Frontiers in Psychiatry*, 25 June.Volume 12.

Mohamed, S.M.H. et al. (2021). Basic and complex cognitive functions in Adult ADHD. *Plos One,* 16(9), p. e0256228.

Precenzano, F. et al. (2020). Electroencephalographic Abnormalities in Autism Spectrum Disorder: Characteristics and Therapeutic Implications. *Medicina (Kaunas),* September.56(9).

Santarone, M.E. et al. (2023). EEG Features in Autism Spectrum Disorder: A Retrospective Analysis in a Cohort of Preschool Children. *Brain Sciences,* 17 February.13(2).

Stein, D.J. et al. (2020). Mental, behavioral and neurodevelopmental disorders in the ICD-11: an international perspective on key changes and controversies. BMC Medicine.18(21 (2020)).

Thapar, A. et al. (2017). Neurodevelopmental disorders. *The Lancet, Psychiatry*, April, 4(4), pp. 339-346.

UNESCO. (1994). *The Salamanca Statement and Framework for Action on Special Educational Needs*. Salamanca: Ministry of Education and Science Spain and UNESCO. Retrieved from: https://unesdoc.unesco.org/ark:/48223/pf0000098427

Zwick, G. P. (2017). Neuropsychological assessment in autism spectrum disorder and related conditions. *Dialogues in Clinical Neuroscience,* December, 19(4), pp. 373-379.

HIGHER EDUCATION TRAINING ACTIVITIES IN INTERNATIONAL ENVIRONMENTS FOR DEVELOPING SKILLS OF CIVIL-MILITARY COOPERATION

Antonino Cambria[1], Marina Marchisio[2] and Enrico Spinello[3]
[1]*High Defence Study Centre, Rome and University of Turin, Italy*
[2]*Department of Molecular Biotechnology and Health Sciences, University of Turin, Italy*
[3]*Education and Training Command and School of Applied Military Studies, Turin, Italy*

ABSTRACT

The educational environment and the panorama of training in the digital age and after the Covid pandemic are dotted with numerous elements and objects, from the traditional to the innovative. In some situations, we see a return to face-to-face teaching, with the teacher identified as a public speaker and facilitator at the same time; in others, we see the creation of specific IT structures for the management of all blended and online teaching. The scenarios in which officers work with civilians have also changed considerably, as they are expected to work together in the context of hybrid warfare. It is important to understand what is the best practice in security and defence education given today's needs. The answer lies in the need to create some learning processes that are usable and flexible in certain contexts, such as laboratories for experimenting with new forms of learning and innovative pedagogies. In Security and Defence education, this is even more important because civilian and military graduates are expected to face ever-changing challenges and to be able to work together. This paper explores how civil-military cooperation skills can be developed in an international context during during the basic training and education at Higher Education. Blended and collaborative learning using a digital environment were the key methodologies for an international school involving civilian and military students.

KEYWORDS

Civil-Military Cooperation, Collaborative Learning, DIGICODE, Security and Defence Education

1. INTRODUCTION

The experience of new methods and technologies for improving the learning processes is vital in education, in particular in Security and Defence Education to develop skills of civil-military cooperation. Collaborative learning in an international context together with the opportunity to work within a digital environment adds an important value to the students' education and training path. The blended intensive programs organized by the European Project Erasmus + DIGItal COmpetencies for improving Security and Defence Education, DIGICODE, could be considered as a laboratory for developing new skills and competencies useful for civilians and military who are supposed to cooperate in international environments during their careers.

In the landscape of various collaborative activities, DIGICODE is a multinational and collaborative experience where interoperability is the keyword. It can be considered one of these laboratories of collaborative learning where new learning methods and good practices are experienced. The main goal of the paper is to study how to develop skills of civil-military cooperation in an international environment during basic training in Higher Education, analyzing feedback collected during an international school for civilian and military students and discussing the add value of similar experiences to personal and professional growth.

2. THEORETICAL FRAMEWORK

In today's Security and Defence environment, there is a need to integrate specialized training and expertise with modern equipment (Wozniak, 2021). In an international view, several programs and funds have been directed towards this sector. It is possible to highlight the Digital Education Action Plan 2021-27 (UE, 2020), and the DEEP (Defence Education Enhancement Programme), proposed by NATO (NATO, 2021). Moreover nowadays, military actions are insufficient if performed alone. The environment wherein resolutive actions are concluded is complex and demands a comprehensive approach with adaptability to all changes occurring. Civil-Military cooperation is vital for the management of complex situations, which should be led efficiently and effectively. The scope is to enable the military to achieve the desired end state with synchronization and coordination of activity amid all sectors of interest, thus merging military operations with political issues. This engagement is oriented to support working relationships among all the actors. Depending on the type of engagement, the levels of interaction range from coexistence to cooperation (CCOE, 2023).

To achieve this result, it is necessary to educate and develop skills that facilitate the civil-military cooperation starting from higher education training. International learning experiences that involve civilian and military students in collaborative learning activities are the vital ingredient to create the above-mentioned skills. Specific forms of training should be the base on which the skills' background and practical knowledge are created (Adler and Pouliot, 2011) (Daniel and Wittichova, 2020). In this scenario of different laboratories, collaborative learning plays a key role, which is much more important than the competitive learning environment (Wilson and Wilson, 2019). In the 20th century, collaboration was the main strategy used to cope with problems. Today's challenges require thinking and working together on issues of critical concern that have spread out (Welch, 1998) shifting the emphasis from individual efforts to workgroup (Leonard and Leonard, 2001). Collaborative learning is an educational approach to teaching and learning in which groups of learners work together to solve a problem and complete a task (Laal, 2012).

In this theoretical framework, the DIGICODE International School represents a valuable laboratory for the development of skills for future generations of leaders and people specialized in the field of cooperation. During the school, group activities were carried out online and in presence, using a digital learning environment. They were asked to solve problems together, civilian and military students, and to discuss the solutions. Teachers played the role of facilitators. The problems were related to logistics in an interdisciplinary scenario.

3. RESEARCH METHODOLOGY

The paper discusses the research on the topic of collaborative learning through a full immersion activity in a civil-military cooperation environment. In particular, the research question is the following:

How to develop skills of civil-military cooperation in an international environment during basic training and education?

In order to answer this question, data were collected through the administration of a survey to the military and civilian students attending the DIGICODE international school in Turin, at the IT-Army Education and Training Command and School of Applied Military Studies, ETC&SAMS. At the end of the week in presence, each group was also supposed to make a SWOT analysis about the experience done. The sample analyzed is composed of 28 students of mixed origin, 12 of whom are civilian students of the Interdepartmental University School for Strategic Sciences, SUISS, of University of Turin. The remaining 16 students are 7 Italian and 9 international military students. The group of 9 international students consists of 2 Romanians, 2 Polish, 2 Bulgarians, 1 Montenegrin, and 2 US officers, with 16 men and 12 women. During the activities, the students were divided into 7 mixed groups each of them including at least one international, one military, and one civilian part. During the different group activities, a participating observation was conducted in order to note and record any details that might be relevant in the context of civil-military cooperation.

4. THE INTERNATIONAL SCHOOL DIGICODE

The DIGICODE project is implemented within the EU strategy to improve the quality of education in the field of Security and Defence through the use of digital education (Marchisio et al., 2023b). It involves several countries such as Bulgaria, Italy, Poland and Romania (Marchisio et al., 2023a). The project aims to promote the effective use of digital tools for teaching in a military context. It is also in line with the idea of strengthening European higher education in the field of Security and Defence through the internationalization programs

(Marchisio and Spinello, 2021) carried out by the Implementation Group of the European Security and Defence College and all European partners providing education and training to young officers).

One of the DIGICODE project results was to study the digital competencies of teachers and students both before and during the COVID-19 pandemic. To achieve this, we conducted two surveys among teachers and students, which assessed various aspects including engagement, communication, development of digital competencies, and achievement of learning outcomes (Marchisio et al., 2022). In the project, four Learning, Teaching, and Training Activities, LTTAs, were organized. The first LTTA was held in Warsaw: in this event, teachers shared their didactic practices and exchanged opinions on the teacher toolkit, which was useful for the second LTTA in Bucharest, for 10 selected international students. The third was again for teachers, in Shumen, and the last is the international school for students in Turin at ETC&SAMS. During this event, a survey was carried out in the field and the data was used for this research.

The topic of the DIGICODE school was "Systems for Command and Control in Security and Defence Field", which involved different disciplines. In order to develop not only disciplinary competencies but also civil-military cooperation skills, the school was organized in the following way. Before teachers and students had an online phase in a digital learning environment integrated with several tools such as an advanced computing environment, an automatic assessment system, a web conference tool, a forum, which allowed to the participants to meet, to work in groups, to share materials, do ask doubts to a tutor, to exchange ideas in an asynchronous way using the forum and to fill the gaps in the prerequisites. These online meetings were important because they allowed the participants to get to know each other and to understand the activities they were supposed to do also during the face-to-face phase. During the school in Turin, the participants were divided into groups to solve problems related to command and control systems and to present and discuss their solutions with the other groups. The teachers involved were from the military academies and universities involved in the project. They played the role of facilitators. Interdisciplinary competence approach, collaborative learning, formative assessment, peer evaluation, discussions on case studies were the key methodologies adopted.

5. RESULTS

Very interesting is the data collected through the SWOT, Strengths, Weaknesses, Opportunities, Threats, analysis, done by each group. This kind of analysis is widely used because in the military field, in particular in activities of civil-military cooperation, the output is a comprehensive situational awareness, which can be used to understand where it is possible to intervene for improving the current situation or to avoid failing to make some decisions. Once the limits have been pointed out, it is possible to find a strategy to overcome them. Once the strengths have been highlighted, it is easier to strengthen more. This analysis assesses the needs, internal resources and external factors in order to choose the best operational strategy. Each team of the DIGICODE international school was asked to reflect on civil-military cooperation during the group activities carried out in the school, on how it helped them in collaborative learning to solve the various problems in the interdisciplinary scenario. The answers are collected in Table 1.

Table 1. Collection of the SWOT Analysis groups' answers

STRENGTHS	WEAKNESSES
Different perspectives Confrontation and Wide points of view (x2) Different problem-solving methods Various backgrounds with a lot of knowledge (x2) Efficiency, deep cooperation, and Interchangeability	Difficulty in integrating both sides Lack of knowledge and understanding of two worlds (x3) Different approaches and mentality Different levels of knowledge Too many background differences
OPPORTUNITIES	**THREATS**
Exchange of opinions and ideas (x2) Mutual interaction (x3) and collaborative learning Improvement of communication skills Sharing experience and knowledge	Common ground in certain things Different dimensions in the cooperation Difficulties in finding a common solution Failing to find a common ground on certain issues

Students perceive the civil-military cooperation implemented in collaborative activities as a point of strength and enrichment and they see opportunities for such collaboration during learning activities. Difficulties in integration also emerge, mainly due to the lack of a common background or, in some cases, different levels of preparation. In the comments, words such as “sharing”, “wide”, “great”, and “expand” recur, all phrases that indicate large spaces that can be filled together. Analyzing the use of words in answers, the idea of the strengths of civil-military cooperation is to go further, to expand one's boundaries of knowledge and learning. The added value of the civil-military cooperation in interdisciplinary activities that require soft skills like problem solving was evidenced, putting the stress on the fact that different backgrounds and different perspectives of civilian and military students helped achieve a deeper collaboration. Civil-military cooperation represents an opportunity for exchanging ideas and opinions, which has an impact on continuous and mutual learning. It is also an opportunity to increase communication skills, and to enrich the way of reasoning and of dealing with a problem. On the contrary, the weaknesses show a constant presence of the word "different", indicating the different levels of knowledge and approaches, which in some cases act as a barrier to integration between civilian and military students. Therefore, mitigating actions need to be implemented to bridge these differences and turn them into strengths. Having different backgrounds and approaches is first and foremost a strength for the environment in which this dimension of civil-military cooperation is created; however, it can become a weakness if not properly considered.

During the SWOT activities, the authors collected some interesting considerations expressed during the collection of feedback, in particular the usefulness of the group activities that allowed the students to distribute the work in an efficient way, and the remark that the competencies were complementary and useful to learning new technical and practical concepts. This shows how military and civilian students in problem-solving activities were able to immediately share and recognize the different skills they had due to their different university paths, thus being able to organize and complete the required tasks in the shortest possible time. In addition, the internationalization of the school allowed students to see and face the tasks in a better way because of the different cultural points of view.

Another group pointed out that, for civilians, the collaboration with military personnel was an added value thanks to the specialized and professional knowledge acquired. For the military, instead, an added value was the level of human factor introduced by the civilian component rather than the professional level. It was also pointed out that in both small classes and groups it is easier to “break the ice” and find common inputs and interests.

The following are some of the points that emerged during the discussion also on how to increase the strengths, deal with the weaknesses, seize the opportunities, and reduce the threats : 1) make more use of gamification in the activities for civilians and officers to increase motivation; 2) make introductory courses and drills for civilians to better understand the military world; 3) the English level has to be similar for everyone in the group; 4) consolidate a common ground of knowledge; 5) clearly state the objective and the outcomes to be achieved; 6) teachers must monitor the students' progress to make sure they are going in the right direction.

6. CONCLUSION

In this paper, we have tried to answer the research question *How to develop skills of civil-military cooperation in an international environment during basic training and education*? In order to do this, we used the experience of the DIGICODE International School. Thanks to the qualitative analysis made on the data collected throughout the school we can say that it is possible to develop skills of civil-military cooperation in an international environment during the basic training and education at Higher Education. Thanks to a full immersion, the students had the opportunity to develop new competencies, to acquire knowledge on different topics, and improve and master skills and abilities that they had only studied and never experienced.

The international school DIGICODE has proven to be an excellent laboratory where civilian and military students, researchers, teachers and military personnel can experience these training and learning activities: namely, it is an international occasion where young officers, future generations of leaders, and civilian personnel learn how to cooperate and gain new capabilities and skills. The students' comments are also a good indication of how being catapulted into a hostile and hard environment, albeit without any real risk, gives them the opportunity to test themselves and develop those extrinsic and intrinsic motivations, that drive the learning process.

Finally, it is very important to organize training activities to develop skills of civil-military cooperation during the basic training and education at Higher Education. It is essential to pay attention to the teaching methodologies adopted and to keep them up to date, for example in the next future we will have to deal with new tools such as gamification or those provided by generative artificial intelligence. It is equally important to carefully design the activities to be carried out, to clearly illustrate the learning outcomes to be achieved and to enable military and civilian students to work together, for example to acquire linguistic and disciplinary skills at the same level.

ACKNOWLEDGEMENT

The research activity described in this paper has been carried out within the Erasmus+ Key Action 2 Strategic Partnership N. 2020-1-PL01-KA226-096192 "Digital Competences for Improving Security and Defence Education – DIGICODE".

REFERENCES

Adler, E. and Pouliot, V., 2011. International Practices: Introduction and Framework. *Cambridge University Press*, Cambridge, United Kingdom, pp. 3–35.

CCOE, 2023. *CIMIC Handbook.* Civil-Military Cooperation Centre of Excellence, USA.

Daniel, J. and Wittichova M., 2020. Forging Civil-Military Cooperation: Domestic and International Laboratories of CIMIC Knowledge and Practice. *Journal of Intervention and Statebuilding*, Vol. 14, No 5, pp. 596-614. https://doi.org/10.1080/17502977.2020.1812962.

Laal, M. and Laal, M., 2012. Collaborative Learning: What is it? *SciVerse ScienceDirect Procedia, Social and Behavioral Sciences*, Vol. 31, pp. 491-495. https://doi.org/10.1016/j.sbspro.2011.12.092.

Leonard, P.E. and Leonard, L.J. 2001. The collaborative prescription: Remedy or reverie? *International Journal of Leadership in Education*, Vol. 4, No 4; pp. 383–399. https://doi.org/10.1080/13603120110078016.

Marchisio, M. and Spinello, E., 2021. Internationalization for enhancing the European Security and Defence higher education. *Proceedings of the 15thInternational Scientific Conference e-Learning (EL 2021),* pp. 99-106. https://doi.org/10.33965/el2021_202104l011.

Marchisio, M. et al, 2022. Teachers' digital competences before and during the COVID-19 pandemic for the improvement of Security and Defence higher education. *Proceedings* of *16th International Conference on e-Learning (EL2022) – Held at the 16th Multi-Conference on Computer Science and Information Systems (MCCSIS2022)*, pp. 68-75.

Marchisio, M., et al., 2023a. EU Security and Defence Students' Perception and Use of Digital Competencies in Higher Education, *Proceedings of the Multi Conference on Computer Science and Information Systems (ELDL 2023)*, pp. 35-42.

Marchisio, M., et al., 2023b. Students' digital competencies in remote and online higher Education in the Security and Defence field. *Proceedings of the European Distance and E-Learning network (EDEN2023).* In press.

NATO, 2021. *Defence Education Enhancement Program - Strategy for distance learning support.* Brussels, Belgium.

UE, 2020. *Digital Education Action Plan.* https://education.ec.europa.eu/document/digital-education-action-plan.

Welch, M., 1998. Collaboration: Staying on the bandwagon. *Journal of Teacher Education*; Vol. 49, No 1, pp. 26–38.

Wilson, K.F. and Wilson, K., 2019. Collaborate to graduate: what works and why? *Higher Education Research & Development,* Vol. 38, No 7, pp. 1504-1518. https://doi.org/10.1080/07294360.2019.1660311.

Wozniak, R.P., 2021. Distance learning in the training of military professionals in the age of the COVID-19 pandemic. *Scientific Journal of the Military University of Land Forces,* Vol. 53, No. 3(201), pp. 602-613.

THE EFFECTS OF LEARNING ANALYTICS-BASED FEEDBACK ON KNOWLEDGE ACQUISITION: THE ROLE OF FEEDBACK LITERACY

Mustafa Tepgeç[1], Joana Heil[1] and Dirk Ifenthaler[1,2]
[1]*University of Mannheim, Mannheim, Germany*
[2]*Curtin University, Australia*

ABSTRACT

This study investigated the impact of different learning analytics (LA)-based feedback conditions on learners' development of declarative and conditional knowledge, as well as the moderating role of feedback literacy (FL) in these relationships. A total of $N = 95$ students enrolled in an Economic and Business Education program at a European University participated in the study. The participants were randomly assigned to one of three groups: (1) process feedback and reviewing exemplars related to cases (PF1), (2) process feedback only (PF2), or (3) outcome feedback (OF). The participants completed a pre-test and post-test on declarative and conditional knowledge, as well as a questionnaire measuring their FL. The results showed that there were no significant differences in learners' progress on declarative knowledge tests among learners in various feedback conditions. However, the results showed that learners in the PF1 and PF2 groups showed a significantly greater mean difference in knowledge transfer performance compared to the OF group. The findings also showed that FL moderated the relationship between feedback conditions and an increase in knowledge transfer test performances.

KEYWORDS

Learning Analytics, Feedback, Knowledge Transfer, Feedback Literacy

1. INTRODUCTION

Learning analytics (LA) is a growing and important aspect in the development and use of digital learning environments (Ifenthaler & Widanapathirana, 2014). LA use both static as well as dynamic data about learners and their environment for analysis and visualization, to inform and support learning processes and environments (Ifenthaler, 2015). In order to make full use of the potential of LA, Clow (2012) described interventions as an essential part of the LA-process to support learners and facilitate further learning through the provision of LA-based feedback. Research shows that learners tend to perceive LA-based feedback positively, increase their motivation, and actively engage with feedback (Lim et al., 2021). A distinction is made between process feedback (PF) and outcome feedback (OF) (Butler & Winne, 1995). PF is a type of feedback given to learners about their performance during the learning process, whereas OF focuses on feedback after the processes have been completed. Previous research has shown that PF has a positive effect on knowledge transfer (Lim et al., 2021b). Furthermore, learners' ability to make use of feedback is dependent on their level of feedback literacy (FL). Aspects of FL in learners are shown as their appreciation of feedback, their ability to make judgments, and manage affect as well as taking actions upon the given feedback (Carless & Boud, 2018). In bringing these two aspects of feedback together, the extent to which different LA-based feedback conditions can impact learning, and how FL can moderate these impacts, remains an open question. Therefore, the aim of the study is to investigate the impact of different LA-based feedback conditions (PF, OF) on learners' development of declarative and conditional knowledge as well as the moderating role of FL in these relationships. Specifically, we focused on four hypotheses as follows: (1) we assume that there are differences in learners' progress on (declarative) knowledge tests among learners in various feedback conditions (Hypothesis 1). (2) We assume that there are differences in learners' progress on knowledge transfer (conditional) tests among learners in various feedback conditions (Hypothesis 2). (3) We assume that feedback literacy moderates the impact of different feedback conditions on learners' progress on knowledge (declarative) tests (Hypothesis 3). (4) We assume that feedback literacy moderates the impact of different feedback conditions on learners' progress on knowledge transfer (conditional) tests (Hypothesis 4).

2. METHOD

A total of $N = 95$ students took part in the experiment. All of them were enrolled in the Economic and Business Education program at a European University. The study was conducted in a supervised laboratory environment. The participants were asked to use a provided computer and interact with an instance of ILIAS which is a learning management system implemented by the university. On the platform, instructors can provide students with materials and use elements such as tests, forums, and videos. On the specific system, a LA application, Learning Analytics Profiles (LeAP), was installed. LeAP allows for progress feedback in the form of dashboards, to visualize the individual progress of the learners. They also have the option to rate materials by the wish for feedback and the grade of difficulty on a scale of one to three. The instructor has insights into the group's progress as well as the feedback on the materials. Furthermore, the application also includes a prompting feature (Schumacher & Ifenthaler, 2021). Instructors can send feedback to students in the form of prompts. These can be carried out manually by the instructors or triggered automatically through the system. Participants were asked to engage with the digital learning environment and to perform predefined tasks. These tasks included filling in questionnaires, completing tests, studying learning materials, and solving cases about instructional problems. The participants were separated into three groups: Group 1 (n=37) received LA-based process feedback and reviewed exemplars related to cases as a FL practice (PF1), Group 2 (n=32) received solely process feedback (PF2) and Group 3 (n=26) received outcome feedback (OF).

The quasi-experiment process consisted of eight phases and a single session lasted 120 minutes. In the first and last phase, a 10-item achievement test developed by the researchers was conducted, and in the first phase, the FL scale developed by Zhan (2022) was also conducted. In the second, fifth and seventh phases, solutions to hypothetical teaching problems were expected to be developed. They were asked to justify their ideas by supporting them with appropriate teaching methods and strategies. In the third phase, they were given instructional materials that provided information about teaching methods and strategies. In the fourth and sixth phases, Group 1 was given exemplars related to cases, while Groups 2 and 3 were given non-related reading materials (cooking and gardening). After each phase, Group 1 and Group 2 received PF prompts, while Group 3 received OF at the end.

3. FINDINGS

Hypothesis 1 assumes that there are differences in learners' progress on (declarative) knowledge tests among learners in various feedback conditions.

ANOVA was conducted to examine differences in the increase in knowledge test performance between pre-test and post-test scores across different experimental groups. The within-subjects factor was time (pre-test vs. post-test), and the between-subjects factor was feedback conditions (PF1, PF2, OF). There was a significant main effect of time, F (1, 92) = 68.129, $p < .05$, $\eta^2 = .425$, indicating an overall increase in performance from the pre-test to the post-test. However, the main effect of the feedback conditions was not significant, F (2, 92) = 1.889, $p > .05$, $\eta^2 = .039$. The interaction effect was also not significant, F (2, 92) = 1.889, $p > .05$, $\eta^2 = .039$, suggesting that the change in performance from pre-test to post-test did not differ significantly across experimental groups. In contrast to Hypothesis 1, the results suggest that there were no significant differences in learners' progress on (declarative) knowledge tests among learners in various feedback conditions, as indicated by the non-significant interaction effect.

Hypothesis 2 assumes that there are differences in learners' progress on (conditional) knowledge transfer tests among learners in various feedback conditions.

ANOVA was conducted to examine the differences in the increase in knowledge transfer performance between First Case and Final Case performance scores across different experimental groups. The within-subjects factor was time (First Case score vs. Final Case score), and the between-subjects factor was feedback conditions (PF1, PF2, OF). There was a significant main effect of time, F (1, 92) = 22.094, $p < .05$, $\eta^2 = .104$, indicating an overall increase in knowledge transfer performance from First Case to Final Case. However, the main effect of feedback conditions was not significant, F (2, 92) = .060, $p > .05$, $\eta^2 = .001$. The interaction effect was significant, F (2, 92) = 3.283, $p < .05$, $\eta^2 = .067$, suggesting that the change in transfer performance from First Case to Final Case differed significantly across experimental groups. To further explore the significant interaction effect, we conducted post-hoc pairwise comparisons using the Tukey test. The results indicated that both Group 1 and Group 2 showed a significantly greater mean difference in knowledge transfer performance compared to Group 3, $p < .05$, with Group 1 having a mean difference of $M = 1.689$ ($SD = 2.454$), with Group 2 having a mean difference of $M = 1.609$ ($SD = 2.509$) and with Group 3 having a mean difference of $M = 0.231$ ($SD = 2.472$) between First Case and Final Case scores. In conclusion, our findings suggest that the change in test performance differed significantly across the three experimental groups, with Group 1 and Group 2 showing a greater improvement compared to Group 3. Specifically, the improvement in test performance was significantly higher in Group 1 and Group 2 compared to Group 3, as evidenced by the significant mean difference in pre-test and post-test scores. Hence, hypothesis 2, which suggests differences in learners' progress on (conditional) knowledge transfer tests among various feedback conditions, has been supported.

Hypothesis 3 assumes that feedback literacy moderates the impact of different feedback conditions on learners' progress on (declarative) knowledge tests.

A moderation analysis was conducted to examine the effect of FL, as a moderator variable on the relationship between feedback conditions and an increase in knowledge test performances. However, the results did not show a significant interaction effect between feedback conditions and FL on increase in knowledge test performances, $\beta = .18$, $F(1, 91) = 1.08$, $p > .05$. Therefore, the hypothesis that FL moderates the relationship between feedback conditions and increase in knowledge test performances was not supported.

Hypothesis 4 assumes that feedback literacy moderates the impact of different feedback conditions on learners' progress on (conditional) knowledge transfer tests.

A moderation analysis was conducted to examine the effect of FL as a moderator variable on the relationship between feedback conditions and increase in knowledge transfer test performances. The results showed a significant interaction effect, $\beta = -0.058$, $t(1, 91) = -2.576$, $p < .05$. This indicates that the relationship between feedback conditions and an increase in knowledge transfer tests is moderated by FL. Simple slope analysis revealed that the relationship between feedback conditions and increase in knowledge transfer test was significant for participants with moderate FL, $t = -3.375$, $p < .05$ and high FL, $t = -4.298$, $p < .05$, but not for those with low FL, $t = .668$, $p > .05$. Overall, these results suggest that FL moderates the relationship between feedback conditions and increase in knowledge transfer test performances, such that the effect of feedback conditions on increase in knowledge transfer test performances is stronger for individuals with moderate and high FL compared to those with low FL.

4. DISCUSSION

The objective of the study was to examine how la-based feedback affects learners' development of declarative and conditional knowledge. The first hypothesis predicted that there would be differences in learners' progress on knowledge tests depending on the feedback they received, while the second hypothesis predicted differences in progress on knowledge transfer tests. The study found that the first hypothesis was not supported, but the second hypothesis was supported.

The results were unexpected because previous research has shown that la-based PF can be effective in enhancing learning performance (Lim et al., 2021). However, this study suggests that different feedback conditions may not be significant in promoting progress on declarative knowledge tests. One possible explanation for this finding could be the nature of the feedback provided. In this study, the feedback presented through the LeAP dashboard provided insights into the participants' interaction with the learning materials during the experimentation process, while the automated feedback included suggestions for improving the case study solutions. Further research could explore the specific features of la-based feedback that are most effective in promoting learners' progress on declarative knowledge.

In contrast, the finding that there were significant differences in learners' progress on conditional knowledge tasks among different feedback conditions supports Hypothesis 2. Specifically, learners who received la-based PF showed greater improvement in knowledge transfer performance compared to learners who received OF. This finding is consistent with previous research that has shown that PF can promote learners' transfer of knowledge to new situations (Paulson Gjerde et al., 2017; Lim et al., 2021). Although FL training is considered essential for enhancing feedback utilization (Carless & Boud, 2018), the study did not observe any effect of such training on the groups that received PF. However, the benefits of FL training may take time to manifest. Therefore, future research could investigate how FL training activities influence the extent to which learners benefit from la-based feedback over an extended period. In this study, analyzing exemplar tasks is presented as a FL training activity. These effects can be observed in subsequent studies with peer feedback, another recommended method for FL development (Carless & Boud, 2018).

In addition, the present study examined whether FL moderates the effects of different feedback conditions. The results showed that FL did not moderate the effects of different feedback conditions on learners' progress on knowledge tests, which did not support Hypothesis 3. However, the results did support Hypothesis 4, which suggests that FL moderates the effects of different feedback conditions on learners' progress on knowledge transfer tests. The relationship between feedback conditions and an increase in knowledge transfer test performances was stronger for individuals with moderate and high FL compared to those with low FL. These findings have important implications for the design and implementation of feedback interventions in educational settings. The results suggest that PF with FL training or PF alone may be more effective in promoting knowledge transfer compared to OF alone. Additionally, the results highlight the importance of considering learners' FL levels when designing feedback interventions, as learners with higher levels of FL may benefit more from feedback interventions than those with lower levels of FL.

5. CONCLUSION

The study aimed to investigate the effects of different feedback conditions on learners' progress on knowledge (declarative) tests and knowledge transfer (conditional) tests, as well as the moderating role of FL in these relationships. The results indicated that the feedback conditions did not have a significant main effect on knowledge test performance, but there was an overall increase in performance from the pre-test to the post-test. However, the feedback conditions did have a significant interaction effect on knowledge transfer performance, with Group 1 and Group 2 showing a greater improvement compared to Group 3. FL was found to moderate the relationship between feedback conditions and an increase in knowledge transfer test performances, with the effect of feedback conditions on an increase in knowledge transfer test performances being stronger for individuals with moderate and high FL compared to those with low FL.

ACKNOWLEDGEMENT

This study is funded by The Scientific and Technological Research Council of Türkiye (TÜBİTAK) 2214/A International doctoral research fellowship program.

REFERENCES

Butler, D. L., & Winne, P. H. (1995). Feedback and self-regulated learning: A theoretical synthesis. *Review of Educational Research,* 65(3), 245–281.

Carless, D., & Boud, D. (2018). The development of student feedback literacy: enabling uptake of feedback. *Assessment & Evaluation in Higher Education*, *43*(8), 1315-1325.

Clow, D. (2012). The learning analytics cycle: closing the loop effectively. *Proceedings of the 2nd international conference on learning analytics and knowledge* (pp. 134-138).

Ifenthaler, D. (2015). Learning analytics. In J. M. Spector (Ed.), *The SAGE encyclopedia of educational technology* (Vol. 2, pp. 448–451). Sage. https://doi.org/10.4135/9781483346397.n187

Ifenthaler, D., & Widanapathirana, C. (2014). Development and validation of a learning analytics framework: Two case studies using support vector machines. *Technology, Knowledge and Learning*, *19*(1–2), 221–240. https://doi.org/10.1007/s10758-014-9226-4

Lim, L. A., Gentili, S., Pardo, A., Kovanović, V., Whitelock-Wainwright, A., Gašević, D., & Dawson, S. (2021). What changes, and for whom? A study of the impact of learning analytics-based process feedback in a large course. *Learning and Instruction*, *72*, 101202.

Paulson Gjerde, K., Padgett, M. Y., & Skinner, D. (2017). The impact of process vs. outcome feedback on student performance and perceptions. *Journal of Learning in Higher Education, 13*(1), 73–82.

Schumacher, C., & Ifenthaler, D. (2021). Investigating prompts for supporting students' self-regulation – A remaining challenge for learning analytics approaches? *The Internet and Higher Education*, *49*, 100791. https://doi.org/10.1016/j.iheduc.2020.100791

Zhan, Y. (2022). Developing and validating a student feedback literacy scale. *Assessment & Evaluation in Higher Education, 47*(7), 1087-1100. https://doi.org/10.1080/02602938.2021.2001430

PROMOTING SOCIO-EMOTIONAL LEARNING WITH A VIRTUAL ROBOT FACILITATOR OF SMALL GROUP DISCUSSIONS: A CROSS-CULTURAL STUDY

Goren Gordon[1*], Laura Di Giunta,[2] Chiara Riccioni[2], Clementina Comitale[2], Giulia Gliozzo[2] and Carolina Lunetti[3]
[1]Curiosity Lab, Department of Industrial Engineering, Tel-Aviv University, Israel
[2]Psychology Department, Sapienza University of Rome, Italy
[3]Guglielmo Marconi University, Rome, Italy

ABSTRACT

In this contribution, we present continued work-in-progress on an innovative system for facilitating small-group online discussions using an avatar during a video conference. Previous studies have shown that the system had an effective, understandable, and more participatory interaction that is sustained during a long-term interaction. Here, we examine long-term, cross-cultural effects on socio-emotional learning (SEL) for 5th and 6th graders in Israel and 3rd,4th, 5th graders in Italy. Eight elaborate activities were designed specifically for this setup to promote SEL in an engaging and collaborative way. Pre- and post-questionnaires regarding SEL were administered to the students, as well as semi-structured interviews. The results of the study show mixed trends, where in the Israel sample students reported a (non-significant) beneficial effect of the activities on their mindset and behavior, while in the Italian sample a different (non-significant) trend was observed. Qualitative analysis of semi-structured interviews after the activities show that children had a noticeable change in their perception of SEL as well as their behaviors. Despite these mixed results, this work-in-progress continues to support the usage of the virtual robot facilitator of small group activities as an effective teaching assistant for school children, even in soft-skills such as socio-emotional learning domains.

KEYWORDS

Virtual Agent, Group Activity, Video Conference, Facilitation

1. INTRODUCTION

Prior to the COVID-19 pandemic, online learning environments for K-12 have not been a mainstream methodology. However, the pandemic has revealed the importance, as well as the advantages and drawbacks of video conferencing technologies, as well as other social educational technologies. Moreover, the pandemic had a drastic negative effect on children's socio-emotional skills (Bayley et al., 2023).

We report the continued evaluation of a system, that aims to facilitate small online group discussions during video conferencing (Mizrahi et al., 2022a), with a new focus on socio-emotional learning (SEL). Students interacted with the system, which consists of: (i) an avatar, a virtual agent, who manages the educational group activity as well as facilitates the online discussion; (ii) Zoom, and (iii) a screen for the educational content, which is produced on an activity site designed for that purpose.

Previous studies found the system to be effective for discussions and engagement in group activities (Mizrahi et al., 2022a) as well as maintain these effects over a long period of time (Mizrahi et al., 2022b). In this new report, we evaluated the effect of a long-term use of the system on children's socio-emotional learning in a cross-cultural study.

In the study, four groups in Israel (three in 5th and one in 6th grade) and twenty groups in Italy (six in 3rd, eight in 4th grade and six in 5th grade) interacted with the system, performing eight carefully tailored activities promoting socio-emotional learning. All the activities were performed with the avatar facilitation.

*Corresponding author: goren@gorengordon.com

Questionnaires regarding SEL were conducted before and after the activities. We also conducted semi-structured interviews with children after the activities.

Our results reaffirm that the long-term use of the system does not suffer from the novelty effect (Mizrahi et al., 2022b), and show mixed (non-significant) trends wherein SEL was improved for some of the children. Results suggest that there is no significant cross-cultural difference in usage and engagement, suggesting that the system can be used in a wide range of locations, but that future studies are needed to solicit site-specific hypotheses and explanations.

This work-in-progress continues to support the concept of a virtual robot facilitator for long-term use in small group online discussions, with an emphasis on promotion of socio-emotional learning.

2. RELATED WORK

Small group learning activities have been considered as a promising education format (Johnson & Johnson, 2009). Small-group activities can enhance student thinking and learning of both formal and informal content and skills, (Hadwin et al. 2018; Webb, 1995).

Studies have shown that personal face-to-face interactions and discussions in small groups have their advantages (Thomas & Thorpe, 2019), also in online settings (Love & Simpson, 2005). The question of scaling-up group facilitation is, thus, of prominent importance. In group activities, the role of group facilitator is important in facilitating learning-related processes (Franco & Nielsen, 2018). This is because when students have a supportive environment it will foster both the understanding of the content learned, the task value, and positive beliefs about the students' abilities and thus their motivation to learn (Pietarinen et al., 2021).

The appearance of virtual visual agents, avatars, has also initiated a wider usage of conversational and social aspects of interaction. While a face of a conversational agent has been shown to increase rapport and other participant-agent-related measures (Shamekhi et al., 2018), it remains an open question of what *educational benefits* such an avatar presents. Although guiding agents may have disadvantages, they have been found to have the ability to manage time better, to be more objective and efficient than a human facilitator (Rosenberg-Kima et al., 2020).

Extensive developmental research indicates that effective mastery of socio-emotional competencies is associated with greater well-being and better school performance, whereas the failure to achieve competence in these areas can lead to a variety of personal, social, and academic difficulties (Durlak et al., 2011; García-Poole et al., 2020). Promoting socio-emotional learning (SEL) refers to promoting adaptive emotion regulation skills (e.g., management of negative emotions, and expression and reinforcement of positive emotions), as well as perspective-taking, interpersonal communication skills, and responsible decision making. Interventions aimed to promote SEL have mostly focused on elementary school children (Holsen et al., 2008).

This study addresses the question of whether a long-term use of an online learning system with video conference guided by a social virtual agent can promote socio-emotional learning in school children.

3. METHODS

THE SYSTEM: The system is composed of a student-centered site, with which the students interact. The site includes: (a) a robotic avatar from SitePal.com (b) a frame with the Zoom web API, that enables gallery view to see all the group members and; (c) an interaction part, which shows the content and enables answering questions (see more details in Mizrahi et al. (2021)). The avatar was programmed with best practices of group facilitation behaviors. An expert group facilitator aided in formalizing the appropriate behaviors, e.g., how to give feedback and how to handle objections, which were then programmed into the avatar.

Figure 1. Examples of some of the vignettes showed to the children during the online activities in the platform

THE ACTIVITIES: The intervention included 8 online sessions focusing – in order – on: anger, sadness, hostile attribution bias, effortful control, positive emotions, empathy, responsible decision making, and a final session retracing the previous ones. The sessions were created following the guidance of the following previously-validated programs aimed at promoting children's SEL-related competences: CASEL (Collaborative for Academic, Social, and Emotional Learning) (CASEL, 2017); CEPIDEA (Promoting Prosocial and Emotional Skills to Counteract Externalizing Problems in Adolescence) (Caprara et al. 2014; 2015); The Coping Cat Program for Anxious Youth (Kendall et al., 2003); Keeping your cool - anger management program (Nelson et al., 2006); Stop & Think Social Skills Program (Knoff, 2001); The Promoting Alternative Thinking Strategies (PATHS) curriculum (Kusche & Greenberg, 1994). Thus, the sessions were inspired by the aforementioned programs, but adapted to be implemented online with small groups of children.

During each session, vignettes created by Laura Di Giunta based on some of the modules of the aforementioned validated protocols and illustrated by Miss Clementina Comitale (**Error! Reference source not found.**), was presented to groups of 3 to 5 children. Participants were asked to reflect and discuss about the story with the other members of the group. Sessions were moderated by the virtual robot who encouraged children to share their opinions about scenes that were presented.

PARTICIPANTS: The study was conducted on 5th and 6th grade students, in an elementary school in Israel, and in two elementary schools in Italy. Israel cohort: four groups, with 5th grade (4 boys, 7 girls), 6th grade (1 boy, 2 girls). Italy cohort: 20 groups, with 3rd grade (12 boys, 8 girls), 4th grade (14 boys, 18 girls), 5th grades (8 boys, 11 girls).

Given the novelty of the tool, meetings were held in the school in timeslots defined in accordance with teachers, to allow the team to monitor and manage any possible malfunctioning. Participants sat far from each other and in different rooms and wore noise-cancelling headphones to avoid distractions and to enable – as much as possible – interactions to occur through the platform only.

All participants' parents signed a consent form. The study was approved by the IRB in both countries and the ministry of education in Israel.

MEASURES: The study was a mixed-study design, with both quantitative and qualitative. Quantitative measures included child-reported pre-post questionnaires that were administered (Social Skill Improvement System SEL Brief, SSIS SELb, Elliott et al., 2020; Academic Self-Efficacy Scale, ASES; Bandura et al., 1996; Pastorelli et al., 2001). Qualitative results came from semi-structured interviews with the children after the activities.

4. RESULTS

SOCIO-EMOTIONAL LEARNING: We performed a repeated-measures analysis of variance, with gender and country as between-subject factors. There were no significant main effects for SSIS SELb and ASES. There was a significant interaction between gender for ASES ($F(78,1)=16.8$, $p<0.001$, Pillai's Trace, Boys: (Post-Pre): $M=-0.23$, $SD=0.11$, Girls: (Post-Pre): $M=0.15$, $SD=0.11$). Importantly, there were no significant effects or interaction with the sample location. We report the trends in the different questionnaires: Israeli sample: SSIS SELb ((Post-Pre): $M=0.10$, $SD=0.59$). Pre: $M=3.89$, $SD=0.59$. Post: $M=3.93$, $SD=0.75$); ASES ((Post-Pre): $M=0.13$, $SD=1.12$). Pre: $M=3.20$, $SD=1.08$. Post: $M=3.32$, $SD=0.84$). Italian sample: SSIS SELb

((Post-Pre): M=-0.06, SD=0.39). Pre: M=4.08, SD=0.43. Post: M=4.02, SD=0.53); ASES ((Post-Pre): M=-0.11, SD=0.62). Pre: M=3.83, SD=0.72. Post: M=3.72, SD=0.80).

QUALITATIVE ANALYSIS: We have conducted semi-structured interviews with the children after the interactions. After transcribing the interviews and aggregating them according to themes, we present the major results. When asked "what did you learn?" a common theme that emerged is how children learned to regulate their emotions ("I learned how to respond and how to moderate my reactions"), but also more general concepts ("it was like a new moral for life, go and help a person in need", "it tried to teach about life, if someone's sad, what to do about it"). When asked "did you change your behaviors?" a common theme was how to approach other people ("when I saw children sitting alone, I went and helped them", "I am more caring for my friends", "it changed my ability to talk and share with my friends").

One interesting theme that emerged, which has been reported with adults before (Rosenberg-Kima et al., 2020), is the children's ability to share more with the virtual robot than with a person ("It speaks one or two words and then we are the ones that talk", "A robot can yell. With a teacher they can yell sometimes." "I'd feel more comfortable with a robot than with you [the experimenter]").

Regarding long-term engagement, when asked "did you get tired after so many activities?", children replied with a negative ("it was fun to continue doing it. Even if it's the same concept", "I didn't get tired, it's fun to do these activities"). Almost all children commented that the activities themselves were fun ("I liked its jokes and storied, and I love the questions, they were intriguing", "It was fun doing these activities, you learn and have fun at the same time").

5. DISCUSSION AND CONCLUSION

This short paper introduces a work-in-progress on the evaluation of a novel system that facilitates small group on-line discussion using video conferencing and best practices. While previous work has demonstrated the viability of the platform, as well as its long-term engagement value, we focused more on the activities themselves and its cross-cultural implementation. Several important issues rose during the study.

First, preparing the activities was a large endeavor, which consolidated many known practices of promotion of SEL (Durlak et al., 2011) and adapting them into the virtual robotator format. Using vignettes was highly appreciated by the students, where we never once encountered children who did not understand the activity itself. Furthermore, promotion of SEL cannot be done with a single lesson, hence previous validation of the system as maintaining long-term engagement (Mizrahi et al., 2022b) was crucial for the development and utilization of eight full activities.

Second, while the size of the cohorts was relatively small, hence not enabling detection of any significant change in attitudes and beliefs, as measured by the pre-post questionnaires, we could see some trends that emerge with a beneficial direction in some of the measures in one of the two cultural contexts. The semi-structured interviews reflected both a change in attitudes, but, more importantly, a change in behavior. We have two hypotheses for the different trend of the results across cultures. The Israeli children were slightly older than the Italian ones, that may lead to the hypothesis that the activities might be more effective in late, rather than middle childhood. Second, in line with previous studies on inter-informant agreement (De Los Reyes & Kazdin, 2005), children may have over-evaluated their own socio-emotional competences in the pre-tests and may have increased their capacities to identify and evaluate their own socio-emotional competences in the post-tests, thanks to the activities they were involved in.

Thirdly, the post-activity interviews taught us about important aspects of the system, such as the fact that the virtual robot may be perceived as a better facilitator for such emotional sharing activities (Rosenberg-Kima et al., 2020). This is partly due to the fact of the unbiased attitude of the robot, as well as the nature of the activities, which encouraged children to share their experiences with others, with no judgement or comments from the facilitator itself.

Finally, the comparison between the two cultural studies showed no significant difference in participation and engagement, but in effects of the activities on SEL. Hence, it partly supports the generalization of the usage of the system in more cultures and a wider range of socio-economic status communities, but certainly needs further examination to soliciting site-specific hypothesis and explanations.

This study had several major limitations, most notably the continued technical difficulties due to low internet connection of the participants, the small number of participants, and the lack of a control group. Nevertheless, the results reaffirm the promise of the novel system as a long-term facilitator of more discussions and more socio-emotional learning in an environment that is becoming more prevalent in the formal educational system.

Future work aims to use the system at a national level, with dozens of schools participating in a large-scale study, sponsored by the Ministries of Education in multiple countries. Moreover, with the appearance of ChatGPT, future developments include introducing speech recognition that will greatly enhance the effectiveness of the discussions.

ACKNOWLEDGEMENT

This research was funded by the Jacobs Foundation, the Israeli Ministry of Education, Sapienza University of Rome, and the Italian Ministry of Education.

REFERENCES

Bandura, A., Barbaranelli, C., Caprara, G. V., & Pastorelli, C. (1996). Multifaceted impact of self-efficacy beliefs on academic functioning. Child development, 67(3), 1206-1222.

Bayley, S., Wole Meshesha, D., Rose, P., Woldehanna, T., Yorke, L., & Ramchandani, P. (2023). Ruptured school trajectories: understanding the impact of COVID-19 on school dropout, socio-emotional and academic learning using a longitudinal design. Longitudinal and Life Course Studies, 14(2), 203-239.

Caprara, G. V., Luengo Kanacri, B. P., Gerbino, M., Zuffiano, A., Alessandri, G., Vecchio, G., ... & Bridglall, B. (2014). Positive effects of promoting prosocial behavior in early adolescence: Evidence from a school-based intervention. International Journal of Behavioral Development, 38(4), 386-396.

Caprara, G. V., Luengo Kanacri, B. P., Zuffianò, A., Gerbino, M., & Pastorelli, C. (2015). Why and how to promote adolescents' prosocial behaviors: Direct, mediated and moderated effects of the CEPIDEA school-based program. Journal of youth and adolescence, 44, 2211-2229.

De Los Reyes, A., & Kazdin, A. E. (2005). Informant discrepancies in the assessment of childhood psychopathology: a critical review, theoretical framework, and recommendations for further study. Psychological bulletin, 131(4), 483.

Durlak, J. A., Weissberg, R. P., Dymnicki, A. B., Taylor, R. D., & Schellinger, K. B. (2011). The impact of enhancing students' social and emotional learning: A meta-analysis of school-based universal interventions. Child development, 82(1), 405-432.

Elliott, S., Anthpny, C.J., DiPerna, J.C., Lei, p.W., Gresham, F.M. (2020). SSIS SEL Brief Scale User Guide & Technical Manual. Multi-Informant Assessment of Students' Socal Emotional Learning Competences. SAIL CoLab.

Franco, L. A., & Nielsen, M. F. (2018, October). Examining Group Facilitation In Situ: The Use of Formulations in Facilitation Practice. Group Decision and Negotiation, 27 (5), 735–756.

Hadwin, A., J¨arvel¨a, S., & Miller, M. (2018). Self-regulation, co-regulation, and shared regulation in collaborative learning environments. In Handbook of selfregulation of learning and performance, 2nd ed (pp. 83–106). New York, NY, US: Routledge/Taylor & Francis Group.

Holsen, I., Smith, B. H., & Frey, K. S. (2008). Outcomes of the social competence program Second Step in Norwegian elementary schools. School Psychology International, 29(1), 71-88.

Johnson, D. W., & Johnson, R. T. (2009, June). An Educational Psychology Success Story: Social Interdependence Theory and Cooperative Learning:. Educational Researcher. (Publisher: SAGE Publications)

Kendall, P. C., Aschenbrand, S. G., & Hudson, J. L. (2003). Child-focused treatment of anxiety. Evidence-based psychotherapies for children and adolescents, 81-100.

Knoff, H.M. (2000). The stop and think social skills program for children and adolescents: Teaching effective interpersonal and self-management skills. (Preschool to early elementary, early elementary to middle elementary, middle to late elementary editions). Tampa, FL: Author.

García-Poole, C., Byrne, S. & Rodrigo, M. J. (2020): Improving adolescent lifestyles by promoting socioemotional competences in a community-based intervention programme, *European Journal of Developmental Psychology*, 17:6, 965-983.

Greenberg, M. T., & Kusché, C. A. (2006). Building social and emotional competence: The PATHS curriculum.

Love, K., & Simpson, A. (2005). Online discussion in schools: Towards a pedagogical framework. *International Journal of Educational Research*, 43(7-8), 446-463.

Mizrahi, E., Danzig, N., & Gordon, G. (2022a). Long-Term Interaction with a Virtual Robot Facilitator of Small Group Discussions. *International Association for Development of the Information Society*.

Mizrahi, E., Danzig, N., & Gordon, G. (2022b). vRobotator: A Virtual Robot Facilitator of Small Group Discussions for K-12. *Proc. ACM Hum.-Comput. Interact*, *6*, Article 472.

Nelson, W. M., Finch, A. J., & Ghee, A. C. (2006). Anger management with children and adolescents. Child and adolescent therapy: Cognitive-behavioral procedures, 114-159.

Pastorelli, C., Caprara, G. V., Barbaranelli, C., Rola, J., Rozsa, S., & Bandura, A. (2001). The structure of children's perceived self-efficacy: A cross-national study. European Journal of Psychological Assessment, 17(2), 87.

Pietarinen, T., Palonen, T., & Vauras, M. (2021, June). Guidance in computer supported collaborative inquiry learning: Capturing aspects of affect and teacher support in science classrooms. International Journal of Computer-Supported Collaborative Learning, 16 (2), 261–287. (Number: 2)

Rosenberg-Kima, R. B., Koren, Y., & Gordon, G. (2020, January). Robot-Supported Collaborative Learning (RSCL): Social Robots as Teaching Assistants for Higher Education Small Group Facilitation. Frontiers in Robotics and AI, 6, 148.

Shamekhi, A., Liao, Q. V., Wang, D., Bellamy, R. K. E., & Erickson, T. (2018, April). Face Value? Exploring the Effects of Embodiment for a Group Facilitation Agent. In Proceedings of the 2018 CHI Conference on Human Factors in Computing Systems (pp. 1–13). New York, NY, USA: Association for Computing Machinery.

Thomas, G., & Thorpe, S. (2019, January). Enhancing the facilitation of online groups in higher education: a review of the literature on face-to-face and online group-facilitation. Interactive Learning Environments, 27 (1), 62–71.

Webb, N. M. (1995). Learning in small groups. Interaction in Cooperative Groups: The Theoretical Anatomy of Group Learning, 102. (ISBN: 052148376X Publisher: Cambridge University Press).

USAGE OF AND ATTITUDES TOWARDS AI-TECHNOLOGY IN THE LEARNING PROCESSES OF FIRST-YEAR STUDENTS

Jan Delcker[1*], Joana Heil[1], Dirk Ifenthaler[2], Sabine Seufert[3] and Lukas Spirgi[3]
[1]*University of Mannheim, Germany*
[2]*University of Mannheim, Germany and Curtin University, Australia*
[3]*University of St: Gallen, Switzerland*

ABSTRACT

Artificial Intelligence (AI) has an increasing impact on human society. The advancements in machine learning, natural language processing and other fields of AI leads to the development of more and more complex algorithms. Machines are able to automatically fulfill tasks which have traditionally been the domain of humans. These machines, so called AI-robots, have lately found their way into education through the introduction of tools such as DeepL, Quillbot and lately ChatGPT. As of now, research on the influence of AI-tools on teaching and learning processes, but also the required competencies to work with those tools, has been scarce. The research work examines the usage of AI-tools and attitudes towards AI-tools of first-years students, considering two main types of AI-tools. These AI-tools can be distinguished as mindful and mindless robots, depending on their functionalities and capabilities. The results show that first-year students prefer mindless AI tools over more human like tools. Additionally, their attitude towards AI technology does not have statistically significant influence of their willingness to use AI technology.

KEYWORDS

Artifical Intelligence, Education Technology, AI Competence, AI-Robots

1. INTRODUCTION

The increasing interaction between humans and robots is a strong indicator for the rising influence of AI-technology on human life (Kim, 2022). Following the definition by Dang and Liu (2022), AI-robots are agents which are programmed to do jobs, which are traditionally done by humans. The programming of AI-robots is characterized by the usage of AI-methods and algorithms, which allows them to fulfill human-like task semi-automated or fully automated. While many machines are easily distinguishable from humans, AI-robots resemble humans due to their similarity in performance or appearance. As a result, humans tend to attribute AI-robots human-like mental capacities or understanding (Roessler at al., 2021). The pervasion of AI-technology in numerous sectors of human life leads to new and changing demands in humans' digital competencies, to enable them to successfully deal with these ongoing changes (Seufert et al., 2022). The European DigComp Framework 2.2 acknowledges the demand for changing digital competencies by integrating AI literacy into the existing DigComp Framework for digital competent citizens (Vuorikari et al., 2022). Within the framework, AI literacy is allocated to knowledge, proficiency and attitudes towards AI-technology. Research work on AI-robots in the field of higher education is scarce, especially because these tools are not widely available in higher education institutions (Kim, 2022; Lim et al., 2023). Currently, there are no conceptional frameworks in the context of human-like AI-technology. The presented research work attempts to close this research gap. Seven existing AI-tools have been conceptualized for their application in the context of higher education. This conceptualization is a helpful differentiation to analyze the intent and frequency of use, as well as ethical considerations towards those tools. The AI-tools can be allocated into two

*delcker@uni-mannheim.de

different types, which are categorized as <<mindful>> (AI-robots with increasingly human characteristics) and <<mindless>> (AI-robots with machine characteristics) (Dang & Liu, 2022).

Mindless AI-tools:

1) Translation text generators: The generation of written text is one of the main most common tasks for students. Oftentimes, student have to write text which is not written in their first language (Galante, 2020). Translation text generators can help with that task, as they are taking in written text and produce a translated version of that text as output. Two of the most prominent translation text generators are Google Translate and DeepL (Martín-Martín et al., 2021)

2) Summarizing/Rephrasing text generators:

Text generators like Quillbot (Fitria, 2021) use written text as input. They can change the structure of the text and generally be used in two ways. They can help to extract critical information, keywords or main concepts out of structured text. In doing so, they can reduce the complexity of the text. Students can then concentrate on the most important information within the text. Reducing text to it's core information can make it easier to understand complex models, frameworks and ideas. The summarization of text is an important learning strategy in the context of higher education (Mitsea & Drigas, 2019). Secondly, there text generators are able to rephrase text input. When students write research assignments, they have to include sources from existing research literature. Indirect citations through rephrasing parts of text is an import step for theoretical research work, as the ability to rephrase and restructure existing research literature is an import learning goals in higher education (Aksnes & Langfeldt, 2019).

3) Writing assistants:

If students want to improve the quality of written assignments, writing assistant prove to be an important tool. Automated, real-time grammar and spelling checks enable an easy inclusion into writing processes. They can give suggestions for alternative formulations to avoid colloquial language and unnecessary iterations. Word processors (e.g. Microsoft Word) often come with built-in writing assistatns, but standalone programs or extensions such as Grammaraly exist as well (Koltovskaia, 2020).

4) Text generators: These tools can be used to automatically generate written text. Text generators take short prompts as input and produce text based on this input. The output text is mostly used for blog entries, text-based social media posts or twitter messages. They can be differentiated from chatbots as they aren't able to produce more complex pieces of text. WriteSonic is a such a text generator tool (Almaraz-López, 2023).

Mindful AI-tools:

5) Chatbot: Chatbots can simulate human interactions (Chong, 2021), where the chatbot is one part of a conversation and a human is the other part. In the context of business, they can be used to automatically answer costumer questions, mainly as digital assistants on web pages (McLean et al., 2020). Chatbots can also help to guide learners through online environments and administrative processes within learning management systems or online classes. A new type of AI-based chatbot was created with ChatGPT. These chatbots are able to produce various outputs formats, including working algorithms, presentations or picture, based on prompts which are very similar to human interactions (Almarez-Lopez et al, 2023; Fauzi et al., 2023; Fuchs, 2023). The output of ChatGPT and similar chatbots can be used by students to generate content which is traditionally being used as part of instructional design, especially final assessments.

6) Virtual avatars: Virtual avatars are digital representations of living beings. They found their way into online classroom settings as representations of teachers and learners. Virtual representations, such as Synthesia, have shown to improve students' learning performance, compared to classes without virtual representation (Herbert & Dolzycka, 2022).

7) Social-humanoid robots: Social-humanoid robots are used as servers in restaurants, and are tested in medical and educational institutions as well (Henschel et al., 2021). These tools are able to do more than a mere simulation of human. In many cases social-humanoid robots are also build close to human complexity, featuring hands, legs and faces (van Pinxteren et al. 2019). They are able to perform human-like mimic to various degree and might be able to act as teachers in a classroom.

The so-called mindful AI-tools can perform more complex tasks, react to the prompts of the users in a more meaningful way and are designed to act and look like humans. The goal of this study is to identify students' usage of AI-tools in their learning processes, as well as the relationships between students' attitudes towards AI-technology and their usage of mindful and mindless AI-tools. Two hypotheses emerge from the theoretical considerations and the research questions.

Hypothesis 1:
Students with a more positive attitude towards AI technology use mindless AI-tools more frequently.

Hypothesis 2:
Students are more willing to use mindless AI-tools than mindful AI-tools.

2. METHOD

An online questionnaire was designed to collect data from first-year students at a German university and a Swiss university. The first part of the instrument comprises items which contain questions regarding knowledge, skills and attitudes regarding AI-technology (Vuorikari et al., 2022). The different AI-tools are presented in part 2 of the questionnaire. For each tool, current and intended usage was gathered, following the unified theory of acceptance and use of technology (UTAUT) (Venkatesh et al., 2003). In addition, ethical considerations for each tool were prompted (Vuorikari et al., 2022). The actual usage of the tools by the students was evaluated with a 6-point likert scale, their potential willingness to use them with the use of a 5-point likert scale.

In total, 638 first-year students participated in the survey. On average, they were 20.62 years old, with a standard deviation of 2.25 years. Out of the 638 students, 309 identified as male, 322 as female and 7 as non-binary. The lowest average usage of the mindless tools could be found in Paraphrasing and Summarizing Tools ($M = 1.13$, $SD = 1.51$). The usage of online writing assistants was slightly higher ($M = 1.94$, $SD = 1.76$), and the highest average usage could be found in online translation tools ($M = 3.53$, $SD = 1.18$). The overall average use of mindless tools was rather low ($M = 2.2$, $SD = 1.05$). The willingness to use the tools ranged from the lowest in virtual avatars ($M = 2.23$, $SD = 1.13$) to the highest in online translation tools ($M = 3.16$, $SD = 1.17$).

Hypothesis 1:
A linear regression was conducted to analyze the relation between students' attitudes towards AI and their usage of mindless AI-tools. Attitude did not significantly predict usage $\beta = .50$, $p = .15$. Attitude does not explain a significant proportion of the variance in AI-competence, $R^2 < .01$, $F(1,636) = 2.13$, $p = .15$.

Hypothesis 2:
A paired t-test was conducted to analyze the differences between students' willingness to choose mindless and mindful AI tools. Students were significantly more willing to choose mindless AI-tools ($M = 2.84$, $SD = .86$) than high-level tools ($M = 2.4$, $SD = .92$). $t(636) = 13.30$, $p < .001$. The effect size is $d = 0.5$, which can be interpreted as a medium effect.

3. CONCLUSION

The analyzed data provides insights into the actual usage and implementation of AI-tools in the learning process of students in their entry phase. So far, mindless AI-tools are favored by the participants compared to mindful tools. These mindless AI-tools provide useful functionalities regarding task which can be considered as typical for higher education programs, such as written papers, presentations, or reports (Flores et al.,2022; Medland, 2014). These functionalities include translations (DeepL) or summaries (QuillBot). The missing relationship between attitudes and usage of mindless AI-tools might indicate an absence in students' awareness about the kind of technology they are using. As a result, students who are generally reluctant towards AI-technology still incorporate it into their learning processes. A second explanation for the missing relationship might be rooted in students' fear of insufficient study performance. As AI-critical students undergo learning processes, their concern about the quality of their learning outcomes outweighs their attitude towards AI-tools. Both considerations are important factors for the future implementation of AI-tools in higher education. First, students need the competences to identify AI-tools and understand their basic functionalities. In return, these skills help them to assess the challenges and chances AI-tools can provide (Roesler et al., 2022, Seufert et al., 2022). The present discussion about ChatGPT and the influence of AI-tools in general on higher education underline the need to educate learners about AI and their respective AI-competencies (Almarez-Lopez et al, 2023; Fauzi et al., 2023; Fuchs, 2023). A second study is currently being conducted to analyze how the introduction of ChatGPT to the public sphere has changed students' attitudes towards AI and their usage of AI tools, both intended and factual. It can be assumed that the powerful tool leads to an increasing awareness towards AI, as well as a broad usage over different study programs and for different tasks within higher education programs.

REFERENCES

Aksnes, D. W. et al 2019. Citations, Citation Indicators, and Research Quality: An Overview of Basic Concepts and Theories. *SAGE Open*, *9*(1), 215824401982957. https://doi.org/10.1177/2158244019829575

Almaraz-López, C. et al (2023. Comparative Study of the Attitudes and Perceptions of University Students in Business Administration and Management and in Education toward Artificial Intelligence. *Education Sciences*, *13*(6), 609. https://doi.org/10.3390/educsci13060609

Chong, T. et al 2021. AI-chatbots on the services frontline addressing the challenges and opportunities of agency. *Journal of Retailing and Consumer Services*, *63*, 102735. https://doi.org/10.1016/j.jretconser.2021.102735

Dang, J., & Liu, L. 2022. Implicit theories of the human mind predict competitive and cooperative responses to AI robots. *Computers in Human Behavior*, *134*, 107300. https://doi.org/10.1016/j.chb.2022.107300

Fauzi, F., Tuhuteru, L., Sampe, F., Ausat, A. M. A., & Hatta, H. R. (2023). Analysing the Role of ChatGPT in Improving Student Productivity in Higher Education. *Journal on Education*, *5*(4), 14886–14891. https://doi.org/10.31004/joe.v5i4.2563

Fitria, T. N. 2021. QuillBot as an online tool: Students' alternative in paraphrasing and rewriting of English writing. *Englisia: Journal of Language, Education, and Humanities*, *9*(1), 183. https://doi.org/10.22373/ej.v9i1.10233

Flores, M.A. et al 2020.Portuguese university students' conceptions of assessment: taking responsibility for achievement. *High Educ* 79, 377–394 . https://doi.org/10.1007/s10734-019-00415-2

Fuchs, K. 2023. Exploring the opportunities and challenges of NLP models in higher education: is Chat GPT a blessing or a curse? *Frontiers in Education*, *8*. https://doi.org/10.3389/feduc.2023.1166682

Galante, A. 2020. Pedagogical translanguaging in a multilingual English program in Canada: Student and teacher perspectives of challenges. *System*, *92*, 102274. https://doi.org/https://doi.org/10.1016/j.system.2020.102274

Henschel, A. et al 2021. What Makes a Robot Social? A Review of Social Robots from Science Fiction to a Home or Hospital Near You. *Current Robotics Reports*, *2*(1), 9–19. https://doi.org/10.1007/s43154-020-00035-0

Kim, J. et al 2022. Learning design to support student-AI collaboration: perspectives of leading teachers for AI in education. *Educ. Inf. Technol*. 27, 6069–6104. https://doi.org/10.1007/s10639-021-10831-6

Koltovskaia, S. 2020. Student engagement with automated written corrective feedback (AWCF) provided by Grammarly: A multiple case study. *Assessing Writing*, *44*, 100450. https://doi.org/10.1016/j.asw.2020.100450

Martín-Martín, A. et al 2021. Google Scholar, Microsoft Academic, Scopus, Dimensions, Web of Science, and OpenCitations' COCI: a multidisciplinary comparison of coverage via citations. *Scientometrics*, *126*(1), 871–906. https://doi.org/10.1007/s11192-020-03690-4

McLean, G., Osei-Frimpong, K., Wilson, A. and Pitardi, V. (2020), "How live chat assistants drive travel consumers' attitudes, trust and purchase intentions: The role of human touch", *International Journal of Contemporary Hospitality Management*, Vol. 32 No. 5, pp. 1795-1812. https://doi.org/10.1108/IJCHM-07-2019-0605

Medland, E. (2016). Assessment in higher education: drivers, barriers and directions for change in the UK. *Assess. Eval. High. Educ*. 41, 81–96. https://doi.org/10.1080/02602938.2014.982072

Mitsea, E., & Drigas, A. 2019. A Journey into the Metacognitive Learning Strategies. *International Journal of Online and Biomedical Engineering (IJOE)*, *15*(14), 4. https://doi.org/10.3991/ijoe.v15i14.11379

Roesler, E. et al 2021. A meta-analysis on the effectiveness of anthropomorphism in human-robot interaction. *Sci. Robot*. 6, eabj5425. https://doi.org/10.1126/scirobotics.abj5425

Seufert, S., and Tarantini, E. 2022. Gestaltung der digitalen Transformation in Schulen: Ein Reifegradmodell für die Berufsbildung. Medien. *Zeitschrift für Theor. und Prax. der Medien*. 49, 301–326. https://doi.org/10.21240/mpaed/49/2022.07.15.X

van Pinxteren, M. M. E. et al 2019. Trust in humanoid robots: implications for services marketing. *Journal of Services Marketing*, *33*(4), 507–518. https://doi.org/10.1108/JSM-01-2018-004

Venkatesh, V. et al 2003. User Acceptance of Information Technology: Toward a Unified View. *MIS Quarterly*, 27(3), 425–478. https://doi.org/10.2307/30036540

Vuorikari, R. et al 2022. DigComp 2.2: The Digital Competence Framework for Citizens - With new examples of knowledge, skills and attitudes, EUR 31006 EN, Publications Office of the European Union, Luxembourg, 2022, ISBN 978-92-76-48882-8, https://doi.org/10.2760/115376

PROFESSIONAL DEVELOPMENT OF FOREIGN LANGUAGE TEACHERS: OPPORTUNITIES, CHALLENGES AND DEVELOPMENT PATHWAYS

Zhang Yajuan, Maria da Piedade Vaz Rebelo and Maria Augusta Pereira Nascimento
University of Coimbra
Rua do Colégio Novo
3000-115 Coimbra, Portugal

ABSTRACT

Currently, new technologies represented by artificial intelligence, Big Data, cloud computing, blockchain, Internet of Things, 5G technology, etc. drive human society to rapidly enter the intelligent era based on digital applications. In this context, digitization has become an important force in generating structural changes in education. As an important subject of educational practice, it is crucial for teachers to conform to the development trend of education in the era of artificial intelligence and improve their own quality. The development of artificial intelligence gives a new concept to the professional development of foreign language teachers in colleges and universities, and at the same time puts forward new challenges and opportunities for it. This paper analyzes the opportunities and challenges of teacher's professional development in the era of artificial intelligence from the structural change of foreign language education caused by artificial intelligence technology, based in a review of papers on the topic. It also studies and explores the ways of professional development of foreign language teachers in colleges and universities: they must update their concepts of education and teaching, improve their professionalism, and promote their professional development through training, school-based research, and reflective teaching.

KEYWORDS

Foreign Language Teachers, Professional Development, Artificial Intelligence

1. INTRODUCTION

The research on "Artificial Intelligence (AI) + Education" is hot in recent years. AI technology has caused structural changes in foreign language education, especially in the teaching and learning environment, teaching methods and teaching assessment tools. In the face of the impact of AI on traditional education, the foreign language teachers neither should get ahead of themselves and have a psychological crisis of worrying that they will be replaced by technology; nor should they be arrogant and underestimate the driving force of technology on education. They should not only objectively view the advantages of AI, but also calmly analyze the limitations of its application, proactively adapt to the challenges and opportunities brought by AI, carry out active and effective foreign language education and teaching activities, and realize the innovation of foreign language teaching concepts and teaching methods, so as to gradually achieve the purpose of professional development. Li Nannan (2021), Lv Jianxiu (2021) and Yang Yang (2018) presented the challenges and opportunities facing the professional development of foreign language teachers in the age of AI, but there is a lack of research exploring the development path of foreign language teachers from a systematic perspective of their professional development. In this paper, we will explore some development pathways of foreign language teachers from the perspective of their professional development in the face of challenges and opportunities in the era of AI, in order to provide reference for foreign scholars to study related topics in China.

2. METHODOLOGY

This study is a preliminary study of the systematic review. The methodology used in this work is theoretical in nature and is based on a multi-reference from the area related to the theme. The timeframe considered for the search for studies covers the years between 2018 and 2023. To define the most suitably terms for the searches, firstly, we determined the following keywords: foreign language teachers, professional development, artificial intelligence and decided to search China National Knowledge Infrastructure (CNKI) and Web of Science. Secondly we conducted selective and exploratory reading of the retrieved articles. As inclusion criteria, we chose to analyze only articles published in journals written in Chinese, Portuguese and English, those that met the research equations in both title and abstract, and those that were available online. The exclusion criteria were articles with no abstract, no full text, and articles on professional development in the field of education that did not deal with teaching in foreign language education. Finally, we analyzed and interpreted the reading to obtain the most relevant articles for our study. The preliminary analysis using content analysis (Bardin, 1979) made it possible to identify three categories: Changes in teaching, Challenges and Opportunities and Professional Development. The analysis also focused on identifying subcategories. These results are presented below.

Table 1. Data base, Articles selected for analysis, Categories e subcategories

DATA BASE	CATEGORIES	SUBCATEGORIES	AUTHOR/YEAR
CNKI	**Changes in teaching**	**Teaching and learning environment**	**Dong, Y. Y. & Li, Z. C. (2018)** **Li, N. N.(2021)**
		Teaching methods	**Lv, J. X. (2021)**
		Teaching assessment tools	**Yang, Y. (2018)**
	Challenges and opportunities	**Challenges**	**Hockly, N. (2023)** **Li, N. N. (2021)**
		Opportunities	**Chen et al. (2020)**
WOS	**Professional development**		**Lv, J. X. (2021)** **Sun, Y. Z., & Tang, J. L. (2022)** **Giannini, S. (2023)**

3. CHANGES IN TEACHING OF FOREIGN LANGUAGE IN THE AGE OF ARTIFICIAL INTELLIGENCE

Throughout the latest research by numerous scholars (Dong & Li, 2018, et al), AI technology will enable foreign language education to further towards deeper structural changes, namely in teaching and learning environment, teaching methods and teaching assessment tools.

3.1 Changes in the Teaching and Learning Environment

The teaching and learning environment in the age of artificial intelligence is becoming increasingly intelligent. The teaching and learning parties utilize hardware devices such as smartphones and software such as learning APPs to provide strong support for teaching activities. The high degree of virtualization of the teaching situation enables teaching activities to break through the limitations of time and physical space to a large extent, forming a dynamic, open, interactive and shared ubiquitous learning environment. Ubiquitous learning emphasizes the creation of intelligent environments, with the goal of creating environments that allow students to learn anytime, anywhere, using any terminal, and realizing student-centered education. In this environment, effective connectivity and interaction between teaching and learning elements can be realized, so as to achieve seamless learning that can be learned at all times and in all places. Learning of "learning all the time, learning everywhere", effectively connect personal learning and public learning space, cross different time and space boundaries, effectively connect on-campus learning and off-campus learning, formal learning and informal learning, learning in the physical world and learning in virtual reality or network. Big Data can create massive and high-quality multimodal teaching resources, realize the common construction and sharing of decentralized resources, and provide content support for students to carry out ubiquitous learning. Relying on clustering and data mining technologies, teachers can easily obtain teaching resources that are suitable for student's abilities and can stimulate their learning interests, and classify them according to the teaching resources, so that multiple forms of media resources can be effectively integrated to help students carry out appropriate learning (Li, 2021).

3.2 Changes in Teaching Methods

Numerous studies (Li, 2021, et al) have concluded that AI will drive the development of precision education: precision diagnosis, precision evaluation, precision tutoring, precision practice, etc., all from the perspective of the actual situation of individual students, and personalized teaching driven by AI. Big Data analysis technology can accurately collect students' learning situations, including learning preferences, learning needs, cognitive characteristics and other data to form a personalized student portrait, and the system automatically matches and pushes teaching resources. Biometrics technology can sense and record students' performance in classroom interaction and group collaboration through motion capture, etc., and track the learning process to produce analysis results. Teachers design personalized and customized learning content and learning methods for each student based on the results of intelligent analysis. Based on the learning data, teachers adjust teaching strategies, update teaching content, give students personalized learning guidance, help them form "adaptive" learning paths, improve learning efficiency, and stimulate learning motivation at a deeper level. In addition, in the age of AI, acquiring the intellectual content of foreign language learning is no longer the primary goal of teaching, Instead, it is the advanced thinking ability and the ability to solve complex problems that students acquire on the basis of knowledge and experience. Therefore, independent cooperative inquiry-based learning will become another typical learning mode in the age of artificial intelligence.

3.3 Changes in Teaching Assessment Tools

The current AI technology in the teaching and learning assessment session utilization has been relatively mature. By taking a picture of the completed assignment and uploading it AI can recognize the wrong questions in a second. The latest achievements in the application of AI in the field of education, including the "intelligent pen and paper classroom", "intelligent homework platform", "intelligent group paper work" to enable teachers to get rid of the pressure of a large number of correction of homework, questions and tests. In the practice of foreign language assessment, speech recognition and easy-to-analyze technology can help to complete the foreign language speaking assessment, and also can correct and improve student's language pronunciation (Yang, 2018).

4. CHALLENGES AND OPPORTUNITIES FOR THE PROFESSIONAL DEVELOPMENT OF FOREIGN LANGUAGE TEACHERS IN THE AGE OF ARTIFICIAL INTELLIGENCE

The era of AI has led to the leap-forward development of foreign language education, and in the face of this situation, the teachers neither should get ahead of themselves and have a psychological crisis of worrying that they will be replaced by technology; nor should they be arrogant and underestimate the driving force of technology on education. It is necessary to look at the advantages of AI objectively, but also we should calmly analyze the limitations of its application, and take the initiative to adapt to the challenges and opportunities brought by AI.

4.1 Challenges

Education in the age of AI is typically a technology-driven form of education at its core, which requires teachers to be technologically competent, transforming from passive recipients to active collaborators and technological innovators with the following three competencies:

First, the ability to apply smart teaching tools. Nowadays, there are numerous smart teaching tools such as cloud classroom, rain classroom, and platform of Chaoxing, etc. Teachers not only need to be proficient in the technology related to smart function modules such as resource sharing, homework correction, and academic performance statistics, but also need to make smart use of these teaching tools to optimize the teaching mode, reconstruct the ecology of teaching, and promote the effective occurrence of learning with the help of technology (Li, 2021, Lv, 2021).

Second, the ability to select and integrate information resources. The era of AI is also the age of knowledge explosion, students are faced with a massive bombardment of information every day, it is easy to lose their way and fall into the learning-roaming predicament. To this end, Li Nannan suggests that teachers should have the ability to dominate information, to be able to judge, filter, refine and integrate massive amounts of information, to teach effectively and to actively guide students to gradually learn to process and use massive amounts of information to meet real learning needs (Li, 2021).

Third, the ability to process and generates Big Data. Li also mentioned that teaching in the age of AI cannot be separated from the support and application of Big Data, where student's learning habits, behaviors and performances will be data mined, with the advantages of efficiency, precision and science. She recommends that teachers should be highly sensitive to data, be able to analyze and process and generate data in a timely manner, integrate data creatively into the overall teaching design and the whole process of teaching, and promote the optimization of teaching and learning through unremitting efforts (Li, 2021).

4.2 Opportunities

With powerful information processing capabilities and technologies such as voice recognition, AI is able to replace teachers' jobs to a certain extent. However, the complexity of the education system inevitably reveals some limitations in the application of AI, because the work of teachers is often non-preset, non-logical, non-linear, and the various contingencies in the education process require a high degree of creativity and artistry. Teachers remain irreplaceable compared to AI because humans have advantages in imagination, creativity, emotion, and intuition that AI does not have. AI can hardly replace the wholeness and unity of human perception and thinking, as well as the emotional and social nature of human beings. Teachers can use AI to improve its effectiveness and efficiency, thereby enriching or improving the quality of teaching. (Chen et al., 2020)

5. PROFESSIONAL DEVELOPMENT PATH FOR FOREIGN LANGUAGE TEACHERS IN THE AGE OF ARTIFICIAL INTELLIGENCE

The process of deep integration of AI and foreign language education is the process of efficient empowerment of foreign language learning by the new generation of information technology. Under the new technology application scenario, the teacher-student relationship will be reshaped, and teachers should follow the trend, actively change their concepts and roles, and seek apt development paths.

Promoting the professional development of foreign language teachers in colleges and universities in the era of AI requires keeping up with the times. In the process of integrating AI technology with education and teaching, teachers face multiple challenges mentioned above. In this regard, Sun Youzhong, Vice President of Beijing Foreign Studies University, proposed that foreign language teachers need to conform to the development trend of the times, embrace new technologies, establish new concepts, explore new methods, take on new roles, improve their informatization and intelligence literacy, change the traditional concepts of teaching, use new technologies to carry out foreign language teaching effectively, and form the "Four New" concepts of professional development, which is based on the core concepts of "New Technology, New Concepts, New Methods, and New Roles". He said that the "Four New" concept of teacher professional development is in line with the integration of technology and education and teaching, focusing on the development of students, through the application of technology, to promote teachers to achieve the innovation of teaching concepts, optimization of teaching methodology and the transformation of the teacher's identity. He suggested that under the guidance of the "Four New" concepts of teacher professional development, combined with the teaching practice, follow the four effective ways of creating an intelligent educational environment, improving teacher's intelligent literacy, innovating teacher development mode and optimizing teacher's data management to make AI boost the professional development of efficient foreign language teachers from external factors (Sun & Tang, 2022).

In her study on a related topic, Lv Jianxiu (2021) mentions four characteristics of change in language teachers in the context of AI: changes in consciousness, which does not necessarily manifest itself in behavior; the change is not necessarily immediate or overnight; some of the changes are quantifiable, while others are not directly accessible; some of the changes tend to be closed, while others are open-ended (Freeman, 1989). The professional development of foreign language teachers in colleges and universities in this context of AI is understood as foreign language teachers proactively integrating information technology into their professional development, improving their professional qualities, expanding and upgrading their teaching abilities by carrying out action research on teaching, reflecting on classroom teaching, evaluating teaching effects, and continuously improving their professional qualities, expanding and upgrading their teaching abilities in the practice of education and teaching, so as to enhance the level of professional development (Lv, 2021).

Considering the internal factors, the development of foreign language teachers in colleges and universities, firstly, should be from the improvement of their own professional knowledge and ability and emotional attitude to make a change; secondly, foreign language teachers should reflect on the process of teaching practice. At the same time, foreign language teachers should be guided by AI ethics in their development. (Giannini, 2023)

6. CONCLUSION

Artificial Intelligence, due to its powerful data, algorithms and application scenarios and other technological applications, will replace a large amount of mechanized and memorized labor and provide effective support and assistance for foreign language teaching. Individual foreign language teachers should, on the basis of fully affirming their own value, objectively understand the new changes brought about by AI to foreign language teaching, and focus their work on creative work and value leadership that cannot be replaced by AI, so as to better satisfy the personalized needs of students and to promote the overall development of students. Foreign language teachers themselves should take the initiative to think, actively adapt and explore the path of human-technical complicity, and have the ability to develop a series of self-regulation and interaction with the outside world, such as independent learning, practicing, reflecting and transforming. Schools should insist on taking informatization as the leading role, focusing on the construction of new digital infrastructure, promoting the integrated development of online and offline education, further promoting education digital transformation, intelligent upgrading, integration and innovation, advancing the common sharing of high-quality educational resources, and constructing a new system of teacher education in the age of intelligence.

REFERENCES

Bardin, L. (1979). *Análise de Conteúdo.*Edição 70.

Chen, L. J., Chen, P. P., & Lin, Z. J. (2020). Artificial Intelligence in Education: A Review. *IEEE Access,* 8, 75264-75278. doi:10.1109/access.2020.2988510

Dong, Y. Y., & Li, Z. C. (2018). “Opportunities and Challenges for Teacher Professional Development in the Age of Artificial Intelligenc”人工智能时代教师专业发展的机遇和挑战. *Digital Teaching in Primary and Secondary Schools*, 6(3), 8-10. DOI:CNKI:SUN:ZSZJ.0.2018-06-003

Freeman D.(1989). Teacher Training, Development, and Decision Making Model: A Model of Teaching and Related Strategies for Language Teacher Education. *TESOL Quarterly*, 23(1), 27-45.

Giannini, S. (2023). Reflections on generative AI and the future of education. *UNESCO* https://unesdoc.unesco.org/ark:/48223/pf0000385877

Hockly, N. (2023). Artificial Intelligence in English Language Teaching: The Good, the Bad and the Ugly. *RELC Journal,* 54(2), 445–451. https://doi.org/10.1177/00336882231168504

Li, N. N.(2021). “Research on the Professional Development of Foreign Language Teachers in Colleges and Universities in the Era of Artificial Intelligence”人工智能时代高校外语教师专业发展研究. *Journal of Chengdu Normal University*, 37(7), 20-26. DOI:10.3969/j.issn.2095-5642.2021.07.004.

Lv, J. X. (2021). “Professional Development of Foreign Language Teachers in Colleges and Universities in the Context of Artificial Intelligence: Definition, Challenges and Development Pathways” 人工智能背景下的高校外语教师专业发展：内涵、挑战及发展途径. *English on Campus 校园英语*, 3, 72-73. https://wenku.baidu.com/view/5bc98692996648d7c1c708a1284ac850ac020441.html?_wkts_=1694767645586&bdQuery=人工智能背景下的高校外语教师专业发展%3A 内涵、挑战及发展途径 lv

Sun, Y. Z., & Tang, J. L. (2022). “Exploring the Path of Foreign Language Teacher Team Construction in Chinese Colleges and Universities in the Era of Artificial Intelligence: The Four New Concepts and the Four Wheel Drive Model” 人工智能时代中国高校外语教师队伍建设路径探索：“四新”理念与“四轮”驱动模式. *Technology Enhanced Foreign Language Education 外语电化教学*, 3, 3-7. https://mp.weixin.qq.com/s?__biz=MjM5NTAwOTgyMA==&mid=2652100647&idx=2&sn=df1d04086839b82fce697213dadff424&chksm=bd187c548a6ff5423cc1977ec3b257ee72e56d0479e652397c1fd6aa44f77d4e4cae3ec0cb20&scene=27

Yang, Y. (2018). “Challenges and Opportunities for Foreign Language Teachers in the Age of Artificial Intelligence” 人工智能时代下外语教师面临的挑战和机遇. *Think Tank Era 智库论坛*, 27, 2. DOI:CNKI:SUN:ZKSD.0.2018-27-157.

Zhao, L. Y. (2022). “Digitization: Empowering Teachers in the Intelligent Era--An Introduction to the Contribution of the New Era Strong Teachers Program to the Reform of Teacher Education” 数字化：为智能时代教师队伍建设赋能——兼谈新时代强师计划对教师教育改革的贡献. *Educational Research 教育研究*, 4, 151-155. https://mp.weixin.qq.com/s?__biz=MzUwOTg0MTcxMA==&mid=2247484929&idx=1&sn=bb1f480fc714ae867dcd78d80c942773&chksm=f90d5e40ce7ad7562dc32150a55efbcd675b6068bf4cc567ededd23ad74ef01832ef4c97af36&scene=27

Policies & Regulations

“Opinions of the Central Committee of the Communist Party of China and the State Council on Comprehensively Deepening the Reform of Teacher Construction in the New Era” 中共中央国务院关于全面深化新时代教师队伍建设改革的意见. https://www.gov.cn/xinwen/2018-01/31/content_5262659.htm

STUDY ON THE TRAINING TO IMPROVE EMPLOYEES' EMOTIONAL WELL-BEING AT WORKPLACE

Anna Vintere
Latvia University of Life Sciences and Technologies
Liela Street 2, Jelgava, Latvia, LV-3001

ABSTRACT

Individuals' emotional well-being is determined by several factors, including the ability to cope with daily stress and the ability to cope with various daily challenges. In recent years, the Covid-19 pandemic was a major challenge that had a significant impact on the working environment. Remote working, which was introduced during the pandemic, is still in use in many industries and companies, leading to a significant increase in the use of technology and changes in communication and collaboration capabilities. This has a negative impact on individuals' work-life balance, limited socializing opportunities, leading to a deterioration in emotional well-being. In these circumstances, the understanding and ability of the management of the company or institution to ensure favorable psycho-emotional and psychosocial conditions within their team is particularly important. However, managers do not always have the knowledge and skills to improve employees' emotional well-being and ensure a positive psycho-emotional and psychosocial environment in the workplace. The solution to the above situation lies in training for managers of companies and institutions to improve the well-being of employees and to increase their competence. In order to define the content of this training, the objectives of this study are to assess the importance of training and identify what kind of training might be useful to ensure a psycho-emotional and psychosocial environment in the workplace. The results show that the most needed training topics are: Time management, Stress management, Relaxation techniques, Respectful communication, Emotional intelligence, etc. This study was carried out as part of the Nordplus project "Dealing with anxiety during a pandemic to enhance adult well-being".

KEYWORDS

Covid-19, Emotional Well-Being, Healthy Workplace, Pandemic, Psychological Well-Being

1. INTRODUCTION

In recent years, the Covid-19 pandemic has changed people's lives around the world and was a major challenge that had a significant impact on the working environment. Remote working, which was introduced during the pandemic, is still in use in many industries and companies, leading to a significant increase in the use of technology and changes in communication and collaboration capabilities. This has a negative impact on individuals' work-life balance, limited socializing opportunities leading to a deterioration in emotional well-being as emotional well-being is as the emotional quality of everyday experiences, the positive and negative affect that makes one's life pleasant or unpleasant (Kahneman & Deaton, 2010).

Several studies have been conducted on the impact of COVID-19 on the workplace and on employee well-being during a pandemic. Many employees experienced sudden changes in the general work situation, which were mandatory and for which they were not prepared (Carillo et al, 2020). Remote work created a high sense of insecurity among employees, increased work-home conflict and led to high levels of stress (Parent-Lamarche et al, 2021), burnout and symptoms of depression and anxiety (Ksinan Jiskrova, 2022).

It has been shown that individuals are more likely to experience negative mental and psychological consequences if they lack adequate resilience and coping skills during times of stress (Labrague, 2021). It has also been shown that social support can increase resilience to stress and help prevent the development of psychological or emotional trauma (Labrague, 2021). Therefore, in conditions of increased stress, peer support is important. The understanding of the management of the company or institution and the ability to ensure favorable psychological and emotional conditions in its team are also particularly important.

Managers of companies and institutions have insufficient skills on how to improve the emotional well-being of employees, reduce anxiety, and ensure a positive psycho-emotional and psychosocial environment in the workplace. The solution to the mentioned situation is the training of managers of companies and institutions in order to increase their management skills in conditions of high emotional risk. Therefore, the Nordplus project "Dealing with anxiety during a pandemic to enhance adult well-being" has been initiated and implemented with the aim of determining the impact of Covid-19, as well as determining the training that would be needed for managers of companies or organizations to promote emotional well-being in the workplace.

In order to define the content of this training, the objectives of this study are:

- Assess the importance of training in increasing the well-being of employees in the workplace, considering the opinions of both employees and employers;
- Identify what kind of training might be useful to ensure a psycho-emotional and psychosocial environment in the workplace.

2. METHODOLOGY OF THE STUDY

To better understand the needs of managers and employees for specific training on mental health and well-being, and to focus training on specific areas, a survey of employees and managers of companies and institutions was carried out. The questionnaire consisted of three sections:

1. Questions about respondents':
2. Assessment of the impact of the COVID-19 pandemic on the psychosocial environment in the workplace and employee well-being;
3. Contains questions aiming to understand the role of training to increase individual resilience of employees.

The design of the questionnaire is based on several theoretical considerations. One of them is the World Health Organization definitions (WHO, 2004):

- Health is "a state of complete physical, mental and social well-being and not merely the absence of disease or infirmity";
- Mental health is "a state of well-being in which the individual realizes his or her own abilities, can cope with the normal stresses of life, can work productively and fruitfully, and is able to make a contribution to his or her community";
- The main focus of positive psychological health is enhancing individuals' well-being, health and satisfaction as an effective way of preventing mental health disorders, and this is extensible to all workplaces.

In line with these definitions, Kotrum (2014) has identified four key aspects of a healthy workplace: the physical work environment, the psychosocial work environment, personal health resources and the company's involvement in the community (Kotrum, 2014). The assessment of the impact of the COVID-19 pandemic on the psychosocial environment in the workplace and employee well-being was developed by adapting ten categories (e.g. job control, workload and work pace, relationship with superiors, etc.) developed in the WHO model on the impact of psychosocial risks on occupational health.

The questionnaire is available here: https://forms.gle/xBW3ePM4dQGo8cbz9 (in English). A total of 335 respondents took part in the study. The survey was conducted in four countries - Estonia, Latvia, Lithuania and Sweden, but this article analyses the data of the survey that was conducted in the author's country.

In total, 80 respondents participated in the survey - 22 managers and 58 employers.

Characteristics of managers who participated in the survey:

- By the gender: female 15, male 7;
- By the age: 30-39 : 2, 40-49: 7, 50-59: 8, 60-69: 5;
- By the management level: top management 8, middle management 9, first line management 5;
- By the education: vocational 2, bachelor`s degree 5, master`s degree 11, doctoral degree 4;
- By the type of organization: private for-profit 9, governmental and public sector 10, non-profit, including tax exempt and charitable organizations 2, other 1;
- The size of organization: micro (1-4 employees) 3, small (5-19 employees) 7, medium-sized (20-49 employees) 8, large (more than 50 employees) 4.

The numbers of employees who responded to the survey:

- By the gender: female 32, male 26;
- By the age: under 20 -1, 20-29: 12, 30-39: 17, 40-49: 9, 50-59: 10, 60-69: 8; above 70 – 1;
- By the education: basic/elementary 1, high school 8, vocational 14, bachelor`s degree 12, master`s degree 15, doctoral degree 8;
- By the type of organization: private for-profit 34, governmental and public sector 23, non-profit, including tax exempt and charitable organizations 1;
- The size of organization: micro (1-4 employees) 12, small (5-19 employees) 8, medium-sized (20-49 employees) 10, large (more than 50 employees) 28.

3. FINDINGS

3.1 Assessment of the Impact of the COVID-19 Pandemic on the Psychosocial Environment in the Workplace and Employee Well-Being

Emotional well-being includes a positive balance of pleasant to unpleasant affect and a cognitive appraisal of satisfaction with life in general (Keyes, 2003). In order to promote work-life balance and increase organizational productivity, it is important to study the impact of COVID-19 on the workplace, in order to find new norms and create workplaces that are more flexible and sustainable (Rahmani & Zeng, 2023). Therefore, this study assessed the impact of the COVID-19 pandemic on the psychosocial environment in the workplace and the well-being of employees.

Respondents were asked to assess the impact of the COVID-19 pandemic on their workplace. The responses are summarized in Table 1.

Table 1. The impact of the COVID-19 pandemic on workplace

Quality	No impact at all	Slight impact	Moderate impact	High impact	Difficult to say
In total	13	27	23	8	8
Female	3	14	16	7	5
Male	10	13	6	1	3
Employees	11	17	16	6	8
Managers	2	10	7	2	1
Large (more than 50 employees)	4	9	10	7	5
Medium-sized (20-49 employees)	3	8	9	0	2
Small (5-19 employees)	4	6	2	1	1
Micro (1-4 employees)	2	5	1	0	1

Women were the most affected by Covid-19. The results show that Covid-19 had the greatest impact on the workplace in large organizations (more than 50 employees). About two thirds of respondents from small (5-19 employees) or micro-organizations (1-4 employees) say there has been slight impact or no impact.

To assess what kind of impact Covid-19 had on the workplace, respondents were given a number of statements that had to be rated on a five-point Likert scale: strongly agree, somewhat agree, difficult to say, somewhat disagree and strongly disagree. The answers summarized in Table 2.

Table 2. Answers to the question "Regarding the impact of COVID-19 pandemic at your workplace, to what extent do you agree or disagree with the following?"

Statement	Strongly agree	Somewhat agree	Difficult to say	Somewhat disagree	Strongly disagree
My work has become meaningless to me (I have no desire or interest to do this work)	2	4	14	7	51
I feel insecure at work, because I have no confidence about the future	5	9	12	18	34
My workload has increased significantly	13	11	12	16	25
I have less control over my work process and tasks	5	10	17	15	32
The conditions of the working environment have deteriorated, they have not been adapted to the changes caused by the pandemic	5	10	17	17	29
The goals of the organization where I work, would now need tc be clearly defined	4	15	30	13	15
Relationships between employees have improved	15	23	25	10	5
Relationships with superiors have improved	14	23	29	6	6
My role in the organization is now more ambiguous, I have nev opportunities for action	12	21	19	13	12
My career development is negatively affected (career opportunities are worse than before the pandemic)	8	9	10	20	31
My work-life balance is negatively affected (I have less time fo home)	11	6	23	16	10

Respondents were also asked to rate the Cpvid-19 pandemic impact their psychological well-being. The answers were as follows:

- Not at all affected (I feel as before COVID-19 pandemic) -35;
- Slightly affected (I feel slightly more anxious than before the COVID-19 pandemic but manageable) – 27;
- Moderately affected (I feel moderately more anxious than before the COVID-19 pandemic, sometimes I can manage but not always) – 10;
- Very affected (I feel anxious very frequently now in comparison with before the COVID-19 pandemic, difficult to manage) - 4;
- Difficult to say – 4.

3.2 Training to Improve Employees' Emotional Well-Being at Workplace

As we know, learning achievement depends on motivation. Therefore, first of all, the opinion of employees and managers of companies and institutions about the role of training was identified. To assess the role of training to increase individual resilience of employees, the respondents were given the question how they seen the role of training, regardless other measures put in place by organization:

- 40 or half of respondents see training as something needed;
- 21 as something to consider;
- – as priority;
- respondents think that training is not needed at all;
- but 11 respondents had no opinion on this topic.

Respondents were asked to rate various training topics on a five-point Likert scale that could:

- Helps reduce anxiety (Table 3);
- Enhance emotional well-being (Table 4);
- Improve the psychological environment (Table 5).

Managers answered this question about their team, while employees - about themselves.

Table 3. Answers to the question "What kind of training could help to reduce anxiety?"

Statements	Very helpful	Somewhat helpful	Difficult to say	Not very helpful	Not at all helpful
Acquire comprehensive knowledge of human health as a whole	5	36	18	17	3
Acquire knowledge of how to better take care of oneself	15	29	16	19	1
Learn and use different relaxation techniques	16	31	14	16	3
Learn and use different stress management techniques	21	25	13	19	2
Learn and use different time management techniques to better manage one's time	14	35	13	15	2
Any other training to reduce anxiety	16	25	15	17	1

Respondents believe that training on the following topics is essential to reduce anxiety: (1) Learn and use different time management techniques to better manage one's time; (2) Learn and use different relaxation techniques and (3) Learn and use different stress management techniques.

Table 4. Answers to the questions "What kind of training could help to enhance emotional wellbeing?"

Statements	Very helpful	Somewhat helpful	Difficult to say	Not very helpful	Not at all helpful
Acquire knowledge of maintaining a positive attitude towards oneself and others	11	33	12	21	2
Acquire knowledge of the nature and impact of negative stereotypes and stigmatization	7	24	17	29	3
Learn communication skills and techniques to better communicate with colleagues	8	33	13	17	7
Learn ways to boost emotional resilience	17	30	14	16	3
Learn and apply techniques to increase self-compassion	10	29	14	18	9
Some other training to increase emotional well-being	3	3	7	1	0

Training on ways how to boost emotional resilience, communication skills and techniques to better communicate with colleagues and acquiring knowledge of maintaining a positive attitude towards oneself and others – are the most important topic to enhance emotional wellbeing.

Table 5. Answers to the question "What kind of training could help improve the psychological environment in the organization?"

Statements	Very helpful	Somewhat helpful	Difficult to say	Not very helpful	Not at all helpful
Acquire knowledge of achieving a healthy balance between professional and private life	11	27	16	25	1
Acquire knowledge of proper workload (when workload is too high, when optimal)	11	29	15	23	1
Acquire knowledge of identifying the need for psychological support (counselling), i.e., when it is needed, in what ways it can help, etc.	8	22	17	25	7
Acquire and use conflict resolution techniques, to learn t resolve conflicts peacefully and effectively	17	23	14	18	6
Get practical guidance on how to deal with bullying and harassment	11	26	17	20	4
Acquire knowledge and practical skills for achieving a healthy compromise between professional and private life	17	21	18	20	4
Acquire knowledge and practical skills for creating a positive atmosphere at the workplace	15	25	18	19	1

The survey results show that there are three topic which could improve the psychological environment in the workplace: Acquire knowledge of proper workload, Acquire and use conflict resolution techniques, to learn to resolve conflicts peacefully and effectively and Acquire knowledge and practical skills for creating a positive atmosphere at the workplace.

4. CONCLUSION

Emotional well-being is the ability to produce positive emotions, moods, thoughts, and feelings, and adapt when confronted with adversity and stressful situations. It includes a positive balance of pleasant to unpleasant affect and a cognitive appraisal of satisfaction with life in general.

A healthy workplace is characterized by four components: physical work environment, psychosocial work environment, personal health resources, and enterprise community involvement.

The survey data show that for the vast majority of respondents, the pandemic has not had a significant impact on their psychological well-being.

Half of the respondents to this study considered Covid-19 to have had a slight (33.75%) or moderate (28.75%) impact on their workplace. Women and large organizations were the most affected by Covid-19. The results show that Covid-19 has improved relations between employees and with their superiors (almost answered "strongly agree" or "somewhat agree"). 65.38% of respondents have a positive impact on their career development.

5% of respondents think training to improve employees' emotional well-being at workplace is a priority, while half - that it is necessary. The most common responses from employees were "not very helpful" or "not helpful at all".

Managers and employees consider various psychological trainings essential. All three questions the managers' and the employees' answers are different. The results show that the most needed training topics are: Time management, Stress management, Relaxation techniques, Respectful communication, How to boost emotional intelligence, etc.

The most common responses from employees were "not very helpful" or "not helpful at all".

This was a case study. It only reflects the views of the respondents who participated in it and could be used to identify problems / directions for in-depth research

ACKNOWLEDGEMENT

The study uses data from the Nordplus project NPAD-2022/10102 "Dealing with anxiety during a pandemic to enhance adult well-being".

REFERENCES

Carillo, K. et al, 2020. Adjusting to epidemic-induced telework: Empirical insights from teleworkers in France. *European Journal of Information Systems*, 30:1, 69-88.

Kahneman, D., and Deaton, A., 2010. High income improves evaluation of life but not emotional well-being. *Psychological and Cognitive Sciences*, 103(38), 16489–16493.

Keyes, C. L. M., 2003. Complete mental health: An agenda for the 21th century. *In C. L. M. Keyes & J. Haidt (Eds.), Flourishing: Positive psychology and the life well-lived*), Washington, DC: American Psychological Association, 293–312.

Kotrum, E., 2014. The WHO global approach to protecting and promoting health at work. *In Biron, C., Burke, R., Cooper, C. (ed.) Creating Healthy Workplace: Stress reduction, Improved Well-being, and Organizational Effectiveness*, London and New York: Routledge Taylor & Francis Group.

Ksinan Jiskrova, G., 2022. Impact of COVID-19 pandemic on the workforce: from psychological distress to the Great Resignation. *J Epidemiol Community Health*, 76, 525-526.

Labrague, L. J., 2021. Psychological resilience, coping behaviours and social support among health care workers during the COVID-19 pandemic: A systematic review of quantitative studies. *Journal of Nursing Management*, 29 (7), 1893-1905.

Parent-Lamarche, A. and Boulet, M., 2021. Workers' Stress During the First Lockdown: Consequences on Job Performance Analyzed with a Mediation Model. *Journal of Occupational and Environmental Medicine*, 63 (6), 469-475.

Rahmani, D. and Zeng, C.,2023. Editorial: The impact of COVID-19 on workplace practices: challenges, changes, and future directions. *Front. Commun.* 8:1207987.

World Health Organization, 2004. *Promoting mental health: concepts, emerging evidence, practice*: summary report / a report from the World Health Organization, Department of Mental Health and Substance Abuse in collaboration with the Victorian Health Promotion Foundation and the University of Melbourne. World Health Organization, https://apps.who.int/iris/handle/10665/42940.

MOBILE SYSTEM FOR SIMULATION OF PHYSICAL CIRCUIT OPERATION AND APPLICATION TO EDUCATION INVOLVING CIRCUIT CONSTRUCTION

Atsushi Takemura
Tokyo University of Agriculture and Technology
2-24-16, Nakacho, Koganei-shi, Tokyo 184-8588, Japan

ABSTRACT

This study proposes a mobile education system for learning experiments involving the design and construction of electronic circuits. The proposed system utilizes novel image processing techniques that employ a machine learning algorithm to automatically recognize the composition of a wide variety of circuits and translate that composition into a standard circuit description language (e.g., simulation program with integrated circuit emphasis (SPICE)). This feature enables a learner to examine and learn the functionality of the constructed physical circuit using a mobile PC. Moreover, the proposed system discovers the errors and inappropriate parts in a constructed circuit that could cause accidents and instruct to correct them. The effectiveness of the proposed system was verified in actual classes by 60 undergraduates. The comparison tests between two groups that comprised students who used or did not use the proposed system demonstrated the effectiveness of the system.

KEYWORDS

Mobile Education System, Circuit Construction, Image Processing, Circuit Simulation

1. INTRODUCTION

A comprehensive understanding of the design and construction of electronic circuits is essential for modern technology education. Recently, several educational support systems have been developed to improve students' understanding of basic electronic circuits, including their construction and experimentation capabilities (Reisslein, 2013; Rodriguez-Sanchez, 2016; Lei, 2021). However, these education systems are limited in scope and are suitable only for basic circuits within a subject area. A circuit simulator using augmented reality has been developed for virtual experiments relating to electronic circuits (Lucas, 2018). However, this virtual learning system lacks the capability to teach the construction of physical circuits. To overcome the disadvantages of these conventional systems, an education system for supporting the physical circuit construction was developed (Takemura, 2018). This system used image processing techniques to automatically recognize circuit compositions and translate them into standard circuit description languages, such as simulation program with integrated circuit emphasis (SPICE) (Rabaey, 2012). This automated translation technique enables learners to investigate the functionality of a circuit using their personal computer (PC) (without laboratory equipment). However, the circuit recognition technique of this system is not applicable to large-scale circuits, including cross-wirings and multidirectional device connections. To overcome this disadvantage of the system, this study improves the image processing techniques of the system using a classifier based on the machine learning algorithm. The improved system is then employed in practical experiments involving the physical construction of practical circuits with operational amplifiers—an essential aspect of science and technology education.

The rest of this paper is organized in the following manner. Section 2 describes the technical features of the proposed system. Section 3 describes the experimental methodology to evaluate the proposed system. Section 4 summarizes the results of the experiments at actual university classes. This section also describes the quantitative evaluation of the proposed system. Finally, Section 5 provides the conclusions.

2. TECHNICAL FEATURES OF THE SYSTEM

To improve the efficiency and safety of experiments involving circuit construction, an education system that uses image processing techniques was proposed in a previous study (Takemura, 2018). This system consists of individual learners' mobile PCs and the remote analysis system. During experiments, the learners transmit the images of their constructed circuits to the analysis system. The analysis system employs image processing techniques, such as segmentation and pattern recognition, on circuit images to automatically recognize the compositions of the circuits. It then translates the circuit composition into the circuit description language SPICE. This circuit translation technique enables learners to simulate and check the functionality of their circuits without laboratory equipment. However, the pattern recognition-based technique was not applicable to the following features that frequently appeared in large-scale circuits and circuits constructed by unskilled learners:

(a) Cross-wiring using insulating cables and multidirectional device connections (Figure 1(a))

(b) Dangerous cross-wiring and inappropriate long wiring using noninsulating cables (Figure 1(b))

To overcome this disadvantage and increase the usefulness of the system, this study developed image processing techniques based on a machine learning algorithm. Moreover, this new function proves valuable in preventing accidents caused by the erroneous operation of a circuit. The processing flow of the proposed technique is shown in Figure 2(a), and each process is described in the subsequent subsections.

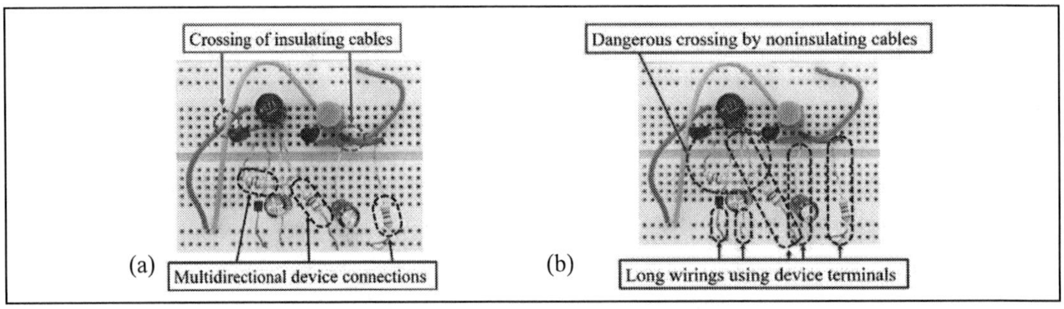

Figure 1. Constructed circuits not applicable to the previous system (Takemura, 2018): (a) circuit including the crossings using insulating cables and multidirectional device connections, and (b) circuits including the dangerous crossings using noninsulating cables and long noninsulating device terminals

2.1 Improvement of the Image Processing Technique for Circuit Recognition

A) Detection of Terminals and Wirings

To automatically detect the terminals and wirings in a circuit image, the analysis system uses mathematical morphology (Sternberg, 1986; Heijmans, 2020). In this system, the structuring elements of the morphological operations are circular with radii ranged 0.7–1.6 mm that match the radii of a terminal hole on a circuit board (breadboard) and the cable thickness, respectively.

B) Recognition of Connected Devices

To automatically recognize the circuit devices connected in a circuit image, this study proposes a machine learning–based ensemble classifier equipped with an effective feature selection process. The proposed classifier is composed using the AdaBoost algorithm (Freund, 1997) and is built by connecting multiple weak classifiers. To improve classification performance, each weak classifier intensively trains the samples misclassified by the previous weak classifier. The proposed system performs device recognition in a circuit image using the feature set extracted from the following statistical attributes of red, green, and blue intensities: (1) average, (2) standard deviation, (3) median, (4) maximum, (5) minimum, (6) kurtosis, and (7) skewness. To distinguish between various circuit devices, the proposed classifier detects the class that yields the minimum Mahalanobis distance between feature vectors extracted from kernel scans in the image and the training samples of circuit devices. To mitigate problems caused by the curse of dimensionality (Duda, 2001), each weak classifier selects an optimal feature vector comprising three features that minimize the classification errors obtained from the training phase. The training data for each device were acquired from a pool of 50 images per device. Moreover, to effectively discriminate multidirectional device connections on a circuit board, the training samples are systematically rotated at 15° intervals during the classification process.

2.2 Generation of a SPICE Netlist Based on the Circuit Recognition

The circuit translation technique, shown in Figure 2(b), plays a vital role within the proposed system. Based on the classification of circuit components obtained from the circuit recognition process, this circuit translation technique generates a SPICE Netlist that describes the composition of the circuit. The SPICE Netlist is a circuit description language that enables the simulation of the functionality of the circuit using a general simulator. The remote system performs an automated translation of the physical circuit into SPICE Netlist and provides the learner with the Netlist and simulation results of the constructed physical circuit.

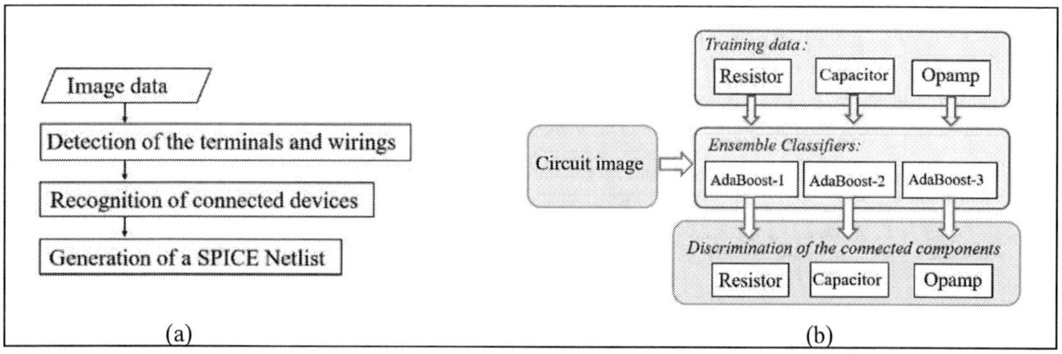

Figure 2. Schematic of the workflow of the image processing-based techniques in the proposed system: (a) flowchart of the proposed techniques using image processing, and (b) new circuit recognition technique based on ensemble classifiers using the AdaBoost algorithm

3. METHODOLOGY FOR EVALUATING THE PROPOSED SYSTEM

The effectiveness of the proposed system was evaluated through a comparative study involving two distinct groups (Group-1 and Group-2) of students aged 19–21 years at the Tokyo University of Agriculture and Technology. Group-1 comprised 30 students who designed and constructed the following circuits under conventional instructor-led guidance: (1) noninverting amplifier (voltage gain 2), (2) 2nd-order Butterworth active low-pass filter (cut-off frequency 0.5 kHz), (3) 2nd-order Butterworth active high-pass filter (cut-off frequency 5 kHz), and (4) 2nd-order Butterworth active band-pass filter (band width 0.5–5 kHz). These circuits hold practical relevance within the category of operational amplifiers and are important for education in the science and technology field. Figure 3(a) shows a diagram of circuit (1). Figure 3(b) shows a diagram of circuit (4), which is composed of circuits (2) and (3).

Group-2 comprised 30 students who performed the same circuit design and construction as those in Group-1 but using the new system. Group-1 and Group-2 were evaluated in 2022 and 2023, respectively. Prior to beginning the experiments, questionnaires were administered to determine each student's degree of experience in the circuit construction. Based on their responses, the students were classified into the following two categories:

A: Experienced in circuit construction, in addition to practice exercises at school.
B: No experience, except for practice exercises at school.

Figure 3(c) shows the number of students belonging to each experience category. The results indicate that the majority of the students fell under category B. Notably, there were no students who had no experience in circuit construction, as all students had learned the construction of elementary circuits as part of mandatory education in junior high schools in Japan.

The students in Group-1 were tasked to design and construct circuits based on the conventional method outlined as follows (T1)–(T5):

(T1) Lecture on the theory and method for constructing circuits using operational amplifiers.

(T2) Circuit design
(T3) Report the designed circuits to the instructor. The instructor examines the design to ensure that they adhere to specifications. If an incorrect part is identified, the student corrects it under the instructor's guidance.
(T4) Circuit construction using the necessary components in the laboratory.
(T5) Report the constructed circuits to the instructor. The instructor inspects the constructed circuit. If an incorrect and dangerous part is discovered, the student corrects it under the instructor's guidance.

The students in Group-2 were tasked to design and construct the same circuits as those in Group-1 but using the proposed new system. Therefore, the tasks (T1), (T3), and (T5) also applied to Group-2 but the tasks of circuit design and construction for Group-2 differed from those denoted as (T2) and (T4) for Group-1, as outlined below:

(T2-G2) Circuit design and confirmation of the characteristics of the designed circuits using the system's simulator.
(T4-G2) Circuit construction using the necessary components in the laboratory. Subsequently, the student assesses the characteristics of the constructed circuits using the system's simulator. If the simulation results do not meet the specified criteria, the student corrects the circuit accordingly.

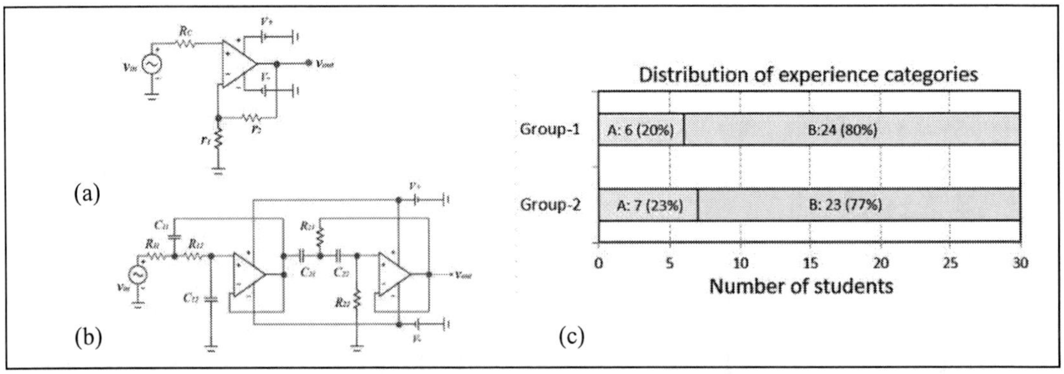

Figure 3. Examples of circuits to be constructed in the experiments and division of groups for evaluation of the proposed system: (a) circuit dialog of a noninverting amplifier, (b) circuit diagram of an active band-pass filter, and (c) division of groups and distribution of experience categories

4. RESULTS AND DISCUSSION

The testing results of Group-1 and Group-2 were compared to demonstrate the impact of the proposed system on the experiment described in Section 3. Figure 4 shows examples of the constructed circuits and the SPICE simulation results based on the circuit translation of the proposed system by a student in Group-2. Figure 4(a) shows an image of the constructed circuit (2nd-order Butterworth active band-pass filter). Figure 4(b) shows the SPICE Netlist obtained using the proposed circuit translation technique. Figure 4(c) shows the SPICE simulation results based on the SPICE Netlist provided by the system. Figure 4(d) shows an image of a correct circuit constructed by another student. From this circuit image, the system automatically detected dangerous crossings by noninsulating cables and long wirings using the noninsulating terminals of the devices. Subsequently, the system highlighted these inappropriate parts to the students using the red dotted lines in the image. This student corrected the inappropriate parts based on the indication from the system.

Figure 5(a) shows that the averages and ranges of the required time for the circuit design and construction in Group-2 were shorter compared to those in Group-1. This result implies that the use of a circuit simulator decreases the time required for circuit design and construction. This is attributed to the students' ability to confirm the functionality of their circuits using their mobile PCs and to independently correct any errors encountered.

Figure 5(b) shows the occurrence of errors in the designed circuits identified by the instructors during the process (T3). As shown in this figure, eight (26%) students in Group-1 had errors in their designed circuits that were observed by the instructor. In Group-2, there were no errors in the circuit design by the students in

Category A, but four (13%) students in Category B had errors. This result indicates that the use of the circuit simulator during the circuit design process reduces the time required to achieve an accurate circuit design. However, the errors were detected in the circuits that were designed by the students who misunderstood the required theories relating to the circuits in Group-1 and -2.

Figure 5(c) shows the occurrence of errors and dangerous parts to be corrected in the constructed physical circuits discovered by the instructors during the process (T5). This figure shows that 11 (37%) students in Group-1 had errors or dangerous parts that were observed by the instructor. Conversely, no errors and dangerous parts in the circuits constructed by the students in Group-2 were noted. This result demonstrates the effectiveness and usefulness of the proposed system for construction of correct circuits without requiring instructor intervention.

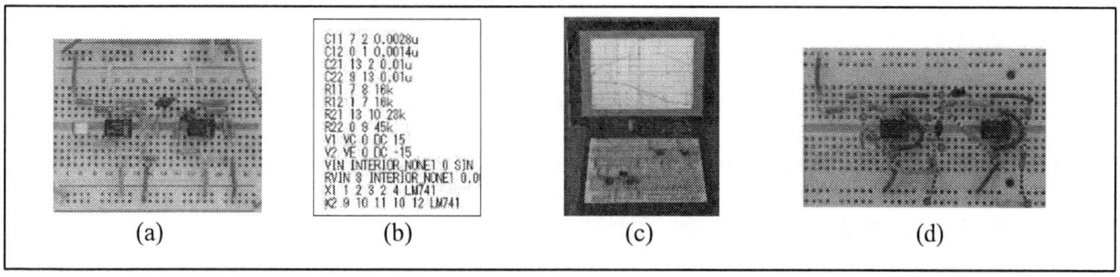

Figure 4. Results of the circuit construction and simulation using the proposed system by the students in Group-2: (a) image of the correct circuit constructed by a student, (b) SPICE Netlist obtained from the system, (c) circuit simulation (frequency characteristics) based on the SPICE Netlist (b), and (d) circuit image with the indication of the unappropriated wirings to be corrected

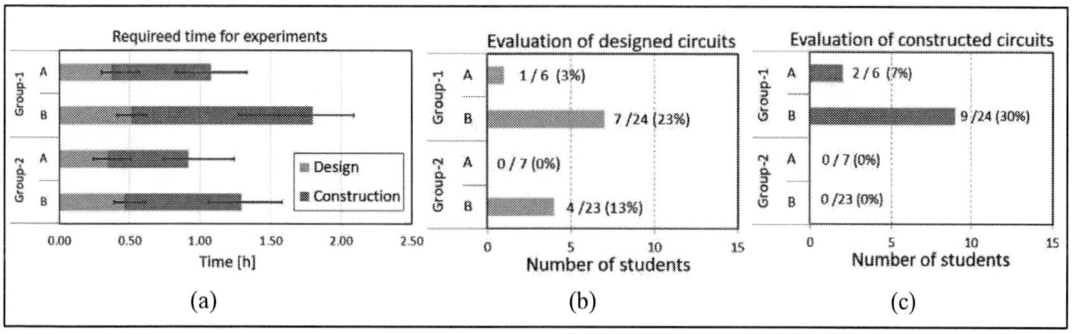

Figure 5. Results of the comparison test between Group-1 and Group-2: (a) average and range of the required time for the circuit construction of each group and experience degree, (b) the number of students whose designed circuits included errors, and (c) the number of students whose constructed circuits included errors and dangerous parts to be corrected

Through the evaluation process, positive responses were obtained from the instructors, which provided further validation of the effectiveness of the proposed system. Their comments highlighted the following key points:

- The use of a circuit simulator is effective in designing a correct circuit and decreases the instructor's load to confirm the designed circuit.
- Automated circuit translation and simulation of the new system are important for avoiding serious errors that could cause accidents (e.g., a short circuit) when operating an incorrect circuit. This function of the new system also decreases the instructors' load to validate the physical circuits constructed by numerous students.

Furthermore, students in Group-2 gave positive responses highlighting the usefulness of the proposed system. These included:

- The automated translation and simulation feature of the physical circuit, accessible using a mobile PC, was convenient because it enables a learner to examine and learn how the functionality of their constructed circuit without relying on laboratory equipment. This function was also effective in preventing accidents that occur as a result of the operation of an incorrect circuit.
- The automated indication of a dangerous and inappropriate part to be corrected in a physical circuit helped to efficiently and safely complete the circuit construction without instruction from an instructor.

To improve the applicability and usefulness of the system, the following studies should be implemented:

- Application to a broad array of circuits (e.g., logic and digital circuits)
- Development of virtual experiments

5. CONCLUSION

In this study, a novel mobile education system for the construction of physical circuits with operational amplifiers, which are essential for science and technology education at the university level, is demonstrated. The proposed system automatically recognizes the image of the constructed physical circuits using a new classification algorithm and enables the student to check the functionality of the circuit based on the automated translation of the circuits. Moreover, this function is effective to prevent accidents caused by the experiments using the incorrect circuits. The effectiveness of the proposed system was demonstrated by the results of a comparison test involving two groups of university students. Further enhancement is required in the image processing and visualization techniques to ensure the applicability of the proposed system to a broad array of circuits. By enhancing these aspects, the system's usefulness and usability can be substantially augmented.

ACKNOWLEDGMENT

This study was partly supported by a Grant-in-Aid for Scientific Research (KAKENHI) 19K03079 and 23K02629 from the Japan Society for the Promotion of Science.

REFERENCES

Duda, R. O., et al., 2001, Pattern classification, Wiley-Interscience, p. 170.

Freund, Y., et al., 1996, Experiments with a new boosting algorithm, *In Proc. 13th International Conf. Machine Learning*, pp.148-156, Bari, Italy.

Garcia-Zubia, J., et al., 2017, Empirical analysis of the use of the VISIR remote lab in teaching analog electronics, *In IEEE Trans. Education*, Vol. 60, No. 2, pp. 149–156.

Heijmans, H.J.A.M,, 2020, Chapter Eleven - Morphology for grey-scale images, *In Advances in Imaging and Electron Physics*, pp. 355-401.

Lei, Z., et al., 2021, 3-d interactive control laboratory for classroom demonstration and online experimentation in engineering education, *IEEE Trans. Educ.*, vol. 64, no. 3, pp. 276–282.

Lucas P., et al., 2018, Virtual Circuits: An Augmented Reality Circuit Simulator for Engineering Students, *In Proc. IEEE 18th International Conference on Advanced Learning Technologies (ICALT)*, pp. 380-384, Mumbai, India.

Rabaey, J. M., The Spice Page, <URL: http://bwrc.eecs.berkeley.edu/Classes/IcBook/SPICE/> (accessed July 18, 2019).

Rachala R. R., et al., 2022, Hand-drawn electrical circuit recognition using object detection and node recognition, *In SN Computer Science*, vol. 3, No. 244.

Rodriguez-Sanchez, M. C., et al., 2016, An embedded systems course for engineering students using open-source platforms in wireless scenarios, *In IEEE Trans. Education*, Vol. 59, No. 4, pp. 248–254.

Sternberg, S.R., 1986, Grayscale morphology, *In Computer Vision, Graphics, and Image Processing*, vol. 35, no. 3, pp. 333-355.

Takemura, A., 2018, e-Learning system for electronic circuit construction using handwriting recognition and mixed reality technique, *Proc. IADIS Conference e-Learning 2018*, pp. 161–166, Madrid, Spain.

EARLY CONCEPT FOR A GENERIC AND DOMAIN AGNOSTIC SERIOUS GAME FRAMEWORK

Daniel Atorf, Sergius Dyck and Ehm Kannegieser
Fraunhofer IOSB
Fraunhoferstr. 1, 76131 Karlsruhe, Germany

ABSTRACT

Educators often struggle or avoid to incorporate digital learning content into their classes because of the lack of matching content available, that fits specific course requirements, high cost of content at hand, that might be fitting and sparse resources to create such material by themselves, without diving into complex tools or lengthy production processes. This paper proposes a twofold solution to this problem by introducing the concept of a serious game framework with pre-made and reusable game mechanics to avoid complex software development in connection with the use of established interoperability standards to link in existing learning content.

KEYWORDS

Digital Game-Based Learning, Serious Game Framework, Interoperability, Reuse Learning Content

1. INTRODUCTION

Educators often face challenges or avoid incorporating digital learning content into their classes due to the limited availability of content that meets specific course requirements. To fill this gap in the education of imagery analysts, the serious game Lost Earth 2307 was developed (Atorf, 2019). It is designed to train individuals in the analysis of aerial and satellite imagery, as well as formal reporting techniques for identified objects using specialized terminology. Due to the complexity of this training domain, individual courses are spread over several months, and instructors are highly motivated to keep students engaged throughout the extended duration.

Once the game was completed, it was evaluated while being used in the classroom. The following key lessons were learned: First, the game should have a stronger connection to the current learning content of the curriculum, making it more easily adaptable and allowing for changes in its sequence if necessary, without requiring changes in the game mechanics. Second, the maintainability of the game should be improved, i.e. changes to the game should not have to be adapted on each individual user client, but should be managed centrally. To specifically address the adaptability aspect, subsequent efforts focused on breaking down tasks into smaller components and formulating a concept for a more streamlined version of the existing game (Atorf, 2020).

This paper goes one step further. The concept presented here not only considers the lessons learned but also outlines a more general approach. The main objective is to create a domain-independent serious game framework that facilitates the development of serious games at the lowest possible cost using existing learning content and interoperability standards.

2. CONCEPT DESIGN

The concept outlined in this paper considers the fundamental requirements derived from the evaluation of Lost Earth 2307, while also extending the scope of these requirements. Essentially, this entails considering the concept not only within the domain of military image analysis applications but also in a more general and versatile manner. By doing so, other domains can benefit from the concept when implementing a serious game component.

Furthermore, like Lost Earth 2307 the concept remains aligned with the principles of Digital Game Based Learning (DGBL) by Prensky (Prensky, 2007) and immersive didactics by Bopp (Bopp, 2006). It aims to facilitate the creation of engaging and immersive serious games that simultaneously facilitate the achievement of learning objectives.

2.1 Base Concept

The primary objective is to assist educators in developing or customizing ad-hoc content for lessons and self-learning sessions. To accomplish this, the concept adopts a generic and modular approach to enhance the interchangeability and adaptability of content. This approach can be likened to a construction kit, where the manifestation of the concept for a specific knowledge domain, such as Lost Earth 2307 as a science fiction game for military image analysis, represents an instance of this construction kit. The construction kit comprises five modules (refer to Figure 1, left). In addition, two distinct roles are established: the author, responsible for initial content creation and authorized to modify all modules, and the teacher with access to the mission module for adapting learning content or creating new learning content for lessons and self-learning sessions.

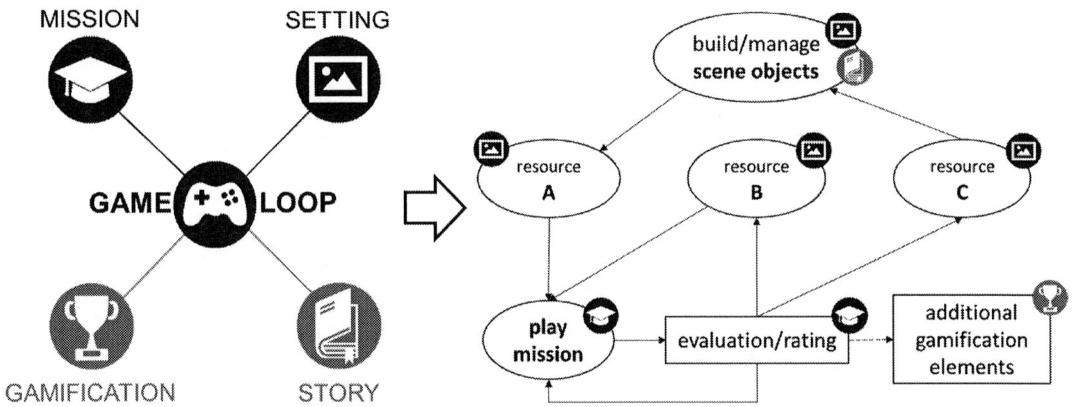

Figure 1. Left: concept modules; right: basic construction and management simulation game loop

The central module is the Game Loop, encompassing general gameplay rules and mechanics. In this concept, the Game Loop embodies a Construction and Management Simulation with Resource Conversion, as proposed by Rollings and Adams (Rollings & Adams, 2003). Progression within the game and the evolution of the game world necessitate the acquisition of certain resources. Successful mission completion yields these resources. However, missions will require the conversion of specific resources before they can be commenced (refer to Figure 1, right). These core game mechanics remain generic and consistent across all instances for specific knowledge domains. The remaining modules are customizable and cater to specific requirements.

The obligatory Setting module defines the game world and the visual aesthetics of the instance. Employing templates and configuration files, authors can define graphical assets, character names, object descriptions, and other game elements. Consequently, these objects are centrally managed. This modular design enables easy modification of settings. For instance, it allows for a transition from the science fiction setting of Lost Earth 2307 to a more realistic setting.

The Story module is optional and dedicated to the role of authors. If deemed necessary, authors can craft a cohesive narrative that spans across all missions within the selected setting. The story incorporates flavor texts, character dialogues, and other textual elements to provide contextualization and motivation for completing mission tasks. Incorporating storytelling within a serious game enables possibilities for deeper immersion (Naul & Liu, 2019). A well-crafted story may engross students, thereby fulfilling learning objectives as they become eager to unravel the narrative's conclusion. It is worth noting that the text elements employed in this module are segregated from mission-related text elements, ensuring the separation of missions from optional storytelling endeavors. For example, the order of missions can be changed without having to adjust the spanning story.

The Gamification module, also optional, is designed to cater to the author role. It offers the ability to introduce additional rewards and achievement goals that extend beyond the basic Game Loop, providing further motivation for players (refer to Gamification option in Figure 1, right)

The Mission module assumes great significance as it encompasses tasks pertaining to the knowledge domain, essential for achieving specific learning objectives. Crucial for providing modularity and adaptability is a modular and independent mission loop (refer to Figure 2). The mission loop is pivotal in facilitating the creation or adaptation of individual missions without requiring modifications to the central game loop or other modules. Consequently, teachers can focus solely on adding or adjusting missions without the burden of aligning them with the overarching story, Gamification elements, graphical assets, or game mechanics. The technical concept of this module presents additional advantages for teachers and authors, elaborated upon in the subsequent chapter.

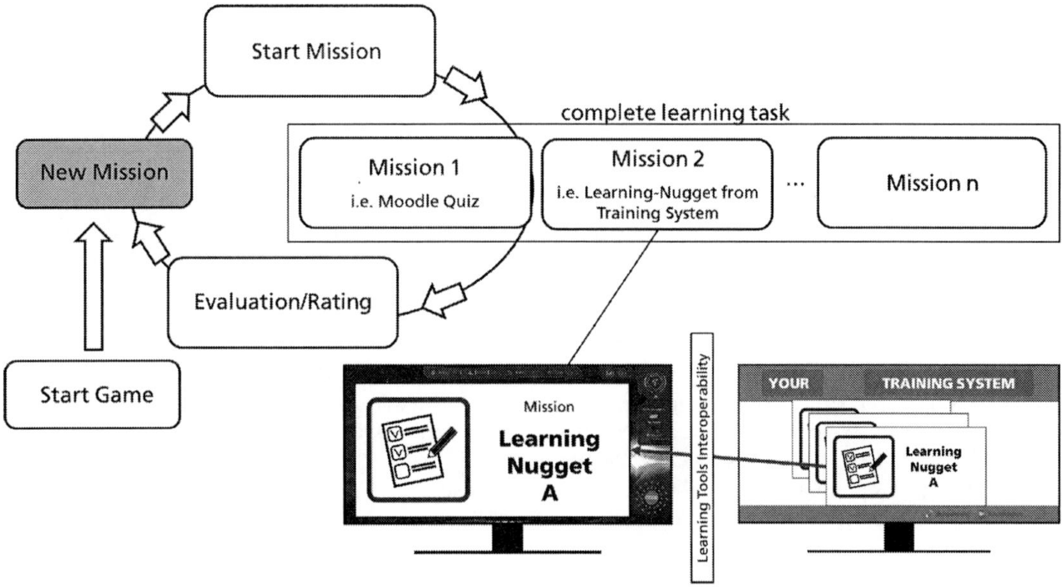

Figure 2. Modular mission loop; each mission contains linked LTI content

2.2 Technical Concept

The Game Loop module, in and of itself, does not inherently provide learning objectives within a specific knowledge domain. The actual learning process occurs within the missions. Successful mission completion serves as the driving force behind game progression and appropriately rewards players.

Therefore, this concept incorporates the integration of existing educational tools, such as learning management systems (LMS), training tools, and simulators. This integration is facilitated through interoperability standards like Learning Tools Interoperability (LTI, see IMS Global, 2023). The LTI embedding of these educational tools makes it look as if the tool is a seamless part of the game (refer to Figure 2). Consequently, a mission could involve completing a learning nugget from an LMS, passing quiz assessments, or engaging with simulation exercises. This integration allows for the seamless accomplishment of learning objectives within missions by utilizing pre-existing educational resources.

The integration of pre-existing educational resources offers two significant advantages. Firstly, authors and teachers are not required to re-create pre-existing content specifically for the game. Existing content can be repurposed and reused. Secondly, authors and teachers do not have to familiarize themselves with new content creation tools, as they can leverage the familiar editors present within the linked educational tools.

The aforementioned LTI interoperability standard necessitates a web-based architecture. This further facilitates improved maintainability and administration. Playing the serious game and accessing content can be accomplished through web browsers. As a result, game instances based on this concept are platform-independent and can be centrally maintained. Maintenance and administration tasks, such as deploying new software versions or adapting content, can be executed centrally on a server, eliminating the need for content deployment on individual desktops.

3. CONCLUSION AND FURTHER WORK

Expert interviews involving students, teachers, and authors were conducted to identify the strengths and weaknesses of the original serious game, Lost Earth 2307, concerning its suitability for lessons and self-learning phases. These assessments revealed specific requirements, particularly the need for more efficient and streamlined content adaptation and creation for classroom use. Additionally, improved maintainability and administrability were deemed essential.

The concept presented in this paper addresses these requirements. The modular mission loop empowers teachers and authors to swiftly adapt individual learning content without the need to alter game mechanics or other game-related components. Employing a construction kit approach with a fixed game loop and modular modules enables the creation of serious game content independent of the military image analysis domain. Elements from the existing Lost Earth 2307 game can be reused or substituted as deemed necessary. As a result, the concept has the potential to evolve into a generic serious game framework, facilitating the creation of serious games within various knowledge domains with less effort and greater efficiency than traditional methods.

However, it is important to note that the concept is still in its early stages. The true efficacy of the described concept as a generic serious game framework catering to multiple knowledge domains can only be ascertained through example implementations and testing. With regard to incorporation of the LTI standard, a first technical proof of concept was conducted (Kannegieser, 2022). The next steps will involve developing further proof of concepts and sample implementations within new knowledge domains. Besides these further technical proofs of concepts, there is a strong need to evaluate if the framework is suitable for other knowledge domains and still meets the requirements of DGBL and immersive didactics. Future evaluations will focus on learning achievements, gaming fun and usability with manifestations of the framework in other knowledge domains, such as Cyber Security or Lean Production.

REFERENCES

Atorf, D. et al, 2019. Balancing Realism and Engagement for a Serious Game in the Domain of Remote Sensing. *In Games and Learning Alliance, Proceedings of the 7th International Conference*, GALA 2018, pp.146-156.

Atorf, D. et al. 2020. Towards a concept for streamlining game design of an existing serious game and preliminary evaluation. *In Proceedings of the IADIS International Conference WWW/Internet 2020*, pp. 155 – 160.

Bopp, M. 2006. Immersive Didaktik und Framingprozesse in Computerspielen. *In Neitzel, B. and Nohr, R.F. Das Spiel mit dem Medium. Partizipation-Immersion-Interaktion. Zur Teilhabe an den Medien von Kunst bis Computerspiel*, pp. 170-186, Schüren, Marburg.

IMS Global (2023). *Learning Tools Interoperability Advantage Implementation Guide*. http://www.imsglobal.org/activity/learning-tools-interoperability. Retrieved 2023-07-11.

Kannegieser, E. et al, 2022. A proof of concept: Cybersecurity learning content in LTI based educational systems. *In Proceedings of the International Conference on Applied Computing 2022 and WWW/Internet 2022*, pp 237 - 240

Naul, E. and Liu, M.. (2019). Why Story Matters: A Review of Narrative in Serious Games. *In Journal of Educational Computing Research*. Vol. 58, No. 3, pp. 687-707.

Prensky, M. (2007). *Digital Game-Based Learning*. Paragon House, St. Paul.

Rollings, A. and Adams, E. (2003). *Andrew Rollings and Ernest Adams on Game Design*. New Riders Publishing. Indianapolis, USA. pp. 417–441.

REFLECTION

THE POWER OF DIGITAL PLATFORMS: FACILITATING THE COLLABORATION OF UNDERGRADUATE COMPUTER SCIENCE PROJECT TEAMS

Margaret R. Scaturro Heil
North Carolina State University – Department of Computer Science
Engineering Building 2-1202A, 890 Oval Drive, Raleigh, NC 27695, USA

ABSTRACT

A required undergraduate computer science 15-week project course at North Carolina State University, Department of Computer Science, USA, has grown rapidly in 29 years from serving 3 student teams to up to 39 teams. To maintain the integrity of the award-winning program and to facilitate the collaboration of hundreds of students in an academic year, the use of digital platforms to augment the face-to-face experience has become necessary. The use of commercial tools (Slack, Zoom, Google Workspace, and Panopto) are described. Customized digital tools to facilitate a feedback loop for student team assignments and to monitor student participation are also outlined. Balancing face-to-face advising with the creative and consistent use of appropriate digital platforms is a necessity for teaching and monitoring effective student collaboration.

KEYWORDS

Computer Science Capstone, Digital Team Collaboration

1. APPROACH TO CAPSTONE PROJECT EXPERIENCE

The North Carolina State University, USA, Computer Science Senior Design Center (SDC) was formed in 1994. The SDC's mission is to educate undergraduate computer science students by providing a real-world software development problem (with industrial partners) and by teaching and integrating the principles of software engineering, teamwork, and professional communication in the solution of that problem. Student teams are expected to collaborate and develop software to solve a problem posed by industrial sponsors.

The SDC offers a 15-week capstone senior design project course taught by instructors with different areas of expertise. The course is team taught by the Director, a technical communicator and teaming specialist (on staff since 1996), and computer science teaching professors who serve as technical advisors to the student teams. Currently 30-40 individual teams (4-5 students/team) are formed each semester. Industrial sponsors provide problem statements and mentors to work with the student teams throughout the semester.

In the beginning, the instructors of the SDC worked with only 3-5 student project teams and senior design was designated as an elective course. By the early 2000s, the course became required for all undergraduate computer science students because it provided a robust communication and teaming experience. In a recent semester, the SDC faculty and staff were required to teach 5 sections; 194 students were placed on 39 teams collaborating on unique problems. Since the inception of the SDC, the teaching team has taught ~800+ teams of students and worked with ~225 different industrial sponsors. The pedagogical approach used in the SDC has been previously described (Carter et al. 2012, Fornaro et al. 2007, Scaturro Heil and Domínguez 2022).

As this experience evolved and grew over the decades, the teaching team was faced with the challenge of managing daily communication with dozens of teams and sponsors as well as hundreds of students. It has been necessary for the teaching team to augment face-to-face student interaction with the use of multiple digital platforms to facilitate collaboration between students, instructors and sponsors. These platforms include email, Slack, Zoom, Google Meet, Panopto, Google Calendar, and a custom-designed document submission system integrated into the course website. While digital tools allow us to accommodate our growing program in many ways, we continue to emphasize the importance of face-to-face communication.

2. FACILITATION OF PROJECT EXPERIENCE WITH DIGITAL TOOLS

2.1 Commercial Tools

Normally, the SDC teaching team meets with students in person twice per week during class time; however, outside communication with teams necessarily occurs on a daily basis. The Pandemic required 100% virtual instruction. This required the use of Panopto, Zoom, Google Workspace, and Slack to replace face-to-face interaction with students. Since the University reopened for in-person instruction and as our enrollment has increased, these tools are being used on a regular basis as a part of the course experience (in addition to face-to-face interaction).

2.1.1 Weekly Industrial Sponsor Meetings

The success of the student project teams is highly correlated to collaborating with industrial sponsors (or mentors) on a regular basis, so the mentors meet with student teams weekly. Many of these weekly meetings are conducted via Zoom or Google Meet; in our case, in one semester, this could total hundreds of meetings. There are many advantages to this method of meeting – it saves travel time to campus for sponsors and allows them to meet with students even if they are out of town, and participants can join when circumstances prevent them from meeting in person. Using digital platforms also allows faculty advisors to more easily join meetings when their expertise is needed. When compared to other semesters when these tools were not used, student teams often ended up not meeting with sponsoring mentors or faculty advisors as often as needed; this created lags in project understanding and progress.

2.1.2 Faculty Advising Sessions with Student Teams & Class Lectures

This senior design experience is most successful if the students attend all class sessions and are actively engaged with the teaching team and each other. Effectively advising dozens of project teams in a 15-week semester is an overwhelming task; the students need assistance with technical details as well as guidance with communication assignments given throughout the semester (i.e., formal presentations and documentation). Recently, the teaching team has relied heavily on digital tools to facilitate such collaboration.

Slack, an instant messaging platform, has proven to be extremely useful when supporting students. For example, in the most recent semester, the Director and Assistant Director each monitored over 90 Slack team channels plus numerous individual channels on a daily basis. Via Slack, the teaching team can quickly answer student questions; in many cases, the instructors collaborate extensively for several hours with student teams, giving them technical tutorials and advice. Slack allows us to create dedicated workspaces for the course and for each team; when compared to using just email (which was the only digital platform used in previous years), Slack is more pointed and efficient. The teaching team is also more readily available to students outside of face-to-face class meetings via Slack; this remote interaction allows productive communication (and usually, improved project progress) in a timelier manner than if only meeting twice/week during class (as in years past).

Zoom or Google Meet are also used for technical advising sessions when face-to-face meetings are not possible. These tools allow instructors to meet with students more easily outside of class time. When needed, instructors also use Zoom or Google Meet to conduct a required teaming project management activity with each team every semester (Heil 2019). As our enrollment numbers have increased, student absenteeism is also on the rise. These digitals tools help to keep students included in activities when they would otherwise not be engaged. This digital inclusiveness has improved the accountability for each team member and hence, in most cases, has increased project productivity.

Lectures included in this course are recorded using Panopto, a video platform that allows the teaching team to securely share on-demand recordings. To encourage collaboration, attendance is required and students who miss lectures are expected to use Panopto to watch any unattended lecture. Panopto monitors whether or not absentee students have downloaded lectures. This tool facilitates students' review of lecture material.

2.2 Custom-Designed Tools

In this project-based course, student teams are expected to provide successively refined versions of a written software development project report and oral progress report presentations. These written and oral reports include extensive details related to Requirements Definition, Design, Implementation and Testing, and they are expected to be completed collaboratively. Electronic and oral feedback from instructors is carefully scheduled and coordinated around due dates of these written and oral deliverables; students are expected to collaborate and respond appropriately to feedback at the next deliverable checkpoint. Each member of the student team is also required to keep an individual log of their personal contribution to the project as well as their activity as a team. Peer evaluations are also required four times during the semester.

2.2.1 Formal Communication Checkpoints

The Assistant Director of the SDC has created an electronic Submission System that allows feedback from multiple instructors to be given to the entire student team on written and oral deliverables. This system allows one instructor to download a document, for example, review, comment, and upload the commented document. The system notifies other instructors on the teaching team who then in turn can download that commented document, review, add additional feedback, and upload for the next instructor. The final reviewer can then electronically open the fully commented document for the student team to review. Before this submission tool was created, students were given handwritten feedback or multiple copies of electronic feedback from various instructors; this sometimes led to inconsistent or untimely feedback and confusion among students, which interrupted the development process. Maintaining the integrity of the SDC while enrollment has increased would not have been realized without this custom-designed digital tool.

2.2.2 Detailed Course Information & Student Logs/Peer Evaluations

The increased enrollment in this robust project course has created challenges related to the consistency of information dissemination. The Assistant Director has created and maintains a course website that is always updated with project listings, information for sponsors, and extensive course guidelines for students (Domínguez 2023). The student tab of the website includes syllabus and assignment rubrics (which are cross-referenced to course pack). Students also use this website to access customized Google calendars/section; the Submission System; class notes and lectures; as well as lab, technology, and testing resources.

Students use the course website to log time and to submit peer evaluations. This facilitates the monitoring of student collaboration and individual accountability, especially with hundreds of students (and enrollment on the rise).

3. CONCLUSION

University enrollments in computer science and information technology disciplines are increasing. The power of using digital tools to facilitate and monitor collaboration among student teams is apparent to those of us who manage 30-40 teams at one given time. There is a concern, however, that these tools could potentially be overused. Digital tools were used exclusively during the Pandemic; when the doors were open again for in-person learning, the SDC teaching team observed that students seemed unusually awkward, uncomfortable, and ineffective when interacting face-to-face. It became apparent that it was essential for our capstone experience to provide young, about-to-become computer science professionals with as many face-to-face learning opportunities as possible. As undergraduate enrollments increase in this discipline, educators must maintain the balance between the convenience of using digital tools and the need to teach foundational skills needed for effective face-to-face communication and collaboration.

REFERENCES

Carter, M. et al., 2012. Creating a Progression of Writing, Speaking, and Teaming Learning Outcomes in Undergraduate CS/SE Curricula. *Proceedings of the World Engineering Education Forum (WEEF), Engineering Education for Sustainable Development and Social Inclusion,* Buenos Aires, Argentina, Abstract p. 262.

Domínguez, I., 2023. NC State University Computer Science Senior Design Center. https://sdc.csc.ncsu.edu/.

Fornaro, R. et al., 2007. Reflections on Ten Years of Sponsored Senior Design Projects: Students Win – Clients Win! *Journal of Systems and Software,* Vol. 80, No. 8, pp. 1209-1216.

Heil, M., 2019. A Project Management Activity for Student Teams in a Computer Science Undergraduate Capstone Project Course: Task Planning. *Proceedings of EduLearn19 Conference,* Palma de Mallorca, Spain, pp. 9072-9077.

Scaturro Heil, M. and Domínguez, I., 2022. A Practical Approach to an Undergraduate Computer Science Senior Design Project Experience: Partnering with Industry to Create an Effective Transition from Academia to the Next Chapter. *Proceedings of International Conference on Interactive Collaborative Learning Conference,* Vienna, Austria, pp. 921-929.

AUTHOR INDEX

Aigner, Wolfgang 3
Ali, Aliza 289
Anastasiou, Vaso 18
Angeli, Charoula 18, 171
Atorf, Daniel 439
Barana, Alice 377
Bender, Beate 125
Bianchi, Robert 142
Blagojevic, Marija 133
Brockmann, Patricia 91
Brucker-Kley, Elke 257
Burkhard, Michael 187
Butz, Andreas 214
Cambria, Antonino 402
Chan, Victor K. Y. 329, 361
Clariana, Roy B. 241
Comitale, Clementina 411
Da Silva, Gustavo Simas 369
De Castell, Suzanne 34, 393
Delcker, Jan 417
Devedzic, Mirjana 133
Devedžic, Vladan 133, 207
Di Giunta, Laura 411
Di Meana, Franco Ripa 25
Diakou, Panayiota 18
Diefenbach, Sarah 214
Doukakis, Spyridon 397
Downes, Stephen 107
Durmus, Dilan 25
Dyck, Sergius 439
Eshet, Yovav 249
Fejzullaj, Selma 142
Georgara, Natalia 397
Ghanam, Ryad 142
Giretti, Alberto 25
Gliozzo, Giulia 411
Gordon, Goren 411
Gramigna, Anita 43
Greubel, André 280
Grinautsky, Keren 249
Guggemos, Josef 51
Guidi, Andrea 25
Hadjerrouit, Said 179, 199
Hansen, Nils Kristian 179
Heil, Joana 407, 417
Heil, Margaret R. Scaturro 445
Hennecke, Martin 280
Hilber, Flurina 257
Ifenthaler, Dirk 345, 407, 417
Iqbal, Huda 142
Ismail, Azleen 163
Jailani, Mohd Azli 84
Jenson, Jennifer 34, 393
Jeong, Allan 233
Jost, Patrick 153
Jüristo, Kristi 133
Kannegieser, Ehm 439
Keller, Thomas 257
Kim, Stella Yun 77
Kittaneh, Khawla 142
Koehler, Adrie 77
Koprivica, Marko 207
Korepanova, Antonina 99
Kossack, Frederike 125
Kostic, Aleksandar 207
Künz, Andreas 153
Leiba, Nathalie 133
Li, Kai 265
Ljubisavljevic, Dragica 207
Loy, Chong Kim 84
Lunetti, Carolina 411
Malik, Mahani Abdul 67
Marchisio, Marina 377, 402
Martens, Alke 337
Matsumoto, Kazunori 273
McKee, Gerard T. 313
Miliou, Ourania 171
Miloševic, Danijela 133
Nascimento, Maria Augusta Pereira 421
Niaz, Afreena 142
Ninggal, Mohd Tajudin Md 163
Nishiguchi, Isoharu 273
Nnagbo, Celestine Ifeanyi 199
Olesova, Larisa 60
Omar, Rohaizak 163
Pantic, Sanja Popovic 133
Pata, Kai 99, 133
Pirnay-Dummer, Pablo 223
Plintz, Nicolai 345
Pohl, Margit 3
Poletti, Giorgio 43
Popp, Tobias Harald 305
Potzmann, Benjamin 3
Radenkovic, Sonja 133
Rangger, Sebastian 153
Rebelo, Maria Da Piedade Vaz 421

Riccioni, Chiara ... 411
Roman, Fabio ... 377
Rosinski, Adam ... 321
Sadaf, Ayesha ... 60, 77
Schätz, Eric ... 337
Schlomske-Bodenstein, Nadine ... 223
Schuhbauer, Heidi ... 305
Seok-Shin, Hyoung ... 233
Sergejeva, Natalija ... 297, 389
Seufert, Sabine ... 417
Siller, Hans-Stefan ... 280
Solnosky, Ryan ... 241
Spinello, Enrico ... 402
Spirgi, Lukas ... 417
Standl, Bernhard ... 223
Steinberger, Pnina ... 249
Stoiber, Christina ... 3
Swanson, Joan Ann ... 353
Takemura, Atsushi ... 433
Tanaka, Hiroshi ... 273
Tanaka, Tetsuo ... 11, 273
Tepgeç, Mustafa ... 407
Tomory, Ibolya ... 116
Tursunkulova, Irina ... 34
Ueda, Mari ... 11, 273
Ulbricht, Vânia Ribas ... 369
Ullrich, Daniel ... 214
Uttich, Eike ... 125
Vaccarini, Massimo ... 25
Vintere, Anna ... 427
Weber, Alan S. ... 142
Wenkmann, Julia ... 280
Yajuan, Zhang ... 421
Yyelland, Byrad ... 142
Zaghouani, Wajdi ... 142
Zambelli, Matteo ... 25
Zapušek, Matej ... 133
Zeidmane, Anda ... 297, 389
Zekry, Dina A ... 313
Zvirgzdina, Liga ... 297